EDUCATIONAL MEDIA AND TECHNOLOGY YEARBOOK

Michael Orey, V. J. McClendon, and Robert Maribe Branch, Editors

2006 Edition Volume 31

Published in cooperation with the Association for Educational Communications and Technology

LIBRARIES
UNLIMITED SERIALS

A Member of the Greenwood Publishing Group

Westport, Connecticut • London

Library of Congress Cataloging-in-Publication Data

Educational media and technology yearbook.—Westport, CT : Libraries Unlimited.
  A Member of the Greenwood Publishing Group, Inc. 1985-
    v.-
  Annual
  2006- vol. 31
  Published in cooperation with the Association for Educational Communications and
  Technology, 1985-
  Continues: Educational media yearbook
  ISBN 1-59158-362-4
  LB1028.3.E372   2006   85643014

British Library Cataloguing in Publication Data is available.

ISBN: 1-59158-362-4

First published in 2006

Libraries Unlimited, 88 Post Road West, Westport, CT 06881
A Member of the Greenwood Publishing Group, Inc.
www.lu.com

Printed in the United States of America

The paper used in this book complies with the
Permanent Paper Standard issued by the National
Information Standards Organization (Z39.48-1984).

10   9   8   7   6   5   4   3   2   1

Contents

Part One: Trends and Issues

Part Two: School and Library Media

Section 1: Performance and Measurement

Section 2: Holistic Approaches to Information Literacy

Part Three: Leadership Profiles

Part Four: Organizations and Associations

Part Five: Graduate Programs

Part Six: Mediagraphy

Preface

This is my fifth year as an editor and my third as senior editor of the *Yearbook*. I go to several conferences each year and try to attend as many sessions as I can. This allows me to gain a sense of the trends in the field. This year, I have noted many trends: gaming, storytelling, technology integration, teacher training and technology integration, handheld technologies, online learning, online learning in instructional technology, multicultural perspectives, portfolios, constructionism, problem-based learning, communities of practice, learning communities, case-based learning, multiple intelligences, experiential learning, mentoring, computer-mediated communication, cooperative learning, motivation, and, finally, cognitive apprenticeships. These were the hot topics from this year's conferences.

The audience for the *Yearbook* consists of media and technology professionals in schools, higher education, and business contexts. Topics of interest to professionals practicing in these areas are broad, as the table of contents demonstrates. The theme unifying each of the following chapters is the use of technology to enable or enhance education. Forms of technology represented in this volume vary from traditional tools such as the book to the latest advancements in digital technology; areas of education encompass widely ranging situations involving learning and teaching.

As in prior volumes, the assumptions underlying the chapters presented here are as follows:

Technology represents tools that act as extensions of the educator.

Media serve as delivery systems for educational communications.

Technology is *not* restricted to machines and hardware but includes techniques and procedures derived from scientific research about ways to promote change in human performance.

The fundamental tenet of the *Yearbook* is that educational media and technology should be used to

achieve authentic learning objectives,

situate learning tasks,

negotiate the complexities of guided learning,

facilitate the construction of knowledge,

support skill acquisition, and

manage diversity.

The *Educational Media and Technology Yearbook* has become a standard reference in many libraries and professional collections. Examined in relation to its companion volumes of the past, it provides a valuable historical record of current ideas and developments in the field. Part One, "Trends and Issues," presents an array of chapters that develop some of the current themes listed here, in addition to others. Part Two, "School and Library Media," concentrates on chapters of special relevance to K–12 education, school learning resources, and school library media centers. In Part Three, "Leadership Profiles," authors provide biographical sketches of the careers of instructional technology leaders. Part Four, "Organizations and Associations in North America," and Part Five, "Graduate Programs in North America," are, respectively, directories of instructional technology-related organizations and institutions of higher learning offering degrees in related fields. Finally, Part Six, the "Mediagraphy," presents an annotated listing of selected current publications related to the field.

The editors of the *Yearbook* invite media and technology professionals to submit manuscripts to be considered for publication. Contact Michael Orey (mikeorey@uga.edu) for submission guidelines.

Michael Orey

Contributors

Barbara Bichelmeyer

Elizabeth Boling

Doris U. Bolliger

Jennifer M. Brill

Gail Bush

Yi-Chia Cheng

Ikseon Choi

Gregory Clinton

Theresa A. Cullen

Lesley S. J. Farmer

Barbara Fiehn

Andrew S. Gibbons

Janette Hill

Stephanie Huffman

Emily Hunter

Jeongwan Kang

Mary L. Kelly

Hyeonjin Kim

Min-Joung Kim

Heng-Yu Ku

Joyce Lee

Linda Lohr

Marcia A. Mardis

Amy McElveen

Michael Molenda

Thomas C. Reeves

Charles Riegeluth

Ellen Rose

Richard Schwier

J. Michael Spector

A. M. Thomas

Walter Wager

Andy Walker

Chun-Min Wang

Jong Won Jung

Part One
Trends and Issues

Introduction

Michael Orey

This is the fifth edition of this book for which I have served as the editor of the Trends and Issues section. It has been my approach to divide the Trends and Issues section into subsections based on whatever I have learned from attending conferences such as the Association for Educational Communications and Technology. Online learning has been a category, in so many words, in each of those issues. I have also tried to ascertain other trends as well. This year, I thought about including sections on online learning,

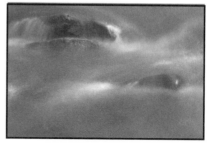

Photo Courtesy of Julie Tallman

ePortfolios, technology integration, gaming, and multicultural perspectives. I have, however, a metaphorical image in my head of the field of instructional technology. Imagine a boulder in the middle of a stream with water rushing over it. The boulder is largely unchanging (although erosion does have a gradual effect), but the water is ever changing. To me, the boulder represents instructional design, instructional theory, and learning theory. These things change slowly in our field. The water represents technology. Technology is changing all the time. To divide the book along the lines described earlier is to divide it largely along the lines of technology. In this volume, I have chosen a few of the theories that seemed to be most popular during the year. These include problem-based learning, case-based learning, cooperative learning, and motivation. Each of these "rocks" has been applied to the prevailing trends in the field.

Bichelmeyer and Molenda provide another overview of the trends in the field from a school, university, and business perspective. Molenda, working with various colleagues, has contributed to this section of this book eight times now. Using my rock in a river metaphor, much of the trend this past year has been on improving and increased spending on the water with little attention to the boulder. With the improvement in the U.S. economy comes more flow in the river. The often-repeated concern in this trends is a suggestion to focus more on the boulder and less on the river.

Bichelmeyer, Boling, and Gibbons focus more directly on instructional design and its role as the rock of the field. Bichelmeyer begins the chapter with a section discussing the idea that instructional design is the core of the field and define that core with the acronym ADDIE: analysis, design, development, implementation, and evaluation. She concludes that this is not a model, however, but a framework around which we in the field can still rally. In the next part of the chapter, Boling suggests that we learn from other design fields how best to teach design but notes that design and the framework of ADDIE is central to the field of IDT. Interestingly, Gibbons proposes a model for research that suggests a flow deflected by an intervention. This fits nicely with the rock and river metaphor: the rock is the intervention, and the flow is how we are using the ever-changing technology.

Perhaps Lee speaks to my metaphor perhaps most directly. She describes how much online learning has grown, but her advice and data suggest that those who wish to teach online ought to consider some fundamental instructional theories. Because of the greater diversity we face in higher education, we must reassert our interest and emphasis in instructional theory. The context has changed, but the theories are like rocks in a river.

1

Kelley, Cullen, and Kim describe a graduate class that makes use of the well-defined theory of problem-based learning (PBL). Using our metaphor, PBL is the rock: the technology is varied, but it involves the use of a variety of technologies to present the problem and have the students work on its solution. The authors also make use qualitative methods in their analysis of the learning experiences of the students. This methodology is becoming increasingly common within the field of instructional technology.

Schwier, Hill, Wager, and Spector's chapter helps us to attend more to the boulder than to the water and instructional models. The first section focuses on practitioners' views of why they do their work. Although this is not well understood within the field, my guess is that it has been fairly persistent, like models of instruction. The "rock" as a change agent, to extend my metaphor, would suggest that the rock changes the water into rapids; with many rocks, the rapids become white water; and the infusion of even more rocks can cause a change in the direction of the river altogether. In the second section, Hill looks at six instructional design technology (IDT) programs seeking a clear description of the "rock." Unfortunately, the only consistent perspective across programs is at the doctoral level. Universities consistently focus on research and theory, however, and this truth exists across most doctoral programs regardless of field. Wager turns back to the instrumental perspective described in the first section and suggests that all IDT programs ought to provide their students with the "tools" to design environments that solve instructional and learning problems. The tools are the rock, and the tools are instructional design models. Schwier and colleagues' look to the future suggests a possible path as the one that moves from IDT to the learning sciences. This puts the rock at the center of our field.

For Thomas, the rock is mentoring, and the water is computer-mediated communication (CMS). This chapter fits well with my metaphor in that Thomas begins his chapter with Odysseus and the *Odyssey* as the roots of mentoring. This is a pretty solid rock. CMC allows new opportunities for mentoring, however. In this case, Thomas considers mentoring in mathematics, sciences, engineering, and teacher education. The rock also changes in that more current theoretical perspectives are woven together to show mentoring as cognitive apprenticeship with scaffolding and coaching as elements of the mentoring process.

Brill and Walker make use of both legitimate peripheral participation and communities of practice to anchor their work in the field. The result is a much more human focus, rather than a focus on technology, but much of what they suggest adapts technology to a more social model of learning. In the flow of all the online technologies is the rock of social learning theory.

Choi, Kim, Jung, and Clinton have come up with an instructional model that fits nicely into a Piagetian notion of learning. Their idea of belief failure is directly related to Piaget's notion of disequilibration. Furthermore, their use of the idea of "Just in Time" learning equates to the scaffolding that is necessary to help learners regain their equilibration. Piaget remains a rock in our field.

Bolliger views constructionism as her rock, while the water is the technology that her students created in a development course. The course attempts to turn over much control to students so they may take charge of their own learning. This new-found power has been met with mixed success in the class.

Ku, Cheng, and Lohr make use of collaborative learning as the rock in the field. The technology in this case is online learning, and the context is an online instructional design class. The authors find that there are some important things that students and online instructors can do to take advantage of the cooperation. For students, they recommend the 5 Cs. For instructors, they recommend ten critical elements to incorporate into the courses.

Rose is also focused on online learning, examining WebCT and Blackboard as teaching tools. In terms of the rock metaphor, this is much more of a critical analysis of the online movement and suggests how the movement is fundamentally behavioral at best and the dumbing of higher education at worst. She warns that we are at risk of having a highly efficient, poorly delivered system of higher education if we do not step up and make sure that we attend to what we know about good instruction and learning. We should focus on the rock, not the water.

Issues and Trends in Instructional Technology: Gradual Growth atop Tectonic Shifts

Barbara Bichelmeyer and Michael Molenda
Indiana University

This is the eighth in a series of reviews begun in 1998, examining the status of instructional technology in the corporate, higher education, and K–12 education sectors in the United States. These reviews draw together quantitative data reported in a wide variety of sources. By tracking the data over a period of years, the authors are able to make some judgments about the direction of change.

The year since the previous review was written (Molenda & Bichelmeyer, 2005) has seen a slight improvement in the economy of the United States after several years of recession. For public K–12 and higher education, the most significant source of financial support is the tax revenue of each state. When state tax revenues fall, schools and colleges compete with other interests for shrinking resources. When institutions' budgets are cut, technology investments decline; when budgets grow, so does technology spending. That is what happened during the dramatic decline—then rebound—in state revenues between 2000 and the beginning of 2005, as shown in Figure 1. In fact, the percentage increase of the first quarter of 2005 compared with the first quarter of 2004 was the largest increase in more than a decade (Jenny, 2005). This increase in state revenues has not immediately found its way to increases in information technology budgets.

Figure 1. Year-over-year percent change in state tax revenues, 2000–2005. Source: Jenny, 2005.

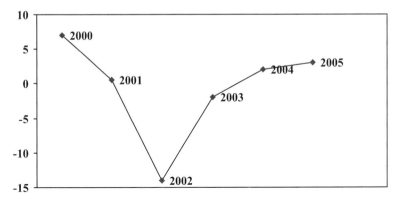

OVERALL DEVELOPMENTS

Over the past year, businesses, colleges, and schools have continued to invest in their technological infrastructure, especially by upgrading their Internet connections to broadband capability and by building wireless networks to complement their wired networks. Such Web-connected networks have become pervasive in the United States, enhancing the opportunities to leverage learning through technology. We have come to learn, though, that pervasive availability does not equal pervasive use. In general, the past decade has seen slow and piecemeal application of information and communications technologies (ICT) in training and education. Change has been evolutionary rather revolutionary, with the ratio of users versus nonusers increasing by single-digit increments per year. At the same time, changes broad enough to be termed tectonic shifts have been taking place beneath the surface. Forces such as global economic competition, advances in ICT hardware and software, changing demographics, government economic policies, and pedagogical reform movements have caused major rearrangement of the landscape even as incremental changes take place in the use of ICT for teaching and learning. In this chapter, we document both the incremental changes and the tectonic shifts, which are less visible to the unaided eye.

One of the traits of current technological evolution is its tendency toward convergence of formats. In the days of analog media, it was easy to distinguish among different media formats—video, film, slide, overhead transparency, audio cassette—but with digital media, it is possible to combine still and moving images, sometimes with sound, in a seamless package. At the same time, functions that were once performed by separate devices—telephone, radio, television, calculating, text messaging—are now converging into a single instrument, usually designed to be handheld. Along the same lines, instructional methods that were once seen as distinct—face-to-face classroom, video, Web-based—are converging into hybrid or blended-learning formats.

The pace of adoption and type of adoption vary from sector to sector because different social and economic forces play out in different ways in the three sectors. This review treats the corporate sector first, the higher education sector second, and the school sector third.

CORPORATE TRAINING AND DEVELOPMENT

The general expansion of business that began in 2004 carried over into 2005, ending the string of years in which corporate spending for training had actually declined. Although spending was not yet rising in 2004 (and was still lower than it had been in 2000), at least the decline had ceased. However, expenditures for off-the shelf training materials continued to decline, being lower in 2004 than in 2000 (Dolezalek, 2004).

We have been tracking the results of the annual survey of corporate training conducted by *Training* magazine since 1997, during which time the survey methodology and response items have been consistent enough to allow reasonable longitudinal comparisons of various media and methods over this eight-year period.

Issue 1: Use of Technology-Based Media for Delivery of Instruction

Live Classroom versus Computer-based Instruction. Despite earlier predictions to the contrary, the learning environment that is most universally used is the face-to-face classroom, currently being used always or often at 85 percent of all companies (Dolezalek, 2004). As shown in Figure 2, this represents a small decline since 1997, although this figure has not otherwise varied far from 90 percent over this period.

A more meaningful figure would be the *proportion* of time that trainees spend in different learning environments. Respondents' reports are a bit difficult to interpret because they are increasingly forced to classify situations that combine different delivery systems, for example, a live instructor who is speaking to one audience face-to-face and another one via videoconference. In any event, the estimate of 70 percent of time spent in face-to-face instruction has also not varied much over the years. At the same time, organizations report that they are making increasing use of Web-based and DVD-based delivery; in 2004, 17 percent of training was delivered by computer with no live instructor (Dolezalek, 2004).

The American Society for Training and Development's annual state of the industry report (Sugrue & Kim, 2004) reports data from a different sample of respondents, with similar findings. They estimate that trainees spent 68 percent of their learning hours in live, instructor-led settings versus 10 percent in self-paced online study and 6 percent in instructor-led remote or online work. This represented a small shift toward technology-based delivery over the previous year. Overall, technology-based methods may be replacing face-to-face methods to some degree, but they appear to be supplementing face-to-face methods to a high degree.

Figure 2. Percentage of organizations using live classroom. (For 1997–2000, figure shows those who use "ever." For 2001–2004, figure shows those who use "always" or "often.") Source: Dolezalek, 2004.

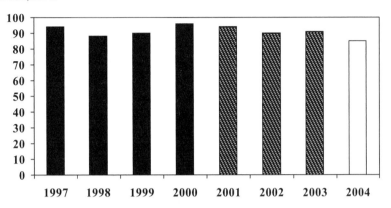

Printed Materials. Manuals and workbooks are alive and well. They were used always or often at 77 percent of businesses (Dolezalek, 2004), indicating a small decline each year since 2002, as shown in Figure 3.[1]

Figure 3: Percentage of organizations using workbook/manual. (For 1997–2000, figure shows those who use "ever." For 2001–2004, figure shows those who use "always" or "often.") Source: Dolezalek, 2004.

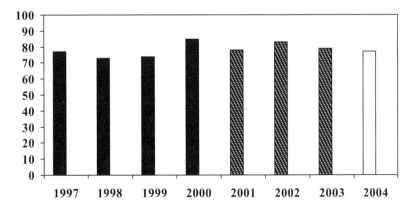

However, the 2004 level of use is virtually the same as in 1997, indicating that there are small yearly fluctuations but not really a trend over this period.

---

[1] Note that the data from 1997 to 2000 are not directly comparable to those from 2001 and later. In the former period, the question was asked simply, "do you use this method or not?" whereas in the latter period, the question was phrased "do you use this method always, often, seldom, or never?"

The dream of a paperless office has been with us since the advent of computers in the 1960s, but thoughtful observers are now talking instead about the *myth* of the paperless office (Sellen & Harper, 2001). Per capita paper consumption actually grew greatly between 1991 and 2001 ("In Praise of Clutter," 2002). Clearly, paper has affordances—things that it allows humans to do—that continue to make it an attractive medium for writing, reading, and studying.

The popularity of print materials suggests that independent self-study might be a rather commonly used method of instruction. Actually, self-study as a method was not included as an option in the *Training* surveys until 2002, where "self-study non-computer" was used always or often at 25 percent of businesses, remaining at about 23 percent in 2003 and 2004 (Dolezalek, 2004), as shown in Figure 4.

Figure 4. Percentage of organizations using self-study, noncomputer "always" or "often." Source: Dolezalek, 2004.

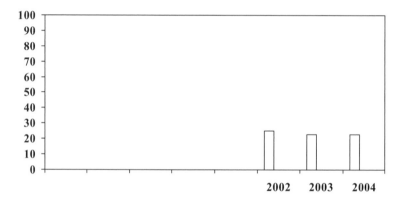

The other category of self-study, "self-study Web-based," was used always or often at 36 percent of responding companies in 2002, rising to 44 percent in 2003 and holding at that level in 2004 (Dolezalek, 2004, p. 32); see Figure 5.

Figure 5. Percentage of organizations using self-study, Web-based "always" or "often." Source: Dolezalek, 2004.

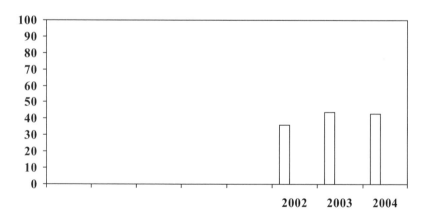

It appears that for several years, more organizations have been making frequent use of the Web for self-directed learning than have been using print materials for self-directed learning, by a ratio of about 2:1. However, this ratio does not seem to be changing dramatically, nor has it affected the overall use of manuals and workbooks. Clearly, manuals and workbooks are used for purposes beyond self-study. They accompany all sorts of classroom and computer-based instruction and are used both as instructional media and as reference materials during and after the training.

Traditional Media. Videotapes are used always or often at 56 percent of responding organizations (Dolezalek, 2004, p. 34). As is shown in Figure 6, this figure has declined a few percentage points in recent years, but the trajectory is not steadily downward.

Figure 6. Percentage of organizations using videotapes. (For 1997–2000, figure shows those who use "ever." For 2001–2004, figure shows those who use "always" or "often.") Source: Dolezalek, 2004.

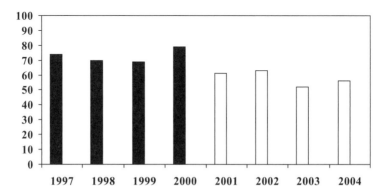

Compared with videotapes, it has been less common for audiotapes to be used as the primary delivery system for prerecorded training modules or courses. Consequently, it is understandable that the reported usage of audiocassettes dropped markedly when the question was changed in the 2001 *Training* survey from "do you use …?" to "how often do you use …?" As shown in Figure 7, only 7 percent of companies used audiocassettes "always" or "often" in 2002, and that figure declined slightly in 2003 and 2004. Some of the drop may also be accounted for by a change in media format; it may be that when audio materials are used they are now more likely to be stored and used in some digital format rather than in tape format.

Figure 7. Percentage of organizations using audiocassettes. (For 1997–2000, figure shows those who use "ever." For 2001–2004, figure shows those who use "always" or "often.") Source: Dolezalek, 2004.

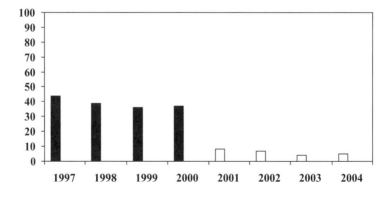

Figure 8. Percentage of organizations using games/simulations, noncomputer. (For 1997–2000, figure shows those who use "ever." For 2001–2004, figure shows those who use "seldom," "always," or "often.") Source: Dolezalek, 2004.

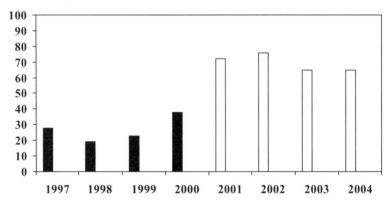

Games and Simulations. It may not make sense to use the same measurement scale to track the adoption of more specialized methods, such as games and simulations. As opposed to training manuals or videos, they are probably not as generically applicable across the whole range of content and objectives. Hence, one would not expect them to be used "always" or even "often" within most organizations' training programs. For this reason, the survey responses are counted a little differently for this category. Usage is counted according to how many respondents report using games and simulations "seldom," "often," or "always." By this measure, the frequency of some usage is quite high—65 percent of companies making some use in 2004 (Dolezalek, 2004, p. 32). As is shown in Figure 8, the reported use of noncomputer games and simulations has declined a bit in the past several years.

Telecommunications Media. A small proportion of organizations use broadcast or satellite television to disseminate training programs to multiple sites. Some 20 percent of respondents reported using broadcast or satellite television in the period of 1998–2000. When the *Training* survey changed the question to measure *frequency* of use, it was found that only around ten percent of companies were using this delivery method "always" or "often." The number has varied only slightly over recent years (Dolezalek, 2004, p. 34), as shown in Figure 9.

Figure 9. Percentage of organizations using broadcast or satellite TV. (For 1997–2000, figure shows those who use "ever." For 2001–2004, figure shows those who use "always" or "often.") Source: Dolezalek, 2004.

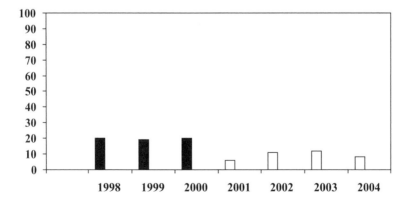

Two-way videoconferences distributed over satellite, cable, or Web are used always or often for training at 19 percent of all organizations (Dolezalek, 2004, p. 34), as shown in Figure 10. This indicates a plateau after an increase over each of the prior three years. However, two-way videoconferences are not used for a large proportion of training time except in the military services. They tend to be used as supplements to other forms of training or for special purposes, such as the introduction of new products or the rollout of new tools at organizations with widely scattered locations.

Figure 10. Percentage of organizations using videoconferencing. (For 1997–2000, figure shows those who use "ever." For 2001–2004, figure shows those who use "always" or "often.") Source: Dolezalek, 2004.

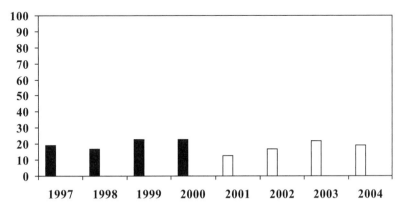

Computer-based Media. Computer-based delivery systems have played a gradually expanding role in training over the past decade. In the early 1990s, this meant modules delivered via floppy disk or local network (LAN). Since then, computer-based material is more likely encountered by means of CD-ROM or DVD modules or by connecting to the Internet or organizational intranet. In the 2004 *Training* survey 60 percent of companies report using instruction in digital storage media "often" or "always," as shown in Figure 11, an increase over the previous year.

Figure 11. Percentage of organizations using digital storage media—diskette, CD, or DVD. (For 1997–2000, figure shows those who use "ever." For 2001–2004, figure shows those who use "always" or "often.") Source: Dolezalek, 2004.

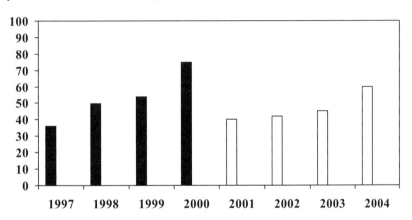

However, 54 percent used Internet or intranet delivery, as shown in Figure 12, a decrease from the previous year, indicating the stalling of a trend of the previous years (Dolezalek, 2004, p. 34). A possible explanation for this reversal is in respondents' perception of what is an "Internet course." The trend has been to combine online and offline activities into new hybrids, possibly reducing the number of training experiences that are exclusively one or the other.

Figure 12. Percentage of organizations using Internet or intranet. (For 1997–2000, figure shows those who use "ever." For 2001–2004, figure shows those who use "always" or "often.") Source: Dolezalek, 2004. Note: in 2001 Internet and intranet listed separately; combined total is shown.

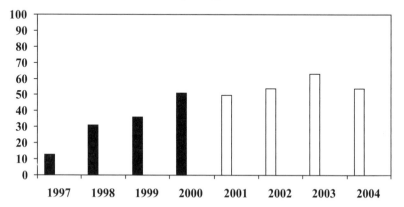

Unexpectedly, the *Training* magazine survey respondents report that the use of computer-based games and simulations has also been stagnant, if not declining, during this same period. As shown in Figure 13, computer-based games and simulations are being used "seldom," "often," or "always" at about 50 percent of all organizations. We suspect that this is something of a definitional issue, because there seems to be an increasing incorporation of Flash-based video simulations in several sorts of training materials, especially computer applications training and soft skills training. It is likely that these simulations are viewed as supplements rather than as the primary medium or method being employed.

Figure 13. Percentage of organizations using games/simulations, computer-based. (For 1997–2000, figure shows those who use "ever." For 2001–2004, figure shows those who use "seldom," "always," or "often.") Source: Dolezalek, 2004.

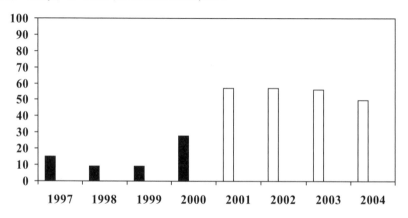

More advanced applications, put under the rubric of "virtual reality," have been tracked by the *Training* survey since 1997. As with games and simulations, it would not be expected that virtual reality media would be applicable across the whole range of training content or objectives. So it probably makes more sense to track how many organizations use it at all, not how many use it often or always. Counted this way, around 20 percent of organizations make some use of virtual reality training methods (Dolezalek, 2004, p. 32), as shown in Figure 14. Unexpectedly, this category shows little evidence of increase over the past several years.

Figure 14. Percentage of organizations using virtual reality. (For 1997–2000, figure shows those who use "ever." For 2001–2004, figure shows those who use "seldom," "always," or "often.") Source: Dolezalek, 2004.

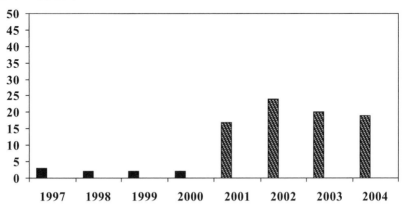

Taken together, information and communications technology (ICT) delivery now accounts for roughly a quarter of the time spent in training. This proportion has not been growing at a steady pace over the years, and some indicators actually fell in the most recent surveys. However, it is predicable that ICT-based instruction will grow, if only because so many companies, in the face of global competition, make changes in their products and services at an accelerating rate. These changes usually entail some employee and customer training, at least of the informational type. This sort of training is highly time-critical, and delivery through an ICT channel can be done faster and cheaper and can be updated more easily than by using live-classroom instruction or print materials sent through the mail.

Issue 2: Constraints on Acceptance and Use of Technology

The global business cycle is probably the largest constraint to rapid expansion of ICT-based learning. The business economy drifted downward after 2000 but was showing continuing recovery in 2004 and 2005. Spending on technology was on the rise again after a period of contraction.

E-learning remains a tempting prospect for improving return-on-investment (ROI) in training. However, there does not seem to be a simple recipe for substituting cheap e-learning for expensive face-to-face instruction. E-learning initiatives require substantial front-end investments in equipment and materials as well as in development time and talent. E-learning obviously works as well as other forms of instruction when the objective is merely information transmission. For more advanced cognitive skills or skills in the interpersonal, affective, and motor domains, more sophisticated pedagogical methods are necessary, whether delivering face-to-face or for ICT formats. The secret still lies in involving learners in engaging, challenging real-world tasks and guiding their budding abilities to accomplish those tasks (Merrill, in press). To the extent that e-learning can provide such a learning environment, it will grow and prosper.

Unfortunately, e-learning courses often suffer a high attrition rate, indicating either that trainees often enter with insufficient reason for staying or that the instructional methods they encounter fail to hold them. A text-heavy, didactic approach is commonly found in e-learning courses, which contrasts sharply with the problem-based, inductive approach advocated for adult learners seeking usable skills.

Issue 3: Challenges to Existing Paradigms

Blended Learning. In the past, trainers tended to classify learning events into discrete categories: face-to-face classroom instruction, online learning, self-directed study, action learning, and so on. In today's corporate training programs, however, learning events increasingly consist of combinations of different formats and methods. An example from management training would be a hybrid course consisting of (1) a kick-off session in a face-to-face setting with a facilitator; (2) a self-study period of four hours of online study to be completed over two weeks; (3) coaching sessions by telephone, one per week, with a mentor; and (4) bimonthly review sessions in which small groups discuss their progress and share ideas.

Such hybrids have come to be recognized as a "third path," referred to as blended learning. The advantages of combining formats are obvious. Online activities offer self-pacing, standardization of information dissemination, and rapid deployment of new material; while face-to-face learning allows practice with feedback, team building, networking, and the other functions that are tied to people's emotional responses.

The trend toward blended learning has been under way for at least five years but is probably still early on the adoption curve, with many organizations still at the awareness or trial stages. There is potential for much more widespread adoption in the coming years. An indicator of the strong foothold of this new paradigm is indicated in the finding cited earlier in this section that face-to-face instruction continues to be employed at as many organizations as ever while *at the same time* e-learning formats are taking off in terms of more and more frequent use. How can both modes be flourishing? By being used as complements to each other in the form of blended learning.

Workflow Learning. Learning needs are escalating while the time available shrinks. Organizations are loath to pay for the downtime involved in sending employees to training. What they learn during formal training doesn't seem to stick or to last very long. What is the answer? Workflow learning, learning that is embedded in everyday work, learning activities available on demand.

This concept came to the fore as the cover story for the February 2005 issue of *Training* magazine, although it had been brewing for some time. As cited earlier, Merrill's (in press) synthesis of instructional principles indicates that at least for cognitive learning, we process and remember best what is relevant to our immediate needs and what is practiced in a realistic setting. So the idea is to embed the training in the job itself.

Cross and O'Driscoll (2005) relate workflow learning to the earlier concept of electronic performance support systems (EPSS): "workflow learning is networked EPSS, operating in an environment where the worker is plugged into the job and learning is delivered in small chunks as it is needed" (p. 32). Although this concept has elements of older, more familiar practices, it can be seen as a whole different paradigm for thinking about training. Instead of starting with the assumption that training takes place away from the job, workflow learning starts with the assumption that learning opportunities can be embedded in the work.

We are still at an early stage of figuring out how to analyze workflow learning needs and then design and develop the mechanisms for facilitating it. This is one of the exciting challenges facing the field.

HIGHER EDUCATION

As we have previously explained, the use of instructional technology in higher education is similar to the corporate sector in that it is affected by both external economic forces and internal sociocultural influences. The downturn of the U.S. national economy beginning in 2000 and continuing through 2003 led to severe shortfalls in state tax revenues, which led to tightening of budgets at most state-supported universities and eventually at private institutions as well. These budget reductions in turn forced cutbacks in planned information technology upgrades or expansions. Although the business cycle began improving in 2004, those improvements had not begun to ripple into college and university budgets by 2005.

Government financial support is not the only economic issue. In any organization, investment in new technology tends to be driven by the expectation of payoffs, particularly economic payoffs—increases in benefits or decreases in costs. In the case of higher education, information technology has begun to pay off in terms of administrative costs and improvement of student services and other auxiliary activities at a more affordable cost. But information technology has not proven to be a cost-reducer on the educational side of operations. Indeed, as long as universities are organized as they are (teacher-centered decision making, professors as independent operators, decentralized academic fiefdoms), there is little possibility to reduce instructional costs. So instructional technology advocates are left with the claim that benefits increase: greater numbers of students reached, students more satisfied, faculty more content or productive (or both), and the like. This benefits argument is not as potent as the economic one, so the provision of technology support tends to be lower in the academic arena than in other parts of the administration.

In any event, the tempo of educational change is driven as much by the dynamics of sociocultural forces within colleges and universities themselves as by economics: by whom instructional decisions are made, whose interests have priority, and how rewards are allocated. In this section, we examine how these forces interact to affect the pace at which technologies are adopted and the manner in which they are used.

Issue 1: Use of Technology-Based Media for Delivery of Instruction

Classroom Media: Analog and Digital Media. In past years, we treated traditional audiovisual media and digital media in two distinct sections. As discussed earlier, one of the overall trends in instructional technology is the convergence of media formats—analog and digital, and higher education has taken a lead in this regard. It has become an increasingly difficult exercise to organize a discussion of media so that analog and digital media are treated separately.

In fact, two important developments in higher education this year are examples of this convergence. One development is the introduction of an Internet-based campus television network. College television stations, which have as long a history (although admittedly a less glamorous) as commercial stations, received a huge boost in distribution and viewership when the Open Student Television Network went online in Spring 2005 (http://www.ostn.tv). The network uses streaming video to air shows from the campus television stations of thirty-three schools that use Internet2's high-speed network (Young, 2005). Although viewership is somewhat limited at this time because of the Internet2 membership requirement, the potential viewership for the college television stations that are involved with this project is still much greater than it would be without the online network, and it will likely grow as more universities become members of Internet2.

The second development will likely be a slower one, and its unclear as yet how issues will be resolved, but the outcome will be important for higher education and interesting to watch. This development has to do with the emergence of electronic books ("ebooks") and the future role of traditional print-based textbooks on college campuses. The ever-increasing costs of textbooks along with the advancement of wireless computing and tablet PCs are key factors that are influencing this situation. The fact that the University of Phoenix, the nation's largest private university, has eliminated print textbooks and replaced them with all digital resources has certainly added urgency to this discussion (Marketwire, 2005). It is not yet clear how rapidly textbooks will become digitized, but the stakes are enormous.

Course Management Systems. The big story in terms of student contact with technology in the classroom is course management systems (CMS). The Market Data Retrieval Service (2005a) reports that virtually all higher education institutions now use course management systems (compared with only 83 percent when they first started collecting such data in 2002). The most popular course management systems continue to be Blackboard, which is supported in 51 percent of higher education institutions, and WebCT, which is adopted by 32 percent of institutions. Blackboard's biggest competitor is viewed by industry watchers at *BusinessWeek* as the open-source software collaborative between Stanford, MIT, Michigan, and Indiana University that has been dubbed "The Sakai Project" (Yang, 2004). As explained in this chapter last year (Molenda & Bichelmeyer, 2005), the goal of the Sakai Project is to provide high-quality open source code for a range of applications, especially a new and improved CMS. Through the shared development process the consortium hopes to innovate more quickly than for-profit competitors and to reduce the costly licensing fees that must be paid by colleges and universities.

In the meantime, college students seem to be relatively satisfied with their experiences using CMSs. Eighty-three percent of respondents to a 2004 EDUCAUSE survey have taken a class that had a course management system, and of those students, 76 percent felt positive or very positive about the experience, whereas 17 percent expressed neutral feelings, and only 7 percent expressed some level of negative feelings about the experience (Kvavik, Caruso, & Morgan, 2004). This seems to be an exceptionally positive response to a software application that is still in its early stages of development, and this bodes well for the future of CMSs.

Emerging Digital Technology. "Clickers" are popping up on college campuses (Wired News, 2005). Personal response systems, also known as audience response systems, are being adopted by many universities for use in the classroom, primarily in the sciences. They are novel enough that there are not yet reliable estimates as to the extent of adoption or how effectively they are being used for improving learning. This is a technology ripe for research. If you are not familiar with what clickers are or how they are used, refer to the K–12 section titled "Emerging Digital Technologies" later in this chapter.

Distance Education. When the dot-com bubble burst in March 2000, it signaled the beginning of the collapse of the most highly touted new U.S. distance education (DE) initiatives. Then in 2004 the major British effort, UK eUniversities Worldwide (UKeU), was dismantled. As further indication of the fading of the land-rush mentality, in EDUCAUSE's annual survey of top issues facing administrators, for "issues with a high potential for becoming significant in the coming year," distance education dropped from first place in 2001 to off-the-chart in 2004 (Spicer et al., 2004).

Curiously, at the same time dot-coms were deteriorating into dot-compost many more modest DE programs were quietly gaining a foothold. Leading the way were proprietary institutions such as University of Phoenix Online, Jones International University, and Capella University. Their initial success in attracting enrollment drew the attention of planners at mainstream residential colleges and universities. They were not only enrolling increasing numbers of students, they were making a profit. This was an enticing prospect for the administrators of not-for-profit institutions, who saw DE as a way to increase their revenue stream and slow the loss of enrollments.

By 2003, the great majority of all residential four-year colleges and universities and two-year community colleges operated DE programs; for large public universities the proportion was about 90 percent. Figure 15 shows the growth between 2002 and 2003 and the breakdown among public and private institutions.

Figure 15. Percent of institutions offering online courses. Source: Allen & Seaman, 2004, p. 6.

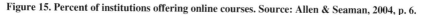

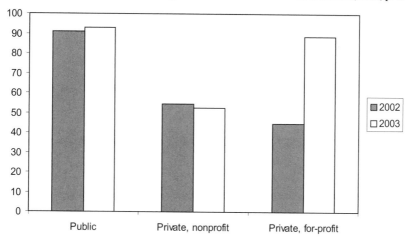

The most comprehensive survey of online enrollments, conducted by the Sloan Consortium in 2004, shows that 1.6 million students in the United States were taking at least one online course in the fall of 2002; by the fall of 2003, this number had grown to 1.97 million, a year-to-year growth rate of 23 percent (Allen & Seaman, 2004). The respondents in this survey also predicted that enrollments would continue to grow at that rate for 2004. Two universities that have reported DE enrollment data for fall 2004 are University of Maryland University College, which grew by 15 percent over the previous year, and University of Illinois Springfield, which grew by 28 percent. These data indicate a continuing healthy increase into 2004. At both these institutions the proportion of students enrolled in online courses versus face-to-face courses is increasing, leading to speculation about an enrollment "tipping point" at which the character of a traditional campus will change (SchWeber, 2005).

Among dual-mode institutions (those with both residential and distance programs), an operational model that appears promising is the consortium approach—a group of universities having a common portal, sharing course development and marketing costs, but facilitating enrollment at any one of the participating schools. Over thirty states have formed such distance learning consortia, and some have experienced growth above the average for individual institutions. For example, UMassOnline enrolled 17,000 students in 2004, up 19 percent over 2003, and Illinois Virtual Campus reported 80,000 enrollments in fall 2004, an increase of 60 percent over fall 2003.

Interestingly, the audience for DE programs at dual-mode universities seems to be shifting. DE programs initially targeted such "nontraditional" niche groups as single mothers, employed adults, people with disabilities, and those living in remote areas. By 2005, these programs were becoming more fully integrated into the universities' traditional programs, drawing many students who are already enrolled in regular on-campus courses of study.

During the years 2000–2005 much of the expansion in online enrollments went to the proprietary, for-profit institutions, but nonprofit institutions have been offering more and more competition, slowing their overall loss of enrollments. The growth of online programs has become so significant that in 2004, for the first time, *US News & World Report* included a section on online graduate programs in its annual college rating issue.

Issue 2: Constraints on Acceptance and Use of Technology

Administrative Issues—Funding. Financial reports for campus instructional technology (IT) have been decidedly bleak since the downturn of the national economy in 2000. In 2004, there were mixed signals regarding the financial condition of campus IT programs. The number of campus IT programs that reported budget cuts for *academic* computing dropped from 41.3 percent in 2003 to 24.3 percent in the 2004 Campus Computing Survey (which is good news). Also, the number of campus IT programs that reported budget cuts for *administrative* computing dropped from 42.3 percent in 2003 to 25.3 percent in 2004 (Campus Computing Project, 2004). Clearly, it would be a more positive report if we were able to say that there have been actual budget gains; however, being able to report decreases in budget cuts is certainly a trend toward the positive. Campus IT budgets are obviously still tight, and for many higher education institutions (more public colleges and universities than private ones), budgets continue to decline.

One result of this ongoing difficult budget situation is, for the third consecutive year, that campus IT officials report IT funding as their main concern and the issue that consumes most of their professional time (Maltz et al., 2005).

Figure 16 reveals a variety of the strategies that Indiana University administrators are considering and planning to implement to contain campus computing costs in their efforts to live within their declining budgets (Goldstein & Caruso, 2004).

Some of the most widely considered strategies that have been considered include sharing of purchases through consortia relationships and shared technology implementation as well as the use of open source programs. The most likely strategies to be used, however, will be across-the-board cuts, cuts in renewal and replacement costs, and cuts in the number of technologies that require support.

Faculty Acceptance of Instructional Technologies. The burgeoning of course management systems (CMS) has triggered an interesting payoff for improved teaching. Most institutions now support a single primary CMS and encourage individual instructors to make at least minimal use of the system. A recent study casts light on the reasons why professors decide to make use of a CMS and the how that adoption decision leads to later pedagogical consequences.

Morgan's (2003) study of 730 faculty members in the University of Wisconsin system, including a survey and further interviews, found that successful adoption took place against a background of active administrative encouragement. Typically, a shell was set up for each course on campus, and faculty were invited to use it or ignore it. Enforced adoption by administrative decree tended to lead to resentment and early abandonment. A more laissez-faire approach allowed curiosity to arise and for peer support to evolve naturally.

Respondents' major explicit reason for using the CMS (chosen by 34 percent) was pedagogical, particularly to 1) increase discussion among students, 2) post grades online, 3) provide additional course materials, or 4) address individual differences. Most users (62 percent) said that their usage increased over time, whereas 33 percent remained at the same level and only 5 percent decreased their usage.

Figure 16. Cost-containment strategies. Source: Goldstein & Caruso, 2004, p. 5.

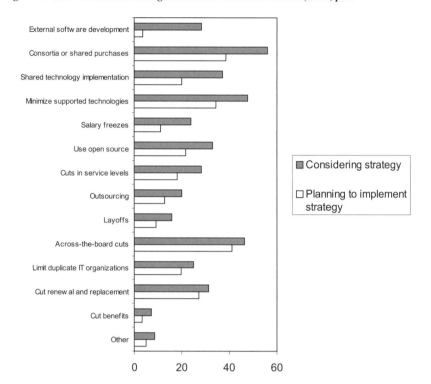

Most interestingly, the findings suggest that the initial level of adoption seems to serve as a wedge that expands to encompass more and larger changes. Professors report that they tend to use the CMS more and more extensively because they gradually see more potential uses of its features. It begins with content presentation tools, and for some it ends there. But many users go on to make use of the discussion forums, quiz tools, and gradebooks. Thus many are drawn step by step into ever more sophisticated uses, uses that yield more learning benefits for students.

For generations, predating the digital age, teachers have been coming to terms with new technologies. Especially at the college level, instructors have traditionally been slow to adopt technologies that require a change in their power relationships or alteration of their teaching routine. Online distance education presents a challenge on both issues because it removes the instructor from face-to-face contact with students, requires the use of methods other than oral presentation, relies on a technical infrastructure that is largely beyond the control of the instructor, and often entails a team effort in development.

Given the extra time demands needed to develop and maintain online courses and the altered role played by the online instructor, it is not difficult to anticipate faculty resistance to distance teaching. Nevertheless, a growing number of faculty do accept this challenge every year. If DE is to continue to grow, it will need to have the support of increasing numbers of faculty, which requires an understanding of the sources of resistance and possible avenues to bypass these barriers. An earlier study of faculty attitudes toward DE (National Education Association, 2000) found that those teaching distance courses received little if any extra compensation and believed that they invested more hours in the job, yet they indicated a high level of satisfaction and willingness to continue.

A more recent study tapped the perceptions of 913 professors teaching online courses in the state of New York system. It found that 90 percent of respondents were satisfied with the course they were teaching, and 96 percent were satisfied with online teaching in general (Shea, Pickett, & Li, 2005). Those who taught residential courses at the same time as distance courses were asked to compare student performance in the online and face-to-face settings. As shown in Figure 17, 48 percent felt there was no difference, and 41 percent felt that the online students actually performed better; only 11 percent rated the in-class students' performance as better. Fully 98 percent said they were willing to teach an online course again!

These happy findings must be read with some caution, however. The response rate to the survey was 34 percent, and there is every reason to suspect that those who responded were those who were more invested in DE. Nevertheless, even among technology enthusiasts this would be quite a ringing endorsement.

Shea et al. (2005) went on to explore the factors that were associated with faculty satisfaction. Their first finding corresponded closely with a finding of the National Education Association study that "high levels of interaction are frequently mentioned as one of the potentially positive aspects of online teaching" (Shea et al., p. 13). In both studies, respondents indicated that they had a higher level of interaction with their online students and tended to form stronger personal bonds with them, and they found this a gratifying outcome. They also found that the new environment of online teaching forced them to reflect more deeply about teaching and to develop new teaching skills. Finally, this group of faculty experienced a course management system that was relatively easy to use and has solid technical support. These conditions contributed significantly to their satisfaction.

Figure 17. Faculty perception of online and live-classroom students' performance. Source: Shea, Pickett, & Li, 2005.

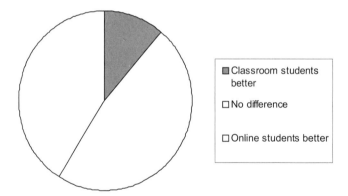

These findings suggest that resistance to online teaching can be overcome and that there are inherent rewards, particularly the gratification of forming close bonds with students and seeing them succeed, that draw professors to online teaching.

Student Acceptance of Instructional Technologies. The EDUCAUSE Center for Applied Research conducted a mixed method study during 2004 that included surveys of nearly 4,500 freshman and seniors at 13 higher education institutions and focus group interviews with 132 students at 6 higher education institutions (Kvavik et al., 2004). Results from the study provide a rich description of students' experiences and attitudes related to campus computing.

The computer applications most commonly used by students are word processing (99.5 percent), electronic mail (99.5 percent), recreational Internet surfing (97.2 percent), and for course activities (96.4 percent). More than 81 percent have broadband access to the

Internet through university or commercial services, and the remainder access the Internet through dial-up modems.

Students rate themselves as highly skilled at using computers for communication, word processing, and the Internet and less skilled at creating and editing audio, graphics, and video. There was some discrepancy between students' self-ratings and interview data, which indicated that, beyond basic functions in Microsoft Office, students have just enough technical knowledge to accomplish their work and are lacking in-depth knowledge of even the most popular computer applications.

Most students prefer that faculty use a moderate amount of technology when teaching their classes, as opposed to extensive use or limited use. The biggest complaints from students about faculty's misuse of computers during courses were 1) overreliance on PowerPoint during presentations, 2) wasting class time while dealing with hardware issues, and 3) requiring online discussions when faculty do not monitor them, provide feedback in the discussion space, or comment about the discussions during class meetings.

The greatest benefit of using computers in classes, according to half of the student respondents, was convenience. Another big benefit that was cited was "saving time." Perhaps the most troubling finding of the study is that only 13 percent of the students cited improved learning as the most valuable benefit of classroom computer use. The problem with educational computing cited by the most students (17 percent) was that using computers "feels like extra work" (p. 13). Fourteen percent of students complained about applications not working on their computers. Thirteen percent of students identified lack of access to printers as a problem. About 10 percent of students said the lack of technical support is a barrier to classroom IT use.

Issue 4: Emerging Themes

IT Accessibility for Students with Disabilities. One unforeseen consequence of the effort of higher education institutions to move more of their classroom and administrative resources onto the Internet is that these same institutions are likely moving further out of compliance with the Americans with Disabilities Act of 1990 and the Rehabilitation Act of 1998, both of which require all public entities and recipients of federal funds to ensure that individuals with disabilities have access to programs and services equal to their nondisabled fellow citizens.

In sum, this means that higher education institutions must make certain that their information technology hardware, software, operating systems, products, programs, services, Web sites, multimedia, and interactive digital materials are fully accessible to individuals with disabilities. This is no small task, and it is an important one. It's also a goal toward which we have a long way to go.

Slightly more than 50 percent of the 91 institutions surveyed as part of an EDUCAUSE study have a staff member dedicated to addressing issues of Web accessibility. Just less than two-thirds of these institutions have Web accessibility policies, and just more than one-third have IT accessibility policies. Figure 18 identifies several promising practices for improving IT accessibility and shows the percent of surveyed institutions that are taking each of these steps (Thompson, 2005).

Figure 18. Percent of institutions taking steps to improve IT accessibility. Source: Thompson, 2005, p. 4.

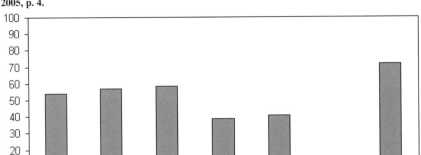

Lest we delude ourselves into thinking this is a problem that only affects a small number of higher education students, Figure 19 shows the number of registered students with disabilities at the thirty-nine institutions that were able to report these data.

Twenty percent of reporting institutions reported have less than 250 registered students with disabilities, 33 percent have between 250 and 499 students with disabilities, 20 percent have between 500 and 750 students with disabilities, and 25 percent have more than 750 registered students with disabilities (Thompson, 2005).

Clearly, this is a large-scale issue that will only become larger as the use of information technology comes to pervade every aspect of life in higher education.

Figure 19. Institution by number of students with disabilities. Source: Thompson, 2005, p. 9.

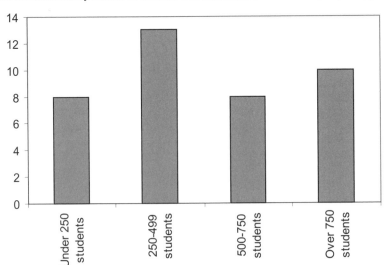

K–12 EDUCATION

In last year's chapter (Molenda & Bichelmeyer, 2005), we noted that, although computers and networks have become ubiquitous in schools, the focus has changed from using computers for teaching and learning to using them for assessment. This shift, driven by President George W. Bush's No Child Left Behind (NCLB) initiative, is a boon to the for-profit educational technology industry, putting the primary focus of computer use on computer-based assessment and the warehousing of assessment results.

This year, we see the natural progression of that initiative, with further forays of the for-profit education industry into the educational technology sector through the development and marketing of test-preparation software. Furthermore, federal funds for educational technology may be redistributed through the elimination of the Enhancing Education Through Technology federal grant program, which will decrease funding for educational technology to cash-strapped states while providing more funds through block grants to for-profit vendors who are aggressively marketing to the poorer school districts that are struggling to meet NCLB requirements.

Issue 1: Use of Technology-Based Media for Delivery of Instruction

The story this year regarding the use of technology for delivery of instruction is that there is no story—or at least not much of a story. Our prediction last year that one consequence of the NCLB legislation would be to increase the use of computers for data warehousing and database management appears to have had merit.

Data Management versus Delivery of Instruction. In a recent survey of state education representatives regarding their state's top two priorities in spending for education technology this year, sixteen listed data management as a priority, the second most frequent response with only professional development receiving more responses (*Education Week,* 2005). Figure 20 shows the relative lack of interest in using technology for instruction, with only five states citing integration of technology with instruction as a priority and four states citing curriculum software as a priority, and two states listed laptop programs as a priority.

Figure 20. State priorities. Source: *Education Week,* May 5, 2005, p. 38.

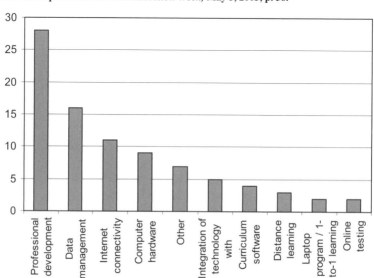

The 2005 *Education Week* Technology Counts issue reported that "educational technology spending priorities of the nations' largest school districts appear to be leaning heavily toward technologies that help educators analyze student-achievement data and then adjust their teaching based on what those results show" (Gehring, 2005, p. 38).

SchoolMatters (http://www.schoolmatters.com), a partnership of nonprofit and for-profit agencies, is one of the first efforts to take advantage of the development of these databases. A $45 million project of the National Education Data Partnership, the goal of the initiative is to make education data such as student demographics, student achievement scores, and school finance figures available to the public.

As the NCLB initiative has turned student assessment into a lucrative market through data warehousing, we predict that we will see more for-profit education technology companies following the lead of the Educational Testing Service, which announced in March 2005 that it will enter the K–12 formative-assessment market (Olson, 2005).

Figure 21. Percentage of schools having wireless networks, by school type. Source: Market Data Retrieval Service, 2005b.

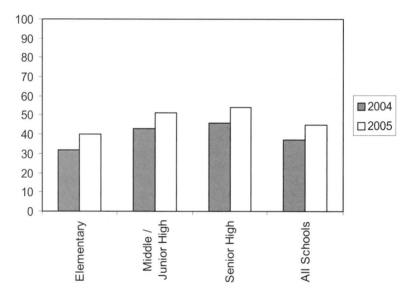

Computer-based Media. Laptop computers and wireless networks were two leading-edge technologies in schools that showed significant growth during the past year. Laptops accounted for a fair amount of new hardware purchases by schools. The overall inventory of laptops in schools increased four percent in just one year, from 13 percent to 17 percent of total computer inventory. Mobile computers were available in 54 percent of all K–12 schools during 2004 (Market Data Retrieval Service, 2005b). At all school levels, the percentage of buildings that have wireless networks continues to grow. Figure 21 shows that secondary schools have the highest percentage of wireless networks (54 percent), whereas 51 percent of middle schools and 40 percent of elementary schools report having wireless networks (Market Data Retrieval Service, 2005b).

The historical benchmark for technology integration in schools has been the "students per instructional computer" ratio, which dropped slightly from 4.0:1 in 2003 to 3.8:1 in 2004, whereas the student-per-Internet-connected computer ratio dropped from 4.3:1 in 2003 to 4.1:1 in 2004 (*Education Week,* 2005). Though *Education Week* reports that these are the recommended ratios of the U.S. Department of Education for technology integration, two-thirds of the teachers who participated in the CDW-G "Teachers Talk Tech" 2004 survey felt that they do not have the right number of computers in their classrooms, and 55 percent felt that the lack of computers for students to use is a "very" or "extremely" serious problem (Rother, 2004, p. 46). The disparity between the Education Department recommendations and these teachers' concerns about student-computer ratios may reflect the long-debated issue of whether computers serve learners better when located in classrooms or in computer labs. We predict that the issue of where computers are located in schools will become less problematic as more schools install wireless networks, because it will become easier to locate Internet-connected computers throughout the building.

Traditional Audiovisual Media. Analog audiovisual (AV) collections are still used in K–12 schools, and they will likely continue to be used as long as the media are in good repair but will eventually be replaced with media in digital AV formats. As we reported previously, new purchases of video tend to be in digital format, so over time we should expect to see the percentage of digital AV materials increasing while analog AV materials will decrease.

This shift from analog to digital audiovisual is also evident in the 2005 Bi-Annual Survey of the National Association of Media & Technology Centers (NAMTC). The forty-eight education service agencies (representing 35 percent of institutional members) that responded to the survey indicated they are taking on increasing responsibility for providing technical support related to technology integration and to the implementation of emerging technologies (Ehlinger, 2005). Figure 22 shows that while video circulation activities continue at a high level without drop-off, services related to tech equipment, video streaming, videoconferencing, and other electronic resources have increased since 2003.

Emerging Digital Technologies. Last year we reported that handheld PCs were finding entry into schools, where students were using them as digital readers and graphing calculators, for word processing and spreadsheet creation, and for specific instructional activities, such as concept mapping.

This year we are seeing the emergence of a more specific type of handheld device that is in keeping with the emphasis on assessment resulting from the NCLB initiative. "Clickers," or personal response systems, are small electronic devices that look similar to a television remote control. Clickers allow students to answer multiple-choice quiz questions during a classroom activity and have the results immediately tallied and presented on a computer screen. Companies such as eInstruction, HyperActive Teaching Technology, Promethean Limited, and Qwizdom market these devices to schools. Clickers are promoted as being valuable for helping students prepare for testing and for providing teachers with immediate feedback on instructional strategies by taking a measure of what students are learning. Critics of this emerging technology are concerned that their emphasis on multiple-choice measures are simplistic and emphasize trivial learning over complex and higher-order thinking (Trotter, 2005).

Teacher Computer Use. The good news according to *Education Week* (2005) is that forty states have technology standards for teachers. Additionally, twenty states have a technology test or technology training as requirements for teachers' initial licensure or endorsement, and ten states have a technology test or technology training as requirements for teachers' recertification. The bad news, according to *Education Week,* is that many of these states do not have enforcement policies to ensure that teachers meet the standards which have been set.

Figure 22. Services provided by Education Service Agencies. Source: Ehlinger, 2005, p. 11.

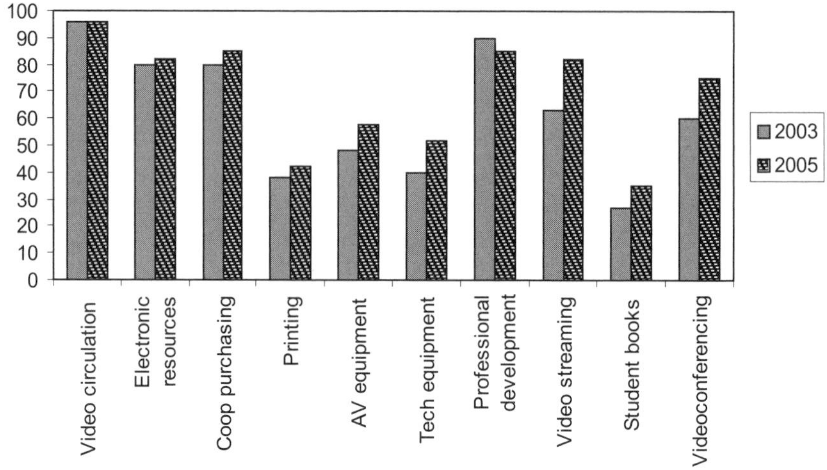

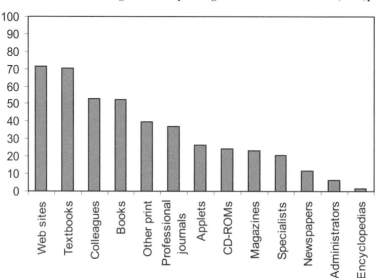

Still, teachers appear to be developing more positive views about the value of technology for helping students learn than they have had in the past. The 2004 "Teachers Talk Tech" survey found that 81 percent of the teachers who participated believe that classroom computer availability increases student academic performance, and 62 percent think that computers help students perform better on standardized tests (Rother, 2004).

The majority of teachers also find benefits in using Web resources for preparation of lesson plans and for teaching in the classroom. A study by Hanson and Carlson (2005) found that teachers use Web sites more than any other resource, including textbooks, for curriculum planning. These teachers also reported using Web sites more than any other resource except textbooks during classroom instruction (see Figures 23a and 23b).

Figure 23a. Resources used during curriculum planning. Source: Hanson & Carlson, 2005, p. 24.

Figure 23b. Resources used during instruction. Source: Hanson & Carlson, 2005, p. 24.

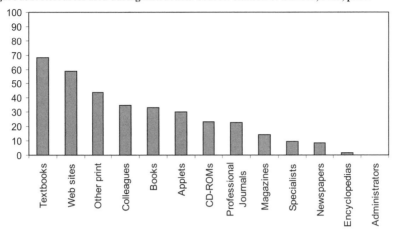

One reason teachers give high marks to Web sites may be because they have less regard for another type of digital resource: the educational software programs available in their schools. Only 45 percent of teachers rated software as "good" or "excellent," and 52 percent rated software as "Just OK" or "poor" (Rother, 2004). Interestingly, one-third of all school districts have a requirement that only software or online content that is backed by scientifically based research may be purchased (Market Data Retrieval Service, 2005b). Again, this reflects current national education policies, the merits of which could be discussed at length.

Student Computer Use. Not surprisingly, research supports the everyday observation that the majority of children and adolescents use computers and the Internet with some frequency. But *which* children use computers and how frequently? Figure 24 shows that children's use of computers begins when they are very young: 67 percent of nursery schoolers and 80 percent of kindergartners are computers users. Twenty-three percent of nursery schoolers and 32 percent of kindergartners also use the Internet. By high school, nearly all students (97 percent) use computers, and a great majority (80 percent) use the Internet (U.S. Department of Education, 2005).

Figure 24. Percentage children enrolled pre-K through 12 using computers and Internet. Source: United States Department of Education (2005), p. 2.

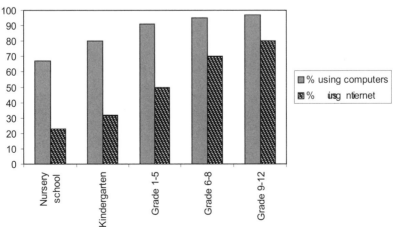

The really interesting story is about *how* adolescents are using computers. Would you believe that young people between the ages of eight and eighteen years old spend an average of nearly *6.5 hours a day* with media? One-third of two thousand third- through twelfth-graders who completed a survey by Kaiser Family Foundation from fall 2003 to spring 2004 are media multitaskers. These children and adolescents describe their media usage as chatting on the phone, surfing the Web, sending instant messages, watching TV, or listening to music "most of the time" while they are also doing their homework (Rideout, Roberts, & Foehr, 2005). The researchers at Kaiser Family Foundation have aptly labeled these young people as "Generation M," with M standing for media.

The imbalance between young people's in-school learning and out-of-school media use is well noted by Komoski (2005), who calculates that children's at-home investment of almost 6.5 hours a day in non-school-related media use, compared with their in-school investment of 3.8 hours a day (five 45-minute periods) in core academic classes during a 180-day school year totaling 700 hours, creates a 3-to-1 imbalance of recreational media use over in-school learning. Komoski presents an even more depressing thought for educators: "if we take into account research by David Berliner and others showing that during the typical 45-minute academic class, students are seldom engaged in on-task learning for more than a third of class time, the 3-to-1 imbalance balloons to 9-to-1. By either measure, this demonstrates a large time-attention learning imbalance for some 50 million 8 to 18 year olds" (p. 37).

If educational technologists are looking for a cause for concern, this would certainly be a good candidate.

Equity in Access. As we reported in the section on student computer use, most students today use computers, so it may be fair to say that we have achieved a measure of equity in that respect. The "new digital divide" has to do with the students who do and do not use the Internet. The majority of students who currently do *not* use the Internet include Black (non-Hispanic) and Hispanic students, students in households where Spanish is the only language spoken, students whose family income is under $20,000, students in poverty, and students whose parents have less than a high school credential (U.S. Department of Education, 2005).

One factor that may be contributing to the new digital divide is likely the mismanagement of the E-rate program, established by Congress in 1996 to provide more than $2 billion per year for Internet access to the poorest schools and libraries in the country. In recent years, the E-rate program has faced allegations of fraud, waste, and abuse, with federal prosecutors bringing charges against schools and districts in Atlanta, New York, San Francisco, and Puerto Rico, among other locales. This situation led to a temporary E-rate freeze and an audit from the U.S. Government Accountability Office (GAO) in 2004. The GAO report released in March 2005 criticized the Federal Communications Commission (FCC), which administers the program, for poor management and lax oversight. The GAO recommended that the FCC create accountability requirements for the E-Rate and establish performance goals and measures for the program (United States Government Accountability Office, 2005). It is hoped that improved management of the E-Rate program will help to minimize the gaps in Internet access that we currently face.

Another concern that has recently emerged related to the equity of technology integration is the targeting by education software vendors of poor schools that are struggling to meet NCLB student achievement requirements. These vendors are promoting sales of what are sometimes referred to disparagingly as "drill and kill" programs that may lead to an achievement gap on standardized tests. If we were to give an Annual Award for Investigative Journalism in Instructional Technology (which we would likely name the "IJIT" award), the winner for 2004 would be the *Baltimore Sun,* for a brilliant exposé in a week-long series of articles about the questionable strategies and tactics of for-profit education software vendors and how these vendors prey on poorer, struggling schools that have access to millions of dollars in federal funding to support their improvement ("Poor Schools, Rich Targets," 2004). The reports include descriptions of all-expense paid international trips for school administrators, riverboat cruises during the National Education Computing Conference in New Orleans, influencing in-school trials of education software, and the trail of money that connects education software vendor companies with elected officials in Washington. If nothing else, this series reveals that big money is linked to the integration of educational technology in public schools.

Issue 2: Constraints on Acceptance and Use of Technology

Funding. Speaking of big money, the big news of the past year was the roller-coaster ride of changing federal positions on funding for educational technology. Along with the E-rate program, the other federal mechanism that provides the majority of educational technology funding to public schools is the Educational Technology State Grants program, also known as the Enhancing Education through Technology (E2T2) program, which was signed into law as part of the No Child Left Behind Act. In late November 2004, Congress passed an omnibus appropriations bill that cut $191 million (27.7 percent) of these educational technology funds for 2005. In January 2005, the U.S. Department of Education released a new National Education Technology Plan that emphasizes the importance of educational technology for preparing learners to meet the challenges of the twenty-first-century global society. On February 7, 2005, President Bush released his 2006 budget proposal with a cut of $500 million to the E2T2 program, in effect eliminating in its entirety the primary source of federal funding for educational technology (eSchool Newsonline, 2005a). On July 12, 2005, the Senate Appropriations Subcommittee on Labor, Health and Human Services, and Education reached a decision to provide $425 million in funding for the E2T2 program for 2006. At the time of this writing, the decision was pending for a vote from the full Senate Appropriations Committee (eSchool Newsonline, 2005c).

Administration officials argued for the proposed elimination of E2T2 because student-computer ratios have reached recommended levels and because they say technology can be better blended into teaching and learning through the use of Title I grants and other federal funds. Critics of the E2T2 cuts argued that schools continue to need funding for replacement and upgrade of computers, as well as for ongoing training of teachers who are still uncomfortable with their computer skills (*Education Week,* 2005).

The current administration's shifting position signals that something different is happening as we continue on our way toward computer integration. After more than fifteen years of focused effort to get computers into schools, during the past year federal officials and school administrators alike have shifted attention from procurement to maintenance of the equipment we have spent past years acquiring. One manifestation of this shift is the increasing popularity among school administrators of a concept known as "total cost of ownership" (TCO). TCO is a calculation taken from business that attempts to determine what the real costs are of implementing technology, by factoring in hidden costs such as support, replacement, retrofitting, connectivity, and software (Hurst, 2005).

Despite the possible cuts in federal funding, a remarkable 30 percent of school districts have projected increases in their technology budgets for 2006 (Market Data Retrieval Service, 2005b). Of course, this also means that 70 percent of school districts project flat or decreased spending, and we all know there is a difference between budget projections and actual funding. Come back next year to see how these districts fared with their projections.

Professional Development. For as long as educators have been working to integrate computers in schools, research and evaluations have shown that not enough money is being spent on teacher professional development and that teachers' perceptions about what little professional development they get are that it is not well-suited to their needs (Bichelmeyer, 1991; eSchool Newsonline, 2005b; Gehring, 2005; Hanson & Carlson, 2005; Maryland

Business Roundtable for Education, 2005; Rother, 2004; U.S. Department of Education, 2003). Sadly, this failing continues.

Barriers to Use of Technology. Not surprisingly, one of the biggest barriers to technology integration in schools is lack of quality professional development for teachers. Other barriers to the use of technology cited by teachers include having too few computers in the classroom and lack of time to plan for computer use, both of which are also perennial issues related to technology integration (eSchool Newsonline, 2005b; Rother, 2004; U.S. Department of Education, 2003).

Technology Support. While we're discussing old news, the amount of technology support provided to support teachers and maintain equipment in schools is still problematic (Hanson & Carlson, 2005). There is, however, an interesting solution to this problem that is becoming popular in many schools. Students are serving as technology support personnel (Borja, 2004a). State funding and grant programs are springing up to train students to provide technical support, set up and maintain equipment, and troubleshoot problems that arise. This seems to be evolving as a win-win solution that helps schools keep equipment up and running while providing skills and experience that help students find good jobs when they leave school.

Issue 3: Challenges to Existing Paradigms

Distance Education. The number and popularity of DE programs at the K–12 level continue to increase, primarily because of the growth of virtual schools. Important stakeholders are not only taking notice, they are jumping on the bandwagon.

In the first large-scale, federal-government-sponsored study of distance education since virtual schools have become an option, the National Center for Education Statistics found that students in more than one-third of public school districts enroll in distance education courses, with greater proportions of these students being from large districts, districts with relatively high socioeconomic status, and from rural areas of the country. Seventy-six percent of students enrolled in distance education are in high school, 15 percent are in combined or ungraded schools, 7 percent are in middle or junior high school, and 2 percent are in elementary schools (Setzer & Lewis, 2005).

The current administration of the U.S. Department of Education has certainly jumped on the bandwagon. During an NCLB Leadership Summit in Orlando in July 2004, a white paper was presented by a consulting group that works in the area of charter schools titled, "How Can Virtual Schools Be a Vibrant Part of Meeting the Choice Provisions of the No Child Left Behind Act?" (Hassel & Terrell, 2004). Last year we raised the possibility that the Bush administration is promoting virtual schools as an opportunity to further its agenda of privatizing education; this white paper seems to provide further evidence of that position.

Other stakeholders who are jumping onto the bandwagon of virtual schools include Michigan Virtual University (Carnevale, 2004); a for-profit cyber school business named Connections Academy (Borja, 2004b); and even the tiny sixty-five-student school district of Branson, Colorado, where district administrators have found that offering online courses has allowed them to boost enrollments by more than one thousand and increase the district's funding by about $15 million since they began the project in 2001 (Dillon, 2005). The rise of virtual schools is also seen as a key factor that has helped the home-schooling movement attract mainstream families (Kumar, 2004). The National Center for Education Statistics reports that there were more than 1.1 million home-schooled students in the United States during 2003 (United States Department of Education, 2004).

Based on these trends, we agree with the technology experts who predicted as part of the Pew Internet and American Life Project (2005):

Enabled by information technologies, the pace of learning in the next decade will increasingly be set by student choices. In ten years, most students will spend at least part of their "school days" in virtual classes, grouped online with others who share their interests, mastery, and skills. (p. vi)

Radio Frequency Identification Devices. One of the more Orwellian developments related to the use of technology in education during 2005 was the case of the Sutter, California, elementary school where the principal implemented a radio frequency identification device (RFID) for taking attendance (Bailey, 2005).

Students were required to wear badges with their photo, name, a tiny computer chip, and an antenna so that when they entered classes, scanners located above the door could pick up the identification information, send it to the school's central database server, and provide a master attendance list for the teacher on a wireless handheld computer. The RFIDs worked very well—at least until parents, the American Civil Liberties Union, and the Electronic Frontier Foundation raised protests about possible misuses of the technology. The protests led the RFID provider to shut down the project, although a company spokesman noted that all the press from the Sutter case had been good for business, with many callers expressing interest in adopting RFID technology for their schools. Based on that interest, we suspect that the use of electronic identification devices in schools is an emerging trend that we will be tracking for some time to come.

CONCLUSION

During the period covered in this review, schools, colleges, and businesses were still suffering from the budget exigencies inflicted by the recession of 2000–2003. Corporate training budgets actually contracted two years in a row and by 2004 had still not matched the level of 2000. In schools and colleges, many information technology operations absorbed budget cuts, working diligently to avoid service reductions. Information technology infrastructure has continued to expand nevertheless, so that access to computers and the networks that connect them has become virtually ubiquitous.

Adoption of new technologies and integration of them into instruction continues at a measured pace. For newer technologies, the pace is fast at the beginning, but then it plateaus. For more mature technologies, adoption moves more slowly as the market becomes saturated. In the public education sector, the marketplace has experienced a major biasing effect in the form of the NCLB initiative, and we continue to see the effects of attempts to privatize and corporative K–12 education.

We must remember that pervasive access to information technology infrastructure does not guarantee its use in teaching, nor any improvements in effectiveness of instruction. Human factors such as resistance to practices that require new ways of working and the need for specialized training impinge on trainers', teachers', and professors' use of ICT. Because of these human factors, as they play out in training and education, it is inevitable that technology use lags behind technology availability.

REFERENCES

Allen, I. E., & Seaman, J. (2004). *Entering the mainstream: The quality and extent of online education in the United States, 2003 and 2004.* Needham, MA: The Sloan Consortium.

Bailey, E. (2005, February 22). Town gives brave new world an F: When an elementary school required students to wear radio frequency IDs, some parents saw the specter of Big Brother. *Los Angeles Times,* p. B1

Bichelmeyer, B.A. (1991). *The pilot implementation of an educational computer resource network: A naturalistic study.* Unpublished Ph.D. dissertation, University of Kansas.

Borja, R. (2004a, November 3). The MOUSE squad. *Education Week,* pp. 32–35.

Borja, R. (2004b, December 8). New player in online school market pursues profits. *Education Week,* p. 8.

Campus Computing Project. (2004). The 2004 National Survey of Information Technology in US Higher Education. Retrieved April 13, 2005, from http://www.campuscomputing.net/summaries/2004/index.html

Carnevale, D. (2004, November 5). Michigan Virtual University shifts its focus to elementary and secondary schools. *Chronicle of Higher Education,* p. A30.

Cross, J., & O'Driscoll, T. (2005, February). Workflow learning gets real. *Training* 42(2), 30–35.

Dillon, S. (2005, February 9). Tiny district finds bonanza of pupils and funds online. *The New York Times,* p. 19.

Dolezalek, H. (2004, October). Industry report 2004. *Training* 41:10, 20–36.

Education Week. (2005, May 5). Technology Counts 2005, 24(35).

Ehlinger, C. (2005, May). 2005 bi-annual survey. National Association of Media and Technology Centers Bulletin, pp. 11–12. Retrieved June 3, 2005, from http://www.namtc.org/pdf/0505_etin.pdf

eSchool Newsonline. (2005a, February 8). $500M ed-tech grant slated for elimination. Retrieved February 11, 2005, from http://www.eschoolnews.com/news/PFshowstory.cfm?ArticleID=5502

eSchool Newsonline. (2005b, June 1). Study: These factors retard digital teaching. Retrieved June 5, 2005, from http://www.eschoolnews.com/news/PFshowStory.cfm?ArticleID=5706

eSchool Newsonline. (2005c, July 13). Senators restore ed-tech funds. Retrieved July 15, 2005, from http:www.eschoolnews.com/news/PFshowStoryts.cfm?ArticleID=5782

Gehring, J. (2005, May 5). Big-district priorities. *Education Week,* Technology Counts 2005, 24(35), 38–39.

Goldstein, P., & Caruso, J. (2004, November). Key findings: Information technology funding in higher education. EDUCAUSE Center for Applied Research. Retrieved January 26, 2005, from http://www.educase.edu/ecar

Hanson, K., & Carlson, B. (2005). Effective access: Teachers' use of digital resources in STEM teaching. Education Development Center, Inc. Retrieved April 15, 2005, from http://www2.edc.org/GDI/publications_SR/EffectiveAccessReport.pdf

Hassel, B., & Terrell, M. (2004). How can virtual schools be a vibrant part of meeting the choice provisions of the No Child Left Behind Act? White Paper presented at Secretary's No Child Left Behind Leadership Summit—Increasing Options through e-Learning, July 12–13, 2004, Orlando, FL. Retrieved December 13, 2004, from http://www.nclbtechsummits.org/summit2/s2-presentations.asp

Hurst, M. (2005, May 5). Schools eye future costs. *Education Week,* Technology Counts 2005, 24(35), 34–39.

In praise of clutter. (2002, December 19). *The Economist.* London. Retrieved from http://www.economist.com/business/displayStory.cfm?story_id=1489224

Jenny, N. W. (2005, June). *2005 opens with strong state tax revenue growth.* Fiscal Studies Program, No. 60. Albany, NY: The Nelson A. Rockefeller Institute of Government.

Komoski, K. (2005, July 13). No child (consumer) left behind: Brining balance to a media generation's in- and out-of-school learning. *Education Week,* pp. 36–37.

Kumar, K. (2004, November 28). Home schooling is attracting mainstream families. *St. Louis Post Dispatch.* Retrieved November 30, 2004, from http://www.stltoday.com/stltoday/emaf.nsf/Popup?ReadForm&db=st

Kvavik, R., Caruso, J., & Morgan, G. (2004). *ECAR Study of Students and Information Technology, 2004: Convenience, connection, and control.* Boulder, CO: EDUCAUSE Center for Applied Research.

Maltz, L., DeBlois, P., & EDUCAUSE Current Issues Committee. (2005). Trends in Current Issues, Y2K–2005. *EDUCAUSE Quarterly, 28*(2).

Market Data Retrieval Service. (2005a). *The College Technology Review.*

Market Data Retrieval Service. (2005b). *K–12 Technology Review.*

Marketwire. (2005, March 29). Conference Keynote to Report on the Demise of the Textbook. Retrieved March 30, 2005, from http://www.marketwire.com/mw/release_html_b1?release_id=83496

Maryland Business Roundtable for Education, Committee on Technology in Education. (2005, March). A Progress Report on Technology Resources in Maryland Schools. Retrieved June 10, 2005, from http://md.ontargetus.com

Merrill, M. D. (in press). First Principles of Instruction. In C. M. Reigeluth & A. Carr (Eds.). *Instructional design theories and models III.* Hillsdale, NJ: Lawrence Erlbaum Associates.

Molenda, M., & Bichelmeyer, B. (2005). Issues and trends in instructional technology: Slow growth as economy recovers. In M. Orey, J. McClendon, & R. M. Branch (Eds.), *Educational media and technology yearbook 2005* (Vol. 30). Westport, CT: Libraries Unlimited.

Morgan, G. (2003, May). *Faculty use of course management systems.* EDUCAUSE Center for Applied Research. Retrieved July 21, 2005, from http://www.educause.edu/ir/library/pdf/ers0302/rs/ers0302w.pdf

National Education Association. (2000). *A survey of traditional and distance learning higher education members.* Washington, DC: National Education Association.

Olson, L. (2005, March 2). ETS to enter formative-assessment market at K–12 level. *Education Week,* p. 11.

Pew Internet & American Life Project. (2005). The Future of the Internet. Retrieved January 25, 2005, from http://www.pewinternet.org/PPF/r/145/report_display.asp

Poor schools, rich targets. (2004). *Baltimore Sun.* Retrieved October 1, 2004, from www.baltimoresun.com/news/education/bal-edsoftware,1,1904249.storygallery?coll=bal-education-storyutil

Rideout, V., Roberts, D., & Foehr, U. (2005, March). Generation M: Media in the Lives of 8–18 Year-Olds. Kaiser Family Foundation. Retrieved July 18, 2005, from http://www.kff.org/entmedia/entmedia030905pkg.cfm

Rother, C. (2004, October). Evaluating technology's role in the classroom: Second annual "teachers talk tech" survey examines the long-term impact of technology on learning. *T.H.E. Journal,* pp. 43–49.

SchWeber, C. (2005, March). A tipping point for education? *Sloan-C View* 4:3, 1, 6.

Sellen, A. J., & Harper, R. J. R. (2001). *The myth of the paperless office.* Cambridge, MA: MIT Press.

Setzer, J., & Lewis, L. (2005). Distance education courses for public elementary and secondary school students: 2002–2003 (NCES 2005-101). Washington, DC: U.S. Department of Education, National Center for Education Statistics.

Shea, P., Pickett, A., & Li, C. S. (2005, July). Increasing access to higher education: A study of the diffusion of online teaching among 913 college faculty. *International Review of research in open and distance learning.* Retrieved from http://www.irrodl.org/content/v6.2/shea.html

Spicer, D. Z., DeBlois, P. B., and the EDUCAUSE Current Issues Committee. (2004). Fifth annual EDUCAUSE survey identifies current IT issues. *EDUCAUSE Quarterly* 27:2, 1–23.

Sugrue, B., & Kim, K.-H. (2004). *State of the Industry 2004.* Alexandria, VA: American Society for Training & Development.

Thompson, T. (2005, June 7). *ECAR Bulletin #12—Information Technology Accessibility in Higher Education: Research and Promising Practices.* Boulder, CO: EDUCAUSE Center for Applied Research.

Trotter, A. (2005, May 11). Technology turns test-prep into clicking experience. *Education Week,* p. 8.

U.S. Department of Education, Office of the Under Secretary, Policy and Program Studies Service. (2003). *Federal funding for educational technology and how it is used in the classroom: A summary of findings from the integrated studies of educational technology.* Retrieved April 18, 2004, from http://www.ed.gov/rschstat/eval/tech/iset/summary2003.pdf

U.S. Government Accountability Office. (2005, February). Greater Involvement Needed by the FCC in the Management and Oversight of the E-Rate Program, GAO-05-151. Retrieved April 15, 2005, from http://www.gao.gov/cgi-bin/getrpt?GAO-05-151

United States Department of Education, Institute of Education Sciences. (2004, July). *1.1 million homeschooled students in the United States in 2003.* National Center for Education Statistics, Issue Brief 2004-115.

United States Department of Education, Institute of Education Sciences. (2005, June). *Rates of computer and Internet use by children in nursery school and students in kindergarten through twelfth grade: 2003.* National Center for Education Statistics, Issue Brief 2005-111.

Wired News. (2005, May 14). No wrong answer: Click it. Retrieved May 17, 2005, from http://www.wired.com/news/print/0,1294,67530,00.html

Yang, C. (2004, September 20). Big program on campus. *BusinessWeek,* pp. 96–98.

Young, J. (2005, April 1). Campus-TV network is now online. *Chronicle of Higher Education,* p. A43.

Instructional Design and Technology Models: Their Impact on Research and Teaching in Instructional Design and Technology

Barbara Bichelmeyer
Indiana University

Elizabeth Boling
Indiana University

Andrew S. Gibbons
Brigham Young University

In conversations with our colleagues, we often express concern about the comparative lack of interest within our field regarding how we actually design and how we should design. This statement may seem naïve, given the reams of literature generated in our field having to do with the design of instruction and models of instructional design. However, when we turn to this literature, it generally has to do with either *what* should be designed (instructional theory and strategies), or it has to do with generalized *models* for design; the literature does *not* have to do with the actual *enterprise* of design. There are some studies that have to do with the degree to which instructional designers adhere to generalized frameworks of design (e.g., LeMaistre, 1998; Wedman & Tessmer, 1993). Yet research and discussion of the enterprise of design work is much more limited, including, for example, Gordon Rowland's (1992) investigation of designers at work, Brent Wilson's (2005) discussion of emotion and aesthetics in instructional design, and Kerr's (1983) comparatively early discussion of the "black box" of design.

The purpose of our chapter is to consider the reasons behind this lack of focus on the enterprise of instructional design in the field of instructional design and technology (IDT), to consider the impact of this lack of focus on the research we do and the ways that we teach, and to propose a way of thinking about what we do as instructional designers that may provide a new perspective about what to research and teach in our field.

THE ADDIE MODEL AS A METAPHOR FOR LACK OF CLARITY IN THE FIELD OF IDT (BICHELMEYER)

Indiana University, where I am an associate professor in the Department of Instructional Systems Technology (IST), has a School of Library and Information Sciences, a Department of Telecommunications, a School of Informatics that was opened several years ago, and a newly launched Ph.D. program in Learning Sciences. The growing number of programs related to the field of IDT is one of the main reasons I am currently experiencing a discomforting level of uncertainty regarding the focus of the field, and I find myself wondering how we who work in the field of instructional design and technology add a unique perspective to the generation of knowledge among all of these related fields.

Concern about Lack of Focus in the Field of IDT

I am not alone in my uncertainty about the boundaries and focus of the field. One of the most well-attended sessions during the 2004 Conference of the Association for Educational Communications and Technology (AECT) in Chicago was a panel discussion between instructional technologists and learning scientists intended to help discern what, if any, are the differences between the two fields of study. The panel discussion was the outgrowth of a special issue of *Educational Technology* magazine edited by Carr-Chellman and Hoadley (2004) that included commentary from academics representing both groups about the commonalities and differences between the two fields.

Academics are not the only group experiencing discomfort and uncertainty about the focus and value of the field of IDT. Practitioners face struggles that result from the lack of congruity between theory, research, and practice in IDT. Schwier, Campbell, and Kenny (2004) note that "much of the extensive work describing theoretical models of instructional design (ID) has not been drawn from the practice of the instructional designer and consequently, instructional design theory is not grounded in practice" (p. 1). Conn and Donaldson (2004) note that there is a lack of clear definition and overlap between competing standards for practitioners. Cox and Osguthorpe (2003) conducted a survey of 142 practitioners to determine how instructional designers spend their time, a study they designed because they had "not been able to locate research that asks designers how they actually spend their professional time" (p. 45). These researchers note that there seems to be a "dearth of ethnographic research on the practice of instructional design" and express their "hope that those in instructional design and technology will become increasingly committed to studying the profession by examining the living practice as it changes and grows" (p. 47).

It should come as no surprise, then, that graduate students in some of the most well-respected programs in the United States join academics and practitioners in their sense of confusion about the focus of the field of instructional design and technology. Smith, Hessing, and Bichelmeyer (2004) administered a survey to 170 graduate students in eight of the oldest and largest IDT programs in the United States and asked respondents to describe what the field of IDT means to them. Data were analyzed using the constant comparative method to identify emergent themes, resulting in 14 categories of responses. By far the greatest number of responses fit into a category labeled by the researchers as "Broad/Non-uniform." A few examples of the types of responses that were grouped into this category are:

- "A really broad group of people trying to be unified when they have very different visions of what IDT really is. Consequently, we struggle to explain to people what exactly it is that we do and what exactly it is that we are and represent."

- "A diverse field where too many individuals try and play too many different roles and end up being master of none. 'Graphic design? Oh yeah, I can do that. Computer science? Yeah, I could figure it out. Information systems? Sure why not I deal with computers.' You get the picture. There are also a lot of feeble attempts when it comes to scientific research."

- "As much as people in the field don't like to admit it, I feel that IDT is really an interdisciplinary field that deals with identifying instructional problems and creating solutions to remedy those problems."

Given the available evidence, it does not seem to be an overstatement to claim that professionals of all types in the field of IDT, including academics, practitioners, and students, do not see the field as having a consensus definition, clear focus, distinct boundaries, established links between research and practice, or any obvious added value when compared with other fields. Given this confused state of affairs, one might legitimately ask, is there any sort of core to the field of IDT that can serve as a foundation on which to build?

The Core of IDT: The ADDIE "Model"

If you believe, as an old proverb claims, that many a truth is spoken in jest, then what are we to make of this joke from Debbie Gulick, a student in Learning and Performance Systems at Pennsylvania State University?

Why did the instructional designer cross the road?

To get to the ADDIE side.

Taken literally, the joke tells us that instructional designers are on the side of ADDIE (which stands for Analysis, Design, Development, Implementation, and Evaluation). Metaphorically, we could interpret this joke to mean that ADDIE is a foundational element of the field of IDT. We don't have to look far to find evidence that supports this interpretation.

The Smith, Hessing, and Bichelmeyer (2004) survey cited earlier provides solid evidence of the close link between the field of IDT and the concept of the ADDIE model. Graduate students' second-most frequent group of responses to the question "what does the field of IDT mean to you?" (following closely on the heels of the "broad/non-uniform" category) was the group of responses labeled as "ADDIE." Responses that were categorized into this group included variants of such statements as "It is the liberal application of ADDIE-like models to training and non-training problems . . ."; and one student's tongue-in-cheek reference to the ADDIE model as a key to ruling the world, writing that the field of IDT is "The systematic approach to design, development, evaluation, and management of everything."

A Google search using the term "ADDIE model" (January 12, 2005) generated more than 32,000 hits. A scan of these hits indicates that the concept of "the ADDIE model" is clearly linked to the field of instructional design. References come from universities, consulting companies, professional organizations, books, presentations, journal articles, and many other sources. The link between the ADDIE model and IDT is described as follows:

- *a key instructional design methodology, the ADDIE model*
  (http://www.stcaustin.org/meetings/sep04_fr.html, retrieved January 12, 2005).

- *the classic A-D-D-I-E model* of Instructional System Design
  (http://www.seslisozluk.com/search/design, retrieved January 12, 2005).

- *the ADDIE instructional design model*
  (http://www.centenarycollege.edu/academics_grad_malearningtech_
  coursedescr.php, retrieved January 12, 2005).

One other piece of evidence of the clear link between IDT and ADDIE is that the formal definition of the field produced by the Association for Educational Communications and Technology references all the words that make up the ADDIE acronym (Reiser & Ely, 1997).

In the current state of confusion regarding the boundaries and focus of the field of IDT, there appears to be some consensus among IDT professionals that the ADDIE model is a foundational element of the field. Perhaps the ADDIE model may be a starting point from which to build a broader consensus that could lead to a clearer, stronger sense of how the field of IDT is unique and adds value among other, newer fields. It seems appropriate, then, to examine the ADDIE model in more detail to help us get a better sense of the core of our field.

Strengths and Limitations of the ADDIE Model

The great strength of the ADDIE model is implied in the title we give it. A model is a template, a structure, an approach to be used. Barbara Grabowski provided a historical context for the value of the ADDIE model by explaining, "I grew up before ADDIE, when there was IDI, ISDP, SET" (these acronyms describe a variety of specific and particular approaches to instructional design). "What ADDIE did for me and other instructional designers was to put all the little pieces of all the different instructional design models into a bigger picture. ADDIE was a nice way of putting my nine steps into five. For its time, what was good about ADDIE was to put discrete bits of information into an overarching framework" (personal communication, February 28, 2004).

Despite its hallowed place in IDT, various members of the field over the years have pointed out a number of compelling criticisms of the ADDIE model. Chief among these criticisms are that the ADDIE model is ineffective and inefficient (Gordon & Zemke, 2000), meaning that it does not necessarily lead to the best instructional solutions, nor does it provide solutions in a timely or efficient manner. In recent years, the ADDIE model has also been criticized because it doesn't take advantage of digital technologies that allow for less linear approaches to instructional design such as rapid prototyping (Tripp & Bichelmeyer, 1990). Perhaps most important, Rowland (1992) has pointed out that the ADDIE model is not really the way instructional designers do their work. Furthermore, Molenda, Pershing, and Reigeluth (1996) warn, "in no case that we know of has an instructional design model been promulgated as a *description* of what expert practitioners do" (p. 268, emphasis in the original).

In summary, these criticisms assert that the primary model of instructional design in the field of IDT does not guarantee quality, is not efficient, is out of date, and doesn't reflect the real work of instructional design. Yet despite such withering criticisms, IDT professionals continue to view the ADDIE model as a foundational element of the field. This paradoxical situation should lead us to ask, what makes the ADDIE model strong enough to withstand such criticism?

What the ADDIE Model Isn't—A Model

To answer the question just above, it is important to know something about the origin and development of the ADDIE model. Unfortunately, this leads us away from the clarity and focus for which we have been striving and back into the murky waters of uncertainty and confusion.

In a 2003 article titled "In Search of the Elusive ADDIE Model," Michael Molenda, associate professor of instructional systems technology at Indiana University and historian of the field, documented his effort to track down the original reference to the ADDIE model and his subsequent reflections about that effort.

Molenda's exhaustive search found no original reference for the ADDIE model—not in any dictionary or encyclopedia, any histories of the field, any textbooks, or in any professor's memory. This lack of an original reference led Molenda to conclude that ADDIE exists as a label rather than as an actual ID model (Molenda, 2003).

By definition, a model is a representation that accurately resembles an existing structure. As mentioned earlier, Rowland and others have criticized the ADDIE model because it is not representative of what instructional designers do. If no original ADDIE model exists, and if ADDIE does not represent what instructional designers do, then we must conclude that ADDIE does not accurately represent an existing structure and therefore is not a model at all. So if ADDIE is not a model, then what is it?

What ADDIE Is—A Conceptual Framework

An answer to the question of what ADDIE is may best be gleaned by considering its purpose rather than its origins or development. In the next section of this chapter, Elizabeth Boling, associate professor of instructional systems technology at Indiana University, who holds a master's degree in fine arts, makes the argument that the ADDIE model is just like every other generic description of the design process in other design fields such as fine arts, architecture, and engineering. Professor Boling says, "To me, [the important] discussion is … not about whether ADDIE stays or goes, but whether or not ADDIE is viewed appropriately——we're trying to make it serve as a road map——you can't use it effectively as a literal road map for ID" (personal communication, February 28, 2004).

Molenda (2003) came to a similar conclusion after his fruitless search for the elusive ADDIE model, stating, "I am satisfied at this point to conclude that the ADDIE model is merely a colloquial term used to describe a systematic approach to instructional design, virtually synonymous with ISD" (Instructional Systems Design) (p. 37).

Despite the vast number of references to "the ADDIE model" on the Internet, in textbooks, journal articles, conference presentations, and professional discourse, we need to recognize that ADDIE is not a model at all. Molenda has concluded that ADDIE is a label, a colloquial term used to describe a systematic approach to instructional design. Boling has referred to ADDIE as a generic description of the design process. One might also think of it as a conceptual framework for instructional design, a mental frame of reference that loosely guides instructional designers as they attempt to approach instructional design problems in a systematic way.

So, ADDIE is a framework, not a model. But really, isn't this just semantics? Who really cares whether we call ADDIE a model or a framework? And really, does such a distinction matter in any important way, after all?

What We Call ADDIE Matters—and Why

Yes, whether we call ADDIE a model or a framework matters. It matters a great deal, actually, and this is why. First, to recap the argument of this chapter: IDT is a field that is being inundated by other fields. Those of us who work in the field of IDT don't have a clear focus or vision of how we are unique and add value in relation to these other fields. One area where there does appear to be a consensus among IDT professionals is that we consider the ADDIE model to be a core element of our field. However, the ADDIE model is criticized as not being effective, efficient, or even what instructional designers really do. The ADDIE "model," which we perceive as a core element of our field, one of the few things that we seem to agree upon, is not what we assume it to be. This might help to explain why we question whether the field adds value. It might explain why we are worried that the field isn't moving forward in any coherent way; how can we hope to build a field based on something that doesn't represent reality?

So, what should we do? We must start by recognizing that ADDIE is not a model but rather a conceptual framework and then begin to explore the many manifestations of this conceptual framework in its everyday settings. In other words, the field of IDT should value and study the actual work that professionals engage in when they design instruction. We should describe what the processes of instructional design actually look like to evaluate the strengths and weaknesses of various processes of instructional design, to explore the causal linkages between the processes of instructional design and the implementation of successful instruction, and, based on such knowledge, to prescribe processes of instructional design that make a real and sustained contribution to education in all its forms.

If those of us in the field of IDT were to pursue this agenda purposefully and programmatically, I believe our preoccupation with how we relate to other fields and our concern about adding value would disappear. If we were to do this, I believe IDT would be a field that addresses an area of study that no other field addresses (Bichelmeyer, 2003), We would be rooted in and focused on a subject at the core of our field—we would be advancing knowledge about the processes of instructional design.

Teaching a Design Model versus Developing Instructional Designers (Boling)

Coming from a background in the visual arts (MFA, printmaking, 1983), I was puzzled when I began to work in instructional design and technology by the apparent centrality of design process models to the overall enterprise. Although every field incorporating design uses and teaches processes for design, most do not seem to view the design process itself as a central object of focus in teaching and learning design. The focus of teaching in these fields is centered on developing habits of mind within those who will be designers, using design activities as the primary focus and design models as one possible support for those activities. In discussions with colleagues in the IDT Futures group, we have speculated on why this may be so—we want to be seen as a scientifically oriented field instead of a craft- or arts-oriented one; we have traditionally embraced systems and communication theory, which tend to place process models front and center; our models started out as conceptual frameworks and were only hijacked later as convenient vehicles for teaching; and, perhaps my favorite, there are simply not many actual designers teaching in our field, so the use of models in the classroom substitutes for the kind of expertise that would allow for any other approach (e.g., apprenticeship). But the discussion begs another question: does it really matter if we teach design differently than they do in other fields? I believe that it does matter to the extent that we are not satisfied with how we teach design and feel the need to examine other options.

Let me say at the outset of this section that the students in our graduate program who are studying to be designers are some of the finest in the world. Although most of them do not bring any formal design experience with them to the program—indeed, many have not even had much informal design experience prior to their studies in instructional design—most of them are clearly eager to be designers of instruction and hungry to be imaginative, creative designers of good instruction, instruction that will do its job well. I admire them for their drive, their intelligence, and their ability to master new concepts and skills. They learn quickly. They study hard. They take whatever is available in the learning environment and wring the juice from it.

I am troubled, however, by some of what I see happening to my students as they move through the program. Generally speaking, they seem to be timid about venturing outside the design process. Some clearly expect the process to yield acceptable results simply because it has been followed rather than because it has been used as a powerful tool. They often ignore their own intuition about what might be important in a design situation and sometimes set aside very thoughtful observations because they cannot cite an author who has validated those observations previously. They have well-functioning imaginations but frequently do not apply them to problem solving, and when asked why not, they reply that they weren't sure a particular innovative approach to the problem would be valid instructional design practice. They do not seek out examples of instructional design and generally do not make any but a small personal collection of cool instructional strategies that they can draw on for new design problems. They invest sparingly in the generation of design alternatives, expecting that they can reason their way to an appropriate design and seeming to regard as a mistake, or a waste, any work that does not feed directly into the finished product. Sadly, they often seem disappointed in their own efforts, dismayed at the gap between what they expected to produce and what actually came to be, and at a loss to turn the current design experience into fruitful learning for the next one. Let me remind the reader:—these are students I respect and students who graduate, I believe, as some of the best-prepared designers in the field. But I want more for them and more for the field.

I have worked on filling in the "black box" in the design process (Kerr, 1983), thinking that when students could separate function from form and manipulate those constructs as a bridge between an instructional strategy and a particular instantiation of the strategy that they would be freed to examine alternatives, generate new forms, and apply their analyses meaningfully. This has been helpful in some ways but has added steps to the process model rather than reducing the tyranny of the model. I have also instituted critiques and design journals (for collecting design examples, reflection on design and sketches—both text and image—of design ideas) as staple activities in my beginning ID and production courses. Students feel some utility from critique—they get feedback—but most are mystified by the design notebooks. The critiques allow us to practice critical review of design and definitely show promise as a teaching tool, but both critique and design notebooks feel incomplete when they are grafted on to an environment in which transformation of the self is not expected. Finally, I have removed the design process model from my initial ID course and recast analysis as a research project in which the students are striving to immerse themselves in understanding the context for the proposed instruction in all its facets. Again, the change shows promise, but the students are probably frustrated because it seems to them as though the process—that central focus of learning ID—is simply getting fuzzier. Bear in mind that these are classes in which the students practice hands-on ID and production. They operate as "novice professionals" and tackle entire design problems, not bits and pieces of the process taken out of context. In other words, I have not been grafting studio-like activities onto a course that is otherwise lecture oriented or that is limited to teaching software applications or single topics (analysis, design, evaluation). So I ask myself, is something else missing in the way that we prepare individuals to be instructional designers? And could we learn something about what might be missing from those who teach designers in other design fields?

First, What Do I Mean by Design?

A misconception that seems to arise when I address the issue of how we teach design is that, because I am a visual designer of media, I must be speaking primarily of visual design—or perhaps message design—when I say "design." A second misconception arises among those who have so little themselves to do with media design that they assume I am speaking of instructional design in the narrowest sense—that of making instructional strategy decisions within a single design effort. In the context of this discussion my intention is to use *design* in a broad sense to encompass the whole enterprise in which instructional designers labor. If one works as an instructional designer, then one's work is fundamentally that of design—when design is defined as the *conscious generation of interventions into the experience of others for specific purposes*. I am drawing here from Andy Gibbon's premise that instructional design might best be seen as a form of engineering, or planned intervention in naturally occurring process to meet a specified goal. The reader should see also Gibbons (2003a) for more on the relationship between IDT and engineering, and Pitt (2001) for a concise discussion of engineering knowledge. However, I use the term "experiences of others" rather than "naturally occurring processes" because the processes in which we intervene as instructional designers are inevitably the experiences of others.

Even if one does not subscribe to Gibbons's view of the instructional technologist, it is possible to place our enterprise within the broad scope of design by examining the models used in other fields where the products of a professional's activity represent an intervention in the lives of others for an intended purpose.

We Are Different but Not Unique among Designers

Instructional design models fall into a family of like models or frameworks developed across a number of fields of endeavor. Even though much time and energy could be spent discussing the variations between these models, they are striking to me in their underlying resemblance to one another. Not every field represents these models explicitly or represents them in spatial form with boxes and arrows, but the basic components are discoverable in explanations of "how we do our work." See Rowe (1987) on *Design Thinking* for an overview of models for architectural design and Mitchell's (2002) *User Responsive Design* for a recent update on user-responsive design for architects and interior designers. See the revision of Dreyfuss's (2003) classic *Designing for People* for an inferred model of what was called industrial design at the time of his first writing and is more usually called product design now. Review the School of Engineering and Advanced Technology, Staffordshire University (2004) Web site, which supports a realistic lab-based experience for students, to get an idea of the underlying process model being used for their instruction. In the field of human-computer interface design, a design field somewhat less established than IDT, see Beyer and Holtzblatt (1997) on *Contextual Design* and compare the major activities described there with those typically covered by ISD models.

Product designers, graphic designers, architects, software interface designers and engineers all carry out analysis in the early stages of their process—analysis of those who will use their designs, of where and how the designs might be used, of the critical versus desirable features for the designs and of the desired outcomes for them. All examine the design alternatives in the light of the analysis data they have collected. All narrow those alternatives through the understanding of constraints—in materials, time, budget, acceptability of certain aspects of a design, mandates from clients, and appropriateness of the solution for the problem specified. All face the transition from concept to instantiation—from design to development and production in our terminology—and all consider the implementation of the design to be part of the process. Although the goals they work toward differ in their character, all these designers incorporate evaluation into both the pre- and post-implementation phases of design (formative and summative), whether their evaluation activities would be considered adequate or on-target by instructional designers or not. (See Table 1 for a comparison of design activities carried out by most designers and instructional designers.)

The emphasis within various parts of the design process is different in each field, as it should be. The detail of terminology is different and can be quite confusing when the same words are used in different ways ("design," for example). But the functional description of what is getting done when a person sits down to create something that will be used by someone else for a certain purpose is pretty much the same.

I do not argue that our process model should be the same as anyone else's, nor theirs the same as ours. I do not argue that the processes in other fields are more or less effective than in ours or that any field has a single model that can be held forth as the one by which it should be judged. I do claim that ADDIE represents just what Walt Wager tells us it was originally meant to be—a conceptual framework for the design enterprise. In fact, although academics would immediately start arguing over the details, ADDIE could be seen equally well in any field of design as the basic conceptual framework for design activity. Even quasi-radical departures from what might be called "traditional ISD process" contain ADDIE components when those components are viewed as constructs that define the purposes of design activities. This being so, I argue further—and in company with Rowland (1992)—that we can learn by examining the practice in other fields of design, including the ways in which they teach people to be designers.

Table 1. Design Activities Carried Out by Most Designers and Instructional Designers

Design Activities Generally Present in the Models	Some Equivalent IDT Activities
Define the problem	Needs analysis, human performance technology analysis, stakeholder analysis
Conduct research	Needs analysis, context analysis, audience analysis, task analysis, content analysis, subject matter expert consultation, technical analysis, comparative product review
Identify potential design solutions	Instructional approach, instructional strategy selection, sequencing instruction, motivational strategy design
Select solutions in accordance with constraints and goals	Prototyping, formative evaluation, expert design review, SME review, media selection, implementation planning, change management planning, technical feasibility tests
Build the design	Development, production
Test	Quality testing
Deliver	Implementation, change management
Refine, redesign	Evaluation, implementation, analysis

Learning to Be a Designer outside of IDT

My own graduate experience in fine arts was an apprenticeship experience (Boling, 2003). See the series of short papers, Design Cultures, in the *IDT Record* at http://www.indiana.edu/~idt/shortpapers/documents/design_cultures.html for additional descriptions of learning and teaching design in various fields. Because of this experience, I am aware of how very different teaching design can be from what I have observed and been part of within the field of instructional design. However, I am not proposing to apply a studio art model directly to instructional design. In this culture, studio art is understood to be driven largely by the personal goals of the artist. Instead, I look to several discussions of learning design in fields where designers are expected to generate interventions for purposes that are either driven by a client or arrived at jointly between a client and a designer. In particular, I consider graphic design (Heller, 1998), engineering (Platts, 2004), and architecture (Anthony, 1999; Lawson, 1997).

In a series of interviews, Heller (1998, pp. 179–207) asks prominent graphic designers how they learned to design and how, if they teach, they teach design. Prominent among their responses is that they learned from role models, either in school or outside school, and that they attempted to emulate the kind of person that the role model was—not necessarily to emulate the designs that person produced. They also said that they learned from their mentors profound insights into the *meaning* of design—not that they learned a *process* of design. These designers mention a mentor who showed them the work of other designers and made them conscious of what was important about that work. They point to the independent thought that was required, to the expectation that they would develop their voices as designers and to the commitment their mentors had to design. In discussing their own teaching, they talk about technical methods but more about teaching designers to be ethical, to define their own talents, to understand the world, have passion for design, acquire their own voices, and be "agents of their own making" (p. 193). Reading these descriptions reminds me of Rick Schwier's investigation of the big vision of instructional design, the overarching passion that he did not always find expressed by the instructional designers who participated in his study. It also pointed to the notion that teaching design in this field is concerned with transforming students into designers, rather than teaching students the process of design. The nature of the change in these students is clearly not a simple accretion of technical skills or process competencies. It is a change in their perspectives, activities and selves.

Platts (2004) introduces a case study describing a learning laboratory at the University of Cambridge with a discussion of the required knowledge and skills for designing manufacturing systems. He explains that both Eurault's type A knowledge, which is declarative (p. 206), and type B knowledge, which is "the knowledge that professionals bring to their practice that enables them to think and perform on the job" (p. 207), are required for engineers in this domain. Also required are "skills of synthesis" that enable them to put what they know together effectively within the constraints of a design situation. The third requirement Platts stresses is judgment. Designers need to judge the reality of a situation, make value judgments about objectives, and make action judgments about what to do (p. 207). The laboratory environment that he describes for teaching these requirements to engineering students places them in charge of designing and running an actual manufacturing system; the students themselves plan and monitor their work, meet their own process requirements, and consult experts with process problems on as as-needed basis. They have to decide what to find out, how to apply what they know, and how to measure their progress. The emphasis is definitely on the development of judgment—which is an aspect of instructional design not covered by process models.

In her discussion of design juries, Anthony (1999) likens the teaching process in architecture to that in fine arts—a studio environment where all students work within the same space, setting their own process and focusing on a variety of activities leading up to the design jury, a public critique and oral defense of their work. In this environment, the student learns what kinds of issues will be addressed in critique through observation and practice, and then uses whatever resources he can learn about or imagine to address those issues during iterative bouts of design. Lawson (1997) has proposed a three-dimensional model of design problems (not design process) that describes the stakeholders involved in a design problem on one axis (designer, client, user, and legislator [decision maker at the level of society]), the source of constraints on another (internal and external), and the aspects of all design problems that must be considered on the third (radical [basic], practical, formal, and symbolic). This model offers the designer a space in which to define the interrelated aspects of the design problem rather than a process by which to tackle the problem and seems to capture the flavor of design learning in the architectural studio. The student sits in the middle of this problem model, responsible for addressing all aspects of the model at a level commensurate with their importance for this project. The brief (or problem statement) from which the student designs does not specify the manner in which this process is to be carried out. Emphasis here is on independent problem solving, generation of previously unknown solutions, and the resourcefulness of the student in assembling a rationale for the design decisions that have been made.

Problems with Teaching Design in Other Fields

As might be expected, no field is entirely content with the way in which its designers are taught—or with the ways in which they practice, for that matter. In fact, Anthony's (1999) primary premise is that the design jury requires major rethinking and revamping to serve effectively the purposes for which it is presumably used. Mitchell (2002) is likewise clear in his description of effective methods for user-responsive design that architects generally do not consider all the issues that they should in designing or in learning to design. Clearly, each design field struggles with how best to prepare its own future professionals. However, these reservations do not negate the potential for us to learn from other fields.

Again in architecture, Rowe (1987) lays out in some detail the failure of process models. He reviews multiple models of creative problem-solving (design) in their historical context, tracing them from the phase or staged-process models "characterized by dominant forms of activity, such as analysis, synthesis, evaluation and so on" (p. 46) to the cognitive models taking the form of decision trees (p. 53) and top-down hierarchies of problem space such as Christopher Alexander's pattern language (1964, p. 71) among others. Among the models he describes, ISD appears to be using primarily those of the staged process variety—even though most of the current models do not expect this process to be *linear*. Rowe's observation about these forms of process models is instructive and thought provoking. He says:

> what seemed necessary [at the time of their development] was a clear and logical procedure for producing designs and plans that could be understood and participated in by all those involved. With respect to the former point, what seemed necessary was a far greater understanding of design processes, in order that procedures could be improved. In spite of the very real contributions that were made, at least to our understanding of these processes, in almost all cases the step beyond description to a normative realm in which process became pursued as an end in itself resulted in abject failure. Attempts to devise *the* process became exercises in inanity when compared to the great subtlety and profundity of observed problem-solving behavior. (p. 74)

At least in one other field, models not unlike those we are teaching with now have been developed, taught, tried and discarded for what sound like problems similar to the ones I worry about in my classes. Although I do not accuse us of using these models for their own sake, I do see that they cannot capture or stimulate the "subtlety and profundity" required for good design to happen. So when we use them as a primary vehicle to teach, or focus on them as the core of design activity, we run the risk of ignoring those qualities *required of the designer*. If we ignore those, then we probably don't teach them. And it is not clear that they can be taught directly. The learning environments in other design fields, for whatever their faults, seem to concentrate on developing self-sufficient individuals who are committed to their work, understand its difficulties in a profound way, make it their business to grapple with the complexities of intervening in other people's experiences and have the courage to innovate with process as well as products. I am coming to the conclusion that we need in the future to teach design more as a vocation and much less as a process.

A MODEL OF TECHNOLOGY CAPABLE OF GENERATING RESEARCH QUESTIONS (GIBBONS)

Several frameworks have been suggested for the generation and prioritization of research questions in the field of instructional technology. These include learning theory, philosophy, systems theory, and instructional theory. A model of technological activity that distinguishes technological from scientific inquiry can also be used to generate research topics, with the advantage that the knowledge produced is in a form more readily usable by the designer. Such a model is illustrated in Figure 1.

Figure 1. A model of technological activity capable of generating research questions for instructional technology.

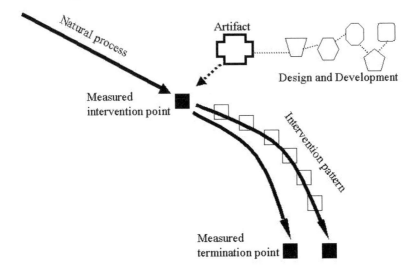

Figure 1 represents ongoing natural processes with a slanted line entering from the left. These processes continue independently of human volition. Left undisturbed, the processes propagate energy and information along natural paths studied by scientists, who attempt to describe and explain them and the forces that drive them (Klir, 1969, 1985). When humans intentionally intervene in these processes to achieve a particular outcome, the path of events may be deflected, which is represented by the arcs moving downward to the right in Figure 1. For the purposes of this chapter, the point of intervention and the course of the resulting events and further interventions constitute the appropriate region for technological study (Gibbons, 2003a; Gibbons & Bunderson, 2004). In this region, although events are driven forward by the same natural processes, there is an added dimension to be studied that consists of theories and principles of planned actions and the deliberate structuring of forces and information. This is the region of designing and design execution; it will be treated in this chapter as the region of technological study.

The elements of a planned intervention illustrated in Figure 1 suggest categories for research and priorities among them. In some cases, the categories described here represent a combination of more traditional research categories or a change of perspective with respect to a traditional research topic. In some cases, the categories represent new ones for technological study that correspond to those used in other design fields. The list of research topics that follows is derived from the narrative sequence of Figure 1. Its categories are suggested in several sources including Alexander (1964), Bucciarelli (1994), Klir (1969), Layton (1992), Schön (1987), Simon (1999), and Vincenti (1990).

Measurement

The intervention point in a deliberate application of technology is a *measured* intervention point. Subsequent intervention points or points of modification of the intervention are also measured, as are the end points at which intervention is terminated. Realizing that decisions during intervention are based on multiple and diverse criteria, this perspective adds breadth to traditional studies of measurement, placing a premium on measurements: (1) that are continuous or frequent and therefore repeatable, (2) that report the performance and response of many aspects of the system influenced by the intervention, (3) that are highly interpreted in terms of motives and degrees of engagement, and therefore (4) that require triangulation of multiple measures under sometimes severe timing constraints (Bunderson, Inouye, & Olsen, 1989). These aspects of measurement depart in an applied direction from traditional measurement research and emphasize application of measurement to influence an ongoing process. The participation of measurement in every aspect of an intervention also gives priority to research on measurement-related topics such as subject-matter analysis, event structure analysis, mental structure analysis, and other topics that provide primitive categories to which intervention-related measurements can be related (see, for instance, Bunderson & Wiley, in preparation).

Intervention Patterns

Figure 1 illustrates the possibility of multiple, measured intervention points. These may represent points at which minor adjustments are made in intervention values or points that mark a major departure in the intervention such as changes of the intervention artifact, the intervention process, or the timing of the intervention. A minor adjustment may involve an increase or decrease in the amount of a medication; a major adjustment may involve the addition of chemicals to a steel melt, followed by molding, quenching, forging, or drawing to determine the crystalline structure of the steel (Misa, 1995). Intervention patterns can be described with reference to stages of progress toward a targeted outcome; each stage may be characterized in terms of measures on the same or on different sets of parameters (e.g., temperature of a melt, chemical composition of a melt, compression of an ingot by forging, rate of drawing, etc.).

Progress toward instructional goals can similarly be characterized in terms of intermediate steps at both macro- and micro-levels. Research on patterns of intervention places emphasis on the description of intermediate stages rather than on single-event outcomes and supports an innovative view of the instructional goal and of methods to guide instructional goal setting. In particular, the notion of single, static goals gives way to the view of dynamic scoping and goal trajectories which cause us to see instruction as a process that can possess and gain momentum. Measurement in this conception is interested in construction of performance curves, trend lines, effect curves, and effect surfaces. Research in this area must also include the computation of probabilities of success of competing possible interventions from a given intermediate point. This recharacterizes instructional strategies as dynamic computations rather than as static formulas or templates and favors the participation of learners in strategic decisions.

Artifact Types and Structures

Interventions are made by the means of artifacts (see Figure 1). Artifacts are structurings of information or force (energy) that work either through injection or catalysis to influence the path of natural processes—in our case, learning processes. A traditional view of instruction as the direct transfer of information structures to the learner's mind has given way to more complex views in which information and forces are made available to the learner as raw materials, to which the learner may respond by constructing understanding, feelings, or performance capability, often based on a multiplicity of inputs. In both cases, the artifacts—(1) the instructional materials and (2) the processes of instructional events—can be seen as attempts to structure information and to awaken motivation, engagement, interest, desire, and other forces that impel the learner forward toward acts of choice that lead to learning. In this process, learners either absorb information and forces or transform them into new organizations. This places emphasis on the study of the transforming processes of learners and the catalysis performed by a full range of time-space and information structurings than the designer can possibly conceive. It subtly shifts emphasis away from study of traditional categories of artifacts, events, and forms and toward new categories based on event structures, information structures, affect and conation states, and an ongoing negotiation of goals and resources in collaboration with learner. This implies the study of instruction as a conversational process in which learners become participants in telling of the subject-matter story and ultimately the managers of their own learning processes (Gibbons, 2004).

Artifact Design and Fabrication Processes and Tools

The traditional approach to an artifact design problem has been to divide the problem by decomposition into subproblems for solution. Over the years, instructional designers have created a standard approach that involves decomposition in terms of design processes, normally referred to as ISD, ADDIE, or a "design model."

An alternative view that may yield new directions for research divides design problems into layers and sublayers representing the *functional partitioning of the designed product* rather than of the design process. In this view, artifact structure is considered in terms of a set of integrated structures operating at different abstract layers, each supporting a particular function of injecting a particular pattern or behavior into the artifact. Single instructional events and material artifacts are thus seen as multiple layers of structures bound together to fill an overall purpose.

This alternative to the subdivision of design problems is consonant with descriptions of design-making in other fields. It also focuses attention on families of design languages used for designing within different layers. Although attention to design languages has led to progress in other design fields, design languages are often not noticed in instructional design (Gibbons & Brewer, 2004). Recognition of these languages has many implications:

- *Notation systems.* Abstract languages are most often represented in a public form by the means of notation systems that aid and are aided by development of the language itself. In many advanced design fields notation systems and languages have been at the root of rapid advances in design technology because they allow symbolic manipulation of the abstract ideas involved in design problem solutions (Waters & Gibbons, 2004). Both languages and notation systems are valuable study topics because they lead to further elucidation of the design activity itself (see Simon, 1999, p. 137).

- *Participatory designs.* Public symbolic notation of abstract design language concepts means that multiple designers can more readily share in designing and design reviews, that designs can become more complex and nuanced, and that design patterns can be lifted or abstracted for future use. Experience in many design fields (Booch, Jacobson, & Rumbaugh, 1998) has shown that designs framed in terms of layers (or "views") usually require multiple design expressions (graphs, views) to create a complete design. Public symbolic notation suggests the possibility of the evaluation of designs within shared work spaces (Fischer & Sullivan, n.d.). This provides additional means for studying the social dimension of design by groups and teams and how not only designs but new design languages emerge under working conditions.

- *Alignment with tool structures.* Design languages existing at different layers of a design imply multiple kinds of structural figures ("building blocks") that are involved in design creation. A rich field of study may be found in the manner of alignment of these abstract sets with the building blocks supplied by software development tools. It is likely that study in this area could result in new tool types and configurations (Gibbons & Fairweather, 2000).

- *Computational leveraging of the language principle.* Existence of languages for expressing designs implies that designs may be generated and manipulated as rule-bound expressions of languages. This principle has been a major factor in rapid advances made in other technology fields over the last 30 years. Generation can include real-time generation of instructional experiences from primitive elements, or real-time assembly of experiences from existing, reusable elements assembled from distant sources. Research on the relationship of design languages and layer designs to these outcomes may be fruitful.

- *Reexamination of principles of design order.* This alternative view of layers and languages challenges us to reexamine the design process itself, looking for a characterization of the process that can be tailored more readily to the needs of individual design projects. Artifact design can be seen as a sequence of decisions that places successive dimensions or constrains on abstract structures (Gross, Ervin, Anderson, & Fleisher, 1987; Layton, 1992). If so, each design decision can be rationalized, ordered, and disciplined by earlier decisions. This presents a new point of view for describing the design process and the order of design decisions.

CONCLUSION

In this chapter, we have considered the notion that the continuing focus in our field on ADDIE as a "model" of instructional design has a detrimental impact on both what we research and what we teach. Additionally, we have argued that our goal as faculty in the field should be to develop instructional designers rather than to teach design models, and we have explored how we might design our programs and curricula to better address this goal. Finally, we have suggested that a model of technological intervention can be used to derive worthwhile research topics and that those topics place a new perspective on traditional research categories; the list of categories presented is not exhaustive, but it does present a new perspective and priorities as well as to identify new opportunities for research in our field.

REFERENCES

Alexander, C. (1964). *Notes on the synthesis of form.* Cambridge, MA: Harvard University Press.

Anthony, K. (1999). *Design juries on trial: The renaissance of the design studio.* Champagne, IL: Kathryn H. Anthony.

Beyer, H., & Holtzblatt, K. (1997). *Contextual design: A customer-centered approach to systems designs.* San Francisco: Morgan Kaufmann.

Bichelmeyer, B. (2003). Instructional theory and instructional design theory: what's the difference and why should we care? *IDT Record.* Retrieved April 15, 2005, from http://www.indiana.edu/~idt/articles/documents/ID_theory.Bichelmeyer.html

Boling, E. (2003). Design culture in fine arts studio programs. *IDT Record,* Short Papers. Retrieved October 14, 2004, from http://www.indiana.edu/~idt/shortpapers/documents/design_culture_boling.html

Booch, G., Jacobson, I., & Rumbaugh, J. (1998). *The unified modeling language user guide.* Reading, MA: Addison-Wesley Professional.

Bucciarelli, L. L. (1994). *Designing engineers.* Cambridge, MA: MIT Press.

Bunderson, C. V., Inouye, D. K., & Olsen, J. B. (1989). *The four generations of computerized educational measurement.* In R. L. Linn (Ed.), *Educational measurement* (3rd ed.). New York: American Council on Education and Macmillan Publishing Company.

Bunderson, C. V., & Wiley, D. A. (in preparation). *Invariant scaling and domain theories: A new foundation for design experiments.*

Carr-Chellman, A. A. (2004). *Instructional Design and the Learning Sciences: A conversation between two communities of practice.* Paper presented at the annual meeting of the Association for Educational Communications and Technology. Chicago, IL.

Carr-Chellman, A. A., & Hoadley, C. M. (2004). Introduction to special issue: Learning sciences and instructional systems: Beginning the dialogue. *Educational Technology, 44*(3), 5–6.

Conn, C., & Donaldson, A. (2004). *Preparing graduates for positions in business and government: a comparison of HPT competencies and ECIT standards.* Paper presented at the annual meeting of the Association for Educational Communications and Technology, Chicago, IL.

Cox, S., & Osguthorpe, R. T. (2003, May/June). How do instructional design professionals spend their time? *TechTrends, 47*(3), 45–47, 29.

Dreyfuss, H. (2003). *Designing for people.* New York: Allworth press.

Fischer, G., & Sullivan, J. F. (n.d.). *Human-centered public transportation systems for persons with cognitive disabilities: Challenges and insights for participatory design.* Retrieved from http://www.cs.colorado.edu/~l3d/clever/assets/pdf/gf-pdc2002-mfa.pdf

Gibbons, A. S. (2003a). The practice of instructional technology: Science and Technology. *Educational Technology, 43*(5), 11–16.

Gibbons, A.S. (2003b, September/October). What and how do designers design: A theory of design structure. *TechTrends, 47*(5), 22–27.

Gibbons, A. S. (2004, June 3–4). *The interplay of learning objects and design architectures.* Paper presented at the Partnership in Global Learning Workshop on e-Learning Objects and Systems, Orlando, FL.

Gibbons, A. S., & Brewer, E. K. (2004). Elementary principles of design languages and design notation systems for instructional design. In M. Spector, C. Ohrazda, A. Van Schaack, & D. Wiley (Eds.), Innovations to instructional technology: Essays in honor of M. David Merrill. Mahwah, NJ: Lawrence Erlbaum.

Gibbons, A. S., & Bunderson, C. V. (2004). Explore, explain, design. In K. Kempf-Leonard (Ed.), *Encyclopedia of social measurement.* San Diego, CA: Academic Press.

Gibbons, A. S., & Fairweather, P. G. (2000). Computer-based instruction. In S. Tobias & J. D. Fletcher (Eds.), *Training and Retraining: A Handbook for Business, Industry, Government, and the Military.* New York: Macmillan Reference USA.

Gordon, J., & Zemke, R. (2000, April). The attack on ISD. *Training,* 43–53.

Gross, M., Ervin, S., Anderson, J., & Fleisher, A. (1987). Designing with constraints. In Y. E. Kalay (Ed.), *Computability of design.* New York: John Wiley & Sons.

Heller, S. (1998). *The education of a graphic designer.* New York, NY: Allworth Press.

Kerr, S. (1983). Inside the black box: Making design decisions for instruction. *British Journal of Educational Technology, 14*(1), 45–58.

Klir, G. J. (1969). *An approach to general systems theory.* New York: Van Nostrand Reinhold.

Klir, G. J. (1985). *Architecture of systems problem solving.* New York: Plenum Press.

Lawson, B. (1997). *How designers think: The design process demystified* (3rd ed.). Oxford, England: Architectural Press.

Layton, E. (1992). Escape from the jail of shape: Dimensionality and engineering science. In P. Kroes & M. Bakker (Eds.), Technological development in the industrial age. Dordrecht, The Netherlands: Kluwer Academic.

LeMaistre, C. (1998). What is an expert instructional designer? Evidence of expert performance during formative evaluation. *ETR&D, 46*(3), 21–36.

Misa, T. J. (1995). *A nation of steel: The making of modern America, 1865–1925.* Baltimore, MD: Johns Hopkins University Press.

Mitchell, C.T. (2002). *New thinking in design: Conversations on theory and practice.* New York: John Wiley & Sons.

Molenda, M. (2003). In Search of the Elusive ADDIE Model. *Performance Improvement, 42*(5), 34–36.

Molenda, M., Pershing, J. A., & Reigeluth, C. (1996). Designing instructional systems. In R. Craig (Ed.), *The ASTD training and development handbook* (4th ed.). New York: McGraw-Hill.

Pitt, J. (2001). What engineers know. *Techné, 5*(3), 17–30.

Platts, K.W. (2004). Developing knowledge and skills in engineers: A learning laboratory. *Education and Training, 46*(4), 206–213.

Reiser, R. A., & Ely, D. P. (1997). The field of educational technology as reflected through its definitions. *Educational Technology Research and Development, 45*(3), 63–72.

Rowe, P. (1987). *Design thinking.* Cambridge, MA: MIT Press.

Rowland, G. (1992). What do instructional designers actually do? An initial investigation of expert practice. *Performance Improvement Quarterly, 5*(2), 65–86.

Schön, D. A. (1987). *Educating the reflective practitioner.* San Francisco: Jossey-Bass.

School of Engineering and Advanced Technology, Staffordshire University. *Design procedures.* Retrieved October 15, 2004, from http://web.staffs.ac.uk/schools/engineering_and_technology/des/aids/procedures/environ.htm

Schwier, R. A., Campbell, K., & Kenny, R. (2004). Instructional designers' observations about identity, communities of practice and change agency. *Australasian Journal of Educational Technology, 20*(1), 69–100. Retrieved September 22, 2004, from http://www.ascilite.org.au/ajet/ajet20/schwier.html

Simon, H. A. (1999). *The sciences of the artificial* (3rd ed.). Cambridge, MA: MIT Press.

Smith, K., Hessing, J., & Bichelmeyer, B. A. (2004). *Graduate students' perceptions and expectations of the field of instructional design and technology.* Paper presented at the annual convention of the Association for Educational Communications and Technology. Chicago, IL.

Tripp, S., & Bichelmeyer, B. (1990). Rapid prototyping: An alternative instructional design strategy. *Educational Technology Research & Development, 38*(1), 31–44.

Vincenti, W. G. (1990). What engineers know and how they know it: Analytical studies from aeronautical history. Baltimore, MD: Johns Hopkins University Press.

Waters, S., & Gibbons, A. S. (2004). Design languages, notation systems, and instructional technology: A case study. *Educational Technology Research and Development, 52*(2), 57–69.

Wedman, J. F., & Tessmer, M. (1993). Instructional designers' decisions and priorities: A survey of design practice. *Performance Improvement Quarterly, 6*(2), 43–57.

Wilson, B. (2005). Four pillars of practice. For inclusion in a special issue of *Educational Technology* on cultural studies, edited by Ellen Rose. Retrieved October 14, 2004, from http://carbon.cudenver.edu/~bwilson/Pillars.html

Under Construction: Scaffolding the Expansion of Online Learning Communities Through Computer-Mediated Communication

Joyce Lee
California State University, Fullerton

INTRODUCTION

In the new millennium, paradigmatic shifts in educational philosophy and technical advances in instructional technology are dramatically altering the theory and practice of distance learning in higher education. If current trends are any indication, the explosive growth of distance learning will keep universities competitive in the global educational marketplace, alleviate campus capacity constraints, and transform teaching and learning (Oblinger & Kidwell, 2000). Tracking distance learning trends is like "taking a snapshot of a cyclone," according to Maeroff (2003, p. xii). Trends in distance learning, compiled by prestigious institutions such as the Institute for Higher Education Policy (2000) in *Quality on the Line: Benchmarks for Success in Internet Distance Education* and the Sloan Consortium (2004), *Entering the Mainstream: The Quality and Extent of Online Education in the United States, 2003 and 2004*, are addressing fundamental questions about the nature and extent of online education. According to the Sloan report, more than 2.6 million students studied online in fall 2004 with a projected annual growth rate of 24.8%. Thus, there is an increased interest in understanding how learning is best facilitated in an online context and what constitutes community in an online environment. According to Dede (1995), "creating a sense of community among a distributed group linked by low-to-moderate bandwidth networking is a complex challenge." Despite the obstacles, research is revealing "a number of positive outcomes for individuals and the learning communities to which they belong" (Romiszowski & Mason, 1996, p. 407).

What is an online learning community? What conditions give rise to online learning communities? How does computer-mediated communication engender community development? What is the future of online learning communities as technology advances? Inquiry into these compelling questions is the principal focus of this chapter, which first introduces readers to the research-based characteristics of effective online learning communities and the relationship of these characteristics to social constructivism, the epistemological foundation from which most online learning communities emerge. Following this, the findings of a qualitative case study, coresearched by this author, illuminate the meaning of an online learning community as it was perceived by 18 students enrolled in an online master's degree program in instructional design and technology. Online learning communities such as these mark the beginning of a trend for anywhere, anytime graduate programs grounded in community consciousness. Yet most online learning communities are still under construction, expanding from essentially modernist and bureaucratic forms of education into postmodernist phenomena through computer-mediated communication. Online learning communities will undergo significant changes in the future, and several of these projected transformations are discussed at the conclusion of this chapter.

REVISING THE BLUEPRINT FOR COMMUNITY CONSTRUCTION

Distance learning is no longer marginalized in higher education; rather, it has become a viable alternative to on-campus options. Faculty are moving from delivering information to remote learners and moving toward constructing community among learners (Bruffee, 1993; Dede, 1995, 2003a, 2003b; Kaye, 1995). The metaphor of community has been used to describe a wide range of scenarios, both real and virtual. According to Schwier (2001), all communities are collections of individuals bound together for some reason, and the reason defines the boundaries of each community. In a postmodern context, community is increasingly difficult to define because human ties are no longer limited by geographic proximity. Several researchers (Anderson & Misanchuck, 2001; Garrison & Anderson, 2003; Jones, 1995; Kollack & Smith, 1997; Paloff & Pratt, 1999, 2003; Rheingold, 1993; Roschelle & Pea, 1999; Rovai, 2001, 2002; Schaefer & Anudsen, 1993; Schuler, 1996; Simonson, Smaldino, Albright, & Zvacek, 2003) share a common interest in defining communities enabled by the Internet. Three terms used interchangeably to refer to different classifications of community include online learning communities (Chang, 2003; Jonassen, 1993, 1994, 2000; Lock, 2002; Palloff & Pratt, 1999), communities of practice (Brown & Issacs, 1995; Johnson, 2001; Rogers, 2000; Wenger, 1998), and virtual communities (Brook & Boal, 1995; Lockhard, 1996; Rheingold, 1993; Schuler, 1996).

Online Learning Communities Defined

A definition by Rovai (2002) captures the essence of an online learning community as "mutual interdependence among members, a sense of belonging, connectedness, spirit, trust, interactivity, common expectations, shared values and goals, and overlapping histories among members" (p. 2). Chang (2003) synthesizes its salient features: "(1) spontaneous learning and active knowledge construction by individual learners; (2) idea sharing and information provision for all members of the learning community; and (3) distributed knowledge and expertise" (p. 27). Effective online learning communities are hospitable environments founded on strong communal ties that increase the flow of information among members who share a sense of well-being derived from peer support. In the realm of higher education, according to Morrison and Shrivastava (2001), academic online communities reflect all of the characteristics mentioned earlier but are also more formalized "groups of learners and instructors, supported by instructional and learning resources, pursuing common knowledge-interests in an online environment" (p. 3). Dede's (2003) succinct definition frames community online as "a culture of learning in which everyone is involved in a collective effort of understanding" (p. 1).

Definitions of online learning communities are tentative and provisional because the learning theories and instructional technologies that shape them change quickly (Dede, 1995; Haythornthwaite et al., 2000; Hiltz et al., 2000; MacNeil, 1997; Palloff & Pratt, 1999; Tu & Corry, 2001, 2002; Tu & McIssac, 2001). There is no purely administrative or technical way of building an online learning community; professional educators cannot manufacture them. Educators can, however, facilitate the development of community consciousness by acting as responsible and effective members of the communities they inhabit and by creating learning environments that are more meaningful, democratic, and enhancing of learning.

BUILDING COMMUNITY ON A CONSTRUCTIVIST FOUNDATION

Some distance learning courses at the graduate level reflect traditional instructional designs in which learning is viewed as an information delivery process. In the push for universities to market Web-based courses, traditional teacher-centered transmission models emphasizing the efficient delivery of content derived from conventional, print-based materials have prevailed. Despite the availability of instructional technologies offering promising prospects for promoting constructivist learning, adult learners have been treated as passive recipients of content in these environments. Dillenbourg, Schneider, and Synteta (2002) found that most e-learning courses reproduce classroom activities online with virtual campuses mirroring physical campuses.

In traditional educational environments, whether real or virtual, the delivery of curriculum and instruction is the central focus of the educational enterprise; the development of community as a foundation for learning is often ignored. Community building must be addressed at the outset of a course or program. Palloff and Pratt (1999) remind distance learning providers that "attention needs to be paid to the developing sense of community within the group of participants in order for the learning process to be successful" (p. 29). Instructors need to actively support "the natural development of relationships" (Schwier, 2001, p. 6) within these learning communities. Applying a traditional paradigm in the design and delivery of online learning communities is tantamount to implementing old solutions to solve new problems.

Constructivism is emerging as the preferred epistemological approach (e.g., theory of knowing) for creating online learning communities (Hung, 2001). The literature contends that communities founded on social constructivist pedagogy (Jonassen, 2000; Schwier & Balbar, 2002; Weasenforth, 2002) create conditions conducive to the development of online learning communities. Constructivism is founded on the principles of social constructivism where the learner is charged with being an active constructor of knowledge within a socially interactive learning environment. Communicative competence becomes the central focus of learning; learners are engaged in open and critical discourse with their peers and instructors. Tam (2000) contends, "Traditional educational values of replicability, reliability, communication, and control contrast sharply with the seven primary constructivist values of collaboration, personal autonomy, generativity, reflectivity, active engagement, personal relevance, and pluralism" (p. 6) typically found in constructivist learning environments.

In constructivist environments, learning is emphasized over teaching. Learners participate actively in learning activities and instructors become facilitators who assist learners to solve ill-structured problems. Dykes and Schwier (2003) highlight important research (Collinson, Elbaum, Haavind, & Tinker, 2000; Salmon, 2000) asserting that the use of online discussion forums supports social constructivist learning (Maor, 2003) by engaging learners actively, asking them to express their knowledge, and interacting with others as they negotiate, co-create, and expand meaning. Constructivism evolved from Vygotsky (1962, 1978), who proposed the zone of proximal development—the gap between the learner's problem-solving abilities when unassisted and those abilities when assisted by a facilitator. Constructivism was also influenced by Lave and Wenger's (1991) notion of legitimate peripheral participation, a theory rooted in social constructivism in which social presence is the "primary, generative phenomenon, and learning one of its characteristics" (p. 34). The literature confirms that in true communities of practice, learning is "distributed among co-participants" (Lave & Wenger, 1991, p. 15). Oftentimes researchers exploring constructivist learning environments report that "there is very little observable teaching; the more basic phenomenon is learning" (Lave & Wenger, 1991, p. 92).

In constructivist environments, given the limitations of time, distance, and access to students, instructors can never truly be "in control" of every learning situation (Simonson et al., 2003). As such, instructors in constructivist learning environments tend to rely on students to maintain focus on the course objectives, guide discussions, and remain integrally connected to the course content as active learners. Palloff and Pratt (1999) reiterate that "key to the learning process are the interactions among students themselves, the interactions between faculty and students, and the collaboration in learning that results from these interactions" (p. 5).

CASE STUDY OF A LEARNING COMMUNITY IN AN ONLINE GRADUATE PROGRAM

An interpretive qualitative case study was conducted during 2003–2004 by an interdisciplinary team of six faculty members, including this author, who teach in an online graduate program within a college of education at a large state university in Southern California enrolling 33,000 students.

Research Question

The coresearchers investigated the question, "How was an effective online learning community (OLC) developed among the first cohort of students in the master's of science in instructional design and technology program?" The online program, focusing on the direct applications of technology for teaching, learning, and curriculum development for professionals in K–12, business, industry, military, and corporate settings, was designed to provide students with a solid background in the field of instructional design with an emphasis on the design and creation of computer-based training and Internet technologies.

Setting

The cohort formed in 2001 in close physical proximity with an intensive, on-campus "Boot-Up Camp" that served as their first bonding experience. When students returned home, they reinvented this physical proximity as virtual proximity enabled by computer-mediated communication. Blackboard's e-learning course management software served as the primary vehicle, with each of its navigation tools fostering community in a unique way. All courses made extensive use of Blackboard's asynchronous and synchronous collaborative tools. Multiple discussion forums related to weekly course topics were created by each course instructor and functioned as a container for all discussions pertaining to course topics. Discussion threads, subsets of each discussion forum, enabled students to branch out from the designated topics, thereby increasing their control over the learning environment.

Methods

The research was designed using the qualitative case study method (Yin, 2003) to research the phenomenon of online community.

A case study is an empirical inquiry that investigates a contemporary phenomenon within its real-life context, especially when the boundaries between the phenomenon and context are not clearly evident, and that relies on multiple sources of evidence, with data needing to converge in a triangulating fashion, and as another result, benefits from the prior development of theoretical propositions to guide data collection and analysis. (Yin, 2003, pp. 13–14)

Faculty reviewed recent distance learning literature related to online learning communities in higher education and categorized the vast array of theoretical propositions into a conceptual framework of representative studies. This conceptual framework served to guide data collection and analysis. Thus, the case study method proved useful "as a receptacle for putting theories to work" (Eckstein, 1975, p. 100).

Data triangulation was accomplished by collecting data primarily from secondary sources consisting of materials integral to program development including planning, design, delivery, and evaluation documents. The core searchers reviewed documents prepared for national, regional, university, and college committees including advisory councils, workgroups, faculty presentations, Academic Senate, and Western Association of Schools and Colleges (WASC) accreditation. At the programmatic level, the core searchers obtained university-approved course proposals and syllabi for 10 courses that comprised the program. Students' verbatim comments were archived from the discussion boards of four 15-week courses. Each course contained approximately 15 asynchronous threaded discussion forums facilitated by the course instructor. This data set included approximately 60 discussion forums with average postings of 125 postings per forum totaling 7,500 messages. Furthermore, students' written comments about their learning goals were obtained during Boot-Up Camp and reflections on their progress were collected at a Midpoint Symposium and made available to the research group. A focus group, conducted by an outside program evaluator in two, 1-hour sessions split into two parts, was followed by a brief, 10-minute questionnaire followed by a 45-minute discussion concerning students' perceptions about the strengths and weaknesses of the program. Both sessions were tape-recorded with the consent of the participants. A faculty focus group was also conducted in a single, 75-minute session and was tape recorded with participants' consent. Results of both evaluations were provided to the students and to the faculty.

A Web-based interview protocol was posted within a week of students' completion of the program. The survey was based on theoretical propositions discussed in the literature related to online learning community characteristics and was designed to elicit thoughtful, in-depth explorations of each student's perceptions about community development. Survey questions consisted of 14, open-ended questions and one question consisting of 21 items configured in a Likert-like scale ranging from "strongly agree, agree, neither agree or disagree, strongly disagree, and no response." Fifteen of the eighteen students submitted the confidential survey online for a response rate of 83%.

Data analysis was achieved by determining to what extent the characteristics of effective online learning communities converged with or diverged from students' perceptions of community in this program. Researchers sorted through raw data from the sources identified searching for correspondences between the theoretical constructs and the data collected. Trustworthiness was arrived at through data triangulation, consensual validation, member checks, and critiques of multiple drafts of scholarly articles.

Findings and Recommendations

"The sense of community seems so obvious and transparent that it's a taken-for-granted assumption in online learning. When we step back for a moment and realize the tremendous impact of our cohort's culture on learning, we begin to realize that learning is not about content—unless we reframe content to include people, places, and things in our learning community." This student's comment synthesized the perception among students that an e-learning community had formed within the program. Ninety-three percent of students reported that the program embodied a community-centered approach in each of the 10 courses across the program in which "a group of learners shared resources, ideas, and learned together for a common purpose." Ninety-three percent of the students agreed that the environment was founded on constructivist principles of mutual interdependence, connectedness, common expectations, and shared goals focused on learning rather than teaching. Eighty-seven percent of the students' perceived their assessments to be learner-centered, ongoing, aligned with program goals, and benchmarks of their progress as reflected in self-assessments, peer assessments, discussion rubrics, and portfolio assessments. Eighty-seven percent of students cited positive interactions among instructors and peers as highly conducive to community building, but these positive interactions did not correlate with increased academic achievement. Eighty percent of students agreed that critical discourse across multiple discussion forums expanded their capacities as critical thinkers which gave rise, eventually, to a knowledge-building community in which meaningful learning took place. Most students said that although the computer-mediated communication tools in Blackboard's course management software provided a generally supportive technological structure for community development, text-based learning was challenging because it was devoid of visual and verbal cues. Thus, this case study confirmed that students transformed from a cohort of loosely connected individuals at the outset of the program to a community of practice by the end of the program.

CONSTRUCTING COMMUNITY THROUGH COMPUTER-MEDIATED COMMUNICATION

How did learning within a computer-mediated communication environment foster community development in this case study? Learners in this context took full advantage of "fourth-generation" distance learning technologies that use reliable and stable Web-based technologies to facilitate learning (Lauzon & Moore, 1989). In fourth-generation learning technologies, the discrepancies among learning theories, technology, and instructional design disappear. Romiszowski and Mason (1996) provide a working definition of computer-mediated communication, a fourth-generation distance learning technology, as "the process by which people create, exchange, and perceive information using networked telecommunications systems that facilitate encoding, transmitting, and decoding messages" (p. 407). Thus, in this context computer-mediated communication was all at once an instructional technology, a medium, and the engine of social relations. It not only structured social relationships, it became the space within which these relations occurred and the tool that individuals used to navigate the environment.

Riel (1996) argues that building a community is not the same thing as building a physical space. Electronic tools do not define community. It is the partnerships and interactions between and among people that foster or hinder community development within an online learning environment. Students rated their satisfaction with Blackboard's e-learning course management software at 3.7 out of a possible 5 (5 = high) because it was accessible, reliable, and easy to navigate. Blackboard's Course Management software provided a common set of asynchronous and synchronous and navigation tools for designing, delivering, managing, and sustaining participation spanning the program. Table 1 illustrates the complex interrelationships among synchronous and asynchronous learning modes, the instructional technologies implemented across the program, and the impact of computer-mediated communication on community development.

UNDER CONSTRUCTION: SCAFFOLDING THE EXPANSION OF ONLINE LEARNING COMMUNITIES

What is the future of online learning communities fostered by computer-mediated communication? Ongoing epistemological shifts in instructional theory and technological advances will require instructional technologists and university faculty to form stronger partnerships to bring new visions of community to fruition. Web-based simulations, visualizations, immersive learning experiences, game playing, intelligent tutors and avatars, and expanded networks of learners using new collaborative tools in productive ways will be implemented in next-generation communities. Dede (2003) envisions three complementary interfaces for shaping how learners will learn in the next two decades:

1) A world to the desktop interface will provide students with access to distant experts and archives, enabling collaborations, mentoring relationships, and virtual communities-of-practice; 2) expansion of the interfaces for ubiquitous computing in which portable wireless devices infuse virtual resources as students move through the real world. The early stages of augmented reality interfaces are characterized by research on the role of smart objects and intelligent contexts in learning and doing; and 3) Alice-in-Wonderland multi-user virtual environments interfaces in which participants' avatars interact with computer-based agents and digital artifacts in virtual contexts. The initial stages of studies on shared virtual environments are characterized by advances in Internet games and work in virtual reality. (Dede, 2003, p. 2)

Table 1. The Impact of Computer-Mediated Communication on Community Development in an Online Learning Community

Learning Mode	Instructional Technologies	Impact
Asynchronous	Internet	**Provided Access** to distance learning provider with medium speed.
	Course Management Software	**Structured Computer-mediated Communication Environment** Environment was password-protected with access restricted to community members. Promoted ease of use and reliable access to the community through a variety of navigation tools:
		Announcements created a sense of community facilitated by the instructor, provided communicative immediacy, contributed to professional identity formation, and promoted social cohesiveness.
		Course Information archived course syllabi, outlined course content, projected learning goals, and set high course expectations for the community focused on student-centered learning.
		Course Documents archived text-based course materials, multimedia materials, narrated lectures, PowerPoint Presentations (e.g., Camtasia), prerecorded streaming video (e.g., Tegrity). File sharing provided the community with a common core of information and materials.
		Assignments published instructor timelines, allowed for pacing, organized learning activities into manageable chunks and projected common learning goals that community members collaborated to achieve.
		E-mail personalized and individualized communication (one-to-one and one-to-many), connected members within small learning groups, and provided students with instructor feedback via e-tutoring, e-coaching, and electronic office hours.
Synchronous		**Discussion Boards** served as containers for discussions in the community, engaged learners in exchanging multiple perspectives, promoted appreciation for diversity, encouraged individual and collective meaning making, sparked critical thinking and critical reflection, tracked individual participation, integrated course content through problem-based and project-based learning activities, documented cohort stages of development, and contributed to the growth and development of knowledge-building communities.
		Discussion Board Threads permitted divergent student-generated discussion topics, convergent and divergent thinking related to course topics, and reflected group stages of development within the community.
	CD-ROM	**Storage medium** for large file formats, graphics, compressed video, student portfolios, and learning objects archived community achievement.
	Software Applications	**Flash, Producer** Enhanced media literacy and design competencies of community members.
	Web Conferencing (pc chat)	**Enabled real-time interactions for learning** Provided written records of meetings for later reflection by the community.

SCAFFOLDING COMMUNITY DEVELOPMENT: THEORETICAL SHIFTS

1. *Instructional Theory.* The misapplication of learning theories such as implementing behavioral approaches instead of constructivist approaches to shape community development remains an obstacle in virtual learning. Instructional approaches will become more learner-centered, recursive, and nonlinear; self-directed; and meaningful from the learner's perspective. Stated differently, "Distance education can be seen to be evolving from an essentially modernist and bureaucratic form of education into a post-modernist phenomenon with a focus on the student as consumer, on flexibility, and global reach" (Rumble, 2001, p. 31). Dillenbourg et al. (2002) view the most promising work in e-learning as investigating functionalities that do not exist in face-to-face interactions.

2. *Designing for Diversity.* The number of online learning communities will increase emanating from a variety of global settings reflecting infinite variations in community sizes, cultures, and intellectual purposes thereby removing some of the barriers to access and equity in higher education. Implementing culturally responsive online learning environments will be essential to meet the needs of learners from different cultural traditions and, perhaps, for promoting social activist agendas. Martin (1994) comments on the hidden curriculum supporting the myth that men are more competent technologically than women or that it will take women longer to learn via the Internet. Educators need to be aware that "our nation was founded on diversity and has always thrived on the introduction of new ideas and viewpoints" (Martin, 1994, p. 226). The cost of suppressing perspectives is high, and there is a risk that students who do not see themselves or their lives and experiences reflected in the curriculum or program will be disenfranchised. There will also be a shift toward increased accessibility for those who are disabled as researchers feel that "e-Learning holds great promise ... for learners with physical and mental challenges" (Frydenberg, 2002, p. 7). Thus, it is critical that distance educators develop a community of inclusion rather than exclusion.

3. *Implementing Adult Learning Theory.* Adult learning theory, initially promulgated by Knowles (1980), directs attention to the wealth of knowledge and experience adults bring to the learning environment that can be used as a rich resource for learning. Knowles found that adults prefer collaborative learning environments, value self-directed learning, gain understanding and meaning through critically reflective dialogue, and apply what they learn to solve practical problems. Self-direction is made more possible in a hypertext environment where adults can choose which pathways they wish to explore. Online learning communities that apply andragogical theories, focus on the art and science of teaching adults rather than pedagogical theories, and focus on the art and science of teaching children create more appropriate online climates for adult learners, as Fidishun (2000) contends. Mezirow (1991) views a learning community as an opportunity for adult learners to experience perspective transformations while Brookfield and Preskill (1999) argue that facilitating dialogue is the most effective way to teach adults, whether on the ground or online. Two concepts likely to emerge in future online learning communities, according to Romiszowski and Mason (1996), are a "break down of the distinction between the teacher and the taught, and the collective construction of the educational course and, more broadly, of new knowledge" (p. 426).

4. *Facilitating Communities of Discourse.* Learning designs reflecting a "shared exploration of thought processes that lie behind ideas, not just the logic and data in isolation, but also at the human needs and relationships that underlie the issues" (Hudson, 2002, p. 54) will characterize future communities of discourse. Scheffel, Omdal, and Usrey (2000) note that "educators need to understand if and how learning is taking place in an online community. Contingency in discourse may be viewed as a characteristic reflecting knowledge construction between participants and inferring resulting cognitive change" (p. 79). Feenberg (1993) proposes that community growth will also be enabled by electronic language made permanent and more easily reflected on than oral discourse in classroom environments.

SCAFFOLDING COMMUNITY DEVELOPMENT: COMPUTER-MEDIATED COMMUNICATION

1. *Increased Applications of Multimedia.* "New technology will transform higher education as we know it today" (Oblinger & Kidwell, 2000, p. 2). Multimedia resources and access to vast collections of newly digitized materials will characterize these expanded environments. Developments in groupware will forge new social structures. Communities may be expected to migrate from e-learning environments where learners are still tied to a place-based mode of educational delivery to mobile access to distance learning. With the rise in use of mobile telephones and their convergence with personal digital assistants, new vistas will open up to increase the personalization and intimacy of learning experiences. Instructional technology functionalities not imagined ten years ago will be achieved. For example, in 2018, it is projected that computers will be able to translate languages in real time with the accuracy and speed necessary for effective communications.

2. *Expanded Computer Networks.* The Internet2, a not-for-profit consortium network dedicated to educational research among 200 universities across the United States and their educational partners, is deploying advanced network applications and technology, accelerating the creation of tomorrow's Internet. With participation by more than 60 leading companies, the Internet2 will recreate new partnerships among academia, industry, and government. Internet2 will not replace the Internet; rather, it will link resources from academia, industry, and government to develop new technologies and capabilities that can then be deployed in the global Internet. Ubiquitous Internet computing and the Internet2 will increase distance learners' access to information exponentially. With all the growth in online learning communities, an increase in course management systems using the Internet2 will become more crucial.

3. *Increased Use of Digital Video.* Although video has been recognized as a powerful instructional medium, it has been marginalized in Web-based instructional environments because compressed video images are small, fuzzy, and jerky. In the future, students will have enhanced access to full motion video resources including Web-based video clips and video streaming of live and prerecorded material. "Internet2 video includes traditional video as well as simulations, animations, virtual reality, movies, images with audio tracks, remote control of microphones and other instrumentations and many other types of digital media objects" (p. 2), according to Mardis and Fox (2002). For instance, students will be able to click on a hot link in their Web-based course and be transferred immediately to an MPEG file resident on a video server where video can be easily viewed, sized, and saved. Students will be able to create an

index of video clips to demonstrate their learning and save their productions to meta-data text files that can be sent to the instructor as e-mail attachments. However, the reapplication of video for distance education cannot be bridged without clarifying what constitutes fair use and intellectual property rights. Digital rights licensing is a relatively new phenomenon, and given the incipient nature of digital media, it will take time for producers to convert analog to digital video for use in this expanding marketplace.

4. *Synchronous Interactions through Desktop Videoconferencing.* A study conducted by Kies, Williges, and Rosson (1997) indicates that "students in real classroom situations may be less critical of poor video quality than in laboratory settings and confirms the results from the laboratory study in that performance does not suffer. However, the current state-of-the-art of video conferencing technology needs to be improved and configured most effectively to support college teaching at a distance" (p. 79). Technological advancements and research into desktop videoconferencing will cause distance educators to question how technologies such as videoconferencing can be applied to improve distributed learning and enhance participation in online learning communities. Increasingly, distance learners will be exposed to learning communities where visual and verbal information will be transmitted via desktop videoconferencing through point-to-point videoconferences, connecting two participants, or through multipoint videoconferences, connecting three or more participants. Desktop videoconferencing, one of the fastest-growing segments of the computer industry, will affect learner satisfaction with distance learning.

CONCLUSION

To summarize, this chapter focused on the dramatic changes taking place in distance learning in higher education where enrollments are surpassing the capacity of traditional infrastructures, learner profiles are reflecting greater diversity, and adult learners are demanding educational practices that meet their needs for professional growth. As this case study demonstrated, self-improving online learning communities are characterized by participants' active knowledge construction, sociocognitive scaffolding, and distributed expertise. As Bates (2003) concludes, "the biggest challenge in distance education is the lack of vision and the failure to use technology strategically" (p. 7).

REFERENCES

Anderson, T., & Misanchuk, M. (2001). *Building community in an online environment.* (ERIC Document Reproduction Services No. ED463-725).

Bates, T. (2003). Higher education and e-learning: Integration or change? University of British Columbia. Retrieved December 18, 2005, from http://www.tonybates.ca/pdf/Integration_or_change.pdf

Brook, J., & Boal, I. A. (Eds.). (1995). *Resisting the virtual life: The culture and politics of information.* San Francisco: City Lights Books.

Brookfield, S. D., & Preskill, S. (1999). *Discussion as a way of teaching.* San Francisco: Jossey-Bass.

Brown, J., & Issacs, D. (1995). Building corporations as communities: The best of both worlds. In K. Gozdz (Ed.), *Community building: Renewing spirit and learning in business.* San Francisco: Sterling and Stone.

Bruffee, K. (1993). *Collaborative learning: Higher education, independence, and the authority of knowledge.* Baltimore: Johns Hopkins University Press.

Chang, C. (2003). Towards a distributed web-based learning community. *Innovations in Education and Teaching International.* London: Routledge.

Collinson, G., Elbaum, B., Haavind, S., & Tinker, R. (2000). *Facilitating online learning: Effective strategies for moderators.* Madison, WI: Atwood.

Dede, C. (1995). The evolution of distance education: Emerging technologies and distributed learning. *American Journal of Distance Education, 10*(2), 4–36.

Dede, C. (2003a). *Distributed learning communities as a model for educating teachers.* Retrieved March 30, 2005 from http://www.gse.harvard.edu/~dedech/505/Distributed-Learning_Communities.pdf

Dede, C. (2003b). Vignettes about the future of learning technologies. In *Visions 2020: Transforming education and training through advanced technologies.* Washington, DC: U.S. Department of Commerce. Retrieved December 18, 2005, from http://www.ta.doc.gov/reports/TechPolicy/2020Visions.pdf

Dillenbourg, P., Schneider, D., & Synteta, V.(2002). *Virtual learning environments: Proceedings of the 3rd Congressional Information and Communication Technologies in Education* (pp. 3–18). Greece: Kostanitos Editions.

Dykes, M., & Schweir, R. (2003). Content and community redux: Instruction and student interpretations of online community in a graduate seminar. *Canadian Journal of Learning and Technology, 29*(2), 79–99.

Eckstein, H. (1975). Case study and theory in political science. In F. I. Greenstein & N. W. Polsby (Eds.), *Strategies of inquiry.* Reading, MA: Addison-Wesley.

Feenberg, A. (1993). Building a global network: The WBSI experience. In L. Harasim (Ed.), *Global networks: Computerizing the international community.* Cambridge, MA: MIT Press.

Fidishun, D. (2000). *Andragogy and technology: Integrating adult learning theory as we teach with technology.* Retrieved March 30, 2005 from http://www.mtsu.edu/~itconf/proceed00/fidishun.htm

Frydenberg, J. (2002, October). Quality standards in e-Learning: A matrix of analysis. International Review of Research in Open and Distance Learning. 3(2). Retrieved December 18, 2005, from: http://www.irrodl.org/content/v3.2/frydenberg.html

Garrison, D. R., & Anderson, T. (2003). *E-learning in the 21st century: A framework for research and practice.* New York: Routedge/Falmer.

Haythornthwaite, C., Kazmer, M., & Robins, J. (2000). Community development among distance learners: Temporal and technological dimensions. *Journal of Computer-Mediated Communication, 16*(1), 431–463.

Hiltz, S., Coppola, N., Rotter, N. Turoff, M., & Benbunan-Fich, R. (2000). Measuring the importance of collaborative learning for the effectiveness of ALN: A multi-measure, multi-method approach. *Journal of Asynchronous Learning Networks, 4*(2). Retrieved October 18, 2004, from http://www.aln.org/alnweb/journal/Vol4_issue2/le/hiltz/le-hiltz.htm

Hudson, B. (2002). Critical dialogue online. In Rudestam, K. E. & Schoenholtz-Read, J. B. (Eds.), *The Handbook of online learning* (pp. 53–90). Thousand Oaks, CA: Sage.

Hung, D. (2001). Theories of learning and computer-mediated instructional technologies. *Education Media International, 38*(4): 283–287.

Institute for Higher Education Policy. (2000, April). *Quality on the line: Benchmarks for success in Internet distance education.* Washington, DC: Author.

Johnson, C. (2001). A survey of current research on online communities of practice. *Pergamon: The Internet and Higher Education, 4*, 45–60.

Jonassen, D. (1993, January). The trouble with learning environments. *Educational Technology Journal, 33*(1), 35–37.

Jonassen, D. (2000). Technology and constructivism. In M. Moore & N. Shin (Eds.), *Speaking personally about distance education: Foundations of contemporary practice.* University Park: Pennsylvania State University.

Jonassen, D., Campbell, J., & Davidson, M. (1994). Learning with media: Restructuring the debate. *Educational Technology Research and Development, 42*(3), 31–39.

Jones, D. (1995). 1000 users on a 486. *Proceedings of AUUG '95 and Asia-Pacific World Wide Web '95 Conference* (pp. 105–120), Sydney.

Kaye, A. (1995). Computer supported collaborative learning. In N. Heap, R. Thomas, G. Einon, R. Mason, & H. MacKay, *Information technology and society* (pp. 192–210). London: Sage.

Kies, J., Williges, R., & Rosson, M. B. (1997, February). Evaluating desktop videoconferencing for distance learning. *Computers and Technology, 28*(2), 79–91.

Knowles, M. (1980). The modern practice of adult education: From pedagogy to andragogy. Chicago: Association Press/Follett.

Kollock, P., & Smith, M. (1997). *Communities in cyberspace: Perspectives on new forms of social organization.* Berkley: University of California Press.

Lauzon, A., & Moore, G.(1989). A fourth generation distance education system: Integrating computer-assisted learning and computer conferencing. *American Journal of Distance Education, 3*(1), 38–49.

Lave, J., & Wenger, E. (1991). *Situated learning: Legitimate peripheral participation.* New York: Cambridge University Press.

Lock, J. (2002). Laying the groundwork for the development of learning communities within online courses. *Quarterly Review of Distance Education, 3*(4), 395–408.

Lockhard, J. (1996). Progressive politics, electronic individualism, and the myth of virtual community. *Berkeley: California University Press.*

MacNeil, T. (1997). Assessing the gap between community development practice and regional development policy. In B. Wharf & M. Clague (Eds.), *Community organizing: Canadian experiences* (pp. 149–163). Toronto: Oxford University Press.

Maeroff, G. (2003). *A classroom of one: How online learning is changing our schools and colleges.* New York: Palgrave/MacMillan.

Maor, D. (2003). The teacher's role in developing interaction and reflection in an online learning community. *Education Media International, 40*(1/2), 127–137.

Mardis, M., & Fox, L. (2002). Viewing the future: Aligning I2 Video to K–12 Curriculum. Retrieved December 18, 2005, from http://vtf.merit.edu/vtfproposal.pdf

Martin, J. R. (1994). *Changing the educational landscape.* New York: Routledge Press.

McIsaac, M., & Gunawardena, C. (1996). Distance education. In D. H. Jonassen (Ed.), *Handbook of research for educational communications and technology* (pp. 403–437). New York: Simon & Schuster Macmillan.

Mezirow (1991). *Transformative Dimensions of Adult Learning.* San Francisco: Jossey-Bass.

Morrison, J., & Shrivastava, P. (2001, March/April). Online communities as a new learning paradigm: An interview with Paul Shrivastava. *The Technology Source.* Retrieved December 18, 2005, from http://www.technologysource.org/article/online_communities_as_a_new_learning_paradigm/

Oblinger, D., & Kidwell, J. (2000, May/June). Distance learning: Are we being realistic? *Educause,* 31–39.

Palloff, R. M., & Pratt, K. (1999). *Building learning communities in cyberspace: Effective strategies for the online classroom.* San Francisco: Jossey-Bass.

Rheingold, H. (1993). *The virtual community: Homesteading on the electronic frontier.* New York: Harper Perennial.

Riel, M. (1996). The Internet: A land to settle rather than an ocean to surf and an new "place" for school reform through community development. Retrieved December 18, 2005, from http://globalschoolhouse.org/gsh/teach/articles/netasplace.html

Rogers, J. (2000). Communities of practice: A framework for fostering coherence in virtual learning communities. *Educational Technology & Society, 3*(3). Retrieved December 18, 2005, from http://ifets.ieee.org/periodical/vol_3_2000/e01.html

Romiszowski, A. J., & Mason, R. (1996). Computer-mediated communication. In D. H. Jonassen (Ed.), *Handbook of research for educational communications and technology* (pp. 438–456). New York: Macmillian LIBRARY Reference USA.

Roschelle, J., & Pea, R. (1999). Trajectories from today's WWW to a powerful educational infrastructure. *Educational Researcher, 8*(5), 22–25.

Rovai, A. P. (2001). Building classroom community at a distance: A case study. *Educational technology research and development, 49*(4), 33–48.

Rovai, A. (2002). Building a sense of community at a distance. *International Review of Research in Open and Distance Learning, 3*(1). Retrieved December 18, 2005, from http://www.irrodl.org/content/v3.1/rovai.htm

Rumble, G., (January, 2001). Reinventing distance education. *International Journal of Lifelong Education, 20*(1–2), 31–43.

Salmon, G. (2000). *E-moderating: The key to teaching and learning online*. London: Kogan Page.

Schaffer, C., & Anudsen, K. (1993). *Creating community anywhere*. New York: Jeremy Tarcher/Perigree Books.

Scheffel, D., Omdal, S., & Usrey, D. (2000, April). *Computer mediated linguistic interaction as a tool for the social construction of knowledge*. Paper presented at the Annual Meeting of the Central States Communication Association, Detroit, Michigan.

Schuler, D. (1996). *New community networks: Wired for change*. New York: Addison-Wesley.

Schwier, R. (2001). Catalysts, emphases, and elements of virtual learning communities: Implications for research and practice. *Quarterly Review of Distance Education, 2*(1), 5–18.

Schwier, R., & Balbar, D. (2002). The interplay of content and community in synchronous and asynchronous communications: Virtual communication in a graduate seminar. *Canadian Journal of Learning and Technology, 28*(2), 21–30.

Simonson, M., Smaldino, S., Albright, M., & Zvacek, S. (2003). *Teaching and learning at a distance: Foundations of distance education* (2nd ed.). Upper Saddle River, New Jersey: Merrill/Prentice Hall.

Sloan Consortium. (2004). *Entering the mainstream: The quality and extent of online education in the United States, 2003 and 2004*. Retrieved from http://www.sloan-c.org/resources/entering_mainstream.pdf

Tam, M. (2000). Constructivism, instructional design, and technology: Implications for transforming distance learning. *Educational Technology and Society*. Retrieved April 21, 2005, from http://ifets.ieee.org/periodical/vol_2_2000/tam.html

Tu, C., & Corry, M. (2001). A paradigm shift for online community research. *Distance Education, 22*(2), 245–263.

Tu, C., & Corry, M. (2002). E-learning communities. *Quarterly Review of Distance Education, 3*(2), 207–218.

Tu, C., & McIssac, M. (2001). *Community of Practice for Mentoring*. Paper presented at the Annual Conference of American Educational Research Association.

Twigg, C. (2001). *Innovations in online learning: Moving beyond no significant difference*. Troy, NY: Center for Academic Transformation.

Vygotsky, L.(1962). *Thought and language*. Cambridge, MA: MIT Press/Harvard University Press.

Vygotsky, L.(1978). *Mind in society: The development of higher psychological processes*. Cambridge, MA: Harvard University Press.

Weasenforth, D. (2002, September). Realizing constructivist objectives through collaborative technologies: Threaded discussions. *Language learning and technology, 6*(3), 58–86.

Wenger, E. (1998). *Communities of practice: Learning, meaning, and identity*. Cambridge, England: Cambridge University Press.

Yin, R. (2003). *Case study research design and methods* (4th ed.). Thousand Oaks, CA: Sage.

Utilizing Multimedia PBL to Engage Preservice Teachers in Multicultural Special Education Decision Making

Mary L. Kelly and Theresa A. Cullen
Indiana University

Min-Joung Kim
Vanderbilt University

INTRODUCTION

The 2004 *Educational Media and Technology Yearbook* stresses accessibility as a growing area of interest in the field of instructional technology (Orey, 2004). This is especially true for K–12 audiences for which state and federal laws have increased requirements for educators, administrators, and parents to be knowledgeable and to promote new and diverse learning environments for students with special needs. These requirements necessitate that innovative ways are developed to provide preservice teachers with experiences to prepare them to address the needs of students with special needs before entering the profession. This study reports the use of a multimedia problem-based learning (PBL) module to help preservice teachers learn about issues involved in identifying and providing services to students with disabilities, including those with limited English proficiency (LEP), collaborating with multiple stakeholders, and using student artifacts to develop a decision-making rationale in the best interests of their students.

Knowledge Required by Teachers

The central educational goal of assisting preservice teachers to foster professional skills is often challenging because students typically do not have sufficient opportunities to gain realistic experiences before becoming teachers (Andrews, 2002). In addition, teaching is a complex, dynamic profession in which challenges regularly occur that require teachers to incorporate new information, make decisions, and problem solve (Howard, 2002; Jonassen & Hernandez-Serrano, 2002).

Teaching students with disabilities represents one such challenge to general education teachers. For example, the Individuals with Disabilities Education Improvement Act of 2004 (IDEA) reaffirms the requirement that students with disabilities receive a free, appropriate public education (FAPE) in the least restrictive environment (LRE). The LRE is an one that best meets students' needs in the most typical educational setting possible. This requirement has resulted in a dramatic transformation whereby a majority of students with disabilities are no longer educated in separate settings but are now educated in typical general education classrooms with special education supports (Hallahan & Kauffman, 2003; Turnbull, Turnbull, Wehmeyer, & Park, 2003). This change requires that general education teachers have sufficient background knowledge and experience with identifying students for special education services. This challenge may be compounded for general education teachers who are working with students who are English language learners (ELL; Tyler & Smith, 2000). Many educators lack the experience to distinguish between academic difficulties resulting from second-language acquisition and those resulting from learning disabilities (Ochoa et al., 2001). This may lead to students with LEP incorrectly being referred to and placed in special education programs (Artiles & Trent, 1994; Ochoa, Kelly, Stuart, & Rogers-Adkinson, 2004). IDEA also requires educators to work collaboratively with other school personnel (e.g., administrators, special educators, school counselors) and parents to evaluate student behavior, work, and other student needs such as language difficulties to design an individualized education program (IEP), a signed legal document that identifies a student's academic accommodations and goals (Hallahan & Kauffman, 2003; Ochoa et al., 2001).

PROBLEM-BASED LEARNING

To be ready to participate in planning for students with special needs, preservice teachers need experiences to prepare them to identify students with disabilities and design appropriate learning accommodations. It is impractical and not always in the best interest of K–12 students to only train preservice teachers in real-life settings for special education-related topics because actual student outcomes are at stake (Andrews, 2002). Opportunities for contextualized learning before having field-based experiences are important, and instructional techniques such as PBL address this need (Baker, 2000). PBL provides meaningful contextualized tasks that serve as a stimulus for knowledge building (Howard, 2002). Situations used in PBL are often called "ill-structured" (Jonassen & Hernandez-Serrano, 2002) and typically mirror imperfect real-life decisions that professionals (e.g., educators, doctors) need to make based on incomplete and constantly changing information (Baker, 2000; Howard, 2002).

Using Technology to Meet Knowledge and Experience Needs

Researchers (Baker, 2000; Langone, Malone, & Clinton, 1999; Ochoa, Vasquez, & Gerber, 1999) have found that the use of technology can enhance the ability of preservice teachers to acquire skills and content knowledge when the computer is used as part of well-designed and well-managed instruction. Furthermore, in an analysis of a video-enhanced case with preservice teachers, Van Den Berg, Jansen, and Blijleven (2004) found that the multimedia components, especially video, not only motivated students but also aided them in transferring the learning to future teaching opportunities. De La Paz, Hernandes-Ramos, and Barron (2004) found that the multimedia presentation of content allowed students to respond more effectively to observations in their field experiences. This benefit of multimedia was especially important given the difficulty in placing students in a variety of field experiences to prepare them for diverse professional settings.

The study presented in this chapter investigates the impact of implementing a multimedia PBL module, titled Multicultural Special Education (MUSE), in a contextualized learning experience for preservice teachers. The MUSE module was developed as part of the CASELINK series of multimedia PBL cases designed by researchers at the University of California at Santa Barbara to train preservice teachers to think about special education issues in realistic, professional contexts (Gerber, English, & Singer, 1999). The main goal of the modules is to give preservice teachers an opportunity to use information and interact with their peers to become self-sufficient, lifelong learners who are able to adapt to new professional situations (Ochoa et al., 2001).

The MUSE module required preservice teachers to complete a number of tasks, including (a) assessing a student named "Andres" who has limited English proficiency and potential learning disabilities; (b) participating on a team to create an educational plan including an IEP, assessment strategies, and a daily schedule; and (c) making decisions about whether to refer Andres for special education services (Ochoa et al., 2004). The module provided information about the student through interviews with school personnel and family representatives, video footage of actual school interactions, artifacts of the student's work (e.g., writing samples, drawings, test results), and background about related special education laws and concepts. In addition, preservice teachers were required to role-play a typical IEP member during the decision-making process to encourage realistic, collaborative problem solving. Roles included a school principal, a special education teacher, a parent representative, a general education teacher, a bilingual education teacher, and a school psychologist. Students were provided with video and audio interviews, documents, and Internet links that described each stakeholder's perspective.

The study presented in this chapter is the qualitative portion of a larger, mixed-methods study. The focus of the study was to investigate whether preservice teachers felt more prepared to be professional educators who could identify, assess, discuss, and recommend services for English language learners and students with disabilities after using the MUSE module. The study also examined the impact of the PBL experience on student learning. Lastly, the study investigated the contribution of multimedia components to the PBL process.

METHOD

Participants

Thirty-three students were enrolled in an introductory course on teaching exceptional learners in elementary education at a large Midwestern university taught by a doctoral student with diverse experiences with special needs students. The students were required to complete the MUSE module as part of the requirements of the course. Twenty-nine students were women and four students were men. Thirty-one students were Caucasian, one was Asian, and one was Hispanic. Ten students were seniors, nineteen were juniors, and four were sophomores. Twenty-nine students were elementary education majors, and four were noneducation majors. The majority of students had some field experiences before enrolling in the class but indicated little or no experience working with students with disabilities, evaluating a student, creating an IEP, or using a PBL-based case.

Setting

During the PBL activity, the class was grouped into six self-formed groups of five to six students. The activities took place over the course of six 75-minute class sessions. The first and last sessions took place in the general classroom and the remaining four took place in a computer lab equipped with 35 computers. The first session provided an introduction to the PBL process. The instructor gave an overview of PBL, and the class discussed PBL concepts. Over the next four classes in a computer lab, the preservice teachers participated in activities that involved both individual and group work. The first activity was an introduction to Andres, the elementary student presented in the module. The activity required individuals to write a brief assessment of the student based on the information provided in the case. The second activity involved investigating the scenario more in-depth and developing a group consensus about the student's situation. The third activity involved individuals selecting a role strand and exploring information from only one stakeholder's perspective and deciding on an IEP goal for the student. The small groups then met, compared information from their various stakeholder perspectives, and developed a common IEP plan and schedule for the student through a process of discussing, negotiating, and problem solving. On the final day, students met again in the regular classroom in their small groups to develop final recommendations on whether the student should be referred to special education or not and then participated in a classwide discussion about their recommendations and their overall thoughts about the PBL module.

Procedures

The study used qualitative methodologies to collect and analyze the data. This methodological approach was useful for gaining a more in-depth understanding of the participants' perspectives about their learning experience (Denzin & Lincoln, 2000). The study used a variety of qualitative data sources to evaluate the research questions to triangulate the findings and increase the internal validity of the data. Data sources included student reflections submitted online to the instructor after the completion of each of the module steps as part of the general course requirements, a voluntary open-ended survey question, as well as observations of the group collaboration process. After student identifiers were removed in accordance with human subjects' approval, the constant comparative method (Glaser & Strauss, 1967) was used to evaluate the data and identify emergent themes from the data.

The following prompt was used to generate student reflections after the completion of each module step: "Reflect on the Andres activities up to now. What are some of your thoughts, concerns, questions, or issues that come to mind? Think about what you're exploring related to Andres as well as the Problem Based Learning (PBL) process itself." After the final session, students were also required to post a response to the following prompt:

> One of the major objectives of this activity was to simulate the dynamics of the interdisciplinary team. What were some of the challenges your group experienced? How did you resolve them? Also, provide any additional overall comments on this activity.

Participants were also given a space to respond to an open-ended question on a survey distributed at the completion of the module. The question asked students to "Please add any additional comments about the Andres activity."

RESULTS AND DISCUSSION

In analyzing the data, several recurrent themes emerged that characterized the preservice teachers' experiences using the multimedia PBL module. The emergent themes have been categorized within the framework of each research question.

Question 1: Do Preservice Teachers Feel More Prepared to Be Professional Educators after Using the MUSE Module?

Q1.A) The experience had real-life applicability to future teaching.

The PBL process involves participants in the process of solving "real-life" problems from which knowledge and experience can be gained (Bridges & Hallinger, 1997). The feedback from the preservice teachers indicated that the sense of authenticity about the characters and team planning process enhanced their learning experience and had real-life applicability for their future teaching. Three primary areas of real-life applicability expressed by the participants included a better sense of understanding the requirements of teaching students with disabilities and English language learners, participating in an IEP team, and being more prepared to assess students.

Specifically, participants indicated that the MUSE case gave them the opportunity to learn more about students with disabilities and LEP and make decisions about the student in the module through observations of his interactions, samples of his academic work, and comments about the student by school personnel and a family representative. Participants indicated that this process gave them an opportunity to get to know how to better meet the needs of students in their future classrooms. Typical responses included those such as, "The Andres case has given me a good perspective of what it would be like to have a child in the classroom that needs special help and also struggles with the English language."

For most of the participants, this was the first time they had exposure to the IEP process, and therefore they found the experience particularly valuable. Typical sentiments are reflected by comments such as, "I believe that it was good for me personally because I got a little taste of what being on an IEP team was like. I feel that now I would be a lot more comfortable being on an actual team in the field where as [sic] before I was really afraid of the possibility of being on a team like this." Involvement in the module provided participants with an opportunity to rehearse being on an IEP team and contribute to special education planning.

In addition to feeling a sense that they gained insight into having a student with special needs in the classroom, the preservice teachers also expressed that they felt better prepared to assess whether a student had a disability through their activities in the MUSE case. Typical comments included ones such as, "I have really enjoyed this exploration. I have learned many things that will help me be able to evaluate students who might need special help." and "Referral is a really tough job to do and as a future educator you want to do what is best for the child. It was really hard, but on the other hand, it gave some really great experience on the evaluation process."

Feeling prepared to assess a student is not a notion often held by novice teachers, especially within general education (Stough & Palmer, 2003). The assessment of a student's learning needs is particularly challenging when a student's first language is different from the teacher's language. The teacher may find it difficult to assess whether learning difficulties are a result of not understanding the language of instruction or from a disability (Rogers-Adkinson, Ochoa, & Delgado, 2003). Student comments such as, "It gave us a really good idea of what we will have to deal with in our classroom. We will have children like that that are really borderline and you are not sure what you should do" reflect a greater awareness of the issues they may face as real teachers in their own classrooms.

Q1.B) Participants developed collaboration skills.

In school settings, collaboration skills are essential (Tschannen-Moran & Woolfolk-Hay, 2000). General education teachers must be skillful in working with special education teachers, parents and caregivers, and other school professionals to meet the needs of their students (Gerber et al., 1999; Matthews & Menna, 2003). Those involved in the decision-making process about students represent different goals and knowledge bases, all of which must come together to ensure that students are being taught the goals identified in the IEP (Gerber et al., 1999; Howard, 2002).

Collaboration is a skill that often is not taught sufficiently in teacher education programs but is an increasingly required skill because of educational reform efforts (Tschannen-Moran & Woolfolk-Hay, 2000). Ge and Land (2004) found several benefits of collaborative problem solving to students including "providing and receiving explanations, co-constructing ideas, resolving conflicts, and negotiating meaning" (p. 10).

The MUSE module provided numerous opportunities for participants to have discussions, negotiate, and work together as part of a team. Once participants acquired their roles and shared their information with their group members, the groups were required to make decisions about the student. Student reflections included numerous comments about the impact of the collaboration process. Typical comments included ones such as, "This activity has been very successful in working as a group with other people in our class. We have learned so much as a group in how to solve problems in the education field with this real situation regarding Andres" and "It was in this exercise that we really came together as a group, all offering our own insight into what would be the best assessments for Andres, as well as important goals for him." This process of information sharing and decision making provided students an opportunity to practice collaborating with colleagues to accomplish their goals.

Question 2: What Are Ways in which PBL Fosters Engagement with Special Education Concepts and Practices for Preservice Teachers?

Q2.A) PBL provided an authentic context for learning.

One of the goals of PBL is to provide an authentic learning experience for participants (Albanese & Mitchell, 1993). This goal is particularly important for preservice teachers who are working to gain skills to make themselves more effective teachers (Bridges & Hallinger, 1997). Issues of meeting the needs of students with special learning needs are of particular concern for preservice teachers (Ochoa et al., 1999). Because each student's individual needs differ greatly, they require individual attention and unique interventions to tailor a plan to create the best environment for their learning (Andrews, 2002).

Participant comments showed empathy, a developing understanding of the student's situation, and a concern for his future. The participants demonstrated that they incorporated material about the student's current level of performance and made inferences about what might happen to him in his future through their successful participation in the module activities. They showed responsiveness to his perceived needs ("if Andres needed us to") and incorporated it into their group plans, as shown by comments such as, "Hopefully we have come up with a plan for Andres that suits him and will help him flourish in the classroom. My fear is that we have not come up with a plan that is BEST for Andres."

Participants' emotional connection to other module characters was particularly evident when they expressed frustration about Andres' general education teacher. Several participant remarks included strongly worded, judgmental comments, especially toward the actions of the classroom teacher. Typical comments included ones such as, "What bothers me most about his situation is his general ed teacher. I don't feel as though she puts 100% effort towards Andres. I understand that she has other students in the classroom, but she doesn't even try to communicate with his parents. The whole situation with her really bothers me" and "How do the teachers think that his performance will improve when they're not changing anything that they are trying with him?" Because the participants were preservice general education teachers, they were particularly sensitive to any shortcomings they perceived in the classroom teacher's actions.

Q2.B) PBL challenged students to resolve ill-structured problems.

One of the key characteristics of the PBL process is working with an ill-structured problem that reflects the messy, real-life complications of problem solving (Howard, 2002; Jonassen & Hernandez-Serrano, 2002). In some PBL structures, such as the one used in this module, the students are expected to solve problems with missing details and with each student having unique pieces of knowledge to contribute to the process. They seek out information from various sources, prioritize relevant information, and filter out irrelevant information to define the problem. After defining the problem, students are expected to make decisions without perfect knowledge and are not provided with the certainty that their decision is the correct one (Duffy & Cunningham, 2001).

The MUSE case provided comprehensive, albeit incomplete, information about the student and his situation. Despite the variety and depth of information provided, a number of the teams expressed frustration at the perceived lack of information. Typical comments included ones such as, "It would have been a better activity if we had more information about Andres [because] I felt for the most part we were really struggling to make a decision because of lack of information."

Despite concerns about the lack of information, participants were required to utilize the resources and information provided and to reach a collaborative solution. It was necessary for the teams to develop a process to use the information they had and overcome their perceptions that it was an inadequate amount from which to make a decision. A number of participants shared their teams' problem-solving strategies with the ill-structured scenario. Typical reflections included sentiments such as,

> We did not feel like we had all the information we wanted to complete the activity. We overcame it by talking it out with each other and using everyone's input to try and complete the information as much as possible ... or at least make up a scenario that was as close as we could get to the actual truth. There were also several times we just disagreed on certain things, but we would talk through them as well. I think our team did an excellent job talking through things and reaching conclusions based on our knowledge.

Despite perceptions that there was insufficient information to make a fully informed decision, all teams completed the module's activities, developed an educational plan for the student, and were able to make a final decision about whether they would recommend that the student be referred to special education. This ability for participants to accomplish the module goals indicates that the PBL module was appropriately ill structured. Students perceived they didn't have all the answers but were able to collaborate successfully and problem solve sufficiently to respond to the module questions. This incomplete problem structure mirrors how a real IEP meeting may progress because each team member brings to the meeting their personal interactions and experiences with the student (Gerber et al., 1999). For example, a teacher would have special insight on classroom behavior, whereas a school psychologist may have one-on-one counseling information about the student.

Question 3: How Does the Use of Multimedia in the Module Impact Satisfaction with the PBL Experience?

Multimedia is a powerful teaching resource (De La Paz et al., 2004). Multimedia can help strengthen students' conceptual understanding of a topic by linking visual imagery and sound to information that is difficult to understand when presented in text alone (Cognition and Technology Group at Vanderbilt University, 1994; Van Den Berg et al., 2004).

Participants responded that the multimedia components (e.g., video, audio, images) had a positive impact on the experience of using the PBL module. Students indicated that it would have been a different experience for them if multimedia had not been used. A typical comment was, "I don't think it would have been as interactive. I wouldn't have been as responsive to it, I don't think. If they just give you paper, it would not have been as much fun." The same student indicated that media increased the connection she felt to the student and helped personalize the context. She described it as, "I could picture kinda what he was thinking. It was easier that way. I could picture him in my head. I could know what he was like and see him.… It definitely made him more interactive knowing what he was like."

CONCLUSION

The results described by this study offer insight into the effectiveness of using multimedia PBL strategies to teach special education concepts to preservice elementary education teachers. Student reactions and insights indicate that the module provided an effective learning experience. Through the rich multimedia content and activities that mirrored an actual IEP negotiation process, students were able to form a connection with a fictional student, experience the difficulties of advocating for him, and negotiate special education policies in a safe environment where actual student outcomes were not at stake. In addition, the context of a student with limited English proficiency also reinforced multicultural goals of the preservice curriculum and likely provided many students with a virtual experience beyond one that might be available to them through their actual field experiences. Their comments indicated that while they grappled with a perceived lack of information, these preservice teachers collectively increased their knowledge of special educational processes, developed collaboration skills, and began to develop a connection with their future professional community. One student summarized it best when she said:

> I really enjoyed this activity. I feel that this will soon affect me as I become a teacher in a year. I think this type of teaching (PBL) is very important in teaching education. This is the sort of stuff we will be involved with and this will help us become more knowledgeable about this subject.

Future studies plan to follow up with preservice teachers who used the module once they enter the profession, which would provide an additional measure of how the use of this case during preservice training influences inservice teacher practice.

ACKNOWLEDGMENTS

The authors acknowledge Dr. Theresa A. Ochoa at Indiana University for her support and training on the use of the module, and Michael M. Gerber and George Singer at the University of California at Santa Barbara for permission to use the *CASELINK* special education module.

REFERENCES

Albanese, M. A., & Mitchell, S. (1993). Problem-based learning: A review of literature on its outcomes and implementation issues. *Academic Medicine, 68,* 52–81.

Andrews, L. (2002). Preparing general education preservice teachers for inclusion: Web-enhanced case-based instruction. *Journal of Special Education Technology, 17*(3), 27–35.

Artiles, A. J., & Trent, S. C. (1994). Overrepresentation of minority students in special education: A continuing debate. *Journal of Special Education, 27,* 410–437.

Baker, E. A. (2000). Case-based learning theory: Implications for instructional design. *Journal of Technology and Teacher Education, 8,* 85–95.

Bridges, E. M., & Hallinger, P. (1997). Using problem based learning to prepare educational leaders. *Peabody Journal of Education, 72,* 131–146.

Cognition and Technology Group at Vanderbilt University. (1994). Multimedia environment for developing literacy in at risk students. In B. Means (Ed.), *Technology and education reform: The reality behind the promise* (pp. 23–56). San Francisco: Jossey-Bass.

De La Paz, S., Hernandez-Ramos, P. F., & Barron L. (2004). Multimedia environments in mathematics teacher education: Preparing regular and special educators for inclusive classrooms. *Journal of Technology and Teacher Education, 12,* 561–575.

Denzin, N. K., & Lincoln, Y. S. (2000). Introduction: The discipline and practice of qualitative research. In N. Denzin & Y. Lincoln (Eds.), *The handbook of qualitative research,* (2nd ed., pp. 1–30). Thousand Oaks, CA: Sage.

Duffy, T. M., & Cunningham, D. J. (2001). Constructivism: Implications for the design and delivery of instruction. In D. Jonassen (Ed.), *The handbook of research for educational communications and technology.* Bloomington, IN: Association for Educational Communications and Technology.

Ge, X., & Land, S. M. (2004).A conceptual framework for scaffolding ill-structured problem-solving processes using question prompts and peer interactions. *Educational Technology Research and Development, 52*(2), 5–22.

Gerber, M. M., English, J., & Singer, G. H. (1999). Bridging between craft and academic knowledge: a computer supported, problem-based learning model for professional preparation in special education. *Teacher Education and Special Education, 22,* 100–113.

Glaser, B. G., & Strauss, A. L. (1967). *The Discovery of Grounded Theory: Strategies for Qualitative Research.* Chicago: Aldine.

Hallahan, D. P., & Kauffman, J. M. (2003). *Exceptional Learners: Introduction to Special Education* (9th ed.). Boston: Allyn and Bacon.

Howard, J. (2002). Technology enhanced project based learning in teacher education: Addressing the goals of transfer. *Journal of Technology and Teacher Education, 10,* 343–354.

Individuals with Disabilities Education Improvement Act, H.R. 1350, 108th Con.., 2nd sess. (2004).

Jonassen, D. H., & Hernandez-Serrano, J. (2002). Case-based reasoning and instructional design: Using stories to support problem solving. *Educational Technology Research and Development, 50,* 65–77.

Langone, J., Malone, D. M., & Clinton, G. N. (1999). The effect of technology-enhanced anchored instruction on the knowledge of preservice special educators. *Teacher Education and Special Education, 22,* 85–96.

Matthews, D., & Menna, R. (2003). Solving problems together: The importance of parent/school/community collaboration at a time of educational and social change. *Education Canada, 43*(1), 20–23.

Ochoa, T. A., Gerber, M. M., Leafstedt, J. M., Hough, S., Kyle, S., Rogers-Adkinson, D. L., & Koomar, P. (2001). Web technology as a teaching tool: A multicultural special education case. *Journal of International Forum of Educational Technology and Society, 4,* 50–60.

Ochoa, T. A., Kelly, M. L., Stuart, S. & Rogers-Adkinson, D. (2004). The impact of PBL technology on the preparation of teachers of English language learners. *Journal of Special Education Technology, 19*(3), 35–43.

Ochoa, T. A., Vasquez, L. R., & Gerber, M. M. (1999). New generation of computer-assisted learning tools for students with disabilities. *Intervention in School and Clinic, 34,* 251–254.

Orey, M. (2004) Part one: Trends and issues: Introduction. In M. Orey, M. A. Fitzgerald, & R. M. Branch, (Eds.), *Educational Media and Technology Yearbook 2004.* Westport, CT: Libraries Unlimited.

Rogers-Adkinson, D. L., Ochoa, T. A., & Delgado, B. (2003). Developing cross-cultural competence: Serving families of children with significant developmental needs. *Focus on Autism and Other Developmental Disabilities, 18*(1), 4–8.

Stough, L. M., & Palmer, D. J. (2003). Special thinking in special settings: A qualitative study of expert special education educators. *Journal of Special Education, 36,* 206–222.

Tschannen-Moran, M., & Woolfolk-Hay, A. (2000). Collaborative learning: A memorable model. *The Teacher Educator, 36,* 148–165.

Turnbull, H. R., Turnbull, A. P., Wehmeyer, M. L., & Park, J. (2003). A quality of life framework for special education outcomes. *Remedial and Special Education, 24,* 67–74.

Tyler, N., & Smith, D. D. (2000). Welcome to the TESE special issue: Preparation of culturally and linguistically diverse special educators. *Teacher Education and Special Education, 23,* 261–263.

Van Den Berg, D., Jansen L., & Blijleven, P. (2004). Learning with multimedia cases: An evaluation study. *Journal of Technology and Teacher Education 12,* 491–509.

Where Have We Been and Where Are We Going?
Limiting and Liberating Forces in IDT

Richard Schwier
University of Saskatchewan

Janette Hill
University of Georgia

Walter Wager and J. Michael Spector
Florida State University

A number of external forces are currently having an impact on the field of instructional design and technology (IDT). Technology is now nearly ubiquitous in all aspects of our daily lives. One consequence of the shift from an industrial society to information society has been the increasing importance of learning in all environments, including workforce training, professional development, and personal development. This infusion of technology combined with greater need for learning represents an unprecedented opportunity for our field.

In a symposium at Pennsylvania State University (PSU) during spring 2004, eight IDT professors met to discuss the current state and the future of our field. We wondered out loud and together about what forces within our field may be affecting how our field is responding to these broader societal changes.

In this chapter, which is based on the PSU symposium, Rick Schwier discusses a study in which he and his colleagues explored what instructional designers perceive as their "grand purpose"; Janette Hill reports findings from her analysis of purpose and goal statements for several instructional design programs and considers what these statements tell us about what we expect instructional designers to know and be able to do. Walt Wager considers the relationship between theories and practice in IDT, and Mike Spector reflects about what questions we should be asking and answering in the field of IDT.

A GRAND PURPOSE FOR ID? (SCHWIER)

If we ask medical doctors what their grand purpose is, they might describe themselves as healers; lawyers might say that they promote a just society and protect the rights of victims and the accused; teachers might describe themselves as advocates for children and learning and, through them, the future of society. But how might we describe the simple grand purpose of instructional designers? What is our larger mission? What is our grand agenda?

As an artifact of a research program I've been working on with colleagues Katy Campbell and Richard Kenny, we tripped across this question. This portion of the chapter describes some of the issues that surfaced from instructional designers when we put the questions to them, and it offers some perspectives on how the questions might be answered.

But why does this matter? What role does a sense of larger purpose play in nourishing a profession and its participants? On an individual basis, a grand purpose is something that sustains us—that gives us a reason to get out of bed in the morning when challenges are overwhelming, or we're just too tired to face another wave of problems. But collectively, shared purpose or vision shapes our professional identities by providing a metaphorical vessel to contain the disparate roles we play in our daily lives. Larger purpose provides perspective and the lynchpins of a professional community.

Background and Context

The program of research that informs this discussion is being conducted by Katy Campbell from the University of Alberta, Richard Kenny from Athabasca University, and Richard Schwier from the University of Saskatchewan. We have been exploring, through a combination of narrative inquiry and grounded theory analysis, the roles played by instructional designers as agents of social change. This led us through a web of interacting variables, including things such as professional identity, experience, institutional change, professional preparation, and professional communities of practice. The brief context that follows borrows directly from that program of research, so in places where I refer to "we," it is to acknowledge the research team that has worked collaboratively to generate these findings.

A considerable amount of writing in the field of IDT worries aloud about who we are and what we do as professionals (Gustafson & Branch, 2002; Merrill, 1996; Reigeluth, 1996; Schwier, Campbell, & Kenny, 2004; Willis, 1998). Early and continuing scholarly efforts focus on developing models of instructional design that make sense out of the complex array of responsibilities performed by instructional designers (Dick, Carey, & Carey, 2005; Morrison, Ross, & Kemp, 2004; Shambaugh & Magliaro, 2005; Smith & Ragan, 2005). Some scholars argue persuasively that we need to reconsider the nature of instructional design, its maturity, and the assumptions that drive it by comparing our work with that of related professions (Gibbons, 2003; Waters & Gibbons, 2004). Recently, research has begun to examine (or reexamine) the nature of actual practice, with attempts to understand the nature of instructional design theory from the perspective of actual practice (Cox, 2003; Cox & Osguthorpe, 2003; Kenny, Zhang, Schwier, & Campbell, 2004; Rowland, 1992; Visscher-Voerman & Gustafson, 2004). Visscher-Voerman and Gustafson, for example, draw a particularly striking and useful categorization of how designers work by proposing that they practice in instrumental, communicative, pragmatic, and artistic ways, depending on a number of contextual and individual variables. Their study considers questions of how and why designers approach problems the way they do. Each of the broad approaches to understanding professional practice—model development, interprofessional comparison, theory grounded in practice—makes important contributions to our thinking about instructional design. We reject outright the notion that there is a "right way" or magical set of answers that will provide clarity to our understanding of our field of study.

In our research, we took a different angle and proposed a view that focuses more clearly on *why* instructional designers practice instead of how they practice. From this angle the instructional designer is viewed as an agent of social change at interpersonal, institutional, and societal levels. Designers act in purposeful, value-based ways with ethical knowledge, in social relationships and contexts that have consequences in and for action (Campbell, Schwier, & Kenny, 2005). We suspected that the social purposes of design loom large in how instructional designers express their own values and convictions through their designs. Ultimately, we suggest that the instructional design process may be a form of learning that leads to cultural change. In other words, instructional designers act as change agents who challenge and shape the institutional and societal discourse about the purposes and forms of learning.

What do we mean by change agency, and what implications does this view have for the practice of instructional design? We view change agency as a moral relationship with others. Fundamentally we believe that instructional design practice is not grounded in instrumental-rational processes as much as in webs of relationships in which social morality is central (Christians, 2000). Practice is embodied in the designer's core values and beliefs and expressed through decisions made during the process of design. Through the very act of discussing with clients the implications of new approaches to learning and negotiating a new approach with them, designers are modifying a social context, and the discussions contribute to personal and social change (Herda, 1999). In this sense, design is not just a technical act but also a process that includes moral and political consequences.

To be agents of social change, designers must be aware of values they hold and be able to articulate the choices for action that embody them. In this view, instructional design is deliberate and critical. Britzman (1991) asserts that acting with moral agency implies that we have an understanding of our own personal history, circumstances, convictions, social context and even our confusion about what it means to be an instructional designer in an institution of authoritative discourse about the monologic sources of knowledge and power and one's role in it. In her discussion of moral agency, Britzman (1991) was talking about teacher education, but her observations are resonant with instructional design. She suggests that acting with moral authority requires a deep knowledge of yourself, including your own values, what you know, and how you see yourself acting in situations of conflict and contradiction.

We further suggest that the relationships inherent in instructional design practice offer opportunities for transforming the participants—particularly their beliefs about learning and learners and their roles as educators. We propose that clients working with instructional designers in development projects are actually engaging, as learners, in a process of professional and personal transformation that has the potential to transform the institution, and by extension, society.

Initial Findings and Implications

The following discussion is based on interviews of approximately 25 instructional designers, primarily across Canada but also including three participants from the United States and Australia. Two researchers independently coded transcripts of each conversation. Transcripts were analyzed using Atlas ti™ software, and as themes emerged, they were shared with the research team and the participants and used to construct networks of meaning. This chapter concentrates on comments related to how designers view their larger purpose and the grand mission of instructional design.

Instrumental Descriptions of Purpose

Most instructional designers interviewed for this study seemed to focus their attention to descriptive rather than interpretive discussions about the practice of ID. When asked directly about the significance of instructional design, this group of designers spoke about their influence on immediate projects or reflected on specific projects they influenced in important ways. There was little discussion of how instructional design might be influencing the future of education or training, at least not specifically. When asked about social change agency and their perceptions of what the role of the instructional designer is in that process, the perspective was primarily on functional aspects of the profession. There was mention of how we contribute to some positive social movements, such as eliminating stereotyping and institutional change, but most comments described functional rather than global concerns. Here is a sample of comments:

- [The goal is t]o ensure that educational resources help people achieve their learning goals.

- The larger purpose or grand mission of ID is to represent learners and to integrate learning theory into the development of learning materials and activities.

- I think the overall mission of ID is to help in the design of learning experiences/resources which facilitate learning easily and effectively.

- I would say the mission of ID is to optimize the effectiveness and enjoyment of the learning experience through thoughtful, well-designed instructional methods and materials. Of course, a less academic sounding one might be "to help people learn well without making them cry . . . or swear."

These instructional designers had a clear sense of identity that was tied to function. Their statements revealed a strong commitment to the learner and an orientation toward empowerment. But that identity is tied to the development of resources and learning systems not to any lofty purpose served by instructional design. In other words, they seemed to want to discuss immediate aspects of practicing their craft and were not explicitly reflective about the implications of that practice. They did not gravitate to questions about where the profession of instructional design is going, its evolution, or its social influence, even when invited. It is likely that this instrumental approach to instructional design is a natural expectation because graduate programs and professional success require skillful professional practice. There is an urgency and immediacy in the practice of instructional design that may be reflected in the observations these designers made.

Agency Descriptions of Purpose

By contrast, other designers hinted at the importance of the profession in creating social change, for leading educators in a mission to improve education, learning, or society. These individuals commented on the social implications of their work, and some suggested that the process of instructional design had transformative value for clients and learners. Here is a sample of comments we coded to "agency."

- I see . . . the same parallel in working on a project in instructional design as doing development work in emerging countries . . . this comes from my studies in global and human rights education and critical theory . . . this has been fundamental in shaping my own philosophy of design and education. Any time (an OECD country) went in and said, 'This is the way we think you should develop.. . . This is the right way, this is our way'. . . there has been no success.. . . Social change requires that people change how they are in the world—their thinking, their feelings, their actions—and this is extremely personal.

- As developers and designers, we then went back and said, "Ok, how can these learners feel valued? What can they bring to the learning that they feel is of value and how as a designer do you build on that?"

- So they were sort of transforming distance education materials and methodology to the local sites. It's been sort of a practice that gets me in hot water now and then, but everybody needs hot water now and then.

- And I think that that's really important and not only because faculty then begin . . . this cross-fertilization, if you will, and a deeper understanding of what the issues are in teaching and learning within a multitude of disciplines.

- I think the effect of that might be that people who maybe have never thought about what their process is to teaching and learning, or how it might be thought or how it might be improved, made it more positive.. . . But what are the values.. . . that work together and [clients] get exposed to—I think this has an opportunity for transformation.

- I think if it is possible maybe through the influence of instructional design we can create learning experiences and learning environments, if that is how we would put it.. . . So that there would be some opportunity for students to be very experienced with what I would call a deep learning rather than a shallow, surface approach to learning.
  . . . to teach a human being

... a human being goes out and changes everything else.

... and changes the organization in which they work in their own community, in their family life, etcetera.

Instructional designers may be acting as change agents more than they realize; they are participants in moving educational agendas and sweeping societal change. However, because understanding of our grand purpose is not shared, instructional designers are not necessarily participating in setting the agenda for change. They often see themselves just as significant participants rather than as leaders, and yet they are somewhat bewildered about why people come to them only as an afterthought.

Is There a Grand Purpose Hiding under That Rock?

To develop a sense of larger purpose and agency in instructional design, we must move beyond lamenting the failure of designers to implement theoretical models of design faithfully at a the microlevel, and inquire into "the epistemology of practice" that is complex, ill-structured, situational, and value-laden. We suspect that graduate programs in instructional design, particularly in North America, do not concentrate on these issues. We are stronger in teaching about how to do instructional design than we are about reflecting on why we do instructional design. So it was probably not surprising that Visscher-Voerman and Gustafson (2004) found that most instructional designers they interviewed used a rational-instrumental approach. We found the same thing. Perhaps our graduate programs are not emphasizing processes that will help instructional designers articulate a grand purpose for their work.

If we are to promote the development of a grand purpose of instructional design, we will need to understand the motivations and values designers bring to their work. We think that some useful clues exist in designers' stories of the transformative influence of their practice and in their descriptions of themselves as change agents at local, institutional, and societal levels. We stop short of proposing what that grand purpose might be, however. For one thing, it is possible that there is more than one grand purpose, and it would be arrogant and presumptuous to suggest what the single best one might be from the data we've gathered so far. As Visscher-Voerman and Gustafson (2004) point out, a postmodern view would hold that "Western scientific thought is flawed with its emphasis on sameness" (p. 83). We do think it is a question worth pursuing, however, so instructional designers will not have to flinch when someone asks, "So what does an instructional designer actually do?" At least it may keep the tone deaf among us away from singing the "Little Boxes" leitmotif suggested by Michael Spector in another section of this chapter.

A DEGREE IN IDT BY ANY OTHER NAME IS STILL A DEGREE IN IDT—OR IS IT? (HILL)

What do we professors of IDT hope our students will be able to do when they finish their degree programs? In other words, what are the purposes and goals of IDT programs? Perhaps by exploring this question, we will gather useful information for revising and expanding our degree programs.

This section presents and discusses the results of an initial study seeking to answer the question about purposes and goals of IDT programs. I first present a brief overview of IDT as an academic discipline. Next, I describe the method I used to gather the data and present and discuss the results of the study. Finally, I explore implications for IDT programs, seeking to provide guidance for continued growth of the profession.

A Brief Historical Overview of IDT as an Academic Discipline

The use of technology for instructional purposes can be dated back to the turn of the 20th century with the use of film for teaching (McNeil, 2004). It is important to note that one of the most influential organizations, the Association for Educational Communications and Technology (AECT), traces its roots back to 1923. Most scholars trace the practice of IT to the 1940s and to training development for the military in World War II. It was during this time that the term *instructional technologist* was first used (Reiser, 2001).

IDT continued to grow throughout the 1950s and 1960s, with the development of instructional design models and evaluation. The study of IT and the rise of IDT as a formal academic discipline did not occur until the late 1960s and early 1970s. This is when academic programs in IDT began to form at major institutions in the United States. For example, the Instructional Systems Design Program was formed at Florida State University in Tallahassee and Instructional Systems and Technology (IST) was formed at Indiana University (IU) in Bloomington at this time (see, for example, Indiana's departmental timeline for details, http://www.indiana.edu/~ist/students/history/timeline.html).

It is difficult to gather information related to the goals and objectives of these academic programs in the 1960s and 1970s. However, the naming of the program at Indiana University provides some insight into where emphasis was placed with IST at IU. As stated on the departmental timeline:

> The word "instructional" was chosen because instruction and instructional management as they are affected by technological processes are the main concern of the division.. . . "Systems" reflects the application of behavioral and cybernetic principles to the design of instruction and instructional programs that are replicable [and] the relationships between components of the system and between components and the system as a whole . . . "technology" means process, product and a facilitating environment that makes the first two not only possible but also desirable. (Indiana University IST Department, 2004)

One may summarize the following as a goal of the IST division at IU in the 1960s and 1970s: to teach learners instructional management techniques using a systems perspective for solving problems using technology. The memo from which the above passage was taken was written in 1969 by Bob Heinich. One might also assume that it is a reflection of cultural needs at the time – and indeed in looking at the larger timeline, the reader can certainly see how this developed. The question that arises is this: have IDT programs continued to reflect cultural needs?

Clearly, academic programs have been in existence for several decades. As Reiser (2001) indicates, there have been many changes in the structures and culture in which IDT operates. My interest in this section of the chapter is to explore current program goals so that we can start to build an understanding of how these goals may or may not be in alignment with current needs of our society in relation to IDT.

Method

To answer the question of interest and to determine the goals and purposes of IDT programs, I engaged in document analysis of the Web sites of several IDT programs.

Participants

I searched the Web sites of the institutions represented in our IDT Futures meeting at Penn State University during spring 2004. In alphabetical order, these included

- Florida State University—http://www.epls.fsu.edu/is/

- Indiana University—http://www.indiana.edu/~ist/

- Pennsylvania State University—http://www.ed.psu.edu/insys/

- University of Georgia—http://it.coe.uga.edu

- University of Saskatchewan—http://www.usask.ca/education/edcur/edcomm/index.htm

- Utah State University—http://it.usu.edu/

Data Sources and Analysis

I focused on two primary areas of information for data gathering: (1) published mission or purpose statements for these IDT programs and (2) information on degrees offered. For this study, the mission or purpose statements were defined as the information found on the first page of the Web sites or under links with titles such as "About This Program." Within the category of degrees offered, I gathered data on the level of the degrees offered (i.e., master's, specialist, doctoral) and area of focus for the degrees (e.g., instructional development, school library media).

The data were copied from the program Web sites and put into a table to facilitate analysis. The data were read several times, and themes were generated based on the review of the information gathered. The results are presented in the following section.

Limitations

It should be noted that this is a small sample of academic programs in IDT. Furthermore, a limited number of variables were taken into account for answering the research question posed (what are professors of IDT hoping students will be able to do when they finish the degree programs?). Future research should expand in both areas.

Results

Mission or Purpose Statements

The mission and statements for all six programs (see Table 1) mention that graduates can go into a variety of settings to apply their skills. Some provide general statements about their programs, such as UGA, which notes that the program "prepares students to improve education in a wide variety of settings." Others, like the statement from IU, include more specific examples of where students might go for employment after completion of the degree: "institutions of higher education, but also in business, industry, government and ministries of education in other countries."

Three of the six statements include information about the larger profession of IDT. For example, the statement from FSU provides information on the fields from which IS was built: "draws upon the fields of psychology, communications and management." The statement from PSU is the most detailed of all, providing a broad overview of what the learner might expect while studying in the program. The statement from Saskatchewan also provides detail about the field.

Table 1. Mission or Purpose Statements

Institution	Mission/Purpose Statement
FSU Instructional Systems	The field of instructional systems is concerned with the improvement of educational and training programs through the application of research and technology. Instructional systems is a relatively new area of specialization which draws on the fields of psychology, communications, and management to improve human performance. Although materials development and the utilization of technology are core skills in the curriculum, students in the instructional systems program also study the theoretical basis for and receive applied training in the total design, development, implementation, and management of education and training programs. Skill areas range from needs assessment and job analysis through system design and evaluation. The use of computers in performance improvement receives significant emphasis in the program.
Indiana University Instructional Systems Technology	We improve human learning and performance in diverse contexts. The Department of Instructional Systems Technology prepares practitioners and researchers to build and test processes, products, systems and services for use in education and training settings. Graduates of our master's degree program typically assume design/development roles in public or private organizations—about half in corporations. Graduates of our doctoral program teach and conduct research in instructional technology—most often in institutions of higher education, but also in business, industry, government, and ministries of education in other countries.
Pennsylvania State University Instructional Systems	Instructional systems graduates are applied psychologists, applying what is known about how people learn to most effectively and efficiently design systems that support learning. Instructional systems students are encouraged to take courses on learning theory from the psychology and the educational psychology. Instructional systems graduates are prepared to be instructional designers. Instructional designers analyze learner needs and learning environments; design and sequence learning tasks; and design and develop effective and efficient learning materials. Developing instructional materials requires knowledge of the strengths and weaknesses, costs, and development time required by various instructional technologies. This knowledge allows graduates to make sound decisions concerning the technologies most appropriate to support learning. Technologies which are emphasized in the INSYS program include computer hardware, software, and the Internet. Instructional systems graduates are not computer scientists; they are computer users and appliers of computer technologies, such as multimedia, interactive video, and computer tools, to support learning. Assessment and evaluation of learner performance and instructional materials allows the graduate student to assess and improve the quality of his or her educational and training designs.

Institution	Mission/Purpose Statement
University of Georgia Instructional Technology	At the University of Georgia, Instructional Technology is a professional program in education and the learning process that prepares students to improve education in a wide variety of settings. Its programs emphasize instructional design and development, materials production and utilization, computer-based education, school media services, technology integration, and research.
Utah State Instructional Technology	The department offers specializations in educational technology, information technology, school library media administration, instructional development for training and education, and interactive learning technologies. A program emphasis in online learning communities in education and training is also offered. *Minors Offered:* Multimedia Development Minor *Certificates Offered:* School Library Media *Endorsements Offered:* Distance Learning Endorsement
University of Saskatchewan Educational Communications and Technology	The educational communications and technology graduate program includes research, study and practice in designing, developing and evaluating educational systems and resources. Typically, educational technologists are concerned with innovative ways of bringing technology to bear on learning problems. Educational technology is multidisciplinary in nature, applying learning theory to the design of learning environments, the development of educational systems, and the improvement of educational communication through the appropriate use of resources. Careers in educational technology include distance education, instructional design, training, educational television, media education, and computer-based learning. Our graduates have followed careers in education, government, and corporate sectors, and some have started their own consultancies and businesses.

Other purpose statements are not as detailed but do provide some insight into what the learner can expect from the program. The statements from UGA and USU focus on emphasis areas in the programs (e.g., educational technology, information technology, school library media administration). The statement from IU was the only one that included a tag line: "We improve human learning and performance in diverse contexts."

Degrees Offered and Areas of Emphasis

Like the mission statements, the degrees offered and areas of emphasis vary across the six programs. The program at Saskatchewan is the only one that does not offer a doctoral degree. Saskatchewan does offer two master's degrees: one with a thesis option and one without. This is not unlike Penn State's master's program, which also has a thesis option.

All of the programs offer a master's degree in IDT. However, the type of master's degree varies, with two programs offering an M.S. (FSU, IU), two programs offering an M.Ed. or M.S. (PSU, USU), and two programs offering an M.Ed. (UGA and USask). See Table 2 for a summary of programs.

Table 2. Summary of Emphasis Areas for IDT Degrees

Degree	Emphasis	Number of Institutions Offering the Emphasis
M.S.	Instructional systems/instructional technology (broadly defined)	3
	Performance systems design	1
	Open and distance learning	
M.Ed.	Instructional systems/instructional technology (broadly defined)	2
	School library media	2
	Technology integration	2
Ed.S.	Instructional systems/instructional technology (broadly defined)	1
	School library media	1
	Technology integration	1
	Interactive instructional tool building	1
	Advanced interactive multimedia design	1
	Advanced interactive multimedia design	1
	Evaluation	1
D.Ed.	Instructional systems/instructional technology (broadly defined)	1
Ph.D.	Instructional systems/instructional technology (broadly defined)	4

Some of the degree descriptions for the master's level make a clear distinction between the two degrees. For example, the PSU master's degree descriptions indicate that "The M.Ed. degree is a practitioner's degree. It is a more appropriate option for those who plan careers as instructional designers and technologists.. . . The M.S. degree is a research degree."

Three of the six programs offer a specialist degree (Ed.S.): FSU, UGA, and USU. As with the master's degrees, the emphasis varies, but all are clear that the goal is to "prepare students with advanced skills in instructional technology beyond those acquired with the master's degree" (USU Web site).

All of the programs in the United States offer doctoral degrees in the IDT programs. Four of the programs offer a Ph.D. only—FSU, IU, UGA, and USU. Almost all of the program Web sites describe the focus of the Ph.D. as research and theory. PSU offers the option of a doctor of education (D.Ed.) or Ph.D., drawing the following distinction between the two: "The D.Ed. typically prepares students for advanced practitioner posts such as curriculum/technology coordinator for public schools, corporate lead instructional designer or consultant. The Ph.D. degree typically prepares students for the professorate or research posts within labs or think tanks."

In addition to traditional degrees, three of the programs (IU, PSU, UGA) indicated offering some form of certificate in IDT. The certificate at IU focuses on a basic grounding in IST but is not licensed by the state of Indiana. The certificate at the University of Georgia is similar, providing a foundation in IT but no licensure by the State of Georgia. PSU offers two certificates (technology specialist and technology supervisor), both of which are issued by the Pennsylvania Department of Education.

The areas of emphasis across the six programs are more varied than the degrees offered. Table 2 provides a tallied summary of the areas of emphasis.

Discussion and Conclusion

What are we hoping students will be able to do when they finish these degree programs? An initial analysis of the mission/purpose statements and degree areas across six IDT programs indicates a variety of purposes and goals in terms of what students will be able to do after completing their studies. The variety is particularly apparent at the master's level. Learners at the master's degree level are being prepared for a variety of professions, ranging from educational contexts (K–12 to higher education) to business and industry to government organizations.

The emphasis areas for the specialist degrees also vary. Learners can choose from school library media to distance education to evaluation. This also enables the learner to choose multiple contexts in which they can work after completing the degree—including education and business and industry.

The variety at the master's and specialist levels clearly reflects the variety of the profession. We have been accused of, and lauded for, being all things to all people. Hannafin and Hannafin (1986) stated almost 20 years ago that the choice to be a field of "jack of all trades" has implications for our growth as a discipline. It would seem that we have continued this trajectory and may still be suffering from the consequences of those decisions.

The greatest consistency in goals and purposes can be found at the doctoral level. All of the doctorate degrees stated that graduates will have the ability to conduct research and build theory in IDT. The types of positions available for learners after completing the degree do vary (higher education, business and industry, government), but the goals are consistent. It may be that this area offers the most promise for providing a collective trajectory for the IDT profession. That said, it may not be the desire of the IDT professoriate to have a collective trajectory. As indicated in the Hannafin and Hannafin (1986) article, this is a question that will need to continue to be explored—with an understanding of the benefits and challenges associated with either decision.

THEORY AND PRACTICE IN INSTRUCTIONAL DESIGN (WAGER)

One has to be struck by the diverse nature of university programs that offer instructional design degrees. We have instructional systems programs, instructional technology programs, and educational technology programs, all with slightly different curricula, drawing students from diverse populations who are headed for different employment venues. Common to all programs is that graduates will be confronted with instructional or learning problems that they will be expected to solve. In solving these problems, some instructional designers will apply a design model they learned in their graduate programs. Others might have to apply a model used by the organization where they work. Still others will engage in evaluation or research projects, where they will have to develop a model to fit the situation.

How can an instructional systems program help prospective graduates to meet each of these challenges?

The thesis of this section is that we must provide our students with a toolbox of both skills and theory that are adaptable to a variety of learning environments. What is in the instructional designer's toolbox? If we look into a carpenter's toolbox, we'd expect to find a square, hammer, saw, tape measure, drills, screwdrivers, and chisels—tools of the trade. These tools do the basic jobs of cutting, shaping, and fastening wood. The basic tasks of an instructional designer are learning task analysis, learner analysis, learning activities (strategies) design, and learning assessment. What do we look for to determine whether our graduates have these tools, and how do we help them acquire them?

Of course it's our desire to prepare our graduates to be productive and employable when they leave our programs with a degree. Master's students are generally viewed as entry-level designers, and doctoral graduates will go into research positions in academia or in business and industry. Each position requires different levels of knowledge and skills. We can teach our students to apply design models, but they must also know why they work. What will prepare them to think most reflectively about what they will be doing? Can our designers answer the question, "Why should the strategies, materials/ methods I am designing using (whatever model), make a difference in how these particular students learn?" To answer these questions, students must have a theory of how people learn and the factors that affect learning.

Legacy Models

It seems we are at no lack for models in instructional systems. Most ID models are based on one or more theories of learning or instruction. For example, linear small frame programmed instruction was B. F. Skinner's expression of behaviorism. The Dick, Carey, and Carey (2005) model is an expression of the information processing model as interpreted by R. M. Gagne. More recently, theories such as situated cognition and authentic learning have led to design models for anchored instruction (Cognition and Technology Group at Vanderbilt, 1992), and social cognition theories underlie models for collaborative learning and learning communities. The questions for designers are how to optimize the effects of the learning environments through the application of the principles derived from the theories.

A cursory Web review of the descriptions and curriculum for ID programs indicate that master's students usually get one survey course in learning and cognition. The learner in these courses is typically exposed to a number of learning theories, but it is not likely that the theories will be translated into instructional design models. Most ID programs have multiple hands-on technology courses. Often, these courses focus on the application of technology or a design model with only a cursory discussion of the underlying theories. Students come away from these courses knowing how to hammer a nail but with little understanding of how a nail holds the wood together. Yet what is the importance of theory in a field mostly dominated by practice? The importance, as expressed by Nealon and Giroux (2003), is that we all have opinions—personal beliefs about the nature and causes of phenomena, but "Unless we can ask theoretical questions … about the origins of knowledges [sic], who holds them, and how such knowledges were formed and might be changed—we're stuck in a go-nowhere exchange of opinions: he said, she said" (p. 4). The importance of theory is that it makes us question our existing opinions. If we believe that how we think determines how we act, the importance of theory becomes clear.

For example, opponents of traditional models of instructional design, such as the Dick, Carey, and Carey model, claim that they are linear and objectivist and that they are somehow inadequate. Some opinions I've heard expressed are "there are too many steps and they are too tedious," "they lead to one-size-fits all instruction," and that "behaviorism is an outdated theory." These are all descriptions based on opinions about the models and global generalizations about the adequacy of their foundations. However, opinions about the models and criticism of the theories are confounded. The logistics of practicing the model shouldn't damn the theory. Just because the model contains "learning objectives" doesn't mean the instruction produced is based on Skinner's model of operant conditioning.

What we think determines what we do. However, if we aren't critical about our opinions or what we do, we don't grow intellectually. Critical thinking is a necessary tool if our students are going to "construct" theory and knowledge from relevant practice. To paraphrase Nealon and Giroux, we are interested in theory as a toolbox of questions and concepts to be built and experimentally deployed rather than as a menu of methods to be chosen and mechanically applied.

Only approximately 50% of respondents in a recent study by Christensen and Osguthorpe (2004) reported using theories in making instructional strategy decisions. Does this mean they don't reflect on the efficacy of their practice? Another interesting finding of their study is that the most frequently cited sources of new instructional theories, trends, and strategies are peers or coworkers. Does this imply our programs need to engage in more continuing education? They also found that, as a group, ID practitioners do not rigidly subscribe to either objectivist or constructivist philosophical biases, from this Christensen and Osguthorpe conclude ID has migrated away from its objectivist roots (p. 64). How might this inform our program decisions?

Changing Paradigms

Recently, it seems, other programs are infringing on what has traditionally been the territory of instructional design. Educational psychology has become learning sciences, library science has become information studies, and communications programs have started teaching courses in multimedia design. Educational psychologists, by designing instructional materials for public schools, have attracted money from the National Science Foundation. Among other things, research money will get the attention of academicians. Cognitive science, as defined in the study of situated cognition and anchored instruction, became an underlying theory for authentic instruction and learning communities. Because instructional design models reflect educational theories, it wasn't long before the methods associated with design began to change to accommodate the new theories. Was instructional design too slow to see new applications, or was it lacking the theoretical perspective to lead this field of inquiry?

How did this affect instructional design? Theories supporting self-paced, replicable instruction are out, collaborative learning is in, and the models of design for individualized learning materials are no longer seen as relevant—how people think affects how they act. Nothing within an established program changes all that quickly, however. Instructional design has never really penetrated public school instruction anyhow, and the legacy models still works in many venues with clear learning outcomes. Instructional designers, at least FSU's master's graduates, mostly go into business and industry to design training, so we still teach the classic models, based mostly on information processing theory. However, the currently popular educational psychology paradigms have become the foundation for new ways to conceive of instructional design, and systems programs have picked up on the need to design learning environments (in the broad sense), and the sociocultural theories have become foundations for new models of design, as suggested by Christensen and Osguthorpe (2000).

"It seems we live in a world of 'posts': we're post-modern, post-industrial, post-feminist, post-colonial, and, given the advent of e-mail, perhaps we're becoming post-post office" (Nealon & Giroux, 2003, p. 125). Nealon and Giroux conclude that it is "some deliberate sense of indeterminacy or uncertainty that would seem to make an artifact postmodern" (p. 129). Are we entering a period of postinstructionalism? Is a postmodern paradigm appropriate for educational institutions that reflect our culture? What does it mean for an educational institution to be " post-modern"?

Professional Identity of Instructional Designers

Our identity as practitioners is reflected in our identity as a discipline. Are we cognitive scientists or materials developers? Are we learning architects or builders of learning environments? Recent discussions on the *ITForum* has addressed the question of whether there is really an identity crises. Andy Gibbons sees us as interventionists, that is, we apply a process to a problem to affect an outcome. Like doctors, when we intervene and what remedy we apply depends on a diagnosis of the symptoms of the patient, the progress of the disease. However, even doctors as practitioners depend on a theory of disease for the design of successful interventions. What are our core theories? How robust are they?

I am currently on a curriculum committee that is considering what the master's program should be. What courses should a student be required to take? What competencies will they have to demonstrate in their portfolio? What should an entry-level instructional designer be able to do? These questions all relate to identity. How do students gain an identity as an instructional designer, and how do we know when they have this identity?

Roles of Instructional Design Programs and Professors

Academic programs in instructional design work at two levels. At the master's level we produce practitioners. They learn the models and some of the related theory, but the emphasis is on the practice. At the doctoral level, the emphasis switches to a more theoretical level, as it should, for the preparation of researchers. Professors author or identify the knowledge we expect our students to know. First, we want them to know what we have found to be useful. Second, we want them to be able to talk and think like we do. When they identify with us they also gain identity as instructional designers, and we validate their knowledge. However, to continue to develop theory, we must be able to question our assumptions and encourage our students to do likewise.

One question we might consider is this: how would we certify an instructional designer who didn't come through one of our formal educational programs? How would we recognize whether they had the skills? What evidence would convince us that this person was truly an "instructional designer"? Of course, every teacher designs instruction, but they aren't "instructional designers." What sets us apart? I'd contend that it is our beliefs about learning and instruction, our theory, as well as our practice or methodology.

A Changing but Resistant Culture

The culture of instructional design has changed and grown from when I first entered the field. The technology has changed, and models of instruction have changed. Information is available from many more sources, and we have production capabilities on our desktops that were unavailable 30 years ago. These technologies extend our capabilities to communicate, publish, and retrieve information. Slower to change are educational institutions, but they are changing. Students are hooked into technology, so they expect more services. Teachers know they can't continue to ignore new technology, and they are no longer the only authoritative source of information.

At the same time new technologies are clashing with traditional structures. Whereas authority used to rest with the teacher in the classroom, it is now moving to a higher level. Legislatures are developing or contracting for exit exams for high school. Check out the accreditation requirements for universities. Look at "academic learning compacts" that require measurable learning outcomes for undergraduate courses. Consider legislative mandates for block tuition and "standardized" university exit exams. Faced with accountability for student performance, how will teachers and designers incorporate new thinking into public education?

ID Career Paths

Instructional designers work in amazingly diverse venues. I am the coordinator of faculty development at FSU. The modest mission of my unit is to improve instruction on the campus of FSU. This means offering personal consultation to faculty and teaching assistants, offering professional development workshops to help faculty integrate technology into their teaching. It involves thinking about instruction and learning, and the effects instructors have on students through their classroom curriculum, policies, and procedures. I often reflect on Carroll's model of school learning and Keller's ARCS models when I attempt to diagnose instructional problems. I don't design instruction for faculty, but I can help them think about what they want their students to accomplish and how they might help them learn.

If using technology can help improve instruction, that's great. Many instructional problems, however, are far more fundamental then technology use, such as creating a syllabus that clearly communicates course expectations, or that explains assessment and grading policies. This requires basic considerations such as determining how instructors communicate respect and concern for their students. My position at FSU has convinced me that theories about organizational behavior, change, and diffusion and adoption are far more relevant to instructional designers than I thought they would be at the time I studied them. I perceive myself, as Rick Schwier described earlier in this chapter, as a change agent. The people I work with acquire new perspectives and reflections on what it means to be a teacher. But changing an individual's present practice is tough. You have to work within the parameters of that person's culture. Helping people change requires good theory and a practical way to apply it and see it work.

I view instructional designers as problem solvers. A good problem solver has a toolbox of knowledge and skills based in theory. A good problem solver learns from experience. A good problem solver knows how to determine the difference between opinion and theory. A good problem solver knows how to use the various tools in the toolbox to effect different results. There is no one best way to do everything, and a good instructional designer can consider the situation, the desired outcomes, and select or develop a means to facilitate the outcomes.

What should an instructional designer know? What should an instructional designer be able to do? These are the questions that require us to investigate our opinions, and the actions we take on them. I never want to be completely comfortable with regard to what I know or what I believe as truth. It doesn't take much to see how quickly knowledge changes. On the other hand, I don't want to discard a good tool simply because a new one is available. I might watch others use it, see what they say. Try it out for myself, see how it works. If it is better than the old tool, keep it and learn to use it wisely. If not, stick with what works. And if I should find something that works better, I'll share it with others.

REFLECTIONS ON THE FUTURE OF INSTRUCTIONAL DESIGN AND TECHNOLOGY (SPECTOR)

The IDT Futures group, an informal group of scholars that has been meeting for a few years, has been discussing the compound question, where are we going, and how will we get there? We have come to ask this question as a result of thinking about where we have been and wondering how we survived. We evolved from early groups working with new (at the time) educational technologies such as the mimeograph and overhead projector and applying systematic engineering processes to the design of instruction and learning environments. We have been affiliated with a number of disciplines including educational psychology, information studies, and library science. We claim to be a discipline that applies theory to practice—learning theory to instructional design practice. The much promised benefit of doing so would be improved learning and more efficient instruction. Well, something always seems to get in the way. Technologies become obsolete, teachers become frustrated, and researchers are lured into industry.

IDT is an interesting and eclectic discipline. We have more instructional design models than there are elements in the periodic chart, which was up to 112 the last time I looked. Just as there are groups of elements (nine by some accounts), the various instructional design models can be grouped by context or setting (see Branch & Gustafson, 2002) or by many other differentiating factors such as underlying learning theory, delivery mode, and so on.

We are so eclectic that we cannot even agree on our most basic terminology. Debates have raged for years over the difference between instructional design and instructional development, each with a small "d" and a capital "D" as well as other variations. Being interesting and eclectic has led to other disputes as well. Some claim that the systems thinking that formed the core of instructional systems development (ISD) is outdated and inappropriate for instructional design and development; what is needed is more rapid prototyping and user-centered design and development. A few go so far as to claim that constructivism is inconsistent with the design of instruction—learners create their own knowledge and in effect design their own learning, according to some accounts. Whether the latter is a descriptive or prescriptive claim is yet another cause for debate within our discipline.

Given such a contentious history, some have chosen to abandon what they perceive to be a sinking ship and join a different community of professional practitioners who call themselves learning scientists. This is a phenomenon more common in North America than in Europe and may be related to the perceived funding favoritism of government agencies (especially NSF) toward learning researchers (primarily psychologists) compared with educators and instructional designers.

Given that brief caricature of the discipline, one might say that IDT has been all over the map and has surprisingly survived a number of intentional and unintentional assaults. I am not certain that the caricature is accurate in relevant ways, nor am I confident that I have captured what is most interesting about the discipline. Nonetheless, I am concerned about the future of our discipline.

First of all, does IDT actually constitute a discipline? The way that academic and professional disciplines are defined is somewhat arbitrary and variable. There was not always a distinction between physicists and chemists or physicians and dentists. These evolved over time and have been modified as knowledge and technology progressed. Given that sort of academic fickleness, it seems perfectly OK to say yes, IDT is a legitimate discipline.

I am inclined to think that we need to establish two additional things to minimize the loss of interesting people to other disciplines and to shore up our own reputation as a serious academic discipline: a unifying theme and a captivating logo. To facilitate the process of developing (or is it designing?) a unifying theme, I propose that we first adopt a theme song. The one that I propose is Malvina Reynolds's "Little Boxes" (see http://www. ocap.ca/songs/littlbox.html). The common refrain in this song is "little boxes make of tickytacky"—this phrase may be used to characterize the various development models. Moreover, given the frequent analogies to architectural models and our concern that the too rigid application of ISD leads to problems, this song, which is about small tract houses all designed the same way for their inhabitants despite the obvious differences that exist, appropriately captures the designer's concern to balance functionality and individuality.

Second, we need a logo that captures our interesting but eclectic vision and the imagination of professional practitioners and interested onlookers. I recommend a logo based on the hummingbird. A hummingbird can beat its wings about 30 to 50 times a second, which is suggestive of the frequency of change in requirements over the life of a design effort. These birds can also fly in all directions, including upside down, which is often a situation in which instructional designers and technologists find themselves.

On a slightly more serious note, I do not think that our primary concern should be about our identity, although that secondary conversation is worth having and should continue in the hallways and next to water coolers. We all have multiple identities. We have multiple roles and engage in a multitude of activities. Our graduates become instructional designers, technology coordinators, training managers, educational researchers, university professors, military training specialists, advisors, consultants, and so on. We should avoid the "tickytacky" nature of rigidly imposed standard solutions and approaches, as Malvina Reynolds reminds us. We are rich in identity and should embrace that richness and diversity.

We should most definitely pursue collaborative efforts with those who consider themselves learning scientists, cognitive psychologists, systems theorists, design specialists, and so on. This is admittedly difficult. An interdisciplinary, international group that involves folks such as Dijkstra, Merrill, Scandura, Seel, Spector, and van Merriënboer held a series of three meetings between 1999 and 2002—one at the University of Twente hosted by Sanne Dijkstra, one at the University of Bergen hosted by Mike Spector, and one at the University of Freiburg hosted by Norbert Seel. These meetings did bring together prominent international scholars in the combined areas of instructional design and the learning sciences. The first and third of these meeting led to special issues of *Instructional Science,* and the second resulted in an edited volume (Spector & Anderson, 2000).

This group has not been able to sustain the face-to-face interdisciplinary, international collaboration that occurred in the period of time between 1999 and 2002. Perhaps this is due to the many other demands from local institutions and primary disciplines placed on individuals. I am not sure. That group is largely responsible for the new journal *Technology, Instruction, Cognition and Learning* (TICL; see http://www.scandura.com/), so it should be considered a success regardless of the lack of recent meetings. One of our goals is surely improved articulation with communities of practice that we believe are closely associated with our own work and interests. This is a reasonable goal, but it appears to be difficult to turn into a meaningful reality on a sustainable and significant scale. We should investigate whether this perception is accurate and what the potential causes might be.

Gibbons (2003) has characterized a framework for thinking about IDT that accommodates behavioral, cognitive, and other perspectives. This framework provides a way to generate more specific instructional design theories and associated research hypotheses and questions. This approach is perhaps more rational than simply generating so many models and seeing which one sells the most copies and will survive. Indeed, the survival value of an instructional design model should be that it generates testable hypotheses. I imagine that this claim might be contentious.

Examining the underlying assumptions of our discipline is likely to prove to be a valuable way to go about envisioning our future. I have written about two sets of assumptions that lead to an atomistic perspective (learners are rational, individuals are the proper unit of analysis, and conditions and methods can be manipulated to effect outcomes) or to a holistic perspective (learners are intermittently rational, language communities are the proper unit of analysis, and learning occurs within the context of dynamic systems; Spector, 2001). These perspectives are not distinct camps or positions. Rather, they are more like points along a continuum.

What strikes me as worth serious consideration is finding out what others think. Jan Visser provided a preliminary view through the "Book of Problems" sessions that he convened at AECT in 2002 and 2003. A compendium of the ideas of leading scholars can be found on the Learning Development Institute Web site (see http://www.learndev.org and click on Book of Problems). This effort was aimed at identifying the most important things about learning that we do not understand. I conclude with a sampling of some of the questions that contributors thought worth exploring.

John Shotter asked in his contribution to the Book of Problems:

- To what extent does our learning depend on our bodily involvement in (and vulnerability to) events that can provoke surprise and wonder, as well as anxiety and risk, in us?

- To what extent is it important that those teaching us have that kind of continuous 'in touchness' with us, so that at various crucial points in their teaching, they are able to say to us: "Attend not to 'THAT' but to 'THIS';" "Do it 'THIS WAY' not 'THAT WAY' "?

- To what extent is our living involvement in a whole situation necessary for us to get an *evaluative* grasp of the meaning for action of a small part of it—as when a music teacher points out a subtle matter of timing, or a painter a subtle change of hew, or a philosopher a subtle conceptual distinction, such as that between, say, a *mistake* and an *accident*?

- Is learning possible without the bodily risk of, at least, disorientation and confusion, and without the *surety* of being able 'to go on" (Wittgenstein), as *guides* to inform us as to the value of our relations to our surroundings?

- And finally, is the *individual* pursuit of truth possible, without being immersed in an ongoing, unending, chiasmically structured dialogue with the others and othernesses about us, given that we all must continually reevaluate our values as the world around us changes and develops, and the order of multiple values we once thought adequate begin to reveal themselves as inadequate?

Vera John-Steiner asked, "How would our understanding of learning be transformed if its purpose were joint discovery and shared knowledge rather than competition and achievement?" Gavriel Salomon concludes that "what we'd need to study is what makes socialization and acculturation so effective and how their 'active ingredients' could be incorporated into instruction." Leon Lederman suggested that we should figure out "how to construct a dossier of misconceptions, of 'natural' assumptions that must be viewed with suspicion."

Basarab Nicolescue posted these seven questions:

1. If we distinguish three types of learning, the mental (cognitive), the feeling (affective) and the body (instinctive), how important are, for a given type of learning, the other two types?

2. How can one reach an equilibrium between the mental, feeling and body learning? Can we assert that this equilibrium corresponds to a new type of learning (a learning that is 'all comprehensive')?

3. What is the role of the traditional methods of meditation and relaxation for the process of learning?

4. Can we imagine that, in the future, learning through initiatives outside formal institutional settings will be more important than in institutional settings? How can one help the development of such an evolution of learning?

5. Are questions more important than answers in the process of learning? How can one generate a science and an art of questioning?

6. What is the practical role of the included middle (paradox, oxymoron, etc.) in the process of learning ? How could the included middle build transcultural and transreligious attitudes?

7. Could life stories stimulate the process of learning?

Federico Mayor observes that we do not know much about "learning *to be*, to transform information into personal knowledge" even though we know a lot about learning to know and learning to do.

David Perkins posed four general questions about learning in his contribution to the Book of Problems:

1. The Question of Mechanism—When we learn, in what form is that learning captured in us and our physical, social, and symbolic surround?—in the form of mental representations, the weightings of neural networks, conditioned reflexes, runnable mental models, priming or expectancy and different degrees of primability, distributed cognition, etc.? ...

2. The Question of Difficulty—When learning is hard, what makes it hard? When learning is easy, what makes it easy? Answers would have to deal with the match between mechanism and the things to be learned. ...

3. The Question of Design—What can we do to make learning something easier? This is the problem of instructional design taken broadly, not just for schools but for groups, teams, families, societies, even for immune systems and genetic codes. ...

4. The Question of Worth—What's worth learning, for whom, for what purposes practical or ideological, at what cost? Do we find the guide to what's worth learning ... in Adler's great books, in Dewey's pragmatism, in Socrates' insistence that we know our own ignorance, in more humble crafts and skills of the kitchen, the tailor's shop, the chemist's laboratory, the accountant's spreadsheet, in the ancient human modes of love, parenting, friendship, ownership, command, peace, war? ...

This is a brief review of what a distinguished group of scholars thinks we ought to be investigating. Some of these questions and concerns may seem more appropriate for investigation by psychologists or sociologists. Some are surely at the heart of instructional design. Regardless, if one is committed to the fundamental transdisciplinarity of instructional design and technology, then such a diverse range of perspectives ought to inform our envisioning of our future.

The faculty who participated in the PSU symposium are pushing in much the same directions as Visser's Book of Problems group and Scandura's TICL group. What I have to contribute to this dialogue are my ears.

REFERENCES

Branch, R. M., & Gustafson, K. L. (2002). *Survey of Instructional Development Models* (4th ed.). Syracuse, NY: ERIC Information and Technology Clearinghouse.

Britzman, D. P. (1991). Practice makes practice: A critical study of learning to teach. Albany, NY: SUNY Press.

Campbell, K., Schwier, R. A., & Kenny, R. A. (2005). Agency of the instructional designer: Moral coherence and transformative social practice. *Australasian Journal of Educational Technology, 21*(2), 242–262.

Christensen, T. K., & Osguthorpe, R. T. (2004). How do instructional design practitioners make instructional strategy decisions? *Performance Improvement Quarterly, 17,* 45–65.

Christians, C.G. (2000). Ethics and politics in qualitative research. In N. K. Denzin & Y. S. Lincoln (Eds.), *Handbook of qualitative research* (2nd ed.; pp. 133–155). London: Sage.

Cognition and Technology Group at Vanderbilt. (1992). The Jasper Series as an example of anchored instruction: Theory, program description, & assessment data *Educational Psychologist, 27,* 291–315.

Cox, S. (2003). *Practices and academic preparation of instructional designers.* Unpublished master's thesis. Brigham Young University, Provo, Utah.

Cox, S., & Osguthorpe, R. T. (2003, May / June). How do instructional design professionals spend their time? *TechTrends, 47*(3), 45–47, 29.

Dick, W., Carey, L., & Carey, J. O. (2005). *The systematic design of instruction* (6th ed.). Boston: Allyn and Bacon.

Gibbons, A. S. (2003). The practice of instructional technology: Science and technology. *Educational Technology, 43*(5), 11–16.

Gustafson, K. L., & Branch, R. M. (2002). What is instructional design? In R. A. Reiser & J. V. Dempsey (Eds.). *Trends and issues in instructional design and technology* (pp. 16–25). Upper Saddle River, NJ: Merrill Prentice Hall.

Hannafin, M. J., & Hannafin, K. (1986). The status and future of research in instructional design and technology. *Journal of Instructional Development, 8*(3), 24–30.

Herda, E. A. (1999). *Research conversations and narrative: A critical hermeneutic orientation in participatory inquiry.* London: Praeger

Hill, J. R., Bichelmeyer, B. A., Boling, E., Gibbons, A. S., Grabowski, B. L., Osguthorpe, R. T., Schwier, R. A., & Wager , W. (2004). Perspectives on significant issues facing instructional design and technology. In M. Orey (Ed.), *Educational media and technology yearbook* (Vol. 29, pp. 23–43). Westport, CT: Libraries Unlimited.

Kenny, R., Zhang, Z., Schwier, R. A., & Campbell, K. (2005). A review of what instructional designers do: Questions answered and not asked. *Canadian Journal of Learning and Technology, 31*(1), 9–16.

McNeil, S. (2004). A hypertext history of Instructional Design. Retrieved October 14, 2004, from http://www.coe.uh.edu/courses/cuin6373/idhistory/index.html

Merrill, M.D. (1996, July/August). What new paradigm of ISD? *Educational Technology, 36*(4), 57–58.

Morrison, G. R., Ross, S. M., & Kemp, J. E. (2004). *Designing effective instruction* (4th ed.). Hoboken, NJ: John Wiley & Sons.

Nealon, J., & Giroux, S. S. (2003). *The theory toolbox.* London: Rowman & Littlefield.

Reigeluth, C. M. (1996, May–June). A new paradigm of ISD? *Educational Technology, 36*(3), 13–20.

Reiser, R. A. (2001). A history of instructional design and technology: Part II: A history of instructional design. *Educational Technology Research & Development, 49*(2), 57–67.

Rowland, G. (1992). What do instructional designers actually do? An initial investigation of expert practice. *Performance Improvement Quarterly, 5*(2), 65–86.

Schwier, R. A., Campbell, K., & Kenny, R. (2004). Instructional designers' observations about identity, communities of practice and change agency. *Australasian Journal of Educational Technology, 20*(1), 69–100. Retrieved October 14, 2004, from http://www.ascilite.org.au/ajet/ajet20/schwier.html

Shambaugh, N., & Magliaro, S. G. (2005). *Instructional design: A systematic approach to reflective practice* (3rd ed.). Boston: Allyn & Bacon.

Smith, P. L., & Ragan, T. J. (2005). *Instructional design* (3rd ed.). Hoboken, NJ: John Wiley & Sons.

Spector, J. M. (2001). A philosophy of instructional design for the 21st century? *Journal of Structural learning and Intelligent Systems, 14*, 307–318.

Spector, J. M., & Anderson, T. M. (Eds.). (2000). *Integrated and holistic perspectives on learning, technology and instruction: Understanding complexity.* Dordrecht, The Netherlands: Kluwer.

Visscher-Voerman, I., & Gustafson, K.L. (2004). Paradigms in the theory and practice of education and training design. *Educational Technology Research and Development, 52*(2), 69–89.

Waters, S. H., & Gibbons, A. S. (2004). Design languages, notation systems, and instructional technology: A case study. *Educational Technology Research and Development, 52*(2), 57–68.

Willis, J. (1998, May/June). Alternative instructional design paradigms: What's worth discussing and what isn't? *Educational Technology, 38*, 5–16.

From Isolation to Legitimate Peripheral Participation: Encouraging a Community of Practice among Teacher Education Students through a Web Resource Database

Jennifer M. Brill
Virginia Tech University

Andy Walker
Utah State University

INTRODUCTION

The purpose of this chapter is to describe how a social theory of learning influenced the redesign of a Web site evaluation assignment for teachers enrolled in a master's degree program from a highly individuated and discrete learning activity to an experience intended to be more inclusive of students as participating and critical members of a professional community. We describe the original assignment within the context of Lehigh University's Technology-Based Teacher Education master's program. We share the vision and rationale for the new assignment. We detail key components of a social theory of learning, including the constructs of legitimate peripheral participation and community of practice, and how such theory serves as a framework for conceptualizing the redesign. We describe the design, implementation, and usage results for the new learning experience and supporting technology tools. We conclude with a discussion of the limitations of the project and prospects for future work.

BACKGROUND

In 2002, one of the main assignments in the first of two core classes (the Core) for the Technology-Based Teacher Education (TBTE) program at Lehigh University (LU) was for students to identify, critique, and annotate Web-based educational resources. This assignment was intended to support the acquisition of identified program competencies including (a) the use and evaluation of educational technologies and (b) the development of a critically reflective teacher practice. In the original design of the assignment, each student identified 10 educational Web sites related to his or her intended professional practice—elementary education, secondary science, and so on. For each Web site, the student provided a written annotation, detailing the content of the site, its strengths and weaknesses, and potential educational uses. As the assignment was designed originally, these annotations were completed, word processed, and submitted electronically to the instructor. The instructor, in turn, would evaluate the assignment according to a rubric and return it, with feedback, to the individual author.

Although this assignment encouraged the use and critical evaluation of educational technologies by individual students, it was deficient in promoting another core ideal of the program, namely, an orientation toward teacher professional practice as a generative practice requiring the collaboration of professional colleagues and the sharing of valued resources for the life of practice. As an "add-on" to the assignment, students would share findings informally with fellow class members in a group setting, although limited available class time and large class sizes often restricted the degree to which students could share resources effectively. Furthermore, students had no common repository to collect identified resources and share them over time. Thus, even though several sections of the

Core classes were taught each semester, the knowledge gained by the individual students, valuable educational Web sites and their critiques, was lost and reinvented every semester. As such, the assignment promoted a discrete, individuated learning exercise. We envisioned it could be improved. We set out to redesign it.

The vision for the redesign was to create a Web-based database that students could use to craft and submit Web site evaluations and, in turn, search and read Web site annotations from fellow students. A Web database seemed the perfect technology in that students were already using the Web to locate educational sites. With the redesign, students could extend their use of the Web to gather and store knowledge and then search on that knowledge, even accessing source material through links integrated in the annotations. Students could also enrich the database by adding an annotation to a Web site already contained in the database or even peer review existing Web site evaluations, commenting on their quality and usefulness for practice.

In sum, the idea was for the database itself to embody a form of socially constructed knowledge that evolves over time and can be accessed as needed by past, current, and future students. More broadly, the database could serve as an impetus for cross-boundary sharing among varied interest groups including students and faculty at LU and teachers and administrators within the K–12 community. Current LU students and faculty might use the database to identify Web resources to use in their instructional planning. School-based practitioners who might otherwise be isolated, either because of geography (a lone math teacher in a rural school district), pedagogy (the only constructivist-minded teacher in a large urban high school), or innovation (a school staff using action research for the first time) might use the database to extend and enrich their professional lives by locating, and even contributing, educational resources.

To realize the vision, one of the instructors for the Core (Dr. Jen Brill) partnered with a colleague responsible for teaching a Web-database integration course (Dr. Andy Walker). At the beginning of the semester, the Core instructor pitched the project to members of the database course. Four students teamed to develop the database, collaborating with the Core instructor who served as a client. The database project was meant to support not only the goal of professional collaboration among teachers in the TBTE program but also learning goals set by the instructor of the database course including the development of project management and client interface skills within an authentic setting. We viewed the redesign as a "win-win" for all concerned.

THEORETICAL FRAMEWORK

In this section, we offer a conceptual framework for thinking about the redesign. First, Wenger's four assumptions undergirding his social theory of learning provide a context at the macro level. In positioning his work, Wenger assumes the following: humans are social beings, and this condition is not trivial but rather central to learning; knowledge is about being competent with regard to valued activities (such as repairing a car, identifying educational resources, etc.); knowing is about participating in such activities, requiring engagement with the world; and "our ability to experience our engagement as meaningful is ultimately what learning is to produce" (Wenger, 1998, p. 4). This macrolevel viewpoint serves as a meaningful backdrop for our efforts and is important to be aware of, but it is too high level to develop a focal point for our discussion. Within this larger context of learning as a fundamentally social endeavor that both transforms the social group and is transformative to the individual participant (Wenger, 1998), we view situated learning as providing a useful midlevel framework for conceptualizing and developing the professional lives of teachers, including those preservice and inservice teachers participating in Lehigh's TBTE master's program. We see specific constructs within situated learning, namely, "legitimate peripheral participation" and "community of practice," as useful in thinking about and articulating underlying intentions of the redesigned activity.

Situated Learning

Emerging from anthropology, sociology, and cognitive science, situated cognition represents a major shift in learning theory away from traditional psychological views of learning as prescribed and individualistic toward perspectives of learning as emergent and social (Greeno, 1998; Lave & Wenger, 1991; Salomon, 1996). Familiar voices in the situated learning literature, Lave and Wenger (1991) describe learning as "an integral part of generative social practice in the lived-in world" (p. 35). Breaking this definition down, the word *generative* implies learning as an act of creation, *social* suggests that at least a portion of learning time occurs in partnership with other people, and *lived-in world* reminds us that learner engagement with real-world tools, practices, and settings heighten the relevance and usefulness of learning.

Appreciating the shift in perspective that situated learning affords, we set out to transition the Web site evaluation assignment from an experience where the instructor directs individual students to produce and deliver highly tailored annotations to one in which students partner to develop a Web-based educational resource larger than the sum of it annotation parts, a resource that varies in quality and quantity based in students' interactions with it and the work of other individuals. We provided tools in the form of the Internet, the Web database, and links in the database to online resources for guiding the evaluation of educational Web sites from three sources (Harmon & Reeves, 1998; Schrock, 2002). We also offered general parameters for completing the work, for example: select sites pertinent to your professional goals (e.g., math education) and current academic work; evaluate and annotate a minimum of six sites (four from the Web and two from the database); use any relevant resources to support your thinking and your work (e.g., Web based, paper based, fellow students, class discussions); peer review six annotations written by other students. As individuals worked with and transformed the database, it was our hope that the interactions with the database and its associated community would have a transformative impact on individuals as well.

Legitimate Peripheral Participation in a Community of Practice

Situated cognition theory's social, evolving, and contextualized view of learning finds its expression as legitimate peripheral participation in a community of practice (Lave & Wenger, 1991). Thus, the main unit of analysis for understanding how people learn, become, and create is not the individual but the communities that individuals form and engage with to varying degrees of participation (Wenger, 1998). Once again, there is a shift in perspective from individual as student to individual as participant in community; from individual behavior or cognitive process to social practice as a focal point for learning. Extending this idea to how a teacher learns, becomes, and creates, the teacher, regardless of developmental level (preservice or inservice, novice or expert) must be understood within the context of the practitioner communities in which he or she participates, for example, the classroom, the school, and any other professional groupings. Applying this idea to the teacher educator, the teacher educator as master is decentered, shifting his or her primary responsibility from instructing to "structuring a community's learning resources" (Lave & Wenger, 1991, p. 94). In the case of the Web site evaluation redesign, each student was no longer selecting and annotating Web sites for the Core instructor but for the community of educational professionals (local and extended) using the Web resource database. By structuring the annotations activity to include sites already in the database, and by adding the peer review component, the idea of contributing to a community resource was highlighted.

Digging deeper, a community of practice is described by Wenger as comprising three dimensions. First, a community of practice pursues a *joint enterprise* that is negotiated by its members and requires mutual accountability. Second, a community of practice is *mutu-*

ally engaged through the actions of its members and the agreed-on meaning of those actions for the group. Third, a community of practice looks to a *shared repertoire* (of tools, stories, artifacts, concepts, etc.) to pursue its practice.

A joint enterprise is a dynamic response by members of a community to its situation. It is dynamic in that it is negotiated continuously by its members as it is pursued. Furthermore, it requires the mutual accountability of members regarding such things as

> what matters and what does not, what is important and why it is important, what to do and not to do, what to pay attention to and what to ignore, what to talk about and what to leave unsaid,… [and] when actions and artifacts are good enough and when they need improvement or refinement. (Wenger, 1998, p. 81)

The "situation" that our community faced was finding high-quality educational Web sites on the Internet, an abundant and relatively new electronic resource for teachers of variable and unregulated quality. By offering guidance on the criteria one might use to evaluate a Web site, we did play a role in influencing what community members might "pay attention to" in critiquing sites. However, we did not mandate that students use a particular set of criteria put forth by a certain expert. Rather, we encouraged students to consider all pertinent resources as they developed their own evaluative criteria. Encouraging such a "critical eye" in the selection and use of resources (including annotations of Web sites already in the database) and incorporating peer reviews into the experience were both meant to support a sense of accountability for the content and quality of the database as a community resource.

The second dimension of a community of practice, mutual engagement, means that people in the community are "engaged in actions whose meanings they negotiate with one another" (Wenger, 1998, p. 73). Furthermore, to have engagement, people must be included in what is important to the community and must regularly influence each other's understanding by talking and working together closely. TBTE students influenced one another (and the Core instructor) in two ways as yet unmentioned. First, students engaged in large and small group dialogue, facilitated by the instructor, to collaborate on identifying what they felt to be the important criteria for evaluating educational Web sites. Second, students initiated spontaneous conversations with one another (and the instructor) as they worked, exchanging information and opinions regarding what they were finding as they search the Web, leads on potentially useful resources, and understandings of how to negotiate the Web database interface.

The development of a shared repertoire is the third dimension of a community of practice. The repertoire is produced or adopted by community members as an integral part of its practice and includes such things as "routines, words, tools, ways of doing things, stories, gestures, symbols, genres, actions, or concepts" (Wenger, 1998, p. 83). TBTE students shared some obvious tools as participants in the redesigned experience, including the Internet and the Web database. Students also shared conceptual understandings as they explored and negotiated evaluation criteria as well as routines as they worked together in the lab during scheduled class meeting times and, often, at times arranged on their own.

In this section, we teased out certain components of situated learning and mapped them to the redesign to make explicit the conceptual intent behind the revisioned experience. Although helpful in communicating about the redesign, we recognize that, in practice, the separations are largely artificial because elements such as mutual engagement and shared repertoire are much more integrated in experience.

WEB DATABASE PROJECT AND SYSTEM OVERVIEW

As mentioned previously, four students from Dr. Walker's Web-database integration class teamed up with Dr. Brill, the instructor for the Core course, to develop the online database which would allow students to submit, search, read, and review Web site annotations from fellow students. Dr. Walker's students had a single semester to conduct an analysis, come up with a design, create storyboards, then develop, test, and provide documentation for a fully functional Web-based application—all of which happened as they were learning a new development environment, Macromedia Cold Fusion. Following is a more detailed description of the system developed.

System Description

The finished system runs on Windows 2000 server with Internet Information Services providing http services, Cold Fusion for server-side scripting and Microsoft Access for the database back end. Figure 1 shows the main features of the system, which are subsequently described.

Figure 1. System architecture: Links between major pages or between data tables are noted with solid lines, links between pages and data tables are noted with dashed lines.

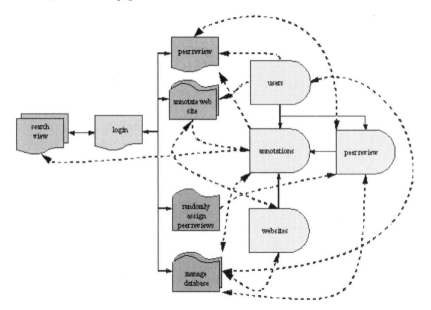

Search and View

A major goal identified by Dr. Brill was to allow for an open access environment. Thus, without logging into the system any user can search the existing set of Web annotations provided by students. Currently all portions of an annotation can be searched using a simple text match. There are two ways to view annotations. If more than one annotation exists for a single Web site, then they can be viewed in aggregate form, allowing the resulting information to be less a reflection of any one individual's perspective and more of a reflection of the community as a whole. The average of the overall rating for the site is shown, along with the total number of descriptors selected by each annotator (possible descriptors include sponsor type, site category, subject area, and educational level). At the bottom of the aggregate annotation is a link to individual annotations (see Figure 2).

Figure 2. Individual Web annotation: To save space, only the sponsor type descriptors are shown.

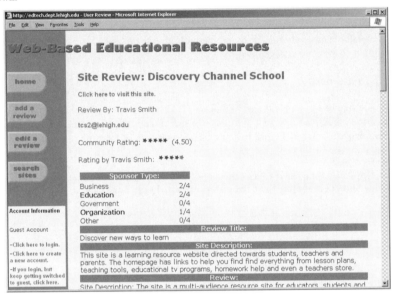

In the individual view, the annotator is identified by name and optionally by e-mail. The five-point rating for the particular annotation is provided and juxtaposed with the average of all other annotations, and site descriptors selected by the individual are placed in bold font alongside a repeat of the total count. The intention of the dual views is to promote the opinions of the larger community while still allowing for individual differences. At the end of the individual annotations is a description of the Web site and then comments that are intended primarily as a review.

Annotate Web Site

If users have created an account and logged into the system, they are given the option to create their own Web site annotations. Students can either start a review on their own by adding a new Web site to the database or, if they are viewing an annotation for a Web site they have not yet annotated themselves, a link is provided to do so. The annotations are entered using the simple Web form shown in Figure 3.

The system uniquely identifies sites by their URL, which introduces a problem of synonymy. Put simply, a set of four students may annotate the same Web site but provide four URLs (Walker, Recker, Lawless, & Wiley, 2004). This would prevent the system from recognizing these as annotations of the same site and providing the aggregate view described previously. In an attempt to circumvent this, users adding new URLs to the database are presented with a list of close matches and asked if one of the matches is in fact the same Web site.

Figure 3. Creating an annotation.

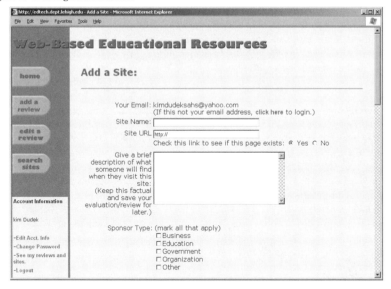

Peer Reviews

In an effort to promote utilization of the Web site annotations, as well as expose students to norms of the community and the hard work of their colleagues, a feature was added in which students could be assigned randomly to review the annotations written by their classmates. Peer reviews consist of a numerical rating and a textual response to the annotation and are utilized as the bulk (80%) of the grade for the Web annotation assignment. When students log into the system, they are presented with a list of annotations to peer review. The process is currently single blind. Reviewers know the authors of the annotations—in large part because the information is public and they could check if they wanted to. The authors, however, are unaware of who peer-reviewed their annotation.

Administrative Options

Users with administrator access are able to take advantage of some basic management tools. They can delete annotations that might be offensive or user accounts that fall into the same category. Administrators also have the ability to combine sets of annotations that point to the same resource but with slightly different URLs, a necessary feature despite the close match prompt shown to users and described previously. Finally, administrators are able to reset forgotten account passwords and prompt the system to randomly assign peer reviews.

USAGE RESULTS

The system was utilized by four iterations of the Core class, with each of the authors teaching two of the classes. A total of 57 students contributed annotations to the system representing a broad range of interests: Educational Leadership ($n = 1$), School Counseling (n = 8), Instructional Design and Development (ID&D; $n = 13$), and TBTE (Secondary and Elementary Education; $n = 35$). Both Core courses were required for TBTE students. Only the first Core course was required for ID&D students. The first course was an elective for students from other disciplines, although a number were advised into the course to meet their

Educational Technology requirement. Because TBTE students were the largest group to populate the Core courses, a preK–12 perspective did pervade these courses and influence the thinking behind the redesign in that teachers were considered the dominant target audience. However, the design of the system did accommodate for other disciplines, something we viewed as an asset in that such disciplinary communities clearly interact with one another in the real world on a regular basis. Thus, in the next section, we report on students' use of and response to the system for all participants in the Core regardless of disciplinary focus.

A total of 307 reviews were entered into the database. Students were required to submit six annotations in all but the final class, for which they were required to submit four. As might be expected, the mean number of annotations submitted, $M = 5.39$ ($SD = 0.90$), approaches the required six. None of the students submitted more annotations than required, but only three students failed to submit all of their annotations. Although the fact that no students used the system beyond the required level is disappointing, it is noteworthy that all but a handful did complete the task. In addition, they tended to devote a good deal of energy to both their annotations and, to a lesser extent, their assigned peer reviews. Table 1 shows the summary statistics for word counts from each of the sections outlined previously in the system description. Note that the decreased N for peer reviews is a result of this feature being unavailable when the system was first utilized.

Table 1. Word Count by Section

Section	N	Min	Max	M	SD
Site description	307	5	284	57.7	38.0
Annotation	306*	21	573	231.6	96.9
Peer review (text)	237	3	372	71.8	57.2

*Note 1 outlier of 880 words was removed from these data.

Perhaps equally important as the summary statistics is a look at the distribution of word counts, which can be seen in Figure 4. To keep things on an equal footing, only the listwise frequencies are shown ($N = 236$ after removal of the same outlier noted previously). The bulk of student efforts were obviously spent in the annotation section (where sites were evaluated), followed by the peer review area and then, lastly, the site description section. This finding is exciting because the richest information in terms of supporting a community of practice would likely come from either descriptions of the strengths, weaknesses, utility, and recommendations for use of a site included in an annotation section or from critiques of an annotation in the peer review area.

Students tended to rate Web sites quite favorably ($M = 3.9$, $SD = 1.1$) on the five-point Likert scale provided. The distribution of ratings shown in Figure 5 is markedly skewed negative. This should not come as much of a shock because students were encouraged to find Web sites that are of use to their current or future practice as professionals. A similar ratings trend has also been found in previous work (Walker et al., 2004) with an audience of exclusively preservice teachers, even when they were rating a mix of self-selected and preselected Web sites.

Figure 4. Distribution of word counts by section.

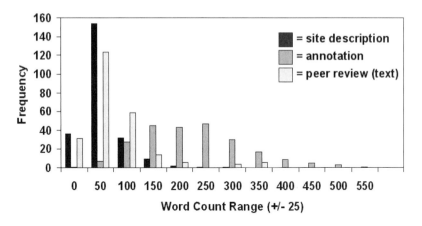

Figure 5. Distribution of ratings for annotations.

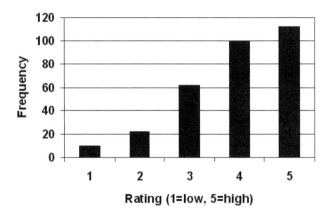

A distribution that is far more markedly skewed can be found in Figure 6 with an examination of peer review ratings. As might be guessed from just a look at the tightly clustered descriptives ($M = 7.5$, $SD = 0.8$), the vast majority of students gave their peers full points for their efforts. It is unclear why this might be the case, perhaps students were unaware that their peer reviews were single blind, perhaps they were unwilling to mark down their colleagues, or perhaps the high scores are truly reflective of the high-quality annotations.

A final interesting feature of the usage statistics is the frequency of annotations per Web site, shown in Figure 7. A handful of Web sites received multiple annotations, the largest of which was 13. The vast majority of Web sites, 132 in all, received just a single review. This result closely follows a Zipf distribution that is commonly found in Internet-related data sets (Heaps, 1978). This has several implications for the ways communities can utilize this kind of information. First, it is unfortunately impossible to get the sense of how the larger community feels about any one single resource. This promotes a kind of "tyranny of the individual" as opposed to a tyranny of the masses. It is, however, not uncommon for individuals within a community of practice to specialize in sources of information and take on a primary role in finding related pieces of information and disseminating them to the larger group (Ehrlich & Cash, 1994). More recently, this concept of pushing information through individuals is embodied with technologies such as blogs and radio blogs.

Figure 6. Distribution of ratings for peer reviews.

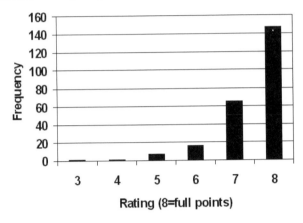

Figure 7. Frequency of annotations per Web site.

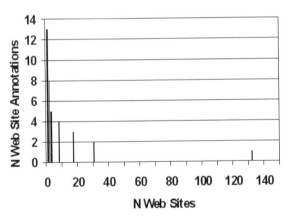

Looking beyond the numbers, students appeared to find some utility in the most important part of the system—the annotations contributed by other students. As one peer reviewer noted, "You ... thought deeply of the applications for the information on this site. I would utilize this information based on your [annotation] in a heartbeat!" Another student wrote, "I agree with your thoughts regarding the Web site. The content and form information you provided about the site is useful. I liked the professional and organized manner in which you portrayed your views. I found the additional link and comment about that link to be useful. I will pass it along to fellow teachers! Thank you!"

It is interesting that students not only found personal utility in reading the Web site annotations but found that utility significant enough to warrant passing it on to their fellow practitioners.

DISCUSSION

We have described how a social theory of learning influenced the migration of a Web site evaluation assignment for teacher education students from a highly prescribed, individualized assignment to one based on the students' creation and use of an online community resource. We also described the design, development, and early usage statistics of the central technology tool supporting this transformation, a Web-based educational resources database. We conclude this chapter with a discussion of the experience, including the limitations of the project and prospects for future work.

Recall that we believed that the original Web site evaluation assignment did support students' use and critical evaluation of educational technologies but did not encourage students' perception of teacher practice as requiring the generative and collaborative sharing of valued educational resources within a professional community. We felt that a rethinking of the assignment could better support such a perspective. In essence, we agree with Wallace, Kupperman, Krajcik, and Soloway (2000) when, in discussing the challenges of promoting inquiry practices with students using the Web, they state: "It matters what students are asked to do and how tools and techniques to accomplish these tasks are provided" (p. 23).

We are unable to claim empirically that the redesigned assignment helped students to orient toward practice as a socially negotiated endeavor. However, we do believe that the new assignment, in striving to reflect a social orientation toward learning, opens up an opportunity for students to experience a shift in that direction. The reframed assignment, by emphasizing the creation, use, and evaluation of a professionally relevant community resource, strives to support that *engagement in a community of practice* of which Wenger and others speak (Brown, Collins, & Duguid, 1989; Greeno, 1998; Kirshner & Whitson, 1997; Lave & Wenger, 1991; Salomon, 1996; Wenger, 1998).

Still, we recognize that one such assignment is only a beginning and is hardly likely to shift one's perspectives toward learning and professional practice in a fundamentally profound way. The redesigned assignment can serve as a stepping stone toward deeper forms of legitimate peripheral participation as TBTE students move forward in their professional development and engage more fully as members of the professional teacher community. For example, those TBTE students who are now more experienced in Web site searching and evaluation and in using the Web resource database could next be asked to develop and implement lessons integrating a Web site identified through searching the database and subsequently report back on their experience in using that site by entering new annotations in the database. In this way, the students use the resource to support their teaching practice but also have an opportunity to reflect on that use and share it with others in the community, enriching the database at the same time. Or, perhaps as part of the student teaching internship, students are asked to design and facilitate an inservice training session for teachers from host schools, teaching them how to use the database as a resource and concurrently extending the community of practice. Such next steps would support what Collins (1991) identified as two potential benefits of a situated learning orientation: the opportunity for individuals to see the implications of knowledge and to develop an understanding of how to structure knowledge in ways appropriate to later use by gaining and working with that knowledge in context.

Examples abound regarding how this simple redesign might be broadened to additional experiences for TBTE students that further embody a social theory of learning. However, we are wary about ending in too prescriptive a fashion because, fundamentally, the concept of legitimate peripheral participation in a community of practice is not meant to be prescriptive but reorientating. In their own words, Lave and Wenger remind us that legitimate peripheral participation "is not an educational form,… a pedagogical strategy or a teaching technique. [Rather] it is an analytical viewpoint on learning, a way of understanding learning ... [that] could inform educational endeavors by shedding a new light on learning processes" (Lave & Wenger, 1991, p. 40). The real story, if you will, in the redesign is about shifting focus toward a certain structure of professional practice, rather that privileging a specific pedagogical practice. In fact, it is likely that embracing a social orientation toward practice could take on many different expressions at the activity level. Thus, rather than advocate for our specific choices in the redesign, what appears most important is a clear understanding of the underlying vision and how that vision might inform how learning takes place and what resources might best support it.

REFERENCES

Brown, J. S., Collins, A., & Duguid, P. (1989). Situated cognition and the culture of learning. *Educational Researcher, 18*(1), 32–42.

Collins, A. (1991). Cognitive apprenticeship and instructional technology. In L. B. Resnick (Ed.), *Knowing, learning, and instruction: Essays in honor of Robert Glaser* (pp. 453–494). Hillsdale, NJ: Lawrence Erlbaum Associates.

Ehrlich, K., & Cash, D. (1994). *I am an information waitress: Bringing order to the new digital libraries* (No. 1994.11). Cambridge, MA: Lotus Research.

Greeno, J. G. (1998). The situativity of knowing, learning, and research. *American Psychologist, 53*(1), 5–26.

Harmon, S. W., & Reeves, T. C. (1998). *Educational WWW sites evaluation instrument*. Retrieved June 19, 2005, from http://it.coe.uga.edu/%7Etreeves/edit8350/wwweval.html

Heaps, H. S. (1978). *Information retrieval: Computational and theoretical aspects*. New York: Academic Press.

Kirshner, D., & Whitson, J. A. (Eds.). (1997). *Situated cognition: social, semiotic, and psychological perspectives*. Mahwah, NJ: Lawrence Erlbaum Associates.

Lave, J., & Wenger, E. (1991). *Situated learning: Legitimate peripheral participation*. Cambridge, England: Cambridge University Press.

Salomon, G. (1996). Unorthodox thoughts on the nature and mission of contemporary educational psychology. *Educational Psychology Review, 8*(4), 397–417.

Schrock, K. (2002). *The ABCs of Web site evaluation*. Retrieved June 19, 2005, from http://school.discovery.com/schrockguide/pdf/weval_02.pdf

Walker, A., Recker, M., Lawless, K., & Wiley, D. (2004). Collaborative information filtering: A review and an educational application. *International Journal of Artificial Intelligence in Education, 14*, 1–26.

Wallace, R. M., Kupperman, J., Krajcik, J., & Soloway, E. (2000). Science on the Web: Students online in a sixth-grade classroom. *Journal of the Learning Sciences, 9*(1), 75–104.

Wenger, E. (1998). *Communities of practice: Learning, meaning, and identity*. New York: Cambridge University Press.

A Case-Based E-Learning Model for Professional Education: Anesthesiology for Dental Students

Ikseon Choi, Hyeonjin Kim, Jong Won Jung, and Gregory Clinton
The University of Georgia

Jeongwan Kang
Yonsei University College of Dentistry, South Korea

INTRODUCTION

Anesthesiology is a relatively new subject added as an introductory course into the dental school curriculum in South Korea. The goal of this introductory course is to teach dental students who will be surgeons to understand all areas of anesthetization and anesthesiologists' decision-making processes to collaborate with them successfully during surgery. However, instructors are often challenged by the fact that a great amount of textbook (decontextualized) information needs to be delivered to the third-year dental students within a limited time (a one credit hour course). Consequently, instructors have observed that students were neither engaged in reflective thinking nor deepening their understanding and problem-solving skills for the topics taught. The knowledge acquired in this class seems to remain as inert knowledge that may not be utilized in real-world situations.

To resolve the time issues and the decontextualized knowledge problem, our main approach is to apply video-based, case-based e-learning environments in which learners can control their learning times (due to e-learning) and have relatively rich experiences with more realistic, authentic contexts (due to real video cases). In the process of transforming the textbook-based instruction into the case-based instruction, we carefully selected cases in order to cover all contents taught before. Our overall design approach of this project is based on the notion of "design experiments" (Brown, 1992; Collins, 1992) because technology-enhanced innovations need to be deployed continually while the innovation (the e-learning environment), students, and instructors (or administrators) adapt themselves in the iterative implementation processes.

The purpose of this chapter is to present an instructional design model that we developed and used for designing a case-based e-learning environment, specifically for training dynamic decision-making skills in anesthesiology. In this chapter, we explain the nature of the task, our assumptions on learning, an e-learning design model, the interface of the product, and our further plans.

DYNAMIC DECISION MAKING IN ANESTHETIZATION

Anesthetization is a complex, dynamic, risky, time pressed, and highly information-loaded task (Gaba & Howard, 1995). For safe patient care, the anesthesiologist's attention needs to be distributed appropriately among the patient, anesthesia equipment, and important clinical activities throughout the entire process of anesthetization (Gaba & Lee, 1990). In this process, a series of decisions are made. The dynamic decision-making cycle has a series of steps: detecting cues from external devices or patient monitoring, identifying problems from the interpretation of cues, predicting future states based on reasoning, planning actions, implementing the actions, monitoring effects of the actions, and evaluating overall results of the decision-making process (Gaba & Howard, 1995). Among decisions being made, we identified two types of occasions in which anesthesiologists are involved in a more clear reasoning process: planning in the preparation stage and (un)expected incidents. In the preparation stage, to develop an operative plan, anesthesiologists gather accurate information about the patient based on the physician's diagnosis and lab test results and about the operation procedures received from the surgeon. In the (un)expected incidents, such as when an anesthesiologist perceives that standard procedures are nonapplicable or unsuccessful, he or she is deeply engaged in reasoning processes about cause-effect or structure-function relationships (Gaba & DeAnda, 1989). Therefore, to teach anesthesiology, including basic medical concepts, we focus on critical decision points within the reasoning and decision-making process. Case selection and development are also conducted according to the decision points.

ASSUMPTIONS ABOUT MEANINGFUL LEARNING: WAYS OF BUILDING EXPERTISE

Belief Failures

We believe that belief failure experienced by a learner is a critical cognitive condition for his or her meaningful learning process (Carlson, 1997; Choi & Jonassen, 2000). Belief failure means a recognized gap or a conflict between what a learner believes and what he or she perceives. Experiencing unexpected things prompts the learner to reflect on his or her belief system (knowledge structure), to realize what she or he needs to know, to seek additional information, and to (re-)sample necessary information available in his or her consciousness in order to (re-)construct his or her belief system (Carlson, 1997; Piaget, 1985). In this case, the learner controls his or her own learning. Thus, belief failure can be seen as a necessary condition for meaningful learning.

If it is true that the belief failure triggers meaningful learning, then meaningful learning environments need to include belief-failure facilitation strategies so that the learner becomes an active information seeker and knowledge constructor within the environments. Among many ways to facilitate learners' experience of belief failures, authentic and complex problems, questions (Jonassen, Peck, & Wilson, 1999), goals or missions (Schank, 1999), and peer challenges (Choi, 2003) are commonly used. In our learning environments, we included realistic cases along with critical decision problems and critical peer review strategies to facilitate learners' belief failure experiences. Details will be explained in the following sections.

Just-in-Time Learning

Just-in-time learning—learning at the moment of need—is one of the most efficient and meaningful types of learning. Once learners experience belief failures, the learners begin to articulate what they need to know through the reflection process. To resolve their knowledge gap, they begin to actively seek additional information. Although learners are motivated to learn something, their efforts will be fruitless if they are not provided with appropriate learning resources such as necessary information, guidance, scaffolding, modeling, and so on. It is important to make appropriate learning resources available to learners at the right moment of need (Gery, 1991). Providing relevant information according to their need is critical for them to construct their knowledge in an efficient, effective, and meaningful way. More important, just-in-time learning allows learning to occur in more meaningful contexts such that students can index their knowledge in more meaningful ways. If the belief failure occurs in an authentic or realistic context, knowledge will be constructed in and indexed by a relevant context so the knowledge can be activated in appropriate situations (Aamodt & Plaza, 1994).

Thus, in our learning environments, we endeavored to make all types of learning resources (or information) available just after or around the learner's belief failure experience. For example, after being exposed to the decision problems through video cases that prompt students to wonder what is going on, students will be provided with an expert's thinking process regarding how he interprets situations and develops solution plans. While the students listen to the expert's reasoning, they become aware of a lack of a particular piece of medical knowledge used in his explanation about the problems. Links to the particular medical references used in the expert's explanation are available for the students to review without any great effort required to search the relevant information.

A CASE-BASED E-LEARNING MODEL

Having learners experience belief failures within realistic contexts (decision making problems through representative cases, real-life stories, and challenge cases) and providing just-in-time learning resources (modeling of expert reasoning, scaffolding of learners' decision-making process, relevant information resources, and interactions in a learning community), as shown in Figure 1, are major instructional strategies we applied in designing each component of our case-based e-learning environment. In this section, details of this environment and design considerations are explained.

Figure 1. A case-based e-learning model.

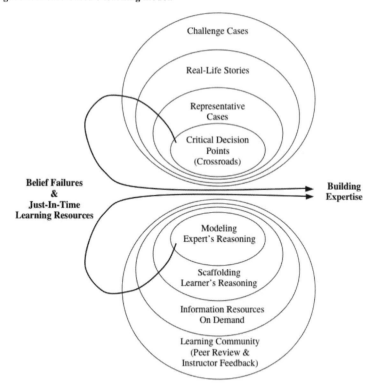

BELIEF FAILURES WITHIN REALISTIC CONTEXTS: ORGANIZATION OF CASES

There are five representative cases in which critical decision points are embedded. As shown in Figure 2, each decision point in each representative case holds two additional layers of cases: real-life stories and challenge cases. The representative cases, critical decision points, real-life stories, and challenge cases are explained in this section.

Figure 2. Case organization in the e-learning model.

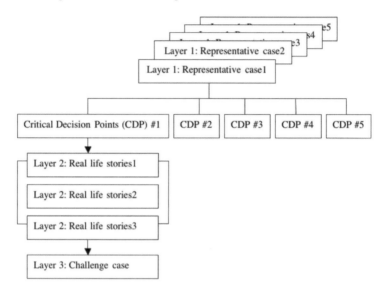

Representative Cases: Performance Video Cases

Contextual knowledge is a part of intellectual skills (Jonassen et al., 1999). Knowledge constructed can be activated in relevant problem situations through processes of matching contextual information perceived and contextual knowledge constructed (Aamodt & Plaza, 1994; Kolodner, 1993). Thus, the overarching purpose of providing these representative cases is creating realistic contexts from which students can build their mental models and manipulate them, construct knowledge on them, and index new knowledge into them for later activation.

Representative cases are actual performance videos of anesthesiologists in various dental surgery cases in operation rooms. These performance-video cases can provide problems and an expert's performance, along with richer contextual information, so students can vicariously experience authentic situations and problems-solving processes that experts deal with in their everyday practices. Five representative types of anesthetization processes were identified. Then we created five realistic scenarios in which we embedded various challenges and problems. Finally, a 10- to 20-minute video clip for each representative case has been developed. In the video productions, the main reason we created realistic scenarios instead of using actual real-life case stories is that after reviewing about 2,000 cases, we struggled to find a single problematic case holding a variety of challenges and problems that we wanted to include.

Learners can get several benefits from these representative cases. First, these expert performance videos provide rich information about what is going on and how anesthesiologists deal with problems in the real operation room. Learners who are not familiar with real situations will be able to build richer mental models for the situations and problems while exploring the video cases. Second, each case encompasses the entire process of anesthetization. Thus, reviewing the videos, learners will gradually be able to understand the general processes of anesthetization. Lastly, the problems embedded within the representative cases will lead to learners' experience of belief failures, whereby they will be motivated to understand situations and solve the problems. They will actively seek additional information to resolve their cognitive dissonance. For that reason, the presentation of the representative cases to the learners is structured around the critical decision points (problems or crossroads).

Critical Decision Points: Crossroads

An anesthetization task consists of a set of decisions being made and actions following the decisions. Some of the decisions, that we are calling critical decisions, are crucial for the success of the task. Anesthesiologists are engaged in serious reasoning processes around the critical decision points to understand problem situations and to generate appropriate courses of actions based on existing medical knowledge. The major goal of this learning environment is to teach experts' reasoning and decision-making skills along with basic medical knowledge related to anesthesiology. Therefore, the critical decision points are major problem units where the learner's attention is focused and where instructional efforts need to be made.

Through a cognitive task analysis process (e.g., Klein, Calderwood, & Macgregor, 1989), we found that most critical decisions are made in the planning stage of anesthetization and during unexpected (or expected) incidents while the surgery is performed. So we designed each representative case to hold five critical decision points. When the video presentation arrives at each critical decision point, the video automatically stops, and further learning resources and activities are provided. In fact, all planned learning experiences will occur around these decision points.

Real-Life Stories: Multiple Cases for Cognitive Flexibility

Experiencing a single case for a particular decision point (problem) may not be enough for learners to develop cognitive flexibility for solving similar problems because the complexities of the ill-structured domains and the dynamic interaction of critical factors in different situations are ignored (Spiro, Feltovich, Jacobson, & Coulson, 1992). Thus, multiple real-life stories are provided to enhance learners' reasoning skills around the critical decision points.

Real-life stories are video clips of an expert's storytelling about his similar experiences related to particular decision points. As shown in Figure 2, each representative case holds five critical decision points (problems), and each decision point in turn has several additional relevant cases. Each real-life story presents a similar problem related to the decision points, and learners must develop reasoning and decision reports for the problems. After students complete their reports, the expert's reasoning and decision video follows in a storytelling format.

Unlike representative cases, the video clips of real-life stories do not present the actual operation process. Although the problems might be more meaningful if they were delivered through video clips of actual performance in the operation room, we used an expert's storytelling video to reduce the developmental cost. However, cost was not the single reason for this decision. The expert storytelling method may also increase efficiency and transfer of learning. We believe that learners who have watched and studied representative cases (actual performance video) for a particular decision point may have a certain level of prior knowledge, so that they will be able to visualize problem situations and build mental models of the problem from simply listening to an expert's narrative story about his experiences. More important, most experts in the real world exchange their experiences and problems through a narrative form, that is, storytelling (Orr, 1996). Therefore, learners can become familiar with building their knowledge through stories.

Challenge Cases

Challenge cases are designed to assess learning outcomes. After studying three real-life stories under each decision point, learners will be given another real-life story video, labeled as a challenge case. Unlike the previous real-life stories, no expert's reasoning and decision story will be provided after the students have completed their reasoning and decision report. Their report will be available for peer review and instructor feedback.

JUST-IN-TIME LEARNING EXPERIENCE: SCAFFOLDING LEARNER'S REASONING

As shown in Figure 1, the other side of our instructional design model represents just-in-time learning resources for scaffolding learners' reasoning. The case-based e-learning environment includes a variety of strategies to scaffold learners' internalization of expert reasoning processes through the entire learning experience: expert reasoning videos, on-demand content information, structured Web page forms for writing decision reports, guiding questions for facilitating student reasoning, comparison tables between the learner's own reasoning reports and the expert's report, and peer review and instructor's feedback. Again, all scaffolding strategies are based on the six steps of decision making as described in the previous sections: identifying problem cues, assessing situations, setting goals, generating solutions, and executing and evaluating the solutions.

After watching each decision problem in a representative case, the learners are given the expert reasoning videos. Then, learners will be asked to summarize the expert's reasoning and decision. Within the decision point, learners will be given three additional real-life stories. When the stories arrive at the problem, students will be asked to write their reasoning and decision reports. After completing them, learners can review experts' stories about their reasoning and decisions. They will also be provided with comparison tables showing their answers and the experts' decisions. After that, a challenge case will be given in the same way. Student answers will be reviewed by a couple of peers, and the peers will give constructive feedback regarding their reasoning and decisions. Learners can revise their answer based on their peers' feedback. All peer interactions and the revision processes will be reviewed by the instructor for his final feedback on the learner's reasoning and decisions.

Modeling Expert's Reasoning: Storytelling about How to Think

We assume that the mind is a tool to interpret the world (Jonassen et al., 1999). Therefore, listening to experts' stories about their interpretations of certain phenomena will help learners to understand the phenomena they are observing. In addition, listening to experts' narrative explanations about how they reason will help learners to model experts' reasoning. When learners watch a problematic situation in the video representative cases, they may be eager to see what is going on. At that time, learners will be given an expert's explanations about how they see and interpret the problems and how they come up with solutions or make decisions.

In this environment, "expert's reasoning" means video clips of experts' narrative storytelling about their internal thought processes when they are faced with a particular problem and have to make critical decisions. The expert's reasoning video usually includes six decision-making steps: identifying problem cues, assessing situations, setting goals, generating solutions, executing the solutions, and evaluating the solutions. Students' experience of these processes will be gradually guided within the problem context while they construct and apply new content knowledge.

Information Resources on Demand

Knowledge should be constructed within authentic contexts (Brown, Collins, & Duguid 1989; Cognition and Technology Group at Vanderbilt, 1990). While reviewing expert reasoning video clips, deploying their reasoning, and making decisions, learners will need a variety of information resources such as textbook information and additional patient records about the problems. Relevant information is provided automatically at the moment of need, so learners construct their knowledge from the given information within their reasoning and decision-making processes. Importantly, existing lecture notes and textbooks are reinterpreted as on-demand information (we call it IOD: Information on Demand) and reorganized to support our case-based learning. That is, decontextualized textbook information is transformed into just-in-time information connected with authentic contexts. Static information becomes dynamic and generative in the case-based learning environment.

To develop IOD, we first divided the existing content into small enough chunks to tailor information to the learner's various needs. Second, to facilitate contextualized understanding of certain theories or concepts, we designed IOD in a pop-up window so that students can use the IOD while watching a case without closing the current Web page (Figure 3). Third, each IOD includes links to relevant cases and other IODs to enable students to connect situations and explore in more flexible ways. Fourth, the IOD interface allows the instructor to add new information in an easy way by providing a template for adding and modifying. The instructor can add recent information or can reorganize some information differently.

Learning Community: Peer Review and Instructor Feedback

Knowledge is constructed and shared within a social context (Greeno, 1997; Lave & Wenger, 1991). Peer review and instructor feedback are also part of scaffolding learners' decision-making skills. However, unlike other scaffolding strategies using multimedia resources, these are asynchronous human communications mediated by the Internet. These activities will help individual learners build their sense of identity as members of their learning community (Wenger, 1998). The confidence they feel about their learning experience will be shared and recognized socially. Another reason we designed this activity to be the last phase of each decision problem set is to reduce the instructor's teaching load. At the beginning of the course, learners will be guided through video modeling, Web forms, written expert reasoning and decisions, and peer feedback. After students have had enough experience on a certain type of decision problem, the instructor can guide only problematic parts of the learners' performances.

THE INTERFACE OF THE CASE-BASED E-LEARNING ENVIRONMENT AND THE LEARNING EXPERIENCE

A sample page from the e-Learning interface is presented in Figure 3. The sample page is the opening screen for one of the representative cases. In this section, we provide a brief overview of how learners explore this learning environment.

Figure 3. Major screen: A representative case.

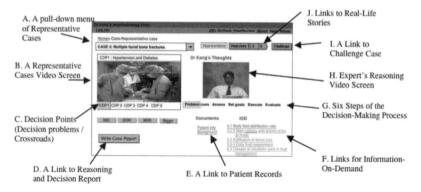

Once a learner enters this main page, he or she selects one of six representative cases in order (A in Figure 3). For example, the learner chooses a representative case titled "Multiple Facial Bone Fractures," at which point the real situation video is played automatically (B). The first of five segments of decision problems for this case is labeled CDP1 (Critical Decision Point 1) and titled "Hypertension and Diabetes" (C). At each decision point, the video stops. The user plays the expert's reasoning video about the decision problem by clicking the Expert's Reasoning video screen (H). The learner watches the expert's reasoning video for each of the six steps of the decision-making process (G). The learner also watches the expert's actual course of action through the representative case video screen (B). Then the learner opens a reasoning and decision report page by clicking the link (D) and summarizes what she or he observed according to the guiding format provided in the reasoning and decision report Web form. While watching representative case videos or expert reasoning videos or while writing reports, learners can access various information resources such as patient records (E) and textbook-like information (F). These information resources are updated according to the current decision problem. Once they have finished the first critical decision point and before moving on to the next decision problem, learners choose three additional real-life stories (J), which present actual problems similar to the situation just experienced. For each real-life story, learners write their own reasoning and decision reports. Upon submitting the reports, they review an expert reasoning and decision video along with an additional comparison table where they can compare easily their answer and the expert's answer. Next, still under the same decision point theme, the learner clicks on the challenge case (I). As with the real-life story, the challenge case requires the learner to submit his or her reasoning and decision reports, which will be reviewed by peers this time. After peer feedback, the student can revise his or her answers. All activities are monitored by the instructor. The instructor's final feedback on a student's reports and peer feedback indicate the end of one decision point theme under a representative case. The learner then moves to the next decision problem segment (crossroads). Overall, the learner will finish one decision problem, three real-life stories, and one challenge case under each decision point, with each representative case having five decision points. During a semester, the learner will finish five of these representative cases.

FURTHER IMPLEMENTATION

As mentioned earlier, the overall approach of this project is based on the notion of "design experiments" (Brown, 1992; Collins, 1992). We believe that technology-enhanced innovations need to be deployed continually while the innovation (the e-learning environment), students, and instructors (or administrators) adapt themselves in the iterative implementation processes. This e-learning environment will be implemented at one of the South Korean dental schools in the context of an introductory course. We will test this innovation and redesign based on feedback from all stakeholders until this implementation is successful. While implementing, we will also try to test the actual learning effectiveness of various instructional strategies embedded in this environment, individually and holistically, so that we can refine these strategies and enhance learning and teaching.

ACKNOWLEDGMENTS

Part of this research was sponsored by Educate Co., Ltd. in Seoul, Korea.

REFERENCES

Aamodt, A., & Plaza, E. (1994). Case-based reasoning: Foundational issues, methodological variations, and systems approaches. *AI Communications, 7*(1), 39–52.

Brown, A. L. (1992). Design experiments: Theoretical and methodological challenges in creating complex interventions in classroom settings. *Journal of the Learning Science, 2*(2), 141–178.

Brown, J. S., Collins, A., & Duguid, P. (1989). Situated cognition and the culture of learning. *Educational Researcher, 18*(1), 32–42.

Carlson, R. A. (1997). *Experienced cognition.* Mahwah, NJ: Lawrence Erlbaum Associates.

Choi, I. (2002). *Effects of peer-challenge support on learning during on-line small group discussion.* Unpublished doctoral dissertation, Pennsylvania State University, University Park.

Choi, I., & Jonassen, D. H. (2000). Learning objectives from the perspective of the experience cognition framework. *Educational Technology, 40*(6), 36–40.

Cognition and Technology Group at Vanderbilt. (1990). Anchored instruction and its relationship to situated cognition. *Educational Researcher, 19*(6), 2-10.

Collins, A. (1992). Toward a design science of education. In E. Scanlon & T. O'Shea (Eds.), *New directions in educational technology* (pp. 15–22). Berlin: Springer-Verlag.

Gaba, D. M., & DeAnda, A. (1989). The response of anesthesia trainees to simulated critical incidents. *Anesthesia and Analgesia, 68*, 444–451.

Gaba, D. M., & Howard, S. K. (1995). Situation awareness in anesthesiology. *Human Factors, 37*(1), 20–31.

Gaba, D. M., & Lee, T. (1990). Measuring the workload of the anesthesiologist. *Anesthesia and Analgesia, 71*, 354–361.

Gery, G. J. (1991). *Electronic performance support systems: How and why to remake the workplace through the strategic application of technology.* Tolland, MA: Gery Performance Press.

Greeno, J. G. (1997). On Claims That Answer the Wrong Questions. *Educational Researcher, 26*(1), 5–17.

Jonassen, D. H., Peck, K. L., & Wilson, B. G. (1999). *Learning with technology: A constructivist perspective.* Upper Saddle River, NJ: Prentice-Hall.

Klein, G., Calderwood, R., & Macgregor, D. (1989). Critical decision method for eliciting knowledge. *IEEE Transactions on Systems, Man, and Cybernetics, 19*(3), 462–472.

Kolodner, J. (1993) Case-Based Reasoning, San Mateo: Morgan Kauffman Publishers.

Lave, J., & Wenger, E. (1991). *Situated learning: legitimate peripheral participation.* Cambridge, England, and New York: Cambridge University Press.

Orr, J. E. (1996). *Talking about machines: An ethnography of a modern job.* Ithaca, NY: Cornell University Press.

Piaget, J. (1985). Equilibration of cognitive structures. University of Chicago Press.

Schank, R. C. (1999). *Dynamic memory revisited.* New York: Cambridge University Press.

Spiro, R. J., Feltovich, P. J., Jacobson, M. J., & Coulson, R. L. (1992). Cognitive flexibility, constructivism, and hypertext: Random access instruction for advanced knowledge acquisition in ill-structured domains. In T. M. Duffy & D. H. Jonassen (Eds.), *Constructivism and the Technology of Instruction: A Conversation* (pp. 57–75). Hillsdale, NJ: Lawrence Erlbaum Associates.

Wenger, E. (1998). *Communities of practice: learning, meaning, and identity.* Cambridge, England, and New York: Cambridge University Press.

Creating Constructivist Learning Environments

Doris U. Bolliger

St. Cloud State University

INTRODUCTION

Constructivism is an educational theory about how reality is created, knowledge is acquired, and individuals learn (Brooks & Brooks, 1993; Marlowe & Page, 1998). The theory is built on the work of Jean Piaget (1954), who is known for his contributions to the field of developmental cognitive psychology. According to Piaget, cognitive structures change when individuals are exposed to the external environment and integrate information by either assimilating or accommodating it.

In the first half of the 20th century, the field of instructional design and technology was dominated by behaviorism (Seels & Richey, 1994). Behaviorists are primarily concerned with the observation of a measurable change in behavior as the result of providing stimuli. In contrast, constructivists provide situated learning experiences that assist learners in the individual sense-making process.

Constructivism has gained acceptance and become highly valued by many educators. Constructivism is about thinking and understanding. Grounded in this theory is the concept that individuals obtain knowledge by creating constructs and by interpreting and reflecting on their experiences (Jonassen, Peck, & Wilson, 1999). Only constructs, which can be a schema or a concept, can be stored when we process information.

Central to this idea are self-regulation, active learning, individual differences, social learning, and reflection (Gagnon & Collay, 2001; Jonassen et al., 1999). Individuals learn by investigating, discovering, and creating structures; actively attaching meaning to a concept; and integrating new or modified constructs into existing knowledge. According to Novak (1998), meaningful learning involves "thinking, feeling, and acting" (p. 9).

A theoretical framework that ties in with constructivism is constructionism. This theory builds on constructivist perspectives and is viewed as an extension of it. Constructionists believe individuals learn not only by doing but also by making (Harel & Papert, 1991). When learners create public artifacts while "working on *personally meaningful* activities and projects," they not only construct new knowledge but new relationships with knowledge (Kafai & Resnick, 1996, p. 2). Persons learn best when they immerse themselves into the material and are connected with the subject (Harel & Papert, 1991).

Constructivists do not argue that constructivist approaches lead to learning and others do not. However, Stahl (2003) points out that everyone is a constructivist because we are constructing knowldege at every conscious moment. Constructivists share the opinion that students have been passive receivers of knowledge for too long (Brooks & Brooks, 1993). Teachers have given too many lectures and have tried transmitting their knowledge to students by acting as *Sage on the Stage*. Yet knowledge cannot be transmitted (Larochelle, Bednarz, & Garrison, 1998). Regrettably, learners memorize facts but, shortly thereafter, forget what they have learned. The transfer that should take place from theory to practice, unfortunately, does not occur.

Constructivism has opened up new, unlimited possibilities (Brooks & Brooks, 1993; Larochelle et al., 1998), and so has constructionism. Instead of using the transmission approach (Berge, 2001) in which students receive knowledge in a top-down delivery system from teachers, constructivists argue students should be actively involved in their learning so that they are able to apply what they have learned. According to DeVries and Kohlberg (1987), Piaget also came to the conclusion that action is instrumental to knowledge acquisition.

Constructivist and constructionist theories can guide educational practice to develop curriculum. Learning can be exciting and should not be dreaded as mindless activity where students end up reciting facts they have stored in short-tem memory. Teachers should ask how they can provide students with environments in which teachers can facilitate student learning so that students (a) can "discover, create, and apply knowledge for themselves," (b) "push themselves," and (c) "truly understand what they learn" (Marlowe & Page, 1998, p. 5). According to Marlowe and Page, components that need revision include terminology, communication between involved parties, learning activities, learning environments, student motivation, and student assessment.

Jonassen et al. (1999) identified several components of constructivist learning environments: (a) an interesting problem, (b) related cases, (c) informational resources, (d) cognitive tools, (e) conversation, and (f) social support. To create constructivist learning environments, teachers can present the big picture to students; ask questions and give students time to respond; encourage questions; probe for student understanding; use primary sources and interactive material; consider students' prior experience and knowledge; be open to and try to understand students' ideas and viewpoints; provide opportunities for exploration, discussion, and reflection; ask for elaboration of responses; allow for flexibility in the use of instructional material; promote group work; serve as a role model and as a coach; and assess student learning with the use of projects and portfolios (Brooks & Brooks, 1993; Jonassen et al., 1999; Wilson, 1996). Constructivist teachers shift from teaching to learning and create safe learning environments (Marlowe & Page, 1998).

The field of instructional technology is suited particularly well for the integration of constructivist and constructionist learning methods. Instructional technology is no longer limited to serve as a delivery tool, but can be used as a "cognitive medium" (Hay & Barab, 2001, p. 281). Courses in many instructional technology degree programs have media development and production requirements. Instructors can require students to work on projects, individually or in groups, and use the technology as tools to construct authentic, meaningful knowledge and gain new skills by creating their own artifacts. This method promotes active learning and problem solving. It can also instill a sense of ownership in the learning process and created artifacts. Students can publicize their final products on Web pages or electronic portfolios that can be shared with interested parties all over the world.

PERCEIVED BARRIERS

Instructors who either wish to use constructivist approaches or have used them in their classrooms face barriers from administration, peers, and students. Administrators are concerned that the integration of constructivist approaches takes too much time. Learner-centered activities such as discussions or group work take more time than lectures. Because of accreditation requirements, instructors must cover content instead of using up valuable time with student-centered approaches.

The roles of instructors and learners shift in the constructivist environment. Instructors become mentors, coaches, and facilitators. It requires teachers to modify existing materials and activities. Some may oppose constructivist approaches because they think this process is too difficult and time-consuming. Others feel their approach has worked well in the past (Brooks & Brooks, 1993). In addition, teachers might not be willing to relinquish classroom control; typically, constructivists surrender some level of control to their students. Instructors who see themselves as the experts in the field may feel threatened if students start questioning them about content or facts.

Roles of students also change. Learners become responsible for their own learning. Many students have been trained to comply with course requirements and have not been taught to think for themselves. Teachers who would like to implement constructivist approaches may find that students resist these changes.

THE STUDY

The purpose of this study was to determine how students would perceive constructivist approaches in the classroom and their own learning. The researcher was particularly interested in (a) how easily students would adapt to the approaches, (b) approaches perceived as useful by students, and (c) approaches that were not effective.

Setting

Nine students were enrolled in a graduate-level instructional media production course during spring 2003 at a Midwestern university. The instruction took place in a classroom-based environment but was enhanced with a course management system (CMS) and a course Web site. Class sessions took place in a Smart Classroom equipped with personal computers, a projector, a visual presenter, and a VCR. Instructors and students had a variety of multimedia software programs available to them. The classroom was in close proximity to an open computer laboratory allowing students access to printers, scanners, digital cameras, and laptop computers.

Constructivist Approaches

Communicating Expectations

During the first class session, the instructor communicated her vision for the course including the fact that the course was not owned simply by her. Students were asked to consider the course to be "their" course because they had a vested interest in their learning. They were given voting rights on certain course requirements (e.g., due dates). After students completed a prerequisite skill questionnaire it was evident that students in this group varied greatly on progress made in their program and, subsequently, varied greatly on existing computer and multimedia authoring skills. However, all students in the course had successfully completed an instructional design course, a prerequisite for the course.

Providing Access

The instructor designed a course Web site that included a syllabus, schedule, assignments, resources, and contact information for all participants. In addition, the course was supplemented by placing course content (e.g., PowerPoint presentations, help notes, and so forth) in the CMS. Other CMS tools utilized were communication and evaluation tools including e-mail, chat, threaded discussions, feedback, and grades.

Providing an Assortment of Tools

Students used a variety of software programs which included Macromedia Dreamweaver, Fireworks, and Flash; the CourseBuilder extension for Dreamweaver; and Microsoft PowerPoint, Word, and Visio. The two textbooks required for the course were a multimedia development text and a Dreamweaver MX self-study text. In addition, students had access to several multimedia development books during class sessions and additional required readings were posted on the syllabus.

Giving Learners Choices

Students completed mandatory and optional assignments. Mandatory assignments made up 80% of the student's grade and included a Web site and all elements of a group-based client project. Optional assignments included other multimedia projects, a final examination, and writing projects.

Jonassen (2000) emphasizes the importance of "grounded educational practices" in the learner-centered environment (p. 11). Instructions for assignments, however, were kept to a minimum. For writing assignments, the instructor purposely did not include any parameters such as paper length, research topics, and so forth. The instructor requested students to submit a proposal outlining the purpose, questions students sought to explore, and a table of contents to provide guidance and feedback to the students who selected these assignments. Specifications for the production of authoring projects were also limited because the instructor did not want to limit the creativity of students.

Creating a Social Learning Environment

During the course of the semester, group members were required to share their work in progress with the class. The instructor provided feedback to the groups at various stages, particularly once they completed the flowcharts and storyboards. To provide students with additional guidance, grading rubrics were posted on the Web for all assignments.

Out-of-class activities included generation of final exam questions, posting to threaded discussions, reading assigned chapters and articles, locating resources for writing assignments, group work related to the client project, and taking the final examination. In-class activities included small group and whole class discussions pertaining to assigned readings, threaded discussions, and writing assignments. Students discussed work in progress and shared experiences. They presented completed assignments after uploading them to their Web sites to the entire class, asked questions of one another, and provided viewpoints and feedback to their peers. Some class time was set aside to work on all elements of the client project.

Providing Freedom with Appropriate Guidance

Lectures were kept to a minimum. During the first four weeks, the Dreamweaver sessions were structured like hands-on training sessions. Students worked through chapters covering basic skills with the instructor. The instructor demonstrated tasks while learners repeated the exercises on their computers. One-on-one assistance was available from the instructor and a graduate assistant. Fireworks and Flash demonstration sessions were less structured because these assignments were optional.

Assigned readings were discussed in either two groups or with the entire class. Students were encouraged to ask questions, share their experiences, express their viewpoints, differentiate concepts, and critique any writings. Only when students could not answer questions raised during the discussions did the instructor provide guidance by clarifying points and concepts.

Research Methodology

The instructor and a graduate assistant observed students during the class sessions. The instructor initiated discussions regarding the assignments and tools used. The students were asked to complete a three-minute evaluation form after each class session to provide feedback to the instructor. The instructor encouraged students to contact her with any questions relating to the course and provided professional and personal contact information on the syllabus. In addition, students had the opportunity to contact a graduate assistant who was available during class and by appointment. The graduate assistant kept the instructor abreast of students who sought his assistance.

In addition, students were asked to provide feedback about the course during a short interview session. Participants were informed that the short session was not a course or instructor evaluation and that the purpose of the interview was not to gather positive feedback. Rather, the interviewer was interested in ascertaining strategies and activities that helped the student learn. The question was as follows: What activities have helped you learn the materials in this course? After students responded to this question, they were asked to complete a questionnaire with a listing of specific course elements and strategies. Individuals indicated which elements were or were not helpful and identified the five most helpful activities.

RESULTS

In-Class Observation

Students voiced confusion during several class sessions. They were not accustomed to having decision-making abilities pertaining to course structure such as deadlines, time management, and assignment parameters. The limited information about assignments particularly confused students even though online grading rubrics were provided on the course Web site. The graduate assistant who observed the same behavior on several occasions confirmed this perception.

Students at first did not actively take responsibility or ownership for their work. For example, they did not ask questions about the first writing assignment and did not follow instructions on the Web site. Several students were surprised by the instructor's feedback.

In one instance, students inquired about the required length of the research paper. The instructor in turn asked them how long they thought the paper should be. Students turned to each other in disbelief. It appeared they were out of their comfort zone regarding this experience. A discussion followed, and participants decided that approximately 10 pages were appropriate.

Another element students were unaccustomed to was that they could select some optional assignments and decide which topics they would like to explore. Several times during class sessions students said that they were used to being told what to do. As the semester progressed students became less confused and took responsibility for their own learning; it appeared that they enjoyed working on their assignments. Not surprisingly, students selected different combinations of assignments, chose a wide variety of topics, and used several tools. For example, tools students used in designing their flowcharts included Word, Visio, or PowerPoint; each group used a different software program.

The instructor was perplexed that students were confused. She expected the students would access the assignment information on the Web. The instructor needed to refer them to the Web site on several occasions when questions pertaining to assignments, grading, and scheduling were raised.

Another concern was whether students were actually learning. Without the use of quizzes and tests, the instructor did not have proof that students were learning at first. However, a few weeks into the semester students conveyed content knowledge and understanding during discussions. They demonstrated that they mastered new skills when they submitted completed assignments. Students actively participated in class. They were asking many questions, shared their experiences and viewpoints, and assisted one another during class sessions.

Occasionally, flexible deadlines caused scheduling problems. Discussions about discussion forums and Show & Tell segments had to be postponed several times because not everyone had completed the assignment by the proposed deadline. The instructor needed to be flexible and adjusted the schedule accordingly. Flexibility was also required in regard to the use of class time. At times, students were so engaged in discussions that other activities needed to be either eliminated or rescheduled. This *structured chaos* in the classroom was responsible for some excellent sessions in which information was truly shared and knowledge individually constructed.

Gathering Student Feedback

One other concern was the quality of the course perceived by students. Because the introduction of change can produce a level of dissatisfaction, the instructor was concerned about learners' perceived course satisfaction. This concern was one of the reasons students were asked to complete a three-minute evaluation at the end of each session. When students expressed concern about a particular class session, the instructor was able to address the issue in the beginning of the next class session. Comments the students provided assisted the instructor in making changes throughout the semester.

Interview Responses

When asked what helped students learn, seven of them reported the hands-on activities were helpful to them because they "learned by doing." The same number of students pointed out that the in-class discussions had helped them learn. Interview participants clarified the interaction was good and that they appreciated discussions about chapters in the Multimedia textbook. One student indicated the class discussions "pulled it all together." These students also enjoyed listening to others' viewpoints and found it helpful to hear what other groups working on the client project were going through.

Six participants mentioned that the group work on the project helped them in their learning process. Students mentioned the perspectives of other group members were particularly helpful, and they were able to balance the workload between group members. Five students considered the workshop-style Dreamweaver sessions held during the first few weeks in the semester helpful.

Even though students were not asked which elements were not helpful in their learning in the interview, four of them shared some of these elements with the interviewer. They were the CMS, the Flash demonstration, the Dreamweaver textbook, and threaded discussions.

Survey Responses

All participants indicated the following course activities had been helpful in their learning: (a) in-class discussions in small groups and as a whole, (b) showing and viewing completed assignments, (c) completing a research paper draft, (d) designing a personal Web page, and (e) working on all parts of the client project (proposal, outline, flowchart, storyboards, and the product itself), (f) providing and receiving feedback in the formative evaluation phase, and (g) presenting the final group project to the class. In addition, all students agreed (a) flexible due dates, (b) online grading rubrics, (c) the freedom to select topics for assignments, (d) resources such as example forms posted online, and (e) instructor feedback had helped them learn.

Students assigned the highest ratings to the following course elements: (1) Web project, (2) hands-on activities, (3) group work, (4) instructor feedback, (5) group discussion, (6) multimedia textbook, (7) selecting assignments, (8) client proposal, and (9) client project.

One activity the majority of the students did not consider helpful was reading assigned chapters in the Dreamweaver textbook. A large percentage of students (44.4%) did not consider the threaded discussions helpful, and 33.3% did not consider the image manipulation project with Fireworks, the final examination, and "our" course attitude as valuable in their learning process.

DISCUSSION AND IMPLICATIONS

The introduction of constructivist approaches in a classroom with learners who are not accustomed to taking responsibility for critical thinking and learning is difficult. The instructor must truly believe in these theories to continue this effort because of the barriers encountered by various constituencies. Instructors must be flexible to accommodate progress, or lack thereof, with course content and requirements.

Many students have been taught to comply with what their instructors tell them without questioning the experts. Critical thinking and reflection can be learned, however. If students have not learned these skills by the time they arrive in our classrooms, we should strive to teach them these skills, because they will need them once they graduate with their college degrees.

It is not surprising that students reported hands-on activities and discussions, whether group discussions or exchanges during which they share their viewpoints, were helpful in their learning. Placing content and learners in the center of the learning experience by engaging students in the learning process, giving them the opportunity to take ownership of ideas and products, and providing them with a learning environment in which expression and reflection are encouraged enables them to form constructs.

Feedback is critical in student learning. Feedback from not only the instructors but also from peers is imperative in the learning process. Learning does not occur in a vacuum; it is truly a social process. Our students are not empty vessels when they arrive on campus. They have acquired knowledge elsewhere and had prior life and professional experiences that they can share with others. Instructors should provide students with the opportunity to revise projects and learn from mistakes to facilitate improvement. Good writers do not write by themselves—professionals use a peer-review process. It is also advantageous for students to build good team working and communication skills. Many projects in the business industry are designed and produced by a team of individuals utilizing and balancing the expertise and skills of its members.

CONCLUSION

The researcher hypothesized that some of the course activities would be more helpful to learners than others. In fact, the researcher expected that certain activities would be clearly identified by all students. Indeed, some of the activities that students were expected to rate highly as being helpful in their learning process were identified as such. However, a wide variety of activities received high ratings. These results indicate that instructors should design a wide variety of activities and assignments to support student learning. Because not all students learn the same way, we need to take individual differences and learning styles into account. This approach is more labor intensive for the instructor, however.

Another hypothesis was that the "our course" attitude would be a successful approach. The instructor expected this would set the stage for a relaxed and supportive learning environment. Students did not report that this approach was considered helpful in their learning. One student wrote on the survey, "Graduate students have learned to do what they are told to do, so this part is difficult to get used to." Perhaps students in this course were not quite prepared to encounter this type of learning environment.

Prepared or not, we should provide students with a safe, supportive environment because some already experience a high level of stress while they attend universities. Fear of failure and lack of control and power is the reality of many students in higher education settings. We should create teachable moments by creating supportive environments in which we can assist learners in creating constructs and internalizing them with the goal to increase retention and transferability so that students can maximize application.

Readers must be careful in generalizing findings in this study to other populations. The study involved a small sample of graduate students at one university in the Midwest. There is a need for replication of the study with other populations and a larger sample size.

REFERENCES

Berge, Z. L. (Ed.). (2001). *Sustaining distance training: Integrating learning technologies into the fabric of the enterprise.* San Francisco: Jossey-Bass.

Brooks, J. G., & Brooks, M. G. (1993). *In search of understanding: The case for constructivist classrooms.* Alexandria, VA: Association for Supervision and Curriculum Development.

DeVries, R., & Kohlberg, L. (1987). *Constructivist early education: Overview and comparison with other programs.* Washington, DC: National Association for the Education of Young Children.

Gagnon, G. W., & Collay, M. (2001). *Designing for learning: Six elements in constructivist classrooms.* Thousand Oaks, CA: Corwin Press.

Harel, I., & Papert, S. (Eds.). (1991). *Constructionism.* Norwood, NJ: Ablex.

Hay, K. E., & Barab, S. A. (2001). Constructivist practice: A comparison and contrast of apprentice ship and constructionist learning environment. *Journal of the Learning Sciences, 10,* 281–322.

Jonassen, D. H. (2000). *Theoretical foundations of learning environments.* Mahwah, NJ: Lawrence Erlbaum Associates.

Jonassen, D. H., Peck, K. L., & Wilson, B. G. (1999). *Learning with technology: A constructivist perspective.* Upper Saddle River, NJ: Prentice Hall.

Kafai, Y., & Resnick, M. (Eds.). (1996). *Constructionism in practice: Designing, thinking, and learning in a digital world.* Mahwah, NJ: Lawrence Erlbaum Associates.

Larochelle, M., Bednarz, N., & Garrison, J. (Eds.). (1998). *Constructivism and education.* Cambridge, England: Cambridge University Press.

Marlowe, B. A., & Page, M. L. (1998). *Creating and sustaining the constructivist classroom.* Thousand Oaks, CA: Corwin Press.

Novak, J. D. (1998). *Learning, creating, and using knowledge: Concept maps as facilitative tools in schools and corporations.* Mahwah, NJ: Lawrence Erlbaum Associates.

Piaget, J. (1954). *The construction of reality in the child.* New York: Ballantine Books.

Seels, B. B., & Richey, R. C. (1994). *Instructional technology: The definition and domains of the field.* Seven Fountains, VA: Association for Educational Communications and Technology.

Stahl, B. (2003, April). *The information-constructivist model of school learning: Implications for teaching, instructional design and testing.* Paper presented at the meeting of the American Educational Research Association, Chicago, IL.

Wilson, B. G. (Ed.). (1996). *Constructivist learning environments: Case studies in instructional design.* Englewood Cliffs, NJ: Educational Technology.

The Cultivation of Group Collaboration in Web-Based Learning Environments

Heng-Yu Ku, Yi-Chia Cheng, and Linda Lohr
University of Northern Colorado

Distance education has developed dramatically during the past few years through the application of learning theory and the delivery of materials. Sims (1999) indicated that interaction serves a variety of functions in the educational transaction, such as allowing for learner control, providing various forms of participation and communication, and aiding in the acquisition of meaningful learning. Interaction is central to the expectations of teachers and learners in distance education and is a primary goal of the educational process (Berge, 2002).

There are four types of interaction identified in the literature (Moore & Anderson, 2003):

1. Learner-content interaction: this type of interaction is one between the learner and the subject of study. With the advance of technology, the interaction of learner and content is getting more diverse ranging from asynchronous to synchronous.

2. Learner-instructor interaction: this type of interaction is between the learner and the expert who prepared the subject materials. Therefore, the instructor is responsible for providing a curriculum, maintaining the learner interest in the content, motivating the student to learn, evaluating the student progress, and providing a supportive environment to each learner.

3. Learner-learner interaction: the third type of interaction is among the learners in group settings with or without the presence of the instructor. The peer groups could interact via discussion boards, chats, or electronic mail.

4. Learner-interface interaction: the fourth type of interaction is defined as a process of employing tools to accomplish a task (Hillman, Willis, & Gunawardena, 1994).

In this study, all four types of interaction in online courses were investigated, but the focus was specifically on the third type of interaction: Learner-learner interaction. In a study conducted by Northrup (2002), it was found that participants enjoyed discussing ideas and concepts as well as sharing information with their peers. Participants considered promoting online collaboration and conversation an important attribute of distance learning. In addition, Berge (2002) mentioned that teamwork or collaboration should be assigned in online classes and that its main goal is to accomplish part or all of the learning goals and to replicate authentic working conditions.

McLoughlin (2002) has suggested that traditional pedagogical approaches in education have decontextualized knowledge and skills from real-world application. Candy, Crebert, and O'Leary (1994) underscored that university education should develop a capacity for and understanding of teamwork along with critical thinking. This situation calls for educators to develop activities that support group collaboration (Bennett, 2004). Working collaboratively provides students with the opportunity to extend and deepen their learning experiences as well as receive critical and constructive feedback. It also helps students develop the skills that will be required to function in a virtual team in real-world contexts (Palloff & Pratt, 2005).

Collaborative learning refers to an instructional method in which small groups of learners mutually engage in the learning environment to accomplish a shared goal (Tu & Corry, 2002). Collaboration should at least contain sharing the learning tasks; combining expertise, knowledge, and skills; and building a learning community. The advantages of collaborative learning include the encouragement of active and constructive learning, deep processing of information, critical thinking, and goal-based learning (Bernard, Rojo de Rubalcava, & St-Pierre, 2000).

Online collaboration can be defined as the collaborative learning that takes place in a distance-learning environment. A critical factor for the success of online collaboration is the learners' experience of engagement in a leaning community (Yang, 2002). Hasler-Waters and Napier (2002) contended that receiving support, getting acquainted, establishing communication, building trust, and getting organized foster successful online teams. Although online group collaboration can generate new knowledge, attitudes, and behaviors, it requires significantly more time and effort than traditional learning (Kulp, 1999).

Previous studies revealed both positive and negative student perspectives toward online collaborative learning. Students have expressed that their communication skills and problem-solving skills were improved through online collaboration (Yang, 2002). However, some described students dissatisfaction regarding the instructional strategies and the delivery methods and disclosed that students tend to resist group collaboration because the outcomes depend on the input of other group members (Kitchen & McDougall, 1999; Ko & Rossen, 2001).

There has been limited research to examine students perceptions and attitudes toward their online collaboration experiences as well as what factors students consider crucial in an online learning environment. What exists has mostly focused on student perspectives on their online learning experiences without collaborative learning components. Thus, this study was designed to examine online collaborating learning experiences from students points of view and instructors' interpretations to provide suggestions and strategies that instructors could implement in their online courses. The following research questions were addressed:

1.   What were student attitudes toward taking an online course in instructional design?

2.   What were student attitudes toward working collaboratively as a group in the online environment?

3.   What elements did students consider critical for a successful online course?

METHOD

Subjects

Participants were 94 Midwestern graduate students enrolled in an online course in instructional design. Sixty-four were female, and 30 were male students. Eighty of the students were American, and 14 were international. Seventy percent of the students were majoring in educational technology or educational media, and less than five percent of these students had experience with taking completely online courses.

Online Course Format

The instructor (the first author in this study) delivered this course using a Web-based course management system called Blackboard. The instructor randomly assigned groups, each of which included three people, using the "Groups" function. From there, group members had access to participating in a synchronous group chat room, posting messages under the group discussion board, sending e-mail to selected group members or the whole group, and posting assignments via file exchange. Each group then discussed and decided on a topic of interest to create a design document and self-paced lesson for that topic throughout the semester. To encourage equal contribution among students, all students were informed in the beginning of the semester that evaluations by the instructor, self, and peers were counted as 20% of their final grade.

In the process of creating a design document of the chosen topic, each group was required to work on the draft design document for three assignments. The first assignment covered needs assessment, learner analysis, and contextual analysis. The second assignment contained task analysis, instructional objectives, and questions and feedback. The third assignment included instructional sequencing, instructional strategies, and message design. Each group worked on its first draft together, provided feedback to and received feedback from its group members, revised its first drafts based on the peer feedback, and posted its revised drafts via file exchange under the "Groups" function. Posting assignments on the file exchange allowed the group members and the instructor to access documents for reading. Following the posting of these drafts, the instructor looked over the revised draft of the assignment and provided feedback to each group. Students then modified drafts based on the instructor's feedback.

The same procedures were repeated for each assignment and each group compiled all revised assignments into a final design document. After all sections of the design process were completed, students developed a self-paced lesson based on the design document that they had been developing. Students then conducted a formative evaluation to test the draft of the self-paced lesson to its target audience and write up an evaluation report. Students then used the evaluation results and learner feedback to revise their self-paced lessons and design documents. Finally, students submitted the final version of the design document and self-paced lesson during the last week of the semester.

Instrument

A student attitude survey with five open-ended questions was designed and used for this study. The survey questions dealt with student perceptions toward online learning environment and online collaborated setting, working on group projects, and suggestions on the important elements that a successful online course should comprise. These questions were as follows:

1. What did you like most about this online course?

2. What did you like least about this online course?

3. Did you like or dislike working collaboratively as a group in an online environment? Why or why not?

4. Do you think you would have learned more in this class if you had done your project alone? Why or why not?

5. In your opinion, what do you consider as a successful online course? What elements should be there?

Procedure

Data were collected from the student attitude survey during the final week of each class across five semesters between the years of 2002 to 2004. In these full-semester courses, students worked collaboratively in small groups to create instructional units. The student attitude survey was distributed as an e-mail attachment to students during the final week of each semester. All participants completed the student attitude survey by responding to the five open-ended questions. They then sent their responses as an e-mail attachment to their instructor by the last day of the semester.

Data Analysis

A thematic analysis was conducted to identify emerging themes and patterns for responses of each of the five open-ended questions. Furthermore, the recurring responses were categorized and counted to provide the framework for discussion.

RESULTS

Student Reponses to Open-Ended Questions

Attitudes toward online course (likes and dislikes)

When asked what students liked most about this online course, the flexibility, convenience, easy communication, semiconstructive nature of the course, group member and instructor feedback, weekly mini-lectures, project examples, and studying at their own pace were what they liked the most about this course. They also liked the instructor posting students' picture and biography on Blackboard for them to know each other and to cultivate an online community.

When asked what students liked least about this course, factors that diminished enjoyment included lack of immediate interaction and feedback, isolation during the learning process, the fact that some group members failed to provide constructive feedback on time, coordinating with group members, technical difficulties, the textbook, and inadequate computer knowledge. They also expressed that they missed the active class atmosphere in which they are able to raise questions in class to discuss responses with classmates and instructors.

Attitudes toward online collaboration (likes and dislikes)

When students were asked whether they liked or disliked working collaboratively as a group in an online environment, 32 students (34%) liked it, 47 students (50%) disliked it, and 14 students (16%) had mixed feelings.

Students who liked working collaboratively as a group appreciated having group members with whom they could share ideas and having opportunities to provide and receive feedback from others. In that way, they felt "forced" and recognized they had responsibilities to read the chapters and course materials thoroughly so they could provide constructive feedback to their group members. Some positive comments from students were the following:

> I really enjoyed working with partners as we bounced ideas and feedback off of each other to create, what I feel, is a quality project. We worked well together and came up with ideas we could not have if we were working independently. Our willingness to work together, combining our resources, greatly helped our overall product.

> I liked the collaborative process because it gave me a chance to work with other students who had knowledge in certain areas that I might not have. I contributed my strengths and they contributed their areas of knowledge, and we came up with a great product.

Students disliked working collaboratively as a group in an online environment because they perceived ineffective and inefficient communication, uneven workloads and efforts, difficulty adjusting to each other's schedules, the time-consuming nature of the class, and arguing with group members on ideas. Negative comments from students included the following:

> I normally work very well in groups and enjoy the group setting. However, it is very hard to be in a group with complete strangers just over the Internet. I felt at times that I was doing most of the work and they weren't putting as much effort into the project as I was.... Communication was also difficult because I couldn't explain my ideas in the way that I would have been if we were to meet face to face. The whole process was very frustrating!

> I liked the online setting, but disliked the collaboration. If you are teamed with people who are shooting for a 'B' or just to pass the class, it is difficult to get an 'A' for a group assignment without taking on the majority of the work. I feel that I shouldered the vast majority of the work for the group. In this way, this online class was far more work than a traditional class. I do not know how I would feel if it was an online, non-collaborative class. It is hard to distribute the work evenly in an online class.

Some comments from students with mixed feelings regarding working collaboratively as a group in an online environment included the following:

> I must admit, at first I absolutely hated it. If the course had not been a requirement, I would have dropped it. Communication felt exasperating. But with time, and getting to know my teammates, it got easier. We worked out the kinks. I had great teammates. When one of us was stuck, one always came through. Now, I miss them. I wrote them yesterday to tell them I thought I was having ID (instructional design) withdrawals!

> At first I really hated it. I found it difficult, mainly due to technology problems, to work with my group. However in the long run, I believe we came up with a better product than any of us would have created alone. In final analysis, I am glad this course forced me into a collaborative learning situation. Many of my initial misgivings were unfounded.

Attitudes toward online collaborated learning

When asked whether students would have learned more in this class if they had done their project alone, 70 students (74%) said "No," 14 students (15%) indicated "Yes," and 10 students (11%) kept their opinion as neutral.

We further categorized students' responses to this question and discovered that for students to work well in an online group collaborative setting, the five Cs (*Communicate, Cooperate, Compromise, Complement, and Commitment*) need to be included and practiced among group members.

The first C, *Communicate*, was derived from the students' responses such as "We instantly established a routine that was very focused on the task at hand; we were able to be honest in working with each other and truly developed a cordial, often fun working relationship" and "by having to work with others, I had to exercise people skills and learn to get along and say things in persuasive rather than confrontative ways."

The second C, *Cooperate*, was based on students' responses such as, "It's always great to have someone else be the sounding board, especially when they have just as much ownership in the assignment," "Having group ideas and a checks and balance system really worked well. I learned more hashing out the details with my group than I would have on my own," and "I really feel our final product was better for the added insights and creativity of three minds instead of one. I think each of us benefited from the camaraderie we experienced, and the support."

The third C, *Compromise*, emerged from students' responses such as, "It meant compromise, especially in the area of topic selection as we all had our own content we wanted to deal with." and "I think being forced together in a group, not of our own choosing, best simulated the business environment. We were forced to cooperate, compromise and communicate with each other in a way that working alone would not allow."

The fourth C, *Complement*, was drawn from students' responses such as, "We all really complemented each other. I must admit I was stuck two times while doing this project. One of the other teammates got the ball rolling, and I think they would say the same thing about me at times when they were stuck." "We had strengths that complemented each other, so we got to see the whole picture and fill in the gaps." and "... when working in a group you can draw on the strengths of the individual group members. In our group one member was a better writer, one had more experience with power point, etc. Plus we could all draw from personal experiences."

The fifth C, *Commitment,* was identified from students' responses such as "Having members that work as hard as you and are as committed makes all the difference" and "Having the advantage of each teammate contributing his/her different perspectives for the project was terrific. Moreover, we supported each other both academically and emotionally, since taking an online course was very challenging to us novices."

Critical Elements in an Online Course

When asked about what students considered as critical elements in a successful online course, their top 10 comments in the order of importance included the following:

1.   Frequent instructor-to-student and peer-to-peer communication (55%)

2.   Clear objectives and course outlines (33%)

3.   Useful mini-lectures (20%)

4.   Strong instructor support (18%)

5.   Opportunities to access and view previous project examples (18%)

6.   User-friendly interface (12%)

7.   Superior organizational skills (12%)

8.   Just-in-time resources (e.g., Web site, books, and references) (11%)

9.   Proficiencies in technology (10%)

10.   Periodic online discussion (10%)

In addition, posting pictures and bios of students and faculty, clarifying project deadlines, and mastering better self-regulation and self-efficacy traits (ranged from 7% to 9%) were other important attributes that student considered as crucial elements in a successful online course.

DISCUSSION AND RECOMMENDATIONS

This study focused on how effectively the instructor integrated teaching and managing strategies into an online instructional design course. The students' attitudes toward this course and strategies for building online collaborative learning communities from both the students' points of view and instructor's interpretations were also discussed. Although many of the findings, such as students' likes and dislikes about the online setting are similar to previous studies, less frequently observed in the literature are the actual comments from students who indicate a dislike of group activity while admitting the importance of it.

Similar to other research findings (Picciano, 2001; Williams, Paprock, & Covington, 1999; Yang, 2002), our results indicate that convenience, flexibility, and easy communication were common themes in the positive student responses regarding the online setting. On the other hand, communication difficulties, lack of face-to-face interaction, and sense of isolation were the overriding negative themes regarding the online setting (Howland & Moore, 2002).

When asked whether students liked or disliked working collaboratively as a group in the online environment, different opinions were noted. Half of the students (50%) indicated they disliked learning in an online collaborative setting, and one-third of students (34%) held the opposite opinion. Interestingly, when asked whether students would have learned more in this class if they had done their project individually, three out of four students (74%) felt that the collaborative environment produced greater learning. Such contrary findings emphasize the usefulness and importance of online collaborative learning while illustrating the difficulties of working in harmony among groups.

The cues derived from the responses to the fourth open-ended question convey to us that the five Cs: Communicate, Cooperate, Compromise, Complement, and Commitment need to be incorporated within the group setting. Practicing these five attributes will enable group members to have better working relationship with each other. From students responses to the fifth open-ended question, we also identified the top-10 critical elements that students considered important in a successful online course. Overall, students concurred that a solid course structure as groundwork to a successful online course (the 10 critical elements), as well as encouraging and supporting collaborative project development (the five Cs), leads to effective learning and better quality of the final project. We believe that the 10 critical elements are the foundation for a successful online course and when the instructor is interested in integrating collaborated learning activities into an online setting, then the five Cs need to be incorporated and practiced among each group. We have provided a framework for online collaborative learning plans as shown in Figure 1.

Figure 1. Online collaborative learning framework.

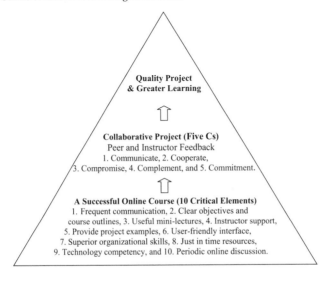

The findings of this study provide recommendations for students who are intending to take online courses as well as instructors who are currently teaching or are planning to teach online courses that involve collaborative learning activities.

Recommendations to Students (The Five Cs)

1. *Communicate.* Take the initiative in online collaborative activities and find opportunities to interact with group members both online and offline. Students should inform their group members if they are going to miss a group meeting or fail to complete the assigned task on time. If group members disappear or do not reply to e-mails for more than three days, the students must report this to the instructor immediately. Students can select a group leader and rotate the leadership role. Group leaders are responsible for resolving disputes among the members. When major problems are encountered within groups, group leaders need to contact the instructor immediately and ask for help.

2. *Cooperate.* Reach team agreement within groups. After forming groups, group members should reach an agreement on strategies for working as well as cooperating better as a group and setting the group rules. It is also suggested that group members need to set group norms on specifying changes and organizing files. Students can use different font colors (or use track changes in Word) to indicate the changes and modifications. To prevent confusion with file names, students should use the name of the assignment and current date to represent the file name (e.g., Assignment1_11_19_2006.doc).

3. *Compromise.* When working collaboratively, students are required to brainstorm ideas and reach an agreement to finalize a topic for the group project. Students also need to accommodate group members schedules and set reasonable deadlines to accomplish reading assignments, post project drafts, and provide peer feedback on time.

4. *Complement.* It was asserted that collaborative learning enhances the opportunity to combine expertise and share skills within a community. Students working in groups are therefore encouraged to identify their own strengths and weaknesses so they can complement each other and contribute different expertise to the group projects.

5. *Commitment.* Students must stay current with their work. Set due dates for all group activities and projects in advance and try to work ahead of time. More time should be devoted to online collaboration because more work is needed in online group works than in traditional classes. It is also critical that students respect their group members and first try to resolve differences of opinions within their group before involving the instructor.

Recommendations to Instructors (The 10 Critical Elements)

Instructors teaching online courses also need to be aware that online learning does not have to take place exclusively in virtual learning environments. Combining virtual learning with face-to-face communication when possible can restore the human moment in the educational process and facilitate student learning. We offer suggestions under each of the 10 most critical elements that student considered important in a successful online course.

1. *Frequent instructor-to-student and peer-to-peer communication.* (a) Establish groups. Ask students to find partners and form groups themselves first to force them to communicate and get to know each other. When students have difficulties finding partners, the instructor can assign groups for them. The instructor should purposely assign international students with American students to form a group (Ku & Lohr, 2003). In terms of group size, three students per group would be ideal, but groups should include no more than four. (b) Communicate with group members. After the group has been formed, ask students to send e-mails to communicate with their group members and also to exchange phone numbers and work schedules. Students can also arrange face-to-face meetings with group members or the instructor. Encourage students to e-mail the instructor when problems persist within the group so that interventions can be made. (c) Provide peer and instructor feedback. Offer opportunities for students to work in small groups for the experience of giving and receiving feedback on their assignments or projects. It is invaluable for the learner to receive guidance and scaffolding from capable peers. After groups post their projects, the instructor should provide feedback to each group.

2. *Clear objectives and course outlines.* (a) Design an orientation packet. The packet should include course introduction, course syllabus, frequently asked questions, and contact information for academic or technical problems. The instructor can mail or e-mail the orientation package to students prior to the course starting date. (b) Set clear expectations. The requirements for online participation, grading rubrics, and deadlines for all projects should be specified on the course syllabi. (c) Establish evaluation criteria. Set specific grading rubrics for each of the assignments so that students know what to expect. When working in groups, ask students to assign a grade to their peers as well as to themselves and indicate their specific contribution or lack of contribution to the project. The instructor can also track students' participation and performance through group online discussion, e-mails, and file exchange.

3. *Useful mini-lectures.* The instructor can post weekly mini-lectures online to summarize the chapter contents for students. Because most of the textbooks were written in academic style that sounded too conceptual and dry to students, the instructor can use a friendly tone or conversational writing style to reinforce learning and reassure students.

4. *Strong instructor support.* (a) Be patient and responsive. When students are working in a group project, sometimes the instructor needs to act as a counselor to deal with complaints or conflict among group members. The instructor should strongly encourage students to contact him or her when problems occur and should respond to students' questions in a timely manner. (b) Be available. The instructor should be able to meet or chat with students as needed and to provide technical as well as pedagogical support to students throughout the project.

5. *Access to previous project examples.* The instructor should provide additional project examples to students. By doing so, students have opportunities to view some best examples of the final project, identify the scope and depth of the final project and frame a big picture in mind of what the instructor expects from them.

6. *User-friendly interface.* The instructor should inform students where they can gain access to an online tutorial and be familiar with the interface of the course. All communication forms in the Web-supporting management tool, such as e-mail, chat room, discussion board, and file exchange should be open to stu-

dents and give time for students to explore the interface and communication tools.

7. *Superior organizational skills.* (a) Require students to log on to the course Web site frequently and regularly. The instructor may want to e-mail students to remind them of new announcements. That way, everyone in the class is informed and students cannot make any excuses when they fail to log on to Blackboard. (b) Get to know the students. Encourage students to send their pictures, background information, and interests, and then post them online. The instructor should set a due date and ask students to submit their bios and pictures via e-mail when the course starts. One reason for doing this is to make sure that the instructor has correct student e-mail addresses. If the instructor has not heard from students, he or she needs to access the registration information and contact the students. This also enables the instructor to build an online community so students can become acquainted. (c) Set consistent due dates. The instructor should set specific and consistent due dates for all assignments and projects. For example, if the instructor decides to set the deadline on Mondays, he or she should keep the same due dates throughout the whole semester so that students can remember better and the due dates can become a ritual for them. For larger-scale group assignments or projects, the instructor can set due dates by midnight on Mondays or Tuesdays because students (including instructors) generally do not like to work on weekends.

8. *Just-in-time resources.* For additional information related to a specific topic, the instructor can post supporting Web links, books, and references under the "Course Material" or "Web Sites" functions in Blackboard. The instructor can also post the "best example" of each assignment to boost morale of groups that have produced quality work and use these examples for other groups to model and revise their work.

9. *Proficiencies in technology.* Give students time to improve their computer literacy skills that are essential in the course. The first two weeks should be more relaxed so that students have time to obtain their login names and passwords to Blackboard, explore the different management tools and functions in Blackboard, and become familiar with the online learning environment.

10. *Periodic online discussion.* The instructor can use the "Groups" function in Blackboard to place students together as one group. From there, group members have access to participating in a synchronous group chat room, posting messages under the group discussion board, sending e-mail to selected group members or the whole group, and posting assignments via file exchange.

In summary, distance learning is gaining in popularity because of the convenience it brings and academic institutions have responded by placing increased emphasis on developing online learning. However, the preparation for teaching online classes takes time, detailed thought, lots of patience, and adequate computer and communication skills. When designing the online teaching materials, instructors have to consider interaction and collaboration and encourage interaction and support communal scaffolding throughout the collaboration process. It is hoped that such acts will motivate students in the online collaboration process and will make the collaboration a worthwhile learning experience for them.

The results of the study have practical significance for both online instructors and students. Guidelines are offered for instructors planning to implement online collaborative learning components as well as students required to work collaboratively in the online environment. Furthermore, it may help instructors to have a more systematic understanding of the pedagogical, technological, and administrative approaches to distance learning. Future research can explore other online teaching strategies to help students work well collaboratively and produce better outcomes in an online learning environment.

REFERENCES

Bennett, S. (2004). Supporting collaborative project teams using computer-based technologies. In T. S. Roberts (Eds.), *Online Collaborative Learning: Theory and Practice* (pp. 1–27). Hershey, PA: Information Science.

Berge, Z. L. (2002). Active, interactive, and reflective e-learning. *Quarterly Review of Distance Education, 3*(2), 181–190.

Bernard, R. M., Rojo de Rubalcava, B., & St-Pierre, D. (2000). Collaborative online distance learning: Issues for future practice and research. *Distance Education, 21*, 260–277.

Candy, P., Crebert, G., & O'Leary, J. (1994). *Developing lifelong learners through undergraduate education.* Canberra, Australia: Australian Government Publishing Service.

Hasler-Waters, L., & Napier, W. (2002). Building and supporting student team collaboration in the virtual classroom. *Quarterly Review of Distance Education, 3*(3), 345–352.

Hillman, D. C., Willis, D. J., & Gunawardena, C. N. (1994). Learner-interface interaction in distance education: An extension of contemporary models and strategies for practitioners. *American Journal of Distance Education, 8*(2), 31–32.

Howland, J. L., & Moore, J. L. (2002). Student perceptions as distance learners in Internet-based courses. *Distance Education, 23*(2), 183–195.

Kitchen, D., & McDougall, D. (1999). Collaborative learning on the Internet. *Journal of Educational Technology Systems, 27*(3), 245–258.

Ko, S., & Rossen, S. (2001). *Teaching online: A practical guide.* Boston: Houghton Mifflin.

Ku, H-Y., & Lohr, L. (2003). A case study on Asian students' attitudes toward their first on-line learning experience. *Educational Technology Research and Development, 51*(3), 95–102.

Kulp, R. (1999). *Effective collaboration in corporate distributed learning: Ten best practices for curriculum owners, developers, and instructors.* Chicago: IBM Learning Services.

McLoughlin, C. (2002). Computer-supported teamwork: An integrative approach to evaluating cooperative learning in an online environment. *Australian Journal of Educational Technology, 18*(2), 227–245.

Moore, M. G., & Anderson, W. G. (2003). *Handbook of distance education.* Mahwah, NJ: Erlbaum Associates.

Northrup, P. T. (2002). Online learners preferences for interaction. *Quarterly Review of Distance Education, 3*(2), 219–226.

Palloff, R. M., & Pratt, K. (2005). *Collaborating online: Learning together in community.* San Francisco: Jossey-Bass.

Picciano, A. G. (2001). *Distance learning: Making connections across virtual space and time.* Upper Saddle River, NJ: Prentice Hall.

Sims, R. (1999). Interactivity on stage: Strategies for learner-designer communication. *Australian Journal of Educational Technology, 15*(3), 257–272.

Tu, C. H., & Corry, M. (2002). eLearning communities. *Quarterly Review of Distance Education, 3*(2), 207–218.

Williams, M. L., Paprock, K., & Covington, B. (1999). *Distance learning: The essential guide.* Thousand Oaks, CA: Sage.

Yang, Y. S. (2002). A case study for promoting collaboration on online project-based learning. *Proceedings of the World Conference on Educational Multimedia, Hypermedia & Telecommunications, USA,* 2107–2112.

"Is There a Class with This Content?" WebCT and the Limits of Individualization

Ellen Rose

University of New Brunswick

This essay traces the provenance of Internet-based course delivery and management systems such as WebCT and Blackboard and thereby seeks insight into the ideologies and assumptions underlying the current diffusion of such systems into institutions of higher education. A historical perspective reveals that these purportedly revolutionary pedagogical tools originated with the low-tech teaching machines with which behaviorists of the 1950s and 1960s sought to individualize instruction. Although widely touted by advocates of programmed instruction as an educational panacea and source of learner empowerment, individualization emerged from a drive to make instruction more efficient by replacing the human teacher with a machine that delivered standardized content to a large number of students. The goal of instructional efficiency underlay further developments in computer-assisted instruction, computer-managed instruction, and integrated learning systems. The potential of contemporary Web-based systems to enhance classroom dynamics in higher education is therefore severely constrained by the legacy of individualization and the long-standing premise, embedded within the design of such systems, that the goal of technology-based instruction is to achieve efficiencies by replacing human interaction in the classroom with access to mediated, individualized content.

Some readers may notice an oblique reference in my title to the title of another essay: Stanley Fish's (1980) "Is There a Text in This Class?"[1] The reference is deliberate but largely whimsical, for although it could be argued that Fish and I share a concern with meaning, text, knowledge, and pedagogy, there the similarity between our essays ends. Fish's purpose in "Is There a Text in This Class?" is to defend reception theory, the notion that a text's meaning is produced by the reader, whereas my objective is to explore the historical and ideological provenance of the Internet-based course delivery and management systems that, according to their promotional materials as well as to more objective sources such as college surveys (Young, 2002, p. A35), have been adopted by thousands of institutions of higher learning in hundreds of countries. Moreover, the question "Is there a text in this class?" is of interest to Fish because it is entirely comprehensible, particularly when addressed by a student to a professor. My title question, on the other hand, is of interest to me as a starting point for a discussion of what it means to adopt Internet-based platforms such as WebCT and Blackboard because, as I write, the state of higher education is still such that most college and university teachers would, I suspect, be at a loss as to how to respond if a student were to ask, "Is there a class with this content?" This may not long be the case, however, given the numerous forces that now require university teaching and learning to become more cost-efficient, "relevant," and amenable to the use of high-tech "solutions." Therefore, unlike Fish, who is concerned to show that the ways in which his title question can be understood are contextually limited, I am interested in exploring, from a historical perspective, the impetus that is imparting new meaning to a hitherto absurd query, such that it may soon become as common and as generally comprehensible as Fish's question.[2]

What is the value of a historical perspective on the new Internet-based tools for course delivery and management? Once, perhaps, the answer to such a question might have seemed self-evident, but that is no longer the case in an age that, as Henry Giroux (1999) puts it, "borders on a crisis of forgetting" (p. 146). After several centuries of rampant technological innovation, the Western world tends to ascribe far less importance to understanding where we have come from than to knowing, or at least purporting to know, where we are headed. Hence, our society's celebration of progress, manifested in the techno-prophet's resolutely forward gaze, goes hand in hand with what Lewis Mumford (1964) calls "an un-concealed hostility to the past" (p. 21), a tendency to dismiss as irrelevant (or, in the oft-quoted terms of industrialist Henry Ford, as "bunk") the values, attitudes, and negotiations from which modern scientific and technological innovations emerge. This is nowhere more true than in the discourses about the role of information technology in education, which are "mostly celebratory of the new approach and strategies rather than historically and institutionally reflective" (Popkewitz & Shutkin, 1993, p. 24). Mumford further asserts that "This failure to recognize the importance of cosmic and organic history largely accounts for the imperious demands of our age, with its promise of instant solutions and instant transformations" (1964, p. 91). In other words, the sophisticated technologies that we regard as the height of human intellectual achievement bear no relationship to wisdom, which requires historical context and understanding. Wise use of today's purportedly "revolutionary" course delivery and management systems begins with an understanding that these systems are not revolutionary at all but are in fact part of an existing trajectory that can best be understood through a historical perspective.

History, of course, is relative. In *Technics and Civilization* (1963), Mumford traces the development of the technological worldview from prehistoric times. I begin with the 1950s, and specifically with Harold Innis's lament in *The Bias of Communication* that university education of the time was increasingly reduced to the mere transmission of mechanized content. According to Innis (1951), with the support of textbook suppliers and other information industries, "Information . . . is disseminated in universities by the new media of communication, including moving pictures, loud speakers, with radio and television in the offing. Staff and students are tested in their ability to disseminate and receive information. Ingenious devices, questionnaires, intelligence tests are used to tell the student where he belongs" (pp. 83–84). More than half a century later, Innis's catalogue of "new" media may seem antiquated, but his reflections on the state of higher education remain enormously prescient and provide an apt starting point for an investigation of the provenance of purportedly revolutionary Internet-based systems such as WebCT.

The situation that Innis lamented in the early 1950s arose in large part from the confluence in educational thinking of the time of three powerful and related forces: behavioral psychology, programmed instruction, and individualization. Originating with turn-of-the-century research of animal psychologists such as Ivan Pavlov and Edward Thorndike, behavioral psychology had, by the 1950s, become an accepted basis for conceptualizing human intelligence and learning. Its leading proponent, Burrhus Frederic Skinner, espoused a radical behaviorism that dismissed as irrelevant the psychological processes taking place within the individual learner's mind. Rather, Skinner suggested that the learner should be regarded as a black box to which one applied stimuli with the expectation that certain predictable and observable responses would be forthcoming. If closely followed by appropriate reinforcement, the desired response would eventually become entrained: learning, in other words, would have occurred.

To achieve the desired behavioral modifications that constituted learning, it was first necessary to break the instructional content into small, carefully ordered pieces that could gradually be imparted to the student through repeated stimulus–response reinforcement sequences. Given this requirement for highly structured content and rigorously controlled delivery, behaviorists believed that their technology of instruction could be best provided not by human teachers but by "devices," such as those Innis itemized. Behaviorists advocated a heavy reliance on media, used in conjunction with specially designed instructional materials that would provide the relevant stimuli and associate those stimuli with appropriate responses (Silverman, 1974, p. 79). The specially designed materials became known as "programmed instruction"—*programmed,* in this context, referring to "the process of constructing sequences of instructional material in a way that maximizes the rate of acquisition and retention and enhances the motivation of the student" (Glaser, 1964, p. 87).

The carefully arranged material, with accompanying questions and reinforcement, could be presented in books ("If you answered 'true,' turn to page 14"); however, given the behaviorists' penchant for mediated instruction, programmed instruction tended increasingly to go hand in hand with the use of "teaching machines," low-tech devices into which one loaded "programs" printed on rolls of paper. The instruction would begin by presenting a frame of content through a translucent window of the teaching machine. After writing a response to a question about the content on a designated area of the paper strip, the learner would turn a crank to advance the program to the next frame, which would typically inform the learner of the correctness of his or her response. Another turn of the crank would advance the program to a new frame of content and a related question. As the name implies, teaching machines were from the outset intended to function as teacher substitutes. The design of deliberately "teacher-proof" instructional machines and materials clearly reflected this conception: "No attempt was made to build flexibility into the devices, since they were never conceived as teaching supplements, but as replacements for human teachers" (Maddux & Willis, 1992, p. 53).

Skinner made no secret of his tendency to privilege mechanical devices over human instructors, nor of the fact that his preference was based largely on the criterion of *efficiency* as a legitimate, and indeed primary, goal of education. Implicit in his call for an "instrumental attack on the *status quo*" (Skinner, 1964, p. 66) were the assumptions, first, that the education system was in need of reform because instructional decision making had been left to educators who did not understand the mechanisms of human learning, and, second, that devices—developed by psychologists who *did* understand human learning—could deliver instruction that would surpass, in efficiency and effectiveness, that which human teachers provided. As Skinner explained in an article titled "Why We Need Teaching Machines," originally published in 1959, it "is far beyond the capacity of teachers" to provide the necessary stimuli and reinforcements for every student with the frequency and subtlety required, but *"relatively simple machines will suffice"* (1964, p. 47, emphasis in original). Research conducted by Skinner and other behaviorists was bound to lend credence to his basic assumptions because the myriad studies of programmed instruction conducted during the 1960s sought to compare "the teacher in the program" with "the teacher in the classroom" (Gotkin, 1964, p. 161) largely on the basis of instructional efficiencies:

> The strategy of these studies has been to pit the classroom teacher against the teacher in the machine. Using the standard of the job being done in the schools, these studies by and large show the teacher in the programed [*sic*] textbook to be *as effective as and more efficient* than the classroom teacher: students learn as much in less time from programed instruction. (Gotkin, 1964, p. 160, emphasis in original)

Skinner's implicit condemnation of ad hoc, heuristic-based classroom methods, and his suggestion that education could be improved (i.e., made more efficient) through the use of a precise technology of instruction was received as common sense by a North American society that, since the advent of Frederick Taylor's principles of scientific management in the early 20th century, had become increasingly prone to regard science and the efficiencies it brought to all areas of human affairs as its sole hope for social progress. In this intellectual environment, it seemed natural that responsibility for the development of learning materials, and indeed decisions about the nature of education as a whole, should increasingly devolve from teachers to the psychologists who strove to create an exact science of human learning (Popkewitz & Shutkin, 1993, p. 20) and, by extension, to the machines that the psychologists developed to achieve this end.

According to Skinner, teaching machines reduced instructional time to half that required to learn the same material in teacher-led classrooms because the devices allowed each student to proceed through the instructional material at his or her own rate: "Holding students together for instructional purposes in a class is probably the greatest source of inefficiency in education" (Skinner, 1964, pp. 52–53). The alternative to holding students together in a class was the third element of the educational triad: individualization. In simple terms, individualized instruction was defined as "adapting instructional practices to individual requirements" (Cooley & Glaser, 1969, p. 95). Technically, this implied allowing each learner to interact with instructional content on his or her own terms, controlling and selecting a variety of variables, including pace of study, learning objectives, scope, media, and instructional strategies (Romiszowski, 1986, p. 21). Given its close association with programmed learning, however, which prescribed all elements of instruction with the exception of pacing, individualization was most commonly understood, during the 1960s and 1970s, as "self-paced individual study of prescribed material (usually common to all the students in a group)" (Romiszowski, 1986, p. 20). In other words, objectives, scope, and strategies were all highly standardized; only the pace of instruction could be adapted to the capabilities and needs of the individual learner, usually through the use of a teaching machine.

Self-pacing, however, seemed to be more than enough for the advocates of programmed instruction and individualization, who touted the enormous benefits to be gleaned from a mode of instruction in which "the student is at the throttle" (Schramm, 1964, p. 7). These benefits went well beyond the instructional efficiencies celebrated by Skinner. Indeed, by the early 1970s, the heritage of efficiency seemed to have been largely forgotten amid a heady new discourse that ironically represented individualization as the antithesis of industrial era approaches to teaching and learning. The argument was that existing teacher-led modes of education had arisen from the need to deliver instruction efficiently to a mass of learners. As a result, "teaching [was] pitched to the average" (Fritz & Levy, 1972, p. 1), and students of differing abilities were compelled to move through the curriculum in lockstep, like widgets on an assembly line, completing the same instructional activities in the same amount of time. Individualization became widely regarded and promoted as the complete opposite of this factory approach, an economically feasible means of replicating the personalized instruction that a good tutor would provide (Romiszowski, 1986, p. 19):

> The fast student need not waste time and the slowest student need not get lost in the shuffle. Like the private tutor, the program presents the next step when the individual student is ready for it, not when the average student is ready. (Markle, 1964, p. 147)

Increasingly, the rhetoric surrounding this new educational "panacea" (Oettinger, 1969, p. 117) suggested that it had less to do with efficiency than with responding to individual needs, helping individuals fulfill their potential, and serving to "dealienate and rehumanize" education (Fritz & Levy, 1972, p. 2). Individualization became transmuted, in the minds of many educators and educational reformers, to an instructional end in itself, with acquired associations to self-development, personal autonomy, and accommodation for individual differences that bore little apparent connection to its origins as a means of increasing instructional efficiency and control:

> [S]omewhere along the line, a word that referred to the use of behavioral modification strategies to enhance the learner's acquisition of pre-packaged knowledge came to connote opportunities for a self-motivated learner to engage in independent discovery. In short, *individualization* became equated with *individualism*, the humanist view that the rational individual's consciousness is the source of all meaning and truth. (Rose, 2000, p. 72)

One adherent went so far as to describe individualization as "a philosophical and professional commitment to the concept of permitting students to have a voice in the learning program in which they participate" (Denton, 1974, p. 55). The assumption seemed to be that the decision-making powers that individualization took from the teacher were conferred upon the student, but the reality was that individualized instruction was neither teacher-centered nor learner-centered but, given its links to behaviorism and programmed instruction, almost entirely *technology*-centered.

Although individualization became, for a time, "high fashion" (Oettinger, 1969, p. 118), it had, from the beginning, its detractors, individuals who saw beyond the hype and offered cogent, if generally overlooked, objections to a view of education as the solitary interface between a "black box" and a mechanical tutor. For example, Herbert Muller (1970) commented that the "so-called 'technological revolution in education' " (p. 215) that was being led by the behaviorists involved such dubious practices as replacing live instructors with packaged, mediated content: "Professors are being put into cans of videotaped lectures, carefully tested by educational psychologists, who refer to them as cans of 'teaching behavior' " (p. 215). Others argued that, far from being the opposite of the factory approach to schooling, individualized instruction was by definition *mass* instruction, its whole point being to replicate the dynamics of one-on-one instruction for a large number of students, with the goal of ensuring that all students ended up in the same place, having mastered the same content:

> Although it is argued that teaching machines provide for individualized instruction by permitting each student to progress at his own rate of speed, programed [*sic*] learning actually represents a mass standardization of content and process in education. The teaching machine requires absolute uniformity of interpretation and response on the part of the learner. (Tanner, 1964, p. 303)

Individualization was, in short, mass production made to *look* like customization—"a fad without deeper significance than Detroit's customizing, namely taking a mass-produced object and stamping it with gold initials or heaping chrome to give the illusion of individual tailoring" (Oettinger, 1969, p. 121). The rhetoric of responsiveness and humanization merely "mask[ed] business as usual: regimentation and the primacy of discipline over intellect or action still prevail" (Oettinger, p. 44).

Observations of this kind signaled a disillusionment with individualization that triggered its eventual decline. In their history of individualized instruction in America, Grinder and Nelson (1985) claim that despite the initial hyperbole about the potential of individualization to revolutionize education, the project soon waned, counting, in the long run, "for little more than a few yahoos in the wilderness" (p. 26). Despite individualization's decline from favor within the educational establishment as a whole, however, extravagant claims about the transformational potential of individualization persisted in the new discourse of computer-based instruction. After all, in the absence of compelling evidence regarding the instructional efficacy of computers, school boards and postsecondary institutions needed something to justify their massive investments in hardware and software. Thus, during the 1970s and 1980s, as teaching machines gave way to more sophisticated digital devices, the primary rationale for the use of computers in the classroom remained their "rich and intriguing potential . . . for answering today's most pressing need in education—the individualization of instruction" (Atkinson & Wilson 1969, p. 3). As late as 1995, University of Toronto professor Robert Logan was still offering the computer as "an ideal medium for delivering and promoting individualized learning" (p. 187), while, a few years later, communications specialist Don Tapscott (1998) concurred that digital media allow schools to make the transformation from mass education to the "individualized approach" (p. 146).

As computers made their way into classrooms, in part on the strength of such hyperbole, it became clear that they served two distinct roles with respect to individualized instruction. First, and most conspicuously, they functioned as sophisticated teaching machines, capable of providing self-paced instructional materials that functioned smoothly and automatically: now there was no need to turn a crank to advance from frame to frame. This use of the computer to present instructional content directly to the learner was referred to as computer-assisted instruction (CAI). However, the computer also had the potential to serve a separate data processing role, purportedly vital when each student proceeded through the material at his or her own pace. The use of the computer to "cope with the mass of detailed information generated by programs of individualized education" (Baker, 1978, p. 15) was referred to as computer-managed instruction (CMI). Whereas the student interacted directly with CAI programs, CMI produced data intended largely for the teacher's eyes: records of student progress, prescriptions for instructional activities, pre- and post-test scores.

During the 1970s, CAI and CMI developed more or less independently and according to markedly different visions of the computer's role in education. CAI researchers tended to perpetuate Skinner's claims, premising their work on the assumption that instruction could be more effective and efficient if it were provided by machines rather than by human teachers. Like the behavioral psychologists before them, CAI innovators sought to make their software "as 'teacher-proof' as possible" (Oettinger, 1969, p. 115). Thus, "a CAI math program, for example, bears its own evaluation, independent of what the teacher thinks of the child" (Olson, 1987, p. 200), and there was rarely any provision for the teacher to have input into either the means of evaluation or the instructional content itself. Computer-managed instruction researchers, on the other hand, seemed at pains to emphasize that, unlike CAI systems that reduced the teacher's role to "either an interested bystander or a resource person to call upon when the CAI system can't get a person to learn" (Baker, 1978, p. 13), computer-based instructional management systems were "designed to fit into existing schools" (Kooi & Geddes, 1970, p. 45), where they would merely assist with the teacher's management functions in a "non-threatening" (Fritz & Levy, 1972, p. 14) way. In short, although the CAI program was represented as a sophisticated "teaching machine," the CMI system was offered as the teacher's humble and tireless "machine servant" (Steffenson & Read, 1970, p. 58).

Underlying this laudable concern with supporting teachers' management efforts was an undeniable self-interest on the part of CMI researchers. By the early 1970s, CAI developers had discovered, to their dismay, that the teachers whom they sought to replace were also the final gatekeepers, capable of "blocking classroom doors" and "preventing the entry of this magical innovation, this panacea for the school's problems" (Cuban, 1986, p, 80). Computer-managed instruction researchers sought to "[alleviate] teacher anxiety" (Kooi & Geddes, 1970, p. 45) because CAI's cool reception had taught them that the "biggest factor in the success of CMI will be the cooperation of the teacher" (Finch, 1972, p. 47). Hence, the tendency of researchers and promoters to describe CMI systems not as intelligent programs capable of autonomous decision making but as tools that supported teachers. The cultivated aura of nonthreatening assistance was supported by the representation of early CMI systems as customized solutions to the problems of specific school districts, schools, or even of specific instructors and groups of students (Baker, 1978, p. 52; Scanlon, 1974, p. 7).

However, despite the rhetoric of personalized accommodation and support, CMI no less than CAI was based upon and carried into the classroom a belief that individualized instruction was something that "could be monitored and steered best by a computer" (Gibbons, Fairweather, & O'Neal, 1993, p. 7). Developments in both CAI and CMI emerged from and perpetuated a tendency to privilege instructional efficiency and precision and, by extension, the technological means by which these rather diminished educational ends could best be achieved. Moreover, if CMI research was not, like much CAI research, premised on an impulse to replace the teacher, it certainly involved a radical revisioning of both the instructional process and the teacher's role, with the latter regarded as something akin to "the production line worker," someone who "provides the student with the raw materials, work sheets, books, etc." (Baker, 1978, pp. 271–272) necessary to support both the student's individualized interaction with prescribed instructional content and the computer's processing demands.

Although CAI and CMI originated and developed separately, there were, from the beginning, efforts to unite these parallel innovations into integrated systems capable of both delivering and managing instruction. The union made perfect sense: the CAI instructional programs could directly provide the CMI module with achievement data that it could use to prescribe another CAI lesson, and so forth. Working together, feeding into each other, and enabling the capture and analysis of every student input, CAI and CMI formed a perfect loop, a bulwark against the follies and inefficiencies of human decision making.

During the 1980s and 1990s, CAI/CMI amalgams, known as *integrated learning systems*, proliferated at all levels of education. Integrated learning systems such as WICAT, Plato, and CCC were defined as " 'individualized' computer software supplied by a single vendor and containing instruction and practice problems covering a multiple-year curriculum sequence. . . . Specific lessons are automatically loaded onto each student's computer when that student 'logs in' based on a continuous assessment of that student's previous accomplishments and current learning needs" (Becker, 1990, p. 1). These "complete teaching/learning package[s]" (Bluhm, 1987, p. 8) were invariably top-down initiatives, introduced into classrooms by school boards and administrators who were pressured by unfavorable media reports and increasingly reform-minded bureaucrats and parents to implement technological "solutions" to the inefficiencies of teacher-led instruction. Like teaching machines and CAI, integrated learning systems were intended to function not as teacher tools and resources but as teacher replacements. Indeed, the prepackaged instruction such systems offered was so closely integrated and tied to the CMI module that it was virtually impossible for the teacher to choose alternative modes of instruction for specific lessons. In effect, choosing to use an ILS entailed handing over "the student's overall learning experience . . . to ILS companies who produce the instructional systems and instructional materials" (Bailey, 1992, p. 3).

Critics of integrated learning systems objected to this loss of teacher control, as well as to the repetitive, "drill-and-kill" instruction (Bailey, 1992, p. 3; White, 1992, p. 49), based largely on behavioral principles, which these systems tended to offer. There was also an increasing realization that the solitary learning promoted by these systems was inconsistent with emerging research suggesting that learning was primarily a social activity (Becker, 1992, p. 7).

Appearing at this point in the history of individualized, technology-based instruction, the Internet was quickly hailed, like other technologies before it, as the new panacea at all levels of education—a source of endless information as well as a means of restoring the social dimension to mediated instruction. The Internet was touted as "revolutionary," an information "highway" with no speed limits; and, given the language of acceleration and urgency surrounding it, there certainly seemed to be little time to reflect on the educational implications of this new, "cutting-edge" technology. K–12 educators and administrators were quick to jump on the careening bandwagon, but postsecondary institutions were even quicker to appreciate the benefits—less, perhaps, to adult learners than to the institutions themselves—of anytime, anywhere online delivery of university courses. From this spirit of haste and rampant opportunity emerged Internet-based platforms such as WebCT and Blackboard, designed to enable colleges and universities to take their place in the new global order. Like the earlier CAI/CMI amalgams such as Wicat and Plato, the new Internet-based platforms were premised on the importance of combining, within one system, the ability both to deliver comprehensive course content and to manage (that is, track and report on) students' progress through it. Unlike those integrated learning systems, however, WebCT and other similar platforms were empty shells into which only the instructor could breathe life.

Emerging from a new paradigm based not on broadcast (or one-way) technologies but on media that enable two-way synchronous and asynchronous dialogues, Internet-based systems would seem, at first glance, to represent the death knell of individualization and all its ramifications: the emphasis on instructional efficiency, the privileging of technological means, the standardization of content, the separation of learning from its social contexts, the reduction of the learner to a "black box," and the marginalization of the inefficient human teacher. Certainly, Web-based course delivery and management systems are promoted as revolutionary tools; the WebCT Web site, for example, claims that this "innovative solution" to the "new demands on higher education" will "transform the educational experience." However, although a superficial examination of these "advanced pedagogical tools" may suggest no kinship to programmed learning and individualization, there is, in fact, a clear line of descent from early attempts to individualize instruction with low-tech teaching machines to the newer, more sophisticated Internet-enabled systems. Consider the following description of the functionality of a "typical learning management system":

> To illustrate how a typical learning management system operates, imagine Alex, a university student, learning from an e-learning course. Alex first logs on to the system and is greeted by a list of courses for which he has signed up. Upon selection of a course from the list, he is brought to a page with an arrangement of icons or buttons, and probably some announcement. He can now access various course materials by clicking on these icons or buttons. Some common materials include course schedule, course information, course materials and documents, a discussion forum, assignments, online assessment, online chat, and reference links. The course materials can range from text documents to interactive tutorials. Upon completing the course content, Alex can choose to do the online assessment and obtain immediate results of his performance. (Tan & Hung, 2002, p. 49)

As this description makes clear, the "interactive" components, such as the links to online resources and communications tools, are frills, nonessential functions of a system that is primarily designed to fill the same "information pumping" (Tan & Hung, 2002, p. 49) role evoked many years ago both by Innis and by Muller's nightmare vision of the "professor in a can."

The authors of the previous passage are not alone in currently striving to discover uses of the Web that transcend the well-established paradigm of technology-mediated content delivery to individual learners. However, just as the potential of the Web in general has been co-opted by commercial interests that regard it as a vast conduit for product and consumer information,[3] so the potential of Web-based systems to enhance classroom dynamics has been severely constrained by the legacy of individualization and the long-standing premise, embedded within the design of such systems, that the goal of technology-based instruction is to achieve efficiencies by replacing teacher-student and student-student interactions in the classroom with access to mediated, "individualized" (i.e., self-paced) content. Today, talk continues to be "all about efficiency and, ultimately, money" (Feenberg, 1999, n.p.), and, as in the days of the teaching machine, such discourse continues to thinly mask a disenchantment with the educational status quo and the limited capabilities of educators to individualize instruction for a mass audience. Hence, rather than serving teachers and learners by pinpointing where instructor interventions are needed, Web-based systems perpetuate the efficient factory model of education, the "Taylorization of instructional labor" (Noble, 2001, p. 88), which gave rise to the teaching machine and which is the essence, and end, of individualization.

Of course, much of the discourse surrounding the use of Web-based course delivery and management systems—like the hype that once surrounded the use of teaching machines—suggests that such systems represent an unavoidable and, in any case, highly desirable evolutionary development toward more personalized, empowering, learner-centered educational environments. However, although it is true that the new platforms function, like the teaching machines of old, to remove teachers from the center of the educational enterprise, we should not assume that this means that the resulting instruction is necessarily learner-centered. Rather, like previous modes of individualized instruction, the Web-based systems are organized around technology and content. This was made overwhelmingly clear to me during a conference on Web-based learning (NAWeb 2002) where although the term "learner-centered" cropped up repeatedly, they focused on high-tech tools that facilitated content manipulation and delivery. The same message was driven home during a faculty workshop on WebCT. The emphasis of the two-day workshop was not on what the system would enable me to do for my students but on what it would enable me to do with my course content. The clear expectation of the workshop providers, and of the designers of WebCT, is that I will "migrate" all of my content—including syllabi, lecture notes, assignments, readings, and assessments—into the WebCT structure, and that, having done so, I will regard this imported content as a *course* (rather than, say, a course resource or supplement).[4] Books and articles on the use of the Internet in higher education perpetuate both the emphasis on content—universities are described, with increasing frequency, as "content providers" or "content producers" (e.g., Duderstadt, 1999, p. 13; Katz, 1999, p. 36), and students become "network-based consumer[s] of higher education intellectual content" (Katz, p. 39)—and the assumption that "content" and "course" are synonymous.

Underlying this vision of a world of online content accessed at the convenience of individual students are at least three problematic assumptions. The first, which I have implicitly challenged throughout this essay, is that what we now call individualization—that is, the use of technological means to enable the mass delivery of self-paced, standardized content—is a viable model of instruction, worth perpetuating with emergent technologies. The corollary assumption, equally dubious, is that classroom instruction is always "lockstep" and in the university generally takes the form of a professor reading from yellowed notes in a lecture hall packed with hundreds of students. It is true that as institutions of higher learning devolve into profit-seeking enterprises, the teacher–student ratio is decreasing; however, as this brief historical survey has suggested, individualized instruction emerged not in opposition to that trend but as part of it and as such cannot be assumed to be inherently more personalized and learner-centered than mass-delivered lectures. It is, however, more *efficient* because it is self-paced. Given that the true end of individualization is neither enhanced learning nor the creation of responsible citizens but increased efficiency, the question becomes this: Is efficiency an appropriate and meaningful end of education? Janice Gross Stein has cautioned that when efficiency "is used as an end in itself, as a value in its own right, and as the overriding goal of public life, it becomes a cult" (2001, p. 6). In education, the cult of efficiency, couched within the terms of a purportedly empowering individualization of instruction, is leading us inexorably to a time when, according to some forecasters, not only the class but the campus as a whole will be obsolete: "Students will pick out courses at an educational equivalent of Blockbuster and 'do' college at home without ever meeting a faculty member or fellow student" (Feenberg, 1999, n.p.).

The second problematic assumption, which also warrants challenge, is that the structure into which teachers are encouraged to import their content is absolutely neutral—just as the teaching machine was assumed to be a value-free product of objective science. In other words, there is no acknowledgment of the fundamental transformations that must be wreaked on content imported into platforms such as WebCT and Blackboard nor of the fact that the very structure of these systems constrains instructional possibilities and decision making. Looking back at the teaching machines of the 1960s and 1970s, it is now apparent that they transformed content by requiring that it be atomized, standardized, and in many cases, trivialized because the structures the teaching machines enforced meant that content that could not be reduced to small, measurable behaviors simply fell out of the viewfinder. Because factual material has always been more amenable to mechanized delivery—and still is, despite the grandiose claims of the promoters of online systems—it is important to ask whether less attention is being given to abstract ideas as more and more faculty members succumb to the pressures to fit their courses (in other words, their course content) into the "predetermined navigation models and course formats" (Storey, Phillips, Maczewski, & Wang, 2002, n.p.) of the new Web-based systems. Moreover, given that what is tested tends to drive what is taught, it is also worth inquiring into whether the efficient multiple-choice tests administered by WebCT and its ilk have the effect of "reduc[ing] the higher learning to the kind of proficiency that can be tested or graded by machines" (Muller, 1970, p. 216). Granted, WebCT also allows for short-answer and other test formats that must be marked by human teachers; but given the unchallenged mandate of efficiency that underlies the design and use of these systems, it is likely that multiple choice tests will "tend to drive out less efficient tests, leaving many important abilities untested—and untaught" (Stein, 2001, p. 157).

The final troubling assumption is that teachers in institutions of higher learning will gladly import their content into the Web-based systems. This assumption has been far more widely problematized and discussed than the previous two because it gives rise to the thorny issue of intellectual property. Rather than delving into the many dimensions and implications of this topic, which others (e.g., Bates, 2000; Noble, 2001) have treated in detail, I point out only that the issue of intellectual property arises because—unlike teaching machines, CAI, and integrated learning systems, which were designed to present learners with predefined instructional content that the teacher usually could not alter—the new Web-based systems are, at least for the time being, empty frameworks.[5] WebCT, for example, contains content pages but no content, a syllabus template but no course information, multiple-choice tests but no questions, a database capable of generating student reports but no student information. Right now, only professors have the wherewithal to feed these content hogs, a situation that would seem to restore power, after 50 years of "teacher-proof" programs, to the instructor. However, power is a function of choice, and the decisions as to whether to place course content online and as to whether it is possible to do so without relinquishing ownership and control of that content is increasingly being withdrawn from instructors by campus administrators who buy into, and must subsequently justify the expense of, ever more exorbitantly priced[6] Web-based course delivery and management systems. The result, as David Noble (2001) observes, is that the dynamics and intellectual activity of the classroom are increasingly being translated into a static package of individualized content—known as "courseware"—that can be marketed to a widely dispersed audience (pp. 26–27). And the question of whether particular content will be accompanied by a class—that is, a group of people who come together to make meaning of that content—is beginning to seem less and less absurd. Indeed, the increasingly accepted view is that, in a world of ATMs, online libraries, and Internet-based commerce, the class itself is an absurd and outmoded social construct, persisting not because of educational necessity but only because of "educational inertia" (Blustain, Goldstein, & Lozier, 1999, p. 54).

Noble (1995) points out elsewhere that when it comes to technology, history is far from inevitable. The ultimate meaning of a technology and the uses to which it is put will have something to do with its inherent affordances but a great deal more to do with human interests, values, and decisions over the years. During the past half century or so, our decisions as a society have tended to privilege technology-mediated instruction and the efficient, individualized content delivery it enables, while pushing away from the center both the classroom practitioner and the forum for communicating meanings in a human context over which the teacher presides. Today, with the advent of Web-based systems, the euphemisms have changed—we now talk, for instance, about instructional "relevance" and the "radical retooling" of higher education—but embedded within such language are the same premises that gave rise to teaching machines and individualization: the belief that education must be made more efficient and the belief that it is imperative, in the interests of enhanced (i.e., more efficient) learning, that more and more instructional decision-making power be transferred from educators to devices and those who make them. In the days of teaching machines, CAI, CMI, and integrated learning systems, hyperbole served as an effective means of overcoming teacher resistance to such premises; today, again thanks to the proliferation of a hyped rhetoric that tends to shut down critical response, many university instructors are willingly, even enthusiastically, participating in their own displacement by the machine. Does this mean that, in years to come, the question "Is there a class with this content?" will be as legitimate and comprehensible, when addressed by a student to a professor, as the question "Is there a text in this class?" is today? The answer, of course, depends on how those of us teaching in institutions of higher learning now choose to confront the increasing presence of, and pressure to use, Web-based systems; it depends, in particular, on how much decision-making power we are willing to relinquish to technological devices and to those who design, program, and implement them within the university.

ENDNOTES

1. My title question also owes something to Brown and Duguid (2000), who observe that as more people pursue distance education, "it becomes increasingly important to ask, 'Is there a class (or community) with this text?'" (p. 223).

2. The questions that we can ask are intimately connected to social (and technological) realities. Fish's title question would certainly have given pause to a university lecturer before the invention of the printing press, when "texts" were what students, taking assiduous notes, produced *during* a course.

3. Many readers may be surprised to discover that there is another little-known Web paradigm that has been around for as many years as the Internet and that resembles, far more than the online shopping mall we now have, the vision held by the Web's early architects. I refer to Wiki, an engine that allows for the creation of Web pages that any user can enter and modify at will. Each page thus functions not as a static piece of information but as the focal point of an ongoing dialogue. For more information on Wiki, see http://www.openwiki.com and http://c2.com/cgi/wiki.

4. MIT's April 2001 announcement that it was placing all of its teaching materials online elicited numerous comments about market implications. However, this OpenCourseWare initiative has not provoked reflections on the significance of the move as a statement about the fundamental difference between content and course, although the point was clearly made by MIT President Charles Vest when he announced the initiative: "Our central value is people and the human experience of faculty working with students in classrooms and laboratories" (Goldberg, 2001, n.p.).

5. This may not long be the case. In its 2002 "Technology Solutions" catalogue, Pearson Education Canada offers "e-packs" for WebCT and Blackboard. E-packs provide "online course content written by academics from reputable higher education institutions. . . . The e-packs offer a wealth of pre-loaded content."

6. It comes as no surprise that, having become established in many institutions, WebCT and Blackboard both announced new high-priced versions of their software: "Colleges that until recently paid a few thousand dollars a year for the companies' products . . . are now being asked to pay tens or even hundreds of thousands for the latest systems" (Young, 2002, p. A35).

REFERENCES

Atkinson, R. C., & Wilson, H. A. (1969). Computer-assisted instruction. In R. C. Atkinson & H. A. Wilson (Eds.), *Computer-assisted instruction: A book of readings* (pp. 3–14). New York: Academic Press.

Bailey, G. D. (1992, September). Wanted: A road map for understanding integrated learning systems. *Educational Technology, 32*(9), 3–5.

Baker, F. B. (1978). *Computer managed instruction: Theory and practice*. Englewood Cliffs, NJ: Educational Technology Publications.

Bates, A. W. (2000). *Managing technological change: Strategies for college and university leaders*. San Francisco: Jossey-Bass.

Becker, H. J. (1990, October). *Computer-based integrated learning systems in the elementary and middle grades: A critical review and synthesis of evaluation reports*. Baltimore, MD: John Hopkins University, Center for Social Organization of Schools. (ERIC Document Reproduction Service No. ED 348 939)

Becker, H. J. (1992, September). A model for improving the performance of integrated learning systems. *Educational Technology, 32*(9), 6–15.

Bluhm, H. P. (1987, January). Computer-managed instruction: A useful tool for educators? *Educational Technology, 27*(1), 7–11.

Blustain, H., Goldstein, P., & Lozier, G. (1999). Assessing the new competitive landscape. In *Dancing with the Devil: Information technology and the new competition in higher education* (pp. 51–71). San Francisco: Jossey-Bass.

Brown, J. S., & Duguid, P. (2000). *The social life of information*. Boston: Harvard Business School Press.

Cooley, W. W., & Glaser, R. (1969). An information and management system for individually prescribed instruction. In R. C. Atkinson & H. A. Wilson (Eds.), *Computer-assisted instruction: A book of readings* (pp. 95–117). New York: Academic Press.

Cuban, L. (1986). *Teachers and machines: The classroom use of technology since 1920*. New York: Teachers College Press.

Denton, J. J. (1974, January). Individualizing instruction via a computer managed instructional approach. *Educational Technology, 14*(1), 55–56.

Duderstadt, J. J. (1999). Can colleges and universities survive in the information age? In *Dancing with the Devil: Information technology and the new competition in higher education* (pp. 1–25). San Francisco: Jossey-Bass.

Feenberg, A. (1999, Summer). Reflections on the distance learning controversy. *Canadian Journal of Communication, 24*(3). Retrieved from http://cjc-online.ca

Finch, J.M. (1972, July). An overview of computer-managed instruction. *Educational Technology, 12* (7), 46-47.

Fish, S. (1980). Is there a text in this class? In *Is there a text in this class?: The authority of interpretive communities* (pp. 303–321). Cambridge, MA: Harvard University Press.

Fritz, K., & Levy, L. (1972, June). *Introduction to computer managed instruction and the automated instructional management system*. Madison: University of Wisconsin Counseling Center. (ERIC Document Reproduction Service No. ED 069 757)

Gibbons, A. S., Fairweather, P. G., & O'Neal, A. F. (1993, May). The future of computer-managed instruction (CMI). *Educational Technology, 33*(5), 7–10.

Giroux, H. A. (1999). *The mouse that roared: Disney and the end of innocence.* Lanham, MD: Rowman & Littlefield.

Glaser, R. (1964). Programed instruction: A behavioral view. In A. de Grazia & D. A. Sohn (Eds.), *Programs, teachers, and machines* (pp. 86–99). New York: Bantam Books.

Goldberg, C. (2001, April 4). Auditing classes at MIT, on the web and free. *New York Times.* Retrieved from http://education.mit.edu/tep/11125/opencourse

Gotkin, L. G. (1964). Programed instruction in the schools: Individual differences, the teacher, and programming styles. In A. de Grazia & D. A. Sohn (Eds.), *Programs, teachers, and machines* (pp. 159–171). New York: Bantam Books.

Grinder, R. E., & Nelson, E. A. (1985). Individualized instruction in American pedagogy: The saga of an educational ideology and a practice in the making. In M. C. Wang & H. J. Walberg (Eds.), *Adapting instruction to individual differences* (pp. 24–43). Berkeley, CA: McCutchan.

Innis, H. A. (1951). *The bias of communication.* Toronto: University of Toronto Press.

Katz, R. N. (1999). Competitive strategies for higher education in the information age. In *Dancing with the Devil: Information technology and the new competition in higher education* (pp. 27–49). San Francisco: Jossey-Bass.

Kooi, B. Y., & Geddes, C. (1970, February). The teacher's role in computer assisted instructional management. *Educational Technology, 10*(2), 42–45.

Logan, R.K. (1995). *The fifth language: Learning a living in the computer age.* Toronto: Stoddart.

Maddux, C. D., & Willis, J. W. (1992, September). Integrated learning systems and their alternatives: Problems and cautions. *Educational Technology, 32*(9), 51–57.

Markle, S. M. (1964). Individualizing programed instruction: The programer's part. In A. de Grazia & D.A. Sohn (Eds.), *Programs, teachers, and machines* (pp. 145–158). New York: Bantam Books.

Muller, H. J. (1970). *The children of Frankenstein: A primer on modern technology and human values.* Bloomington: Indiana University Press.

Mumford, L. (1963). *Technics and civilization.* New York: Harcourt, Brace & World.

Mumford, L. (1964). *The myth of the machine: The pentagon of power.* San Diego, CA: Harcourt Brace Jovanovich.

Noble, D. F. (1995). *Progress without people: New technology, unemployment, and the message of resistance.* Toronto: Between the Lines.

Noble, D. F. (2001). *Digital diploma mills: The automation of higher education.* New York: Monthly Review Press.

Oettinger, A. G. (1969). *Run, computer, run: The mythology of educational innovation.* Cambridge, MA: Harvard University Press.

Olson, C. P. (1987). Who computes? In D. L. Livingstone (Ed.), *Critical pedagogy and cultural power* (pp. 179–204). Toronto: Garamond Press.

Popkewitz, T. S., & Shutkin, D. S. (1993). Social science, social movements and the production of educational technology in the US. In R. Muffoletto & N. N. Knupfer (Eds.), *Computers in education: Social, political, and historical perspectives* (pp. 11–36). Cresskill, NJ: Hampton Press.

Romiszowski, A. J. (1986). *Developing auto-instructional materials: From programmed texts to CAL and interactive video.* London: Kogan Page.

Rose, E. (2000). *Hyper texts: The language and culture of educational computing.* London, Canada: Althouse Press.

Scanlon, R. G. (1974, November). Computer-managed instruction: Present trends and future directions. In H. E. Mitzel (Ed.), *Conference Proceedings: An examination of the short-range potential of computer-managed instruction* (pp. 4–8). Chicago: National Institute of Education. (ERIC Document Reproduction Service No. ED 112 943)

Schramm, W. (1964). The stage setting for programed instruction. In A. de Grazia & D. A. Sohn (Eds.), *Programs, teachers, and machines* (pp. 3–15). New York: Bantam Books.

Silverman, R. E. (1974). Using the S-R reinforcement model. In E. W. Eisner & E. Vallance (Eds.), *Conflicting conceptions of curriculum* (pp. 64–79). Berkeley, CA: McCutchan.

Skinner, B. F. (1964). Why we need teaching machines. In A. de Grazia & D. A. Sohn (Eds.), *Programs, teachers, and machines* (pp. 43–66). New York: Bantam Books.

Steffenson, R. G., & Read, E. A. (1970). A computer program for management of student performance information. *Audio-Visual Instruction, 15*(5), 56–59.

Stein, J. G. (2001). *The cult of efficiency.* Toronto: Anansi.

Storey, M.A., Phillips, B., Maczewski, M., & Wang, M. (2002). Evaluating the usability of Web-based learning tools. *Educational Technology and Society, 5*(3). Retrieved from http://ifets. ieee.org/periodical/vol_3_2002/storey.html

Tan, S. C., & Hung, D. (2002). Beyond information pumping: Creating a constructivist e-learning environment. *Educational Technology, 42*(5), 48–54.

Tanner, D. (1964). The machine teacher and the human learner. In A. de Grazia & D. A. Sohn (Eds.), *Programs, teachers, and machines* (pp. 300–309). New York: Bantam Books.

Tapscott, D. (1998). *Growing up digital: The rise of the net generation.* New York: McGraw-Hill.

White, M. A. (1992, September). Are ILSs good education? *Educational Technology, 32*(9), 49–50.

Young, J. R. (2002). Pricing shifts by Blackboard and WebCT cost some colleges much more. *Chronicle of Higher Education, 48*(32), A35.

Technology: Friend or Foe of Mentoring Relationships?

A. M. Thomas
University of Georgia

THE ORIGINS OF MENTORING

The term *mentor* originated in Greek mythology. Homer coined the term mentor in his epic, *The Odyssey*. In that work, Mentor was a good friend to Odysseus, the king. When Odysseus left to fight in the Trojan War, Odysseus left the training and counsel of his son, Telemachus, in the hands of Mentor. From the basis of this story, mentoring embodies an individual that acts as a role model, counselor, and guide.

The world of the ancient Greeks may seem like an odd place to consider technology, but the potential impact of technology on Mentor's and Telemachus's relationship provides a background in addressing the title question of the chapter. Without the aid of telecommunications technology, mentoring relationships of the ancient Greeks were limited to face-to-face contact. How would e-mail, instant messaging, or video teleconferencing have affected Mentor and Telemachus's interaction? Physical separation would no longer constrain the possibilities for interaction, but what might they lose?

Additionally, while fighting in the Trojan War, could Odysseus have used computer-mediated communication (CMC) to connect to Telemachus? Some might say a computer-mediated relationship between Odysseus and Telemachus may eliminate the need for Mentor. Some might say CMC may create the possibilities for Telemachus to receive dual mentoring from both Mentor and Odysseus. As we consider these possibilities, we must not lose sight of the ultimate goal of Telemachus's mentoring relationship: to prepare him to be the next king. The manner in which CMC would enhance or constrain Telemachus's and Mentor's relationship lies in the capability of CMC to meet the goal of preparing Telemachus to be the next king.

The purpose of this chapter is to describe the application of CMC into mentoring relationships in today's world. I describe the goals of mentoring relationships. Additionally, I introduce four theoretical frameworks for researching mentoring relationships conducted through CMC. I use these theoretical frameworks to offer some suggestions for the development of mentoring relationships using CMC.

GOALS OF MENTORING PROGRAMS

Jacobi (1991) provided a listing of several definitions of mentoring from the research literature. Two important goals are contained in these definitions. First, mentors should provide emotional or psychosocial support to protégés. Second, mentors should help protégés develop skills for professional development. Although these are important goals of mentoring programs, I propose two additional goals in light of the challenges some professions face. A third goal is that mentoring relationships should address problems of high attrition that exist in some professions. In addition, mentoring programs should help professions that lack diversity in terms of gender, race, or ethnic origin.

Providing Emotional Support

Newcomers to a profession are bound to face some stresses as they encounter new environs (Millinger, 2004). Pressures for the newcomer to the profession to make a good initial impression are strong. In dealing with these stresses, newcomers desire the emotional support a mentor can provide. When this is missing, protégés often notice the importance of this missing element. For example, Murrell (1999) found that many women lack the emotional and psychosocial support they desire in mentoring relationships.

Definitions of mentoring from the research literature describe the importance of the mentor providing emotional support to the protégé. Olian, Carroll, Giannantonia, and Feren (1988) defined a mentor as "a senior member of the profession who ... shares emotional support" (p. 16). Several of the definitions of mentoring contained in Jacobi (1991) used terms such as *supportive, psychosocial support,* and *nurturing.*

Helping Individuals Perform Successfully in a Profession

Mentors are often seen in the role of providing emotional support (Jacobi, 1991; Murrell, 1999). Although the value of emotional support is important, we must not neglect other measures of a valuable mentoring relationship. For instance, Wang and Odell (2002) noted that many teacher mentoring programs focus on providing emotional support at the expense of preparing teachers to learn to teach. Marra and Panghorn (2001) described the need for mentors of engineers to encourage a wider base of learning than mathematics and science alone. In their view, engineering mentors should encourage undergraduate engineers to build skills in writing and reading as well as calculus and physics. These skills will allow the engineer to communicate effectively with nonengineers. The mentor must help the protégé develop the necessary skills to function within the profession (Billingsley, 2004; Haack & Smith, 2000; Millinger, 2004).

King and Denecke (2003) noted the importance of the academic advisor's role as mentor in helping graduate students build necessary research skills. They stated, "Rather than being concerned solely with the student's completing the dissertation or developing technical competence, the mentor is concerned with promoting a broader range of psychological, intellectual, and professional development" (p. 15). They further described some specific skills the advisor-mentor should build such as writing grants and managing budgets. This is important because numerous research studies have found that graduate students are poorly prepared to teach; are unfamiliar with faculty governance and service; have no idea what is involved in managing a lab, procuring grants, managing budgets, or directing student research; and are unable to explain their research to anyone outside their own discipline (King & Denecke, 2003, pp. 18–19).

High Attrition Rates in a Profession

High attrition rates plague a number of professions and present concerns for these professions in planning for the future. The teaching profession is estimated to lose anywhere between 30% and 40% of teachers within their first five years of teaching (Dove, 2004; McGlamery & Edick, 2004). Several researchers (e.g., Billingsley, 2004; Dove, 2004; McGlamery & Edick, 2004; Millinger, 2004) have described the value of mentoring in relieving some of the stress that beginning teachers face.

The issue of high attrition rates is an ongoing issue for doctoral programs (Golde, 2000; Johnson, Green, & Kluever, 2000; Moyer & Salovey, 1999; Nolan, 1999). Herzig (2002) cited that the estimated proportion of mathematics students who do not complete their doctorate ranges from 30% to 70%. High attrition rates were compounded by the fact that 20% of all doctoral students who do not complete their degrees are in the dissertation phase of their studies.

Mentoring offers some possibilities in addressing the high attrition rates of doctoral students. In a study conducted by Moyer and Salovey (1999) to address high attrition rates of doctoral students, 13% of respondents suggested improvements to the mentoring process. Herzig (2002) also described the benefits of mentoring to dealing with the high attrition rates of doctoral students in mathematics. By acting as role models, he believed that mentors could visually display the skills necessary to be successful as a mathematical researcher.

Encouraging Underrepresented Groups

Underrepresentation of demographic groups within some professions presents special challenges. For instance, underrepresentation of women in mathematics and science is an ongoing problem (Holland & Eisenhart, 1990). This disparity is particularly glaring when we compare the gender breakdown of physical sciences to biological sciences. In 2000, approximately 45% of biologists were women. In contrast, that same year, approximately 9% of engineers were women (U.S. Census Bureau, 2002). Disparities within a profession may limit the diversity of ideas that exist within that community.

This disparity is not a recent phenomenon. Holland and Eisenhart (1990) explored the gender disparity that existed in mathematics and science in the 1980s. Although the bulk of their study focused on the culture of romance that existed within the undergraduate setting, they did find that mentoring was a useful piece of the puzzle in addressing gender disparity. They found that the women most likely to remain in science career fields were those who formed mentoring relationships with their professors.

This is not to deny that several issues present themselves with respect to using mentoring to help underrepresented groups. In many cases, the persons in senior positions to mentor women are men (Hansman, 2002). Although men can serve as mentors to women, we should consider some things. Crotty (1998) stated that some feminists believe men do not have the experiences of women to understand fully the issues facing women. Holland and Eisenhart (1990) noted that the possibility for misunderstanding regarding romantic overtures is always present in crossgender mentoring relationships as well. Some of the women in their study described experiences of unwanted sexual overtures from men while serving as mentors. A male mentor should actively seek to understand the unique challenges his female protégé faces.

COMPUTER-MEDIATED COMMUNICATION FOR MENTORING IN TODAY'S WORLD

The use of computer-mediated communication (CMC) in mentoring relationships is generally referred to as online mentoring or telementoring. Bierema and Merriam (2002) defined online mentoring as the "use of e-mail or computer conferencing systems to support a mentoring relationship when a face-to-face relationship would be impractical" (p. 214). Although the amount of face-to-face contact can vary, a totally online mentoring relationship would involve no face-to-face contact. Ensher, Heun, and Blanchard (2003) placed the degree in which CMC is used in online mentoring relationships along a continuum with four categories:

1. Totally face-to-face

2. CMC-supplemental: In this relationship, the bulk of the interaction is face-to-face with small amounts of online communication. An example of this would be when the mentor and protégé meet weekly face-to-face. They periodically communicate via e-mail to share electronic documents or schedule meeting times.

3. CMC-primary: In this relationship, the bulk of the interaction is online with small amounts of face-to-face communication. An example of this type of relationship is one in which the mentor and protégé communicate on a weekly basis via e-mail. They may meet once a year at conference.

4. Totally Online

Computer-mediated communication (CMC) affects many facets of our daily lives including communicating with friends, family, and colleagues; making online reservations; and searching for information. Mentoring relationships are not excluded from the increasing application of CMC. Ensher et al. (2003) found the number of online mentoring programs grew by 500% in a 2-year time frame. Table 1 provides five examples of online mentoring programs.

Table 1. Examples of Online Mentoring Programs

Program	Web Site	Purpose	Literature References
Electronic Emissary	http://emissary.wm.edu	Subject matter expert provides real-world information to K–12 students and teachers via e-mail	Harris, 1994; Sanchez & Harris, 1996
Mentornet	http://www.mentornet.net	Encourage women to enter careers in math, science and engineering through mentoring relationships with professions in these fields via e-mail exchange for eight months	Kasprisin, Boyle, Single, & Muller, 2003; Mueller, 2004
Guardian Angel System (GANS)	http://inet2002.org/ CD-ROM/lu65rw2n/ papers/ipv64-bi.pdf	Expert medical personnel provide guidance to emergency personnel in the field via video teleconferencing	Information Society Technologies, 2000
Welcoming Interns and Novices with Guidance and Support Online (WINGS)	http://wings.utexas.org/	Experienced teachers at a distance provide support to beginning teachers in the state of Texas via e-mail	
Women in Coaching	http://www.coach.ca/ WOMEN/e/mentor/ index.htm	Women coaches provide support to other women coaches via e-mail	Marshall, 2001

The five online programs described in Table 1 are only a small sample of online mentoring programs that exist. I choose these particular online mentoring programs for four reasons:

1. I am a member of two of the programs listed (Electronic Emissary and Mentornet).

2. Two of the programs (Mentornet and Women in Coaching) address similar concerns to differing professional communities. Mentornet and Women in Coaching seek to provide support to women in engineering and coaching, respectively (fields traditionally underrepresented by women).

3. Aside from GANS, each of the online mentoring programs predominately uses e-mail for communication between the mentor and protégé. GANS provides an example of the use of video telecommunication between experienced doctors and emergency medical personnel. GANS illustrates that other forms of computer-mediated communication (CMC) beyond e-mail are possible in online mentoring relationships.

4. The diversity of the professional communities (teachers, emergency medical personnel, and engineers) in the list helps illustrate that the application of online mentoring is not limited to a single profession.

With the proliferation of online mentoring programs, I now turn to some techniques for researching online mentoring programs.

RESEARCH AGENDA FOR ONLINE MENTORING

Despite the growth in applications of online mentoring programs, much of the evidence surrounding online mentoring programs is anecdotal (Bierema & Merriam, 2002). Ensher and colleagues (2003) developed several research propositions that are a useful starting point for researching online mentoring programs. Two of these research propositions are listed next. Thomas (2005) considered these two research propositions with respect to pre- and inservice teachers.

The Impact of Previous Mentoring and Computer-Mediated Communication Experiences

Ensher et al. (2003) hypothesized that previous online relationships and mentoring experiences significantly predict the chances of whether a person is willing to participate in an online mentoring program. One issue that must be resolved is how we measure previous online relationships and mentoring experiences. What questions reliably measure one's previous online relationships and mentoring experiences?

The Impact of Online Mentoring on Access to Mentors

Ensher et al. (2003) believed that online mentoring will increase the number of contacts an individual has within a profession. Online mentoring has the potential to increase one's ability to network within the professional community. In theory, online mentoring extends the boundaries of contacts outside one's own local area. In addition, Ensher et al. (2003) found that those engaged in online mentoring relationships often gain a desire to meet face-to-face. In what ways does CMC affect access to mentors?

Other Opportunities and Challenges

Ensher et al. (2003) hypothesized that online mentoring offers several opportunities. Each of these is worth further research. First, they proposed that online mentoring would result in reduced costs than traditional face-to-face mentoring programs. If so, this may encourage more businesses to use online mentoring. Second, online mentoring may reduce the initial salience of demographics (gender, race, and age). If so, this feature of online mentoring may provide greater access to the other members of a professional community for underrepresented groups.

In contrast, Ensher et al. (2003) described some challenges that online mentoring programs pose. First, they believed that online mentors will have greater difficulty in acting as a role model. Second, they proposed that online mentors will have greater difficulty in providing psychosocial support than face-to-face mentors. Third, they believed that concerns regarding trust and security are more challenging in an online mentoring relationship. We should engage in further research to assess the extent of these challenges for mentoring relationships.

THEORETICAL FRAMEWORKS FOR RESEARCHING ONLINE MENTORING PROGRAMS

This section describes four theoretical frameworks that are useful for researching online mentoring programs. These theoretical frameworks can also guide the process of design, development, and evaluation of online mentoring programs. These four theoretical frameworks are as follows: social exchange theory, cognitive apprenticeships, the distribution of power in the mentoring relationship, and social presence.

Social Exchange Theory

Social exchange posits that benefits must be mutually beneficial between mentor and protégé for the mentoring relationship to last (Ensher et al., 2003; Jacobi, 1991; Vo-Thanh-Xuan & Rice, 2000; Wilson & Elman, 1990). Jacobi (1991) defined the notion of social exchange theory as "The mentor as well as the protégé derives benefits from the relationship, and these benefits may be either emotional or tangible" (p. 513). Vo-Thanh-Xuan and Rice (2000) observed social exchange theory at work in a study in which grandparents mentored their grandchildren. The grandchildren (protégé) benefited by getting to know their grandparents better. The grandparent's self-esteem improved as they realized they could make a positive contribution to society. Schrum, Skeele, and Grant (2002/2003) noted the reciprocity present in many teacher education programs. Cooperating teachers shared their experience with preservice teachers, and preservice teachers taught inservice teachers about technology.

In using social exchange theory, we should seek to gain an understanding of the benefits that participants in online mentoring relationships seek. Aryee and Chay (1996) researched the motivation of managers to participate in mentoring relationships. Extrinsic motivators were employee development-linked reward systems and opportunities for interactions on the job. Intrinsic motivators were the altruism and positive affectivity. Positive affectivity is the ability to maintain a positive outlook despite external circumstances.

Cognitive Apprenticeship

The terms *mentoring* and *apprenticeship* are often used interchangeably (Clark, 1997; Hill, Wiley, Nelson, & Han, 2004; Selwa, 2003). For instance, Hill et al. (2004) described electronic mentoring as a "one-to-one link between an apprentice and expert" (p. 448). Selwa (2003) noted the need for a mentor in the medical field to follow the apprenticeship model. We should ponder the tenets of cognitive apprenticeship in relation to online mentoring programs.

Lave and Wenger (1991) developed three useful notions from cognitive apprenticeship that we should consider in online mentoring programs. First, legitimate peripheral participation implies that the initial tasks performed by the apprentice (protégé) do not demand high levels of responsibility. At the same time, these initial tasks are required within the particular profession. For example, a preservice teacher that takes the class roll for the inservice teacher is an example of legitimate peripheral participation.

Second, scaffolding is an important component in cognitive apprenticeship. Scaffolding is "support for the initial performance of tasks to be later performed without assistance (the scaffold)" (Lave & Wenger, 1991, p. 48). Prior to starting a student teaching experience, a preservice teacher might receive a booklet containing photos and description of students in the classroom (scaffold). Once the preservice teacher learns the members in the class, she will no longer need this particular scaffold.

Last, the mentor should serve as a coach to the protégé. As coach, the mentor seeks to help the protégé understand his or her own assumptions. In the initial phase of a student teaching experience, a coach might ask the preservice teacher to compare the student teaching experience to what she thought it would be like.

Structure of Power in Mentoring Relationships

We must consider the balance of power between mentor and protégé. In an ideal world, the mentor and protégé would have equal levels of power. Of course, we do not live in an ideal world, so we must deal with imbalances of power that exist between mentor and protégé. Because of the structure of some professions, the mentor may come from the dominant group (Hansman, 2002). Hansman experienced difficulties when she and her male mentor had competing definitions of success. He defined success in terms of moving up the organizational ladder. She, in turn, defined success in terms of balancing work and family life.

Lave and Wenger (1991) considered relationships in which protégés served in positions of involuntary servitude. Historically, apprenticeship programs originally failed because of the coercive nature of the relationship. Snell (1996) noted that apprentices in the 1200s could not purchase land or marry. These coercive experiences dramatically hinder the learning process as well as limit the possibilities the protégé can participate fully in a particular profession (Lave & Wenger, 1991).

Darder (1996) described the link between power and truth. In particular, he noted the dominant group has the power to define truth within the function of society. Herring (2003) noted the power men held in the course of online dialogue. She described this situation as "The contentiousness of many male messages tends to discourage women from responding, while women's concerns with considerateness and social harmony tend to be disparaged as a 'waste of bandwidth' in male-authored netiquette guidelines" (p. 624).

Postman (1992) presented a case regarding the power the dominant group has to define the use of technology within society. He stated, "Those who have control over the workings of a particular technology accumulate power" (p. 9). We must also keep in mind when underrepresented groups may lack access to technological resources to reap the benefits of online mentoring relationships (Guy, 2002).

Social Presence

Social presence denotes the sense of being together (De Greef & Ijsselsteijn, 2001) or a feeling of community among individuals in a learning environment (Conrad, 2002). De Greef and Ijsselsteijn (2001) considered face-to-face communication as the baseline for evaluating the sense of being together. In comparing audio to video communication, they found video communication had the highest degree of social presence. Mutual respect between participants is also an important consideration within social presence studies. For instance, Conrad (2002) found students in an online course under study "wanted to behave well online and they did not want to offend other group members" (p. 202).

Perhaps, the nature of social presence in online settings is evolving. Earlier findings regarding social presence by Sproull and Kiesler (1986) were much different from those of

Conrad (2002). Respondents in Sproull and Kiesler's study reported flaming (speaking in a fanatical manner or being insulting) occurred on average 33 times per month via e-mail versus 4 times per month face-to-face. Have we learned the rules of proper online behavior since the 1980s? Are there other reasons to explain the differences between these two studies? Sproull and Kiesler's (1986) findings were based on a business organization, whereas Conrad's (2002) work involved an online class.

The manner in which we portray ourselves in online settings is an important element of social presence. Turkle (1995) stated that heavy Internet users "exist(s) in many worlds and play(s) many roles at the same time" (p. 14). I should note that the setting of her study did not involve formal online learning settings (e.g., an online class). Conrad (2002) noted this pattern of multiple roles played by online participants is less likely to occur in formal online learning settings. The five online mentoring programs described in Table 1 are intended to help the online protégé learn, but they are not formal online classes as considered in Conrad (2002). Because online mentoring programs do not directly fall in line with either Turkle's (1995) or Conrad's (2002) study setting, we should conduct further research on the impact of multiple roles in online mentoring programs.

CONSIDERING THE RANGE OF COMPUTER-MEDIATED COMMUNICATION

As shown in Table 1, e-mail is a common technology for online mentoring programs. The ubiquity of e-mail makes it an easy choice to use, but there are other computer-mediated choices (e.g., instant messaging, video teleconferencing, chat rooms) that we should consider in online mentoring relationships. Cuban (2001) considered the lack of effective integration of technology into the curriculum of kindergarten through universities in Silicon Valley. We might extend this idea to consider whether we are integrating technology into mentoring relationships to the fullest extent possible.

As we consider deploying a wider range of computer-mediated communication (CMC) tools, we must assess the potential for differences between how mentors versus protégés use CMC tools. Gal-Ezer and Lupo (2002) found that it was more difficult for students in introductory science classes to use the Internet to learn new material. In their study, advanced students were the most likely group to use the Internet. We should therefore compare the comfort level of using various forms of CMC (e-mail, instant messaging, chat rooms, discussion boards, and video teleconferencing) for online mentors and protégés.

Additionally, online mentors and protégés may use CMC tools at different rates. Ferneding-Lenert and Harris (1994) noted the frustrations experienced by an online mentor when he received no responses from his class for over three weeks. He normally checked his e-mail daily. In contrast, the teacher of the class only checked her e-mail biweekly. Contrasting patterns of CMC use between the online mentor and protégé can create feelings of being ignored.

DISCUSSION

The title of the chapter posed the question of whether the use of computer-mediated communication is a friend or foe to mentoring relationships. In other words, does CMC enhance or undermine the desired goals of a mentoring relationship? Online mentoring should meet one or more of the four primary goals for mentoring relationships. As we look at online mentoring programs, we must ask the following questions:

1. Does the online mentoring program provide emotional or psychosocial support?

2. Does the online mentoring program promote the development of skills for members of the professional community?

3. Does the online mentoring program treat issues of high attrition within the professional community?

4. Does the online mentoring program provide support to underrepresented groups within the professional community?

As we assess the possibilities of online mentoring, four theories are useful considerations. First, we should consider whether the online mentoring relationship provides benefits to both mentor and protégé (social exchange theory). Second, we should address the possibilities of cognitive apprenticeship in online mentoring relationships. In particular, we should seek to incorporate features of legitimate peripheral participation, scaffolding, and coaching into online mentoring experiences. Third, we should consider the balance of power between the online mentor and protégé. Does the online mentoring experience exploit the wishes of either the mentor or protégé? Last, we should consider the identity or behavior patterns individuals take in online mentoring relationships.

Because the overall mentoring goals defined earlier are so broad and diverse, no one mentor can realistically meet all of these goals in either a face-to-face or an online relationship. Burlew (1991) defined three types of mentors for business organizations: the training mentor, educational mentor, and development mentor. Peyton, Morton, Perkins, and Dougherty (2001) defined five types of mentors for graduate students in gerontology: the information mentor, the peer mentor, the competitor mentor, and the grandfather or grandmother mentor.

Because of the diversity of mentoring goals and skills, research suggests the value of having multiple mentors. Johnson, Settimi, and Rogers (2001) noted the value of multiple mentors in the medical field due to the wide range of paths a medical student could take. Zachary (2000) noted multiple mentors may minimize the chances of a single mentor becoming overwhelmed. In addition, she found that three-quarters of Generation Xers liked the idea of having multiple mentors. Although these studies focused on traditional face-to-face mentoring, the value of multiple online mentors is a useful consideration as well.

We should begin to assess the value of all forms of CMC to meet the goals of mentoring relationships. A comparison of CMC puts many of these goals in tension. Ensher et al. (2003) proposed that CMC, like e-mail, may reduce the initial salience of demographics (race, gender and age) of the mentor and protégé. This is important because mentoring relationships are often established on perceived similar characteristics (Ensher & Murphy, 1997). E-mail, in this light, could potentially provide a wider range of mentoring opportunities to women and people of color. The online mentor and protégé could use e-mail to focus on similar interests rather than similar demographics.

E-mail presents challenges to online mentoring relationships, however. The lack of visual cues decreases the opportunities for the mentor to role model. In combating this, we might turn to video teleconferencing such as WebCAM. Because video teleconferencing provides visual information, the mentor may have a greater opportunity to role model and coach. Conversely, video teleconferencing will increase the salience of demographics.

This chapter presented four theoretical frameworks to establish a set of questions for consideration in the design, development, and evaluation of online mentoring programs. From social exchange theory, we should begin to question the benefits online mentors and protégés seek from these relationships? From cognitive apprenticeship, how might we incorporate legitimate peripheral participation into online mentoring relationships? How is power used in online mentoring relationships? Using social presence, how do different forms of CMC influence the manner in which the online mentor or protégé interact or treat with one another?

REFERENCES

Aryee, S., & Chay, Y. W. (1996). The motivation to mentor among managerial employees. *Group & Organizational Management, 21*(3), 261–277.

Bierema, L. L., & Merriam, S. (2002). E-mentoring: Using computer mediated communication to enhance the mentoring process. *Innovative Higher Education, 26*(3), 211–227.

Billingsley, B. S. (2004). Special education teacher retention and attrition: A critical analysis of the research literature. *Journal of Special Education, 38*(1), 39–55.

Burlew, L. D. (1991). Multiple mentor model: A conceptual framework. *Journal of Career Development, 17*(3), 213–221.

Clark, B. R. (1997). The modern integration of research activities with teaching and learning. *Journal of Higher Education, 68*(3), 241–255.

Conrad, D. (2002). Inhibition, integrity and etiquette among online learners: The art of niceness. *Distance Education, 23*(2), 197–212.

Crotty, M. (1998). *The foundations of social research: Meaning and perspective in the research process.* London: Sage.

Cuban, L. (2001). *Oversold & underused: Computers in the classroom.* Cambridge, MA: Harvard University Press.

Darder, A. (1996). *Culture and power in the classroom.* Westport, CT: Bergin & Garvey.

De Greef, P., & Ijsselsteijn, W. A. (2001). Social presence in a home tele-application. *Cyberpsychology & Behavior, 4*(2), 307–315.

Dove, M. K. (2004). Teacher attrition: A critical American and international education issue. *Delta Kappa Gamma Bulletin, 71* (1), 8–14.

Ensher, E. A., Heun, C., & Blanchard, A. (2003). Online mentoring and computer-mediated communication: New directions in research. *Journal of Vocational Behavior, 63*(2), 264–288.

Ensher, E. A., & Murphy, S. E. (1997). Effects of race, gender, perceived similarity, and contact on mentor relationships. *Journal of Vocational Behavior, 50,* 460–481.

Ferneding-Lenert, K., & Harris, J. B. (1994). Redefining expertise and reallocating roles in text-based asynchronous teaching/learning environments. *Machine-Mediated Learning, 4*(2&3), 129–148.

Gal-Ezer, J., & Lupo, D. (2002). Integrating Internet tools into traditional CS distance education: Students' attitudes. *Computers & Education, 38*(4), 319–329.

Golde, C. M. (2000). Should I stay or should I go? Student descriptions of the doctoral attrition process. *Review of Higher Education, 23*(2), 199–227.

Guy, T. C. (2002). Telementoring: Sharing mentoring relationships in the 21st century. In C. A. Hansman (Ed.), *Critical perspectives on mentoring: Trends and issues* (pp. 27–37). Columbus, OH: ERIC.

Haack, P., & Smith, M. V. (2000). Mentoring new music teachers. *Music Educators Journal, 87*(3), 23–27.

Hansman, C. A. (2002). Diversity and power in mentoring relationships. In C. A. Hansman (Ed.), *Critical perspectives on mentoring: Trends and issues* (pp. 39–48). Columbus, OH: ERIC.

Harris, J. (1994). The Electronic Emissary: Bringing together students, teachers, and subject matter experts. *Computing Teacher, 22*(1), 60–63.

Herring, S. C. (2003). Computer-mediated discourse. In D. Schiffrin, D. Tannen, & H. E. Hamilton (Eds.), *The handbook of discourse analysis* (pp. 612–634). Malden, England: Blackwell.

Herzig, A. H. (2002). Where have all the good students gone? Participation of doctoral students in authentic mathematical activity as a necessary condition for persistence toward the Ph.D. *Educational Studies in Mathematics, 50*(2), 177–212.

Hill, J. R., Wiley, D., Nelson, L. M., & Han, S. (2004). Exploring research on Internet-based learning: From infrastructure to interactions. In D. H. Jonassen (Ed.), *Handbook of Research on Educational Communications & Technology* (pp. 433–460). Mahwah, NJ: Lawrence Erlbaum Associates.

Holland, D. C., & Eisenhart, M. A. (1990). *Educated in romance: Women, achievement, and college culture.* Chicago: University of Chicago Press.

Information Society Technologies. (2000). IPv6 wireless initiative: Guardian angel system. Retrieved January 14, 2004, from http://inet2002.org/CD-ROM/lu65rw2n/papers/ipv64-bi.pdf

Jacobi, M. (1991). Mentoring and undergraduate academic success: A literature review. *Review of Educational Research, 61*(4), 505–532.

Johnson, E. M., Green, K. E., & Kluever, R. C. (2000). Psychometric characteristics of the revised procrastination inventory. *Research in Higher Education, 41*(2), 269–279.

Johnson, T., Settimi, P. D., & Rogers, J. L. (2001). Mentoring in the health professions. In A. G. Reinarz & E. R. White (Eds.), *Beyond teaching to mentoring: New directions for teaching and learning* (Vol. 85, pp. 25–33). San Francisco: Jossey-Bass.

Kasprisin, C. A., Boyle, P., Single, R. M., & Muller, C. B. (2003). Building a Better Bridge: Testing e-training to improve e-mentoring programmes in higher education. *Mentoring and Tutoring: Partnerships in Learning, 11*(1), 67–78.

King, M. F., & Denecke, D. D. (2003). *On the right track: A manual for research mentors.* Washington, DC: Council of Graduate Schools.

Lave, J., & Wenger, E. (1991). *Situated learning: Legitimate peripheral participation.* Cambridge, England: Cambridge University Press.

Marra, R. M., & Panghorn, R. N. (2001). Mentoring in the technical disciplines: Fostering a broader view of education, career, and culture in and beyond the workplace. In A. G. Reinarz & E. R. White (Eds.), *Beyond teaching to mentoring: New directions for teaching and learning* (Vol., 85, pp. 35–41). San Francisco: Jossey-Bass.

Marshall, D. (2001). Mentoring as a development tool for women coaches. *Canadian Journal for Women in Coaching, 2*(2), 1-13.

McGlamery, S., & Edick, N. (2004). The CADRE project: A retention study. *Delta Kappa Gamma Bulletin, 71*(1), 43–46.

Millinger, C. S. (2004). Helping new teachers cope. *Educational Leadership, 61* (8), 66–69.

Moyer, A., & Salovey, P. (1999). Challenges facing female doctoral students and recent graduates. *Psychology of Women Quarterly, 23*(3), 607–630.

Mueller, S. (2004). Electronic mentoring as an example for the use of information and communications technology in engineering education. *European Journal of Engineering Education, 29*(1), 53–63.

Murrell, A. J. (1999). *Mentoring dilemmas: Developmental relationships within multicultural organizations.* Mahwah, NJ: Lawrence Erlbaum Associates.

Nolan, R. E. (1999). Helping the doctoral student navigate the maze from beginning to end. *Journal of Continuing Higher Education, 48*(3), 27–32.

Olian, J. D., Carroll, S. J., Giannantonia, C. M., & Feren, D. B. (1988). What do proteges look for in a mentor: Results of three experimental studies. *Journal of Vocational Behavior, 33,* 15–37.

Peyton, A. L., Morton, M., Perkins, M. M., & Dougherty, L. M. (2001). Mentoring in gerontology education: New graduate student perspectives. *Educational Gerontology, 27*(5).

Postman, N. (1992). *Technopoly: The surrender of culture to technology.* New York: Vintage Books.

Sanchez, B., & Harris, J. (1996). Online Mentoring: A success story. *Learning and Leading with Technology, 23*(8), 57–60.

Schrum, L., Skeele, R., & Grant, M. (2002/2003). One college of education's effort to infuse technology: A systematic approach to revisioning teaching and learning. *Journal of Research on Technology in Education, 35*(2), 256–271.

Selwa, L. M. (2003). Lessons in mentoring. *Experimental Neurology, 184,* S42–S47.

Snell, K. D. M. (1996). The apprenticeship system in British history. *History of Education, 25*(4), 303–321.

Sproull, L., & Kiesler, S. (1986). Reducing social context cues: Electronic mail in organizational communication. *Management Science, 32*(11), 1492-1512.

Thomas, A. M. (2005). *Using technology in mentoring relationships: Considerations of online mentoring for professional development.* Unpublished doctoral dissertation, University of Georgia, Athens.

Turkle, S. (1995). *Life on the screen: Identity in the age of the Internet.* New York: Simon & Schuster.

U.S. Census Bureau. (2002). *Labor force, employment, and earnings: Statistical abstract of the United States.* Retrieved January 14, 2004, from http://www.census.gov/prod/2002pubs/01statab/labor.pdf

Vo-Thanh-Xuan, J., & Rice, P. L. (2000). Vietnamese-Australian grandparenthood: The changing roles and psychological well-being. *Journal of Cross-Cultural Gerontology, 15,* 265–288.

Wang, J., & Odell, S. J. (2002). Mentoring learning to teach according to standards-based reform: A critical review. *Review of Educational Research, 72*(3), 481–546.

Wilson, J. A., & Elman, N. S. (1990). Organizational benefits of mentoring. *Academy of Management Executive, 4*(4), 88–94.

Zachary, L. J. (2000). *The mentor's guide: Facilitating effective learning relationships.* San Francisco: Jossey-Bass.

Part Two
School and Library Media

Introduction

V. J. McClendon

In 2005, assessment and performance measures remain driving forces in all levels of education, shaping the way libraries develop and deliver services to user populations. This ever-increasing scrutiny on performance outcomes has clear implications for funding and its rationale. Regardless of administrative demands for demonstrable outcomes, library professionals continue to recognize the qualitative nature of their work. At the heart of libraries is the desire to support the natural human curiosity, the love of reading, and other mediums of information and art. So we continue to dance along the fine line between answering administrative agendas and developing programs and materials to meet actual user needs.

As a result of increased pressure on materials and personnel budgets, research continues to illustrate the critical nature of libraries and information access for students. Following the lead of the Lance (1994) study, researchers have continued to seek methods to measure the effectiveness of libraries and their impact on users. Scholastic Research (2004), examining the last 15 years of library research, provide a cogent argument not only for the support of the library as a place but also illustrate that significant student achievement is fostered best by a realization that the library is not only a set of materials, not only a place, but also a professional staff coordinating and driving collaboration with teachers and other professionals. Studies repeatedly illustrate the ways libraries support the curriculum, promote critical thinking, assist problem-solving behaviors, and bring creative approaches to addressing the needs of students, parents, teachers, and administration (Baxter & Smalley, 2003; Lance, Rodney, & Hamilton-Pennell, 2005; Todd & Kuhlthau, 2004; Woolls, 2004).

Reflecting these trends and issues in U.S. libraries and media centers, there are five articles in this segment of the *Educational Media and Technology Yearbook,* which is divided into two areas: "Performance and Measurement" and "Holistic Approaches to Information Literacy." In the first section, we see ways in which libraries and media centers continue to seek a vision for increased performance and usability. In the second section, we explore ways library leadership seeks holistic ways to view the cycle of student and teacher learning and information access. Both sections demonstrate an awareness that approaches adopted must match needs for internal workflow as well as the demand for increased and measurable productivity with discernable contributions to institution- and district-wide achievement. At the same time, library professionals remain aware of the more qualitative needs of students as they leverage the strengths of the media center to promote a view of the learner as a holistic being rather than a single indicator on the line of school progress. Thus, the library professional seeks a balance between interpreting state and local guidelines and meeting individual needs of patrons and stakeholders.

PERFORMANCE AND MEASUREMENT

The first article in the first section is "Science Teacher and School Library Media Specialist Roles: Mutually Reinforcing Perspectives as Defined by National Guidelines" by Marcia A. Mardis. As an educator, researcher, and consultant, Mardis adopted a wide lens for seeking greater collaboration by examining the relations between existing national guidelines for both science and libraries. She makes an insightful observation that library goals and the roles of library professionals are consistent with other national interest groups—in this case, science professionals. As a group, science teachers have traditionally underutilized the school library media center, seeing their teaching roles as more fact driven and related more to lab work. However, this vision ignores the wealth of science research and resources readily available thorough the library. Mardis makes a coherent argument for the alignment of goals of both library and science professionals.

The second and third chapters in the "Performance and Measurement" section provide methods for implementing useful assessment techniques that actually work for the library professional to illustrate its productivity and increase opportunities to visualize and plan for change. Stephanie Huffman's chapter, "Technology Planning for the School Library Media Center: The SIMPLE Model," provides an excellent paradigm called SIMPLE, an acronym, representing six areas that should be addressed when developing and implementing technology for strategic planning within an organization: (1) staff and student assessment, (2) inventory, (3) measurement, (4) planning, (5) leadership, and (6) evaluation.

Feihn's chapter on total quality management (TQM) in the media center pairs this technique with annual planning and reporting. Her strong contribution is the use of flow charts, consensograms, control charts, affinity charts, and customer feedback to bring a concrete sense of workable application for practitioners. Her study examined 23 schools implementing the TQM model and discusses the results of their trial. The result is a handy toolkit for those seeking systemic planning and improvement which reaches from administration to student input.

HOLISTIC APPROACHES TO INFORMATION LITERACY

Section 2 of this segment looks at two very different issues in literacy education as they relate to the media center. First is Farmer's study, which examined information literacy and socioemotional behaviors among a population of high school students. In this study, Farmer made an interesting attempt to understand the relative levels of independence and problem-solving ability among a selected group of 9th and 11th graders as correlated to information literacy and success in locating and evaluating information for school research. Implications of her study suggest that socioemotional well-being does play a role in student success.

Finally, in the second chapter in Section 2, Bush provides a novel look at new ways to incorporate creativity and a willingness to encourage creativity into the media center. In her position paper, the author suggests that creativity literacy can and should incorporate synectics or problem solving combined with active creative thinking, metaphorical thinking, lateral thinking, analogies, or problem reversal. She issues a challenge to the findings of Sternberg's (1998) study, which found that teachers prefer to teach students with high intelligence quotients rather than students with high creativity quotients. Bush suggests that divergent learning skills can provide a new window on our world and provide new approaches to old and new problems alike. She provides some excellent guidelines for considering what creativity literacy might imply for materials and services within the school library media center.

The works included here suggest that although resources continue to shrink, library professionals continue to work in multiple directions to meet the needs of patrons. Studies of students and schools continue to illustrate the pivotal role played by the media center and its professionals in creating success for the individual learner as well as the institution. In addition, as a central location for school-wide curriculum, media centers and their professionals have an opportunity to focus on extending broader district and school agendas as well as looking for alternative methods to approach student needs.

REFERENCES

Baxter, S. J. & Smalley, A. W. (2003). *Check it out! The results of the school library media program census, final report.* St. Paul, MN: Metronet.

Lance, K. C. (1994). The impact of school library media centers on academic achievement. *School Library Media Quarterly 22*(3), 167–170, 172.

Lance, K. C., Rodney M. J., & Hamilton-Pennell, C. *Powerful libraries make powerful learners: The Illinois Study.* Canton: Illinois School Library Media Association, 2005. Retrieved from http://www.islma.org/resources.htm

Scholastic Research. (2004). *School libraries work!* Danbury, CT: Scholastic Library Publishing. Retrieved from http://www.scholastic.com/librarians/printables/slp_rfp_804.pdf

Sternberg, R. (Ed.). (1998). *Handbook of creativity.* Cambridge, England: Cambridge University Press.

Todd, R. J., & Kuhlthau, C. C. (2004). *Student learning for Ohio school libraries: The Ohio Research Study.* Ohio Educational Library Media Association. Retrieved from www.oelma.org/studentlearning.htm

Woolls, B. (2004). *The school library media manager* (3rd ed.). Westport, CT: Libraries Unlimited.

Science Teacher and School Library Media Specialist Roles: Mutually Reinforcing Perspectives as Defined by National Guidelines

Marcia A. Mardis

Wayne State University and University of Michigan

Although many studies have found a strong connection between school library media programs and student reading achievement, little research has focused on the ability of the school library to support science learning. In addition, science teachers and school library media specialists (SLMSs) rarely collaborate and learn about one another's professional roles. In an effort to gain more understanding into ways in which science educators and school librarians can work together effectively, this chapter explores the professional guidelines expressed in the National Science Education Standards and Information Power (American Association of School Librarians [AASL] and the Association for Educational Computing and Technology [AECT], 1998) for overlap and points of mutual reinforcement.

A substantial amount of research documents the relationship between strong school library media programs and student achievement in reading. The Colorado Study (Lance, Welborn, & Hamilton-Pennell, 1993) and subsequent replications (Baughman, 2000; Lance, Hamilton-Pennell, Rodney, Peterson, & Sitter, 2000; Lance, Rodney, & Hamilton-Pennell, 2000a, 2000b, 2001, 2002; Rodney, Lance, & Hamilton-Pennell, 2002, 2003) have all shown a positive correlation between school library media programs and reading achievement, but school library media specialist practitioner and scholarly literature rarely addresses support of science achievement (Mardis, 2005b). Good science teachers and strong school media specialists have been independently linked to student achievement, but no research has examined the two roles in conjunction (Ercegovac, 2003; Sosa, 1999; Whelan, 2004). The lack of cooperation between school library media specialists (SLMSs) and science teachers is a challenging issue. These positions in the school community have great potential to be mutually reinforcing, but little interaction occurs between them (Abilock, 2003; Ercegovac, 2003; Valentine, 2003; Whelan, 2004).

In many educational organizations, the relationship between science education and school library media programs has attained a "chicken or the egg"-type of cycle: science teachers do not often use the school library because they do not feel that the school librarian has the resources or the skills to help them; the school librarian doesn't develop the skills or resources to help science educators because they are not frequent users of the school media program (Mardis, 2005a). The purpose this chapter is to begin to explore ways to improve the relationship between science achievement and school library media programs through an examination of professional standards in both areas.

BACKGROUND LITERATURE

Science education and school library media programs have practical and philosophi-cal commonalities that justify an exploration of their link. Science education includes many integrated components that are compatible with *Information Power* (AASL/AECT, 1998) principles and common practices in school library media programs. These primary compo-nents are "(1) science processes, (2) scientific knowledge gathered by applying various processes, and (3) values and attitudes undergirding scientific inquiry" (Churton, Cranston-Gingras, & Blair, 1998). These authors argue that science learning is intricately linked to technology and that understanding and using technology is connected to modern living. As Lance (2001) and Todd (2003) point out, the school library media center is often the hub of technology for the school. Vassila (2005) points out that both the inquiry process and the information process can be used complementarily to promote deep understanding and deep knowledge. The focus of this chapter is primarily on school library media programs; it is not meant to be an exhaustive investigation of science curriculum content or science teaching practices but rather is intended to inform both library and science professionals of the potential for collaboration.

More teachers are out-of-field in science than in any other area of K–12 education (Ellis, 2003; U.S. Department of Education, 2000). Perhaps the lack of experience with science topics combined with the importance of science achievement accounts for many teachers' reliance on science textbooks (Stern & Roseman, 2004; Ulerick, n.d.). However, Stern and Roseman (2004) reviewed middle school science textbooks and found that leading textbook series rarely presented important ideas in ways that challenged students to construct knowledge and gain deep topical understanding. Some material conveyed through textbooks, then, may counter the goals of inquiry-based, constructivist learning advocated by the *National Science Education Standards* (National Research Council, 1996) and related federal initiatives (Ellis, 2003).

Science students benefit from consistently delivered instruction and solid prior knowledge that allows them to deliver replicable frameworks for problem solving. Yet science instruction is often implemented without specific instruction to students in strategies unique to science learning (Churton et al., 1998). Many learning problems in science can be traced back to lack of background knowledge, lack of ability to contrast new ideas to existing ones, and lack of ability to devise learning techniques to process scientific information. Teachers and students of science need support.

Krajcik and other researchers from the Center for Highly Interactive Computing in Education (hi-ce) at the University of Michigan (Kracjik, Blumenfeld, Marx, & Soloway, 1999) concluded that both teachers and students need considerable amounts of scaffolding to engage with science material effectively. Science teachers can gain support through professional development provided by the school district that focuses on curriculum goals and tools for more effective teaching (Supovitz, 2003). Teacher confidence is encouraged by collaborative teaching relationships that take place in the classroom, in other school settings, or in informal learning spaces such as museums and field environments (Drayton & Flick, 2000).

Students likewise benefit from extensive instructional support. They often need help in the metacognitive processes of inquiry (Novak, 1998), especially in formulating rich questions, collecting quality and appropriate substantiating evidence, and communicating results clearly (Abbas, Norris, & Soloway, 2003; Kracjik et al., 1999). Because questioning and the ability to conduct problem-solving processes are essential to science learning (Churton et al., 1998), SLMSs can support science learning through their teaching of information literacy and student research skills (McKenzie, 2002). Strong information literacy and research skills support student learning in authentic means and contexts and can help students develop multiple literacies with data, technologies, and communication media simultaneously (Lemke, 2000).

In Australia, Todd, Lamb, and McNicholas (1993) studied Year 7 and Year 11 students and found that collaborative integration of information skills had a positive impact on student learning, including better understanding of subject content and improved test scores. Todd (1995) analyzed the impact of integrated information skills instruction in a Year 7 science class. The two treatment classes recorded significantly higher annual science scores than did the control classes.

Ample evidence suggests that reading capabilities are tied to science achievement. Problems with science learning often stem from problems with reading. Churton and colleagues (1998, p. 173) delineated common learning problems associated with science:

1. The inability to learn and assimilate new knowledge due to lack of opportunities designed to contrast current beliefs with new information.

2. Poor comprehension of science textbooks due to high readability or difficulty level and lack of instruction in comprehension strategies to understand science reading.

3. Poor performance in reading short, specific selections such as reading to follow directions in performing a science experiment or interpreting an explanation of graphic material.

4. The inability to apply learned concepts to new situations.

5. The inability to master specialized vocabulary common to all science areas at all grade levels.

Three of the five most common difficulties in science learning that students encountered were linked to reading skills. As Churton et al. (1998) demonstrated, effective science education is supported by a variety of strategies and media. In line with *Information Power* (AASL/AECT:9, 1998) principles and goals, effective science learning is composed of a blend of hands-on activities and active reading in a variety of sources so that students can construct science concepts and knowledge.

THE CONVERGENCE OF PROFESSIONAL STANDARDS FOR SCIENCE AND SCHOOL MEDIA

An examination of the professional guidelines that have been developed for both science teachers and media specialists will show that despite the lack of current cooperation, these roles stem from similar beliefs about the school community and student learning. These similarities can form the basis for further investigation into the depth of their complementarity as well as into the barriers to collaboration.

Overview of Science Teaching and Standards

Teaching philosophy influences instructional practice, but other forces such as teacher preparedness and preservice teacher education affect the classroom environment. Teachers at all levels report feeling unprepared to teach life, earth, or physical science, with elementary teachers at a particular disadvantage (Horizon Research, 2002; Weiss, Banilower, McMahon, & Smith, 2001). Preservice science teachers are also not uniformly receiving the exposure to science teaching methods and approaches that allow them to develop their own perspectives on teaching and learning (Baker, 2002).

In an effort to give science teachers, with their diverse backgrounds and experiences, a common language, multiple efforts have been undertaken to create instructional guidelines and goals. The American Association for the Advancement of Science (AAAS) established Project 2061, a long-term initiative to improve science literacy, and the National Science Teachers Association (NSTA) contributed to benchmarking and dissemination efforts. Finally, in 1996, the National Research Council (NRC) unified the AAAS and NSTA products into the *National Science Education Standards* (NSES). These standards proceed from their beliefs in high student expectations, teaching for depth of understanding, science literacy, and active learning; the NSES recognize that diversity in approaches and perspectives will exist within its framework (Ellis, 2003). The standards also strongly promote professional development to increase awareness of different teaching and learning ideas.

The *National Science Teaching Standards*, in its segment on classroom practice, begin with encouraging teachers to develop a long-term plan for science teaching that facilitates inquiry-based learning, includes formative and summative assessments, and creates a conducive physical setting (NRC, 1996). Although the imperative to balance and integrate immediate demands (such as state-mandated standardized tests) with these professional standards will be an ongoing challenge, the *National Science Teaching Standards* do give educators a lens through which to examine their own practice as well as their role in the school community.

Overview of School Library Media Practice and Principles

The American Library Association (ALA) has been releasing standards for school libraries since 1925, with the publication of *Elementary School Library Standards*. Subsequent publications refined and expanded ALA's vision for school libraries and culminated in the publication of *Information Power* in 1988. This collaboration between the members of the American Association of School Librarians (AASL) and the Association for Educational Computing and Technology (AECT) gave guidelines to school librarians who wanted to take advantage of the increasing amount of print and electronic information in their practice. In these guidelines, school librarians were encouraged to involve themselves in new areas of decision making and facilitate the access to and use of information by students, teachers, and parents.

In 1998, *Information Power* was revised and expanded to reflect the explosion of knowledge made possible by advances in information technology in schools and the increased opportunities access brings to the school library media program. In *Information Power*, authors from AASL and AECT state that

> The library media program combines effective learning and teaching strategies and activities with information access skills. Information availability will undoubtedly continue to mushroom in the next century, which will make a strong school media program even more essential to help its users acquire the skills they will need to harness and use information in everyday life. (p. 1)

Three themes for practice are established for the media specialist in *Information Power*: collaboration, leadership, and technology. The collaborative theme recognizes the influence of collaborative teaching on student achievement (Lange, Magee, & Montgomery, 2003); the leadership theme recognizes that steady and visionary leadership is widely evident in effective school media programs (Lance, 2001); and the technology role recognizes that access to and facility with information technology is essential (Kulhthau, 1997).

Often, discussions of school library media centers are treated as synonymous with discussions of educational technology because media centers are often the location of the majority of the school's technology equipment (Lance & Loertscher, 2001). However, technology is merely a vehicle for the delivery of information in the school library whether it be via telephone and fax machine, cable television, the online catalog and circulation data, electronic periodicals and texts, access to the Internet, or software applications (AASL/AECT, 1998). It is essential that discussions of technology and the school library media center focus on both access to and use of technology to locate information and to construct knowledge.

Reinforcing Aspects of Science Teaching and School Media Practice

Both sets of guidelines are founded on an idea of literacy. "Information literacy is the ability to recognize when information is needed and have the ability to locate, evaluate and use effectively the needed information" (AASL/AECT, 1998, p.1). According to the NSES (NRC, 1996),

> Scientific literacy is the knowledge and understanding of scientific concepts and processes required for personal decision making, participation in civic and cultural affairs, and economic productivity. People who are scientifically literate can ask for, find, or determine answers to questions about everyday experiences. They are able to describe, explain, and predict natural phenomena. (p. 1)

Both literacies require learners to be able to identify a problem, systematically investigate the problem by gathering information, and assess the problem with the gathered information.

The vision of both sets of guidelines is to promote research-based contemporary learning theories. Both *Information Power* and the NSES emphasize that the active building of knowledge through construction and inquiry is the key to the authentic learning modern education seeks to promote.

An overview of the roles and their mutually reinforcing nature is depicted in Figure 1. Each of the National Science Teaching Standards is delineated across the top of the figure; each of the *Information Power* roles is listed across the bottom of the figure. Connections between the two sets of standards are indicated by double-ended arrows.

Figure 1. Mutually reinforcing roles as defined by science teaching and school library media specialist standards.

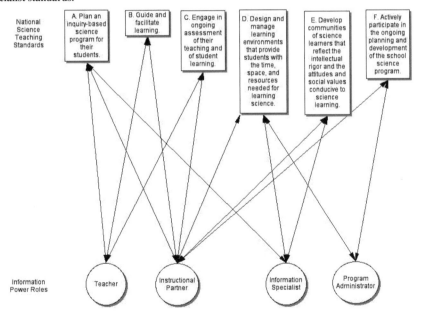

This graphical representation illustrates that the roles of the science teacher and of the SLMS enjoy a fair amount of commonality. Depending on the school context in which these educators work, the overlap may be even greater. These relationships are described in more detail in the subsequent paragraphs.

Within each of these sets of guidelines, activities for science teachers and SLMS are broken down into role elements. In Teaching Standard A, science teachers are to plan inquiry-based science programs for their students. In doing this, teachers will develop a framework of yearlong and short-term goals for students; select science content and adapt and design curricula to meet the interests, knowledge, understanding, abilities, and experiences of students; select teaching and assessment strategies that support the development of student understanding and nurture a community of science learners; and work together as colleagues within and across disciplines and grade levels (NRC, 1996).

To meet Teaching Standard B, science teachers are to guide and facilitate learning. Teachers should focus and support inquiries while interacting with students; orchestrate discourse among students about scientific ideas; challenge students to accept and share responsibility for their own learning; recognize and respond to student diversity and encourage all students to participate fully in science learning; and encourage and model the skills of scientific inquiry, as well as the curiosity, openness to new ideas and data, and skepticism that characterize science (NRC, 1996).

Teachers are often caught between the conflicting demands of needing to prepare students for high-stakes tests, the extra planning time required by inquiry-based activities, and the desire to integrate NSES principles (Humphrey & Carver, 1998). The SLMS may be able to provide crucial support to the teacher in this situation. In the Teacher role, the SLMS is knowledgeable about current research on teaching and learning and skilled in applying its findings to a variety of situations and works with students to access, evaluate, and use information from multiple sources to learn, to think, and to expand their general understanding of information issues (AASL/AECT, 1998). Especially using information technology, SLMSs can help students learn how to effectively complete classroom tasks with school library resources. In the Instructional Partner role, the SLMS is committed to the process of collaboration (AASL/AECT, 1998). SLMSs can share the burden of instructional planning and allow the teacher to focus on his or her instructional expertise.

To address Teaching Standard C, teachers of science are to engage in ongoing assessment of their teaching and of student learning. In doing this, teachers should use multiple methods and systematically gather data about student understanding and ability; analyze assessment data to guide teaching; and guide students in self-assessment. Teachers should use student data, observations of teaching, and interactions with colleagues to reflect on and improve their teaching practice. By using student data, observations of teaching, and interactions with colleagues, science teachers should to report student achievement and opportunities to learn; this information should be disseminated to students, teachers, parents, policy makers, and the general public (NRC, 1996).

Student assessment is also an area in which the SLMS has expertise. As Teacher, the SLMS collaborates with members of the learning community to analyze learning and information needs, to locate and use resources that will meet those needs, and to understand and communicate the information the resources provide (AASL/AECT, 1998). By interacting with the media specialist to discuss information needs, subject areas, and activities that require resource support, teachers can reflect on their own practice and identify possible solutions to student learning problems.

In the Instructional Partner role, the SLMS works closely with individual teachers in the critical areas of designing authentic learning tasks and assessments and integrating the information and communication abilities required to meet subject matter standards (AASL/AECT, 1998). With the assistance of the media specialist, teachers can undertake more informal and observational assessment techniques as well as work in collaboration with media specialists to perform assessment activities. This cooperation can improve the quality of assessment by including multiple viewpoints and by having external validation of instruments.

To meet Teaching Standard D, teachers of science are to design and manage learning environments that provide students with the time, space, and resources needed for learning science. In doing this, teachers structure the time available so that students are able to engage in extended investigations; create a setting for student work that is flexible and supportive of science inquiry; ensure a safe working environment; make the available science tools, materials, media, and technological resources accessible to students; identify and use resources outside the school; engage students in designing the learning environment; and develop environments that enable students to learn science (NRC, 1996).

In the Information Specialist role, the SLMS provides leadership and expertise in acquiring and evaluating information resources in all formats and in modeling for students and others strategies for locating, accessing, and evaluating information within and beyond the library media center (AASL/AECT, 1998). The media specialist can form a critical link not only to resources held by the media specialist but also to informal learning contexts such as museums and zoos as well as to experts and mentors in the community and available through the Internet.

As Program Administrator, the SLMS manages staff, budgets, equipment, and facilities to ensure that the media center environment meets the needs of teachers (AASL/AECT, 1998). Collection development can be influenced by the science teacher, but so can the physical layout of the media center and class scheduling to provide a site for group work and discussion.

In Teaching Standard E, teachers of science are to develop communities of science learners that reflect the intellectual rigor of scientific inquiry and the attitudes and social values conducive to science learning. In doing this, teachers display and demand respect for the diverse ideas, skills, and experiences of all students; enable students to have a significant voice in decisions about the content and context of their work and require students to take responsibility for the learning of all members of the community; nurture collaboration among students; structure and facilitate ongoing formal and informal discussion based on a shared understanding of rules of scientific discourse; and model and emphasize the skills, attitudes, and values of scientific inquiry (NRC, 1996).

As Instructional Partner, the SLMS leads the development of policies, practices, and curricula that guide students to develop the full range of information and communication abilities (AASL/AECT, 1998). In this role, the media specialist can promote resource evaluation and ethical use of information. Students can learn not just what information is available to them but how to judge its quality and its appropriateness to their needs.

As Information Specialist, the SLMS has a mastery of sophisticated electronic resources and maintains a constant focus on the nature, quality, and ethical use of information available in these and in more traditional tools (AASL/AECT, 1998). With the media specialist, students can learn when to refer to print resources and when to use electronic sources, as well as how to locate information in these resources quickly and effectively. With the use of digital libraries and other online community-building and research tools, library media specialists can provide access to unique tools that support the inquiry process and promote principles of investigation, analysis, and critical literacy (Bell, 2004).

To meet Teaching Standard F, teachers of science are to participate actively in the ongoing planning and development of the school science program. In doing this, teachers plan and develop the school science program; participate in decisions concerning the allocation of time and other resources to the science program; participate fully in planning and implementing professional growth and development strategies for themselves and their colleagues (NRC, 1996).

In the Instructional Partner role, the SLMS joins with teachers and others to identify links across student information needs and curricular content (AASL/AECT, 1996). With an overall view of the curriculum, SLMSs are well-positioned to help science teachers identify activities in other curricular areas that complement and reinforce student learning.

A barrier to standards-based teaching is the difficulty teachers face in locating and managing instructional materials (Weiss et al., 2001). As Program Administrator, the SLMS works collaboratively with members of the learning community to define the policies of the library media program and to guide and direct all activities related to it (AASL/AECT, 1998). The school media center's ability to support the science program with adequate resources depends on the strength of communication between the school library media specialist and the science teacher. This communication can ensure that a sufficient portion of the budget is earmarked for the acquisition, maintenance, replacement, and management of print and electronic science teaching resources in the media center's collection.

CONCLUSION

The comparisons presented in this chapter are intended to begin defining common ground between science teaching and school library media practice. Although science teachers and school library media specialists do not often collaborate at present, an examination of the professional principles and guidelines for the two roles indicates that a strong potential for productive, mutually reinforcing activity exists. Although movements toward federal- and state-mandated testing suggest that inquiry will be increasingly underemphasized, the two approaches are actually compatible (Linn, Davis, & Bell, 2004) and can best be accomplished through collaboration between the SLMS and the science teacher. By working together, these educators can transform the school library media program from "the information place to the knowledge space" (Todd, 2001, n.p.). More research, then, is needed into specific factors of school library media programs that affect science achievement as well as into extrinsic and intrinsic barriers to collaboration among science teachers and media professionals.

REFERENCES

Abbas, J., Norris, C., & Soloway, E. (2003). Teacher effect in system use within the Artemis digital library. In M. Mardis (Ed.), *Developing digital libraries for K–12 education*. Syracuse, NY: ERIC Clearinghouse on Information & Technology.

Abilock, D. (2003, January/February). Collaborating with science teachers. *Knowledge Quest, 31,* 8–9.

American Association of School Librarians and the Association for Educational Computing and Technology. (1998). *Information Power: Building partnerships for learning*. Chicago: American Library Association.

Baker, P. (2002). More content courses? Maybe not! *ENC Focus, 9*(3), 38–39.

Baughman, J. C. (2000, October 26). School libraries and MCAS scores: A paper presented at a symposium sponsored by the Graduate School of Library and Information Science, Simmons College. Retrieved January 3, 2004, from http://web.simmons.edu/~baughman/mcas-school-libraries/BaughmanPaper.pdf

Bell, P. (2004). The educational opportunities of contemporary controversies in science. In M. C. Linn, E. A. Davis, & P. Bell (Eds.), *Internet Environments for Science Education* (pp. 233–260). Mahwah, NJ: Lawrence Erlbaum Associates.

Churton, M. W., Cranston-Gingras, A., & Blair, T. R. (1998). *Teaching children with diverse abilities*. Needham Heights, MA: Allyn & Bacon.

Drayton, B., & Flick, K. (2000, May 3). Collaboration. In *Teacher change through collaboration with scientists: The model and "how-to."* Retrieved July 17, 2004, from http://www.terc.edu/papers/tepe/chapter7.html

Ellis, J. D. (2003). The influence of the National Science Education Standards on the science curriculum. In K. S. Hollweg & D. Hill (Eds.), *What is the influence of the National Science Education Standards? Reviewing the evidence, a workshop summary* (pp. 39–63). Washington, DC: National Academies Press.

Ercegovac, Z. (2003). Bringing the library into the lab: How information literacy skills make better science students. *School Library Journal, 49*(2), 52–55.

Horizon Research. (2002). The influence of the National Science Education Standards on teachers and teaching practice. In K. S. Hollweg & D. Hill (Eds.), *What is the influence of the National Science Education Standards? Reviewing the evidence, a workshop summary* (pp. 91–107). Washington, DC: National Academies Press.

Humphrey, D. C., & Carver, R. (1998). A case study if New York's SSI (NYSSI), 1993–1997. In A. A. Zucker & P. M. Shields (Eds.), *SSI case studies, cohort 3: Arkansas and New York*. Menlo Park, CA: SRI International.

Kracjik, J., Blumenfeld, P., Marx, R., & Soloway, E. (1999). Instructional, curricular, and technological supports for inquiry in science classrooms. In J. Minstell & E. Van Zee (Eds.), *Inquiry into inquiry: Science learning and teaching* (pp. 283–315). Washington, DC: American Association for the Advancement of Science Press.

Kulhthau, C. C. (1997). Learning in digital libraries: An information search process approach. *Library Trends, 45*(4), 708–724.

Lance, K. C. (2001). *Proof of the power: Recent research on the impact of school library media programs on the academic achievement of U.S. public school students*. Syracuse, NY: ERIC Clearinghouse on Information & Technology. (Eric Digest No. EDO-IR-2001-05)

Lance, K. C., Hamilton-Pennell, C., Rodney, M. J., Peterson, L., & Sitter, C. (2000). *Information empowered: The school librarian as an agent of academic achievement in Alaska schools*. Juneau: Alaska State Library.

Lance, K. C., & Loertscher, D. V. (2001). *Powering achievement: School library programs make a difference: The evidence*. San Jose, CA: Hi Willow Research.

Lance, K. C., Rodney, M. J., & Hamilton-Pennell, C. (2000). *How school librarians help kids achieve standards: The second Colorado study*. Denver: Colorado State Library, Colorado Board of Education.

Lance, K. C., Rodney, M. J., & Hamilton-Pennell, C. (2000). *Measuring up to standards: The impact of library programs & information literacy in Pennsylvania schools*. Harrisburg: Pennsylvania Department of Education.

Lance, K. C., Rodney, M. J., & Hamilton-Pennell, C. (2001). *Good schools have good librarians: Oregon school librarians collaborate to improve student achievement*. Portland: Oregon Educational Media Association.

Lance, K. C., Rodney, M. J., & Hamilton-Pennell, C. (2002). *How school libraries improve outcomes for children: The New Mexico study*. Santa Fe: New Mexico State Library.

Lance, K. C., Welborn, L., & Hamilton-Pennell, C. (1993). *The impact of school media centers on academic achievement*. Castle Rock, CO: Hi Willow Research.

Lange, B., Magee, N., & Montgomery, S. (2003). Does collaboration boost student learning? *School Library Journal, 49*(6), 4.

Lemke, J. (2000). Multimedia literacy demands of the science curriculum. *Linguistics and Education, 10*(3), 247–271.

Linn, M. C., Davis, E. A., & Bell, P. (2004). Inquiry and technology. In M. C. Linn, E. A. Davis, & P. Bell (Eds.), *Internet Environments for Science Education* (pp. 3–27). Mahwah, NJ: Lawrence Erlbaum Associates.

Mardis, M. (2005a). *The Relationship between School Library Media Programs and Science Achievement in Michigan Middle Schools*. Unpublished doctoral dissertation, Eastern Michigan University, Ypsilanti.

Mardis, M. (2005b). *Science-related topics in school library media periodicals: An analysis of citation content from 1998–2003*. Paper presented at the Centre for Studies in Teacher Librarianship Research Retreat, April 9–10, 2005, Canberra, Australia.

McKenzie, J. (2002). *Beyond technology: Questioning research and the information literate school*. Bellingham, WA: From Now On Press.

National Research Council. (1996). *National Science Education Standards*. Washington, DC: National Academies Press.

Novak, J. D. (1998). Metacognitive strategies to help students: Learning how to learn, *Research Matters—to the Science Teacher*. Retrieved January 3, 2006, from http://www.educ.sfu.ca/narstsite/publications/research/Metacogn.html

Rodney, M. J., Lance, K. C., & Hamilton-Pennell, C. (2002). *Make the connection: Quality school library media programs impact academic achievement in Iowa*. Bettendorf, IA: Mississippi Bend Area Education Agency.

Rodney, M. J., Lance, K. C., & Hamilton-Pennell, C. (2003). *The impact of Michigan school librarians on academic achievement: Kids who have libraries succeed*. Lansing: Library of Michigan.

Sosa, M. (1999). Inquiry-based learning in the library. In M. Sosa & T. Gath (Eds.), *Exploring science in the library* (pp. 131–160). Washington, DC: American Association of the Advancement of Science Press.

Stern, L., & Roseman, J. E. (2004). Can middle-school science textbooks help students learn important ideas? Findings from Project 2061's curriculum evaluation study: Life science. *Journal of Research in Science Teaching, 41*(6), 538–568.

Supovitz, J. (2003). Evidence of the influence of the National Science Education Standards on the professional development system. In K. S. Hollweg & D. Hill (Eds.), *What is the influence of the National Science Education Standards? Reviewing the evidence, a workshop summary* (pp. 64–75). Washington, DC: National Academies Press.

Todd, R. (1995). Integrated information skills instruction: Does it make a difference? *School Library Media Quarterly, 23*(2), 133–138.

Todd, R. (2001, July 9). Keynote paper: Virtual conference session. Transitions for preferred futures of school libraries: Knowledge space, not information place; Connections, not collections; Actions, not positions; Evidence, not advocacy. Retrieved July 15, 2005, from http://www.iasl-slo.org/virtualpaper2001.html

Todd, R. (2003). *Student learning through Ohio school libraries: A summary of the Ohio research study*. Columbus: Ohio Educational Library Media Association.

Todd, R., Lamb, L., & McNicholas, C. (1993). Information skills and learning: Some research findings. *Access, 7*(1), 14–16.

U.S. Department of Education. (2000, September). Before it's too late: A report to the nation from the National Commission on Mathematics and Science Teaching for the 21st century. from http://www.ed.gov/americacounts/glenn

Ulerick, S. L. (n.d.). Using textbooks for meaningful learning in science. Retrieved July 12, 2004, from http://www.educ.sfu.ca/narsite/publications/research/textbook2.htm

Valentine, D. (2003, January/February). School library media specialists and science teachers: Untapped potential for collaboration. *Knowledge Quest, 31,* 37–39.

Vassila, H. (2005). The information process supporting investigating scientifically. *Scan, 24*(11), 16–21.

Weiss, I. R., Banilower, E. R., McMahon, K. C., & Smith, P. S. (2001). *Report of the 2000 National Survey of Science and Mathematics Education*. Chapel Hill, NC: Horizon Research.

Whelan, D. L. (2004). A golden opportunity: Why "No Child Left Behind" is your chance to become indispensable. *School Library Journal, 50*(1), 40–42.

Technology Planning for the School Library Media Center: The SIMPLE Model

Stephanie Huffman
University of Central Arkansas

INTRODUCTION

The use of technology in education is increasing at an ever accelerating rate. Submitting assignments via e-mail, developing dynamic multimedia projects, and downloading documents are just a few of the activities students engage in across the country. Students demand for 24-7 access is only the tip of the iceberg. The need to have the equipment and training to remain one step ahead of the Generation Next students is a driving force behind technology planning (Anderson, 1995). The one area in a school setting that usually houses the majority of the technology is the library media center. It is the heart and soul of the information processing cycle of the school. The need for information access and the need for production materials and equipment are critical to the success and failure of our students (Lemke & Coughlin, 1998). Regardless of the size of the educational institution, the challenge remains the same: how does the library media center (LMC) help to meet the technological needs of the teachers and students? A conscious effort must be made on a continuous basis to focus on the need of both faculty and students, thus affecting current and future decisions (Fisher, 1995). The use of strategic planning generates an outline/guide for the LMC to use in making current and future decisions. Selecting the appropriate strategic planning model for technology planning sets the tone for the direction in which the LMC is headed.

When addressing LMC technology needs and selecting a strategic planning model, it is imperative to remember that technology integration begins in the classroom with the teacher. If the concerns of the faculty have not been addressed, then all the technology available will make no difference (O'Neil, 1995). Computers, printers, and scanners can become large paperweights collecting dust in the LMC. The basic reservations haunting the faculty can often be dealt with by involving them in the technology planning process for the center. Faculty will be more willing to undertake the changes that inevitability face them if jointly engaged in the technology planning process (Baule, 2001). Because the LMC services the entire school and the community, it is important to involve as many stakeholders as possible in its development and decision making (Baule, 1995).

In regard to the use of technology, the majority of students' today tower above their counterparts of 10 years ago, and this disparity in knowledge grows substantially each year. They are ravenous users demanding high-tech equipment, conveniences, and flexibility (Gordon, 2000). It is a given that LMC must provide quality hardware and software, yet it is nonetheless a struggle. The LMC wrestles to support the technical needs of the schools curriculum and to bridge the gap in the digital divide for those students who are technologically illiterate.

Tackling this massive task involves strategic planning—specifically, developing a technology plan for the LMC. The individual plan for the LMC should not conflict with the overall technology plan for the school or district but should represent a cornerstone in the foundation. There are many models available to aid in the evolution of an institution's technology plan. All too often, organizations sidestep this fundamental building block and unwittingly watch hundreds of thousands of dollars go to waste on poorly chosen technology (Hoffman, 1995). The LMC is not innocent in the wasting of funds. Money is spent on poorly chosen databases, little used equipment (often due to lack of training), and little used software. The SIMPLE model represents the best ideas and techniques for tackling the overwhelming job of planning for the technological needs of a school library media center (see Figure 1).

Figure 1. The SIMPLE model.

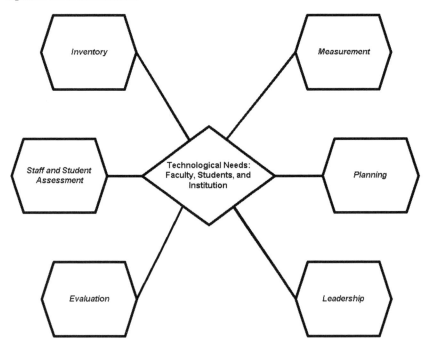

SIMPLE is an acronym representing six areas that should be addressed in developing and implementing a technology plan for the LMC. The six areas are as follows: (1) staff and student assessment, (2) inventory, (3) measurement, (4) planning, (5) leadership, and (6) evaluation (Huffman & Rickman, 2003). The SIMPLE technology planning model is a valuable tool for addressing the needs of faculty and students, as well as serving as a guide for the LMC. It was developed through an extensive seven-year review of research and literature on the subject.

Staff and Student Assessment

In developing a technology plan, it is essential to first appraise the situation. Three types of assessment should be conducted. The first should determine the technological skills and abilities of the LMC staff. This assessment should include a hardware and software ability survey. This assessment instrument will shed light on the training needed to ensure the day-to-day operation of the center. The second assessment should determine the technological skills and abilities of the faculty and students served by the LMC. This assessment should include a hardware and software ability survey. It is vital to determine the skill level of patrons of the LMC, because this will directly affect future decisions in the planning process and the selection of items for collection development. The third type of assessment should determine what technology is needed to support school curriculum. This assessment must address both present and future curricular technological deficiencies.

From these instruments a wealth of knowledge can be gleaned. Each establishes a fundamental baseline for the LMC helping the library media specialist (LMS) responsible for the planning process delineate the gaps that currently exist (Huffman & Rickman, 2003). Resources for developing technology assessment instruments are numerous and can easily be found online. The following are a few suggested sites:

- The *Effective Teaching with Technology Assessment* Web site (http://www.setda.org/nli2002/CD/EET/) was developed by the State Educational Technology Directors Association (SETDA). SETDA's membership includes educational technology directors and staff from the state departments of education of all 50 states, the District of Columbia, and the Bureau of Indian Affairs.

- The *CEO Forum on Education and Technology* Web site (http://www.ceoforum.org/) was founded in the fall of 1996 to help ensure that U.S. schools effectively prepare all students to be contributing citizens and productive workers in the 21st century. To meet this objective, the forum issued an annual assessment of the nation's progress toward integrating technology into U.S. classrooms.

- The *WWW 4 Teacher: Technology Assessment and Impact* Web site (http://www.4teachers.org/4teachers/intech/index.shtml) The High Plains Regional Technology in Education Consortium (HPR*TEC) is responsible for the development of this site. The site is an effort designed to meet the needs of K–12 teachers.

Inventory

Once staff and student assessment is addressed, a complete inventory of existing (in-house) hardware and software should be done. Hardware inventory should encompass all types, such as computers, peripheral devices, and networking equipment, the relative age of the equipment, the industry suggested useful life, and the last time any upgrades were completed (Ocasio et al., 1995). Common elements found on a hardware inventory form are (1) model and serial number, (2) purchase price, (3) date acquired and vendor information, (4) activity status and location, (5) description, and (6)comments.

Software inventory should include all LMC networking, application, and operating system software, relative age of each set of software, and version. Common elements found on a software inventory form are the following: (1) program title, (2) version, (3) license number and expiration date, (4) media format, (5) purchase price, (6) date acquired and vendor, (7) location and description of product, and (8) comments (Picciano, 2001). Collecting this data provides valuable insight into the planning and selection process. From this process several questions should be answered:

1. What hardware and software is currently available for faculty and student use in the LMC?

2. What hardware should be upgraded to expand its useful life?

3. What hardware and software is obsolete?

4. What are the fundamental baseline hardware and software needs to maintain the current technological status of the LMC?

5. Based on the data collected from both the inventory and the curricular needs assessment, what must be purchased to meet future curricular needs of the institution supported by the LMC?

Measurement

Measurement focuses on a spectrum of issues within the LMC, such as the following: (1) measurement of current LMC media (hardware and software); (2) measurement of current and future curricular needs based on state, regional, and national technology standards; (3) measurement of available new technologies; (4) measurement of standards (i.e., International Society for Technology Education, North Central, American Association of School Librarians, Association for Educational Computing and Technology, or other accrediting body); and (5) measurement of financial issues. In this instance measurement is defined as *sizing up* or determining *what areas are being met versus what is actually needed.* Applying this definition to each measurement issue sheds light onto pivotal areas where decisions must be made. The measurement element should be utilized in conjunction with both the staff and student assessment element and the inventory element, which is reflected by the inclusion of *measurement of current LMC media (hardware and software).* Even though these data were collected within the inventory element, its inclusion in the measurement element provides a bridge or link when determining what is needed to meet state, regional, and national technology standards when evaluating new technologies for selection, when addressing accreditation issues, and when targeting financial issues (budget and collection development). By pulling these three elements (staff and student assessment, inventory, and measurement) together a complete technological picture of the LMC is generated, thus answering vital questions and providing direction for future technology selection decisions. To address technology planning adequately, measurement must take place (Ferguson, 2000). Fundamental questions would target the following:

1. Does the current hardware and software meet the current needs of the LMC? Of the patrons serviced by the LMC? If not, where do the deficiencies lie?

2. Does the current hardware and software meet the standards as outlined based on state, regional, and national technology curriculum?

3. What new technologies are available to target deficiencies?

4. What funding or resources (or both) are available to meet the financial requirements?

Planning

Regarding planning, input from all parties and stakeholders (i.e., students, teachers, community members, parents, and administration) involved is valued (O'Neil, 1995). Technology plans are usually developed for a 3- or 5-year time span with major adjustments taking place at the end of the scheduled time period (Hoffman, 2002). The LMC technology plan should parallel the school/district plan. The planning component includes the following: (1) creation of a LMC technology mission statement; (2) development of technology goals and objectives; (3) creation of a technology committee; (4) training for deficient technology areas—LMC staff; (5) rotation of inventory—purchasing new, upgrading old, and replacement issues; (6) future academic challenges of the LMC based on the school/district technology plan; (7) funding issues—technology budget, grants, and community partnerships; and (8) policy development—selection, use, and possible inventory handling. There are a variety of planning forms styles available. Figure 2 characterizes a typical planning form but is based on the SIMPLE.

Student and staff assessment, inventory, and measurement are the driving force behind planning. Those three areas represent the data and information needed to develop a comprehensive technology plan for the LMC. These areas provide the data and analysis that fuel the decisions made during the planning component. Without those three areas, the planning phase is moot, leading to arbitrary decisions that do not target or address the LMC, parallel the technology plan, or the organization as a whole.

Figure 2. SIMPLE model technology planning form.

SIMPLE Model Technology Planning Form				
SIMPLE Planning Elements	*Issue*	*Planning Year*	*Due Date*	*Comments*
Staff & Student Assessment	Develop Staff Survey			
	Develop Student Survey			
	Data Analysis: Survey Results			
Inventory Control	Hardware			
	Software			
	Rotation Schedule			
Measurement	Develop Curricula Planning Instrument			
	State Standards			
	Regional Standards			
	National Standards			
	Data Analysis: Target Deficiencies			
Planning	Technology Committee			
	Mission			
	Goals			
	Objectives			
	Staff Development			
	Funding Issues			
Leadership	Technology Support Specialist			
	Technology Coordinator			
	Development of Technology Leadership Skills: Classroom Teacher			
Evaluation	Data Analysis: Annual Evaluation			
	Report Deficient Areas			
	Revise Overall Technology Plan			
	Revise Timeline			

Leadership

Leadership is the one area that is often underdeveloped. Technology leadership is vital. Leadership in the LMC begins with the LMS. The LMS should have a hand on the pulse of patrons, on curricula needs, and on the technology training needs of the LMC staff. With the guidance of the LMS, technology utilization and information access in the LMC opens up a fountain of ever-flowing knowledge (American Association of School Librarians and Association for Educational Computing and Technology [AASL/AECT], 1998). Technology is change; problems arise when the LMS staff is fearful of change. When such a problem arises, leadership issues weigh more heavily on the LMS. The LMS's guidance is pivotal and serves as a shining example for all. He or she must secure technology support for adequately training LMC staff, thus resulting in proper scaffolding for patrons lacking information access skills.

Tossing money at a one-time 1- to 3-day inservice workshop does not equate adequate training. Dedication by the LMS and central administration to providing comprehensive training on a yearly basis is the only viable option and should be unified with the overall school/district technology training plan. This helps to circumvent budgetary problems that might arise if the unit acted independently (Uebbing, 1995). It is essential that training not focus solely on hardware and software skills. The primary focus of any technology training is on the application process (Joseph, 1995). In this case, integration of technology and information access stimulates the curriculum. Furthermore, LMC staff need to be knowledgeable in technology areas to improve their productivity and to understand how to help patrons with technology integration and information access issues (AASL/AECT, 1998).

1. How can this piece of hardware or software be used to enhance the existing curriculum?

2. What hardware and software is needed to support the curriculum?

3. How will this hardware or software effect student learning?

4. What do my students and I need to know to use this hardware or software effectively?

If technology integration and information access is not the primary focus, then the technology becomes an add-on to the curriculum instead of an element of the curriculum (AASL/AECT, 1998).

Once training has been initiated, a network of support must be put in place for the faculty. A fundamental part of the network is acquiring a working relationship with the technology coordinator and a technology support specialist (Huffman & Rickman, 2003). The technology coordinator's primary functions are to seek out new sources of funding, to lead the technology planning process, and to cultivate a training program. The technology support specialist's principal areas of concern are to maintain the hardware and software and to provide input in the purchasing and functionality of new hardware and software. These two individuals provide support in technical areas for the LMS and can help the LMS align the LMC technology plan with the broader school/district plan.

The primary function of the LMS is to help colleagues on a daily basis with curriculum development in relation to technology utilization for information access and media development. It is not the responsibility of the LMS to be a technology expert but simply to provide guidance and support in the integration of media into the curriculum, which includes computer access. Yet it is essential that the LMS lead by example, by improving essential technology skills and abilities thus demonstrating to the LMC staff the importance of technology as an information access point. In addition, technology leadership should also be so far reaching as to include parent and community organizations. Setting up partnerships with these valuable groups can lead to strong advocates for the LMC program, a source of funding and volunteers, and a wealth of technology knowledge and experience (Fisher, 1995).

Evaluation

Finally, evaluation is the end of one cycle and the beginning of another. Every technology plan should allow for annual evaluation. This allows for minor adjustments in the overall plan (Baule, 2001). The evaluation should address the goals and objectives of the technology plan as to whether the goals and objectives were met for the year. Evaluation should also be comprehensive within each area of the LMC—inventory, selection, staffing, patrons, and training (Van Orden, 2001). A thorough evaluation of the entire plan should be completed at the end of the planning cycle, thus allowing for any overlooked opportunities to be addressed during the next cycle. Keep in mind the LMC technology plan should be a cornerstone in the school/district technology plan and should follow its evaluation cycle. Even if the school/district plan calls for an evaluation every only 2 to 3 years, a thorough annual evaluation should take place during the LMC's year-end review.

CONCLUSIONS

Regardless of the approaches chosen to meet the needs of faculty and students, the LMC must be dedicated to providing the equipment, software, and training needed to build the technology backbone for the programs and curriculum it supports. Flexibility and convenience is essential to maintaining student and faculty morale. The best way to address these areas is through strategic planning. Technology is an essential component of everyday life in the 21st century. When used appropriately and wisely, LMCs are transformed, and the flow of information never ceases. The technology planning process often focuses on acquiring hardware and software. Entire ranges of curriculum and instructional areas may be overlooked. The SIMPLE model provides a structure for developing a systematic analysis of existing resources while defining a successful technology plan, as well as identifying links between each component part. SIMPLE helps the planner maintain focus on the critical issues, thus meeting the technological needs of the LMC while simultaneously addressing the technology needs of the institution.

REFERENCES

American Association of School Librarians and Association for Educational Computing and Technology. (1998). *Information Power: Building partnerships for learning.* (1998). Chicago: American Library Association.

Anderson, L. S. (1995). Making dreams come true! How to write a technology plan. *Multimedia Schools*, 2(5), 15–19.

Baule, S. M. (1995). Planning for technological support: Help! Why isn't the smiley face smiling? *Technology Connection, 2* (2), 12.

Baule, S. M. (2001). *Technology planning for effective teaching and learning.* Worthington, OH: Linworth.

Ferguson, D. B. (2000). Moving beyond the shopping-cart mentality. *Curriculum Administrator, 36*(7), 52–55.

Fisher, F. (1995). *Growing healthy technology: A process for developing effective strategies to integrate education and technology.* Yakima, WA: Educational Technology Support Center.

Gordon, D. T. (2000). *The digital classroom: How technology is changing the way we teach and learn.* Boston: Harvard Education Letter.

Hoffman, B. (1995). Integrating technology into schools: Eight ways to promote success. *Technology Connection, 2*(6), 14–15.

Hoffman, R. (2002). Strategic planning lessons learned from a big-business district. *Technology & Learning, 22*(10), 26–38.

Huffman, S. P., & Rickman, W. A. (2003, Spring). Keep it SIMPLE: Technology planning strategy. *Proceedings of Society of Information Technology and Teaching*, International Conference, Albuquerque, NM.

Huffman, S. P., & Rickman, W. A. (2004, August). Technology planning: The SIMPLE Model. *Educational Technology , 44*(4), 36–40.

Joseph, L. (1995, March/April). Cyberneting: Staff development makes the difference. *Multimedia Schools*, 36–39.

Lemke, C., & Coughlin, E. (1998). *Technology in American Schools: Seven dimensions for gauging progress.* Santa Monica, CA: Milken Foundation.

O'Neil, J. (1995). Teachers and technology: Potential and pitfalls. *Educational Leadership, 53*(2), 10–12.

Ocasio, L., et al. (1995, April). Great technology plans. *Electronic Learning*, 31–38.

Picciano, A. G. (2001). *Educational leadership and planning for technology* (3rd ed.). New York: Prentice Hall

Uebbing, S. J. (1995). *Planning for technology. The Executive Educator, 17*(11), 21–23.

Van Orden, P. J., & Bishop, K. (2001). *The collection program in schools: Concepts, practices, and information sources* (3rd ed.). Westport, CT: Libraries Unlimited.

Van Orden, P. (2000). *Selecting books for the elementary school library media center : a complete guide.* New York: Neal-Schuman.

TQM—Continuous Improvement in the School Library Media Center

Barbara Fiehn
Northern Illinois University

School library media specialists are facing changes in school management processes as school administrators move their schools toward more accountable management systems. These systems are frequently labeled Quality Schools, Total Quality Management, Data-Driven Decision Making, and Continuous Improvement. Quality Schools is part of the William Glasser Institute, and Total Quality Management is based on the work of W. E. Deming; both philosophies use processes based on Data-Driven Decision Making to improve the quality of education (Bonstingl,1996).

Continuous improvement is an underlying theme of Total Quality Management, which is described as "a philosophy and a set of graphical problem-solving tools"(Jurow & Barnard, 1993, p. 4). This philosophy leads individuals or organizations to adopt "methods and measurements to systematically collect and analyze data for the purpose of improving the processes identified as critical to the organization's mission" (Jurow & Barnard, 1993, p. 4). An example of a continuous improvement process is the Plan, Do, Study, Act (PDSA) cycle. This process asks that an improvement be planned and tried, that results be studied by collection data during the trial, and that action be based on the study data. A variety of tools are used to collect data. This chapter discusses the use of flow charts, consensograms, control charts, affinity charts, and customer feedback. "These techniques are used in determining the present status and then generating options for improvement" (Carson & Smith, 1993, p. 36).

This research report focuses on specific uses of continuous improvement found to be effective by participants. The library media specialists' application of continuous improvement in instruction is primary in this report. Application of continuous improvement in the management and consultative roles is briefly discussed here.

THE STUDY

Beginning in the fall of 1998, the research focused on 18 library media specialists in Minnesota who were learning about continuous improvement (CI) and were determining how a CI program could be implemented in their media centers. It began as a district initiative and ended as the researcher's doctoral dissertation. The purpose of the study was to understand how continuous improvement processes and tools could be used in library media centers. This was a qualitative (phenomenological) study. As the Media Services Coordinator, the researcher-author was able to visit buildings to see these efforts in action. During observations, documentation regarding continuous improvement processes was made. Notes, interviews, photos, and artifacts collected during the observations provided rich documentation for analysis, interpretation, and reporting.

Research Questions

The research questions were as follows: How is continuous improvement being used in the instructional, consultative, and management processes of the media center program? How has continuous improvement affected student achievement? Library literature indicated that TQM and continuous improvement had worked well in academic and public libraries. There is limited literature indicating that there were also school library media applications, particularly articles by Rux (1993, 1995). In beginning this research, the assumption was that continuous improvement would work in school library media centers even in the absence of available school library media center models with which to work.

Participants and Demographics

The school district consisted of 23 school buildings, 3 high schools, 4 middle schools (6–8), 1 K–8 school, each with one media specialist. There were also 15 elementary schools (K–5). The eight smallest elementary schools, with a total of fewer than 500 students, were paired and each pair was assigned one media specialist. The remaining units each had a full-time media specialist. The district student enrollment was 15,877; 23.3% of them received free and reduced meals, 20.54%, were non-Caucasian, 12.4% had limited English proficiency, and 10.4% received special education services.

All of the media specialists except one had a master's degree in school library media. Four of the library media specialists had three to five years of media center experience; nine had six to nineteen years of experience; and five had twenty or more years of media center experience. All participants had experience as classroom teachers before becoming library media specialists. There was one male participant, a high school media specialist. Within this report non-gender-specific pseudonyms are used for all media specialists.

Training

The Quality Academy program, designed for the Pinellas County school district, consisted of two separate two-day training sessions. The first two-day session introduced the historical and philosophical foundations of Total Quality Management, the Total Quality Schools system terminology, and basic quality tools. The second two-day training focused on classroom applications, development of classroom and school improvement plans, and use of system checklists based on the Baldrige Educational Criteria for Performance Excellence. The Baldrige criteria, based on the Baldrige National Quality Program, "provide a systems perspective for understanding performance management. They reflect validated, leading-edge management practices against which an organization can measure itself" (National Institute of Standards and Technology, 2002, para. 2). Most of the media specialists enrolled in the training as a cohort group; the first two-day training occurred during the fall semester, and the second two-day training took place during the beginning of spring semester.

District-provided training created a common knowledge base for the media specialists. Reinforcing the training, the media specialists participated in brainstorming, experimentation, and sharing sessions during district department meetings and in small groups. These sessions provided ongoing support and encouragement.

During the period of investigation, the media specialists concentrated their efforts on applying continuous improvement tools and principles to the school district's goals:

- High student achievement
- Safe and welcoming environment
- Effective and efficient operations

Working toward these goals, the media specialists focused on the CI principles of

- Meeting customer needs
- Students taking responsibility for their learning
- Streamlining processes

Using the CI Process

The media specialists tried a variety of continuous improvement tools in their efforts to collect data and measure the effectiveness of interactions with students and teachers. The experiences were shared at monthly media services departmental meetings. The monthly sharing helped spread CI innovations from media center to media center within the district. The sharing also provided a supportive environment in which problems and suggestions could be discussed.

As a means of validating observational and anecdotal data, the library media specialists were asked to reflect on their interactions with CI training and implementation. Reflective of a general consensus, one participant, Casey, stated, "Media staff in some areas are learning, planning, and using the training in isolation. Each building needs to commit to learning and using this system." It was easier for media specialists to work with continuous improvement in school buildings where administration and staff were using CI. In buildings that did not actively adopt CI, the lack of understanding of terminology, processes, and tools created barriers to be overcome.

Reflecting on three plus years of CI implementation, Pat stated:

> The thing continuous improvement left with me, in my head, was how you help the kids to help themselves. And so, that is a dramatic way of looking at it. In that way, it is easier to come up with ideas. How do you keep them engaged, how do you keep them responsible for their own learning, how do you keep them interested in what they are going to accomplish?

And Jordan noted, "I guess I am trying to find ways to be more efficient because we just don't have time to waste."

The library media specialists were working with continuous improvement in their library media centers, within the Media Services department, and for some, within their buildings. This variety of CI involvement created a variety of experiences and responses. Casey summarized the general feeling about the effect on the department by stating:

> Media personnel have grown together. Department communication has improved. Delineating our service, goals, and processes has helped the cohesiveness and interdependence of all of us. Bringing our issues forward and airing them with the whole group has put us all on the same page.

Other participants also indicated that the department members were sharing more and that the sharing of data was helpful. Alex said, "It would have been so helpful to have had the increased sharing earlier. We save so much time by not reinventing the wheel." Pat concurred, saying, "I enjoyed sharing ideas and curriculum plans with other media specialists."

Continuous Improvement Tool or Process

Existing models for the educational implementation of CI were based on classroom instruction. The lack of media center application models resulted in the media specialists experiencing frustration when trying to select appropriate tools or processes for specific application. Most library media specialists relied on the Process Improvement Tools handbook (Pinellas County Schools, 1998) received during training and on the ideas shared between library media specialists. Some of the media specialists also used the set of CI resource books purchased for each building by the Media Services department.

Jordan, one of the library media specialists who always searched for new applications of continuous improvement, said:

> You have to be creative; I keep the books on my headboard of my bed cause every once in a while I'll think of something and then refer to that. And I have some [books] in the professional collection at school and some in my office. I don't use them as often as I used to. Like last year, I used them more than this year. Some of it I have engrained; you don't have to go to the tools resources for some cases.

Many of the library media specialists expressed a desire for additional models of tool use specifically designed for application in the library media center. Because such models are not found in the professional literature, the library media specialists need to continue developing their own models and sharing them within the Media Services department.

Continuous Improvement in the Library Media Center Program

As described in *Information Power* (American Association of School Librarians and Association for Educational Communications and Technology, 1998), the library media specialist's instructional role is primary and involves helping students develop information literacy skills and life-long reading habits. The consultative role encourages collaborative planning of lessons with classroom teachers, team teaching of students, and assistance in locating and developing learning resources. The management role consists of all tasks necessary for the effective operation of the library media center. In this research study, media specialists found ways to apply continuous improvement processes and tools within each of these roles.

Instructional Use of Continuous Improvement

The researcher observed CI tools and processes used by library media specialists within their teaching processes and collected artifacts that represented that use when possible. The CI tools were identified by library media specialists during interviews as being important in gathering data for decision making about instructional needs, curriculum development, and student learning. Kris said, "It [data collection] really has been helpful, just in the way I deal with the kids and trying to make sure they can get what I am trying to teach them." Successful use of CI tools and processes was shared between the library media specialists. Analysis of research data showed that most library media specialists used only a few tools with which they had become very comfortable. These tools included affinity charts, consensograms, control charts, and flow charts.

Affinity Charts

An affinity chart is used to organize large groups of ideas into logical order. Encouraging students to read is a key activity of the library media specialist. Many participants looked at ways the continuous improvement process could help increase reading and meet students' reading interests. Trish talked about how she was "using affinity charts to get opinions on what students prefer to read and to aid in purchasing."

Sidney applied the affinity cart in another way. "I wanted the students to tell me what they need/want to learn more about pertaining to library 'stuff'. We used the results to do some lesson planning. This gave the students some input into what they were learning."

Consensograms

A consensogram is used to quickly obtain information for decision making or to get a feeling for how a group values issues or topics. Jordan detailed the use of consensograms to determine student reading tastes:

> During February I made several very large posters with "I love to read FICTION" and other genres and popular types of books. Each student, K–5, was given special colored dot stickers. For example, red hearts for kindergarten, blue dots for second grade. Students were given an opportunity to vote the way they felt about the heading on the poster. The fourth grade girls who suggested that I total each poster for each grade level added up these posters. This has helped me in ordering new materials throughout the school year. These posters were put on display in the media center afterwards for all to see.

The idea of using affinity charts and consensograms was adopted by many of the media specialists. Jordan brought masters of her designs to a department meeting for each of the media specialists. Several of the media specialists used these as models for similar data collection.

Sidney commented on her consensogram application to reading, "After book talks on Maud Hart Lovelace selections, students marked the one that they are most interested in reading. In the spring after reading the books, they [students] compared their fall selections to how well they actually liked the books." This comparison provided information to students about the perceived "good read" quality of the books, while giving the library media specialist added insight into the student's reading tastes. Pat took a slightly different approach to the technique:

> I wanted to advertise the Maud Hart Lovelace contest. Each time a kid reads a book on the contest list, he could put a sticker on the graph. We have a running tally of what is read. Also, the kids can keep a running tally of the book they liked best so far using another chart.

The consensogram was one of the most frequent CI tools employed by the library media specialists. It was the tool most often discussed in interviews, observed hung in library media centers, and collected as artifacts. The library media specialists noted that consensograms are easy to construct and administer, they provide a quick visual analysis, and students are willing participants in consensogram activities. While talking about quality tools, Corey said, "The quality tools I found most helpful were the affinity diagram and consensogram. Students responded well to these, and I liked having immediate results that students can easily see and understand." Many of the library media specialists developed creative adaptations of the consensogram chart process. These creative forms helped to keep the technique fresh and exciting for both students and media center staff.

Instead of the traditional column approach of a consensogram, one media specialist designed a tree with large leaves to represent the consensogram choices. Each leaf on the tree represented a book award nominee. Students signed their names by the appropriate leaf after reading a book. This not only tracked which books were most popular but also identified the students who were reading them.

Control Charts

A control chart is a graph that allows analysis of data about a specific process over time. Pat described a monthly graph showing which class had the most overdue books. "Overdue books are of course a big problem in all libraries. I thought a graph that visualized overdues by classroom would keep the problem visible for all the kids, yet would not shame anyone in particular." At the secondary level, Dylan said, "I am working on a chart for overdues. I did a graph chart. I am really frustrated by the high number of overdue materials."

Other library media specialists used control charts to track class behavior during times when the students were in the library media center while teachers had planning time. This helped the students assess their own behavioral record and identify when control measures needed to be taken.

In general, control charts worked well as a means of making behaviors visible. Students liked seeing improvements displayed and worked with each other to keep the chart data moving in a positive direction.

Flow Charts

A flow chart is a graphic representation of the steps in a process. Sidney integrated a curriculum goal with this quality tool. After helping students to depict the process of selecting and checking out a book through flow charts, Jordan said:

> Creating a flow chart is a fifth grade objective. This gave the students a real life application and helped the media center at the same time. We have a flow chart to show students the steps on how to check out materials using the laser gun at the desk. I would like to make more flow charts: how to find a book on the computer and on the shelves, how to use the index of a book, etc. The students like having the guide at hand if they forget.

Making a flow chart into a large poster for display was accomplished by using a poster maker owned by the school district. Although flow charts were not frequently observed in library media centers, they were often mentioned in interviews. Printed materials within the school district commonly included flow charts of processes. Many media specialists and their paraprofessionals constructed flow charts in order to evaluate procedures, routines, and tasks for effectiveness and efficiency. These flow charts led to revision of procedures and routings. One media specialist revised all processes at her checkout desk. This resulted in a redesign of the whole checkout area and much more efficient operations.

Obtaining Feedback from Customers

Evaluating a lesson or an activity is often difficult within a library media center because students are scheduled for a limited amount of time. As a result, quickly taking the "pulse" of a class is crucial. The *fist to five* evaluation asks for a vote to be indicated by using one hand held high. A fist indicates a negative response or zero, whereas five fingers indicates strong agreement. Using this tool, media specialists were able to evaluate student feelings about participation activities.

The "plus/delta process" is used with groups to identify two or three things that worked well and deserve continuation versus things that worked poorly and need to be changed to increase success. The plus/delta can be conducted using chart paper with columns, one each for plus and delta. This method works well with seated and large groups. The plus/delta can also be conducted orally and easily as students are lining up. In either case, the leader asks "what was a plus today." After obtaining two or three answers, the leader asks, "what were the deltas?" Shannon discussed using plus/delta at the end of a class:

> I'd like to think that I am responsive to the reactions of students to the lessons and projects. I know that I am always revamping lessons based on how I perceived it was going. Having the student impressions helps. Getting that imme-

diate feedback takes only a minute or two and allows me to adjust before I do the lesson with another class.

Many of the media specialists liked using the plus/delta strategy as well as using the fist to five voting technique to get quick, immediate feedback. Bailey said, "It's not that it's a bad idea, I'm just usually running too fast to query my customers."

Another method of obtaining feedback from students and staff is through use of an Issue Bin (Figure 1). The Issue Bin is usually a poster, but it may also be a jar, box, or other container used for collecting notes. A pen or pencil and a pad of sticky notes located near the Issue Bin facilitates the communication process. These Issue Bin notes can be suggestions for improvement of the media center, problems that need attention, requests of many types, and occasionally a "pat on the back." Issue Bins are also excellent to use in lengthy meetings or training sessions as a vehicle to allow participants to ask questions or make suggestions.

Figure 1. Student using the "Issue Bin" to leave a note for the library media center staff.

Setting Expectations

In order for learning to take place efficiently, students must understand what is expected of them. During CI training, the need for students to take responsibility for how the classroom operates was emphasized. Sidney worked with the students in each of the classrooms in her building to help them set their own expectations for behavior in the library media center. Sidney found "students know what they want for the environment. When they set the rules, they follow them better." At one elementary school, the library media specialist used a rain stick (a dried cactus stem that, when turned on end, causes seeds slowly to cascade inside, thus creating a rain-like sound) to alert students to undesirable behavior with a noticeable but pleasant sound. Jordan said:

> I think it made kids more accountable; they knew if I turned over the rain stick someone was misbehaving and it wasn't pointed out to the class they just knew it was like every time I turned over the rain stick each kid was self

checking themselves—there was no issue with it. I can turn over the rain stick without stopping my lesson. It is unobtrusive.

Many of the media specialists provided opportunities for students to set behavior expectations, which were then posted in the media center. One middle school made table tents with the media center rules posted on them as illustrated in Figure 2. Table tents are heavy paper, folded in half to form a "tent" when placed on a table.

Figure 2. Table tent used as part of behavior management in a middle school library media center.

The middle school developed this table tent to use when students need reminders about behavior. The library media center staff can either point to the part of the card that describes the undesired behavior or quietly ask the student to think about behaviors for improvement.

Scaffolds for Student Independence

One goal set by the media specialists was to promote independent use of libraries and information by students. Students can often work independently in the library media center with the assistance of job aids, checklists, charts, signs, and other assistance techniques. These scaffolds provide temporary prompts for students while reducing the time the library media center staff spends repeating directions and providing assistance for repetitive questions. Using scaffolds helps students to develop their independent work skills. Media center staff reported that use of scaffolds gave them more time to work with students and other staff needing their assistance.

The library media specialists improved shelf labeling and section labeling in order to enhance student and staff ability to find materials independently. This simple scaffolding technique was well received at all levels. Money was allocated from the Media Services department's supply budget to support the purchase of shelf and section labeling supplies. The funding encouraged library media specialists to undertake the evaluation of signage throughout their media centers. In addition to labeling shelving, some library media specialists added room maps, hanging signage, and other directional information to assist patrons. Improved shelf and section labeling made finding materials more efficient not only for students and teachers, but also for parents and volunteers working in the library media centers.

A variety of task aids and rubrics also help students work independently in the media center. Taylor defined this scaffold for independence by stating:

> [It is] when kids have rubrics [with] steps they need to go through to accomplish the product.... There is not a whole lot of question about what they need to do.... That keeps kids more focused, and also deadlines are [defined]. They can have two days in here. This is what you need to do. Here are the tools that you have to use: there are books, there are Internet sites… I'd say most of the kids are good about doing that.

Other scaffolds provided by library media specialists included guides for research, bibliographic citations and bibliographies, website lists, and general information about using library resources. Frequently, library media specialists and teachers jointly developed scaffolds to support curriculum assignments. In the computer lab, one media specialist developed a URL wall, which listed in large print the URLs of frequently requested sites.

Promoting Student Responsibility

A foundational concept in continuous improvement as applied to school environments involves turning over to students as much responsibility for their own learning as possible. The library media specialists actively searched for methods through which responsibility could be shifted from the media center staff to the students.

Like other schools, Jordan's media center converted to student self-checkout because of the belief that making students more responsible helps them develop social responsibility. Allowing students to check out their own materials and to check on what materials they have out, as well as when they are due, provides a sense of ownership and responsibility for the library materials. Jordan stated, "The side benefit is the saving of a great deal of staff time so that we can do other things."

The self-checkout process varied from school to school. On the elementary levels, student library cards containing barcode, name, and picture were prepared for each student. The cards were then kept in the library media center or classroom, or were given to the student. Some of the elementary media specialists color-coded student library cards by grade level. Others developed library card wall charts to store student library cards. Students placed their library card under the laser scan gun to bring up their library account in the automation system. Cards at the checkout station labeled "Check Out," and "Clear" allowed students to conduct their transactions.

Many of the elementary library media specialists adopted the use of student self-checkout and reported an overwhelmingly positive student response. Students were observed efficiently conducting their business at the checkout station and moving on to other activities. During one researcher observation, Jordan pointed out a recent innovation in the process. Because elementary students had begun crowding the checkout station, a colorful, seasonal floor mat had been placed on the floor. Only the student working at the station could stand on the mat. Other students were required to stay outside of the mat area. As Jordan said, the "mats are inexpensive and can be changed frequently to match curriculum, holiday, or seasonal themes." They instantly solved the crowding problem and added a festive quality to that area of the media center.

The library automation system used in the secondary media centers did not allow student self-checkout of materials. Secondary students were required to use their student ID cards as their library cards as well. Use of the ID card helps speed up checkout time. Student workers man the circulation desk, thus relieving the media center staff and allowing them more time to work on other tasks.

Another innovation came from analysis of a problem with reserved materials. Jordan explained:

> We have a small white board by the checkout computer that we use to list the names of students who have a book on reserve that is waiting for them to pick up. We found that several of our classroom teachers did not give the students our reserve note or gave it to them too late. We hold reserves for three days. This white board works better than notes! Kids can check it to see if the book they have on reserve is in. Other kids will tell student[s] their names are on this list.

After sharing the white-board technique in a department meeting, several media specialists tried the process in their media centers and reported that the solution worked well for them also. During researcher observations, white boards were in a number of media centers. Not only were they being used to alert students about the availability of requested materials but they also found use for posting other types of notices. The small white boards were inexpensive to purchase and easy to hang or display in strategic locations within the media centers.

Students frequently move from classroom or study hall to the library media center on a pass system. As an extension of this concept, the number of students in the library media center can be controlled through the pass system. This is particularly important on days or during class periods when several classes are using the facility. The use of pass systems varies greatly between school buildings. One system that seemed to work very well in the secondary buildings involved students signing up for the day and class period they wanted to be in the media center in advance. The students took a pass that validated their transition from classroom or study hall to the media center. These signup sheets can be used to limit passes by crossing off signup slots when space is reserved for class use. Putting the responsibility on the student to schedule a media center pass requires advanced planning on the part of the student, and the use of a regular number of signup slots eliminates haggling over times, dates, and regularity regarding library use. Thus, this preplanning also seems to decrease the number of students who use the media center as a place to "hang out."

The goal of controlling students flowing to and from the media center is to provide the greatest possible overall access, control the number of people in the media center at any one time, help students use their time effectively, and reduce the number of students "wandering the halls." Casey worked with a student to develop a poster for each of the study halls to help students remember the process involved in obtaining a pass to the library media center. These posters reduced the number of students making extra trips from study hall to the library media center in order to get a pass. The posters also helped remind study hall supervisors that students must preplan their library media center visits. Overall, Casey's building seems to have found a workable solution to the media center pass problem.

Improving Instruction

The media specialists are constantly seeking new or better methods of instruction. Many of the media specialists commented on keeping lesson plan files with notes detailing both the things that went well and those that needed improvement for future use. Feedback from students and teachers formed the basis for suggested changes. The sharing with and suggestions from other media specialists contributed to the constant search for instructional improvement. Alex talked about a primary strategy for improving instruction:

> At the end of the year, I always do a plus/delta; then I go back and talk to the other media specialists. For example, I haven't found the perfect way to teach the Dewey Decimal system that will attract tons of kids clapping and

hurrahing over that concept, so that was one of the things that came out as a delta. I went back to the group, the media group, and asked "what are you doing to teach the Dewey Decimal system so that kids will sit down and listen and really learn?" So there is always that sharing that I think is really important and then going back and saying "that really worked, that idea really worked."

Other library media specialists mentioned getting useful ideas from professional journals, conferences, taking classes, and talking to library media specialists from outside the district. Building a repertoire of instructional strategies and evaluative techniques is necessary for meeting the instructional needs of the wide variety of students using a library media center.

Consultative Applications

In the consultative role, the library media specialists worked closely with teachers to improve instruction and learning. This role relies on good communication skills. The library media specialist not only provides materials to support classroom curriculum but also works with the teachers as part of a teaching team. As teacher and library media specialist work together exchanging instructional methodologies, brainstorming assists in developing instructional plans, and the library media specialist readily suggests ways in which his or her role can assist the teacher achieve instructional goals (Turner, 1993).

The teachers frequently ask for consultation and planning with media specialists. Taylor is noted for having extensive knowledge of young adult literature; teachers take advantage of this knowledge:

Sometimes I work with the teachers in developing the rubrics; it depends on what it is. A lot of times, in language arts I do, especially if it is a book that they are doing that I have read. Also, I have teacher [Internet] sites that they can go to pull lesson plans from different places.

Owing to budget reductions, the elementary library media program changed beginning in the fall of 2001 from flexible scheduling to fixed scheduling. As a result, the consultative role became increasingly complex. Sidney commented on this problem: "Keeping up the dialogue with teachers especially now that we are on fixed schedule and keeping that open so that they aren't just using us as a place to drop the kids off" is a challenge under the new policy. Pat has tried to reduce this problem through careful planning:

Every year I am very clear with the teachers about what I can do with their kids and what my curriculum goals are for the year. I ask them what they want me to do. I get a lot of response from the teachers. Part of the continuous improvement is just knowing what needs to be done and having it clearly stated. It was helpful to me to decide for each grade what needed to be done and have it in writing.

All of the elementary library media specialists commented on how drastically this change had altered not only their teaching but their ability to meet and plan with teachers. They expressed frustration with having students scheduled for classes while teachers had planning time. They indicated that it is difficult to get teams to meet before or after school. Frequently, the time for teachers and the library media specialist to plan is "on the run" as they pass within the building.

The secondary library media specialists also saw the effect of budget reductions. Bailey commented on the effect of losing elementary flexible scheduling:

I think we are going to see the problems and the negative results of our elementarys [library media specialists] being prep providers. The skills the kids come in with now are without the conductivity to an assignment that they were providing before. Now they're just providing it [skills instruction] because they have to have the kids in there [the library media center], where before it was a meaningful experience. They are trying their darnedest to make it meaningful. But you know what, it's a different egg. I think we are going to reap what we sow in that it's not going to be as nice for the students and the staff trying to educate them in the higher levels.

The secondary media specialists noted the lack of planning time with teachers since their paraprofessional work time has been reduced 50 percent. Within their buildings department planning time had been virtually eliminated, reducing even more their chance for planning with teachers.

Administrative Applications

Several of the media specialists made specific attempts to apply continuous improvement processes to the management areas of their media center. Tory was concerned about her "follow-through on concerns" expressed by customers. A solution was to keep a log of concerns and notes about how they were handled. Tory felt less likely to forget or put off dealing with a concern if records were kept.

During this initial period of the continuous improvement program, two of the library media centers were being refurbished. Tory had new carpeting installed. This provided the chance to "relocate materials for most efficient access for student, teachers, and staff." After requesting user suggestions, Tory developed a new floor plan. As Tory worked on the floor plan, consideration was given to traffic flow, instructional space, and recreational reading areas, and additional display shelving was added with the innovative use of plastic rain gutters.

The ceiling, lighting, windows, and carpeting in Austin's library media were replaced. Austin said, "Because the books and other library material will be boxed and moved, I have the opportunity to rearrange the location of materials to provide the most efficient access for students, teachers, and library staff." Austin and her paraprofessional had design input on a new circulation desk that, in Austin's words, "will streamline the workflow as well." They analyzed what was not working in the media center, and they made changes to help that system function more efficiently.

At this same time, Tory's paraprofessional resigned, leading to the hiring of a new paraprofessional. As Tory stated, the "new paraprofessional gave me the opportunity to rethink tasks and decide who should perform each task. The creation of a flow chart for the most efficient use of library staff time [including student media aides and volunteers] was very useful."

Taylor was concerned about meeting the expectations of the teaching staff, a primary user group:

I did the affinity chart [What are your expectations of the media center/media specialist?] in the mailroom with post-it notes and a pencil attached. The pluses were it was anonymous, so staff could be open and honest. I received good suggestions about atmosphere. They also gave me ideas to build into my web page. The delta is I didn't get the suggested book club up and running.

This researcher heard from Taylor's principal and teachers that Taylor more than met their expectations.

Alex, like many of the library media specialists, kept track of activity in the library media center:

> I keep charts in my files to see units that have[been] done… I kind of graph it so I can know where my heaviest load is going to be…for certain kinds of books. I am doing projections.

The tracking of classes taught, classes using the library media center, circulation, and other time-use activities was mentioned by many media specialists. In addition, many also mentioned using this data to keep their principal, staff, and parents informed about the library media center's activities.

Tracking lessons and requests from teachers and students is an important part of the administrative role of the library media specialist. This tracking provides important data for improving service delivery and program development. Finding effective and efficient modes of operation creates an environment in which customer needs are met with less effort and better quality.

CI's Effect on Student Achievement

Student achievement is a primary goal set forth by the American Association of School Librarians' *Information Power* (1998). This goal provides a strong focus for the school library media professional. Library media specialists in this study focus most of their instructional, collaborative, and management efforts on helping students reach high levels of achievement in reading at grade level and research skills.

Reading

Within the first year of continuous improvement, the library media specialists observed definite growth in student interest in reading. The library media specialists felt that the increased efforts to promote reading and to pay greater attention to students' expressed reading choices accounted for the increase in reading interest. All library media centers provided more frequent displays of popular books with reading lists and other reading promotions.

Sam discussed the goal of having students read at grade level:

> [All] students know what their reading score is so they know what books to choose. We have a Degrees of Reading Power program (DRP). If a student comes in and wants to check the reading level of a book, we can check the DRP to see if it is at [his or her] reading level. Students can use it any time. Our circulation has gone up because of this emphasis.

Since reading at grade level is a district goal, the media specialists have looked for ways to record what students are reading and to stimulate increased reading. Pat described student reactions to her charting efforts:

> The kids look at the reading charts and really talk about what they are reading and ask one another about the books they have read. I guess instructionally it would be that component of getting kids engaged with reading. Charting what they read and checking the diversity of reading by genres, award winners, etc.

Helping students identify interesting books at their reading level is an important part of increasing reading proficiency. Using a variety of techniques to chart reading interests, the media specialists have gathered information to develop the book collections with the specific idea of encouraging reading. At the same time, they have attempted to coordinate their purchases with curriculum needs. Bailey described a discussion she had with the building improvement committee:

> You are talking about boosting reading and math. I've started a collection specifically for those children. For math I've purchased those books that give kids the visual of what they are working on. They are working on fractions; here is a story the teacher can read to them. They will benefit twofold, they hear the language and see the pictures, and they are also getting a better understanding of that math skill.

The library media specialists' efforts to promote reading were observed in all library media centers. Reading lists, book displays, reading charts, as well as reading promotion programs, were ongoing, observable elements of the library media program. Figure 3 provides an example of the promotional effort to engage students in reading. This reading quilt filled a wall near the main building entrance. Students designed and contributed a quilt square based on the theme: *Grow with Reading*. This bright display announced to all a buildingwide emphasis on reading.

Figure 3. Grow with reading bulletin board made by elementary students to encourage reading in their school.

Research Skills

Closely connected with the library media program is the development of research skills. Conducting and presenting research are complex skills that are difficult for students and teachers to manage. Jordan commented, "I think graphing can apply well to the research model. They can see how they are progressing in the research. Are they on time, are they doing all the steps?" She developed a chart for each step in the process. As illustrated in Figure 4, students tracked their progress by moving a sticky note with their name from chart to chart. This approach allows students to see where they are, and it also helps the library media specialist and teacher be aware of how individual students and the class as a whole are progressing.

Figure 4. Elementary students tracking sticky notes on a search process chart.

EFFECTS OF CI STUDENT ACHIEVEMENT

When Corey was asked about the effect of continuous improvement on student achievement, he responded as follows:

> There is a positive effect on students because of the organization that is involved in it and the idea of always improving yourself. How can I make this better? How can I improve on this, not just in a lesson or unit but as a live long learning? I like the organization of it. Students become more conscious of the step-by-step things they do to solve a problem or to create a product or whatever they are doing. I see that as a positive learning.

The library media specialists' efforts to implement continuous improvement seem to have positively affected student achievement. Although there is no statistical baseline from which to gauge this positive effect over the district, evidence exists at the building level from increases in book circulation, increased reading test scores, and the observations made by students and teachers about increased success.

SUMMARY

Beginning with theory and classroom application models for using CI, the 18 media specialists in this study experimented with the application of CI in the school media centers. Evidence collected during this study indicates that the library media specialists discovered how to use CI in their library media center programs. Consistent applications of CI tools were visible in library media centers across the school district. The media specialists were able to identify how using CI had positive effects on student achievement, interactions with teachers, and the operation of their media centers. The use of CI in reading and research skills was particularly noted. All of the participating media specialists indicated that they would continue to use consensograms, control charts, affinity charts, and customer feedback. They also wanted to continue learning new applications of CI.

The need for accountability in K–12 education is not likely to go away. Media specialists in this study found that using CI processes and tools allowed them to document the media center program in new and effective ways. The research presented in this report provides a small window into the CI processes. Using CI is not a matter of just tools but a whole way of thinking about and documenting how media specialists should function. Since the end of the study, the researcher has shared with school library media students some of the processes and tools of continuous improvement. These students have reported their own success with using the continuous improvement strategies.

REFERENCES

American Association of School Librarians and Association for Educational Communications and Technology. (1998). *Information Power: Building partnerships for learning.* Chicago: American Library Association.

Bonstingl, J. J. (1996). *Schools of quality: An introduction to total quality management in education* (2nd ed.). Alexandria, VA: Association for Supervision and Curriculum Development.

Bradburn, F. B. (1999). *Output measures for school library media program.* New York: Neal-Schuman.

Carson, B. B., & Smith, J. B., (Eds.). (1993). *Renewal at the schoolhouse.* Englewood, CO: Libraries Unlimited.

Jurow, S., & Barnard, S. B., (Eds.). (1993). *Integrating total quality management in a library setting.* New York: Haworth Press.

Laughlin, S., Shockley, D., & Wilson, R. (2003) *Library's continuous improvement fieldbook: 29 ready-to-use tools.* Chicago: ALA.

National Institute of Standards and Technology. (2002, February 1, 2005). *Education Criteria for Performance Excellence* [Web site]. Retrieved July 15, 2005, from http://www.quality.nist.gov/Education_Criteria.htm

Pinellas County Schools. (1998). *Process improvement tools.* Largo, FL: Quality Academy.

Rux, P. (1993). TQM for libraries. *Book Report, 11*(4), 39.

Rux, P. (1995). Managing the trends with a little help from TQM and Taoism. *Book Report, 13*(4), 11–13.

Turner, P. M. (1993). *Helping teachers teach: A school library media specialist's role* (2nd ed.). Englewood, CO: Libraries Unlimited.

RECOMMENDED RESOURCES FOR CI TOOLS AND PROCESSES

Bonstingl, J. J. (1996). *Schools of quality: An introduction to total quality management in education* (2nd ed.). Alexandria, VA: Association for Supervision and Curriculum Development.
 Bonstingl provides practical tools and examples for applying the philosophy of quality to every level of the school. The strategies in this book are designed to help educators establish processes that foster continuous improvement for everyone involved in schooling. The book explains how educators have used philosophy to guide strategic planning, communicate more effectively with parents, improve students' learning strategies, and build a community of learners based on mutual respect and clearly defined aims. *Schools of Quality* is now available in a third edition.

Bradburn, F. B. (1999). *Output measures for school library media program.* New York: Neal-Schuman.
 A user-friendly "how-to" book shows how to take data already collected by library media specialists, use that data to talk about existing programs, and document the need for program change. Information, illustrated by examples and charts, explains which data will best support a given need, how to collect data so that they are reliable and useful, and how to interpret and use data effectively. Readers are also warned about problems in the use of these statistics. Case studies show the use of output measures.

Carson, B. B., & Smith, J. B., (Eds.). (1993). *Renewal at the schoolhouse.* Englewood, CO: Libraries Unlimited.

 Twelve authors offer strategies, based on their area of expertise, for effective management in the areas of personnel, time, finances, technology, change, and communication. The work is based on the concept that library media specialists are in a partnership with administrators and teachers focused on student achievement and the revitalization of schools. Charts, vignettes, cartoons, and memorable quotations emphasize key points.

Cleary, B. A., & Duncan, S. J. (1997). *Tools and techniques to inspire classroom learning.* Milwaukee, WI: ASQ Quality Press.

 Each chapter introduces a quality tool and provides several examples for classroom application at different grade levels. Each chapter focuses on the benefits to be gained by a classroom when the tool is used. Includes glossary.

Cleary, B. A., & Duncan, S. J. (1999). *Thinking tools for kids: An activity book for classroom learning.* Milwaukee, WI: ASQ Quality Press.

 Using scenarios from the classroom, Cleary presents an introduction to quality tools with clear guidance for selecting the right tool for the problem. Includes exercises, illustrations to help clarify concepts, a glossary, and suggestions on how to apply concepts to home situations.

Laughlin, S., Shockley, D., & Wilson, R. (2003) *Library's continuous improvement fieldbook: 29 ready-to-use tools.* Chicago: ALA.

 Provides an introduction to CI tools, when and how to use them, and examples of use in a library.

McClanaham, E., & Wicks, C. (1993). *Future force: Kids that want to, can, and do!* Chino Hills, CA: PACT Publishing.

 The tools and techniques of TQM translated for use by teachers to assist them in showing students to work with the concepts of continuous improvement. Presented as an interactive learning process, this book enables students to apply analytical and technical tools and social skills in the classroom.

Tague, N. R. (1995). *The quality toolbox.* Milwaukee, WI: ASQ Quality Press.

 This easy to use resource provides instructions for using more than 50 tools. Included are matrices and flow charts, data collection and analysis techniques, and other tools for analyzing processes, discovering causes, and generating ideas. It also includes many diagrams, charts, and checklist examples, as well as a tool matrix chart to help users find the right tool for a particular situation.

An Examination of the Correlation of Research Information Literacy Competence and Socioemotional Behavior among High School Students

Lesley S. J. Farmer

California State University, Long Beach

INTRODUCTION

The purpose of this research was to investigate the degree of correlation of information literacy competency and socioemotional behavior of high school students. Specifically, three assessment instruments were administered to a sample of 9th- and 11th-grade students in Orange County, California. Respondents indicated the relative degree of their information literacy competency and socioemotional behavior. Sample research reports of those students were rated by their teachers. Correlation statistics tested hypotheses linking literacy and behavior. Persistence and "getting along" were the best predictors of information literacy and research success.

K–12 library media programs are attempting to establish correlations between well-implemented library service and student achievement. In terms of curriculum, school librarians tend to focus on information literacy. In attempts to measure information literacy competency, professionals are examining student research processes and developing corresponding rubrics (see Appendix for an example). School librarians are using those rubrics more specifically to assess student work, although such work is difficult to generalize and extrapolate or perform on a large scale.

These assessments tend to focus on cognitive skills, with little regard to students' socioemotional-motivational competence. Conducted by Carol Kuhlthau (1983), one seminal work in this area tracked students' emotional status during their research process. However, little research has been conducted in the area of emotional readiness with respect to information literacy. Just as with reading readiness, there may be a developmental and psychological aspect that influences student success with regard to information literacy.

Ellis and Bernard (1983) have led the research in socioemotional behavior therapy, which examines students' affective-motivational characteristics as contributing independently from students' cognitive characteristics to student achievement. On a broader scale, the Collaborative to Advance Social and Emotional Learning (2003) have identified key social and emotional competencies, which include many that align with information literacy, such as problem identification and solving, communication skills, and social skills of cooperation and help seeking. Thus, as students exhibit positive socioemotional behavior, they may be more likely to achieve information literacy competency.

Based on these premises, this research investigated the correlation of socioemotional behavior and information literacy competencies of sample high school students. The goal was to determine whether affective domain factors needed to be considered when teaching these competencies to students.

RESEARCH QUESTIONS

Based on the statement of the problem, the guiding research questions were as follows:

1. To what degree does a correlation exist between students' socioemotional behavior status and students' research information literacy competence?

2. To what degree does a correlation exist between students' socioemotional behavior status and students' research project quality?

If a significant correlation exists, then the next step in socioemotional behavior therapy may be investigated. Specifically, school librarians would focus on critical affective and behavior competencies within the information literacy framework and provide effective interventions so that students would have opportunities to learn and practice these behaviors during the research process.

This research builds on the research that American Association of School Librarians (AASL) is conducting to ensure high-quality library media programs that support the mission of assuring that students and staff are effective users of ideas and information. It also builds on Farmer's (2003) research regarding the perceptions of school community members toward the AASL factors. The project also links to various research correlating information literacy standards and student achievement (Goodin, 1991; Harada & Yoshina, 1997; Lance, 2002).

METHODOLOGY

The strategy for answering the research questions consisted of administering three assessment instruments to 72 9th graders and 41 11th graders in an Orange County high school. The 9th-grade classes were designated as gifted and talented, and the 11th-grade classes were not so designated.

One instrument consisted of a research process rubric adapted from Colorado's (Colorado State Library and Adult Education Office and Colorado Educational Media Association, 1997) and Grover's (Grover, Lakin, & Dickerson, 1997) work on information literacy competency. A parallel rubric, measuring the quality of a research product, was also adapted from these sources and the AASL/Association for Educational Communications and Technology (AASL/AECT; 1998). The instruments were used and validated by the investigator for the Tamalpais Union High School District (Redwood High School Research Study Group, 1999). The research product instrument was used to analyze sample student research reports as a cross-validation of student self-assessment of research information literacy competency. The Students' Foundation for Achievement and Socioemotional Well-Being Inventory (Bernard & Laws, 1988) was used as a third instrument; it has been validated for use with 10 to 17 year olds.

Specifically, at the beginning of a research project, four 9th-grade classes (all with Teacher A) and two 11th-grade classes (both with Teacher B) self-completed the Students' Foundation for Achievement and Socioemotional Well-Being Student Form (Bernard, 2003) and the Research Process Rubric (Redwood High School Research Study Group, 1999). At the end of the research project, the teacher completed the Research Product Rubric (Redwood High School Research Study Group, 1999).

The scores were coded and entered into a spreadsheet. The process rubric was coded from 1 (*emerging*) to 4 (*exceptional*), and the product rubric was coded from 1 (*unsatisfactory*) to 6 (*exceptional*); these scores were treated as ordinal numbers. Grade level and gender were also coded and entered. A code number was generated for each student to link the three instruments while insuring confidentiality. The data were then imported into SPSS version 12 (2003).

Exploratory statistics were generated to reveal potential patterns. It was suspected that gender and grade might be significant factors, so the data were desegregated by these two factors as well.

FINDINGS

Socioemotional Well-Being

Before determining the degree of correlation between socioemotional well-being and research processes or products, the investigator examined patterns within this 25-factor set of measurements. Bernard (2003) statistically analyzed the 25 factors, dividing them into five distinguishing attributes: confidence (A1), persistence (A2), organization (A3), getting along (A4), and emotional resilience (A5). Confidence applied to new experiences, meeting people, communicating, and doing homework. Persistence applied to concentrating, trying even when work is hard, and checking one's work. Organization dealt with writing down directions, planning, and having needed sources for doing homework. Getting along referred to listening, following directions, cooperating, and begin sensitive to others. Emotional resilience dealt with self-control and overcoming upsetting situations.

Initially, an independent samples *t* test was conducted on these five attributes to determine whether boys and girls represented the same population, which they did. When the data for the two grades were compared, it was found that 9th graders rated themselves significantly higher/more mature than 11th grades for persistence (7.82 vs. 7.29 with .033 significance) and organization (8.16 vs. 7.51 with .026 significance), which was entirely accounted for by the 9th-grade girls' responses. Initial data analysis of the five attributes did not reveal enough differentiation, so individual factors were analyzed.

Gender

An independent samples *t* test was conducted to determine whether boys and girls represented the same population. For each gender as a whole, there was no difference in process and product. Three socioemotional factors were found to be significantly different:

- F11: I make sure I understand the teacher's instructions before beginning to work.
- F17: I listen and do not interrupt when someone else is speaking.
- F18: I am sensitive to the feelings of others, and I volunteer to help others in need.

In each case, girls indicated that they exhibited these behaviors more than boys.

Factor	Girls' Mean	Boys' Mean	Significance*
11	8.10	6.47	.002
17	8.23	7.65	.018
18	8.60	6.58	.000

Correlation is significant at the .01 level (two-tailed) or significant at the .05 level (two-tailed) for this and the following tables.

When the data for the two grades were treated separately, results were different. Among the 11th graders, there was no significant difference in socioemotional well-being factors. However, the girls exhibited significantly more mature behaviors than boys along seven factors:

- F6: I continue to try, even when schoolwork is hard.
- F11: I make sure I understand the teacher's instructions before beginning to work.
- F13: I write down assignments and when they have to be completed.
- F15: I am organized in doing schoolwork.
- F18: I am sensitive to the feelings of others, and I volunteer to help others in need.
- F22: I am good at controlling my temper.

Factor	Girls' Mean	Boys' Mean	Significance
F6	8.53	7.26	.045
F11	8.50	6.94	.000
F13	8.39	5.53	.007
F15	8.37	6.76	.041
F18	8.53	7.15	.015
F22	7.68	6.76	.003

Research process behavior self-assessment and teacher-assessed research products were also analyzed using independent samples *t* tests. In terms of gender, 11th-grade girls outperformed boys in terms of adhering to the assignment (3.45 girls' mean vs. 3.16 boys' means with a .036 significance). Among the 9th graders, there was no significant difference in process or product.

To see whether grade level made a difference in the findings about gender, independent samples *t* tests were performed for boys and for girls. There was no significant difference between 9th-grade boys and 11th-grade boys. Between 9th-grade girls and 11th-grade girls, there was no significant difference in socioemotional attributes, but in terms of products, 9th-grade girls performed significantly better (correlation at the .01 level of confidence) for research product indicators. Additionally, they self-assessed their research process skills significantly higher (correlation at the .01 level of confidence) than 11th-grade girls in terms of

- determining information need,
- developing search strategy,
- assessing an comprehending information, and
- interpreting and organizing information.

Grade

Seeing these results, the investigator used an independent samples *t* test to determine whether there was a significant difference between 9th graders and 11th graders in terms of the measures of the three instruments.

The following individual socioemotional factor means differed significantly between the two grades:

- F1: I volunteer to participate in a new activity/experience.
- F6: I continue to try, even when schoolwork is hard.
- F7: I concentrate well when working.
- F9: I put in the effort necessary to complete difficult class and homework assignments.
- F10: I am persistent in doing schoolwork.
- F11: I make sure I understand the teacher's instructions before beginning to work.
- F17: I listen and do not interrupt when someone else is speaking.
- F19: I understand that by following important rules, I help make my world a safer and better place to live and learn.
- F20: I get along well with others.
- F24: When I get upset about something, I am good at being able to calm down quickly.

In each case, the 9th graders rated themselves more positively than the 11th graders.

Factor	9th Graders' Mean	11th Graders' Mean	Significance
F1	6.68	5.41	.024
F6	7.93	7.22	.023
F7	7.28	6.44	.050
F9	7.96	7.05	.002
F10	8.22	7.10	.010
F11	7.76	6.59	.004
F17	8.25	7.46	.037
F19	8.20	7.49	.000
F20	8.42	8.20	.006
F24	6.72	6.34	.018

In terms of research processes, 11th graders self-assessed their skill significantly higher than 9th graders for the following:

- Process 1: Determines information need
- Process 2: Develops search strategy
- Process 5: Interprets and organizes information

Ninth graders self-assessed their skill significantly highly than eleventh graders for Process 7: Evaluates product and process.

Process	9th Graders' Mean	11th Graders' Mean	Significance
1	3.29	3.90	.011
2	3.31	4.00	.008
5	3.32	4.07	.012
7	3.31	2.95	.004

The teacher evaluated the students' work using the research product rubric. For three of the five target indicators, 9th graders outperformed 11th graders to a significant degree:

- Indicator 1: Adherence to assignment
- Indicator 2: Organization
- Indicator 3: Proof and justification

Indicator	9th Graders' Mean	11th Graders' Mean	Significance
1	4.31	3.32	.046
2	4.64	3.10	.000
3	4.78	3.05	.001

Well-Being and Research

On the face of it, it appeared that older students were less mature; they conducted research more effectively and yet wrote poorer research products. However, the differences in research product may be attributed to differences in the assignment and differences in the teachers' scoring of the product.

Thus, a follow-up Kendall tau test was used to determine the degree of correlation among the following:

- socioemotional well-being and research processes,
- socioemotional well-being and research product, and
- research processes and research product.

First, the five socioemotional attributes were correlated to processes and product indicators. There was a significant positive correlation between socioemotional well-being and the research process overall:

Attribute	Correlation Coefficient	Significance
Persistence	.141	.034
Getting along	.247	.000
Emotional Resilience	.175	.009

Among 11th graders, the correlations were as follows:

Attribute	Correlation Coefficient	Significance
Persistence	.290	.012
Getting along	.300	.008

In contrast, the correlation between socioemotional well-being and the research process overall (using Kendall tau test) generated these findings for 9th graders:

Attribute	Correlation Coefficient	Significance
Self-confidence	.256	.003
Persistence	.191	.024
Getting along	.307	.000
Emotional Resilience	.253	.003

Next, the seven research processes were analyzed separately to determine finer distinctions in the correlations. Overall findings were as follows:

	Process 6: Communicate	Process 7: Evaluate
Attribute	Correl. Coef./Significance	Correl. Coef./Significance
Self-confidence	.297/.001	.236/.002
Persistence	.345/.000	.273/.000
Organization	.013/.890	.225/.003
Getting Along	.389/.000	.231/.002
Emotional Resilience	.315/.001	.256/.001

Grade level seemed to be a significant variable, so a follow-up Kendall tau test was used to analyze the data. For 9th graders, the results were as follows:

	Self-confidence	Persistence	Organization	Getting Along	Emotional Resilience
Process Indicator	Correl. Coef./Signif.	Correl. Coef. /Signif.	Correl. Coef. /Signif.	Correl. Coef./ Signif.	Correl. Coef./ Signif.
ID task	NS	.205/.027	NS	.206/.026	.237/.011
Strategize	NS	.188/.044	NS	.215/.021	NS
Comprehend	.330/.000	NS	NS	.289/.002	.217/.019
Interpret	.268/.004	NS	NS	.289/.002	NS
Communicate	.203/.031	NS	.240/.009	.245/.009	.236/.012
Evaluate	.197/.037	.244/.010	.200/.033	.228/.016	.273/.004

Note: NS = nonsignificant.

For 11th graders, the results were as follows:

	Persistence	Getting Along	Emotional Resilience
Process Indicator	Correl. Coef./Signif.	Correl. Coef./ Signif.	Correl. Coef./Signif.
Communicate	.332/.008	.287/.023	.284/024
Evaluate	.300/.018	NS	NS

Note: NS = nonsignificant.

To determine whether individual socioemotional behaviors correlated with research processes, follow-up Kendell tau tests were administered. The most highly correlated behaviors were as follows:

- 1: Confidence: I volunteer to participate in a new activity/experience.
- 6: Persistence: I continue to try, even when schoolwork is hard.
- 8: Persistence: I check my work when finished to make sure it's correct.
- 9: Persistence: I put in the effort necessary to complete difficult class and homework assignments.
- 10: Persistence: I am persistent in doing schoolwork.
- 15: Organization: I am organized in doing schoolwork.
- 16: Getting along: I am good at working cooperatively with my classmates on projects [only for 11th graders].

- 23: Emotional resilience: When I get upset about something, I am good at being able to calm down quickly.

- 24: Emotional resilience: I am good at bouncing back from something that happens that upsets me.

Behavior	Overall	9th Grade	11th Grade	Girls	Boys
1	C6: .187/.016 C7: .273/.000		C7: .399/.002	C6: .227/.033 C7: .292/.007	C7: .245/.032
6	C6: .201/.011 C7: 209/.009		C6: .304/.021 C7: .276/.007		C6: .284/.014
8	C6: .183/.017 C7: .269/.001	C6: .197/.042 C7: .264/.007		C7: 258/.019	C7: .272/.016
9	C6: .227/.004 C7: .264/.001	C7: .249/.013	C6: .442/.001 C7: .262/.047	C7: .350/.002	C6: .345/.003
10	C6: .249/.002 C7: .239/.003		C6: .400/.002 C7: .285/.031	C7: .301/.007	C6: .316/.006
15	C6: .208/.008 C7: .273/.002	C6: .259/.009 C7: .272/.006		C7: .273/.015	C6: .233/.040 C7: .202/.023
16	C6: .270/.001		C6: .438/.001	C6: .293/.009	C6: .242/.036
23	C6: .300/.000 C7: .265/.001	C6: .226/.021 C7: .241/.014	C6: .426/.001 C7: .306/.020	C6: .352/.001 C7: .283/.010	C6: .275/.017 C7: .290/.011
24	C6: .266/.001 C7: .252/.001	C6: .271/.006 C7: .244/.013	C6: .263/.045 C7: .272/.038	C6: 221/.040	C6: .307/.007 C7: .288/.011

Note: C6 = Process 6: Communicate; C7 = Process 7: Evaluate. Correlation Coefficient/Significance in terms of level of confidence.

Next, to determine the degree to which there was a correlation between socioemotional attributes and research product, a Kendall tau test was used. The attribute average in relationship to the research product average resulted in a .228 correlation coefficient (significance at the .020 level of confidence). By separate attributes in relationship to the research product average, only persistence was significantly correlated (.312 correlation coefficient with significance at the .01 level of confidence).

When the data were examined by grades, the differences emerged. For 9th graders, there was no significant correlation between:

- overall well-being and research product average or
- any one attribute and research product average.

In contrast, for 11th graders, the findings were as follows. The attribute average in relationship to the research product average resulted in a .275 correlation coefficient (significance at the .017 level of confidence). More specifically:

Research Product Indicator	Persistence	Getting Along	Emotional Resilience
Average	.242/.036	.325 /.005	.247 /.033
Organization	.285/.085	NS	NS
Proof and Justification	NS	.335/.009	.338/.007

Note: NS = nonsignificant. Correlation Coefficient/Significance in terms of level of confidence.

The most highly correlated research product indicator was proof/justification. Again, Kendall tau tests were used to determine the degree to which correlations existed between individual socioemotional behaviors and research product indicators. It was found that examining correlations by gender and grade level was more informative than obtaining correlations for the entire population, particularly because each subgroup had unique correlations that crossed research product indicators. The most significant individual behaviors were as follows:

Behavior	9th Graders	11th Graders	Girls	Boys
Confident meeting new people	D1: −.226/.017 D3: −.242/.012 D4: −.249/.011			
Check work when finished to make sure it's correct		D1: 304./.020 D2: .322/.014 D3: .297/.023		D1: .292/.008 D2: .290/.008 D3: .250/.018 D4: .234/.034
Put in effort needed to complete difficult assignments		D1: .344/.011		D1: .423/.000 D2: .280/.012 D3: .352/.001 D4: .378/.001 D5: .270/.015
Work cooperatively on projects	D2: −.278/.004 D3: −.280/.004	D2: .278/.039 D3: .340/.011 D4: .274./043		

Follow important rules for safety and have better world				D1: .231/.037 D2: .239/.031 D3: .324/.003 D4: .313/.005 D5: .310/005
Get along well with others	D1: −.245/.012 D3: −.283/.004 D4: −.271/.007	D1: .300/.026 D3: .340/.010	D2: −275/.012 D3: −231/.029 D4: 251/.020 D5: .236/.029	

Note: D1: Adherence to Assignment; D2: Organization; D3: Proof and Justification; D4: Language & Strategy Use; D5: Spelling & Grammar. (Correlation Coefficient/Significance in terms of level of confidence.)

The most surprising findings, however, were in regard to the degree of correlation between the research process (which was self-assessed) and research product (which was assessed by the teacher). Overall, there was no significant difference between the research process and product average. When individual indicators were compared, however, the findings were significant for most:

Process Indicators	Adherence to Assignment	Organization	Proof and Justification	Language and Strategy Use	Spelling and Grammar
ID Task	−.257/.001	−.366/.000	−.341/.000	−.365/.000	−.361/.000
Strategize	−.333/.000	−.449/.000	−.422/.000	−.438/.000	−.411/.000
Locate	−.223/.000	−.277/.001	−.294/.000	−.273/.001	−.252/.002
Comprehend	−.352/.000	−.432/.000	−.433/.000	−.411/.000	−.408/.000
Interpret	−.308/.000	−.444/.000	−.452/.000	−.484/.000	−.462/.000
Communicate	NS	NS	NS	NS	NS
Evaluate	.190/.020	.261/.001	.272/.001	.210/.010	.251/.002

Note: NS = nonsignificant.

For 9th graders, there was a significant *negative* correlation between the process average and the product average: –.321 with .000 significance. More specifically:

Process Indicators	Adherence to Assignment	Organization	Proof and Justification	Language and Strategy Use	Spelling and Grammar
ID Task	–.210/.038	–.222/.029	–.220/.032	–.267/.010	–.249/.015
Strategize	–.251/.014	–.271/.008	–.281/.006	–.306/.003	–.244/.018
Locate	NS	–.224/.031	–.288/.005	–.261/.013	MS
Comprehend	–.363/.000	–.336/.001	–.396/.000	–.355/.001	–.333/.001
Interpret	–.215/.034	–.235/.021	–.286/.005	–.373/.000	–.322/.002
Communicate	–.213/.037	–.228/.007	–.251/.016	–.281/.007	NS
Evaluate	NS	NS	NS	NS	NS

Note: NS = nonsignificant.

In contrast, for 11th graders, most correlations were either not significant or were positive:

Process Indicators	Adherence to Assignment	Organization	Proof and Justification	Language and Strategy Use	Spelling and Grammar
Communicate	.418/.003	NS	.467/.001	.337/.020	.333/.019
Evaluate	.341/.018	.559/.000	.570/.000	.506/.001	.337/.019

When gender was taken into effect, it was found that on the whole, girls' scores accounted for the results, particularly for 9th-grade girls (in contrast, for 9th-grade boys the only significant correlation between process and product was Interpreting and Language/Strategy Use, which had a –.374 correlation coefficient and .016 significance).

DISCUSSION

This study intended to answer the following research questions:

1. To what degree does a correlation exist between students' socioemotional behavior status and students' research information literacy competence?

2. To what degree does a correlation exist between students' socioemotional behavior status and students' research project quality?

It also examined the possible correlation between students' self-perceptions of their ability to follow a research process and teachers' perception of students' research products.

It was found that gender and grade made a significant difference in terms of self-perceptions and teachers' evaluations relative to these behaviors and products.

Instrumental Inner-Correlations

Socioemotional Well-Being

Before looking at the correlations, it was useful to examine students' self-perceptions about their socioemotional well-being. 9th graders tended to rate their behaviors more highly, mainly for the attributes of persistence, organization, and getting along; in particular, 9th-grade girls rated their behavior higher than their male peers as well as their 11th-grade female counterparts. The factors that were found to be significant followed the expected behavior styles of females: waiting to understand teachers' instructions, not interrupting, and being sensitive to others' feelings. However, by 11th-grade, boys' and girls' self-perceptions of behaviors did not differ significantly. When comparing *all* girls and *all* boys, though, girls self-reported more mature socioemotional behaviors in terms of trying hard, being organized, and self-regulating emotions. When these results are examined in light of the students' research product as assessed by teachers, it appears that the study's 11th-graders self-assessed their behaviors more accurately and realistically than did the 9th graders. Because the 9th graders were designated as gifted and talented, they may have an elevated sense of well-being. Alternatively, 11th graders may find their studies more challenging than in freshman year and so self-assess themselves less optimistically. It would be useful to have parallel classes to test this hypothesis.

Research Processes

In terms of research processes, 11th graders self-assessed their skills significantly higher for the steps of determining information need, developing a search strategy, and interpreting/organizing information. Ninth graders thought that they did a better job of evaluating product and process. Gender did not seem to be a significant factor in self-reporting of research processes, but between 9th-grade and 11th-grade girls, 9th-grade girls thought they were more capable in determining an information need, strategizing, comprehension, and interpretation of information. Again, 9th-grade self-perceptions could have been accounted for by their gifted/talented designation, or it could be due to perceptions shaped by experience in high school courses that were more difficult and nuanced than middle school work.

Research Product

The 9th-grade teacher assessed the students' research product significantly higher than the 11th grader teacher relative to adherence to assignment, organization, and proof and justification. However, because the two assignments were different, it is difficult to determine the relative complexity of each aspect of the product let alone the teachers' differences in assessment. What *can* be examined, however, is the relative level of performance within each grade.

Socioemotional Well-Being and Research Processes

A significant positive correlation was found between socioemotional attributes and self-perceptions about the ability to conduct research. Overall, getting along and emotional resilience were found to be significant at the .01 level of confidence, and persistence was found to be significant at the .05 level. The two research process indicators that correlated most closely with socioemotional well-being were communicating findings and evaluating the process/product; for the population as a whole, all attributes except organization *as a whole* were found to be significantly correlated positively at the .01 level of confidence.

The subgroup that reflected the highest correlations for several of the attributes and processes was 9th-grade girls. Overall, the data seem to indicate that research can be a frustrating process, so being able to deal with obstacles emotionally and intellectually and to revise the work to a satisfactory conclusion are important socioemotional skills across grades and gender.

Communicating the Information

Persistently putting in the effort to complete difficult work was a significant factor to communicating the information, particularly for 11th-grade boys. For 9th graders, being organized in doing schoolwork was also clearly correlated with communicating. For 11th graders, working cooperatively with classmates on projects was another highly significant factor, particularly for girls. Being able to calm down quickly and bounce back when upset was significantly correlated for all subgroups.

Evaluating Product and Process

For 11th graders, particularly girls, evaluating the research process and product correlated closely with risk taking (willingness to participate in new activities and to try even when schoolwork is hard). Because girls in general are less likely to take risks, helping them develop this willingness will pay off in the research process. Checking work when finished to make sure it is correct appears to be more important for 9th graders. Being able to bounce back when upset is another significant factor, particularly for 9th graders.

Thus, teachers of 9th graders can help their students with basic study skills of organization and checking over completed schoolwork to make sure it is correct and adheres to the assignment. Teachers should also help students become more adept in their self-evaluations by taking "reality checks" of their work habits and reflecting on the repercussions of their behaviors on their final work. They can also help them with emotional skills of getting back on task when upset or frustrated. I-search research projects are a good way to incorporate this kind of emotive-metacognitive approach to learning; this kind of project consists of traditional research procedures and personal journaling of students' thoughts and feelings throughout the process. For 11th graders, teachers can help them take more intellectual risks and keep trying as part of a general strategy to aim for high-quality results.

Socioemotional Well-Being and Research Products

The potential correlation between socioemotional well-being and research project is particularly interesting because it compares students' self-assessment of their personal behaviors and the teachers' assessment of their academic work. For this population, the most highly correlated research product indicator relative to socioemotional well-being was "proof and justification."

For 9th graders, the behaviors that correlated negatively with research product indicators clustered around human relationships. Thus, those students who were more social tended to adhere less to the assignment, were less organized, had less substantial proof and justification, and exhibited less sophisticated language and search strategies. It could well be that they were distracted by their peers or asked peers rather than the teacher for advice. Eleventh graders, on the other hand, leveraged their social skills to improve their research project.

For 11th graders, persistence behaviors of checking over work correlated highly with adherence to assignments, and putting in the needed effort to complete difficult assignments related to organization, proof and justification, and use of language and strategies. Interestingly, these behaviors were positively correlated with the evaluation step of research processes for 9th graders, but they did not translate into significant correlations with research product indicators. Still, the finding indicates that high school teachers would do well to reinforce behaviors of persistence, revising, and checking final work to make sure all directions are followed.

There was one socioemotional behavior that boys exhibited that correlated significantly across all research product indicators: following rules. This finding would indicate that teachers should help boys in particular see the benefits of such behavior, that it has a good payoff.

Research Processes and Products

It was anticipated that students who were competent in research processes would produce high-quality research projects. For 11th graders, strong positive correlations exist between the research processes of communication and evaluation and research products. However, significantly *negative* correlations between research processes and products tended to apply to 9th graders. In a follow-up communication with the school library media teacher, these 9th graders tended to overestimate their abilities. Indeed, the more highly they rated their research process expertise, the more likely that teachers would consider their work lower quality. Thus, as mentioned before, teachers of 9th graders need to help students learn how to self-assess accurately by objectively linking their research behavior with their output as they conduct research projects. Because boys' behaviors tended to remain stable over the grades, particular attention needs to be made to 9th grade girls' self-perceptions. This finding aligns with competency theory as researched by Dunning, Johnson, and Ehrlinger (2003). They posited that incompetent individuals do not self-assess themselves accurately and do not improve by seeing models of competency. They need to be explicitly taught the skills that render them competent.

CONCLUSIONS

This exploratory study examined students' socioemotional well-being and its possible correlation with research processes and products. Because it was limited to one site, it could control to some extent school expectations, but the students studied in this investigation represent two curricular "tracks," which limited comparisons. Additionally, having one teacher per grade also compromised the data. Still, the investigation unearthed some interesting patterns and suggested some directions to take.

At the very least, this study shows the correlation between socioemotional well-being and information literacy as defined as research processes and products. In short, library media teachers and classroom teachers should pay attention to the social and emotional skills of students. Teachers need to address listening accuracy explicitly; one practice is to have students check their own work to see whether it adheres to the teachers' directions. Both library media teachers and classroom teachers should encourage students to persist in their research efforts; classroom teachers can emphasize the benefits of revising research questions, interpretation and manipulation of information, and communication of findings. Library media teachers can help students rethink key words, broaden their research strategies, and recycle the research process to refine questions and answers. Both classroom and library media teachers can help students by telling them frankly that conducting research can be a frustrating experience for students as well as information professionals and that students should try to think of different approaches when they hit the wall and to keep on refocusing to find satisfying solutions to research questions.

On the positive side, the AASL included social skills (i.e., collaborative work) in its information literacy standards. What needs to be addressed, as revealed in this study, is the need for teachers to help students differentiate between social interaction and academically focused collaboration. Although it appears that this issue is resolved by 11th grade, teachers can recognize freshman developmental behaviors and facilitate their actions to align more closely to academic demands. In addition, 9th-grade teachers can help students think about how their behaviors impact their academic performance by using metacognitive exercises that concretely illustrate the relationship between socioemotional behavior and research processes. This reality check can help students become more objective and accurate in their self-assessments. Peer review of these self-reflections can offer a socially acceptable and developmentally appropriate way to examine research efforts.

Particular attention should be made to gender-specific issues. For example, girls should be encouraged to take intellectual risks, and boys should be encouraged to follow directions, both with the goal of producing more accurate and substantive work. These issues can be expressed to the entire class because the ones who need that particular encouragement can apply that information and those who already follow those ideas will be affirmed in their behavior.

This study raises several questions, which call for further research:

- How do different populations (gifted, average, at risk) reflect different socioemotional well-being as well as research processes and products?

- Do other high schools exhibit similar behaviors and performances?

- How do other teachers assess research products? What roles can library media teachers play in assessment of research products?

- Other theories of socioemotional well-being and self-determination should be examined (e.g., Wehmeyer, 2003) in light of research processes and products.

- What impact would interventions have, as suggested earlier, in students' research processing and products?

In the final analysis, conducting research is an emotional and social process as much as it is an intellectual one. Therefore, library media and classroom teachers should pay attention to these dynamics in a proactive way so students will be more successful in each of these developmental domains.

REFERENCES

American Association of School Librarians/Association for Educational Communications and Technology. (1998). *Information power.* Chicago: American Library Association.

Bernard, M. (2003). *You can do it!* New York: Time Warner.

Bernard, M., & Laws, W. (1988, August). *Childhood irrationality and mental health.* Paper presented at the 24th International Congress of Psychology, Sydney, Australia.

Collaborative to Advance Social and Emotional Learning. (2003). *SEL competences.* Chicago: Collaborative to Advance Social and Emotional Learning. Retrieved April 15, 2005, http://www.casel.org/about_sel/SELskills.php

Colorado State Library and Adult Education Office and Colorado Educational Media Association. (1997). Rubrics for the assessment of information literacy. In California Library Media Association (Ed.), *Form library skills to information literacy* (2nd ed.). San Jose, CA: Hi Willow.

Dunning, D., Johnson, K., & Ehrlinger, J. (2003, June). Why people fail to recognize their own incompetence. *Current Directions in Psychological Science, 12*(3), 53–57.

Ellis, A., & Bernard, M. (Eds.) (1983). *Clinical applications of rational-emotive therapy.* New York: Plenum Press.

Farmer, L. (2003, October). *Degree of library media program implementation and student achievement.* Paper presented at the American Association of School Librarians conference, Kansas City, Missouri.

Goodin, M. (1991). The transferability of library research skills from high school to college. *School Library Media Quarterly, 20,* 33–42.

Grover, R., Lakin, J., & Dickerson, J. (1997). An interdisciplinary model for assessing learning. In L. Lighthall & K. Haycock (Eds.), *Information rich but knowledge poor?* Seattle, WA: International Association of School Librarianship.

Harada, V., & Yoshina, J. (1997, July). Improving information search process instruction and assessment through collaborative action research. *School Libraries Worldwide, 3,* 41–55.

Kuhlthau, C. (1983). The library research process: Case studies and interventions with high school seniors in advanced placement English classes using Kelly's theory of constructs, *Dissertation Abstracts, 44,* 1961 (AAT 8325888).

Lance, K. (2002, February). Proof of the power. *Teacher Librarian, 29*(2), 29–34.

Redwood High School Research Study Group. (1999). *Research handbook.* Larkspur, CA: Tamalpais Union High School District.

Wehmeyer, M. (2003). *Theory in self-determination.* New York: Thomas.

RESEARCH PROCESS RUBRIC

Your Grade: _____ Your Gender: M or F   Your Birth Date: ____ / ____ / ____ (in the form of 01/29/86)

DIRECTIONS: Please check the box ☑ of the group of sentences for each indicator (such as Indicator I. Determine information needs) that most accurately represents your action when doing a research project. You should have 7 ☑ (one per indicator) when done reading the rubric.

TARGET INDICATORS	EMERGING	NEARLY PROFICIENT	ACCOMPLISHED	EXCEPTIONAL
1. Determines information need	☐ Someone else defines the topic and what information I need.	☐ Someone else defines the topic. I can identify, with help, some of the information I need.	☐ I determine a topic and identify the information I need.	☐ I determine a manageable topic and identify the kinds of information I need to support it
2. Develops search strategy	☐ Someone else selects the resources I need and shows me how to find the information. Someone also develops my plan and timeline. I don't know what to record.	☐ I select resources but they aren't always appropriate. I have an incomplete plan and timeline, but don't always stick to them. I return to the same source to find bibliographic details.	☐ I use a variety of information strategies and resources. I have a complete plan and stay on my timeline. I sometimes record bibliographic information.	☐ I always select appropriate strategies and resources. I have a complete plan and can adjust my timelines when needed. I always record bibliographic information for all my sources.
3. Locates and accesses sources	☐ I don't understand how to use information resources.	☐ I don't use a variety of information resources.	☐ I prefer to limit the number of information resources I use.	☐ I am comfortable using various information resources.
4. Accesses and comprehends information	☐ Someone else helps me extract details from sources. I have no way to determine what information to keep and what to discard.	☐ I can extract details and concepts form one type of information source. I sometimes apply appropriate criteria to decide which information to use.	☐ I extract details and concepts from different types of sources. I examine my information and apply criteria to decide what to use.	☐ I extract details and concepts from all types of sources. I effectively apply criteria to decide what information to use.
5. Interprets and organizes information	☐ I need help to find which sources to use. I don't know how to use facts. I have trouble processing and organizing information. I need to be reminded to credit sources.	☐ I use the minimum sources assigned. I just list the facts. I know some ways to organize information. I can use 1–2 very well. Sometimes I credit sources appropriately.	☐ I create and improve my product by using a variety of resources from school. I organize information in different ways. I usually credit sources appropriately.	☐ I compare/contrast facts from a variety of sources found both in and out of my community. I use various media for products and audiences. I organize information to best meet my information needs. I always credit sources appropriately.
6. Communicates the information	☐ I'm not sure what actions to take based on my info needs. My product is incomplete. I don't revise	☐ I know what to do with the information I find. I complete my product, but need help revising.	☐ I act based on the information I have processed, according to my needs. I complete, practice and revise my product.	☐ I act independently on the relevant info I've processed, and explain my actions clearly. I complete, practice and revise my product several times. I ask for feedback.

RESEARCH PROCESS RUBRIC

DIRECTIONS: Please check the box ☑ of the group of sentences for each indicator (such as Indicator I. Determine information needs) that most accurately represents your action when doing a research project. You should have 5 ☑ (one per indicator) when done reading the rubric.

TARGET INDICATORS	ADHERENCE TO ASSIGNMENT	ORGANIZATION	PROOF AND JUSTIFICATION/ COMMENTARY	USE OF LANGUAGE AND STRATEGIES	SPELLING AND GRAMMAR
6. Exceptional	☐ All aspects of assignment covered in depth. Bibliography and citations done according for format without errors. Assignment is free of plagiarism.	☐ Well-organized structure and paragraphs that support insightful, defined thesis.	☐ Substantial and appropriate proof with convincing justification & commentary.	☐ Language is mature & clear; sentence structure is varied and well-developed.	☐ Errors are rare
5. Accomplished	☐ All aspects of assignment covered. Bibliography and citations done according for format with few or no errors. Assignment is free of plagiarism.	☐ Organized structure and paragraphs that support clearly defined thesis.	☐ Suitable proof with convincing justification and commentary.	☐ Language is effective and clear; sentence structure is varied.	☐ Errors are infrequent.
4. Competent	☐ Most aspects of assignment covered. Bibliography and citations done according for format with some errors. Assignment is free of plagiarism.	☐ Organization and paragraphs that support simplistic thesis.	☐ Adequate proof with somewhat convincing justification and commentary.	☐ Language is adequate; sentence structure varies somewhat.	☐ Errors appear occasionally.
3. Emerging	☐ Some important aspects of assignment are missing. Bibliography and citations contain frequent, distracting errors. Assignment is free of plagiarism.	☐ Unorganized structure and paragraphs with underdeveloped or vague thesis.	☐ Inadequate proof with underdeveloped or vague justification and commentary.	☐ Language is awkward; sentence structure is simplistic.	☐ Errors appear often and distract the reader.
2. Rudimentary	☐ Many important aspects of assignment are missing. Bibliography & citations incomplete. Assignment contains uncited information.	☐ Unorganized structure and paragraphs with no apparent thesis or focus.	☐ Inadequate proof with little clear or related justification or commentary.	☐ Language is unclear or repetitive; sentence structure is simplistic and lacks control.	☐ Errors appear continuously and distract the reader.
1. Unsatisfactory	☐ Most important aspects of assignment are missing. Bibliography and citations missing or incomplete. Assignment contains plagiarism.	☐ No organization is present; product lacks thesis.	☐ Clearly lacking proof with little or no justification or commentary.	☐ Language is ineffective or repetitive; sentence structure is confused.	☐ Errors make comprehension difficult.

Creativity Literacy in the School Library: Tapping Our Inner Resources

Gail Bush
Dominican University

THE CREATIVE ENTERPRISE WRIT SMALL

In his introduction to *Creating Minds: An Anatomy of Creativity Seen through the Lives of Freud, Picasso, Stravinsky, Eliot, Graham, and Gandhi*, Howard Gardner (1993a) describes one of his goals as seeking "conclusions about the nature of the Creative Enterprise writ large" (p. 7). Certainly we could take the principles that Gardner uncovers as those that govern creative human activity and apply them to novel situations. Vera John-Steiner (1997), Mihaly Csikszentmihalyi (1996), and other scholars focus on studying creative genius. What is of interest to educators about studying creativity beyond discovering the habits and predilections of Mozart, Einstein, Cassatt, and Picasso is the connection we can make to creating a learning environment that fosters creativity literacy learning in our students.

The focus for this chapter is on creativity writ small—writ just about the size of our students. Let us investigate those habits, characteristics, and tool sets that foster creativity in learners. In addition, the chapter focuses on the context of the school library and how we can use what we do and what we know to develop a culture of creativity within our existing learning environments. If education is light, let our light be one that illuminates creativity and wonderment in learning.

This focus on creativity puts a new spin on one of our core values in library service—the concept of equitable access to resources. It requires a broadening of our concepts regarding resources and generating ideas for increasing those available to our students. Conversely, we must encourage and stimulate their own stores of inner resources to be called on in providing these learners with fresh ideas and encouraging appetites for greater intellectual adventures. Educators and administrators alike will find that students who feel stimulated to think creatively will feel ownership for their learning, will be engaged learners, and thus perhaps increase performance on accountability measures.

CREATIVITY LITERACY INSTRUCTIONAL STRATEGIES

The constructivist theory of learning is well-suited to the creativity literacy learner. Focus on learning experiences that

- Are framed around an essential question

- Have problem- or inquiry-based scenario

- Require students to define their information and learning needs

- Have a mix of independent and social learning opportunities

- Encourage use of resources outside traditional library or school resources

- Are authentically assessed

- Provide a variety of end products that satisfy the learning outcomes.

CREATIVITY LITERACY INNER RESOURCES

Creativity literacy learners are able to dig deeply into their childhood memories for inspiration and ideas. Mozart returned to his store of memories again and again. Einstein played with ideas as a child plays with toys. Poets and writers listen to their inner voice. Scientists and mathematicians refer back to strong childhood impressions of observing nature and patterns. There are invisible tools within us all that facilitate the creative process; creativity is a self-reflective process (John-Steiner, 1997). Inner resources include memories, intellectual hunger, psychological safety in the learning environment and a well-honed discipline for one's creative work.

A critical resource for many creativity-literate learners is a strong mentor who is invested in the learner's development. Independent and intellectually curious learners who engage and receive responses from creative mentors are encouraged to think creatively. Teachers who collaborate with creative school library media specialists will undoubtedly feel more confident in creating units and lessons that include instructional strategies that will enhance the creativity literacy of their students.

In his article "Unleashing Creativity," Kraft (2005) states that "the ability to create is one of the outstanding traits of human beings ... originality is not a gift doled out sparingly by the gods. We can call it up from within us through training and encouragement" (p. 18). Examine the following list and find your creative strengths in and consider playing with ideas pairing some of the other attributes in your role in the library media center:

Twelve Characteristics of the Creative Library Media Specialist

1. Adaptability—makes changes to fit new situation
2. Flexibility—bends without yielding
3. Fluidity—grace under pressure
4. High energy
5. Independent thinker
6. Divergent thinker
7. Often toils alone yet seeks to exchange ideas
8. Playful while responsible
9. Seeks future challenges
10. Passionate about one's work
11. Displays a sense of unbridled wonder
12. Has many ideas, some better than others (Bush, 2001, p. 21).

TOWARDS A DEFINITION OF CREATIVITY

You probably do not need help defining creativity as you see it exhibited in school projects and course deliverables. Like good art, you know it when you see it. Often in student work, it is easy to make a distinction between creative representations of learning and those that simply meet rubric guidelines but lack real creativity. The creative thinking that we identify fits into the larger concept of creativity. Creative thinking does have a set of thinking skills or techniques that can be nurtured in schools and in libraries such as synectics (problem solving combined with active creative thinking), metaphorical thinking, lateral thinking, analogies, and problem reversal.

When attempting to capture the grand meaning of creativity, we often refer to our own chosen model of a creative work or one that is world renowned. When attempting to isolate the elements of its design which lead you to define a thing as creative, we may begin with such things as beautiful, elegant, simple, or complex in design. It might have various aesthetic values and might be so unique as to seem original or a novel response to a directive. Regardless of the criteria you apply to your exemplar, the likelihood is that you are thinking of some representative work. It is a product of the mind. Creative people are productive, and in fact, most are prolific. Creative work requires that the learner understand how to achieve the creation of the product and to be accomplished at this process (Eisner, 1964).

Creative products move beyond the ordinary. There must be an underlying comprehension within the given domain of what would be considered adequate for the task in order to take that next creative step. In relation to our studies in school, a student would need to have a basic understanding of relevant concepts to take the content a step further. Otherwise, we would not consider the product creative, and it would miss the mark in some obvious way. Perhaps this essential element of requiring comprehension of content before creativity is fostered is an approach worth considering in our curricular studies. Having creative ideas that do not move beyond that ideation stage or those that do not have a solid context are neither seen nor can they be judged. In considering creativity, we focus on the product within a context or domain, the process, and the one who creates.

Beginning in the middle of the 20th century, psychologist J. P. Guilford (1950) measured abilities he determined needed to be present for creativity to occur. In his work, he correlated results with various abilities and found that persons who scored highly on one ability test were more likely to score high on another. Naturally this research suggested more questions, and one question rested on the relationship between creativity and intelligence. During the 1960s, University of Chicago educational psychologists Philip Jackson and Jacob Getzels (1962) took creativity testing to the next level which was commonly measured in standardized IQ tests. Their research found that while there is a positive relationship between creativity and intelligence, it was not a strong one (Jackson & Getzels, 1962). Based on their results, they viewed creativity and IQ as different attributes requiring different types of abilities. They continued to study creativity and chose to test the relationship between creativity and academic achievement (Eisner, 1964).

Creativity and IQ discussions become more interesting when you add academic achievement to the equation. Sternberg's (1998) study found that teachers prefer to teach students with high intelligence quotients rather than students with high creativity quotients. High IQ students responded more traditionally to questions of future careers; they were easier to handle in classroom situations and performed well on measures regardless of the quality of teaching. Creative students might not perform consistently well on tests, questioned the status quo, and looked for ambiguity (Eisner, 1964). Within the literature, it is not clear whether there was any relationship between teachers' attitudes regarding and comfort levels with highly creative students especially among those who do not feel particularly creative.

Interestingly, academic achievement was found to be equal among high IQ and highly creative students even though the creative students often had a much lower intelligence quotient (Sternberg, 1998). This leads to a new level of inquiry: can high creativity possibly facilitate learning? Does the student understand that he or she needs to comprehend the content within the curriculum to then take it to a creative level? Whatever the motivation, the academic achievement of highly creative students exceeded what would be thought of as normal in light of their intelligence quotients (Sternberg, 1998). These are interesting ideas to ponder, especially for school library media specialists who have a learning laboratory primed to serve our students in the best manner possible for improved learning.

CONSIDERING CREATIVE THINKING SKILLS

As educators, we have a paradox to consider between the subject-centered curriculum and the learner-centered curriculum. Traditionally, subjects or content areas have been treated as fodder to fill the vessel, or the learner. The learner was intended to absorb information in the best manner possible to ease the retrieval of the information for testing purposes. Year after year of this absorption and retrieval trains the learner and skills that develop are directed at convergent thinking so that the end result is a correct answer (McGilly, 1994).

In today's information society redolent with an abundance of useful data, it seems obvious that no one can have a complete comprehension of every fact and event in each content area, field, or domain. Current trends in learning direct us to learn basic underlying general principles that apply within most contexts (Eisner, 1964). In doing so, we identify areas of interest that require more in-depth study that lead us to divergent perspectives pointing various fields. We develop skills whereby we analyze, synthesize, draw conclusions, ask relevant probing questions, and consider future implications of a variety of resolutions. Consider who among our students will be most adept in handling the ambiguity that colors our information world. In teaching future generations, would we not rather paint that ambiguity as a beautiful kaleidoscope that illuminates divergent points of view rather than a confusing, dark shadow obscuring understanding? The paradigm of continuing to teach to the correct answer in the context of the 21st century is no longer appropriate for today's students.

The irony about the paradox is that the situation we find ourselves in regarding creative thinking skills is one of our own making. Children come into school highly creative as a whole, and our traditional teaching philosophy retrains them to think convergently in an attempt to find *correct* answers (Gardner, 1993b). Flexible, original, creative thinking abounds in young children. Children at play create masterpieces of imagination and creativity. Our challenge is to foster creativity while responsibly educating students with a goal of their improved learning and academic success.

The skills that define creative thinking reside in the process element of creativity and fall into the three learning domains of cognitive, affective, and metacognitive. Cognitive skills include creativity literacies of originality, flexibility, fluency, and elaboration among others. Affective skills include tolerance for ambiguity, open-mindedness, risk-taking behaviors, playfulness, and curiosity. Metacognitive skills include goal setting, predicting, diagnosing, considering feedback, and awareness of one's creativity (Puccio & Murdock, 2001).

Problem solving is the closest relative to creative thinking in schools today. Imagine a successful problem solver who does not exhibit some of the creative thinking skills mentioned above. Many instructional manuals offer problem solving along with creative thinking projects for young students (see, among others, Meador, 1997; Wilks, 1995). Creativity identifies problems where others do not see them, or at least before others may recognize them. Problem finding is evidence of creativity because it is the creative individual who notices and who makes connections among divergent issues.

Helping students to exercise problem-finding skills might include encouraging multiple representations of the problem in words or actions; examining it from many angles and vantage points; attempting different solutions; considering various implications or results for various solutions; not stopping at a single solution. Once problem finding is accepted as an instructional method, creative students will have an outlet for extending beyond the established curriculum. Skills used in content areas can transfer and students can be encouraged to make interdisciplinary connections. Engaging these students can naturally inspire their classmates and the learning environment can be enriched for all students.

TOWARD A DEFINITION OF CREATIVITY LITERACY

We are awash in information; we dabble with visual, media, technology, computer literacy, and all literacies that help us to "read the world" we inhabit (Freire, 1998). What will it take to equip our future leaders completely to consider the unseen? Needless to say, this is an impossible question to answer, or, at best, it has many answers. We as educators develop models of literacies that represent bodies of literature and science substantiating the need to read, comprehend, compute, connect, and create effectively.

Here, then, are the characteristics of creativity that add up to a creativity literacy that allows for the process, the product, and the creative spirit to emerge:

Creativity Literacy

Flexibility   **Ambiguity**

Problem Acumen
Fluency
Redefinition
Originality

Elaboration   **Reflection**

Propensities of Creativity-Literate Learners
Autonomy and Independence
Wonderment and Playfulness
Humor and Wit
Persistence and Prolificacy

Flexibility—New perspectives are seen when thinkers are flexible; when habits of mind are not limiting but illuminating; when new information does not find old constructs in which to settle. Flexible thinkers play with information before relegating it to categorization and storage. Psychological safety is necessary for creativity-literate learners to thrive (Eisner, 1964).

Ambiguity—More than simply a tolerance but a welcoming for exposure to new and unfamiliar stimuli that may cause new responses to information (Langer, 1997). Confidence in one's own intuition, although an important trait, is comfortably set aside while the learner remains open to varieties of exposure.

Problem Acumen—Sensitivity to problems including solving, finding, and redefining; problem acumen includes the following elements:

- *Fluency*—Idea after idea after idea after solution after problem with no limits or boundaries. Bad ideas, good ideas, some ideas that seem at first flush to be completely off the mark. The creativity-literate learner questions the delineation of that which is acceptable and may expand those boundaries.

- *Redefinition*—Perhaps the problem is in need of refitting; shedding a new light requires redefinition of the problem (as researchers are well aware). Confidence in one's creative abilities is required to presume to redefine a problem that has been presented to a learner.

- *Originality*—Even those who hold that there are no new ideas under the sun will agree that there are an infinite combinations of ideas under the sun. Consider an artist's rendering, a musician's song, a poet's ode, or a choreographer's dance. It is unimaginable that we would ever live without such creative perspectives. Our culture depends on inventors, discoverers, and explorers for future problems and reasons unimagined today. Those learners who are in touch with their inner resources can respond in more personal ways and value their own particular perspective. The unique response of an individual to a given situation is by definition an example of originality.

Elaboration—Takes an idea, an event, a product, and embellishes it in a unique way. In many cases we have snippets of information from historical times; think about the task of the archaeologist, biblical scholars, or present-day event planners. Elaboration may have original ideas but often require much process for those ideas to be expanded upon and contributions to come to fruition. Contrary to thoughts of sloppy, inattentive acts of creativity, elaboration takes focus and dedicated attention to meticulous detail beyond the norm.

Reflection—Momentary but essential, reflection fits into the metacognitive skill set. The creativity-literate learner knows that she is merely standing in the river at a particular moment in time with a particular resolution. Could her response be different, better, more? Yes, and perhaps it will be for the next challenge. Ask an artist about a book written years ago or a sculpture or a composition. She reads the words, hears the music, or views the sculpture as if someone else created it because the artist is a different person now than she was then. The momentary reflection asks the self-aware creator if the product reflects her inner resources at that time. If so, she might ponder other results or products as a self-evaluative strategy but will be only momentarily satisfied and will be eager to begin the next creative process.

PROPENSITIES OF CREATIVITY-LITERATE LEARNERS

Autonomy and Independence—It takes a strong belief in the value of one's ideas to follow through on the creative process from redefinition to originality to elaboration. That confidence is evidence of an independent thinker who seeks autonomy of thought. Autonomy and independence may be challenges to teachers who do not closely adhere to a constructivist theory of teaching. Teachers who understand that some students need that sense of self as a learner will have an easier time supporting autonomous, independent learners.

Wonderment and Playfulness—Creativity-literate learners play with information and scenarios and wonder "what if." Learners feel at ease pondering the mysteries of life and wondering about them. They are intellectually curious, inventive, and eager to explore; they turn given assumptions upside down and inside out. They imagine and play with ideas, combine and dissect our known world; they bring a store of concepts together that might seem related only to them. They feel passion and joy in the act of creation.

Humor and Wit—It is not the humor of another's misfortune but the playful twisting of words, ideas, and situations that intrigue creativity-literate learners. Ambiguity and incongruity provide opportunities for relating disparate elements in society. Irony, puns, wit, satire, and all forms of intellectual chuckles are food for thought since they inspire further novel combinations of ideas. Humor has vitality, enabling us to see ordinary things in new ways; wit helps us think about the mundane and commonplace as juxtaposed with unordinary ideas.

Persistent and Prolific—Creativity-literate learners are driven and tenacious. They commit to a task and are driven by the creative process. The downside of this persistence may be that transitions do not come easily as they think deeply and inwardly as they create. They have many ideas and produce many creative products as they continue to strive toward greater challenges. They do not tend to dwell on past creations but have new directions in which to grow as artists, writers, thinkers. Because they are continually growing as learners, they look for opportunities to use their newly acquired knowledge in innovative ways.

PROMOTING CREATIVITY LITERACY IN THE SCHOOL LIBRARY MEDIA CENTER

Learners who produce creative work know how to apply themselves to their task. Even when they appear to be daydreaming, they may be contemplating a potential solution. They comprehend the requirements of a task and have the insight to produce beyond the expected. Where does the insight come from? How can we, as educators, nurture that development? More specifically, how do the unique trappings of the school library media center fit the needs of a well-oiled learning laboratory for creativity to thrive? Fostering and promoting a learning environment that welcomes creativity helps to level the playing field for students who might not have literacy-rich home environments. Providing as many relevant and appropriate resources in a variety of formats to not only support the curriculum but to feed the creativity-literate learner fulfills the mission of the school library media program.

CREATIVITY LITERACY RESOURCES

Think broadly, deeply, and creatively. Consider every community resource that might provide an additional landscape for your students: schools, colleges, and universities; public library; historical society; park district; senior and child-care centers; museums; faith-based organizations; local service clubs; performing arts groups; local businesses and chamber of commerce.

Creativity-literate learners require multiple representations of concepts and information. Include a wide variety of formats and types of materials in your library collection. Include the arts whenever possible. Photographs, political cartoons, songs, and slogans interest students by presenting information in creative representations. You are more likely to engage students in their research tasks by offering them a wide range of materials than if you have limited resources available.

INTERNET RESOURCES

Creative Thinking Techniques by Robert Harris: http://www.virtualsalt.com/crebook2.htm

Critical and Creative Thinking: Georgia Critical Thinking Skills Program: http://eduscapes.com/tap/topic69.htm

Teaching Thinking Skills: NW Regional Education Laboratory: http://www.nwrel.org/scpd/sirs/6/cu11.html

REFERENCES AND ADDITIONAL READING

American Association of School Librarians and Association for Educational Communications and Technology. (1998). *Information Power: Building partnerships for learning.* Chicago: American Library Association.

Bush, G. (2001). Just sing: Creativity and technology in the school library media center. *Knowledge Quest, 30*(2),18–21.

Bush, G. (2002). *The school buddy system: The practice of collaboration.* Chicago: American Library Association.

Callison, D. (1998). Creative thinking. *School Library Media Activities Monthly, 15*(4), 41–44.

Cameron, J. (1992). The *artist's way: A spiritual path to higher creativity.* New York: Putnam.

Costa, A., ed. (2001). *Developing minds: A resource book for teaching thinking* (3rd ed.). Alexandria, VA: Association for Supervision and Curriculum Development.

Costa, A., & Kallick, B., eds. (2000). *Discovering & exploring: Habits of mind.* Alexandria, VA: Association for Supervision and Curriculum Development.

Csikszentmihalyi, M. (1996). *Creativity: Flow and the psychology of discovery and invention.* New York: HarperCollins.

de Bono, E. (1970). *Lateral thinking: Creativity step by step.* New York: Harper & Row.

Dewey, J. (1938). *Experience and education.* New York: Macmillan.

Eisner, E. (1964). *Think with me about creativity.* Dansville, NY: Owen.

Fletcher, J. M. (1934). *Psychology in education with emphasis on creative thinking.* Garden City, NY: Doubleday.

Friere, P. (1998). *Teachers as cultural workers: Letters to those who dare to teach: Critical studies in educational theory* (D. Mancelo, D. Koike, & A. Oliveira, Trans.). Boulder, CO: Westview Press.

Gardner, H. (1993a). *Creating minds: An anatomy of creativity seen through the lives of Freud, Picasso, Stravinsky, Eliot, Graham, and Gandhi.* New York: Basic Books.

Gardner, H. (1993b). *The unschooled mind: How children think and how schools should teach.* New York: Basic Books.

Grudin, R. (1990). *The grace of great things: Creativity and innovation.* New York: Ticknor & Fields.

Guilford, J. P. (1950). Creativity. *American Psychologist, 5,* 444–454.

Jackson, P. W., & Getzels, J. W. (1962). *Creativity and intelligence.* New York: John Wiley & Sons.

John-Steiner, V. (1997). *Notebooks of the mind: Explorations of thinking* (2d ed.). New York: Oxford University Press.

John-Steiner, V. (2000). *Creative collaboration.* New York: Oxford University Press.

Kraft, U. (2005). Unleashing creativity. *Scientific American Mind, 16*(1), 16–23.

Langer, E. J. (1997). *The power of mindful learning.* Cambridge, MA: Perseus.

May, R. (1975). *The courage to create.* New York: Norton.

McGilly, K. (Ed.). (1994). *Classroom lessons: Integrating cognitive theory.* Cambridge, MA: MIT Press.

Meador, K. S. (1997). *Creative thinking and problem solving for young learners.* Englewood, CO: Libraries Unlimited.

Perkins, D. & Tishman, S. (1995). *The thinking classroom: Learning and teaching in a culture of thinking.* Needham Heights, MA: Allyn and Bacon.

Puccio, G. J., & Murdock, M.C. (2001). Creative thinking: An essential life skill. In A. Costa (Ed.), *Developing minds: A resource book for teaching thinking* (3rd ed., (pp. 67–71). Alexandria, VA: Association for Supervision and Curriculum Development.

Sternberg, R. (1988). *The nature of creativity.* Cambridge, England: Cambridge University Press.

Sternberg, R. (1995). *Defying the crowd: Cultivating creativity in a culture of conformity.* New York: Free Press.

Sternberg, R., ed. (1998). *Handbook of creativity.* Cambridge, England: Cambridge University Press.

Torrance, E. P. (1962). *Guiding creative talent.* Englewood Cliffs, NJ: Prentice-Hall.

Torrance, E. P., & Safter, H.T. (1999). *Making the creative leap beyond.* Buffalo, NY: Creative Education Foundation.

Wilks, S. (1995). *Critical & creative thinking: Strategies for classroom inquiry.* Portsmouth, NH: Heinemann.

Part Three
Leadership Profiles

Introduction

Robert Maribe Branch

The purpose of this section is to profile individuals who have made significant contributions to the field of educational media and communication technology. Leaders profiled in the *Educational Media and Technology Yearbook* have typically held prominent offices, composed seminal works, or made significant contributions that have influenced the contemporary vision of the field. The people profiled in this section have often been directly responsible for mentoring individuals who have themselves become recognized for their contributions in one way or another.

There are special reasons to feature people of national and international renown. This volume of the *Educational Media and Technology Yearbook* profiles two people who continue to uphold the tradition of leadership in educational media and communication technology. The leaders profiled this year are Michael Molenda and Ronald Oliver.

The following people (listed alphabetically) were profiled in earlier volumes of the *Educational Media and Technology Yearbook*:

John C. Belland	Roger Kaufman
Robert K. Branson	Jean E. Lowrie
James W. Brown	Wesley Joseph McJulien
Bob Casey	M. David Merrill
Betty Collis	Robert M. Morgan
Robert E. De Kieffer	Robert Morris
Robert M. Diamond	James Okey
Walter Dick	Tjeerd Plomp
Frank Dwyer	Rita C. Richey
Donald P. Ely	Paul Saettler
James D. Finn	Wilbur Schramm
Robert Mills Gagné	Charles Francis Schuller
Castelle (Cass) G. Gentry	Don Carl Smellie
Thomas F. Gilbert	Howard Sullivan
Kent Gustafson	William Travers
John Hedberg	Constance Dorothea Weinman
Robert Heinich	Paul Welliver
Stanley A. Huffman	Paul Robert Wendt
Harry Alleyn Johnson	

Those profiled in this section are usually emeritus faculty who may or may not be active in the field. There is no formal survey or popularity contest to determine the persons for whom the profiles are written. You are welcome to nominate individuals to be featured in this section. Your nomination of someone to be profiled must be accompanied by the name of the person who agrees to compose the leadership profile. Please direct comments, questions, and suggestions about the selection process to the senior editor.

Leadership Profile

Michael Molenda

Indiana University

Charles Riegeluth

Michael Molenda was born November 19, 1941, in South Bend, Indiana, two years after his sister, Julieann. His parents were children of immigrants, his father's family from Poland, his mother's from the Trentino region of northern Italy. Because they grew up during the Depression, neither parent finished high school. His father, Henry, spent most of his working life in the fermenting cellars at Schlitz Brewery in Milwaukee, the city where Michael and his sister grew up. His mother, Helene, was a devoted homemaker, who, after the children grew up, purchased and managed a food store and later became a teacher of fur remodeling in the adult education program of Milwaukee Public Schools.

Helene made sure that Michael received the best education available in Milwaukee —at Marquette University High School, a Jesuit school that required a competitive exam to enter. There he majored in classics and developed a lifelong interest in the Greek and Latin literatures and cultures. The logical next step was Marquette University. His interest in writing took him first to journalism and ultimately to a double major in english and radio-television. Another important source of education was his part-time job as information clerk at the Greyhound bus terminal in downtown Milwaukee, a great place to interact with people of every possible variety.

After completing his bachelor's degree in 1963, mentored by Professor Ray Bedwell, he competed successfully for a National Defense Education Act (NDEA) doctoral fellowship to study instructional technology at Syracuse University. The NDEA program was one of those "radical social experiments" of the federal government that bore abundant fruit, anticipating the need for college faculty in the burgeoning area of using media and technology to improve education.

Mike's mentor at Syracuse, Donald P. Ely, helped him gain another step up the ladder, a Ford Foundation internship at the National Education Association in Washington, D.C., in 1965, at the height of President Lyndon Johnson's monumental education initiatives. It was an exciting place to be and fortunate time to be there! Through his work as a Washington intern, Mike gained visibility and made contacts that helped him to contribute at the national and international levels for the rest of his career.

One of those contacts was Robert O'Kane, dean of the School of Education at University of North Carolina at Greensboro (UNC-G). In 1968, he offered Mike a position as director of a new instructional media center that was to be built in the coming year. Going to Greensboro directly from his doctoral studies at Syracuse, Mike got a postdoctoral education on the job, figuring out how to do audiovisual facilities planning, curriculum and course development, and administration of a growing media center. In the fall of 1969, he found himself standing in front of a class teaching for the first time, in a room he designed, equipped with audiovisual equipment and materials he had acquired. He was teaching a course that was new to UNC-G, part of a curriculum that was also new to the university. Fortunately, he again benefited from sterling mentoring, this time by Professor Mary Frances "Frankie" Johnson, a flawless colleague and superlative professional.

His work at UNC-G brought him to visibility in the major professional association, the Department of Audio-Visual Instruction (later the Association for Educational Communications and Technology—AECT), where an Indiana University professor Mendel Sherman served as president in 1965 (Mike's internship year), his Syracuse mentor Donald Ely served as president in 1966, and another IU professor, Robert Heinich, served as president in 1971.

Through these professional relationships, Mike was invited to join the Instructional Systems Technology faculty at Indiana University in 1972. At that time, the department was recognized as the Mecca of the field, so he did not hesitate to accept. For the next 10 years, he worked closely with Bob Heinich, teaching courses related to applications of media in education and co-directing the School of Education's instructional development center. There he encountered Amos Patterson, then a graduate assistant and later a leading professor and administrator at the University of Toledo, who became a valued colleague and mentor regarding management of instructional development projects—more on-the-job learning.

The most important project during this period was the creation of a two-day workshop on Evaluation and Change Management as part of the nationally distributed Instructional Development Institute. This workshop featured many innovative hands-on activities for teachers, including a large-scale simulation game, *The Diffusion Simulation Game*. The game was recognized by the National Society for Performance and Instruction (NSPI) as a finalist for Instructional Development Product of the Year in 1977. It became widely used at other universities in instructional technology graduate programs and continued to be used in the following decades. It also spawned a dozen variants including *Spiegeldorf*, used for many years at IU in modern European history courses, and *Making Change*, distributed by The Network, Inc.

His second decade at IU featured the publication of a textbook with Bob Heinich and James D. Russell of Purdue University, *Instructional Media and the New Technologies of Instruction*. To the surprise of everyone, including the publisher, when the book reached the market in 1982, it immediately became the most widely adopted textbook for instructional media courses, displacing two rivals that had shared the market for a generation. The eighth edition, published in 2005, continues to be widely adopted. In such a rapidly changing field, the content evolved greatly, but the book was highly regarded for its clarity and exemplary pedagogical design. The first edition won the Publication of the Year award from AECT and NSPI, and in 2004 the book was recognized as Outstanding Book in Educational Technology and Teacher Education by the teacher education division of AECT. It was used in universities around the world, with authorized translations in Spanish and Chinese.

Mike served a term as department chair from 1988 to 1991, a crucial time for the Instructional Systems Technology department, as the last of the Old Guard were retiring, so replacements had to be found and the curriculum had to be restructured. He was instrumental in convincing me to go to Indiana University in 1988, and he initiated the process of establishing a highly innovative, integrated, project-based core curriculum for the IU master's and doctoral programs.

His work brought him to international attention, leading to consulting and lecturing in Europe (the Netherlands, Spain, and Poland); in Latin America (Venezuela, Peru, and Puerto Rico); in many of the countries in the Middle East; in Africa (Egypt and Swaziland); and in Asia (Japan, China, Korea, and Indonesia). Beginning in 1992, he was involved more intensively in Korea, collaborating with Professor James A. Pershing of Indiana University in a five-year project of summer institutes for Korean training managers. In collaboration with these successive teams of managers, Molenda and Pershing developed a conceptual schema to integrate instructional design with other sorts of performance interventions, the Strategic Impact Model.

These contacts with Asian leaders in educational technology led to his selection to be the founding editor in 2003 of the *Asia-Pacific Cybereducation Journal*, published online and in print form by APEC, the Asia-Pacific Economic Cooperation, the international body dedicated to facilitating economic growth, cooperation, trade, and investment in the Asia-Pacific region. The journal aims to promote appropriate use of technology to improve education in the member countries through scholarly exchange.

Another acknowledgment of his standing in his field is the number of commissions he received to author articles for encyclopedias, giving authoritative definitions and descriptions of instructional technology, instructional design, audiovisual media, educational technology in elementary–secondary education, Dale's Cone of Experience, and Association for Educational Communications and Technology (AECT), among others. He played leadership roles in AECT's "definition" projects in the 1970s, in 1994, and again in 2003–2005. He was a passionate advocate that the definition of the field must acknowledge its core values, arguing that instructional technology was distinguished from related concepts by its commitment to improving access to learning and to creating learning environments that were more efficient, effective, and humane than those others had devised.

Throughout his career he has been a leader in AECT, sometimes behind the scenes as an advisor in the national headquarters and sometimes in formal offices, such as president of the international division and member of the national board of directors. In the 1970s, he conducted a series of annual opinion surveys among members, which provided critical information to guide the association as it considered major restructuring in the face of seismic shifts on the national scene. Because of his deep involvement over the years since 1965, he was asked to write a history of the association for use on its Web site, which was published in 2005.

Because of his status as high-level observer of the field, each year beginning in 1998 and continuing through the present (including 2006) he was invited to author or coauthor an annual review of the state of instructional technology in the United States for the *Educational Media and Technology Yearbook*. This "issues and trends" review covered growth and change in the use of technology in the corporate, higher education, and K–12 sectors.

All of this work was really an extension of teaching, which he always gave top priority and which he always approached with enthusiasm and a high degree of organization. One of his students once commented to the department chair, "If Dr. Molenda had been in charge of Robert E. Lee's logistics, the Confederate Army might still be fighting." In his last decade of teaching, he focused on the department's core courses, which are the first ones taken by new graduate students, and a doctoral reading seminar, which is the last course taken by doctoral students. This has offered grad students a "Molenda sandwich" and increased their chance to benefit from his mentoring, as he had benefited from his mentors. Among the recognitions he received for his teaching was a Student Choice teaching award, chosen solely by students across the university.

He retired from teaching in 2005 with plans to continue work related to the historical and theoretical foundations of the field and, he hopes, to return to study of the Greek and Latin classics—reading Homer, as he started to do in high school but without the benefit of life experience. On the Latin front, he is enthralled with the Stoic philosophers and those who put their teachings into practice, such as Marcus Aurelius and Hadrian. He will remain in Bloomington where his wife, Janet Stavropoulos, practices law and where his two grown sons and stepdaughter enjoy returning to the family nest.

Leadership Profile

Ron Oliver

Foundation Professor of Interactive Multimedia
Edith Cowan University, Perth, Western Australia

Thomas C. Reeves

Real generosity toward the future lies in giving all to the present.

—Albert Camus

The long and rich history of distance education in Australia began as early as 1910 with teaching notes mailed to parents schooling their children in remote areas of Queensland and Western Australia. In the late 1940s, distance education progressed from postal correspondence to shortwave radio with the establishment of the famous Alice Springs School of the Air. Over the last fifty years, Australians have explored the application of virtually every new technology for distance education, and as a result, Australia is widely recognized today as a leader in the provision of distance and flexible learning, employing online technologies to enable tens of thousands of students to pursue primary, secondary, and higher education as well as professional training around the globe.

Any discussion of contemporary online learning in Australia acknowledges the enormous contributions of Ron Oliver, Foundation Professor of Interactive Multimedia, at Edith Cowan University in Perth, Western Australia. A household name "Down Under," Professor Oliver has recently become recognized as one of the most important scholars in the global educational technology community.

Ron was born in 1955 in the rural shire of Kojonup in the Great Southern region of Western Australia. Growing up, Ron and his family lived in several small towns of rural South West Australia as his father, a primary school principal, was promoted to various schools by the Ministry of Education for Western Australia. After paying their dues in the Bush, most Western Australian educators gradually work their way to the state capital, and

241

thus ten year-old Ron and his family moved to Perth in 1965. Ron graduated from high school in that most geographically isolated of major modern cities in 1972.

After completing a degree in mathematics at the University of Western Australia, Ron commenced his teaching career as a "Maths" teacher in rural Western Australia schools in 1977. Microcomputers were just becoming available in schools, and Ron was a pioneer in using computers to motivate his rural students, encouraging them to consider opportunities beyond their pastoral roots. Recognizing that there was more to teaching and learning than his formal mathematics education had provided, Ron completed a bachelor in education degree in 1980 via a distance program from Murdoch University. Ever thirsty for new knowledge and skills, he next completed two more graduate diplomas (computing in 1981 and science education in 1985) and a master's of applied science in 1985, all from the Western Australian Institute of Technology (which became Curtin University of Technology in 1986). Throughout these postgraduate studies, Ron continued to explore the educational uses of microcomputers at various schools where he was employed, and he actually cowrote his first educational computing book in 1981!

In 1984, Ron shifted his career from primary schools to tertiary (postsecondary) education as a lecturer in computer education at the Western Australian College of Advanced Education (which became Edith Cowan University in 1991). His formal education ended with a Ph.D. from the Curtin University of Technology in 1990. In his doctoral dissertation, Ron explored the efficacy of an alternative constructivist-based approach to teaching introductory programming. The theoretical foundations for much of Ron's work today remains grounded in constructivist learning theories and as well as the principles of social cognition and authentic learning tasks.

With respect to scholarly contributions, summing up Ron's many contributions is a task fit for a professional accountant. Here are just a few impressive figures:

Ron has published 70 papers in refereed journals ranging from the *Research in Science Education* journal in 1986 to the *Journal of Computing in Higher Education* in 2005. In addition, he has published more than 70 articles in nonrefereed publications.

Ron has published nearly 100 books, monographs, edited proceedings, and book chapters. The 30 plus "how-to" books that Ron cowrote with his Edith Cowan University colleague, Paul Newhouse, and his wife, Helen Oliver, have helped two generations of Australian teachers integrate computing and other technologies into education.

In addition to being a frequently invited speaker in all eight Australian states and territories, Ron has given keynotes, workshops, and invited presentations in numerous other countries including Austria, Canada, England, Germany, Japan, Malaysia, the Netherlands, Scotland, Singapore, Switzerland, South Africa, and the United States. His presentations are an appealing combination of substantive content and practical examples delivered with disarming charm and a slightly wicked sense of humor.

Ron has attracted millions of dollars of research and development funding to Edith Cowan University. Among his most notable projects is his involvement in the National Flexible Toolboxes project (see http://www.flexiblelearning.net.au/toolbox/), ongoing since 1999. This large-scale project is a global model for a nationally coordinated effort to develop online materials to enhance the quality of e-learning.

Ron has supervised the doctoral dissertations of nearly a dozen members of the next generation of educational technology leaders "Down Under." For example, Associate Professor Jan Herrington of Wollongong University completed her dissertation titled "Authentic Learning in Interactive Multimedia Environments" under Ron's guidance, and she was subsequently selected as the Young Researcher of the Year in 1999 by the Association for Educational Communications and Technology and as a Fulbright Scholar in 2002.

In recent years, Ron has taken on more administrative duties. He is now the associate dean (Teaching and Learning) in the Faculty of Communications and Creative Industries (see http://www.cci.ecu.edu.au/) and chair of the Academic Board at Edith Cowan University. Thanks largely to Ron's leadership, Edith Cowan University has become one of the top-10 institutions researching online learning in the world.

On the international stage, Ron is chair of the steering committee for the increasingly worthy series of international ED-MEDIA conferences (see http://aace.org/conf/ edmedia/), Executive Member of the Asia Pacific Chapter of the Association for the Advancement of Computers in Education, and a member of the editorial boards of several journals including the *British Journal of Educational Technology*, *Journal of Educational Media and Hypermedia*, *Distance Education*, *Journal of Interactive Learning Research*, *Australian Journal of Educational Technology*, *Australian Educational Computing*, and *ALT-J- Research in Learning Technology*.

With so many academic achievements, it is difficult to conceive that Ron could have "a life," but his lovely wife, Helen, and his talented children, Tim and Sally, can attest that he is a super husband and dad. When they leave their home in the Perth suburb of Booragoon, the Olivers' favorite retreat is their country home located on 50 hilly acres surrounded by Jarrah forests (see http://www.wafa.org.au/aboutjarrah.htm) near the historic town of Dwellingup, 97 kilometers south of the capital. In addition, Ron and Helen have often taken their children abroad, including a six-month length stay in Japan in 1996 when Ron was a visiting scholar at the National Institute for Multimedia Education (NIME; see http://www.nime.ac.jp/).

My own experience with Professor Oliver began in 1993, when I spent five months as a visiting professor at Edith Cowan University. What began as a collegial relationship quickly grew into an international collaboration and personal friendship. Today, Ron, Jan Herrington, and I are conducting a long-term research collaboration related to authentic task design for Web-based learning environments (see http://www.authentictasks. uow.edu.au/). But this is just one of Ron's current initiatives. In addition to the authentic tasks project and the aforementioned National Flexible Toolboxes project, Ron and Professor Barry Harper, dean of the Faculty of Education at the University of Wollongong, have co-led an important effort to define innovative technology-based learning designs for higher education with funding from the Australian Department of Education, Science, and Training (see http://www.learningdesigns.uow.edu.au/).

Anyone who knows Ron has experienced his extraordinary generosity. This is exemplified in many ways, not least in his development of "RonLine" (see http://aragorn.scam. ecu.edu.au/ronline/ronline.php). This Web site provides teachers around the world with free access to a valuable suite of interactive online learning support tools developed by Ron and his colleagues at Edith Cowan University. The spirit of open sharing that exemplified the earliest days of the World Wide Web continues to flourish here and there because of rare people like Ron.

The accomplishments summed up in this tribute would be remarkable for someone nearing the end of a career, but Ron Oliver is only at the midpoint of his and indeed may be just hitting his stride as he approaches the age of fifty. Increasingly, experienced and novice educators from many nations look to Australia for inspiration and guidance in distance and flexible learning, and it is no exaggeration to state that all of Australia looks westward to Professor Ron Oliver for their own homegrown source of educational technology expertise.

Part Four
Organizations and Associations

Introduction

Emily Hunter and Amy McElveen, Editors

Part Four includes annotated entries for associations and organizations, most of which are headquartered in North America, whose interests are in some manner significant to the fields of instructional technology and educational media. For the most part, these organizations consist of professionals in the field or agencies which offer services to the educational media community. Entries are separated into sections for the United States and Canada. The U.S. organizations are also organized into a classified list designed to facilitate location of organizations by their specialized interests or services. (The Canadian section is small enough not to need such a list.) In addition, one organization based in Cape Town, South Africa is named.

Information for this section was obtained through e-mail directing each organization to an individual web form through which the updated information could be submitted electronically into a database created by Dr. Mike Orey. Although the section editors made every effort to contact and follow up with organization representatives, responding to the annual request for an update was the responsibility of the organization representatives. The editing team would like to thank those respondents who helped ensure the currency and accuracy of this section by responding to the request for an update. So that readers can judge the accuracy of information provided by each entry, a "last updated" date has been provided at the end of entries. Figures quoted as dues refer to annual amounts unless stated otherwise. Where dues, membership, and meeting information is not applicable, such information is omitted. Readers are encouraged to contact the editors with names of unlisted media-related organizations for investigation and possible inclusion in the 2007 edition.

Classified List

Adult and Continuing Education

(ALA Round Table) Continuing Library Education Network and Exchange (CLENERT)

Association for Continuing Higher Education (ACHE)

Association for Educational Communications and Technology (AECT)

National Education Telecommunications Organization & Education Satellite Company (NETO/EDSAT)

National University Continuing Education Association (NUCEA)

Network for Continuing Medical Education (NCME)

PBS Adult Learning Service (ALS)

University Continuing Education Association (UCEA)

Children- and Youth-Related Organizations

American Montessori Society

Association for Childhood Education International (ACEI)

Association for Library Service to Children (ALSC)

(CEC) Technology and Media Division (TAM)

Children's Television International, Inc.

Close Up Foundation

Computer Learning Foundation

Council for Exceptional Children (CEC)

National Association for the Education of Young Children (NAEYC)

National PTA

Young Adult Library Services Association (YALSA)

Communication

Association for Educational Communications and Technology (AECT)

Health Science Communications Association (HeSCA)

International Association of Business Communicators (IABC)

Lister Hill National Center for Biomedical Communications of the National Library of Medicine

National Communication Association (NCA)

National Council of the Churches of Christ

Computers

(AECT) Division of Interactive Systems and Computers (DISC)
Association for the Advancement of Computing in Education (AACE)
Association for Computers and the Humanities (ACH)
Computer Learning Foundation
Computer-Using Educators, Inc. (CUE)
International Society for Technology in Education (ISTE)
Online Computer Library Center (OCLC)
Society for Computer Simulation (SCS)

Copyright

Association of American Publishers (AAP)
Association of College and Research Libraries (ACRL)
Copyright Clearance Center (CCC)
Hollywood Film Archive
International Copyright Information Center (INCINC)
Library of Congress
Multimedia Education Group (MEG), University of Cape Town

Distance Education

Community College Satellite Network (CCSN)
Instructional Telecommunications Council (ITC)
International Society for Technology in Education (ISTE)
International Telecommunications Satellite Organization (INTELSAT)
National Education Telecommunications Organization & EDSAT Institute
    (NETO/EDSAT)

Education—General

American Society of Educators (ASE)
Association for Childhood Education International (ACEI)
Association for Experiential Education (AEE)
Council for Basic Education
Education Development Center, Inc.
Institute for Development of Educational Activities, Inc. (I|I|D|E|A|)
Minorities in Media (MIM)
National Association of State Textbook Administrators (NASTA)
National Clearinghouse for Bilingual Education
National Council for Accreditation of Teacher Education (NCATE)
National School Boards Association (NSBA) Institute for the Transfer of
    Technology to Education (ITTE)
The Learning Team (TLT)

Education—Higher

American Association of Community Colleges (AACC)
American Association of State Colleges and Universities
Association for Continuing Higher Education (ACHE)
Association for Library and Information Science Education (ALISE)
Community College Association for Instruction and Technology (CCAIT)
Consortium of College and University Media Centers (CCUMC)
Multimedia Education Group (MEG)
Northwest College and University Council for the Management of Educational Technology
PBS Adult Learning Service
University Continuing Education Association (UCEA)

Equipment

Association for Childhood Education International (ACEI)
Educational Products Information Exchange (EPIE Institute)
ITA
Library and Information Technology Association (LITA)
National School Supply and Equipment Association (NSSEA)
Society of Cable Telecommunications Engineers (SCTE)

Film and Video

Academy of Motion Picture Arts and Sciences (AMPAS)
(AECT) Division of Telecommunications (DOT)
(AECT) Industrial Training and Education Division (ITED)
Agency for Instructional Technology (AIT)
American Society of Cinematographers
Anthropology Film Center (AFC)
Association for Educational Communications and Technology (AECT)
Association of Independent Video and Filmmakers/Foundation for Independent Video and Film (AIVF/FIVF)
Cable in the Classroom
Central Educational Network (CEN)
Children's Television International, Inc.
Close Up Foundation
Community College Satellite Network
Council on International Non-theatrical Events (CINE)
Film Advisory Board
Film Arts Foundation (FAF)
Film/Video Arts, Inc.
Great Plains National ITV Library (GPN)

Hollywood Film Archive
International Teleconferencing Association (ITCA)
International Television Association (ITVA)
ITA
National Aeronautics and Space Administration (NASA)
National Alliance for Media Arts and Culture (NAMAC)
National Association of Broadcasters (NAB)
National Education Telecommunications Organization & Education Satellite Company (NETO/EDSAT)
National Endowment for the Humanities (NEH)
National Film Board of Canada (NFBC)
National Film Information Service (offered by AMPAS)
National Information Center for Educational Media (NICEM)
National ITFS Association (NIA/ITFS)
National Telemedia Council, Inc. (NTC)
The New York Festivals
Pacific Film Archive (PFA)
PBS Adult Learning Service (ALS)
PBS VIDEO
Public Broadcasting Service (PBS)
Society of Cable Telecommunications Engineers (SCTE)

Games, Toys, Play, Simulation, Puppetry

Puppeteers of America, Inc. (POA)
Society for Computer Simulation (SCS)
USA-Toy Library Association (USA-TLA)

Health-Related Organizations

Health Science Communications Association (HeSCA)
Lister Hill National Center for Biomedical Communications
Medical Library Association (MLA)
National Association for Visually Handicapped (NAVH)
Network for Continuing Medical Education (NCME)

Information Science

Association for Library and Information Science Education (ALISE)
Freedom of Information Center
International Information Management Congress (IMC)
Library and Information Technology Association (LITA)
Lister Hill National Center for Biomedical Communications
National Commission on Libraries and Information Science (NCLIS)

Innovation

> Institute for Development of Educational Activities, Inc. (I|D|E|A|)
> Institute for the Future (IFTF)
> World Future Society (WFS)

Instructional Technology, Design, and Development

> (AECT) Division of Educational Media Management (DEMM)
> (AECT) Division of Instructional Development (DID)
> Agency for Instructional Technology (AIT)
> Association for Educational Communications and Technology (AECT)
> Community College Association for Instruction and Technology (CCAIT)
> International Society for Performance and Instruction (ISPI)
> Professors of Instructional Design and Technology (PIDT)
> Society for Applied Learning Technology (SALT)
> The Learning Team (TLT)
> Multimedia Education Group, University of Cape Town (MEG)

International Education

> (AECT) International Division (INTL)
> East-West Center
> International Association for Learning Laboratories, Inc. (IALL)
> International Visual Literacy Association, Inc. (IVLA)
> National Clearinghouse for Bilingual Education (NCBE)

Language

> International Association for Learning Laboratories, Inc. (IALL)
> National Clearinghouse for Bilingual Education (NCBE)

Libraries—Academic, Research

> American Library Association (ALA)
> Association of College and Research Libraries (ACRL)

Libraries—Public

> American Library Association (ALA)
> Association for Library Service to Children (ALSC)
> Library Administration and Management Association (LAMA)
> Library and Information Technology Association (LITA)
> Public Library Association (PLA)
> Young Adult Library Services Association (YALSA)

Libraries—Special

American Library Association (ALA)
Association for Library Service to Children (ALSC)
Association of Specialized and Cooperative Library Agencies (ASCLA)
Medical Library Association (MLA)
Special Libraries Association
Theater Library Association
USA Toy Library Association (USA-TLA)

Libraries and Media Centers—School

(AECT) Division of School Media Specialists (DSMS)
(ALA Round Table) Continuing Library Education Network and Exchange (CLENERT)
American Association of School Librarians (AASL)
American Library Association (ALA)
American Library Trustee Association (ALTA)
Association for Educational Communications and Technology (AECT)
Association for Library Collections and Technical Services (ALCTS)
Association for Library Service to Children (ALSC)
Catholic Library Association (CLA)
Consortium of College and University Media Centers
International Association of School Librarianship (IASL)
Library of Congress
National Alliance for Media Arts and Culture (NAMAC)
National Association of Regional Media Centers (NARMC)
National Commission on Libraries and Information Science (NCLIS)
National Council of Teachers of English (NCTE), Commission on Media
On-Line Audiovisual Catalogers (OLAC)
Southeastern Regional Media Leadership Council (SRMLC)

Media Production

(AECT) Media Design and Production Division (MDPD)
American Society of Cinematographers (ASC)
Association for Educational Communications and Technology (AECT)
Association of Independent Video and Filmmakers/Foundation for Independent Video and Film (AIVF/FIVF)
Film Arts Foundation (FAF)
International Graphics Arts Education Association (IGAEA)

Museums and Archives

(AECT) Archives

Association of Systematics Collections
George Eastman House
Hollywood Film Archive
Library of Congress
Museum Computer Network (MCN)
Museum of Modern Art
National Gallery of Art (NGA)
National Public Broadcasting Archives (NPBA)
Pacific Film Archive (PFA)
Smithsonian Institution

Photography

Electronic Camera Repair, C&C Associates
George Eastman House
International Center of Photography (ICP)
National Press Photographers Association, Inc. (NPPA)
Photographic Society of America (PSA)
Society for Photographic Education (SPE)
Society of Photo Technologists (SPT)

Publishing

Graphic Arts Technical Foundation (GATF)
International Graphics Arts Education Association (IGAEA)
Magazine Publishers of America (MPA)
National Association of State Textbook Administrators (NASTA)

Radio

(AECT) Division of Telecommunications (DOT)
American Women in Radio and Television (AWRT)
Corporation for Public Broadcasting (CPB)
National Endowment for the Humanities (NEH)
National Federation of Community Broadcasters (NFCB)
National Public Broadcasting Archives (NPBA)
National Religious Broadcasters (NRB)
Western Public Radio (WPR)

Religious Education

Catholic Library Association (CLA)
National Council of the Churches of Christ in the USA
National Religious Broadcasters (NRB)

Research

(AECT) Research and Theory Division (RTD)
American Educational Research Association (AERA)
Appalachia Educational Laboratory, Inc. (AEL)
ECT Foundation
Education Development Center, Inc.
Mid-continent Regional Educational Laboratory (McREL)
Multimedia Education Group (MEG), University of Cape Town
National Center for Improving Science Education
National Education Knowledge Industry Association (NEKIA)
National Endowment for the Humanities (NEH)
National Science Foundation (NSF)
The NETWORK
North Central Regional Educational Laboratory (NCREL)
Northwest Regional Educational Laboratory (NWREL)
Pacific Regional Educational Laboratory (PREL)
Research for Better Schools, Inc. (RBS)
SouthEastern Regional Vision for Education (SERVE)
Southwest Educational Development Laboratory (SEDL)
WestEd

Special Education

Adaptech Research Project
American Foundation for the Blind (AFB)
Association for Experiential Education (AEE)
Association of Specialized and Cooperative Library Agencies (ASCLA)
Council for Exceptional Children (CEC)
National Association for Visually Handicapped (NAVH)
National Center to Improve Practice (NCIP)
Recording for the Blind and Dyslexic (RFB&D)

Telecommunications

(AECT) Division of Telecommunications (DOT)
Association for the Advancement of Computing in Education (AACE)
Association of Independent Video and Filmmakers/Foundation for Independent Video and Film (AIVF/FIVF)
Community College Satellite Network (CCSN)
Instructional Telecommunications Council (ITC)
International Telecommunications Satellite Organization (INTELSAT)
International Teleconferencing Association (ITCA)
Library and Information Technology Association (LITA)

National Education Telecommunications Organization & Education Satellite Company (NETO/EDSAT)

Research for Better Schools, Inc. (RBS)

Teachers and Writers Collaborative (T&W)

Television

American Women in Radio and Television (AWRT)

Central Educational Network (CEN)

Children's Television International, Inc. (CTI)

Corporation for Public Broadcasting (CPB)

International Television Association (ITVA)

National Cable Television Institute (NCTI)

National Federation of Community Broadcasters (NFCB)

Society of Cable Telecommunications Engineers (SCTE)

Training

(AECT) Industrial Training and Education Division (ITED)

American Management Association (AMA)

American Society for Training and Development (ASTD)

Association for Educational Communications and Technology (AECT)

Federal Educational Technology Association (FETA)

International Society for Performance Improvement (ISPI)

Alphabetical List

UNITED STATES ORGANIZATIONS

Academy of Motion Picture Arts and Sciences (AMPAS). 8949 Wilshire Blvd, Beverly Hills, CA 90211-1972. (310) 247-3000. Fax: (310) 859-9351. E-mail: answers@oscars.org. Web site: http://www.oscars.org. Bruce Davis, Exec. Dir. An honorary organization composed of outstanding individuals in all phases of motion pictures. Seeks to advance the arts and sciences of motion picture technology and artistry. Presents annual film awards; offers artist-in-residence programs; operates reference library and National Film Information Service. *Membership: 6,000. Publications: Annual Index to Motion Picture Credits; Academy Players Directory.*

AEL, Inc. P.O. Box 1348, Charleston, WV 25325-1348. (304) 347-0400, (800) 624-9120. Fax: (304) 347-0487. E-mail: ael.org. Web site: http://www.ael.org. Dr. Doris L. Redfield, President and CEO. AEL is a catalyst for schools and communities to build lifelong learning systems that harness resources, research, and practical wisdom. To contribute knowledge that assists low-performing schools to move toward continuous improvement, AEL conducts research, development, evaluation, and dissemination activities that inform policy, affect educational practice, and contribute to the theoretical and procedural knowledge bases on effective teaching, learning, and schooling. Strategies build on research and reflect a commitment to empowering individuals and building local capacity. AEL serves Kentucky, Tennessee, Virginia, and West Virginia. *Publications:* The AEL Electronic Library contains links to free online tools and information created by staff on a wide array of education-related topics. In addition there are the online versions of AEL's newsletters. *The Link* is a free quarterly publication that provides helpful information to practitioners about trends in education, and *TransFormation* is written for those interested in policy related to education.

Agency for Instructional Technology (AIT). Box A, Bloomington, IN 47402-0120. (812) 339-2203. Fax: (812) 333-4218. E-mail: info@ait.net. Web site: http://www.ait.net. Charles E. Wilson, Executive Director. The Agency for Instructional Technology has been a leader in educational technology since 1962. A nonprofit organization, AIT is one of the largest providers of instructional TV programs in North America. AIT is also a leading developer of other educational media, including online instruction, CDs, videodiscs, and instructional software. AIT learning resources are used on six continents and reach nearly 34 million students in North America each year. AIT products have received many national and international honors, including an Emmy and Peabody award. Since 1970, AIT has developed 39 major curriculum packages through the consortium process it pioneered. American state and Canadian provincial agencies have cooperatively funded and widely used these learning resources. Funding for other product development comes from state, provincial, and local departments of education; federal and private institutions; corporations and private sponsors; and AIT's own resources. No regular public meetings. Updated: 3/4/04. Cheri Harris, charris@ait.net

American Association of Colleges for Teacher Education (AACTE). 1307 New York Ave., NW, Ste. 300, Washington, DC 20005-4701. (202) 293-2450. Fax: (202) 457-8095. Web site: http://www.aacte.org/. David G. Imig, President and Chief Executive Officer. Adjunct to the ERIC Clearinghouse on Teaching and Teacher Education. AACTE provides leadership for the continuing transformation of professional preparation programs to ensure competent and caring educators for all America's children and youth. It is the principal professional association for college and university leaders with responsibility for educator preparation. It is the major voice, nationally and internationally, for American colleges, schools, and departments of education, and is a locus for discussion and decision-making on professional issues of institutional, state, national and international significance. *Membership:* more than 2,400 members. Membership in AACTE is institutional and there are three categories: regular, affiliate, and candidate. Regular membership is available to four-year degree-granting colleges and universities with significant commitment to the preparation of education personnel, which meet all the criteria for regular or candidate membership. Affiliate membership is available to not-for profit two-year or four year degree-granting foreign institutions of higher education; not-for-profit two-year domestic degree-granting institutions of higher education; and not-for profit organizations, state education associations, regional education laboratories, university based research or policy centers, and other not-for profit education associations as identified by the AACTE Board of Directors. Many meetings, including the New Deans Institute. See http://www. aacte.org/Events/default.htm. *Publications:* AACTE publishes books and other publications in a range of areas that address key issues related to teacher education. We have more than 70 titles available on a variety of subject areas. Updated: 5/22/03.

American Association of Community Colleges (AACC). One Dupont Circle, NW, Ste. 41, Washington, D.C. 20036-1176. (202) 728-0200. Fax: (202) 833-9390. E-mail: nkent@aacc.nche.edu. Web site: http://www.aacc.nche.edu. George R. Boggs, President and CEO. AACC is a national organization representing the nations more than 1,100 community, junior, and technical colleges. Headquartered in Washington, D.C., AACC serves as a national voice for the colleges and provides key services in the areas of advocacy, research, information, and professional development. The nations community colleges serve more than 10 million students annually, almost half (44%) of all U.S. undergraduates. *Membership:* 1,151 institutions, 31 corporations, 15 international associates, 79 educational associates, 4 foundations. Annual convention held April of each year. *Publications: Community College Journal* (bimonthly); *Community College Times* (biweekly newspaper); *College Times*; *Community College Press* (books, research and program briefs, and monographs). Updated: 7/7/04. Mary Latif, Director of Administrative Services

(AACC) Community College Satellite Network (CCSN). One Dupont Cir. NW, Ste. 410, Washington, DC 20036. (202) 728-0200. Fax: (202) 833-2467. E-mail: CCSN@AACC.NCHE.EDU. Web site: http://www.aacc.nche.edu. Monica W. Pilkey, Dir. An office of the American Association of Community Colleges (AACC), CCSN provides leadership and facilitates distance education, teleconferencing, and satellite training to the nation's community colleges. CCSN offers satellite training, discounted teleconferences, free program resources, and general informational assistance in telecommunications to the nation's community colleges. CCSN meets with its members at various industry trade shows and is very active in the AACC annual convention held each spring. CCSN produces a directory of community college satellite downlink and videoconference facilities. *Membership:* 150. *Membership:* $400 for AACC members; $800 for non-AACC members. *Publications: Schedule of Programming* (2/year; contains listings of live and taped teleconferences for training and staff development); *CCSN Fall & Spring Program Schedule* (listing of live and taped teleconferences for training, community and staff development, business and industry training, and more); *Teleconferencing at U.S. Community Colleges* (directory of contacts for community college satellite downlink facilities and videoconference capabilities). A free catalog is available.

American Association of School Librarians (AASL). 50 E. Huron St., Chicago, IL 60611-2795. (312) 280-4386, (800) 545-2433, ext. 4386. Fax: (312) 664-7459. E-mail: aasl@ala.org. Web site: http://www.ala.org/aasl. Julie A. Walker, Exec. Dir. A division of the American Library Association, AASL is interested in the general improvement and extension of school library media services for children and youth. Activities and projects of the association are divided among 30 committees and 3 sections. *Membership:* 9,800. Personal membership in ALA (1st year, $50; 2nd year, $75; 3rd and subsequent yrs., $100) plus $40 for personal membership in AASL. Inactive, student, retired, unemployed, and reduced-salary memberships are available. National conference every two years. *Publications: School Library Media Research* (electronic research journal, Web site: http://www.ala.org/aasl/SLMR/). *Knowledge Quest* (print journal; online companion at Web site: http://www.ala.org/aasl/kqWeb/). *AASL Hotlinks* (e-mail newsletter). Nonserial publications (http://www.ala.org/aasl/pubs_menu.html). Updated: 2/18/05. Robin Ely, rely@ala.org, (312) 280-4382

American Association of State Colleges and Universities (AASCU). One Dupont Cir., NW, Ste. 700, Washington, D.C. 20036-1192. (202) 293-7070. Fax: (202) 296-5819. E-mail: currisc.aascu.org. James B. Appleberry, Pres. Membership is open to regionally accredited institutions of higher education (and those in the process of securing accreditation) that offer programs leading to the degree of bachelor, master, or doctor, and that are wholly or partially state-supported and state-controlled. Organized and operated exclusively for educational, scientific, and literary purposes, its particular purposes are to improve higher education within its member institutions through cooperative planning, studies, and research on common educational problems and the development of a more unified program of action among its members; and to provide other needed and worthwhile educational services to the colleges and universities it may represent. *Membership:* 393 institutions (university), 28 systems, and 10 associates based on current student enrollment at institution. *Publications: MEMO: To the President; The Center Associate; Office of Federal Program Reports; Office of Federal Program Deadlines.* (Catalogs of books and other publications available upon request.)

American Educational Research Association (AERA). 1230 17th St., NW., Washington, DC. 20036-3078. (202) 223-9485. Fax: (202) 775-1824. E-mail: outreach@aera.net. Web site: http://www.aera.net. Marilyn Cochran-Smith, President of the Board, 2004–2005, cochrans@bc.edu. AERA is an international professional organization with the primary goal of advancing educational research and its practical application. Its members include educators and administrators; directors of research, testing, or evaluation in federal, state, and local agencies; counselors; evaluators; graduate students; and behavioral scientists. The broad range of disciplines represented includes education, psychology, statistics, sociology, history, economics, philosophy, anthropology, and political science. AERA has more than 145 Special Interest Groups, including Advanced Technologies for Learning, Computer Applications in Education, Electronic Networking, Instructional Systems and Intelligent Tutors, Instructional Technology, and Text, Technology and Learning Strategies. *Membership:* 23,000, dues vary by category, ranging from $20 for students to $45 for voting members, for one year. See AERA Web site for complete details: www.aera.net. *Publications: Educational Researcher; American Educational Research Journal; Journal of Educational and Behavioral Statistics; Educational Evaluation and Policy Analysis; Review of Research in Education; Review of Educational Research.* Books: *Handbook of Research on Teaching,* 2001 (rev., 4th edition); *Ethical Standards of AERA, Cases and Commentary,* 2002; *Standards for Educational and Psychological Testing* (rev. and expanded, 1999). Copublished by AERA, American Psychological Association, and the National Council on Measurement in Education. Updated: 7/7/04. Marilyn Cochran-Smith, cochrans@bc.edu

American Foundation for the Blind (AFB). 11 Penn Plaza, Ste. 300, New York, NY 10001. (212) 502-7600, (800) AFB-LINE (232-5463). Fax: (212) 502-7777. E-mail: afbinfo@afb.net. Web site: http://www.afb.org/default.asp. Carl R. Augusto, Pres.; Kelly Parisi, Vice Pres. of Communications. AFB is a leading national resource for people who are blind or visually impaired, the organizations that serve them, and the general public. A nonprofit organization founded in 1921 and recognized as Helen Keller's cause in the United States, AFB's mission is to enable people who are blind or visually impaired to achieve equality of access and opportunity that will ensure freedom of choice in their lives. AFB is headquartered in New York City with offices in Atlanta, Dallas, Huntington (West Virginia), and San Francisco. A governmental relations office in AFB is headquartered in Washington, DC. *Membership:* The American Foundation for the Blind is not a membership organization. *Publications: AFB News* (free—online only); *Journal of Visual Impairment & Blindness; AFB Press Catalog of Publications* (free). *AccessWorld* (free-online only). Subscriptions to JVIB: Tel: (800) 232-3044 or (412) 741-1398. E-mail: afbsub@ abdintl.com. Updated: 4/11/05. Ellen Couch, Manager Information & Referral

American Library Association (ALA). 50 E. Huron St., Chicago, IL 60611. (800) 545-2433. Fax: 312-440-9374. E-mail: ala@ala.org. Web site: http://www.ala.org. Keith Michael Fiels, Exec. Dir. The ALA is the oldest and largest national library association. Its 64,222 members represent all types of libraries: state, public, school, and academic, as well as special libraries serving persons in government, commerce, the armed services, hospitals, prisons, and other institutions. The ALA is the chief advocate of achievement and maintenance of high-quality library information services through protection of the right to read, educating librarians, improving services, and making information widely accessible. See separate entries for the following affiliated and subordinate organizations: American Association of School Librarians, American Library Trustee Association, Association for Library Collections and Technical Services, Association for Library Service to Children, Association of College and Research Libraries, Association of Specialized and Cooperative Library Agencies, Library Administration and Management Association, Library and Information Technology Association, Public Library Association, Reference and User Services Association, Young Adult Library Services Association, and Continuing Library Education Network and Exchange Round Table. *Membership:* 64,222 members at present; everyone who cares about libraries is allowed to join the American Library Association. *Membership:* Professional rate: $50 first year; $75 second year; third year and renewing, $100. Student members: $25. Retirees: $35. International librarians: $60. Trustees: $45. Associate members (those not in the library field): $45. Annual Conference. *Publications: American Libraries; Booklist; Choice; Book Links.* Updated: 3/9/05. Karen Muller, library@ala.org

American Library Trustee Association (ALTA). 50 E. Huron St., Chicago, IL 60611. (312) 280-2161. Fax: (312) 280-3257. E-mail: kward@ala.org. Web site: http://www. ala.org/alta. Susan Roman, Exec. Dir. A division of the American Library Association, ALTA is interested in the development of effective library service for people in all types of communities and libraries. Members, as policymakers, are concerned with organizational patterns of service, the development of competent personnel, the provision of adequate financing, the passage of suitable legislation, and the encouragement of citizen support for libraries. *Membership:* 1,710. *Membership:* $50 plus membership in ALA. Held in conjunction with ALA. *Publications: Trustee Voice* (quarterly newsletter); professional monographs and pamphlets.

American Management Association International (AMA). 1601 Broadway, New York, NY 10019-7420. (212) 586-8100. Fax: (212) 903-8168. E-mail: cust_serv@amanet.org. Web site: http://www.amanet.org. Barbara M. Barrett, Pres. and CEO. Founded in 1923, AMA provides educational forums worldwide where members and their colleagues learn superior, practical business skills, and explore best practices of world-class organizations through interaction with each other and expert faculty practitioners. AMA's publishing program provides tools individuals use to extend learning beyond the classroom in a process of lifelong professional growth and development through education. AMA operates management centers and offices in Atlanta, Boston (Watertown), Chicago, Hamilton (NY), Kansas City (Leawood), New York, San Francisco, Saranac Lake (NY), and Washington, DC, and through AMA/International, in Brussels, Tokyo, Shanghai, Islamabad, and Buenos Aires. In addition, it has affiliated centers in Toronto, Mexico City, Sao Paulo, Taipei, Istanbul, Singapore, Jakarta, and Dubai. AMA offers conferences, seminars, and membership briefings where there is an interchange of information, ideas, and experience in a wide variety of management topics. *Membership:* over 75,000. *Membership:* corporate, $595–$1645; growing company, $525–$1845; indiv., $165 plus $40 per additional newsletter. *Publications: Management Review* (membership); *Compensation & Benefits Review; Organizational Dynamics; HR Focus; President; Getting Results.;* and *The Take-Charge Assistant.* Also 70 business-related books per year, as well as numerous surveys and management briefings. Other services offered by AMA include FYI Video; Extension Institute (self-study programs in both print and audio formats); AMA Interactive Series (self-paced learning on CD-ROM); Operation Enterprise (young adult program); AMA On-Site (videoconferences); the Information Resource Center (for AMA members only), a management information and library service; and six bookstores.

American Montessori Society (AMS). 281 Park Ave. S, New York, NY 10010. (212) 358-1250. Fax: (212) 358-1256. E-mail: mimi@amshq.org. Web site: http://www.amshq.org. Eileen Roper Ast, Executive Director. Dedicated to promoting better education for all children through teaching strategies consistent with the Montessori system. Membership is composed of schools in the private and public sectors, teacher education programs, Montessori credentialed teachers, parents, and other individuals. It serves as a resource center and clearinghouse for information and data on Montessori education, prepares teachers in different parts of the country, and conducts a consultation service and accreditation program for school members.

The mission of the American Montessori Society is to promote high-quality Montessori education for all children by providing service to parents, teachers, and schools. Membership includes schools, teachers, parents, school heads, and friends of Montessori. This total is approximately 11,000. Dues vary based on membership. Membership is available for Certified Montessori Teachers, Montessori Schools, and General Members (includes those who are not certified Montessori Teachers, parents, friends of AMS). Three regional and four professional development symposia under the auspices of the AMS Teachers' Section. *Publications: AMS Montessori LIFE* (quarterly); *Schoolheads* (newsletter); *Montessori in Contemporary American Culture,* Margaret Loeffler, Editor; *Authentic American Montessori School; AMS The Montessori School Management Guide;* AMS position papers; and the following AMS *Publications: Montessori Teaching A Growth Profession; The Elementary School Years 6-12; Your Child Is in an Accredited School; Some Considerations in Starting a Montessori School; Montessori Education Q&A; The Early Childhood Years, 3–6; Attracting and Preparing Montessori Teacher for the 21st Century; Adolescent Programs; The Kindergarten Experience; Some Comparisons of Montessori Education with Traditional Education; Helping Children Become All They Can Become; The Montessori Family: A Parent Brochure; Tuition and Salary Surveys.* Updated: 5/13/03. Carol Monroe, Director of Finance & Administration, (212) 358-1250, ext. 203.

American Society for Training and Development (ASTD). 1640 King St., Box 1443, Alexandria, VA 22313. (703) 683-8100. Fax: (703) 683-1523. E-mail: customercare@ astd.org. Web site: http://www.astd.org. Tony Bingham, President and CEO. Founded in 1944, ASTD is the world's premiere professional association in the field of workplace learning and performance. *Membership:* ASTD's membership includes more than 70,000 people in organizations from every level of the field of workplace performance in more than 100 countries. Its leadership and members work in more than 15,000 multinational corporations, small and medium-sized businesses, government agencies, colleges, and universities. ASTD is the leading resource on workplace learning and performance issues, providing information, research, analysis, and practical information derived from its own research, the knowledge and experience of its members, its conferences and publications, and the coalitions and partnerships it has built through research and policy work. ASTD has a board membership of 16 and staff of 90 to serve member needs. There are 70,000 National and Chapter members. The Classic Membership ($150.00) is the foundation of ASTD member benefits. Publications, newsletters, research reports, discounts and services and much more, are all designed to help you do your job better. Here's what you have to look forward to when you join: Training and Development—Monthly publication of the *Industry*. Stay informed on trends, successful practices, public policy, ASTD news, case studies and more. *Performance in Practice*—Quarterly newsletter offers articles written by members for members. "Hot Topics"—ASTD's online reading list gets you up to speed on leading edge issues in the training and performance industry. Database and Archive Access—FREE online access to Trainlit, ASTD's searchable database featuring products reviews, book and article summaries and archived articles. *Learning Circuits*—Monthly Webzine features articles, departments and columns that examine new technologies and how they are being applied to workplace learning. *Human Resource Development Quarterly*— In depth studies and reports on human resource theory and practice give you a scholarly look at the training profession. HRDQ is available ONLY online with archives dating back to 1998. *ASTD News Briefs*—Weekly news briefs relating to the training and performance industry. Special Reports and Research—*Trends Report, State of the Industry, Learning Outcomes and International Comparison Report. Training Data Book*—An annual publication, now online, draws on ASTD research and highlights the nature and magnitude of corporate investment in employer-provided training. Research Assistance— ASTD provides an Information Center that can provide you with the research you're looking for while you're on the phone. You can also send your research request through the Web site. Just provide your member number! Membership Directory—Online directory and searchable by a variety of criteria. Access to the Membership Directory is for Members Only, and is being enhanced for future networking capabilities. Buyers Guide & Consultants Directory—A one-stop resource for information on over 600 suppliers of training and performance products and services. We also have several segments that you can add on to your Classic Membership. Membership Plus: Your choice of 12 info lines or four prechosen ASTD books ($79.00). Training Professionals: Includes an annual subscription to *Info-lines, Pfeiffer's Best of Training,* and the *ASTD Training and Performance Yearbook* ($130.00). Organizational Development/Leadership Professionals: Includes *Pfeiffer's Consulting Annual, Leader to Leader and Leadership in Action* ($200.00). Consulting: Includes annual subscription to *C2M* (quarterly journal) and *Pfeiffer's Consulting Annual* ($75.00). E-Learning: Includes *Training Media Review Online* (Database and newsletter that evaluates audio, video, software and online products 6/year e-mail newsletters year) and *ASTD Distance Learning Yearbook* ($175.00). International Conference. *Publications: Training & Development Magazine*; *Info-Line*; *The American Mosaic*: An In-depth Report of Diversity on the Future of Diversity at Work; *ASTD Directory of Academic Programs in T&D/HRD; Training and Development Handbook*; Quarterly publications: *Performance in Practice; National Report on Human Resources; Washington Policy Report.* ASTD also has recognized professional forums, most of which produce newsletters. Updated: 7/7/04. CustomerCare@astd.org, (703) 683-8100.

American Society of Cinematographers (ASC). 1782 N. Orange Dr., Hollywood, CA 90028. (213) 969-4333, (213) 876-4973, (213) 882-6391. E-mail: suzanne.lezotte @creativeplanet.com. Victor Kemper, Pres. ASC is an educational, cultural, and professional organization. *Membership:* 336. Membership is by invitation to those who are actively engaged as directors of photography and have demonstrated outstanding ability. Classifications are Active, Active Retired, Associates, and Honorary. Book Bazaar (Open House); Awards Open House; Annual ASC Awards. *Publications: American Cinematographer Video Manual; Light on Her Face;* and *American Cinematographers Magazine.*

American Society of Educators (ASE). 1429 Walnut St., Philadelphia, PA 19102. (215) 563-6005, (215) 587-9706. E-mail: tatjana@media-methods.com. Web site: http://www. media-methods.com. Michele Sokolof, Publisher and Editorial Director. American Society of Educators publishes *Media & Methods Magazine,* the recognized authoritative publication dedicated to exemplary teaching practices and resource materials for K–12 educators. Full of pragmatic articles on how to use today's instructional technologies and teaching tools, *Media & Methods* is the flagship magazine of practical educational applications specifically for school district technology coordinators, media specialists, school librarians, administrators, and teachers. A long-respected and treasured magazine focusing on how to integrate today's tools for teaching as well as for administrative and library management in K–12 schools. Individuals subscribe to *Media & Methods Magazine.* Meetings occur at national education conferences. *Media & Methods Magazine* is published 7 times a year. Cost: $33.50 per year. Updated: 7/7/04/. Tatjana Miloradovic, tatjana@media-methods. com

American Telecommunications Group (ATG). 1400 E. Touhy, Ste. 260, Des Plaines, IL 60018-3305. (847) 390-8700. Fax: (847) 390-9435. E-mail: gerie@atgonline.org. Web site: http://www.itmonline.com/Marketplace/atg.htm. James A. Fellows, President. The American Telecommunications Group serves as am umbrella framework for six entities that are organized to provide and support educational and programming services, professional development and policy development for public broadcasting, educational telecommunications and related public service media: American Center for Children and Media—a professional development and resource center for people who create, commission, distribute and study children's TV and digital media; Center for Education Initiatives—supports distance learning, adult training, and evaluation of new technology initiatives in education; Central Educational Network—a nonprofit executive-level association of public broadcasting licensees that undertakes joint activities and services, administers program funds and awards, and conducts leadership exchanges; Continental Program Marketing—distributes quality programming to U.S. public television stations; The Hartford Gunn Institute —assists in developing fundamental plans for building the second generation of public telecommunications; The Higher Education Telecommunications Consortium—assists colleges and universities in managing telecommunications operations and advances the expansion and development of higher education–based telecommunication services. *Membership:* Membership in the CEN component of ATG is available to public television and telecommunications organizations and agencies. Membership in The Higher Education Telecommunications Consortia is available to public television stations that are licensed to colleges and universities. *Publications: Close Up Online* is a periodic briefing that keeps readers informed about the various services and activities of the organizations that are a part of the ATG. *Close Up Online* also reports on noteworthy people and activities throughout our nationwide constituency. Updated: 7/7/04. Marilyn Price, marilyn@ atgonline.org

American Women in Radio and Television (AWRT). 8405 Greensboro Drive, Ste. 800, McLean, VA 22102. (703) 506-3290, (703) 506-3266. E-mail: info@awrt.org. Web site: http://www.awrt.org. Maria E. Brennan. American Women in Radio and Television is a national, nonprofit organization that extends membership to qualified professionals in the electronic media and allied fields. AWRT's mission is to advance the impact of women in the electronic media and allied fields by educating, advocating and acting as a resource to its members and the industry. Founded in 1951, AWRT has worked to improve the quality of broadcast programming and the image of women as depicted in radio and television. 40 chapters. *Membership:* Student memberships available, $125. Annual Leadership Summit, Annual Gracie Allen Awards. *Publications: News and Views; Resource Directory; Careers in the Electronic Media; Sexual Harassment;* Mentoring Brochure (pamphlet). Updated: 3/1/05. info@awrt.org

Anthropology Film Center (AFC). #5 Paseo Sin Nombre, Valencia, NM 87535-9635. (505) 757-2219. Mailing address: HC70 Box 3209, Glorieta, NM 87535-9635. E-mail: anthrofilm.org. Web site: http://www.anthrofilm.org. Carroll Williams, Dir. Offers the Ethnographic/Documentary Film Program, a 32-week full-time course for 16mm film, CD, and DVD production and theory. Workshops are offered as well. AFC also provides consultation, research facilities, and a specialized library. Workshops in visual anthropology are offered. September and June starts. We do not have memberships. No dues. A filmography for American Indian Education. Updated: 3/16/05. Carla McClure, mcclurec@ael.org, (800) 614-9120.

Association for Childhood Education International (ACEI). 17904 Georgia Ave., Ste. 215, Olney, MD 20832. (301) 570-2111. Fax: (301) 570-2212. E-mail: ACEIHQ@aol. com. Web site: http://www.acei.org. Executive Director, Jerry Odland. ACEI publications reflect careful research, broad-based views, and consideration of a wide range of issues affecting children from infancy through early adolescence. Many are media-related in nature. The journal (*Childhood Education*) is essential for teachers, teachers-in-training, teacher educators, day care workers, administrators, and parents. Articles focus on child development and emphasize practical application. Regular departments include book reviews (child and adult); film reviews, pamphlets, software, research, and classroom idea-sparkers. Six issues are published yearly, including a theme issue devoted to critical concerns. *Membership:* 12,000. *Membership:* $45, professional; $29, student; $23, retired; $80, institutional. 2006 Annual Conference, San Antonio, TX. *Publications: Childhood Education* (official journal) with *ACEI Exchange* (insert newsletter); *Journal of Research in Childhood Education;* Professional Focus Quarterlies (*Focus on Infants and Toddlers, Focus on Pre-K and K, Focus on Elementary, Focus on Middle School, Focus of Teacher Education,* and *Focus on Inclusive Education*). Numerous books, including new titles such as: *Childrens Fears of War and Terrorism: A Resource for Teachers and Parents; The Developmental Benefits of Playgrounds, Chinese American Children & Families: A Guide for Educators & Service Providers; Creative Construction of Mathematics and Science Concepts in Early Childhood;* and *Developmental Continuity Across Preschool and Primary Grades: Implications for Teachers* (position paper); and pamphlets. Updated: 2/22/05. Marilyn Gardner, Director of IT, Membership.

Association for Computers and the Humanities (ACH). c/o Stéfan Sinclair, Exec. Secretary of ACH, SOTA, McMaster University, 1280 Main Street West, Hamilton, ONL8S 4M2 Canada. (905) 525-9140 ext. 23930. Fax: (905) 527-6793. E-mail: sgsinclair@gmail.com. Web site: http://www.ach.org. Stéfan Sinclair, Exec. Secretary. The Association for Computers and the Humanities is an international professional organization. Since its establishment, it has been the major professional society for people working in computer-aided research in literature and language studies, history, philosophy, and other humanities disciplines, and especially research involving the manipulation and analysis of textual materials. The ACH is devoted to disseminating information among its members about work in the field of humanities computing, as well as encouraging the development and dissemination of significant textual and linguistic resources and software for scholarly research. *Membership:* 300. *Membership:* Individual regular member, US $65. Student or Emeritus Faculty member, US $55. Joint membership (for couples), add US $7. Annual meetings held with the Association for Literary and Linguistic Computing. *Publications: Computers and the Humanities; Humanist.* Updated: 4/5/05. Stéfan Sinclair (contact as above).

Association for Continuing Higher Education (ACHE). Trident Technical College, P.O. Box 118067, CE-M, Charleston, SC 29423-8067. (803) 574-6658. Fax: (803) 574-6470. E-mail: irene.barrineau@tridenttech.edu. Web site: http://www.acheinc.org/. Dr. Pamela R. Murray, President; Ms. Michele D. Shinn, Executive Vice President. ACHE is an institution-based organization of colleges, universities, and individuals dedicated to the promotion of lifelong learning and excellence in continuing higher education. ACHE encourages professional networks, research, and exchange of information for its members and advocates continuing higher education as a means of enhancing and improving society. *Membership:* 1,950 individuals in 640 institutions. *Membership:* $60, professional; $260, institutional. For a list of Annual and Regional Meetings, see http://www. acheinc.org/ calendar_of_events.html. *Publications: Journal of Continui*ng Higher Education (3/year); *Five Minutes with ACHE* (newsletter, 10/year); *Proceedings* (annual).

Association for Educational Communications and Technology (AECT). 1800 N Stonelake Dr., Ste. 2, Bloomington, IN 47404. (812) 335-7675. Fax: (812) 335-7678. E-mail: aect@aect.org. Web site: http://www.aect.org. Phillip Harris, Executive Director. AECT is an international professional association concerned with the improvement of learning and instruction through media and technology. It serves as a central clearinghouse and communications center for its members, who include instructional technologists, library media specialists, religious educators, government media personnel, school administrators and specialists, and training media producers. AECT members also work in the armed forces, public libraries, museums, and other information agencies of many kinds, including those related to the emerging fields of computer technology. Affiliated organizations include the Association for Media and Technology in Education in Canada (AMTEC), Community College Association for Instructional and Technology (CCAIT), Consortium of College and University Media Centers (CCUMC), International Association for Learning Laboratories (IALL), International Visual Literacy Association (IVLA), Minorities in Media (MIM), National Association of Regional Media Centers (NARMC), New England Educational Media Association (NEEMA), and the Southeastern Regional Media Leadership Council (SRMLC). Each of these affiliated organizations has its own listing in the Yearbook. The ECT Foundation is also related to the Association for Educational Communications and Technology and has an independent listing. Divisions (10) are as follows: Instructional Design & Development, Information & Technology Management, Training & Performance, Research & Theory, Systemic Change, Distance Learning, Media & Technology, Teacher Education, International, and Multimedia Production. *Membership:* 3,000 members in good standing from K–12, college and university, and private sector/government training. Anyone interested can join. There are different memberships available for students, retirees, corporations, and international parties. We also have a new option for electronic membership for international affiliates. *Membership:* $95.00 standard membership. Discounts are available for students and retirees. Additional fees apply to corporate memberships or international memberships. Summer Institute held each July. Annual Conference each year in late October. *Publications: TechTrends* (6/year, free with membership; $55 nonmembers); *Educational Technology Research and Development* (quarterly, $35 members; $75 nonmembers); *Quarterly Review of Distance Education* (quarterly, $55 members); many books & videotapes. Updated: 3/10/05. Phillip Harris, pharris@aect.org

AECT Archives (AECT). University of Maryland, Hornbake Library, College Park, MD 20742. (301) 405-9255. Fax: (301) 314-2634. E-mail: tc65@umail.umd.edu. Web site: http://www.library.umd.edu/UMCP/NPBA/npba.html. Thomas Connors, Archivist, National Public Broadcasting Archives. A collection of media, manuscripts, and related materials representing important developments in visual and audiovisual education and in instructional technology. The collection is housed as part of the National Public Broadcasting Archives. Maintained by the University of Maryland in cooperation with AECT. Open to researchers and scholars. Updated: 2/27/03. Tom Connors, tc65@umail.umd.edu

(AECT) Division of Design and Development (D&D). 1800 N. Stonelake Dr. Ste. 2, Bloomington, IN 47408. (315) 443 1362. Fax: (315) 443 1218. E-mail: eboling@ indiana.edu. Web site: http://aect-members.org/dd/. Elizabeth Boling, President. D&D is composed of individuals from business, government, and academic settings concerned with the systematic design of instruction and the development of solutions to performance problems. Members interests include the study, evaluation, and refinement of design processes; the creation of new models of instructional development; the invention and improvement of techniques for managing the development of instruction; the development and application of professional ID competencies; the promotion of academic programs for preparation of ID professionals; and the dissemination of research and development work in ID. *Membership:* Approximately

750. Membership is open to any AECT member. Division membership can be indicated when joining or renewing AECT membership or any time thereafter and has no additional cost associated. Meeting held in conjunction with the annual AECT Convention. *Publications:* D&D listserv with an occasional D&D newsletter and papers. Members regularly contribute to and read *Educational Technology Research & Development* and *TechTrends*. Division news can be found at: http://aect-members. org/dd/. Updated: 2/19/05. Trey Martindale, treymartindale@gmail.com

(AECT) Division of Learning and Performance Environments (DLPE). 1025 Vermont Ave. NW, Ste. 820, Washington, DC 20005. (202) 347-7834. Fax: (928) 523-7624. E-mail: sschaff@purdue.edu. Web site: http://www.aect.org/T&P/index.htm. Scott Schaffer, President; Pam Loughner, President-Elect. Supports human learning and performance through the use of computer-based technology; design, development, evaluation, assessment, and implementation of learning environments and performance systems for adults. A Division of AECT. *Membership:* See www.aect.org for membership information. One division membership included in the basic AECT membership; additional division memberships $10. Held in conjunction with the annual AECT Convention. *Publications: TechTrends* in coordination with AECT. Updated: 2/19/05. Connie Tibbitts, ctibbits@mindspring.com

(AECT) Division of School Media and Technology. DSMT. 1800 N. Stonelake Dr., Ste. #2, Bloomington, IN 47404. (812) 335-7675, (812) 335-7678. E-mail:aect@aect.org. Web site: http://www.aect.org/Divisions/mt.asp and Web site: http://www.coe.ecu.edu/aect/dsmt/Default.htm. Lois Wilkins, Pres., lwilkins@tapnet.net, and Nancy Reicher, Sec., nreichkc@pei.edu. The School Media and Technology (K–12) Division provides leadership in educational communications and technology by linking professionals holding a common interest in the use of instructional technology and its application to the learning process in the school environment. This division of AECT is of special interest to School Library Media Specialists and others who work with technology in a K–12 environment. *Membership:* One division membership is included in the basic AECT membership, which is $95 for regular status and $130 for comprehensive status; additional division memberships $10. DSMT meets in conjunction with the annual AECT National Convention. *Publications: DSMT Update* is now published in electronic format. The *Update* editors are Mary Alice Anderson and Mary Ann Fitzgerald. Please direct all content questions and comments to them. E-mail to: mfitzger@coe.uga.edu or maryalic@wms.luminet. net. In addition, *TechTrends* is published 6 times annually.

(AECT) International Division (INTL). 1025 Vermont Ave. NW, Ste. 820, Washington, DC 20005. (202) 347-7834. E-mail: khanb@gwis2.circ.gwu.edu. Badrul Khan, Pres. INTL encourages practice and research in educational communication and distance education for social and economic development across national and cultural lines, promotes international exchange and sharing of information, and enhances relationships among international leaders. *Membership:* 295. One division membership included in the basic AECT membership; additional division memberships $10. Meeting held in conjunction with the annual AECT Convention. *Publications:* Newsletter.

(AECT) Media Design and Production Division (MDPD). 1025 Vermont Ave. NW, Ste. 820, Washington, DC 20005. (202) 347-7834. E-mail: chuck@cc.usu.edu. Chuck Stoddard, Pres. MDPD provides an international network that focuses on enhancing the quality and effectiveness of mediated communication, in all media formats, in educational, governmental, hospital, and corporate settings through the interaction of instructional designers, trainers, researchers, and evaluators with media designers and production team specialists who utilize state-of-the-art production skills. *Membership:* 318. One division membership included in the basic AECT membership; additional division memberships $10. Meeting held in conjunction with annual AECT Convention. *Publications:* Newsletter.

(AECT) Research and Theory Division (RTD). 1800 N. Stonelake Dr., Ste. 2. Bloomington, IN 47404. (812) 335-7675. Fax: (812) 335-7678. E-mail: aect@aect. org. Web site: http://www.aect.org. Phil Harris, AECT Executive Director. Seeks to improve the design, execution, utilization, and evaluation of educational technology research; to improve the qualifications and effectiveness of personnel engaged in educational technology research; to advise the educational practitioner as to the use of the research results; to improve research design, techniques, evaluation, and dissemination; to promote both applied and theoretical research on the systematic use of educational technology in the improvement of instruction; and to encourage the use of multiple research paradigms in examining issues related to technology in education. *Membership:* 452. One division membership included in the basic AECT membership; additional division memberships $10. Meeting held in conjunction with annual AECT Convention. *Publications:* Newsletter. Updated: 2/27/03. Phil Harris, aect@aect.org

(AECT) School Media and Technology Division (SMT). 1800 N. Stonelake Dr. Ste. 2, Bloomington, IN 47408. (877) 677-AECT. Fax: (912) 267-4234. E-mail: susan.stansberry@okstate.edu. Web site: http://www.aect-members.org/smt/. Dr. Carol Brown, President; Dr. Susan Stansberry, President-elect; Chwee Beng Lee, Board representative; Chien Yu, Secretary. The School Media and Technology (K–12) Division provides leadership in educational communications and technology by linking professionals holding a common interest in the use of instructional technology and its application to the learning process in the school environment. *Membership:* Members of this division are primarily School Library Media Specialists, K–12 teachers, Instructional Technology Coordinators in K–12 school districts, and Higher Ed Teachers preparing people to work in Library Media programs. Division membership included in the basic AECT membership. Held in conjunction with the annual AECT Convention. No publications at this time.

(AECT) Systemic Change in Education Division (CHANGE). 1800 N. Stonelake Dr. Ste. 2, Bloomington, IN 47408. (877) 677-AECT. Fax: (812) 335-7675. E-mail: frick@indiana.edu. Web site: http://ide.ed.psu.edu/change/. Roberto Joseph, President. CHANGE advocates fundamental changes in educational settings to dramatically improve the quality of education and to enable technology to achieve its potential. Members of the Association for Educational Communications and Technology (AECT) are welcome to join the CHANGE Division. *Membership:* In March 2004, there were approximately 2,500 members of AECT, and of those about 150 are members of CHANGE. Membership in AECT is required. Once an AECT member, one can join the CHANGE Division at no extra cost. Meeting held in conjunction with annual AECT Convention. See the Web site: http://ide.ed.psu.edu/change/. Updated: 3/5/04. Theodore W. Frick, frick@indiana.edu

(AECT) Training & Performance (T&P). 1800 North Stonelake Drive, Ste. 2, Bloomington, IN 47408. (812) 335-7675. Fax: (812) 335-7678. Cynthia.Conn@nau.edu. Web site: http://www.aect.org/T&P/. Cynthia Conn, President; Angela Benson, President-Elect; Pam Loughner, Past-President; Scott Schaffer, Board Representative; Ana Donaldson, VP-Communications. AECT's Training & Performance (T&P) Division serves members from government, business and industry, and academic communities. Its members are training, performance, and education professionals interested in applying current theory and research to training and performance improvement initiatives. Topics of interest to T&P Division members are real world solutions that intersect the use of hard technologies (e.g., computers, the Internet), soft technologies (e.g., instructional design and performance technology processes and models), and current learning and instructional theories (e.g., constructivism, problem-based learning). The Training & Performance Division resulted from the 2000 merger of the former Industrial Training and Education Division (ITED) and the Division for Learning and Performance Environments (DLPE). If you are a training, performance, or education professional who values the application of theory and research to practice, join Association for Educational Communications and Technology (Web site: http://www.aect.org/Membership/) and be sure to specify Training & Performance as one of the divisions you would like to join. *Membership:* Training & Performance Division membership is free with your AECT membership. Meetings are held in conjunction with the annual AECT Conference. Updated: 3/11/05. Cynthia Conn, Cynthia.Conn@nau.edu, (928) 523-7624.

Association for Experiential Education (AEE). 3775 Iris Avenue, Ste. 4, Boulder, CO 80301-2043. (303) 440-8844. Fax: (303) 440-9581. E-mail: aee.org. Web site: http://www.aee.org. Kristin E. Von Wald, Ph.D., Executive Director. AEE is a nonprofit, international, professional organization committed to the development, practice, and evaluation of experiential education in all settings. AEE's vision is to be a leading international organization for the development and application of experiential education principles and methodologies with the intent to create a just and compassionate world by transforming education and promoting positive social change. *Membership:* More than 1,200 members in more than 30 countries including individuals and organizations with affiliations in education, recreation, outdoor adventure programming, mental health, youth service, physical education, management development training, corrections, programming for people with disabilities, and environmental education. *Membership:* $55 student; $95 individual; $125 family; $240 organizational. AEE Annual Conference is in November. Regional Conferences are from February through April. *Publications: The Journal of Experiential Education* (3/year); *Adventure Therapy: Therapeutic Applications of Adventure Programming*; *Manual of Accreditation Standards for Adventure Programs, Vol III*; *The Theory of Experiential Education,* 3rd ed.; *Ethical Issues in Experiential Education,* 2nd ed.; *The K.E.Y. (Keep Exploring Yourself) Group: An Experiential Personal Growth Group Manual*; *Book of Metaphors, Volume II*; *Women's Voices in Experiential Education*; *A Guide to Women's Studies in the Outdoors*; *Administrative Practices of Accredited Adventure Programs.* New publications since last year: *Adventure Program Risk Management Report, Volume 3*; *The Back Door Guide to Short-term Job Adventures*; *Body Stories: Research & Intimate Narratives on Women*; *Coming of Age: The Evolving Field of Adventure Therapy*; *A Discussion of Parallels between Experiential Education and Quaker Education*; *The Game and Playleaders Handbook*; *Lessons Learned: A Guide to Accident Prevention and Crisis Response*; *QRAI Cards: 50 Ideas for Raising Quality and Role Awareness*; *Reflective Learning: Theory & Practice; Rethinking High School: Best Practices on Teaching, Learning & Leadership*; *Teamwork & Teamplay*; *Therapy within Adventure*; *Turth Zone: An Experiential Approach to Organizational Development*; *Under Cottonwoods: A Novel of Friendship, Fly Fishing and Redemption.* Updated: 3/16/05. Christine Day, Membership Manager.

Association for Information and Image Management (AIIM International). 1100 Wayne Avenue, Ste. 1100, Silver Spring, MD 20910. (301) 587-8202. Fax: (301) 587-2711. E-mail: pwinton@aiim.org. Web site: http://www.aiim.org/. John Mancini, President. AIIM International is the industry's leading global organization. We believe that at the center of an effective business infrastructure in the digital age is the ability to capture, manage, store, preserve, and deliver enterprise content to support business processes. The requisite technologies to establish this infrastructure are an extension of AIIM's core document and content technologies. These Enterprise Content Management (ECM) technologies are key enablers of e-Business and include: Content/Document Management, Business Process Management, Enterprise Portals, Knowledge Management, Image Management, Data Warehousing, and Data Mining. AIIM is a neutral and unbiased source of information. We produce educational, solution-oriented events and conferences, provide up-to-the-minute industry information through publications and our online ECM Resource Center, and are an ANSI/ISO-accredited standards developer. *Membership:* Trade Membership: $1,000/yr; New Professional Membership: $62.50; Renewal Professional Membership: $125. *Publications:* AIIM Content Management Solutions Seminars, AIIM Service Company Executive Forum. *AIM E-DOC Magazine*; *DOC.1* e-Newsletter. Updated: 5/13/03. Beth Mayhew; bmayhew@aiim.org

Association for Library Collections & Technical Services (ALCTS). 50 E. Huron St., Chicago, IL 60611. (312) 280-5038. Fax:(312) 280-5033. E-mail: alcts@ala.org. www.ala.org/alcts. Charles Wilt, Executive Director; Carol Pitts Diedrichs, President (2004–2005); Brian E. C. Schottlaender, Past-President (2004–2005). A division of the American Library Association, ALCTS is dedicated to acquisition, identification, cataloging, classification, and preservation of library materials; the development and coordination of the country's library resources; and aspects of selection and evaluation involved in acquiring and developing library materials and resources. Sections include Acquisitions, Cataloging and Classification, Collection Management and Development, Preservation and Reformatting, and Serials. *Membership:* 5,091. Membership is open to anyone who has an interest in areas covered by ALCTS. $45 plus membership in ALA. *Publications: Library Resources & Technical Services* (quarterly); *ALCTS Newsletter Online* (6/yr). Updated: 3/4/04. Laura Schulte-Cooper, (312) 280-2165 or lschulte@ala

Association for Library and Information Science Education (ALISE). 11250 Roger Bacon Drive, Ste. 8, Reston, VA, 20190-5202. (703) 234-4146. Fax: (703) 435-4390. E-mail: alise@drohanmgmt.com. Web site: http://www.alise.org. Louise Robbins, Professor and Director. Seeks to advance education for library and information science and produces annual *Library and Information Science Education Statistical Report. Membership:* Open to professional schools offering graduate programs in library and information science; personal memberships open to educators employed in such institutions; other memberships available to interested individuals. *Membership:* 500 individuals, 73 institutions. Institutional, sliding scale, $325–$600; $200 associate; $125 international; personal, $90 full-time; $50 part-time; $40 student; $50 retired. *Publications: Journal of Education for Library and Information Science; ALISE Directory and Handbook; Library and Information Science Education Statistical Report.* Updated: 5/21/03.

Association for Library Service to Children (ALSC). 50 E. Huron St., Chicago, IL 60611. (312) 280-2163. Fax: (312) 944-7671. E-mail: alsc@ala.org. Web site: http://www. ala.org/alsc. Malore I. Brown. Who We Are: The Association for Library Service to Children develops and supports the profession of children's librarianship by enabling and encouraging its practitioners to provide the best library service to our nation's children. The Association for Library Service to Children is interested in the improvement and extension of library services to children in all types of libraries. It is responsible for the evaluation and selection of book and nonbook library materials and for the improvement of techniques of library service to children from preschool through the eighth grade or junior high school age, when such materials and techniques are intended for use in more than one type of library. Committee membership is open to ALSC members. *Membership:* 3,600. $45 plus membership in ALA. Annual Conference and Midwinter Meeting with ALA National Institutes. *Publications: Children and Libraries: The Journal of the Association for Library Service to Children* (3x per year); *ALSConnect* (quarterly newsletter). Updated: 3/4/04. Laura Schulte-Cooper, (312) 280-2165 or lschulte@ala

Association for the Advancement of Computing in Education (AACE). P.O. Box 2966. Charlottesville, VA 22902. (804) 973-3987, (804) 978-7449. E-mail: aace@virginia.edu. Web site: http://www.aace.org. Gary Marks, Exec. Dir.; April Ballard, contact person. AACE is an international educational and professional organization dedicated to the advancement of learning and teaching at all levels with information technology. AACE publishes major journals, books, and CD-ROMs on the subject and organizes major conferences. AACE's membership includes researchers, developers, and practitioners in schools, colleges, and universities; administrators, policy decision-makers, trainers, adult educators, and other specialists in education, industry, and the government with an interest in advancing knowledge and learning with information technology in education. *Membership:* 6,500. Basic membership of $75 includes one journal subscription and *Educational Technology Review* subscription. Annual SITE Conference held every March (2006: Orlando, Florida; 2007: San Antonio, Texas). *Publications: Educational Technology Review* (ED-TECH Review) (2 or 3 times yearly); *Journal of Computers in Mathematics and Science Teaching* (JCMST); *Journal of Computing in Childhood Education* (JCCE); *Journal of Educational Multimedia and Hypermedia* (JEMH); *Journal of Interactive Learning Research* (JILR) (formerly *Journal of Artificial Intelligence in Education*); *Journal of Technology and Teacher Education* (JTATE); *International Journal of Educational Telecommunications* (IJET). A catalog of books and CD-ROMs is available upon request or by visiting the Web site: http://www.aace.organize/conf/pubs.

Association of American Publishers (AAP). 50 F Street, NW, Ste. 400, Washington, DC 20001. (202) 347-3375. Fax: (202) 347-3690. E-mail: kblough@publishers.org. Web site: http://www.publishers.org. Patricia S. Schroeder, Pres. and CEO (DC); Judith Platt, Dir. of Communications/Public Affairs. The Association of American Publishers is the national trade association of the U.S. book publishing industry. AAP was created in 1970 through the merger of the American Book Publishers Council, a trade publishing group, and the American Textbook Publishers Institute, a group of educational publishers. *Membership:* AAP's approximately 300 members include most of the major commercial book publishers in the United States, as well as smaller and nonprofit publishers, university presses, and scholarly societies. AAP members publish hardcover and paperback books in every field and a range of educational materials for the elementary, secondary, postsecondary, and professional markets. Members of the Association also produce computer software and electronic products and services, such as online databases and CD-ROMs. AAP's primary concerns are the protection of intellectual property rights in all media, the defense of free expression and freedom to publish at home and abroad, the management of new technologies, development of education markets and funding for instructional materials, and the development of national and global markets for its members products. *Membership:* Regular Membership in the Association is open to all U.S. companies actively engaged in the publication of books, journals, loose-leaf services, computer software, audiovisual materials, databases and other electronic products such as CD-ROM and CD-I, and similar products for educational, business and personal use. This includes producers, packagers, and co-publishers who coordinate or manage most of the publishing process involved in creating copyrightable educational materials for distribution by another organization. "Actively engaged" means that the candidate must give evidence of conducting an ongoing publishing business with a significant investment in the business. Each Regular Member firm has one vote, which is cast by an official representative or alternate designated by the member company. Associate Membership (nonvoting) is available to U.S. not-for-profit organizations that otherwise meet the qualifications for regular membership. A special category of associate membership is open to nonprofit university presses. Affiliate Membership is a nonvoting membership open to paper manufacturers, suppliers, consultants, and other nonpublishers directly involved in the industry. *Membership:* Assessed on the basis of annual sales revenue from the print and electronic products listed above (under Regular Membership), but not from services or equipment. To maintain confidentiality, data is reported to an independent agent. Annual Meeting (February), Small and Independent Publishers

Meeting (February), School Division Annual Meeting (January), PSP Annual Meeting (February). *Publications: AAP Monthly Report.*

Association of College and Research Libraries (ACRL). 50 E. Huron St., Chicago, IL 60611-2795. (312) 280-2523. Fax: (312) 280-2520. E-mail: dconnolly@ala.org. Web site: http://www.ala.org/acrl.html. Frances Maloy, President, libfm@emory.edu. An affiliate of the American Library Association, ACRL provides leadership for development, promotion, and improvement of academic and research library resources and services to facilitate learning, research, and the scholarly communications process. It provides access to library standards for colleges, universities, and two-year institutions, and publishes statistics on academic libraries. Committees include Academic/Research Librarian of the Year Award, Appointments, Hugh C. Atkinson Memorial Award, Budget and Finance, Colleagues, Committee on the Status of Academic Librarians, Bylaws, Copyright, Council of Liaisons, Doctoral Dissertation Fellowship, Government Relations, Intellectual Freedom, International Relations, Samuel Lazerow Fellowship, Media Resources, Membership, Nominations, New Leader Orientation, Professional Development, Publications, Racial and Ethnic Diversity, Research, K. G. Saur Award for the Best C&RL Article, Scholarly Communication, Standards and Accreditation, Statistics. The association administers 15 awards in three categories: Achievement and Distinguished Service Awards, Research Awards/Grants, and Publications. *Membership:* over 11,000. *Membership:* $35 (in addition to ALA membership). 2007 ACRL National Conference, Apr 29–May 1, Baltimore, MD. *Publications: College & Research Libraries* (6/year); *College & Research Libraries News* (11/year); *RBM: A Journal of Rare Books, Manuscripts, and Cultural Heritage* (2/yr); *CHOICE Magazine: Current Review for Academic Libraries* (11/year). *CLIP Notes* (current issues are nos. 16, 17, 20-26). Recent titles include *Making the Grade; Literature in English; The Collaborative Imperative; Assessing Information Literacy Programs* (CLIP Note 32); *Library Web Site Policies* (CLIP Note 29); *Academic Library Trends and Statistics*; and *Proceedings of the 10th ACRL National Conference.* A free list of materials is available. ACRL also sponsors an open discussion listserv, ACRL-FRM@ALA.ORG. Updated: 7/7/04. David Connolly, dconnolly@ala.org

Association of Independent Video and Filmmakers/Foundation for Independent Video and Film (AIVF/FIVF). 304 Hudson St., 6th Floor, New York, NY 10013. (212) 807-1400. Fax: (212) 463-8519. E-mail: info@aivf.org. Web site: http://www.aivf.org. Beni Matias, Interim Executive Director, AIVF. AIVF is the national trade association for independent video and filmmakers, representing their needs and goals to industry, government, and the public. Programs include screenings and seminars, insurance for members and groups, and information and referral services. Recent activities include seminars in filmmaking technology, meets with distributors, and regular programs on related topics. AIVF also advocates public funding of the arts, public access to new telecommunications systems, and monitoring censorship issues. *Membership:* Membership includes annual subscription to the Independent magazine; AIVF trade discounts; online and phone information service; Web members-only area; discounted admission to events, etc. *Membership:* $55, indiv.; $75, library; $100, nonprofit organization; $150, business/industry; $35, student. Annual membership meeting. *Publications: The Independent Film and Video Monthly; The AIVF Guide to International Film and Video Festivals; The AIVF Guide to Film and Video Distributors; The Next Step: Distributing Independent Films and Videos; AIVF Self Distribution Toolkit & the AIVF Film & Video Exhibitors Guide.* Updated: 7/7/04. Sonya Malfa, sonia@aivf.org

Association of Specialized and Cooperative Library Agencies (ASCLA). 50 E. Huron St., Chicago, IL 60611. (800) 545-2433, ext. 4398. Fax: (312) 944-8085. E-mail: ascla@ala.org. Web site: http://www.ala.org/ascla. Cathleen Bourdon, Exec. Dir. A division of the American Library Association, ASCLA represents state library agencies, multitype library organizations, independent libraries, and libraries serving special populations to promote the development of coordinated library services with equal access to information and material for all persons. The activities and programs of the association are carried out by 21 committees, 4 sections, and various discussion groups. *Membership:* 917. *Membership:* Join ALA and ASCLA—new member $90; student member $40 ($25 for ALA plus $15 for ASCLA); trustee and associate member $85 ($45 for ALA plus $40 for ASCLA); add ASCLA to current ALA membership $40; renew ALA and ASCLA membership $140 ($100 for ALA plus $40 for ASCLA). ASCLA meets in conjunction with the American Library Association. *Publications: Interface* (quarterly); see Web site: http://www.ala.org/ascla for list of other publications. Updated: 4/27/04. Eileen Hardy, ehardy@ala.org

Cable in the Classroom (CIC). 1724 Massachusetts Avenue, NW, Washington, DC 20036. (202) 775-1040. Fax: (202) 775-1047. E-mail: cic@ciconline.org. Web site: http://www.ciconline.org. Peggy O'Brien, Ph.D., Executive Director. Cable in the Classroom represents the cable telecommunications industry's effort to use cable content and new technologies to improve teaching and learning for children in schools, at home, and in their communities. By focusing on five essential elements of a good education in the 21st century—visionary and sensible use of technologies, engagement with rich content, community with other learners, excellent teaching, and the support of parents and other adults—the cable industry works for positive change in education locally and nationally. Cable in the Classroom is a consortium of more than 8,500 local cable companies and 40 national cable-programming networks. Local cable companies provide free basic cable service to all accredited K–12 schools passed by cable. Cable networks offer free educational programming with no commercials or viewing requirements and with extended copyright clearances so teachers can tape for classroom use. In addition, cable companies and networks create print and online resources to help teachers use the resources effectively in the classroom. *Publications: Cable in the Classroom Magazine* (monthly). Updated: 7/7/04. Windy Wiener, wwiener@ciconline.org

Catholic Library Association (CLA). 100 North St., Ste. 224, Pittsfield, MA 01201-5109. (413) 443-2CLA. Fax: (413) 442-2CLA. E-mail: cla@vgernet.net. Jean R. Bostley, SSJ, Exec. Dir. Provides educational programs, services, and publications for Catholic libraries and librarians. *Membership:* approx. 1,000. *Membership:* $45, indiv.; special rates for students and retirees. Meetings are held in conjunction with the National Catholic Educational Association in April. *Publications: Catholic Library World* (quarterly); *Catholic Periodical and Literature Index* (quarterly with annual cumulations).

Children's Television International (CTI) /GLAD Productions, Inc. (CTI/GLAD). P.O. Box 87723, San Diego, CA 92138. (619) 445-4647. Fax: (619) 445-2813. E-mail: cti-gladprod@worldnet.att.net. Web site: worldnet.att.net. Tim Gladfelter, Pres. and Dir. of Customer Services. An educational organization that develops, produces, and distributes a wide variety of color television and video programming and related publications as a resource to aid the social, cultural, and intellectual development of children and young adults. Programs cover language arts, science, social studies, history, and art for home, school, and college viewing. *Publications:* Teacher guides for instructional series; *The History Game: A Teachers Guide;* complementary catalog for educational videos. Updated: 5/13/03. Tim Gladfelter by phone or e-mail.

Close Up Foundation (CUF). 44 Canal Center Plaza, Alexandria, VA 22314. (703) 706-3300. Fax: (703) 706-0000. E-mail: alumni@closeup.org. Web site: http://www.closeup.org. Stephen A. Janger, CEO. A nonprofit, nonpartisan civic education organization promoting informed citizen participation in public policy and community service. Programs reach more than a million participants each year. Close Up brings 25,000 secondary and middle school students and teachers and older Americans each year to Washington for weeklong government studies programs and produces television programs on the C-SPAN cable network for secondary school and home audiences. *Membership:* Any motivated 10th–12th grade or 6th–8th grade student who wants to learn about government and American history is eligible to come on the program. There are no dues. Tuition is required to participate on Close Up educational travel programs. A limited amount of tuition assistance is available to qualified students through the Close Up Fellowship program. With a designated number of students, teachers receive a fellowship that covers the adult tuition and transportation price. Please contact (800) CLOSE UP (256-7387), ext. 606, for more information. Meetings are scheduled most weeks during the academic year in Washington, DC, all with a government, history, or current issues focus. *Publications: Current Issues; The Bill of Rights: A Users Guide; Perspectives; International Relations; The American Economy;* documentary videotapes on domestic and foreign policy issues. Updated: 3/5/03. Kimberly Ash, ashk@closeup.org

Community College Association for Instruction and Technology (CCAIT). New Mexico Military Institute, 101 W. College Blvd., Roswell, NM 88201-5173. (505) 624-8382. Fax: (505) 624-8390. E-mail: klopfer@yogi.nmmi.cc.nm.us. Jerry Klopfer, Pres. A national association of community and junior college educators interested in the discovery and dissemination of information relevant to instruction and media technology in the community environment. Facilitates member exchange of data, reports, proceedings, and other information pertinent to instructional technology and the teaching-learning process; sponsors AECT convention sessions, an annual video competition, and social activities. *Membership:* 250; $20. *Publications:* Regular newsletter; irregular topical papers.

Computer Assisted Language Instruction Consortium (CALICO). 214 Centennial Hall, Texas State University, 601 University Dr., San Marcos, TX 78666. (512) 245-1417. (512) 245-9089. E-mail: calico.org. Web site: http://calico.org. Robert Fischer, Exec. Dir. CALICO is devoted to the dissemination of information on the application of technology to language teaching and language learning. *Membership:* 1,000 members from United States and 20 foreign countries. Anyone interested in the development and use of technology in the teaching/learning of foreign languages are invited to join. *Membership:* $50 annual/individual. 2005, Michigan State University, East Lansing, MI. *Publications: CALICO Journal* (three times a year), CALICO Monograph Series. Updated: 2/18/05. Esther Horn, info@calico.org

Computer-Using Educators, Inc. (CUE). 1210 Marina Village Parkway, Ste. 100, Alameda, CA 94501. (510) 814-6630, (510) 814-0195. E-mail: cueinc@cue.org. Web site: http://www.cue.org. Bob Walczak, Exec. Dir. CUE, a California nonprofit corporation, was founded in 1976 by a group of teachers interested in exploring the use of technology to improve learning in their classrooms. The organization has never lost sight of this mission. Today, CUE has an active membership of 11,000 professionals worldwide in schools, community colleges, and universities. CUE's 23 affiliates in California provide members with local year-round support through meetings, grants, events, and mini-conferences. Special Interest Groups (SIGs) support members interested in a variety of special topics. CUE's annual conferences, newsletter, advocacy, Web site, and other programs help the technology-using educator connect with other professionals. *Membership:* 11,000 individual, corporate, and institutional members. *Membership:* $30. Annual Conference (see Web site). *Publication: CUE NewsLetter.*

Consortium of College and University Media Centers (CCUMC). 1200 Communications Bldg., ITC, Iowa State University, Ames, IA 50011-3243. (515) 294-1811. Fax: (515) 294-8089. E-mail: ccumc@ccumc.org. Web site: http://www.ccumc.org. Donald A. Rieck, Exec. Dir. CCUMC is a professional group of higher education media personnel whose purpose is to improve education and training through the effective use of educational media. Assists educational and training users in making films, video, and educational media more accessible. Fosters cooperative planning among university media centers. Gathers and disseminates information on improved procedures and new developments in instructional technology and media center management. *Membership:* 750 individuals at 325 institutions/corporations. Institutional Memberships: Individuals within an institution of higher education who are associated with the support of instruction and presentation technologies in a media center and/or technology support service. Corporate Memberships: Individuals within a corporation, firm, foundation or other commercial or philanthropic whose business or activity is in support of the purposes and objectives of CCUMC. Associate Memberships: Individuals from a public library, religious, governmental, or other organization not otherwise eligible for other categories of membership. Student Memberships: Any student in an institution of higher education who is not eligible for an institutional membership. *Membership:* $325 institutional; $325, corporate; $55, student; $325, associate. Annual meeting: 2006, Austin, TX, Oct. 12–16; 2007. Gainesville, FL, Oct. 18–22. *Publications: College & University Media Review* (journal, semiannual). *Leader* (newsletter, 3 issues annually in electronic format). Updated: 3/15/05. Don Rieck, Executive Director, (515) 294-1811.

Continuing Library Education Network and Exchange Round Table (CLENERT). 50 E. Huron St., Chicago, IL 60611. (800) 545-2433. E-mail: wramsey@cml.lib.oh.us. Web site: http://www.ala.org. Wendy Ramsey. An affiliate of the American Library Association, CLENERT seeks to provide access to quality continuing education opportunities for librarians and information scientists and to create an awareness of the need for such education in helping individuals in the field to respond to societal and technological changes. *Membership:* 350; open to all ALA members. *Membership:* $15, indiv.; $50, organization. *Publication: CLENExchange* (quarterly), available to nonmembers by subscription at $20.

Copyright Clearance Center, Inc. (CCC). 222 Rosewood Drive, Danvers, MA 01923. (978) 750-8400. Fax: (978) 750-0347. E-mail: marketing@copyright.com. Web site: http://www.copyright.com. Joseph S. Alen, Pres. CCC is the world's largest licenser of text reproduction rights and provider of many licensing services for the reproduction of copyrighted materials in print and electronic formats. Formed in 1978 to facilitate compliance with U.S. copyright law, CCC manages the rights relating to more than 1.75 million textbooks, newspapers, magazines, and other copyrighted works. CCC-licensed customers in the U.S. number over 10,000 corporations and subsidiaries (including most of the Fortune 100 companies), as well as thousands of government agencies, law firms, document suppliers, libraries, academic institutions, copy shops and bookstores. CCC's licensing services include the following: (1) Annual Authorizations Service (AAS) —a blanket annual photocopy license for companies with more than 750 employees, as well as law firms of any size. Their employees can photocopy content for distribution in-house. (2) Photocopy Authorizations License (PAL) —the same as the AAS license, but for companies with fewer than 750 employees. (3) Digital Repertory Amendment—a blanket annual license that provides companies with the rights to copy copyrighted content for distribution in-house via e-mail, intranet sites, and other digital formats. (4) Multinational Repertory License—a blanket annual photocopy license that covers U.S. companies' employees working in other countries. (5) Multinational Digital Repertory Amendment—a similar license to the Digital Repertory Amendment, but for U.S. companies with employees working outside of the U.S. (6) Transactional Reporting Service (TRS) —an online "pay as you go" service that enables customers to acquire photocopy permissions on an as-needed basis for library reserves, interlibrary loans, as well as general photocopy needs. Customers also use TRS to report their photocopying activity. (7) Republication Licensing Service (RLS) —an online service that provides customers with permissions to reproduce copyrighted materials for the purpose of republishing that content into a variety of formats, such as Web sites, brochures, books, ads, etc. (8) Academic Permissions Service (APS) —an online permissions service that colleges and universities can use to get the rights to photocopy copyrighted content for use in coursepacks. (9) Electronic Course Content Service (ECCS) —an online service that colleges and universities can use to acquire permissions to reproduce copyrighted content for use in electronic coursepacks and reserves, as well as for distance learning. (10) Digital Permissions Service (DPS) —a transactional service that customers can use to order permissions to reproduce and distribute copyrighted content electronically either in-house or outside of their organizations. (11) Rightslink—a digital rights management service that licenses, packages and delivers digital content from publishers' Web sites. (12) Foreign Authorizations Service (FAS)—authorizes photocopying of U.S. copyrighted materials in foreign countries and distributes royalties collected by foreign reproduction rights organizations to U.S. publishers, authors and other rights holders. (13) Federal Government Photocopy Licensing Service—a blanket annual license that provides rights for federal government employees to photocopy content for in-house use. Updated: 4/5/05. Colleen Cosgrove

Corporation for Public Broadcasting (CPB). 401 9th St., NW, Washington, DC 20004-2037. (202) 879-9600. Fax: (202) 879-9700. E-mail: cpb.org. Web site: http://www. cpb.org. Robert T. Coonrod, Pres. and CEO. A private, nonprofit corporation created by Congress in 1967 to develop noncommercial television, radio, and online services for the American people. CPB created the Public Broadcasting Service (PBS) in 1969 and National Public Radio (NPR) in 1970. CPB distributes grants to more than 1,000 local public television and radio stations that reach virtually every household in the country. The Corporation is the industry's largest single source of funds for national public television and radio program development and production. In addition to quality educational and informational programming, CPB and local public stations make important contributions in the areas of education, training, community service, and application of emerging technologies. CPB has more than 100 employees. *Publications:* Annual Report; *CPB Public Broadcasting Directory.* 5/19/03. Valerie Johnson, vjohnson@cpb.org

Council for Basic Education (CBE). 1319 F St., NW, Ste. 900, Washington, DC 20004-1152. (202) 347-4171. Fax: (202) 347-5047. E-mail: jkeiser@c-b-e.org. Web site: http://www.c-b-e.org. A. Graham Down, Acting CEO, gdown@c-b-e.org. CBEs mission is to strengthen teaching and learning of the core subjects (mathematics, English, language arts, history, government, geography, the sciences, foreign languages, and the arts) to develop the capacity for lifelong learning and foster responsible citizenship. As an independent, critical voice for education reform, CBE champions the philosophy that all children can learn, and that the job of schools is to achieve this goal. CBE advocates this goal by publishing analytical periodicals and administering practical programs as examples to strengthen content in curriculum and teaching. CBE is completing a kit of Standards for Excellence in Education, which includes a CD-ROM; guides for teachers, parents, and principals, and a book of standards in the core subjects. *Publications: Basic Education: A Journal of Teaching and the Liberal Arts:* journal was suspended as of September 2003. Copies of past issues are still available for ordering. (Single copy $10 which includes shipping and handling; contact CBE for bulk orders; issues of BE before September 2002 are only $4 a copy; change price on order form.) Each issue contains analyses, opinions, and reviews of the key issues in K–12 education. Updated: 7/7/04. J. Keiser, jkeiser@c-b-e.org

Council for Exceptional Children (CEC). 1110 N. Glebe Rd., #300, Arlington, VA 22201. (703) 620-3660. TTY: (703) 264-9446. Fax:(703) 264-9494. E-mail: cec@cec. sped.org. Web site: http://www.cec.sped.org. Nancy Safer, Exec. Dir. CEC is the largest international organization dedicated to improving the educational success of students with disabilities and/or gifts and talents. CEC advocates for governmental policies supporting special education, sets professional standards, provides professional development, and helps professionals obtain conditions and resources necessary for high-quality educational services for their students. Teachers, administrators, professors, related services providers (occupational therapists, school psychologists.), and parents. *Membership:* CEC has approximately 50,000 members. *Membership:* $89 a year. Annual Convention & Expo attracting approximately 6,000 special educators. *Publications:* Journals, newsletters books, and videos with information on new research findings, classroom practices that work, and special education publications. (See also the ERIC Clearinghouse on Disabilities and

Gifted Education.) Updated: 3/12/03. Lynda Van Kuren, lyndav@cec.sped.org, (703) 264-9478

(CEC) Technology and Media Division (TAM). 1920 Association Dr., Reston, VA 20191-1589. (703) 620-3660. TTY: (703) 264-9446. Fax: (703) 264-9494. E-mail: cec@cec.sped.org. Web site: http://www.cec.sped.org. The Technology and Media Division (TAM) of the Council for Exceptional Children (CEC) encourages the de-velopment of new applications, technologies, and media for use as daily living tools by special populations. This information is disseminated through professional meet-ings, training programs, and publications. *Publications:* TAM members receive four issues annually of the *Journal of Special Education Technology* containing articles on specific technology programs and applications, and five issues of the TAM news-letter, providing news of current research, developments, products, conferences, and special programs information. *Membership:* 1,700. Dues; $10 in addition to CEC membership.

Council on International Non-Theatrical Events (CINE). 1112 16th Street, N.W., Ste. 510, Washington, DC 20036. (202) 785-1136. Fax: (202) 785-4114. E-mail: cine.org. Web site: http://www.cine.org. Carole L. Feld, President. CINE's mission is to discover, reward, educate, and support professional and new emerging talent in the film and video fields. It accomplishes its mission through major film and video competitions that recognize and celebrate excellence, and through various educational programs. CINE is best known for its prestigious CINE Golden Eagle competitions, culminating annually in a gala Awards Cere-mony in Washington, D.C. Awards are given in 20 major categories, encompassing all gen-res of professional and pre-professional film and video production. CINE also facilitates entry into worldwide film festivals for its own competition winners; at the same time, it has reciprocal arrangements whereby distinguished works from outside the United States achieve CINE recognition and viewership in the U.S. *Membership:* CINE is not at this time a membership organization. CINE Showcase and Awards held annually in Washington, DC. *Publications:* CINE Annual Yearbook of Film and Video Awards; Worldwide Direc-tory of Film and Video Festivals and Events. Updated: 7/7/04. David L. Weiss

East-West Center. 1601 East-West Rd., Honolulu. HI 96848-1601. (808) 944-7111. Fax: (808) 944-7376. E-mail: EastWestCenter.org. Web site: http://www.eastwestcenter.org/. Dr. Charles E. Morrison, Pres. The U.S. Congress established the East-West Center in 1960 with a mandate to foster mutual understanding and cooperation among the governments and peoples of Asia, the Pacific, and the United States. Officially known as the Center for Cultural and Technical Interchange Between East and West, it is a public, nonprofit institu-tion with an international board of governors. Funding for the center comes from the U.S. government, with additional support provided by private agencies, individuals, and corpo-rations, and several Asian and Pacific governments, private agencies, individuals, and cor-porations. The center, through research, education, dialog, and outreach, provides a neutral meeting ground where people with a wide range of perspectives exchange views on topics of regional concern. Scholars, government and business leaders, educators, journalists, and other professionals from throughout the region annually work with Center staff to address issues of contemporary significance in such areas as international economics and politics, the environment, population, energy, the media, and Pacific islands development. Updated: 3/4/04.

ECT Foundation (ECT). c/o AECT, 1800 N. Stonelake Drive, Ste. 2, Bloomington, IN 47404. (812) 335-7675. Fax: (812) 335-7678. E-mail: aect@aect.org. Web sites: http://www.aect.org, http://www.ect.net. Hans-Erik Wennberg, Pres. The ECT Foundation is a nonprofit organization whose purposes are charitable and educational in nature. Its op-eration is based on the conviction that improvement of instruction can be accomplished, in part, by the continued investigation and application of new systems for learning and by periodic assessment of current techniques for the communication of information. In addition to awarding scholarships, internships, and fellowships, the foundation develops and conducts leadership training programs for emerging professional leaders. Its operations are closely allied to AECT program goals, and the two organizations operate in close conjunction with each other. The Foundation is currently engaged in a $50,000 capital campaign to increase both the number of and amount of support to students and professionals in the instructional technology area. The ECT Foundation is managed by a 16-member board of trustees. It makes its scholarships and leadership grants available to any member of the Association for Educational Communications and Technology. Semiannual meetings are held at the International Conference of AECT and the AECT Summer Conference. Updated: 3/10/05. Hans-Erik Wennberg, wennberg@etown.edu

Educational Communications, Inc., Environmental and Media Projects of. P.O. Box 351419. Los Angeles, CA 90035. (310) 559-9160. Fax: (310) 559-9160. E-mail: ECNP@aol.com. Web site: www.ecoprojects.org. Nancy Pearlman, Executive Director and Producer. Educational Communications is dedicated to enhancing the quality of life on this planet and provides radio and television programs about the environment. Serves as a clearinghouse on ecological issues. Programming is available on 100 stations in 25 states. These include: ECONEWS television series and Environmental Direction radio series. Services provided include a speakers' bureau, award-winning public service announcements, radio and television documentaries, volunteer and intern opportunities, and input into the decision-making process. Its mission is to educate the public about both the problems and the solutions of the ecological crisis. Other projects include the Ecology Center of Southern California (a regional conservation group), Project Ecotourism, Take-to-the-Hills, and Earth Cultures (providing ethnic dance performances). Nonmembership except for the Ecology Center of Southern California. *Membership:* $20 for regular. All donations accepted. *Publications: Compendium Newsletter* (bi-monthly); *Directory of Environmental Organizations.* ECOVIEW newspaper articles. 500 television shows and documentaries on videocassettes. 1,500 radio shows on audio cassettes. Updated: 2/18/05. Nancy Pearlman, ECNP@aol.com

Education Development Center, Inc. 55 Chapel St., Newton, MA 02458-1060. (617) 969-7100. (617) 969-5979. E-mail: comment@edc.org. Web site: http://www.edc.org. Janet Whitla, Pres., Jwhitla@edc.org. EDC is a nonprofit research and development organization that works in the United States and worldwide in the fields of education, health, and human development. Active projects include curriculum development, teacher and administrator professional development, materials development, research and evaluation. EDC seeks to bridge research and practice in order to improve education at all levels by providing services to the school and the community. EDC produces interactive Web sites, CD-ROMs, DVDs and videocassettes, primarily in connection with curriculum development and teacher training. *Publications:* Annual Report; Detailed Web site with vast archive of publications, technical reports, and evaluation studies. Updated: 3/10/05. Eric Marshall, emarshall@edc.org

Educational Products Information Exchange (EPIE Institute). 103 W. Montauk Highway, Hampton Bays, NY 11946. (516) 728-9100. Fax: (516) 728-9228. E-mail: kkomoski@optonline.net. Web site: http://www.epie.org. P. Kenneth Komoski, Exec. Dir. Assesses educational materials and provides consumer information, product descriptions, and citations for virtually all educational software and curriculum-related Web sites. All of EPIE's services are available to schools and state agencies as well as parents and individuals. Online access is restricted to states with membership in the States Consortium for Improving Software Selection (SCISS). *Publications:* The Educational Software Selector Database (TESS), available to anyone. All publication material available on CD-ROM. Updated: 5/27/03. Kenneth Komoski, kkomoski@optonline.net

Eisenhower National Clearinghouse for Mathematics and Science Education (ENC).
1929 Kenny Road, Columbus, OH 43210-1079. (800) 621-5785, (614) 292-7784. Fax:
(614) 292-2066. E-mail: enc.org. Web site: http://www.enc.org. Dr. Len Simutis, Director.
The Eisenhower National Clearinghouse for Mathematics and Science Education (ENC) is
located at the Ohio State University and funded by the U.S. Department of Educations Office of Elementary and Secondary Education (OESE). ENC provides K–12 teachers and
other educators with a central source of information on mathematics and science curriculum materials, particularly those that support education reform. Among ENC's products
and services are *ENC Online*; 12 demonstration sites located throughout the nation; and a
variety of publications (including the *Guidebook of Federal Resources for K–12 Mathematics and Science,* a listing of federal resources in mathematics and science education;
ENC Focus, a free online and print magazine on topics of interest to math and science educators; and professional development CD-ROMs). *Membership:* Users include K–12
teachers, other educators, policy makers, and parents. Magazine subscriptions are free, and
there are no fees for any ENC services. *ENC Focus* magazine has more than 130,000 subscribers, mostly K–12 math and science teachers. *ENC Online* is available at
http://www.enc.org). Updated: 3/11/04. Melanie Shreffler, mshreffler@enc.org

Federal Communications Commission (FCC). 445 12th St., S.W, Washington, DC
20554. (888) 225-5322. Fax: (202) 418-1232. E-mail: fcc.gov. Web site: http://www.fcc.
gov. Michael Powell, Chairman. The FCC is an independent U.S. government agency, directly responsible to Congress. The FCC was established by the Communications Act of
1934 and is charged with regulating interstate and international communications by radio,
television, wire, satellite and cable. The FCC's jurisdiction covers the 50 states, the District
of Columbia, and U.S. possessions. Updated: 3/17/04. fccinfo@fcc.gov

Film Arts Foundation (Film Arts). 145 9th St., #101. San Francisco, CA 94103. (415)
552-8760. Fax: (415) 552-0882. E-mail: filmarts.org. Web site: http://www.filmarts.org.
Film Arts is a service organization that supports and promotes independent film and video
production. Services include low-cost 16mm, Super-8, and dV equipment rental; online
and offline editing including AVID, Final Cut, 16mm flatbeds, as well as a Pro Tools with
5.1 Dolby Digital Surround sound room and Optical Printer; resource library; group legal
and Dental insurance plans; monthly magazine; seminars; grants program; annual film and
video festival; nonprofit sponsorship; exhibition program; and advocacy and significant
discounts on film- and video-related products and services. *Membership:* 3,500+. *Membership:* $45 for supporter level benefits including monthly magazine and access to libraries
and online databases. $65 for filmmaker benefits including above plus access to equipment
and post production facilities, discounts on seminars, nonprofit fiscal sponsorship, group
legal and Delta Dental plans, Annual Festival, Annual membership meeting, and Network
events. *Publications: Release Print* (magazine); *Answer Print* (e-mail blast once per
month); *Rushes* (e-mail blast with last-minute notices). Updated: 3/10/05. Eric,
erich@filmarts.org

Film/Video Arts (F/VA). 462 Broadway, Ste. 520, New York, NY 10013. (212) 941-8787.
Fax: (212) 219-8924. E-mail: education@fva.com. Web site: http://www.fva.com. Eileen
Newman, Exec. Dir. Film/Video Arts has come a long way since its founding in 1968 when
educators Rodger Larson and Lynne Hofer in collaboration with filmmaker Jaime Barrios
introduced 16mm motion picture equipment to Latino youth on the Lower East Side. Operating out of a storefront just off the Bowery, the teenagers were soon making highly personal films, mostly concerned with growing up in the neighborhood.

In 1968, the organization was officially incorporated as the Young Filmakers Foundation, to encourage filmmaking as an artistic, educational and vocational experience for
young people. A major grant in 1970 made it possible for Young Filmakers to stabilize and
expand its programs citywide.

In 1971, in collaboration with the New York State Council on the Arts, Young Filmakers established the first public media equipment access center in a basement on West 53rd Street, known as Media Equipment Resource Center (MERC), this program served film and video makers of all ages with production and postproduction services free of charge. In 1973, the activities of the organization were consolidated in a loft building at 4 Rivington Street. By 1978, Young Filmakers had introduced modest fees and redirected its focus to adults.

In 1985, Young Filmakers changed its name to Film/Video Arts and relocated to 817 Broadway. The new location and major equipment upgrades enabled the organization to evolve from a set of experimental programs to an established service institution. In 1997, Film/Video Arts built the Digital Studio and initiated the Digital Arts Certificate Program. Consequently, a new generation of digital media producers were emerging from Film/Video Arts with the benefit of having equal access to necessary resources. In 2001, Film/Video Arts relocated to its present address at 462 Broadway (corner of Grand Street). The future of the Film/Video Arts at its new location holds forth many possibilities as the organization continues to grow with the emergence of newer technologies.

Drawing from its rich history Film/Video Arts has steadily evolved, all the time maintaining its staunch commitment to supporting the needs of independent film, video and digital media producers. The founders' mission, to make the tools and skills of the media arts available to those who might otherwise not have access to them, remains the guiding force behind all Film/Video Arts activities and programs. Join Film/Video Arts today and become a part of a thriving community of independent film, video and multimedia producers. A Film/Video Arts membership allows one to take courses, receive fiscal sponsorship and mentorship and receive access to the postproduction facilities for affordable rates.

Membership contributions help support Film/Video Arts equipment purchases and low service fees. Memberships are valid for one year from the date of issue. Contributions are tax-deductible to the full extent of the law. To become a member fill out the Membership Application and submit it to Film/Video Arts (with membership payment) via e-mail or regular mail. *Membership:* Individual $75/Organization $95. Access to Film/Video Arts courses, production equipment rentals and postproduction services at affordable rates.

Fiscal Sponsorship: Referrals for affordable premiums on General Liability and Production Insurance. Opportunities to exhibit work in Members Screenings. A subscription to *Film/Video Arts Email Newsletter.* Enrollment in Film/Video ARts Membership Discount Program which entitles F/VA members to savings at several film and video service providers. Note: Individual membership is for one person only. An organizational membership is for two authorized individuals.

Fiscal sponsorship program: This program serves the independent producer who is seeking funding for projects. Film/Video Arts will act as a fiscal sponsor for independent producers in cases where a donor (such as a governmental body, nonprofit organization, an individual or other entity) stipulates in their funding guidelines that the recipient have nonprofit status under 501(c) 3 of the Internal Revenue Code. In such cases Film/Video Arts can use its nonprofit status to receive and administer grants, gifts or donations that are made in the name of the producers project. As a Fiscal Sponsor, Film/Video Arts does not supervise the actual production of projects, but is responsible for monitoring their progress. To apply to the program, individuals must complete and send in the Fiscal Sponsor Application accompanied by a project proposal which includes a detailed description/treatment of the project, fundraising and distribution plan, résumés of key personnel, a list of project advisors (as applies), a budget and a sample reel. A nonrefundable membership fee of $75 is required for review of the project proposal. The proposal will be reviewed by a Film/Video Arts screening committee. The review process takes approximately two weeks.

Once a project is accepted into Film/Video Arts Fiscal Sponsor Program, Film/Video Arts will then administer and turn over all funding raised by the producer after deducting a

6% administrative fee. *Membership:* $75, indiv., $95, organization. Updated: 3/5/04: Guil Parreiras

Freedom of Information Center (FOI Center). 127 Neff Annex, University of Missouri, Columbia, MO 65211-0012. (573) 882-4856. (573) 882-9002. E-mail: FOI@missouri.edu. Web site: http://www.missouri.edu/~foiwww. Dr. Charles N. Davis, Director; Kathleen Edwards, Manager; Robert W. Anderson, Web Manager. Located in the Missouri School of Journalism, the Freedom of Information Center is an academic research facility specializing in educational advocacy. The collection focuses on the centrality of open government to its role in fostering democracy. The center staff assists the public with requests or questions about freedom of information with the help of an extensive archive of materials dating from the FOI movement's inception. The center's operating hours are Monday through Friday, 8:00 a.m. to 5:00 p.m., excluding University holidays. *Membership:* The FOI Center does not offer memberships. The center serves approximately 23,000 researchers annually through its Web page and through individual contacts. No dues charged. Minimal fees may be charged for research. The FOI Center meets annually with the National Freedom of Information Coalition. *Publications:* Access to Public Information: A Resource Guide to Government in Columbia and Boone County, Missouri, a directory of public records, and the FOI Advocate, a periodic electronic newsletter. Both publications are linked to the center's Web page. Some older publications are available for sale by contacting the center. Updated: 7/7/04. K. Edwards, edwardsm@missouri.edu.

George Eastman House International Museum of Photography and Film (GEH). 900 East Ave., Rochester, NY 14607. (585) 271-3361, (585) 271-3970. E-mail: tbannon@geh.org. Web site: http://www.eastmanhouse.org. Anthony Bannon, Dir. World-renowned museum of photography and cinematography established to preserve, collect, and exhibit photographic art and technology, film materials, and related literature, and to serve as a memorial to George Eastman. Services include archives, traveling exhibitions, research library, school of film preservation, center for the conservation of photographic materials, and photographic print service. Educational programs, exhibitions, films, symposia, music events, tours, and internship stipends offered. Eastman's turn-of-the-century mansion and gardens have been restored to their original grandeur. *Membership:* 8,000. *Membership:* $40, library; $50, family; $40, indiv.; $36, student; $30, senior citizen; $75, Contributor; $125, Sustainer; $250, Patron; $500, Benefactor; $1,000, George Eastman Society. *Publications: 1000 Photo Icons* (with Taschen); *Image* magazine; Newsletter/film calendar; *Annual Report: The George Eastman House and Gardens;* and exhibition catalogs. Updated: 3/10/05. Dresden Engle, PR Mgr., dengle@geh.org

The George Lucas Educational Foundation (GLEF). P.O. Box 3494, San Rafael, CA 94912. (415) 507-0399. Fax: (415) 507-0499. E-mail: edutopia@glef.org. Web site: http://glef.org. Milton Chen, PhD., Exec. Dir. *Mission:* The George Lucas Educational Foundation (GLEF) is a nonprofit operating foundation that documents and disseminates models of the most innovative practices in our nation's K–12 schools. We serve this mission through the creation of media—from films, books, and newsletters to CD-ROMS. GLEF works to provide its products as tools for discussion and action in conferences, workshops, and professional development settings. *Audience:* A successful educational system requires the collaborative efforts of many different stakeholders. Our audience includes teachers, administrators, school-board members, parents, researchers, and business and community leaders who are actively working to improve teaching and learning. *Vision:* The Edutopian vision is thriving today in our country's best schools: places where students are engaged and achieving at the highest levels, where skillful educators are energized by the excitement of teaching, where technology brings outside resources and expertise into the classroom, and where parents and community members are partners in educating our youth. Annual Advisory meeting. *Edutopia Online:* The Foundation's Web site (www.glef.org) celebrates the unsung heroes who are making Edutopia a reality. All of GLEF's multimedia content dating back to 1997 is available on its Web site. A special feature, the Video Gallery, is an archive of short documentaries and expert interviews that allow visitors to see these innovations in action and hear about them from teachers and students. Detailed articles, research summaries, and links to hundreds of relevant Web sites, books, organizations, and publications are also available to help schools and communities build on successes in education. *Publications: Edutopia: Success Stories for Learning in the Digital Age*—This book and CD-ROM include numerous stories of innovative educators who are using technology to connect with students, colleagues, the local community, and the world beyond. The CD-ROM contains more than an hour of video footage. Published by Jossey-Bass. *Teaching in the Digital Age (TDA)* Videocassettes—This video series explores elements of successful teaching in the Digital Age. The project grows out of GLEF's belief that an expanded view is needed of all our roles in educating children and supporting teachers. The series explores school leadership, emotional intelligence, teacher preparation, and project-based learning and assessment. *Learn & Live*—This documentary film and 300-page companion resource book showcases innovative schools across the country. The film, hosted by Robin Williams, aired on public television stations nationwide in 1999 and 2000. The *Learn & Live* CD-ROM includes digital versions of the film and book in a portable, easy-to-use format. *Edutopia Newsletter*—This free, semiannual print newsletter includes school profiles, summaries of recent research, and resources and tips for getting involved in public education. Updated: 7/7/04. K. Meredith

Great Plains National ITV Library (GPN). P.O. Box 80669, Lincoln, NE 68501-0669. (402) 472-2007, (800) 228-4630. Fax: (800) 306-2330. E-mail: gpn@unl.edu. Web site: http://gpn.unl.edu. Stephen C. Lenzen, Executive Director. Produces and distributes educational media, video, CD-ROMs and DVDs, prints and Internet courses. Available for purchase for audiovisual or lease for broadcast use. *Membership:* Membership not required. There are no dues required. There are no meetings. We do attend subject specific conventions to promote our products. *Publications:* GPN Educational Video Catalogs by curriculum areas; periodic brochures. Complete listing of GPN's product line is available via the Internet along with online purchasing. Free previews available. Updated: 7/7/04. Connie Hoerle, gpn@unl.edu

Health Sciences Communications Association (HeSCA). One Wedgewood Dr., Ste. 27, Jewett City, CT 06351-2428. (203) 376-5915. Fax: (203) 376-6621. E-mail: keven@hesca.org. Web site: http://www.hesca.org/. Ronald Sokolowski, Exec. Dir. An affiliate of AECT, HeSCA is a nonprofit organization dedicated to the sharing of ideas, skills, resources, and techniques to enhance communications and educational technology in the health sciences. It seeks to nurture the professional growth of its members; serve as a professional focal point for those engaged in health sciences communications; and convey the concerns, issues, and concepts of health sciences communications to other organizations that influence and are affected by the profession. International in scope and diverse in membership, HeSCA is supported by medical and veterinary schools, hospitals, medical associations, and businesses where media are used to create and disseminate health information. *Membership:* 200. *Membership:* $150, indiv.; $195, institutional ($150 additional institutional dues); $60, retiree; $75, student; $1,000, sustaining. All include subscriptions to the journal and newsletter. Annual meetings: May-June. *Publications: Journal of Biocommunications; Feedback* (newsletter). Updated: 2/21/05. Keven, keven@hesca.org

Hollywood Film Archive (HFA). 8391 Beverly Blvd., #321, Hollywood, CA 90048. (323) 655-4968. Fax: (323) 555-4321. E-mail: hfa.com. Web site: http://www.hfa.com. D. Richard Baer, Dir. Archival organization for information about feature films produced worldwide, from the early silent films to the present. Comprehensive movie reference works for sale, including *Variety Film Reviews* (1907–1996) and the *American Film Institute Catalogs* (1893–1910, 1911–20, 1921–30, 1931–40, 1941–50, 1961–70), as well as the *Film Superlist* (1894–1939, 1940–1949, 1950–1959) volumes, which provide information both on copyrights and on motion pictures in the public domain; *Harrison's Reports and Film Reviews* (1919–1962). Updated: 5/23/03. Richard Baer, (323) 655-4968

The Institute for the Advancement of Emerging Technologies in Education at AEL (IAETE). P.O. Box 1348, Charleston, WV 25325-1348. (304) 347-1848. Fax: (304) 347-1847. E-mail: iaete.org. Web site: http://www.iaete.org. Dr. John D. Ross, Director. The mission of the Institute for the Advancement of Emerging Technologies in Education (IAETE) is to support the purposeful use of new and emerging technologies to improve teaching, learning, and school management. IAETE is committed to providing unbiased, research-based information to the education community as well as to product developers. Annual National Conference. *Publications:* IAETE publishes several white papers, briefs, and reports annually in both print and electronic format. All address new and emerging technologies and their impact on teaching, learning, and school management. For more information, please visit www.iaete.org. Updated: 2/22/05. John Ross, rossj@iaete.org

Institute for Development of Educational Activities, Inc. (I|D|E|A|). 259 Regency Ridge, Dayton, OH 45459. (937) 434-6969. Fax: (937) 434-5203. E-mail: IDEADayton @aol.com. Web site: http://www.idea.org. Dr., Steven R. Thompson, Pres. I|D|E|A| is an action-oriented research and development organization originating from the Charles F. Kettering Foundation. It was established in 1965 to assist the educational community in bridging the gap that separates research and innovation from actual practice in the schools. Its goal is to design and test new responses to improve education and to create arrangements that support local application. Activities include developing new and improved processes, systems, and materials; training local facilitators to use the change processes; and providing information and services about improved methods and materials. I|D|E|A| sponsors an annual fellowship program for administrators and conducts seminars for school administrators and teachers.

Institute for the Future (IFTF). 2744 Sand Hill Rd., Menlo Park, CA 94025-7020. (650) 854-6322. Fax: (650) 854-7850. E-mail: iftf.org. Web site: http://www.iftf.org. Robert Johansen, Pres. The cross-disciplinary professionals at IFTF have been providing global and domestic businesses and organizations with research-based forecasts and action-oriented tools for strategic decision making since 1968. IFTF is a nonprofit, applied research and consulting firm dedicated to understanding technological, economic, and societal changes and their long-range domestic and global consequences. Its work falls into four main areas: Strategic Planning, Emerging Technologies, Health Care Horizons, and Public Sector Initiatives. IFTF works with clients to think systematically about the future, identify socioeconomic trends and evaluate their long-term implications, identify potential leading-edge markets around the world, understand the global marketplace, track the implications of emerging technologies for business and society, leverage expert judgment and data resources, offer an independent view of the big picture, and facilitate strategic planning processes.

Instructional Technology Council (ITC). One Dupont Cir., NW, Ste. 410, Washington, DC 20036-1176. (202) 293-3110. Fax: (202) 833-2467. E-mail: cdalziel@aacc.nche.edu. Web site: http://www.itcnetwork.org. Christine Dalziel, Executive Director. An affiliated council of the American Association of Community Colleges established in 1977, the Instructional Technology Council (ITC) provides leadership, information, and resources to expand access to, and enhance learning through, the effective use of technology. ITC represents higher education institutions in the United States and Canada that use distance learning technologies.

ITC members receive a subscription to the ITC News and ITC listserv with information on what's happening in distance education, participation in ITC's professional development audioconference series, distance learning grants information, updates on distance learning legislation, discounts to attend the annual Telelearning Conference which features more than 80 workshops and seminars, discounts to downlink PBS/ALS videoconferences, and a free copy of ITC publications and research.

Members include single institutions and multicampus districts; regional and state-wide systems of community, technical and two-year colleges; for-profit organizations; four-year institutions; and nonprofit organizations that are interested or involved in instructional telecommunications. Members use a vast array of ever-changing technologies for distance learning. They often combine different systems according to students needs. The technologies they use and methods of teaching include: audio and video conferences, cable television, compressed and full-motion video, computer networks, fiber optics, interactive videodisc, ITFS, microwave, multimedia, public television, satellites, teleclasses, and telecourses. *Membership:* $450, Institutional; $750, Corporate. Holds the annual Telelearning Conference. *Publications: Quality Enhancing Practices in Distance Education: Vol. 2, Student Services; Quality Enhancing Practices in Distance Education: Vol. 1 Teaching and Learning; New Connections: A Guide to Distance Education* (2nd ed.); *New Connections: A College President's Guide to Distance Education; Digital Video: A Handbook for Educators; Faculty Compensation and Support Issues in Distance Education; ITC News* (monthly publication/newsletter); ITC Listserv. Updated: 5/13/03. Christine Dalziel, (202) 293-3110

International Association of Business Communicators (IABC). One Hallidie Plaza, Ste. 600, San Francisco, CA 94102. (415) 544-4700. Fax: (415) 544-4747. E-mail: service_centre@iabc.com. Web site: http://www.iabc.com. Julie Freeman, Pres. and CEO. IABC is the worldwide association for the communication and public relations profession. It is founded on the principle that the better an organization communicates with all its audiences, the more successful and effective it will be in meeting its objectives. IABC is dedicated to fostering communication excellence, contributing more effectively to organizations goals worldwide, and being a model of communication effectiveness. *Membership:* 13,500+. *Membership:* $209 in addition to local and regional dues. Holds an International Conference (2006: June 4–7, Vancouver, Canada). Publication: *Communication World.* Updated: 4/5/05. pclifton@iabc.com

International Association for Language Learning Technology (IALLT). Instructional Technology Services, Concordia College, Moorhead, MN 56562. (218) 299-3464. Fax: (218) 299-3246. E-mail: business@iallt.org. Web site: http://iallt.org. Peter Liddell President; Ron Balko, Treasurer. IALLT is a professional organization whose members provide leadership in the development, integration, evaluation and management of instructional technology for the teaching and learning of language, literature and culture. *Membership:* 500 members. *Membership/Subscription Categories:* Educational Member—for people working in an academic setting such as a school, college, or university. These members have voting rights. Full-time Student Member—for full-time students interested in membership. Requires a signature of a voting member to verify student status. These members have voting rights. Commercial Member—for those working for corporations interested in language learning and technology. This category includes for example language laboratory vendors, software and textbook companies. Library Subscriber—receive our journals for placement in libraries. *Membership:* 1 year—$50, voting member; $25, student; $60, library subscription; $75 commercial. 2 year—$90, voting member; $140 commercial. Biennial IALLT conferences treat the entire range of topics related to technology in language learning as well as management and planning. IALLT also sponsors sessions at conferences of organizations with related interests, including CALICO and ACTFL. *Publications IALLT Journal of Language Learning Technologies* (twice annually); materials for language lab management and design, language teaching and technology. Visit our Web site for details: http://iallt.org. Updated: 3/10/05. Ron Balko, business@iallt.org

International Association of School Librarianship (IASL). Box 34069, Dept. 962, Seattle, WA 98124-1069. (604) 925-0266. Fax: (604) 925-0566. E-mail: iasl@rockland.com. Web site: http://www.iasl-slo.org/. Dr. Penny Moore, Exec. Dir. Seeks to encourage development of school libraries and library programs throughout the world; promote professional preparation and continuing education of school librarians; achieve collaboration among school libraries of the world; foster relationships between school librarians and other professionals connected with children and youth and to coordinate activities, conferences, and other projects in the field of school librarianship. *Membership:* 900+. *Membership:* $50 Zone A (e.g., United States, Canada, Western Europe, Japan); $35 Zone B (e.g., Eastern Europe, Latin America, Middle East). $20 Zone C (e.g., Angola, India, Bulgaria, China). Zone based on GNP. Annual Conference: 2006, July 3–7, Lisbon, Portugal. *Publications: IASL Newsletter* (3/year); *School Libraries Worldwide* (semiannual); *Conference Professionals and Research Papers* (annual); *Connections: School Library Associations and Contact People Worldwide; Sustaining the Vision: A Collection of Articles and Papers on Research in School Librarianship; School Librarianship: International Issues and Perspectives; Information Rich but Knowledge Poor? Issues for Schools and Libraries Worldwide: Selected Papers from the 26th Annual Conferences of the IASL.* Updated: 6/4/03. Michelle Rudert

International Center of Photography (ICP). 1114 Avenue of the Americas, New York, NY 10036. (212) 857-0001. Fax: (212) 857-0091. E-mail: icp.org. Web site: http://www.icp.org. Willis Hartshorn, Dir.; Phyllis Levine, Dir. of Public Information. A comprehensive photographic institution whose exhibitions, publications, collections, and educational programs embrace all aspects of photography from aesthetics to technique; from the 19th century to the present; from master photographers to newly emerging talents; from photojournalism to the avant-garde. Changing exhibitions, lectures, seminars, workshops, museum shops, and screening rooms make ICP a complete photographic resource. ICP offers two options of Graduate Study in conjunction with New York University: (1) a Master of Fine Arts in Studio Art with a concentration in Media Studies (1 year, 60-point program). (2) a master in studio art with a concentration in photography (36-point program) and one-year certificate programs in documentary photography and photojournalism and general studies in photography. *Membership:* 6,000. $60, indiv.; $75, double; $150, Supporting Patron; $300, Photography Circle; $600, Silver Card Patron; $1,200, Gold Card Patron;$3,000 Benefactor; corporate memberships available. The 18th Annual ICP Infinity Awards. *Publications: Telling Tales, Kiki Smith, Reflections in a Glass Eye; Images from the Machine Age: Selections from the Daniel Cowin Collection; Library of Photography; A Singular Elegance: The Photographs of Baron Adolph de Meyer; Talking Pictures: People Speak about the Photographs That Speak to Them; Encyclopedia of Photography: Master Photographs from PFA Collection; Man Ray in Fashion;* Quarterly Program Guide; Quarterly Exhibition Schedule. Updated: 7/7/04. Suzanne Nicholas, (212) 857-0051.

International Council for Educational Media (ICEM). Hanns-Fay Strasse 1, Frankenthal D67227, Germany. (+49) 6233 46051. Fax: (+49) 6233 46355. secretariat@icem-cime.com. Web site: http://www.icem-cime.com. Dr. Marina McIsaac, Pres. and U.S. member, Margo Van Sluizer, Secretary General. The objectives of ICEM are to provide a channel for the international exchange of information and experience in the field of educational technology, with particular reference to preschool, primary, and secondary education, technical and vocational training, and teacher and continuing education; encourage organizations with a professional responsibility for the design, production, promotion, distribution, and use of educational media in member countries; promote an understanding of the concept of educational technology on the part of both educators and those involved in their training; contribute to the pool of countries by the sponsorship of practical projects involving international cooperation and co-production; advise manufacturers of hardware and software on the needs of an information service on developments in educational technology; provide consultancy for the benefit of member countries; and cooperate with other international organizations in promoting the concept of educational technology. ICEM has established operational relations with UNESCO. There are national memberships as well as those for individuals, students, academic institutions and corporate entities. Membership is open those who work in the area of educational and instructional media, grades 12–Adult. *Membership:* There are presently 30 member nations in ICEM and 195 individual members. *Membership:* National Members are 2,500 Swiss francs (SF) per year and may be paid in either Swiss francs or US Dollars. Individual dues are $85 or 125 SF. Students and retired individual dues are $40 or 58 SF. Primary and Secondary School dues are $135 or 200 SF. Public and nonprofit organization dues are $205 or 300 SF (includes government departments, foundations, associations, universities, etc.). Commercial organization dues are $275 or 400 SF (producers, distributors, manufacturers, etc.). *Publications: Educational Media International,* a quarterly refereed journal. The Editor-in-Chief is Dr., John Hedberg, Faculty of Education, University of Wollongong, Wollongong, NSW 2522 AUSTRALIA, john_hedberg@uow.edu.au. Updated: 2/27/03.

International Graphics Arts Education Association (IGAEA). 1899 Preston White Drive, Reston, VA 20191-4367. (703) 758-0595. E-mail: gcc@teched.vt.edu. Web site: http://www.igaea.org. Mark Sanders, gcc@teched.vt.edu. IGAEA is an association of educators in partnership with industry, dedicated to sharing theories, principles, techniques, and processes relating to graphic communications and imaging technology. Teachers network to share and improve teaching and learning opportunities in fields related to graphic arts, imaging technology, graphic design, graphic communications, journalism, photography, and other areas related to the large and rapidly changing fields in the printing, publishing, packaging, and allied industries. *Membership:* Approx. 600 members. Open to educators, middle school through college and university, who teach graphic arts, graphic communications, printing and publishing, desktop publishing, multimedia, and photography. *Membership:* $20, regular; $12, associate (retired); $5, student; $10, library; $50-$200, sustaining membership based on number of employees. See Web site for information: http://www.igaea.org. *Publications: The Communicator; Visual Communications Journal* (annual). Updated: 7/7/04.

International Recording Media Association (IRMA). 182 Nassau St., Princeton, NJ 08542-7005. (609) 279-1700, (609) 279-1999. E-mail: recordingmedia.org. Web site: http://www.recordingmedia.org. Charles Van Horn, President; Phil Russo, Exec. Director. IRMA is the advocate for the growth and development of all recording media and is the industry forum for the exchange of information regarding global trends and innovations. Members include recording media manufacturers, rights holders to video programs, recording and playback equipment manufacturers, and audio and video replicators. For more than 30 years, the association has provided vital information and educational services throughout the magnetic and optical recording media industries. By promoting a greater awareness of marketing, merchandising, and technical developments, the association serves all areas of the entertainment, information, and delivery systems industries. *Membership:* 450 corporations. Corporate membership includes benefits to all employees. *Membership:* Corporate membership dues based on sales volume. *Publications:* IRMA Executive Forum; IRMA Marketing Summit; DVD Entertainment; Membership Quarterly Magazine; Seminar Proceedings; International Source Directory, Marketing Statistics. Updated: 3/12/03.

International Society for Performance Improvement (ISPI). 1400 Spring Street, Ste. 260, Silver Spring MD 20910. (301) 587-8570. (301) 587-8573. E-mail: ispi.org. Web site: http://www.ispi.org. Richard D. Battaglia, Exec. Dir. Founded in 1962, the International Society for Performance Improvement (ISPI) is the leading international association dedicated to improving productivity and performance in the workplace. ISPI represents more than 10,000 international and chapter members throughout the United States, Canada, and 40 other countries. ISPI's mission is to develop and recognize the proficiency of our members and advocate the use of Human Performance Technology. Assembling an Annual Conference & Expo and other educational events like the Institute, publishing books and periodicals, and supporting research are some of the ways ISPI works toward achieving this mission. *Membership:* 10,000, including performance technologists, training directors, human resources managers, instructional technologists, human factors practitioners, and organizational consultants are members of ISPI. They work in a variety of settings including business, academia, government, health services, banking, and the armed forces. *Membership Categories and Membership:* Active Membership ($145 annually). This is an individual membership receiving full benefits and voting rights in the Society. Student Membership ($60 annually). This is a discounted individual full membership for full-time students. Proof of full-time enrollment must accompany the application. Retired Membership ($60 annually). This is a discounted individual full membership for individuals who are retired from full-time employment. Special Organizational Membership Categories: These groups support the Society at the top level. Sustaining Membership ($950 annually). This is an organizational membership and includes five active memberships and several additional value-added services and discounts. Details available on request. Patron Membership ($1,400 annually). This is an organizational membership and includes five active memberships and several additional value-added services and discounts. Details available upon request. Conferences: Annual International Performance Improvement Conference & Exposition held each April, Performance-Based Instructional Systems Design Conference each September, various Human Performance Technology Institutes throughout the year. *Publications: Performance Improvement Journal* (10/yr): The common theme is performance improvement practice or technique that is supported by research or germane theory. *PerformanceXpress* (12/yr): Monthly newsletter published online. *Performance Improvement Quarterly*: PIQ is a peer-reviewed journal created to stimulate professional discussion in the field and to advance the discipline of HPT through publishing scholarly works. ISPI Bookstore: The ISPI online publications and book catalog. Updated 6/5/03.

International Society for Technology in Education (ISTE). 480 Charnelton Street, Eugene, OR 97401. (800) 336.5191 (U.S. & Canada), (541) 302.3777 (Intl.). Fax: (541) 302.3780. E-mail: iste@iste.org. Web site: http://www.iste.org. Don Knezek, CEO; Cheryl Williams, Co-President; Cathie Norris, Co-President. As the leading organization for educational technology professionals, the International Society for Technology in Education is a professional organization that supports a community of members through research, publications, workshops, symposia, and inclusion in national policy making through ISTE-DC. Home of the National Center for Preparing Tomorrows Teachers to Use Technology (NCPT3), ISTE works in conjunction with the U.S. Department of Education and various private entities to create and distribute solutions for technology integration. ISTE's National Educational Technology Standards (NETS) for students and teachers have been adopted by hundreds of districts nationwide. ISTE is also the home of NECC, the premier U.S. educational technology conference, is a forum for advancing educational philosophies, practices, policies, and research that focus on the appropriate use of current and emerging technologies to improve teaching and learning in K–12 and teacher education. ISTE members are leaders. ISTE members contribute to the field of educational technology as classroom teachers, lab teachers, technology coordinators, school administrators, teacher educators, and consultants. ISTE provides leadership and professional development opportunities for its members. In addition to other benefits, ISTE members can participate in ISTE-sponsored invitational events at the National Educational Computer Conference (NECC), join one of ISTEs many Special Interest Groups (SIGs), and test and evaluate the latest in educational technology products and services through the ISTE Advocate Network. ISTE Members also enjoy subscriptions to *ISTE Update* and *Learning & Leading with Technology* or the *Journal for Research on Technology in Education.* In the member's areas of the ISTE Web site, ISTE members can join discussion lists and other on-line forums for participation, review a database of educational technology resources, network with a cadre of education professionals, and review online editions of ISTE publications. *Membership:* Annual dues for individual ISTE members are $58. Membership to SIG communities are $20 for ISTE members. Contact iste@iste.org to become a member. Annual dues for ISTE 100 members are $50,000. Contact iste100@iste.org for more information. Group discounts are available. To see if you qualify, contact groupdiscounts@iste.org. National Educational Computing Conference (NECC). *Publications: ISTE Update* (online member newsletter); *Learning & Leading with Technology*; *Journal of Research on Technology in Education* (quarterly; formerly *Journal of Research* *on Computing in Education*); and books about incorporating technology in the K–16 classroom. Updated: 5/21/03.

International Telecommunications Satellite Organization (INTELSAT). 3400 International Dr., NW, Washington, DC 20008. (202) 944-7500. (202) 944-7890. Web site: http://www.intelsat.int. Conny L. Kullman, Dir. Gen. and CEO; Tony A. Trujillo, Dir., Corporate Communications. INTELSAT owns and operates a global communications satellite system providing capacity for voice, video, corporate/private networks, and Internet in more than 200 countries and territories. In addition, the INTELSAT system provides educational and medical programming via satellite for selected participants around the world.

International Teleconferencing Association (ITCA). 100 Four Falls Corporate Center, Ste. 105, West Conshohocken, PA 19428. (610) 941-2015. Fax: (610) 941-2015. E-mail: staff@itca.org and president@itca.org. Web site: http://www.itca.org. Henry S. Grove III, Pres.; Eileen Hering, Manager, Member Services; Rosalie DiStasio, Asst. Manager, Member Services. ITCA, an international nonprofit association, is dedicated to the growth and development of teleconferencing as a profession and an industry. ITCA provides programs and services that foster the professional development of its members, champions teleconferencing and related technology as communications tools, recognizes and promotes broader applications and the development of teleconferencing and related technologies, and serves as the authoritative resource for information and research on teleconferencing and related technologies. ITCA represents more than 1,000 teleconferencing professionals throughout the world. ITCA members use teleconferencing services to advise customers and vendors, conduct research, teach courses via teleconference, and teach about teleconferencing. They represent such diverse industry segments as health care, aerospace, government, pharmaceutical, education, insurance, finance and banking, telecommunications, and manufacturing. *Membership:* 6,250, Platinum Sustaining; $2,500, Gold Sustaining; $1,250, Sustaining; $625, Organizational; $325, small business; $125, indiv.; and $35, student. Conferences: Spring and fall MultimediaCom Shows; spring show in San Jose, fall show in Boston, August 30–September 2. *Publications:* Forum newsletter; *Member Directories*; White Paper; *Teleconferencing Success Stories.*

International Visual Literacy Association, Inc. (IVLA). Navarro College, 3200 W. 7th Ave., Corsicana, TX 75110. (903) 875-7441. Fax: (903) 874-4636. E-mail: darrell. beauchamp@navarrocollege.edu. www.ivla.org. Darrell Beauchamp, IVLA Treasurer. IVLA provides a multidisciplinary forum for the exploration, presentation, and discussion of all aspects of visual learning, thinking, communication, and expression. It also serves as a communication link bonding professionals from many disciplines who are creating and sustaining the study of the nature of visual experiences and literacy. It promotes and evaluates research, programs, and projects intended to increase effective use of visual communication in education, business, the arts, and commerce. IVLA was founded in 1968 to promote the concept of visual literacy and is an affiliate of AECT. *Membership:* 500, mostly from academia and from many disciplines. We are an international organization and have conferences abroad once every third year. Anyone interested in any visual-verbal field should try our organization: architecture, engineering, dance, the arts, computers, video, design, graphics, photography, visual languages, mathematics, acoustics, physics, chemistry, optometry, sciences, literature, library, training, education, etc. *Membership:* $40 regular; $20 student and retired; $45 outside United States; corporate memberships available; $500 lifetime membership. Yearly conference usually Oct./Nov. in selected locations. *Publications: The Journal of Visual Literacy* (bi-annual; juried research papers); *Selected Readings from the Annual Conference*; and *The Visual Literacy ReView* (newsletter 4 times per year). Updated: 7/7/04.

Learning Point Associates. 1120 East Diehl Road, Ste. 200. Naperville. IL. 60563-1486. (630) 649-6500, (800) 356-2735. (630) 649-6700. E-mail: ann.kinder@learningpt.org. Web site: www.learningpt.org. Gina Burkhardt, CEO. Learning Point Associates is a mission-driven nonprofit organization that offers research-based educational resources, products, and services. We work together with schools, districts, and states to build capacity in the following areas: adolescent literacy; after-school programming; curriculum alignment and classroom-based assessments; information systems for school improvement; K–12 comprehensive school improvement; leadership development; teaching and teacher quality; and technology integration, standards and assessment. Based in Naperville, Illinois, with offices in Chicago and Washington, D.C., Learning Point Associates delivers knowledge, strategies, and results. In 1984, Learning Point Associates was founded as the North Central Regional Educational Laboratory (NCREL), one of the 10 regional educational laboratories funded by the U.S. Department of Education. The organization was chartered to perform and deliver research, development, technical assistance, and policy activities to address critical education issues for the seven-state Midwest region (Illinois, Indiana, Iowa, Michigan, Minnesota, Ohio, and Wisconsin). NCREL continues as a wholly owned subsidiary of Learning Point Associates. With more than 130 staff, Learning Point Associates is a resource for all education stakeholders and work directly with K-16 practitioners, policymakers, and funders to build research- and technology-based products, tools, and resources; deliver capacity-building professional services and technical assistance; and conduct high-integrity evaluation and policy research. Annual Conference and a variety of Education Policy meetings. NCREL's Learning Point magazine; Policy Issues; Viewpoints; Center for Comprehensive School Reform and Improvement Newsletter.

The Learning Team. TLT. Ste. 204 84 Business Park Drive, Armonk, NY 10504. (914) 273-2226. Fax: (914) 273-0936. E-mail: NMcLaren@LearningTeam.org. Web site: http://www.learningteam.org. Tom Laster, Executive Director. The Learning Team is a not-for-profit company that is focused on publishing inquiry-based, supplementary, technology resources for science education. The multimedia resources include science, mathematics and utilities software and videos. Science subjects include physics, physical sciences, biology, earth sciences (geosciences), environmental sciences, general science, chemistry, energy use, and culture and technology. Software includes inquiry-based student resources, teacher resources, and professional development. Resources available include *High School Geography Product* (HSGP), *Intermediate Science Curriculum Study* (ISCS), *Man: A Course of Study* (MACOS), and *Human Sciences Project* (HSP). Most of the resources come from National Science Foundation (NSF) funding and have been done in conjunction with institutions such as the American Association of Physics Teachers (AAPT), the American Institute of Physics (AIP), and American Geological Institute (AGI). Although the term "membership" does not apply specifically to our organization, it loosely applies to the range of licensors, collaborators, and colleagues that cooperate with us and are active in the area of science education, as appropriate. *Publications: Physics InfoMall; CPU—Constructing Physics Understanding; Exploring the Nardoo; Investigating Lake Iluka; The Dynamic Rainforests; Insects—Little Creatures in a Big World; Culture & Technology; Enhanced Science Helper; Enhanced Science Helper Videos; The Green Home; The Sun's Joules; Whelmers; EarthView Explorer; GETIT—Geosciences Education Through Interactive Technology; Crossword Wizard; Cloze Word Wizard; Maths Worksheet Wizard.* Updated: 5/6/02. Neil McLaren, (914) 273-2226, ext. 585

Library Administration and Management Association (LAMA). 50 E. Huron St., Chicago, IL 60611. (312) 280-5032. (312) 280-5033. E-mail: lama@ala.org. Web site: http://www. ala.org/lama. Lorraine Olley, Executive Director; Paul Anderson, President. A division of the American Library Association, LAMA provides an organizational framework for encouraging the study of administrative theory, improving the practice of administration in libraries, and identifying and fostering administrative skills. Toward these ends, the association is responsible for all elements of general administration that are common to more than one type of library. Sections include Buildings and Equipment Section (BES);

Fundraising & Financial Development Section (FRFDS); Library Organization & Management Section (LOMS); Human Resources Section (HRS); Public Relation and Marketing Section (PRMS); Systems & Services Section (SASS); and Measurement, Assessment and Evaluation Section (MAES). *Membership:* 4,800. *Membership:* $50 regular (in addition to ALA membership); $65 organizations and corporations; $15, library school students. ALA Annual Conference 2006, New Orleans, June 22–28. *Publications:* Library Administration & Management (quarterly); LEADS from LAMA (electronic newsletter, irregular). 3/4/04. Lorraine Olley, lolley@ala.org

Library and Information Technology Association (LITA). 50 E. Huron St., Chicago, IL 60611. (312) 280-4270, (800) 545-2433, ext. 4270. Fax: (312) 280-3257. E-mail: lita@ala.org. Web site: http://www.lita.org. Mary C. Taylor, Exec. Dir., mtaylor@ala.org. An affiliate of the American Library Association, LITA is concerned with library automation; the information sciences; and the design, development, and implementation of automated systems in those fields, including systems development, electronic data processing, mechanized information retrieval, operations research, standards development, telecommunications, video communications, networks and collaborative efforts, management techniques, information technology, optical technology, artificial intelligence and expert systems, and other related aspects of audiovisual activities and hardware applications. LITA's members come from all types of libraries and institutions focusing on information technology in libraries. They include library decision makers, practitioners, information professionals and vendors. *Membership:* Approximately 5,400. *Membership:* $35 (first time) plus membership in ALA; $25, library school students; $35, first year; renewal memberships $45 plus ALA cost. Conferences: National Forum, fall. *Publications: LITA Newsletter* (electronic only; see Web site). *Information Technology and Libraries* (ITAL: Contains the table of contents, abstracts and some full-text of *ITAL*, a refereed journal published quarterly by the Library and Information Technology Association. *Technology Electronic Reviews* (*TER*): *TER* is an irregular electronic serial publication that provides reviews and pointers to a variety of print and electronic resources about information technology. LITA Publications List: Check for information on LITA Guides and Monographs. Updated: 6/10/03.

Library of Congress (LOC). James Madison Bldg., 101 Independence Ave., SE, Washington, DC 20540. (202) 707-5000. Fax: (202) 707-1389. E-mail: pao@loc.gov. Web site: http://www.loc.gov. Dr. James Billington, Librarian of Congress. The Library of Congress is the major source of research and information for the Congress. In its role as the national library, it catalogs and classifies library materials in some 460 languages, distributes the data in both printed and electronic form, and makes its vast collections available through interlibrary loan, on-site to anyone over high school age, and through its award-winning Web site at www.loc.gov. The Library is the largest library in the world, with more than 126 million items on 532 miles of bookshelves. The collections include nearly 19 million cataloged books, 2.6 million recordings, 12 million photographs, 4.8 million maps, and 56 million manuscripts. It contains the world's largest television and film archive, acquiring materials through gift, purchase, and copyright deposit. In 2002, some 23 million items (discs, cassettes, Braille materials) produced by the Library in Braille and recorded formats for persons who are blind or physically challenged were circulated to a readership of more than 500,000. The collections of the Motion Picture, Broadcasting and Recorded Sound Division include nearly 900,000 moving images. The Library's public catalog, as well as other files containing copyright and legislative information, are available on the Library's Web site. In 2000, the Library launched the Americas Library Web site for children and families. This easy-to-use, interactive site (www.americaslibrary.gov) allows children to "have fun with history." The site receives more than 150 million hits annually. See list on Library's Web site. Updated: 5/23/03.

Lister Hill National Center for Biomedical Communications (LHNCBC). National Library of Medicine, 8600 Rockville Pike, Bethesda, MD 20894. (301) 496-4441. Fax: (301) 402-0118. E-mail: nlm.nih.gov. Web site: http://www.nlm.nih.gov. Robert Mehnert, Director of Communications, mehnert@nlm.nih.gov. The Lister Hill National Center for Biomedical Communications is a research and development division of the National Library of Medicine (NLM). The center conducts and supports research and development in the dissemination of high-quality imagery, medical language processing, high-speed access to biomedical information, intelligent database systems development, multimedia visualization, knowledge management, data mining, and machine-assisted indexing. The Lister Hill Center also conducts and supports research and development projects focusing on educational applications of state-of-the-art technologies including the use of microcomputer technology incorporating stereoscopic imagery and haptics, the Internet, and videoconferencing technologies for training health care professionals and disseminating consumer health information. The center's Collaboratory for High Performance Computing and Communication serves as a focus for collaborative research and development in those areas, cooperating with faculties and staff of health sciences educational institutions. Health profession educators are assisted in the use and application of these technologies through periodic training, demonstrations and consultations. High Definition (HD) video is a technology area that has been explored and developed within the center, and is now used as the NLM standard for all motion imaging projects considered to be of archival value. Advanced three dimensional animation and photorealistic rendering techniques have also become required tools for use in visual projects within the center. Updated: 3/9/05.

Magazine Publishers of America (MPA). 810 Seventh Ave, New York, NY 10019. (212) 872-3700. Fax: (212) 753-2768. infocenter@magazine.org. Web site: http://www.magazine.org. Nina Link, Pres. MPA is the trade association of the consumer magazine industry. MPA promotes the greater and more effective use of magazine advertising, with ad campaigns in the trade press and in member magazines, presentations to advertisers and their ad agencies, and magazine days in cities around the United States. MPA runs educational seminars, conducts surveys of its members on a variety of topics, represents the magazine industry in Washington, DC, and maintains an extensive library on magazine publishing. *Membership:* 240 publishers representing more than 1,500 magazines. Conferences: American Magazine Conference, The Magazine Lifetime Achievement Awards, The Retail Conference. See Web site for more details. *Publications: Newsletter of Consumer Marketing*; *Sales Edge*; *Newsletter of International Publishing*; *Washington Newsletter*; *MPA Market Profiles.* Updated: 2/22/05.

Media Communications Association—International (MCA-I). 7600 Terrace Avenue, Ste. 203, Middleton, WI 53562. (608) 827-5034. Fax: (608) 831-5122. E-mail: mca-i.org. Web site: http://www.mca-i.org. Susan Rees, Executive Director—The Rees Group. Formerly the International Television Association. Founded in 1968, MCA-I's mission is to provide media communications professionals opportunities for networking, forums for education and resources for information. MCA-I also offers business services, such as low-cost insurance, buying programs, etc., to reduce operating costs. MCA-I also confers the highly acclaimed Media Festival awards (The Golden Reel is back!) on outstanding multimedia productions. Visit MCA-I's Web site for full details. *Membership:* More than 3,000 individual and corporate members. Membership programs also are available to vendors for relationship and business development. $160, individual.; $455, organizational; PLATINUM—$7,500; GOLD—$5,500; SILVER—$2,500; BRONZE—$1,250. Various Partnerships with Association Conferences. *Publications: MCA-I News* (quarterly newsletter); *MCA-I Member2Member E-News* (6/year); *Membership Directory* (annual). Updated: 4/5/05.

Medical Library Association (MLA). 65 E. Wacker Pl., Ste. 1900. Chicago, IL 60601-7298. (312) 419-9094. Fax: (312) 419-8950. E-mail: mlahq.org. Web site: http://www.mlanet.org. Carla J. Funk, MLS, MBA, CAE, Executive Director. MLA is an educational organization of more than 1,000 institutions and 3,800 individual members in the health sciences information field. MLA members serve society by developing new health information delivery systems, fostering educational and research programs for health sciences information professionals, and encouraging an enhanced public awareness of health care issues. *Membership:* MLA is an educational organization of more than 1,000 institutions and 3,800 individual members in the health sciences information field. MLA fosters excellence in the professional achievement and leadership of health sciences library and information professionals to enhance the quality of health care, education, and research. *Membership categories:* Regular, Institutional, International, Affiliate, Student. *Membership:* $135, regular; $90, introductory; $210–$495, institutional, based on total library expenditures, including salaries, but excluding grants and contracts; $90, international; $80, affiliate; $30, student. National annual meeting held every May; most chapter meetings are held in the fall. *Publications: MLA News* (newsletter, 10/year); *Journal of the Medical Library Association* (quarterly scholarly publication.); MLA DocKit series, collections of representative, unedited library documents from a variety of institutions that illustrate the range of approaches to health sciences library management topics; MLA BibKits, selective, annotated bibliographies of discrete subject areas in the health sciences literature; standards; surveys; and copublished monographs. Updated: 4/26/04.

Mid-continent Research for Education and Learning (McREL). 2550 S. Parker Rd., Ste. 500. Aurora, CO 80014. (303) 337-0990. Fax: (303) 337-3005. E-mail: mcrel.org. Web site: http://www.mcrel.org. J. Timothy Waters, Exec. Dir. McREL is a private, nonprofit organization whose purpose is to improve education through applied research and development. McREL provides products and services, primarily for K–12 educators, to promote the best instructional practices in the classroom. McREL houses 1 of 10 regional educational laboratories funded by the U.S. Department of Education, the Institute for Educational Science. The regional laboratory helps educators and policy makers work toward excellence in education for all students. It also houses 1 of 10 Eisenhower Regional Consortia for Mathematics and Science Education. McREL has particular expertise in standards-based education systems, leadership for school improvement, effective instructional practices, teacher quality, mathematics and science education improvement, early literacy development, and education outreach programs. *Membership:* Not a membership organization. No dues. Annual conference. *Publications: Changing Schools* (quarterly newsletter); *Noteworthy* (annual monograph on topics of current interest in education reform). Numerous technical reports and other publications. Check Web site for current listings. Updated: 2/22/05. Linda Brannan, Info. Resource Mgr. E-mail: mcrel.org

Minorities in Media (MIM). 1800 N. Stonelake Dr., Ste. 2, Bloomington, IN 47408. (703) 993-3669. Fax: (313) 577-1693. E-mail: moorejoi@missouri.edu. Joi Moore, President. MIM is a special interest group of AECT that responds to the challenge of preparing people of color for an ever-changing international marketplace and recognizes the unique educational needs of today's diverse learners. It promotes the effective use of educational communications and technology in the learning process. MIM seeks to facilitate changes in instructional design and development, traditional pedagogy, and instructional delivery systems by responding to and meeting the significant challenge of educating diverse individuals to take their place in an ever-changing international marketplace. MIM encourages all of AECT's body of members to creatively develop curricula, instructional treatments, instructional strategies, and instructional materials that promote an acceptance and appreciation of racial and cultural diversity. Doing so will make learning for all more effective, relevant, meaningful, motivating, and enjoyable. MIM actively supports the Wes McJulien Minority Scholarship, and selects the winner. Contact MIM president. *Membership:* $10, student; $20, faculty or professional. During AECT conference. *Publications:* Newsletter is forthcoming online. The MIM listserv is a membership benefit. Updated: 4/5/05. Joi Moore, moorejoi@missouri.edu

Museum Computer Network (MCN). 65 Enterprise, Aliso Viejo, CA 92656. (877) 626-3800. Fax: (949) 330-7621. E-mail: membership@mcn.edu. Web site: http://www. mcn.edu. Leonard Steinbach, Pres 2001–2002; Fred Droz, Admin. MCN is a nonprofit organization of professionals dedicated to fostering the cultural aims of museums through the use of computer technologies. We serve individuals and institutions wishing to improve their means of developing, managing and conveying museum information through the use of automation. We support cooperative efforts that enable museums to be more efficient at creating and disseminating cultural and scientific knowledge as represented by their collections and related documentation. MCN members are interested in building databases complete with images and multimedia components for their collections, in using automated systems to tract membership, manage events and design exhibits, in discovering how multimedia systems can increase the effectiveness of educational programs, and in developing professional standards to ensure the investment that information represents. *Membership:* MCN's membership includes a wide range of museum professionals representing more than 600 major cultural institutions throughout the world. The primary job duties of our membership include 33% Registrar/Collection Managers; 33% IT professionals; and the remaining third is comprised of administrator, curators, and education professionals. Our membership comes from all sorts of cultural heritage organizations, including art, historical and natural history museums, and academia. Each member receives a complimentary issue of *Spectra* (published three times a year), a discount on conference fees, can subscribe to MCN-L, the online discussion list, and can join, at no additional cost, any of our Special Interest Groups which focus on such topics as intellectual property, controlled vocabulary, digital imaging, IT managers, and data standards. *Membership:* $300, corporate; $200, institution; $60, individual. Conferences: Annual Conference, held in the fall; educational workshops. *Publications: Spectra* (newsletter), published three times a year. Subscription to *Spectra* is available to libraries only for $75 plus $10 surcharge for delivery. *eSpectra* is a monthly electronic magazine featuring online links to information of interest to the museum computing community, job openings, and a calendar of museum-related events, such as workshops, conferences, or seminars. Updated: 6/12/02. fred.droz@mcn.edu

Museum of Modern Art, Circulating Film and Video Library (MoMA). 11 W. 53rd St., New York, NY 10019. (212) 708-9530. Fax: (212) 708-9531. E-mail: circfilm@moma.org. Web site: http://www.moma.org. William Sloan, Libr. Provides film and video rentals and sales of over 1,300 titles covering the history of film from the 1890s to the present. It also includes an important collection of work by leading video artists and is the sole distributor of the films of Andy Warhol. The Circulating Film and Video Library continues to add to its holdings of early silents, contemporary documentaries, animation, avant-garde, independents and video and to make these available to viewers who otherwise would not have the opportunity to see them. The Circulating Film and Video Library has 16mm prints available for rental, sale, and lease. Some of the 16mm titles are available on videocassette. The classic film collection is not. The video collection is available in all formats for rental and sale. The Library also has available a limited number of titles on 35mm, including rare early titles preserved by the Library of Congress. They also now distribute some films on art and artists formally handled by the American Federation of the Arts as well as the film work of contemporary artists such as Richard Serra and Yoko Ono. *Membership:* No membership. *Publications:* Information on titles may be found in the free Price List, the Documentaries on the Arts brochure and the Films of Andy Warhol brochure, all available from the Library. Circulating *Film and Video Catalog Vols. 1 and 2,* a major source book on film and history, is available from the Museum's Mail Order Dept. (To purchase by mail order, a form is included in the Price List.) Updated: 4/27/04. Kitty Cleary, Kitty_Cleary@moma.org

National Aeronautics and Space Administration (NASA). NASA Headquarters, Code N, Washington, DC 20546. (202) 358-1525. Fax: (202) 358-3032. E-mail: shelley. canright@nasa.gov. Web site: http://education.nasa.gov. Dr. Adena Williams Loston, Chief Education Officer. To develop the next generation of explorers, NASA must do its part to inspire and motivate students to pursue careers in science, technology, engineering, and mathematics. NASA's mission to understand and explore depends upon educated, motivated people with the ingenuity to invent tools and solve problems and with the courage to always ask the next question. It is not enough to depend on the excitement generated by NASA's images of its achievements in space and on Earth; NASA must capitalize on that interest to provide meaningful education programs that will benefit the Agency and the Nation. To meet this challenge, education has become a core part of NASA's mission, and education programs are an integral part of every major NASA activity. To ensure a pipeline of highly trained people prepared to meet mission requirements within NASA, as well as in industry and academia, NASA must: motivate students to pursue careers in science, technology, engineering, and mathematics; provide educators with unique teaching tools and compelling teaching experiences; ensure that public resources are invested wisely; and fully engage minority and under-represented students, educators, and researchers in NASA's education programs. The Office of Education will strive to reach the masses of young people in the Nation to connect with, excite, and inspire the next generation of scientists, inventors, technicians, and explorers. For more information see: Web site: http://education.nasa.gov/ and visit the NASA Portal at Web site: http://www.nasa.gov/. Web site: http://www.nasa.gov/audience/foreducators/topnav/materials/about/index.html. Updated: 2/20/05. Shelley Canright (see above)

National Alliance for Media Arts and Culture (NAMAC). 145 9th Street, Ste. 250. San Francisco, CA 94103. (415) 431-1391. Fax: (415) 431-1392. E-mail: namac@namac.org. Web site: http://www.namac.org. Helen DeMichel, Co-Director; Jack Walsh, Co-Director. NAMAC is a nonprofit organization dedicated to increasing public understanding of and support for the field of media arts in the United States. Members include media centers, cable access centers, universities, and media artists, as well as other individuals and organizations providing services for production, education, exhibition, distribution, and preservation of video, film, audio, and intermedia. NAMAC's information services are available to the general public, arts and non-arts organizations, businesses, corporations, foundations, government agencies, schools, and universities. *Membership:* 200 organizations, 150 individuals. *Membership:* $75–$450, institutional (depending on annual budget); $75, indiv. Biennial Conference. *Publications: Media Arts Information Network;* annual anthology of case-studies, *A Closer Look*; periodic white paper reports; *Deep Focus: The Future of Independent Media.* Updated: 4/12/05. Daniel Schott, dan@namac.org

National Association for the Education of Young Children (NAEYC). 1509 16th St., Washington, DC 20036-1426. (202) 232-8777. Fax: (202) 328-1846. E-mail: naeyc@naeyc.org. Web site: http://www.naeyc.org. Mark R. Ginsberg, Ph.D., Exec. Dir.; Alan Simpson, Communications. Dedicated to improving the quality of care and education provided to young children (birth–8 years). *Membership:* NAEYC has more than 100,000 members, including teachers and directors in child care, preschool and Head Start programs, and in classrooms from kindergarten through third grade. Other members include researchers, professional development experts, and parents. Anyone who is interested in improving early childhood education is welcome to join NAEYC. Most members join NAEYC as well as state and local affiliates in their area. *Membership:* vary according to which affiliates you join. Generally, dues range between $45 and $75 annually, with lower rates for full-time students. Annual Conference. *Publications: Young Children* (journal); more than 100 books, posters, videos, and brochures. Updated: 3/5/03. Alan Simpson, ext. 11605

National Association for Visually Handicapped (NAVH). 22 West 21st St., 6th Floor, New York, NY 10010. (212) 889-3141 or 255-2804. Fax: (212) 727-2931. E-mail: staff@navh.org. Web site: http://www.navn.org. Dr. Lorraine H. Marchi, Founder/CEO; Cesar Gomez, Executive Director. Making the difference in the lives of people with low vision, the HARD OF SEEING—that has been NAVH's Mission for more than 50 years. Serves the partially seeing (not totally blind). Offers all type of optical and visual aids, personal items, and more. We have the things to make your life a lot easier. Also informational literature about vision and vision impairment for the layperson and the professional, most in large print. Maintains a national free-by-mail large print loan library of more than 9,000 titles. A resource for visual aids counseling, use and distribution. Provides emotional support and guidance, advocacy, and referrals for the visually impaired and their families, and the professionals and paraprofessionals who work with them. *Membership:*15,000, but it is not mandatory to became a member to receive our services. *Membership:* $50 indiv.; sliding scale or no fee for those unable to afford membership. Seniors support group 2 times at month; Yearly Medical Advisory Board meetings at the Amer. Acad. of Ophthalmology Annual Meetings. *Publications:* Newsletter updated quarterly, distributed free throughout the English-speaking world; *navhUPDATE* (quarterly); Visual Aids magnifiers to writing aids, personal items, and more. *Visual Aids and Informational Material Catalog; Large Print Loan Library Catalog;* informational pamphlets on topics ranging from diseases of the macula to knitting and crochet instructions. Updated: 4/5/05. Dr. Lorraine H. Marchi, Founder/CEO, (212) 889-3141

National Association of Media and Technology Centers (NAMTC). 7105 First Ave., SW, Cedar Rapids, IA 52405. (319) 654-0608. Fax: (319) 654-0609. E-mail: bettyge@ mchsi.com. Web site: www.namtc.org. Betty Gorsegner Ehlinger, Executive Director. NAMTC is committed to promoting leadership among its membership through networking, advocacy, and support activities that will enhance the equitable access to media, technology, and information services to educational communities. *Membership:* open to regional, K–12, and higher education media centers that serve K–12 students as well as commercial media and technology centers. Institutional and corporate members numbering approximately 225. *Membership:* $80, institutions; $300, corporations. Annual NAMTC Leadership Summit; www.NAMTC.org for details. *Publications:* Membership newsletter is *ETIN*, a quarterly publication. Updated: 2/21/05. Betty Gorsegner Ehlinger, bettyge@mchsi.com

National Association of State Textbook Administrators (NASTA). 120 S. Federal Place, Room 206, Santa Fe, NM 87501. (505) 827-1801. Fax: (505) 827-1826. E-mail: president@nasta.org. Web site: http://www.nasta.org. David P. Martinez, President. NASTA's purposes are to (1) foster a spirit of mutual helpfulness in adoption, purchase, and distribution of instructional materials; (2) arrange for study and review of textbook specifications; (3) authorize special surveys, tests, and studies; and (4) initiate action leading to better quality instructional materials. Services provided include a working knowledge of text construction, monitoring lowest prices, sharing adoption information, identifying trouble spots, and discussions in the industry. The members of NASTA meet to discuss the textbook adoption process and to improve the quality of the instructional materials used in the elementary, middle, and high schools. NASTA is not affiliated with any parent organization and has no permanent address. *Membership:* Textbook administrators from each of the 21 states that adopt instructional material at the state level on an annual basis. *Membership:* $25 annually per individual. NASTA meets annually during the month of July. *Publication:* Manufacturing Standards and Specifications for Textbooks (MSST). Updated: 6/9/03. Ali Ahmed, ali.ahme@uwlax.edu

The National Center for Improving Science Education. 1726 M Street, NW, #704, Washington, DC 20036. (202) 467-0652. Fax: (202) 467-0659. E-mail: ncise.org. www.wested.org. Senta A. Raizen, Dir. A division of WestEd (see separate listing) that works to promote changes in state and local policies and practices in science curriculum, teaching, and assessment through research and development, evaluation, technical assistance, and dissemination. *Publications: Science and Technology Education for the Elementary Years: Frameworks for Curriculum and Instruction; Developing and Supporting Teachers for Elementary School Science Education; Assessment in Elementary School Science Education; Getting Started in Science: A Blueprint for Elementary School Science Education; Elementary School Science for the 90s; Building Scientific Literacy: Blueprint for the Middle Years; Science and Technology Education for the Middle Years: Frameworks for Curriculum and Instruction; Assessment in Science Education: The Middle*

Years; Developing and Supporting Teachers for Science Education in the Middle Years; The High Stakes of High School Science; Future of Science in Elementary Schools: Educating Prospective Teachers; Technology Education in the Classroom: Understanding the Designed World; What College-Bound Students Abroad Are Expected to Know About Biology (with AFT); Examining the Examinations: A Comparison of Science and Mathematics Examinations for College-Bound Students in Seven Countries. Bold Ventures series: Vol. 1: Patterns of U.S. Innovations in Science and Mathematics Education; Vol. 2: Case Studies of U.S. Innovations in Science Education; Vol. 3: Case Studies of U.S. Innovations in Mathematics. A publications catalog and project summaries are available on request.

National Center to Improve Practice (NCIP). Education Development Center, Inc., 55 Chapel St., Newton, MA 02458-1060. (617) 969-7100, ext. 2387. TTY (617) 969-4529. Fax: (617) 969-3440. E-mail: jzorfass@edc.org. Web site: http://www.edc.org/FSC/NCIP. Judith Zorfass, Project Dir. NCIP, a project funded by the U.S. Department of Education's Office for Special Education Programs (OSEP), promotes the effective use of technology to enhance educational outcomes for students (preschool to grade 12) with sensory, cognitive, physical, social, and emotional disabilities. NCIP's award-winning Web site offers users online discussions (topical discussions and special events) about technology and students with disabilities, an expansive library of resources (text, pictures, and video clips), online workshops, "guided tours" of exemplary classrooms, "spotlights" on new technology, and links to more than 100 sites dealing with technology and/or students with disabilities. NCIP also produces a series of videos illustrating how students with disabilities use a range of assistive and instructional technologies to improve their learning. NCIP presented sessions at various educational conferences around the country. *Publications and Products: Video Profile Series: Multimedia and More: Help for Students with Learning Disabilities; Jeff with Expression: Writing in the Word Prediction Software; "Write" Tools for Angie: Technology for Students Who Are Visually Impaired; Telling Tales in ASL and English: Reading, Writing and Videotapes; Welcome to My Preschool: Communicating with Technology.* Excellent for use in training, workshops, and courses, videos may be purchased individually or as a set of five by calling (800) 793-5076. A new video to be released this year focuses on standards, curriculum, and assessment in science.

National Clearinghouse for Bilingual Education (NCBE). The George Washington University, 2011 I Street NW, Ste. 200, Washington, DC 20006. (202) 467-0867. Fax (800) 531-9347, (202) 467-4283. E-mail askncbe@ncbe.gwu.edu. Web site: http://www.ncbe. gwu.edu. Dr. Minerva Gorena, Interim Dir. NCBE is funded by the U.S. Department of Education's Office of Bilingual Education and Minority Languages Affairs (OBEMLA) to collect, analyze, synthesize, and disseminate information relating to the education of linguistically and culturally diverse students in the United States. NCBE is operated by the George Washington University Graduate School of Education and Human Development, Center for the Study of Language and Education in Washington, DC. Online services include the NCBE Web site containing an online library of hundreds of cover-to-cover documents, resources for teachers and administrators, and library of links to related Internet sites; an e-mail-based, biweekly news bulletin, Newsline; an electronic discussion group, NCBE Roundtable; and an e-mail-based question answering service, AskNCBE. *Publications:* short monographs, syntheses, and reports. Request a publications catalog for prices. The catalog and some publications are available at no cost from the NCBE and other Web sites. Updated: 5/23/02. Judy Zorfass jzorfass@edc.org

National Clearinghouse for English-Language Acquisition and Language Instruction Educational Programs (National Clearinghouse). The George Washington University, 2121 K Street NW, Ste. 260, Washington, DC 20037. (800) 321-6223, (202) 467-0867. Fax: (800) 531-9347, (202) 467-4283. E-mail: askncbe@ncbe.gwu.edu. Web site: http://www.ncbe.gwu.edu. Dr. Minerva Gorena, Director. The National Clearinghouse for English Language Acquisition and Language Instruction Educational Programs is funded by the U.S. Department of Education's Office of English Language Acquisition, Language

Enhancement and Academic Achievement for Limited English Proficient Students (OELA) to collect, analyze, synthesize, and disseminate information relating to the education of linguistically and culturally diverse students in the United States. Online services include a Web site containing an online library of hundreds of cover-to-cover publications, resources for teachers and administrators; links to related Web sites; a weekly e-mail news bulletin, *Newsline*; a monthly e-mail magazine, *Outlook*; and an e-mail question answering service. The National Clearinghouse is operated by the George Washington University Graduate School of Education and Human Development, Center for the Study of Language and Education in Washington, DC. The National Clearinghouse is funded by the U.S. Department of Education. *Membership:* There is no membership, and services are provided no cost. *Publications:* Short monographs, syntheses, and reports. Request a publications catalog for prices. The catalog and most publications are available at no cost from the National Clearinghouse Web site. Updated: 4/11/02. Anneka Kindler, akindler@ncbe.gwu.edu

National Commission on Libraries and Information Science (NCLIS). 1110 Vermont Ave. NW, Ste. 820, Washington, DC 20005-3552. (202) 606-9200. Fax: (202) 606-9203. E-mail: nclis.gov. Web site: http://www.nclis.gov. Robert S. Willard, Exec. Dir. A permanent independent agency of the U.S. government charged with advising the executive and legislative branches on national library and information policies and plans. The commission reports directly to the president and Congress on the implementation of national policy; conducts studies, surveys, and analyses of the nation's library and information needs; appraises the inadequacies of current resources and services; promotes research and development activities; conducts hearings and issues publications as appropriate; and develops overall plans for meeting national library and information needs and for the coordination of activities at the federal, state, and local levels. The commission provides general policy advice to the Institute of Museum and Library Services (IMLS) director relating to library services included in the Library Services and Technology Act (LSTA). *Membership:* 16 commissioners (14 appointed by the president and confirmed by the Senate, the Librarian of Congress, and the director of the IMLS). Average three meetings a year with a combined meeting of NCLIS/IMLS. *Publications:* Annual Report. Updated: 5/8/02. Kim Miller; kmiller@nclis.gov

National Communication Association (NCA). 1765 N Street NW, Washington, DC 20036. (202) 464-4622. Fax: (202) 464-4600. E-mail: memberservice@natcom.org. Web site: http://www.natcom.org. Roger Smitter, Exec. Dir. A voluntary society organized to promote study, criticism, research, teaching, and application of principles of communication, particularly of speech communication. Founded in 1914, NCA is a nonprofit organization of researchers, educators, students, and practitioners whose academic interests span all forms of human communication. NCA is the oldest and largest national organization serving the academic discipline of communication. Through its services, scholarly publications, resources, conferences and conventions, NCA works with its members to strengthen the profession and contribute to the greater good of the educational enterprise and society. Research and instruction in the discipline focus on the study of how messages in various media are produced, used, and interpreted within and across different contexts, channels, and cultures. *Membership:* 7,000 individual, plus departmental members. Any individual who supports the mission of the association is welcome to join. Student membership is $65/year; regular membership is $155/year. Additional memberships (including life memberships) also available. Annual National Conference held in November. *Publications:* *Spectra* Newsletter (mo.); *Quarterly Journal of Speech*; *Communication Monographs*; *Communication Education*; *Critical Studies in Mass Communication; Journal of Applied Communication Research; Text and Performance Quarterly; Communication Teacher; Index to Journals in Communication Studies through 1995; National Communication Directory of NCA and the Regional Speech Communication Organizations* (CSSA, ECA, SSCA,

WSCA). For additional publications, request brochure or check Web site. Updated: 3/2/05. Dennis Wallick, dwallick@natcom.org

National Council for Accreditation of Teacher Education (NCATE). 2010 Massachusetts Ave. NW, Ste. 500. Washington, DC 20036. (202) 466-7496. Fax: (202) 296-6620. E-mail: ncate@ncate.org. Web site: http://www.ncate.org. Arthur E. Wise, Pres. NCATE is a consortium of professional organizations that establishes standards of quality for and accredits professional education units in schools, colleges, and departments of education. *Membership:* Members include 34 National Professional organizations. NCATE accredits colleges of education in more than 550 higher education institutions and over 100 institutions are in candidacy. See Web site: http://www.ncate.org/accred/fees.htm; http://www. ncate.org/ partners/meetings.htm. *Publications: Standards*; *Quality Teaching* (newsletter, twice yearly; online resources for institutions and the public; *NCATE Speakers Guide*; *Handbook for Accreditation Visits. Publications:* Check our Web site for the complete publications list. Updated: 2/27/03. ncate@ncate.org

National Council of the Churches of Christ in the USA (NCC). Communication Commission, 475 Riverside Dr, New York, NY 10115. (212) 870-2574. Fax: (212) 870-2030. E-mail: dpomeroy@ncccusa.org. Web site: http://www.ncccusa.org. Wesley M. "Pat" Pattillo, Director of Communication. Ecumenical arena for cooperative work of Protestant and Orthodox denominations and agencies in broadcasting, film, cable, and print media. Offers advocacy to government and industry structures on media services. Services provided include liaison to network television and radio programming; film sales and rentals; information about telecommunications; and news and information regarding work of the National Council of Churches, related denominations, and agencies. Works closely with other faith groups in the Interfaith Broadcasting Commission. Online communication Web site: www.ncccusa.org. 36 denominations. *Publications: EcuLink.* Updated: 4/12/02. Dave Pomeroy dpomeroy@ncccusa.org

National Council of Teachers of English: Commission on Media, Committee on Instructional Technology, Assembly on Media Arts (NCTE). 1111 W. Kenyon Rd., Urbana, IL 61801-1096. (217) 328-3870. Fax: (217) 328-0977. E-mail: ncte.org. Web site: http://www.ncte.org. Kent Williamson, NCTE Executive Director; Bruce David, Commission Director; Rae C. Schipke, Committee Chair; Alan Teasley, Assembly Chair. The NCTE Commission on Media is a deliberative and advisory body which each year identifies and reports to the NCTE Executive Committee on key issues in the teaching of media; reviews what the council has done concerning media during the year; recommends new projects and persons who might undertake them. The commission monitors current and projected NCTE publications (other than journals), suggests topics for future NCTE publications on media, and performs a similar role of review and recommendation for the NCTE Annual Convention program. Occasionally, the commission undertakes further tasks and projects as approved by the executive committee. The NCTE Committee on Instructional Technology studies emerging technologies and their integration into English and language arts curricula and teacher education programs; identifies the effects of such technologies on teachers, students, and educational settings, with attention to people of color, handicapped, and other students not well served in current programs; explores means of disseminating information about such technologies to the NCTE membership; serves as liaison between NCTE and other groups interested in computer-based education in English and language arts; and maintains liaison with the NCTE Commission on Media and other Council groups concerned with instructional technology. The NCTE Assembly on Media Arts promotes communication and cooperation among all individuals who have a special interest in media in the English language arts; presents programs and special projects on this subject; encourages the development of research, experimentation, and investigation in the judicious uses of media in the teaching of English; promotes the extensive writing of articles and publications devoted to this subject; and integrates the efforts of those with an interest in this subject. The National Council of Teachers of English, with 75,000 individual and institutional members worldwide, is dedicated to improving the teaching and learning of English and the language arts at all levels of education. Members include elementary, middle, and high school teachers; supervisors of English programs; college and university faculty; teacher educators; local and state agency English specialists; and professionals in related fields The members of the NCTE Commission on Media and Committee on Instructional Technology are NCTE members appointed by the director and chair of the groups. Membership in the Assembly on Media Arts is open to members and nonmembers of NCTE. Membership in NCTE is $40 a year; adding subscriptions to its various journals adds additional fees. Membership in the Assembly on Media Arts is $10 a year. Annual convention: 2006, November 16–21, Nashville, Tennessee; see http://www.ncte.org/conventions/. *Publications:* NCTE publishes about 20 books a year. Visit http://www. ncte.org/books/ and http://bookstore.ncte.org. NCTE's journals include *Language Arts; English Journal; College English; College Composition and Communication; English Education; Research in the Teaching of English; Teaching English in the Two-Year College; Voices from the Middle; Primary Voices, K–6; Talking Points; Classroom Notes Plus; English Leadership Quarterly;* and *The Council Chronicle* (included in NCTE membership). Journal information is available at http://www.ncte.org/journals/. The Commission on Media and Committee on Instructional Technology do not have their own publications. The Assembly on Media Arts publishes *Media Matters,* a newsletter highlighting issues, viewpoints, materials, and events related to the study of media. Assembly members receive this publication. Updated: 2/23/05. Lyndsey Tate, public_E-mail: ncte.org

National Education Knowledge Industry Association (NEKIA). 1718 Connecticut Avenue, NW, Ste. 700, Washington, DC 20009-1162. (202) 518-0847. Fax: (202) 785-3849. E-mail: nekia.orgab. Web site: http://www.nekia.org. James W. Kohlmoos, Pres. Founded in 1997, NEKIA is a nonpartisan, nonprofit trade association representing the emerging knowledge industry. In the same way that research and development are crucial to the sciences, manufacturing and agriculture, research and development is vital to the field of education. In recent years, a new field—the education knowledge industry—has emerged to provide structure, quality, and coherence to education practices, policies and products. The members of this industry include researchers, educational developers, service providers, and a rapidly increasing number of entrepreneurs. Together, they work across the education spectrum from research to development to dissemination to practice. NEKIA brings educational innovation and expertise to all communities while providing its members with leadership, policy development, advocacy, professional development, and the promotion of quality products and services. NEKIA's mission is to advance the development and use of research based knowledge for the improvement of the academic performance of all children. The association's members are committed to finding new and better ways to support and expand high-quality education research, development, dissemination, technical assistance, and evaluation at the federal, regional, state, tribal, and local levels. Annual Legislative and Policy Conference; Annual Meeting. *Publications: Plugging In: Choosing and Using Educational Technology; Probe: Designing School Facilities for Learning; Education Productivity; Technology Infrastructure in Schools.* Updated: 5/12/03. John Waters; may be reached using info above.

National Education Telecommunications Organization & EDSAT Institute (NETO/EDSAT). 1899 L Street NW, Ste. 600, Washington, DC 20036. (202) 293-4211. Fax: (202) 293-4210. E-mail: neto-edsat@mindspring.com. Web site: http://www. netoedsat.org. Shelly Weinstein, Pres. and CEO. NETO/EDSAT is a nonprofit organization bringing together U.S. and non-U.S. users and providers of telecommunications to deliver education, instruction, health care, and training in classrooms, colleges, workplaces, health centers, and other distance education centers. NETO/EDSAT facilitates and collaborates with key stakeholders in the education and telecommunications fields. Programs and services include research and education, outreach, seminars and conferences, and newsletters. The NETO/EDSAT mission is to help create an integrated multitechnology infrastructure, a dedicated satellite that links space and existing secondary access roads (telephone and cable) over which teaching and education resources are delivered and shared in a user-friendly format with students, teachers, workers, and individuals. NETO/EDSAT seeks to create a modern-day "learning place" for rural, urban, migrant, suburban, disadvantaged, and at-risk students that provides equal and affordable access to and utilization of educational resources. *Membership:* More than 60 U.S. and non-U.S. school districts, colleges, universities, state agencies, public and private educational consortia, libraries, and other distance education providers. *Publications:* NETO/EDSAT *UPDATE* (newsletter, quarterly); *Analysis of a Proposal for an Education Satellite, EDSAT Institute, 1991; Global Summit on Distance Education Final Report, Oct 1996; International Report of the NETO/EDSAT Working Group on the Education and Health Care Requirements for Global/Regional Dedicated Networks, June 1998.*

National Endowment for the Humanities (NEH). Division of Public Programs, Media Program, 1100 Pennsylvania Ave., NW, Room 426, Washington, DC 20506. (202) 606-8269. Fax: (202) 606-8557. E-mail: publicpgms@neh.gov. Web site: http://www. neh.gov. Nancy Rogers, Director, Division of Public Programs. The NEH is an independent federal grant-making agency that supports research, educational, and public programs grounded in the disciplines of the humanities. The Media Program supports film and radio programs in the humanities for public audiences, including children and adults. Nonprofit institutions and organizations including public television and radio stations. Visit the Web site (http://www.neh.gov) for application forms and guidelines as well as the Media Log, a cumulative listing of projects funded through the Media Program. Updated: 3/2/05. Margaret Scrymser, mscrymser@neh.gov

National Federation of Community Broadcasters (NFCB). 1970 Broadway, Ste. 1000. Oakland, CA 94612. (510) 451-8200. Fax: (510) 451-8208. E-mail: nfcb@aol.com. Web site: http://www.nfcb.org. Carol Pierson, President and CEO. NFCB represents noncommercial, community-based radio stations in public policy development at the national level and provides a wide range of practical services, including technical assistance. *Membership:* 200. Noncommercial community radio stations, related organizations, and individuals. *Membership:* range from $200 to $3,000 for participant and associate members. Annual conference: http://www.nfcb.org/conference/communityradioconference.jsp. *Publications: Public Radio Legal Handbook; AudioCraft; Community Radio News; Let a Thousand Voices Speak: A Guide to Youth in Radio Projects.* Updated: 2/22/05. Ginny Z. Berson; ginnyz@nfcb.org

National Film Board of Canada (NFBC). 1123 Broadway, Ste. 307, New York, NY 100010. (212) 629-8890. Fax: (212) 629-8502. E-mail: j.sirabella@nfb.ca. Web site: http://www.nfb.ca. John Sirabella, U.S. Marketing Mgr./Nontheatrical Rep. The National Film Board of Canada has been producing and distributing films for over sixty years and has become particularly well known for its insightful point of view documentaries and creative auteur animation. The NFBC has made more than 10,000 original films which have won more than 4,000 prizes, including eleven Academy Awards. Updated: 3/10/05. Lisa Malcolm, l.malcolm@nfb.ca

National Film Information Service (NFIS). Center for Motion Picture Study, 333 So. La Cienega Blvd., Beverly Hills, CA 90211. (310) 247-3000. Fax: (310) 657-5597. E-mail: nfis@oscars.org. Web site: http://www.oscars.org/mhl/nfis.html. The fee-based National Film Information Service of the Margaret Herrick Library can answer queries from patrons outside of a 150-mile radius from the Fairbanks Center for Motion Picture Study. NFIS can accept inquiries via e-mail, fax or letter but all work undertaken by NFIS requires payment in advance. Requests for information should be as specific as possible. Updated: 6/5/03.

National Gallery of Art (NGA). Department of Education Resources, 2000B South Club Drive, Landover, MD 20785. (202) 842-6273. Fax: (202) 842-6935. E-mail: EdResources @nga.gov. Web site: http://www.nga.gov/education/classroom/loanfinder/. Leo J. Kasun, Education Resources Supervisory Specialist. This department of NGA is responsible for the production and distribution of 120+ educational audiovisual programs, including interactive technologies. Materials available (all loaned free to individuals, schools, colleges and universities, community organizations, and noncommerical television stations) range from videocassettes and color slide programs to videodiscs, CD-ROMs, and DVDs. A free catalog of programs is available upon request. All videodiscs, CD-ROMs, DVDs, utilizing digitized images on the gallery's collection are available for long-term loan. *Membership:* We have no members. However, last year we provided programs to over one million borrowers. Our programs are available to anyone who requests them. *Publications: Extension Programs Catalogue.* Updated: 2/22/05.

National Information Center for Educational Media (NICEM). P.O. Box 8640, Albuquerque, NM 87198-8640. (505) 265-3591, (800) 926-8328. Fax: (505) 256-1080. E-mail: nicem@nicem.com. Web site: http://www.nicem.com. Roy Morgan, Exec. Dir.; Marjorie M. K. Hlava, Pres., Access Innovations, Inc. The National Information Center for Educational Media maintains an international database of information about educational nonprint materials for all age levels and subject areas in all media types. NICEM editors collect, catalog, and index information about media that is provided by producers and distributors. This information is entered into an electronic masterfile. Anyone who is looking for information about educational media materials can search the database by a wide variety of criteria to locate existing and archival materials. Producer and distributor information in each record then leads the searcher to the source of the educational media materials needed. NICEM makes the information from the database available in several forms and through several vendors. CD-ROM editions are available from NICEM, SilverPlatter, and BiblioFile. Online access to the database is available through NICEM, EBSCO, SilverPlatter, and The Library Corporation. NICEM also conducts custom searches and prepares custom catalogs. NICEM is used by college and university media centers, public school libraries and media centers, public libraries, corporate training centers, students, media producers and distributors, and researchers. *Membership:* NICEM is a nonmembership organization. There is no charge for submitting information to be entered into the database. *Publications:* Corporate members of AECT, AIME, NAMTC, CCUMC. A-V Online on SilverPlatter; NICEM A-V MARC by BiblioFile; NICEM Reference CD-ROM; NICEM MARC CD-ROM; NICEM Producer & CD-ROM.

National ITFS Association (NIA). 77 W. Canfield, Detroit, MI 48201. (313) 577-2085. Fax: (313) 577-5577. E-mail: p.gossman@wayne.edu. Web site: http://www.itfs.org. Patrick Gossman, Chair, Board of Directors; Don MacCullough, Exec. Dir. Established in 1978, NIA is a nonprofit, professional organization of Instructional Television Fixed Service (ITFS) licensees, applicants, and others interested in ITFS broadcasting. ITFS is a very high frequency television broadcast service that is used to broadcast distance learning classes, two way internet service and data service to schools and other locations where education can take place. The goals of the association are to gather and exchange information about ITFS, gather data on utilization of ITFS, act as a conduit for those seeking ITFS information, and assist migration from video broadcast to wireless, broadband Internet services using ITFS channels. The NIA represents ITFS interests to the FCC, technical consultants, and equipment manufacturers. The association uses its Web site and Listserv list to provide information to its members in areas such as technology, programming content, FCC regulations, excess capacity leasing and license and application data. *Membership:* The current membership consists of Educational Institutions and nonprofit organizations that hold licenses issued by the Federal Communications Commission for Instructional Television

Fixed Service (ITFS). We also have members that have an interest in ITFS and members such as manufacturers of ITFS related equipment and Law firms that represent licensees. We have two main types of memberships: Voting memberships for ITFS licensees only, and nonvoting memberships for other educational institutions and sponsors. See the Web site (http://www.itfs.org) for details. Annual Member Conference, January/February. Updated: 5/13/03. Orville Thein, VP of the NIA, (319) 398-5663

National Press Photographers Association, Inc. (NPPA). 3200 Croasdaile Dr., Ste. 306. Durham, NC. 27705. (919) 383-7246. Fax: (919) 383-7261. E-mail: president@nppa.org. Web site: http://www.nppa.org. Todd Stricker, President. An organization of professional news photographers who participate in and promote photojournalism in publications and through television and film. Sponsors workshops, seminars, and contests; maintains an audiovisual library of subjects of media interest. *Membership:* 9,000. *Membership:* $90, domestic; $120, international; $55, student. An extensive array of conferences, seminars, and workshops are held throughout the year. *Publications: News Photographer* (magazine, mo.); *The Best of Photojournalism* (annual book). Updated: 3/5/04.

National PTA (NPTA). 541 N. Fairbanks Court, Ste. 1300, Chicago, IL 60611. (312) 670-6782. Fax: (312) 670-6783. E-mail: pta.org. Web site: http://www.pta.org. Linda Hodge (July 2003–June 2005); Anna Weselak, President-elect (2005–2007); Warlene Gary, Chief Executive Officer. Advocates the education, health, safety, and well-being of children and teens. Provides parenting education and leadership training to PTA volunteers. National PTA partners with the National Cable & Telecommunications Association on the "Taking Charge of Your TV" project by training PTA and cable representatives to present media literacy workshops. The workshops teach parents and educators how to evaluate programming so they can make informed decisions about what to allow their children to see. The National PTA in 1997 convinced the television industry to add content information to the TV rating system. *Membership:* 6.2 million. Membership open to all interested in the health, welfare, and education of children and support the PTA mission— http://www.pta.org/aboutpta/mission_en.asp. *Membership:* Vary by local unit—national dues portion is $1.75 per member annually. National convention, held annually in June in different regions of the country, is open to PTA members; convention information available on the Web site. Publication: *Our Children* (magazine) plus electronic newsletters and other Web-based information for members and general public. Updated: 3/14/05. Customer Service Department—E-mail: pta.org

National Public Broadcasting Archives (NPBA). Hornbake Library, University of Maryland. College Park, MD 20742. (301) 405-9255. Fax:(301) 314-2634. E-mail: tc65@umail. umd.edu. Web site: http://www.library.umd.edu/UMCP/NPBA/npba.html. Thomas Connors, Archivist. NPBA brings together the archival record of the major entities of non-commercial broadcasting in the United States. NPBA's collections include the archives of the Corporation for Public Broadcasting (CPB), the Public Broadcasting Service (PBS), and National Public Radio (NPR). Other organizations represented include the Midwest Program for Airborne Television Instruction (MPATI), the Public Service Satellite Consortium (PSSC), Americas Public Television Stations (APTS), Children's Television Workshop (CTW), and the Joint Council for Educational Telecommunications (JCET). NPBA also makes available the personal papers of many individuals who have made significant contributions to public broadcasting, and its reference library contains basic studies of the broadcasting industry, rare pamphlets, and journals on relevant topics. NPBA also collects and maintains a selected audio and video program record of public broadcastings national production and support centers and of local stations. Oral history tapes and transcripts from the NPR Oral History Project and the Televisionaries National History Project are also available at the archives. The archives are open to the public from 9 a.m. to 5 p.m., Monday through Friday. Research in NPBA collections should be arranged by prior appointment.

For further information, call (301) 405-9988. Updated: 2/27/03. Tom Connnors, tc65@umail.umd.edu

National Religious Broadcasters (NRB). 9510 Technology Dr., Manassas, VA 20110. (703) 330-7000. Fax: (703) 330-7100. E-mail: atower@nrb.org. Web site: http://www.nrb.org. Dr., Frank Wright, President, fwright@nrb.org. National Religious Broadcasters is a Christian international association of radio and TV stations, Webcasters, program producers, consultants, attorneys, agencies, and churches. NRB maintains rapport with the FCC, the broadcasting industry, and government bodies. NRB encourages growth of Christian communications through education, professional training, publications and networking opportunities. The association maintains relationships with other media associations to promote cutting-edge technology and practice. NRB fosters high professional standards through its Code of Ethics and Statement of Faith. *Membership:* 1,500 members who are organizations and individuals representing Christian TV, radio and internet stations and broadcasters, program producers, churches, agencies, consultants, attorneys, and companies who are directly or indirectly related to Christian broadcasting.

Intercollegiate Religious Broadcasters (IRB) is a chapter of NRB for colleges and universities who have a student run broadcast. Membership is open for both faculty and students. based on broadcast related expenses—associate members have fixed rates. Annual NRB Convention and Exhibition, 5 regional conventions held during summer and fall. *Publications: NRB magazine* (10 issues a year); *Directory of Religious Media and CD Rom; Inside NRB* (for members only), an e-mail broadcast; *Convention News,* a daily newspaper at national convention. Updated: 6/10/03. Anne Tower, VP of Membership, atower@nrb.org

National School Boards Association/ITTE: Education Technology Programs (NSBA/ITTE). 1680 Duke St., Alexandria, VA 22314. (703) 838-6722. Fax: (703) 548-5516. E-mail: itte@nsba.org. Web site: http://www.nsba.org/itte. Ann Lee Flynn, Director, Education Technology. ITTE was created to help advance the wise uses of technology in public education. ITTE renders several services to state school boards associations, sponsors conferences, publishes, and engages in special projects. The Technology Leadership Network, the membership component of ITTE, is designed to engage school districts nationwide in a dialogue about technology in education. This dialogue is carried out via newsletters, meetings, special reports, projects, and online communications. The experience of the network is shared more broadly through the state associations' communications with all school districts. *Membership:* Approximately 400 school districts in 47 states and Canada. Membership includes mostly public school districts, though private schools are eligible as well. Contacts include technology directors, superintendents, board members, curriculum directors, library/media specialists, and teachers. *Membership:* Based on the school district's student enrollment. *Publications: Virtual Realities: A School Leaders Guide to Online Education; Connecting Schools and Communities through Technology; Technology Professional Development for P–12 Educators; Legal Issues and Education Technology: A School Leader's Guide,* 2nd edition; *Education Leadership Toolkit: A Desktop Companion; Plans and Policies for Technology in Education: A Compendium,* 2nd edition; *Models of Success: Case Study of Technology in Schools; Investing in School Technology: Strategies to Meet the Funding Challenge/School Leader's Version; Leadership and Technology: What School Board Members Need to Know; Technology Leadership Newsletter; Technology & School Design: Creating Spaces for Learning.* Updated: 3/8/04. Ann Flynn, itte@nsba.org, (703) 838-6764

National School Supply and Equipment Association (NSSEA). 8300 Colesville Rd., Ste. 250, Silver Spring, MD 20910. (301) 495-0240. Fax: (301) 495-3330. E-mail: nssea@aol.com. Web site: http://www.nssea.org. Tim Holt, Pres. A service organization of more than 1,600 manufacturers, distributors, retailers, and independent manufacturers' representatives of school supplies, equipment, and instructional materials. Seeks to maintain open communications between manufacturers and dealers in the school market and to encourage the development of new ideas and products for educational progress. *Publication: Annual Membership Directory.*

National Science Foundation (NSF). 4201 Wilson Blvd. Arlington, VA 22230. (703) 292-5111. E-mail: lboutchy@nsf.gov. Web site: http://www.nsf.gov/start.htm. Mary Hanson, Chief, Media Relations and Public Affairs. Linda Boutchyard, Contact Person. NSF, an independent federal agency, funds research and education in all fields of science, mathematics and engineering. With an annual budget of about $5 billion, NSF funds reach all 50 states, through grants, contracts, and cooperative agreements to more than 2,000 colleges, universities and other institutions nationwide. NSF receives more than 50,000 requests for funding annually, including at least 30,000 new proposals. Applicants should refer to the NSF Guide to Programs. Scientific material and media reviews are available to help the public learn about NSF-supported programs. NSF news releases and tip sheets are available electronically via *NSFnews.* To subscribe, send an e-mail message to listmanager@nsf.gov; in the body of the message, type "subscribe nsfnews" and then type your name. Also see NSF news products at Web site: http://www.nsf.gov/od/lpa/news/start.htm, http://www.eurekalert.org/, and http://www.ari.net/newswise. In addition, NSF has developed a Web site that offers information about NSF directorates, offices, programs, and publications at http://nsf.gov. Updated: 5/8/02. Linda Boutchyard, Contact Person.

National Telemedia Council Inc. (NTC). 1922 University Ave., Madison, WI 53705. (608) 218-1182. Fax: (608) 218-1183. E-mail: NTelemedia@aol.com. Web site: http://www.nationaltelemediacouncil.org. Dr. Martin Rayala, President; Marieli Rowe, Exec. Dir. The NTC is a national, nonprofit professional organization dedicated to promoting media literacy, or critical media viewing skills. This is done primarily through work with teachers, parents, and caregivers. NTC activities include publishing *Telemedium: The Journal of Media Literacy,* the *Teacher Idea Exchange* (T.I.E.), the Jessie McCanse Award for individual contribution to media literacy, assistance to media literacy educators and professionals. Our membership is open to all those interested in media literacy. *Membership:* $30, basic; $50, contributing; $100, patron. No meetings scheduled for members. *Publications: Telemedium; The Journal of Media Literacy* (quarterly newsletter). Updated: 4/15/02. Jaci Kotzum, (608) 218-1182

Native American Public Telecommunications (NAPT). 1800 North 33rd St., P.O. Box 83111, Lincoln, NE 68501-3111. (402) 472-3522. Fax: (402) 472-8675. E-mail: native@unl.edu. Web site: http://nativetelecom.org. Frank Blythe, Exec. Dir. The mission of NAPT is to inform, educate, and encourage the awareness of tribal histories, cultures, languages, opportunities, and aspirations through the fullest participation of America Indians and Alaska Natives in creating and employing all forms of educational and public telecommunications programs and services, thereby supporting tribal sovereignty. *Membership:* No membership. *Publication: The Vision Maker* (newsletter).

Natural Science Collections Alliance (NSC Alliance). 1725 K St., NW, Ste. 601, Washington, DC 20006. (202) 835-9050. Fax: (202) 835-7334. E-mail: general@nscalliance.org. Web site: http://www.nscalliance.org. Fosters the care, management, and improvement of biological collections and promotes their utilization. Institutional members include freestanding museums, botanical gardens, college and university museums, and public institutions, including state biological surveys and agricultural research centers. The NSC Alliance also represents affiliate societies, and keeps members informed about funding and legislative issues. *Membership:* 85 institutions, 31 affiliates, 120 individual and patron members. *Membership:* depend on the size of collections. Annual Meeting (June). *Publications: Alliance Gazette* (newsletter for members and nonmember subscribers, quarterly); *Guidelines for Institutional Policies and Planning in Natural History Collections; Global Genetic Resources; A Guide to Museum Pest Control.* Updated: 5/20/03. Karen Kajiwara, (202) 835-9050

NCTI. 8022 Southpark Circle, Ste. 100, Littleton, CO 80120. (303) 797-9393. Fax: (303) 797-9394. E-mail: ncti.com. Web site: http://www.ncti.com. Tom Brooksher, President and CEO; Alan Babcock, Chief Learning Officer. Located in the Denver area, NCTI provides workforce performance products, services, and education to the cable and broadband industry. NCTI offers extensive and up-to-date training in electronic, instructor-led, paper-based and Web-delivery formats; services such as customized curriculum development, performance assessment and testing; and professional development through college credit and industry certification. Since 1968, system operators, contractors, and industry vendors have turned to NCTI to train more than 250,000 industry professionals. By creating innovative products that develop and improve skills; services that evaluate, identify, and improve workforce competencies; and education that advances careers; NCTI remains committed to providing individuals and their employers the knowledge they need to succeed in the broadband industry. For more information, please visit www.ncti.com. Updated: 5/20/03. Michael Guilfoyle, michaelg@ncti.com

Network for Continuing Medical Education (NCME). One Harmon Plaza, 6th Floor, Secaucus, NJ 07094. (201) 867-3550. Produces and distributes videocassettes, CD-ROMs & Web Based Programs to hospitals for physicians' continuing education. Programs are developed for physicians in the practice of general medicine, anesthesiology, emergency medicine, gastroenterology, and surgery. Physicians who view all the programs can earn up to 25 hours of Category 1 (AMA) credit and up to 10 hours of Prescribed (AAFP) credit each year. *Membership:* More than 1,000 hospitals provide NCME programs to their physicians. Subscription fees: VHS—$2,160/year. *Publications:* Sixty-minute videocassettes & CD-ROMs are distributed to hospital subscribers every 18 days.

The NETWORK, Inc. (NETWORK). 136 Fenno Dr., Rowley, MA 01969-1004. (800) 877-5400, (978) 948-7764. Fax: (978) 948-7836. E-mail: davidc@thenetworkinc.org. Web site: www.thenetworkinc.org. David Crandall, President. A nonprofit research and service organization providing training, research and evaluation, technical assistance, and materials for a fee to schools, educational organizations, and private sector firms with educational interests. The NETWORK has been helping professionals manage and learn about change since 1969. Our Leadership Skills series of computer-based simulations extends the widely used board game versions of *Making Change* and *Systems Thinking/Systems Changing* with the addition of *Improving Student Success: Teachers, Schools and Parents* to offer educators a range of proven professional development tools. *Publications: Making Change: A Simulation Game* (board and computer versions); *Systems Thinking/Systems Changing: A Simulation Game* (board and computer versions); *Improving Student Success: Teachers, Schools and Parents* (computer based simulation); *Systemic Thinking: Solving Complex Problems; Benchmarking: A Guide for Educators.* Updated: 3/14/05. David Crandall, davidc@thenetworkinc.org

New England Educational Media Association (NEEMA). c/o Charles White, Executive Director, 307 Cumberland Terrace, 5C, Myrtle Beach, SC 29572. (203) 545-0251. Fax: (617) 559-6191. E-mail: charliewvt@aol.com. Web site: www.neema.org. Charles White, Executive Director. An affiliate of American Association of School librarians and the Association for Educational Communications and Technology (www.aect.org), NEEMA is a regional professional association dedicated to the improvement of instruction through the effective utilization of school library media services, educational media, and technology applications. For more than 80 years, it has represented school library media professionals through activities and networking efforts to develop and polish the leadership skills, professional representation, and informational awareness of the membership. The board of directors consists of departments of education as well as professional leaders of the region. An annual conference program and Leadership Program is offered in conjunction with the various regional state association conferences. A bimonthly publication (*NEEMA Views*) is available electronically at the Web site. NEEMA focuses on school library media issues among the six New England states; consequently, membership is encouraged for school library media specialists in this region. *Membership:* Annual membership $30; dual member (state and NEEMA): $20. If you are already a member of your state organization, you can join NEEMA at a reduced rate this year. Student (fte) and retiree: $15. (Make checks payable to NEEMA and return to: Carolyn Markuson, Membership Chair, 61 Hickory Road, Sudbury, MA 01776.) Annual Leadership Conference and Business Meeting. *Publication: NEEMA Views.* Updated: 3/15/05. Charles White charliewvt@aol.com

New York Festivals (NYF). 7 West 36th Street, 14th Floor, New York, NY 10018. (212) 643-4800. Fax: (212) 643-0170. E-mail: newyorkfestivals.com. Web site: http://www. newyorkfestivals.com. Tara Dawn, Executive Director. The New York Festivals (NYF) oversees six international awards competitions: Film & Video; Television Programming and Promotion; Radio Programming and Promotion; Television and Radio Advertising; Design, Print & Outdoor Advertising; and Interactive Media. Entries to each of these competitions are judged in the United States and around the world by panels of peers in their respective industries. Founded in 1957, the New York Festivals now has representation in 62 countries. Categories in the New York Festivals annual international Film & Video Awards cover both industrial and educational film and video productions, filmstrips and slide programs, multi-image business theater and interactive multimedia presentations, short films and home videos. The 2006 competition will be open for entry from July 2005. Entry fees begin at $225 for a single entry. For more information visit http://www.newyorkfestivals. com. No membership feature. The competition is open to any one who produces industrials, educational or informational films, DVDs, CD-ROMs, Web sites, Home Videos, short films, multi-image or business theatre productions. Winners are posted on our Web site at www.newyorkfestivals.com, and details are released to trade publications in North America, Europe and throughout the world through our network of international representatives. Updated: 3/30/05. Anne White, Marketing Director, awhite@newyorkfest

NJS Logistics. Holladay Blvd., #230. Salt Lake City, UT 84117. (801) 277-9821. Fax: (801) 365-9707. E-mail: njs@fiber.net. Web site: http://www.powerdown.net. Neal J. Stevens. NJS Logistics specializes in Supply Chain Management training. There are four modules: (1) *Shipping and Receiving for Warehouse Staff*—teaches proper receiving techniques used to spot costly problems and identify fraudulent practices. (2) *Purchasing Techniques and Documentation for Buyers*—because buyers have control over all purchasing transactions, we show them how to make decisions and provide them with instructions that will guarantee lowest landed cost on everything they buy. (3) *Accounting*—accounts payable reviews every invoice before it is paid. Proper scrutiny will reduce costs and recover losses due to vendor noncompliance of shipping and purchasing instructions. (4) *Traffic* —the traffic manager negotiates rates, charges, and services. We teach cost-cutting methods to reduce costs, and eliminate transportation wastage charges. Each dollar wasted is a profit dollar lost.

Northwest College and University Council for the Management of Educational Technology (NW/MET). c/o WITS, Willamette University, 900 State St., Salem. OR 97301. (503) 370-6650. Fax: (503) 375-5456. E-mail: mmorandi@willamette.edu. Web site: http://www.nw-met.org. Tom Matney, Director; Marti Morandi, Membership Chair. NW/MET is a group of media professionals responsible for campus-wide media services. Founded in 1976, NW/MET is comprised of members from three provinces of Canada and four northwestern states. Membership is restricted to information technology managers with campus-wide responsibilities for information technology services in the membership region. Corresponding membership is available to those who work outside the membership region. Current issues under consideration include managing emerging technologies, distance education, adaptive technologies, staff evaluation, course management, faculty development, copyright, and other management/administration issues. Organizational goals include identifying the unique status problems of media managers in higher education. *Membership:* approx. 75. *Membership:* $35. An annual conference and business meeting are held each year, rotating through the region. *Publications:* An annual newsletter and

NW/MET Journal. Updated: 2/27/03. Marti Morandi by e-mail at mmorandi@ willamette.edu

Northwest Regional Educational Laboratory (NWREL). 101 SW Main St., Ste. 500, Portland, OR 97204. (503) 275-9500. Fax: (503) 275-0448. E-mail: nwrel.org. Web site: http://www.nwrel.org. Dr. Carol Thomas, Exec. Dir. One of 10 Office of Educational Research and Improvement (OERI) regional educational laboratories, NWREL works with schools and communities to improve educational outcomes for children, youth, and adults. NWREL provides leadership, expertise, and services based on the results of research and development. The specialty area of NWREL is school change processes. *Membership:* It serves Alaska, Idaho, Oregon, Montana, and Washington, 856 organizations. Holds the Education Now and in the Future Conference. *Publications: Northwest Report* (newsletter); *Northwest Education* (quarterly journal). Updated: 4/26/04. Jennifer Railsback, Resource Advisor, (503) 275-0454.

Online Audiovisual Catalogers, Inc. (OLAC). E-mail: neumeist@buffalo.edu. Web site: http://www.olacinc.org/. In 1980, OLAC was founded to establish and maintain a group that could speak for catalogers of audiovisual materials. OLAC provides a means for exchange of information, continuing education, and communication among catalogers of audiovisual materials and with the Library of Congress. While maintaining a voice with the bibliographic utilities that speak for catalogers of audiovisual materials, OLAC works toward common understanding of AV cataloging practices and standards. *Membership:* 645. Dues, U.S./Canada: Personal Memberships—one year $20.00, two years $38.00, three years $55.00. Institutional Memberships—one year $25.00, two years $48.00, three years $70.00. Dues, Other Countries: All Memberships one year $25.00; two years $48.00, three years $70.00. *Publications: OLAC Newsletter* (biannual). Updated: 4/5/05. Sue Neumeister, neumeist@buffalo.edu

Online Computer Library Center, Inc. (OCLC). 6565 Frantz Rd., Dublin, OH 43017-3395. (614) 764-6000. Fax: (614) 764-6096. E-mail: oclc@oclc.org. Web site: http://www.oclc.org. Jay Jordan, President and CEO. Founded in 1967, OCLC is a nonprofit, membership, computer library service and research organization dedicated to the public purposes of furthering access to the world's information and reducing information costs. More than 50,000 libraries in 94 countries and territories around the world use OCLC services to locate, acquire, catalog, lend and preserve library materials. Researchers, students, faculty, scholars, professional librarians and other information seekers use OCLC services to obtain bibliographic, abstract and full-text information. OCLC and its member libraries cooperatively produce and maintain WorldCat—the OCLC Online Union Catalog. OCLC FOREST PRESS, a division of OCLC since 1988, publishes the Dewey Decimal Classification. Digital Collection and Preservation Services, a division of OCLC since 1994, provides digitizing, microfilming and archiving services worldwide. OCLC's netLibrary provides libraries with eContent solutions that support Web-based research, reference and learning. OCLC welcomes information organizations around the world to be a part of our unique cooperative. A variety of participation levels are available to libraries, museums, archives, historical societies and professional associations. *Membership:* represents more than 50,000 libraries in 94 countries and territories around the world. OCLC also has 66 Members Council delegates who are elected by and represent the OCLC member libraries in their respective regions. OCLC Members Council (3/year) held in Dublin, Ohio. *Publications: Annual Report* (1/year); *OCLC Newsletter* (4/year); *OCLC Abstracts* (1/week, electronic version only). Updated: 2/22/05. Carrie Lauer, OCLC Communications: lauerc@oclc.org

Pacific Film Archive (PFA). University of California, Berkeley Art Museum, 2625 Durant Ave., Berkeley, CA 94720-2250. (510) 642-1437 (library); (510) 642-1412 (general). Fax: (510) 642-4889. E-mail: pfalibrary@uclink.berkeley.edu. Web site: http:// www.bampfa.berkeley.edu. Edith Kramer, Dir. and Curator of Film; Nancy Goldman,

Head, PFA Library and Film Study Center. Sponsors the exhibition, study, and preservation of classic, international, documentary, animated, and avant-garde films. Provides on-site research screenings of films in its collection of over 7,000 titles. Provides access to its collections of books, periodicals, stills, and posters (all materials are noncirculating). Offers BAM/PFA members and University of California, Berkeley, affiliates reference and research services to locate film and video distributors, credits, stock footage, etc. Library hours are 1 p.m.-5 p.m. Mon.–Thurs. *Membership:* Membership is through our parent organization, the UC Berkeley Art Museum and Pacific Film Archive, and is open to anyone. The BAM/PFA currently has over 3,000 members. Members receive free admission to the museum; reduced-price tickets to films showing at PFA; access to the PFA Library & Film Study Center; and many other benefits. Applications and more information is available at http://www.bampfa.berkeley.edu/membership/index.html. *Membership:* $40 indiv. and nonprofit departments of institutions. *Publications: BAM/PFA Calendar* (6/yr). Updated: 3/13/03. Nancy Goldman, e-mail: NLG@uclink.berkeley.edu

Pacific Resources for Education and Learning (PREL). 900 Fort Street Mall, Ste. 1300. Honolulu, HI 96813. (808) 441-1300. Fax: (808) 441-1385. E-mail: askprel@prel.org: Web site: http://www.prel.org/. Tom Barlow, President and Chief Executive Officer. PREL is a nonprofit 501(c) (3) corporation dedicated to helping educators and policy makers solve educational problems in their schools. Using the best available research and the expertise of professionals, PREL helps to implement new approaches in education and provides training to teachers and administrators. The PRELStar program utilizes telecommunications technology to provide distance learning opportunities to the Pacific region. The Pacific Regional Technology in Education Consortium program builds local school and community capacity to acquire and utilize technology to improve teaching and learning. NEARStar provides an interactive, Web-based supplemental early reading program for English language learners. The Ethnomathematics Digital Library provides high-quality educational resources online about ethnomathematics worldwide, with emphasis on the Pacific. The first three projects are funded by the US Department of Education, and the latter by the National Science Foundation. PREL serves teachers and departments and ministries of education in American Samoa, Commonwealth of the Northern Mariana Islands, Federated States of Micronesia (Chuuk, Kosrae, Pohnpei, and Yap) Guam, Hawaii, the Republic of the Marshall Islands, and the Republic of Palau. PREL supports the annual Pacific Educational Conference, held each July. *Publications:* Publications are listed on the PREL Web site at Web site: http://ppo.prel.org/. Most are available in both PDF and HTML format. Updated: 3/10/05. Janis Michael, askprel@prel.org

Penn State Media Sales (PSMS). 118 Wagner Building, University Park, PA 16802. (800) 770-2111, (814) 863-3102. Fax: (814) 865-3172. E-mail: MediaSales@outreach.psu.edu. Web site: http://www.MediaSales.psu.edu. Denise Hartman, Interim Marketing Director. Distributor of educational video with a primary audience of postsecondary education. One of America's largest collections on historic psychology, including Stanley Milgrams experiments, psychosurgery, and early mental illness treatments. Other categories are anthropology, including the Mead/Bateson studies, primatology, sciences, agriculture, and training. Closed-circuit television, broadcast and footage use available on many titles. Call for more information. *Publication:* Product catalog. Updated: 3/11/05. Roberta Stover, rls46@psu.edu or (814) 865-3333 ext. 250

Photographic Society of America (PSA). 3000 United Founders Blvd., Ste. 103. Oklahoma City, OK 73112. (405) 843-1437. Fax: (405) 843-1438. E-mail: hq@psa-photo. org. Web site: http://www.psa-photo.org. Linda Lowery, operations manager. A nonprofit organization for the development of the arts and sciences of photography and for the furtherance of public appreciation of photographic skills. Its members, largely advanced amateurs, consist of individuals, camera clubs, and other photographic organizations. Divisions include electronic imaging, color slide, video motion picture, nature, photojournalism, travel, pictorial print, stereo, and techniques. Sponsors national, regional, and local meetings, clinics, and contests. *Membership:* 5,500. *Membership:* $42, North America; $48 elsewhere. 2002 International Conference of Photography. *Publications: PSA Journal.* Update: 4/24/02. Linda Lowery, Operations manager, PSA.

Printing Industries of America/Graphic Arts Technical Foundation (PIA/GATF). 200 Deer Run Road. Sewickley, PA 15143-2600. (412) 741-6860. Fax: (412) 741-2311. E-mail: piagatf.org. Web site: http://www.gain.net. George Ryan, Executive Vice President and Chief Operating Officer. The Printing Industries of America (PIA)/Graphic Arts Technical Foundation (GATF) along with its affiliates, delivers products and services that enhance the growth, efficiency and profitability of its members and the industry through advocacy, education, research and technical information. *Membership:* 13,000 corporate members, 520 teachers, 100 students. *Membership:* $49, teachers; $49, students; corporations pay dues to regional printing organizations affiliated with PIA/GATF. See http://www.gain.net. *Publications:* PIA/GATFPress publishes books relating to graphic communications. PIA/GATF's Publications Catalogs promotes approximately 150 books, reports, and training curriculum, 100 of which are published by PIA/GATF. Recent publications include *Sheetfed Offset Press Operating* (3rd ed.); *Binding, Finishing, and Mailing* (2nd ed.); *Careers in Printing; Field Guide to Color Reproduction; PDF Print Production Guide* (2nd ed.); *GATF Guide to Troubleshooting for the Web Offset Press;* and the *Ergonomics Guidebook.* Updated: 3/10/05. Thomas M. Destree, tdestree@piagatf.org

Professors of Instructional Design and Technology (PIDT). Instructional Technology Dept., 220 War Memorial Hall, Virginia Tech., Blacksburg, VA 24061-0341. (540) 231-5587. Fax: (540) 231-9075. E-mail: moorem@VT.EDU. Web site: https://www.conted.vt.edu/ssl/pidt-reg.htm. Dr. Mike Moore or Dr. Ed Caffarella, contact persons. An informal organization designed to encourage and facilitate the exchange of information among members of the instructional design and technology academic and corporate communities. Also serves to promote excellence in academic programs in instructional design and technology and to encourage research and inquiry that will benefit the field while providing leadership in the public and private sectors in its application and practice. Faculty employed in higher education institutions whose primary responsibilities are teaching and research in instructional technology, their corporate counterparts, and other persons interested in the goals and activities of the PIDT. *Membership:* No formal membership. Contact either Dr. Mike Moore (moorem@vt.edu) or Dr. Ed Caffarella (CAFFAREL@unco.edu) to be added to listserv for announcements of meeting times, location and conference registration. Cohosts alternate between Virginia Tech and University of Northern Colorado and meetings alternate annually between Virginia and Colorado. Meeting usually is around the middle of May and usually runs from Friday P.M. to Monday A.M. There are no dues, officers, bylaws, or formal organization. Updated: 5/8/02. Mike Moore, moorem@vt.edu

Public Broadcasting Service (PBS). 1320 Braddock Pl. Alexandria, VA 22314. Web site: http://www.pbs.org. Ervin S. Duggan, CEO and Pres. National distributor of public television programming, obtaining all programs from member stations, independent producers, and sources around the world. PBS services include program acquisition, distribution, and scheduling; development and fundraising support; engineering and technical development; and educational resources and services. Through the PBS National Program Service, PBS uses the power of noncommercial television, the Internet, and other media to enrich the lives of all Americans through quality programs and education services that inform and inspire. Subsidiaries of PBS include PBS Adult Learning Service, and PBS Video, which are described below. PBS is owned and operated by local public television organizations through annual membership fees and governed by a board of directors elected by PBS members for three-year terms.

PBS Adult Learning Service (ALS). 1320 Braddock Place, Alexandria, VA 22314-1698. (800) 257-2578, (703) 739-8471. E-mail: als@pbs.org. Web site: http://www.pbs.org/als/. Clinton O'Brien, Senior Director. The PBS Adult Learning

Service is a provider of course content to colleges and universities nationwide. Offerings include Web-based online courses and video-based telecourses. Content is developed by prominent educators and producers and designed for college-credit use. Public television stations nationwide cooperate with colleges that offer PBS courses to reach local populations of adult learners. A pioneer in the widespread use of video in college-credit learning, PBS first began distributing telecourses in 1981. Since that time, more than 3 million students have earned college credit through telecourses from PBS. *Membership:* Nearly 500 institutions are PBS Associate Colleges. These members save on licensing and acquisition fees for PBS courses and are entitled to discounts on related services such as Web-based scheduling, master broadcast tape duplication, and educational videotape purchase. Nonmembers still have access to the same content and services; they simply pay higher fees. *Membership:* $1,500. Multicollege and consortium rates are available. PBS Adult Learning Service Course Catalog. *Publication: PBS Course Bulletin* (monthly e-mail update for course faculty and administrators). Updated: 5/29/02. Kathy Dunne, kdunne@pbs.org

PBS VIDEO. 1320 Braddock Pl., Alexandria, VA 22314. (703) 739-5380; (800) 344-3337. Fax: (703) 739-5269. E-mail: jcecil@pbs.org. Web site: http://shop2.org/pbsvideo/. Jon Cecil, Dir. PBS VIDEO Marketing. Markets and distributes PBS television programs for sale on videocassette and DVD to colleges, public libraries, schools, governments, and other organizations and institutions. *Publications: PBS VIDEO Catalogs of New and Popular Video* (4/yrs). Web site: PBS VIDEO Online Catalog at Web site: http://shopPBS.com/teachers. Updated: 5/13/03. Jon Cecil, (703) 739-5157 or jcecil@pbs.org

Public Library Association (PLA). 50 E. Huron St., Chicago, IL 60611. (312) 280-5PLA. (312) 280-5029. E-mail: pla@ala.org. Web site: www.pla.org. Greta Southard, Exec. Dir. A division of the American Library Association, PLA is concerned with the development, effectiveness, and financial support of public libraries. It speaks for the profession and seeks to enrich the professional competence and opportunities of public librarians. *Membership:* 9,940 as of 2/2002. Any member of the American Library Association is eligible to join PLA. *Membership:* $50, open to all ALA members. *Publications: Public Libraries* (bi-monthly); electronic newsletter sent to members. Updated: 4/10/02. Greta Southard, (800) 545-2433 ext. 5028.

(PLA) Audiovisual Committee. 50 E. Huron St., Chicago, IL 60611. (312) 280-5752. James E. Massey, Chair. Promotes use of audiovisual materials in public libraries.

(PLA) Technology in Public Libraries Committee. 50 E. Huron St., Chicago, IL 60611. (312) 280-5752. William Ptacek, Chair. Collects and disseminates information on technology applications in public libraries.

Puppeteers of America, Inc. (POA). PO Box 29417, Parma, OH 44129-0417. (888) 568-6235. Fax: (440) 843-7867. E-mail: PofAjoin@aol.com. Web site: http://www.puppeteers.org. Joyce and Chuck Berty, Membership Officers. Formed in 1937, POA holds festivals for puppetry across the country, supports local guilds, presents awards, sponsors innovative puppetry works, provides consulting, and provides research materials through the Audio-Visual Library. A National Festival is held in the odd number years and Regional Festivals are held in the even number years at various locations around the United States. The group supports a National Day of Puppetry the last Saturday in April. Local celebrations of the Art of Puppetry are held throughout the United States. The Puppetry Store is an invaluable source of books and miscellaneous printed materials for Puppeteers or anyone interested in Puppetry. The Puppetry Journal is the magazine published quarterly for the members of the organization and Playboard is the Bi-Monthly newsletter. *Membership:* more than 2,200 memberships from people around the world interested in the art of puppetry. Membership includes performing professionals, librarians, storytellers, and people interested in the art of puppetry. *Membership:* We offer subscription memberships to Libraries and discounted memberships to Seniors and Youths. $40, Single Adult; $50, couple; $20, youth (17—6); $25 Full-time Student; $25 Senior (65 and over); $60, family; $70 Company or Business; $35, Journal subscription available to libraries. *Publications: The Puppetry Journal* (quarterly) A quarterly magazine published only for our membership. It is the only publication in the United States dedicated to Puppetry in America. *Playboard* is a bimonthly newsletter published to up-date the voting membership on the business of the organization. Updated: 4/10/02. Joyce Berty, e-mail pofajoin@aol.com or phone.

Recording for the Blind & Dyslexic (RFB&D). 20 Roszel Road. Princeton, NJ 08540. (609) 452-0606. Customer Service (800) 221-4792. Fax: (609) 987-8116. E-mail: information@rfbd.org. Web site: http://www.rfbd.org. John Kelly, President & CEO. Recording for the Blind & Dyslexic (RFB&D), a national nonprofit volunteer organization founded in 1948, is the nation's educational library serving people who cannot read standard print effectively because of a learning disability, visual impairment or other physical disability. RFB&D operates 29 recording studios and offices across the country. Our library of more than 104,000 volumes contains a broad selection of titles, from literature and history to math and the sciences, at all academic levels, from kindergarten through postgraduate and professional. RFB&D offers individual and institutional Learning Through Listening memberships, scholarship programs, a reference service and a custom recording service. RFB&D also offers for nonprofit sale a variety of playback devices and accessories. RFB&DS materials are for people who cannot read standard print because of visual impairment, learning disability or physical disability. Potential individual members must complete an application form, which contains a "disability verification." *Membership:* 137,025 individual and institutional members. *Membership:* The cost of an individual membership is $35 per year, plus a one-time $65 registration fee for qualified individuals. Fees for institutional membership vary based on level of membership chosen. (Contact Customer Service). *Publications: RFB&D Learning through Listening Impact Newsletter.* Updated: 3/15/05. Mark Zustovich, mzustovich@rfbd.org

Recording Industry Association of America, Inc. (RIAA). 1330 Connecticut Ave. NW #300, Washington, DC 20036. (202) 775-0101. Fax: (202) 775-7253. E-mail: aweiss@riaa.com. Web site: http://www.riaa.com/. Hilary Rosen, Chairman and CEO. Founded in 1952, RIAA's mission is to promote the mutual interests of recording companies, as well as the betterment of the industry overall through successful government relations (both federal and state), intellectual property protection, and international activities; evaluating all aspects of emerging technologies and technology-related issues; and promoting an innovative and secure online marketplace. RIAA represents the recording industry, whose members create and/or distribute approximately 90 percent of all legitimate sound recordings produced and sold in the United States. RIAA is the official certification agency for gold, platinum, and multi-platinum record awards. *Membership:* Over 250 recording companies. Updated: 5/24/02. Amanda Collins, (202) 775-0101.

Reference and User Services Association (RUSA). 50 E. Huron St., Chicago, IL 60611. (800) 545-2433, ext. 4398. Fax: (312) 944-8085. E-mail: cbourdon@ala.org. Web site: http://www.ala.org/rusa. Cathleen Bourdon, Exec. Dir. A division of the American Library Association, RUSA is responsible for stimulating and supporting in every type of library the delivery of reference information services to all groups and of general library services and materials to adults. *Membership:* 4,900. *Membership:* Join ALA and RUSA $95; RUSA membership $45 (added to current ALA membership); student member $45 ($25 for ALA and $20 for RUSA). Meetings are held in conjunction with the American Library Association. *Publications: RUSQ* (quarterly), information provided on RUSA Web site:

www.ala.org/rusa. Other select publications. Updated: 4/27/04. Eileen Hardy, ehardy@ala.org

Research for Better Schools, Inc. (RBS). 112 North Broad Street, Philadelphia, PA 19102-1510. (215) 568-6150. Fax: (215) 568-7260. E-mail: rbs.org. Web site: http:// www.rbs.org/. Keith M. Kershner & Louis Maguire, Co-Executive Directors. Research for Better Schools is a nonprofit education organization that has been providing services to teachers, administrators, and policy makers since 1966. Our mission is to help students achieve high learning standards by supporting improvement efforts in schools and other education environments. The staff are dedicated to and well experienced in providing the array of services that schools, districts, and states need to help their students reach proficient or higher learning standards: (1) technical assistance in improvement efforts; (2) professional development that is required for the successful implementation of more effective curricula, technologies, or instruction; (3) application of research in the design of specific improvement efforts; (4) evaluation of improvement efforts; (5) curriculum implementation and assessment; and (6) effective communication with all members of the school community. RBS has worked with a wide range of clients over the years, representing all levels of the education system, as well as business and community groups. *Membership:* No membership. Research for Better Schools sponsors an annual regional conference. *Publications:* RBS publishes a newsletter, available in print, online, and delivered via e-mail (Web site: http://www.rbs.org/currents/index.shtml). RBS also publishes an electronic newsletter (Web site: http://www.rbs. org/archives/riptides.html).The catalog for RBS Publications is online (http://www.rbs.org). Updated: 3/2/05. Louis Maguire, maguire@ rbs.org

Smithsonian Institution. 1000 Jefferson Drive SW, Washington, DC 20560. (202) 357-2700. Fax: (202) 786-2515. E-mail: info.si.edu. Web site: http://www.si.edu. I. Michael Heyman, Sec. An independent trust instrumentality of the United States that conducts scientific, cultural, and scholarly research; administers the national collections; and performs other educational public service functions, all supported by Congress, trusts, gifts, and grants. Includes 16 museums, including the National Museum of Natural History, the National Museum of American History, the National Air and Space Museum, and the National Zoological Park. Museums are free and open daily except December 25. The Smithsonian Institution Traveling Exhibition Service (SITES) organizes exhibitions on art, history, and science and circulates them across the country and abroad. *Membership:* Smithsonian Associates. $24–$45. *Publications: Smithsonian; Air & Space/Smithsonian; The Torch* (staff newsletter, mo.); *Research Reports* (semitechnical, quarterly); Smithsonian Institution Press Publications, 470 L'Enfant Plaza, Ste. 7100, Washington, DC 20560.

Society for Applied Learning Technology (SALT). 50 Culpeper St., Warrenton, VA 20186. (540) 347-0055. Fax: (540) 349-3169. E-mail: lti.org. Web site: http:// www.salt.org. Raymond G. Fox, Pres. The society is a nonprofit, professional membership organization that was founded in 1972. Membership in the society is oriented to professionals whose work requires knowledge and communication in the field of instructional technology. The society provides members with a means to enhance their knowledge and job performance by participation in society-sponsored meetings, subscription to society-sponsored publications, association with other professionals at conferences sponsored by the society, and membership in special interest groups and special society-sponsored initiatives. In addition, the society offers member discounts on society-sponsored journals, conferences, and publications. *Membership:* 350. *Membership:* $55. *Publications: Journal of Educational Technology Systems; Journal of Instruction Delivery Systems; Journal of Interactive Instruction Development.* Send for list of available publications. Updated: 5/14/03. Yvonne Beichner, yvonne@lti.org

Society of Cable Telecommunications Engineers (SCTE). 140 Philips Rd., Exton, PA 19341-1318. (610) 363-6888. Fax: (610) 363-5898. E-mail: scte.org. Web site: http://www.scte.org. John Clark, Pres. & CEO. The Society of Cable Telecommunications Engineers is a nonprofit professional organization committed to advancing the careers of cable telecommunications professionals and serving their industry through excellence in professional development, information and standards. *Membership:* SCTE currently has approximately 14,000 members from the U.S. and 70 countries worldwide and offers a variety of programs and services for the industry's educational benefit. SCTE has more than 70 chapters and meeting groups and has technically certified more than 3,000 employees of the cable telecommunications industry. *Membership:* $58 Individual; $350 Sustaining Members; $29 Full-time Student, Unemployed, or Retired (one-year). *Publications:* Interval Membership Directory; *SCTE Monthly*; *Credentials; Standards Bulletin; Leadership Forum.* Updated: 5/4/04. Sandra L. Ray, e-mail: sray@scte.org

Society for Computer Simulation (SCS). P.O. Box 17900. San Diego, CA 92177-7900. (619) 277-3888. Fax: (619) 277-3930. E-mail: scs.org. Web site: http://www.scs.org. Bill Gallagher, Exec. Dir. Founded in 1952, SCS is a professional-level technical society devoted to the art and science of modeling and simulation. Its purpose is to advance the understanding, appreciation, and use of all types of computer models for studying the behavior of actual or hypothesized systems of all kinds and to sponsor standards. Additional office in Ghent, Belgium. *Membership:* 1,900. *Membership:* $75 (includes journal subscription). Local, regional, and national technical meetings and conferences. *Publications: Simulation* (mo.); Simulation series (quarterly); *Transactions of SCS* (quarterly).

Society for Photographic Education (SPE). Dept. of Art, 110 Art Building, Miami University. Oxford, OH 45056. (513) 529-8328. Fax: (513) 529-9301. E-mail: speoffice@spenational.org. Web site: http://www.spenational.org. Jennifer P. Yamashiro, Executive Director. An association of college and university teachers of photography, museum photographic curators, writers, publishers, and students. Promotes discourse in photography education, culture, and art. *Membership:* 1,800. *Membership:* for the calendar year, January through December, 2005–2006. $90—Regular Membership; $50—Student Membership; $600—Corporate Membership; $400—Institutional Membership; $380—Collector Membership (with print); $150—Sustaining Membership $65—Senior Membership. 43rd SPE National Conference, Chicago, IL, March 23–26, 2006. *Publications: Exposure* (Photographic Journal; biannual); quarterly newsletter. Updated: 3/24/05. Kelly O'Malley, Admin. Asst., speoffice@spenational

Society of Photo Technologists (SPT). 11112 S. Spotted Rd., Cheney, WA 99004. (888) 662-7678 or (509) 624-9621. Fax: (509) 624-5320. E-mail: cc5@earthlink.net. Web site: http://www.spt.info/. Chuck Bertone, Executive Director. An organization of photographic equipment repair technicians, which improves and maintains communications between manufacturers and repair shops and technicians. *Publications:* We publish *Repair Journals, Newsletters, Parts & Service Directory and Industry Newsletters.* We also sponsor SPTNET (a technical e-mail group), remanufactured parts and residence workshops. Members also enjoy discounts on Manufactured Parts. *Membership:* 1,000 shops and manufactures worldwide; eligible people or businesses are any who are involved full or part time in the camera repair field. *Membership:* $97.50–$370 depending on the size/volume of the business. Most one-person shops are Class A/$170 dues. Those not involved full time in the field pay $95.50/Associate Class. See our Web site or e-mail us for enrollment details. *Publications: SPT Journal; SPT Parts and Services Directory; SPT Newsletter; SPT Manuals —Training and Manufacturer's Tours;* journals and newsletters. Updated: 2/22/05. Chuck Bertone. cc5@earthlink.net or (800) 624-9621

Southeastern Regional Media Leadership Council (SRMLC). Virginia State University, P.O. Box 9198. Petersburg, VA 23806. (804) 524-5937. Fax: (804) 524-5757. Dr.

Vykuntapathi Thota, Director. An affiliate of AECT, the purpose of the SRMLC is to strengthen the role of the individual state AECT affiliates within the Southeastern region; to seek positive change in the nature and status of instructional technology as it exists within the Southeast; to provide opportunities for the training and development of leadership for both the region and the individual affiliates; and to provide opportunities for the exchange of information and experience among those who attend the annual conference.

Southeastern Regional Vision for Education (SERVE). SERVE Tallahassee Office, 1203 Governor's Square Blvd., Ste. 400. Tallahassee, FL 32301. (800) 352-6001, (904) 671-6000. Fax: (904) 671-6020. E-mail: wmccolsk@serve.org. Web site: http://www. serve.org/. Wendy McColskey, Program Director. SERVE is a regional educational research and development laboratory funded by the U.S. Department of Education to help educators, policy makers, and communities improve schools so that all students achieve their full potential. The laboratory offers the following services: field-based models and strategies for comprehensive school improvement; publications on hot topics in education, successful implementation efforts, applied research projects, and policy issues; database searches and information search training; a regional bulletin board service that provides educators electronic communication and Internet access; information and assistance for state and local policy development; and services to support the coordination and improvement of assistance for young children and their families. The Eisenhower Mathematics and Science Consortium at SERVE promotes improvement of education in these targeted areas by coordinating regional resources, disseminating exemplary instructional materials, and offering technical assistance for implementation of effective teaching methods and assessment tools. For dates and topics of conferences and workshops, contact Gladys Jackson, (800) 755-3277. *Publications: Reengineering High Schools for Student Success; Schools for the 21st Century: New Roles for Teachers and Principals* (rev. ed.); *Designing Teacher Evaluation Systems That Promote Professional Growth; Learning by Serving: 2,000 Ideas for Service-Learning Projects; Sharing Success: Promising Service-Learning Programs; Future Plans* (videotape, discussion guide, and pamphlet); *Future Plans Planning Guides.* Updated: 5/22/03.

Southwest Educational Development Laboratory (SEDL). 211 E. 7th St., Austin, TX 78701-3253. (512) 476-6861. Fax: (512) 476-2286. E-mail: sedl.org. Web site: http://www.sedl.org. Dr., Wesley A. Hoover, Pres. and CEO. The Southwest Educational Development Laboratory (SEDL) is a private, not-for-profit education research and development corporation based in Austin, Texas. SEDL has worked in schools to investigate the conditions under which teachers can provide student-centered instruction supported by technology, particularly computers alone with other software. From field-based research with teachers, SEDL has developed a professional development model and modules, which resulted in the production of Active Learning with Technology. Active Learning with Technology is a multimedia training program for teachers. Using the modules, videotapes, and CD, teachers can learn how to apply student-centered, problem-based learning theory to their instructional strategies that are supported by technologies. Copies of Active Learning can be ordered from the SEDL Web site (http://www.sedl.org/pubs/catalog/items/tec30.html) or through SEDL's Office of Institutional Communications at (800) 476-6861, x201 or (512) 476-6861, x201. SEDL also operates the SouthCentral Regional Technology in Education Consortium (SouthCentral RTEC), which seeks to support educational systems in Arkansas, Louisiana, New Mexico, Oklahoma and Texas in the use of technology to foster student success in achieving state content standards. A particular focus is on schools serving high populations of disadvantaged students. The RTEC delivers research-based professional development and information resources to teachers, college faculty, district and state level staff developers, as well as local and state decision makers. *Publications: SEDL LETTER,* other newsletters, and documents are available for free general distribution in print and online at http://www.sedl.org/pubs/welcome.html. Topic-specific publications related to educational change, education policy, mathematics, language arts, science, and disability research are also accessible on the SEDL Web site at http://www.sedl.org/pubs/ welcome.html. Publications catalog is available on the SEDL

Web site at Web site: http://www.sedl.org/pubs. Updated: 3/18/05. Nancy Reynolds, (nreynold@sedl.org)

Special Libraries Association (SLA). 331 South Patrick Street, Alexandria, VA 22314-3501. (703) 647-4900. Fax: (703) 647.4901. E-mail: sla@sla.org. Web site: http://www.sla.org. Janice R. Lachance, Executive Director. The Special Libraries Association (SLA) is a nonprofit global organization for innovative information professionals and their strategic partners. SLA serves about 12,000 members in 83 countries in the information profession, including corporate, academic, and government information specialists. SLA promotes and strengthens its members through learning, advocacy, and networking initiatives. For more information, visit www.sla.org. *Membership:* About 12,000. Dues (U.S. dollars): Full Member, $125; Organizational Member, $500; Student Member, $35. SLA 2006 Annual Conference, Baltimore, MD, June 11–14, 2006. *Publication: Information Outlook,* monthly glossy magazine that accepts advertising. Updated: 4/6/05. Karen Santos Freeman (kfreeman@sla.org)

Teachers and Writers Collaborative (T&W). 5 Union Square W, New York, NY 10003-3306. (212) 691-6590, (888) 266-5789. Fax: (212) 675-0171. E-mail: twc.org. Web site: http://www.twc.org and http://www.writenet.org. Nancy Larson Shapiro, Dir. Teachers & Writers Collaborative (T&W) provides a link between New York City's rich literary community and the public schools, where the needs for effective ways to teach writing and for programs that support innovative teaching are greater than ever. T&W not only places professional writers and artists into schools and other community settings, but also publishes books on teaching writing—books that provide sound theory and practical curriculum ideas for the classroom. In our welcoming Center for Imaginative Writing on Union Square, writers and educators come together for workshops, readings, and seminars, and through our Youth Speaks program we hold free after-school writing workshops for students. The National Endowment for the Arts has called T&W the nations group that is "most familiar with creative writing/literature in primary and secondary schools." *Membership:* T&W has more than 1,000 members across the country. *Membership:* The basic membership is $35; patron membership is $75; and benefactor membership is $150 or more. Members receive a free book or T-shirt; discounts on publications; and a free one-year subscription to *Teachers & Writers* magazine. (Please see Web site: http://www. twc.org/member.htm.) T&W is seeking general operating support for all of our programs and program support for specific projects, including: (1) T&W writing residencies in New York City area schools; (2) T&W publications, books and a bimonthly magazine, which we distribute across the country; (3) Youth Speaks, T&Ws free after-school writing and performance workshops for teens; and (4) WriteNet, T&Ws Internet programs for teachers, writers, and students. Grants to T&Ws Endowment support the stability of the organization and help to guarantee the continuation of specific programs. T&W offers year-round public events in our Center for Imaginative Writing in New York City. For a list of events, please see http://www.twc.org/events.htm. *Publications:* T&W has published more than 60 books on the teaching of imaginative writing, including *The T&W Handbook of Poetic Forms; The Dictionary of Wordplay; The Story in History; Personal Fiction Writing; Luna, Luna: Creative Writing from Spanish and Latino Literature; The Nearness of You: Students and Teachers Writing On-Line.* To request a free publications catalog, please send e-mail to E-mail: twc.org or call 888-BOOKS-TW. (Please see http://www.twc.org/tpubs.htm.) Updated: 2/27/03. Bruce Morrow, bmorrow@twc.org

Theatre Library Association (TLA). 149 W. 45th St., New York, NY 10036. (212) 944-3895. (212) 944-4139. kwinkler@nypl.org. Web site: http://www.brown.edu/Facilities/University_Library/beyond/TLA/TLA.html. Maryann Chach, Exec. Sec. Seeks to further the interests of collecting, preserving, and using theater, cinema, and performing arts materials in libraries, museums, and private collections. *Membership:* 500. *Membership:* $30, indiv.; $30, institutional; $20, students and retirees. *Publications: Performing Arts Resources* (membership annual, Vol. 20, Denishawn Collections).

USA Toy Library Association (USA-TLA). 1326 Wilmette Ave., Ste. 201. Wilmette, IL 60091. (847) 920-9030. Fax: (847) 920-9032. E-mail: usatla@aol.com. Web site: http://usatla.deltacollege.org. Judith Q. Iacuzzi, Exec. Dir. The mission of the USA-TLA is to provide a networking system answering to all those interested in play and play materials to provide a national resource to toy libraries, family centers, resource and referrals, public libraries, schools, institutions serving families of special need, and other groups and individuals involved with children; to support and expand the number of toy libraries; and to advocate for children and the importance of their play in healthy development. Individuals can find closest toy libraries by sending an e-mail or written inquiry in a self-addressed stamped envelope. *Membership:* 80 institutions, 150 individuals. Members receive a subscription to the quarterly newsletter *Child's Play,* reduced fees on conferences, workshops, books, videos and other publications and products sold by the USA Toy Library Association. Comprehensive members receive a bonus gift each year. *Membership:* $165, comprehensive; $55, basic; $15, student. Regional workshops in the spring and fall. *Publications: Child's Play* (quarterly newsletter); *How to Start and Operate a Toy Library; Play Is a Child's Work* (videotape); other books on quality toys and play. Updated: 4/22/02. Judith Iacuzzi (usatla@aol.com)

University Continuing Education Association (UCEA). One Dupont Cir. NW, Ste. 615, Washington, DC 20036. (202) 659-3130. Fax: (202) 785-0374. E-mail: shirley@ucea.edu. Web site: http://www.ucea.edu/. Kay J. Kohl, Executive Director, kjkohl@ucea.edu. UCEA is an association of public and private higher education institutions concerned with making continuing education available to all population segments and to promoting excellence in continuing higher education. Many institutional members offer university and college courses via electronic instruction. *Membership:* 425 institutions, 2,000 professionals. *Membership:* vary according to membership category; see: Web site: http://www. ucea.edu/membership.htm. UCEA has an annual national conference and several professional development seminars throughout the year. See: http://www.ucea.edu/page02.htm. *Publications:* monthly newsletter; quarterly; occasional papers; scholarly journal, *Continuing Higher Education Review; Independent Study Catalog.* With Peterson's, *The Guide to Distance Learning; Guide to Certificate Programs at American Colleges and Universities;* UCEA-ACE/Oryx Continuing Higher Education book series; *Lifelong Learning Trends* (a statistical factbook on continuing higher education); organizational issues series; membership directory. Updated: 5/22/03.

WestEd. 730 Harrison St., San Francisco, CA 94107-1242. (415) 565-3000. Fax: (415) 565-3012. E-mail: cmontoy@WestEd.org. Web site: http://www.WestEd.org. Glen Harvey, CEO; Richard Whitmore, Chief Financial Officer; Sri Ananda, Chief Development Officer. WestEd is a nonprofit research, development, and service agency dedicated to improving education and other opportunities for children, youth, and adults. Drawing on the best from research and practice, WestEd works with practitioners and policymakers to address critical issues in education and other related areas, including accountability and assessment; early childhood intervention; curriculum, instruction, and assessment; the use of technology; career and technical preparation; teacher and administrator professional development; science and mathematics education; safe schools and communities. WestEd was created in 1995 to unite and enhance the capacity of Far West Laboratory and Southwest Regional Laboratory, two of the nation's original education laboratories. In addition to its work across the nation, WestEd serves as the regional education laboratory for Arizona, California, Nevada, and Utah. A publications catalog is available and WestEd.org has a comprehensive listing of services offered. *Publications:* Various, relating to our work, plus quarterly board meetings. See WestEd Products & Resources at http://www.wested. org/cs/we/print/docs/we/products.htm. Updated: 2/21/05. Colleen F. Montoya, cmontoy@WestEd.org

Western Public Radio (WPR). Ft. Mason Center, Bldg. D, San Francisco, CA 94123. (415) 771-1160. Fax: (415) 771-4343. E-mail: wprsf@aol.com. Karolyn van Putten, Ph.D., Pres./CEO; Lynn Chadwick, Vice Pres./COO. WPR provides analog and digital audio production training, public radio program proposal consultation, and studio facilities for rent. WPR also sponsors a continuing education resource for audio producers, www. radiocollege.org.

World Future Society (WFS). 7910 Woodmont Ave., Ste. 450, Bethesda, MD 20814. (301) 656-8274. Fax: (301) 951-0394. E-mail: wfs.org. Web site: http://www.wfs.org. Edward Cornish, Pres. Organization of individuals interested in the study of future trends and possibilities. Its purpose is to provide information on trends and scenarios so that individuals and organizations can better plan their future. *Membership:* 30,000. *Membership:* $39, general; $95, professional; call society for details on all membership levels and benefits. Annual conference. *Publications: The Futurist: A Journal of Forecasts, Trends and Ideas about the Future; Futures Research Quarterly; Future Survey.* The society's bookstore offers audio- and videotapes, books, and other items.

Young Adult Library Services Association (YALSA). 50 E. Huron St., Chicago, IL 60611. (312) 280-4390. Fax: (312) 664-7459. E-mail: yalsa@ala.org. Web site: http://www.ala.org/yalsa. Beth Yoke, Exec. Dir.; David Mowery, Pres.; Pam Holley, Pres. Elect. A division of the American Library Association, YALSA seeks to advocate, promote, and strengthen service to young adults as part of the continuum of total library services, and assumes responsibility within the ALA to evaluate and select books and nonbook media and to interpret and make recommendations regarding their use with young adults. Committees include Best Books for Young Adults, Popular Paperbacks, Quick Picks for Reluctant Young Adult Readers, Intellectual Freedom, Outreach to Young Adults with Special Needs, Outstanding Books for the College Bound, Youth Participation, Technology for Young Adults, Publishers Liaison, and Selected DVDs & Videos for Young Adults. *Membership:* 4,469. YALSA members may be young adult librarians, school library media specialists, library directors, children's librarians, publishers, English teachers, or anyone for whom library service to young adults is important. *Membership:* $40 (in addition to ALA membership); $15, students. Two conferences yearly, Midwinter (January or February) and Annual (June or July). *Publications: Young Adult Library Services* (quarterly print journal). YAttitudes (quarterly electronic newsletter for members only). Updated: 2/22/05. Beth Yoke, (800) 545-2433, ext. 4391.

CANADA

Access Network. 3720–76 Ave., Edmonton, AB, T6B 2N9 Canada. (403) 440-7777. Fax: (403) 440-8899. E-mail: promo@ccinet.ab.ca. Dr. Ronald Keast, Pres.; John Verburgt, Creative Services Manager. The ACCESS Network (Alberta Educational Communications Corporation) was purchased by Learning and Skills Television of Alberta in 1995. The newly privatized network works with Alberta's educators to provide all Albertans with a progressive and diverse television-based educational and training resource to support their learning and skills development needs using cost-effective methods and innovative techniques, and to introduce a new private sector model for financing and efficient operation of educational television in the province.

Adaptech Research Network. Dawson College, 3040 Sherbrooke St., West Montreal, QC, H3Z 1A4 Canada. (514) 931-8731, ext. 1546. Fax: (514) 931-3567. E-mail: catherine.fichten@mcgill.ca. Web site: http://www.adaptech.org. Catherine Fichten, Ph.D., Co-director; Jennison V. Asuncion, M.A., Co-Director; Maria Barile, M.S.W., Co-Director. Based at Dawson College (Montreal), we are a Canada-wide, grant-funded team conducting bilingual empirical research into the use of computer, learning, and adaptive technologies by postsecondary students with disabilities. One of our primary interests lies in issues around ensuring that newly emerging instructional technologies are accessible to learners with disabilities. Our research team is composed of academics, practitioners, students, consumers and others interested in the issues of access to technology by students with disabilities in higher education. Membership is upon invitation. Interested individuals can join our listserv by e-mailing Adaptech moderator Jennison Asuncion (asuncion@ alcor.concordia.ca). *Publications:* Fichten, C. S., Asuncion, J. V., Barile, M., Fossey, M. E., Robillard, C., Judd, D., Wolforth, J., Senécal, J., Généreux, C., Guimont, J. P., Lamb, D., & Juhel, J-C. (2004). Access to information and instructional technologies in higher education I: Disability service providers' perspective. *Journal of Postsecondary Education and Disability, 17*(2), 114–133. Asuncion, J. V., Fichten, C. S., Barile, M., Fossey, M. E., & Robillard, C. (2004). Access to information and instructional technologies in higher education II: Practical recommendations for disability service providers. *Journal of Postsecondary Education and Disability, 17*(2), 134–137. Jorgensen, S., Fichten, C. S., Havel, A., Lamb, D., James, C., & Barile, M. (2003). Students with and without disabilities at Dawson College graduate at the same rate. *Journal for Vocational Special Needs Education, 25*(2 & 3), 44–46. Retrieved August 2, 2004, from Web site: http://www. specialpopulations.org/By_Chapters/09Jorgensen.pdf. Fichten, C. S., Asuncion, J. V., Barile, M., Robillard, C., Fossey, M. E., & Lamb, D. (2003). Canadian postsecondary students with disabilities: Where are they? *Canadian Journal of Higher Education, 33*(3), 71–114. Updated: 2/20/05. Catherine Fichten (catherine. fichten@mcgill.ca)

Association for Media and Technology in Education in Canada (AMTEC). 3-1750 The Queensway, Ste. 1318. Etobicoke, ON, M9C 5H5 Canada. (902) 457-6165. Fax: (902) 457-2618. E-mail: Paul.Poirier@MSVU.Ca. Web site: http://www.amtec.ca. Gail Saunders: Past President; Rik Hall: Pres.; Paul Poirier: Sec./Treas. AMTEC is Canada's national association for educational media and technology professionals. The organization provides national leadership through annual conferences, publications, workshops, media festivals, and awards. It responds to media and technology issues at the international, national, provincial, and local levels, and maintains linkages with other organizations with similar interests. *Membership:* AMTEC members represent all sectors of the educational media and technology fields. *Membership:* $101.65, Canadian regular; $53.50, student and retiree. Annual Conferences take place in late May or early June. *Publications: Canadian Journal of Learning and Technology* (a scholarly journal published 3 times a year); *Media News* (3/year); *Membership Directory* (with membership). *Publications:* 2/22/05. Paul Poirier, (902) 457-6165, Paul.Poirier@MSVU.Ca

Canadian Broadcasting Corporation/Société Radio-Canada (CBC/SRC). P.O. Box 500, Station A, Toronto, ON, Canada. E-mail: fortinj@toronto.cbc.ca. Web site: http://www.cbc.ca. The CBC is a publicly owned corporation established in 1936 by an Act of the Canadian Parliament to provide a national broadcasting service in Canada in the two official languages. CBC services include English and French television networks; English and French AM mono and FM stereo radio networks virtually free of commercial advertising; CBC North, which serves Canada's North by providing radio and television programs in English, French, and eight native languages; *Newsworld* and its French counterpart, *Le Réseau de l'information* (RDI), 24-hour national satellites to cable English-language and French-language news and information service respectively, both funded entirely by cable subscription and commercial advertising revenues; and Radio Canada International, a shortwave radio service that broadcasts in seven languages and is managed by CBC and financed by External Affairs. The CBC is financed mainly by public funds voted annually by Parliament.

Canadian Education Association, Association canadienne d'éducation (CEA). 317 Adelaide Street West, Ste. 300, Toronto, ON, M5V 1P9 Canada. (416) 591-6300. Fax: (416) 591-5345. E-mail: cea-ace@acea.ca. Web site: http://www.acea.ca. Penny Milton, Executive Director, Valérie Pierre-Pierre, Research Officer. CEA is a national, bilingual, charitable organization that advances public commitment to education by engaging diverse perspectives in finding common ground on issues that affect the learning of all children and youth in our society. Current issues include ICT and learning; social equity; school improvement. *Membership:* Sustaining Members—provincial, territorial departments of education, and federal government. Organization Members—Nonprofit: educational institutions, research organizations, stakeholder associations. For profit: firms with interests in the education sector. Individuals—educators, researchers. *Membership:* $120, indiv.; $360, not-for-profit organizations; $500, for profit organizations; school boards, based on enrollment. *Publications: Technology Summit; National Education Forum; Superintendents Forum; CEA Handbook; Education Canada* (quarterly); *CEA Newsletter* (8/year); Connections Series. Updated: 4/11/02. Penny Milton (pmilton@acea.ca)

Canadian Library Association (CLA). 328 Frank Street, Ottawa, ON, K2P 0X8 Canada. (613) 232-9625. Fax: (613) 563-9895. E-mail: cla.ca. Web site: http://www.cla.ca. Linda Sawden Harris, Manager of Financial Services. The mission of the Canadian Library Association is to provide leadership in the promotion, development, and support of library and information services in Canada for the benefit of Association members, the profession, and Canadian society. In the spirit of this mission, CLA aims to engage the active, creative participation of library staff, trustees, and governing bodies in the development and management of high-quality Canadian library service; to assert and support the right of all Canadians to the freedom to read and to free universal access to a wide variety of library materials and services; to promote librarianship and to enlighten all levels of government as to the significant role that libraries play in educating and socializing the Canadian people; and to link libraries, librarians, trustees, and others across the country for the purpose of providing a unified nationwide voice in matters of critical concern. *Membership:* 2,300 individuals, 700 institutions, 100 Associates and Trustees. *Membership:* $50-$300. Annual Conference. *Publications: Feliciter* (membership magazine, 6/yr). Updated: 5/6/02. Peter Wilson, pwilson@cla.ca

Canadian Museums Association/Association des musées canadiens (CMA/AMC). 280 Metcalfe St., Ste. 400. Ottawa, ON, K2P 1R7 Canada. (613) 567-0099. Fax: (613) 233-5438. E-mail: museums.ca. Web site: http://www.museums.ca. John G. McAvity, Exec. Dir. The Canadian Museums Association is a nonprofit corporation and registered charity dedicated to advancing public museums and museum works in Canada, promoting the welfare and better administration of museums, and fostering a continuing improvement in the qualifications and practices of museum professionals. *Membership:* 2,000 museums and individuals, including art galleries, zoos, aquariums, historic parks, etc. *Membership:* Individual, $75 (for those who are or have been associated with a recognized museum in Canada). Affiliate, $100 (for those outside the museum community who wish to support the aims and programs of the Association). Foreign $100 (For individuals and institutions, residing or based outside Canada). Institutional/Association: For all recognized Canadian museums that are nonprofit, have a collection and are open to the public. Fee is 0.001 (one tenth of one percent) of operating budget (e.g, if your budget is $150,000, you would pay $150). The minimum fee payable is $100, and the maximum, $2,500. Corporate, $250 (For corporations wishing to support the aims and programs of the Association while developing opportunities within the museum community). Student, $50 (special rate for students). Please enclose a photocopy of your student ID. Senior, $50 (for those who are retired and have been associated with a recognized museum in Canada). CMA Annual Conference, spring. *Publications: Muse* (bi-monthly magazine, color, Canada's only national, bilingual, magazine devoted to museums, it contains museum-based photography, feature articles, commentary, and practical information); *The Official Directory of Canadian Museums and Related Institutions* (online directory) lists all museums in Canada plus information on government departments, agencies, and provincial and regional museum associations. Updated: 5/20/03. L. McConnell (lmcconnell@museums.ca)

Canadian Publishers Council (CPC). 250 Merton St., Ste. 203, Toronto, ON, M4S 1B1 Canada. (416) 322-7011. Fax: (416) 322-6999. E-mail: pubadmin@pubcouncil.ca. Web site: http://www.pubcouncil.ca. Jacqueline Hushion, Exec. Dir. CPC members publish and distribute an extensive list of Canadian and imported learning materials in a complete range of formats from traditional textbook and ancillary materials to CDs and interactive video. The primary markets for CPC members are schools, universities and colleges, bookstores, and libraries. CPC also provides exhibits throughout the year and works through a number of subcommittees and groups within the organization to promote effective book publishing. CPC was founded in 1910. *Membership:* 27 companies, educational institutions, or government agencies that publish books as an important facet of their work. *Membership:* To be assessed when a membership application form is submitted for consideration. *Publications:* Please visit the CPC Web site at www.pubcouncil.ca for various publications. Updated: 3/13/03. Lydia Pencarski, (416) 322-7011, ext. 221.

Consortium for Computers in the Humanities/Consortium pour ordinateurs en sciences humaines (COCH/COSH). Arts 200, UofA, Edmonton, AB, T6G 2E6 Canada. (780) 492-6768. Fax: (780) 492-9106. E-mail: ss@huco.ualberta.ca. Web site: http://coch-coch.ca/. Ray Siemens (President-English), Jean-Claude Guédon (President-French), Geoffrey Rockwell (Vice President), Stéfan Sinclair (Secretary). The Consortium for Computers in the Humanities is a Canada-wide association of representatives from Canadian colleges and universities that began in 1986. Our objective is to foster communications about, and sharing of, information technology developed by Canadian institutions for the betterment of postsecondary education across Canada. Le Consortium pour ordinateurs en sciences humaines, fondé en 1986, est une association constituée de représentants de colléges et d'universités du Canada. Notre but est d'encourager la dissemination d'information sur les technologies nouvelles développées par les organisations canadiennes et ainsi de contribuer á lavancement des études supérieures partout au Canada. *Membership:* 120. *Membership:* Annual, $65 CDN. Annual meeting each May, with the HSSFC Congress. *Publications:* COCH/COSH has formal affiliation with the journals *Text Technology*, *Computing in the Humanities Working Papers*, *Surfaces*; it is pleased to have also enjoyed publications relationships with Early Modern Literary Studies. Updated: 3/4/04. Stéfan Sinclair, e-mail above.

National Film Board of Canada (NFBC). 350 Fifth Ave., Ste. 4820, New York, NY 10118. (212) 629-8890. Fax:(212) 629-8502. E-mail: NewYork@nfb.caab. Web site: http://www.nfb.ca. John Sirabella, U.S. Marketing Mgr./Nontheatrical Rep. Established in 1939, the NFBC's main objective is to produce and distribute high-quality audiovisual materials for educational, cultural, and social purposes. Updated: 3/12/03. Tim Sheehy, through contact e-mail above.

Ontario Film Association, Inc. (also known as the Association for the Advancement of Visual Media/L'association pour l'avancement des médias visuels). 100 Lombard St., 303. Toronto, ON, M5C 1M3 Canada. (416) 363-3388, (800) 387-1181. E-mail: accessola.com. Web site: http://www.accessola.org. Lawrence A. Moore, Exec. Dir. A membership organization of buyers, and users of media whose objectives are to promote the sharing of ideas and information about visual media through education, publications, and advocacy. *Membership:* 112. *Membership:* $120, personal membership; $215, associate membership. OFA Media Showcase, spring.

SOUTH AFRICA

Multimedia Education Group, University of Cape Town (MEG). Hlanganani Building, Upper Campus University of Cape Town, Rondebosch, Cape Town, 7700, South Africa. (+27) 21-650-3841. Fax: (+27) 21 650 3841. E-mail: lcz@its.uct.ac.za. Web site: www. meg.uct.ac.za. Directors Laura Czerniewicz. MEG aims to research and harness the potential of interactive computer-based technologies and approaches (ICBTA) to support effective learning and teaching. Our work focuses on meeting the needs of South African students from diverse backgrounds, particularly those at the University of Cape Town. We employ multimedia researchers and developers with strong educational interests in diversity, redress, and access. See our Web site: http://www.meg.uct.ac.za. Updated: 5/20/03. Laura Czerniewicz, lcz@ched.uct.ac.za

Part Five
Graduate Programs

Introduction

Amy McElveen and Emily Hunter, Editors

This directory describes graduate programs in instructional technology, educational media and communications, school library media, and closely related programs in the United States. Masters, specialist, and doctoral degrees are combined into one unified list.

Entries provide as much of the following information as furnished by respondents: (1) name and address of the institution; (2) chairperson or other individual in charge of the program; (3) types of degrees offered and specialization, emphases, or tracks, including information on careers for which candidates are prepared; (4) special features of the degree program; (5) admission requirements; (6) degree requirements; (7) number of full-time and part-time faculty; (8) number of full-time and part-time students; (9) types of financial assistance available; and (10) the number of degrees awarded by type in 2004. All grade-point averages (GPAs), test scores, and degree requirements are minimums unless stated otherwise. The Graduate Record Examination, Miller Analogies Test, National Teacher's Examination, and other standardized tests are referred to by their acronyms. The Test of English as a Foreign Language (TOEFL) appears in many of the *Admission Requirements,* and in most cases this test is required only for international students. Although some entries explicitly state application fees, most do not. Prospective students should assume that most institutions require a completed application, transcripts of all previous collegiate work, and a nonrefundable application fee.

Directors of advanced professional programs for instructional technology or media specialists should find this degree program information useful as a means of comparing their own offerings and requirements with those of institutions offering comparable programs. This listing, along with the Classified List, should also assist individuals in locating institutions that best suit their interests and requirements. In addition, a comparison of degree programs across several years may help scholars with historical interests trace trends and issues in the field over time.

Information in this section can be considered current as of early 2005 for most programs. Information for this section was obtained by e-mail directing each institution to an individual Web form through which the updated information could be submitted electronically. Although the section editor made every effort to contact and follow up with program representatives, it is up to the program representatives to respond to the annual request for an update. The editing team would like to thank those respondents who helped ensure the currency and accuracy of this section by responding to the request for an update.

Additional information on the programs listed, including admission procedure instructions, may be obtained by contacting individual program coordinators. General or graduate catalogs and specific program information usually are furnished for a minimal charge. In addition, most graduate programs now have e-mail contact addresses and Web sites that provide a wealth of descriptive information.

Again, we are greatly indebted to those individuals who responded to our requests for information. Although the editors expended considerable effort to ensure currency and completeness of the listings, there may be institutions within the United States that now have programs of which we are unaware. Readers are encouraged to furnish new information to the publisher who, in turn, will contact the program for inclusion in the next edition of *EMTY.*

Alphabetical List

Alabama

Alabama State University. Department of Instructional Support Programs, 915 South Jackson Street Montgomery, AL 36101-0271. (334) 229-6829. Fax: (334) 229-6904. Web site: http://www.alasu.edu. Dr. Agnes Bellel, Coord., Instructional Technology and Media. abellel@asunet.alasu.edu. School media specialist preparation (K–12) only; master's and specialist degrees. The applicant must hold a bachelor's degree from an accredited institution. All admission requirements for graduate programs in education should be completed prior to registration for courses. Application forms should be secured from and returned to the School of Graduate Studies. Full admission status should be granted to persons who meet all applicable admission requirements prior to enrollment. Under extraordinary circumstances, a student may be considered as conditionally admitted, but in all circumstances, the requirements for admission to graduate program in education must be met during the FIRST ENROLLMENT PERIOD. When such requirements are met, the student's status will be changed from conditional to full admission, retroactive to the beginning of the enrollment period. A special status may be granted to those persons who do not wish to pursue a degree program but who wish to enroll in a limited number of graduate classes.

Admission to a master's degree program requires that the applicant: hold a class B Certificate, general counseling does not require a teacher's certificate; take and attain satisfactory scores on specified national tests (Graduate Record Examination [GRE] or Miller Analogy Test [MAT]); for all graduate programs, the applicant must submit two letters of recommendation from persons who are qualified to evaluate an applicant's ability to do graduate work; hold a Class A Certificate in a teaching field (for admission to a certification program in Administration and Supervision only). Master's degree in library/media. *Admission Requirements:* education.

Admission to an Education Specialist degree program requires that the applicant: 1. Hold professional certification and a master's degree in the area they want to pursue an Education Specialist degree in. 2. Have at least two years of successful work experience. 3. Must have a 3.25 GPA on master's degree. 4. Make a satisfactory score on the GRE or MAT. 5. AA Certification Programs require a 3.25 graduate GPA, appropriate Class A Certification, and approval of the major department. *Degree Requirements:* Master's: 33 semester hours with 300 clock-hour internship. Specialist: 36 semester hours in 600-level courses. Master's: 50 part-time students; Specialist: 8 part-time. *Financial Requirements:* Student loans and scholarships: 15 M.Ed., 1 Ed.S. Updated: 7/7/04.

Auburn University. Educational Foundations, Leadership, and Technology. 4036 Haley Center, Auburn, AL 36849-5216. (334) 844-4291. Fax: (334) 844-4292. Web site: http://education.auburn.edu/academics/depts/eflt/academicprograms/librarymediatechnology/index.html. Susan H. Bannon, Associate Professor & Program Coordinator. bannosh@auburn.edu. *Specializations:* M.Ed. (nonthesis) and Ed.S. for school library media certification. *Features:* The Department of Educational Foundations, Leadership & Technology (EFLT) prepares exemplary educational practitioners and develops cooperative partnerships with university departments, schools, community agencies, and business and industry to provide high-quality educators, trainers and leaders. Faculty members are committed to guiding students toward becoming competent and professional educational leaders. This department ensures that students will participate in theoretical, applied and practitioner-based research enhancing the fields of Adult Education, Educational Leadership, Educational Media/Technology and Educational Psychology. Outreach partnerships are continually established in these respective fields to provide students with an informative and experiential curriculum. All programs emphasize interactive technologies and computers. *Admission Requirements:* All programs: graduate school admission—GRE test scores less than 5 years old; 3 letters of recommendation; bachelor's degree from accredited institution; and teacher certification at least at bachelor's level. *Degree Requirements:* Library Media Master's: 33 sem. hours. Specialist: 30 sem. hours. *Students:* Master's 3 full-time, 2 part-time. Specialist: 15 part-time. *Financial Assistance:* Graduate assistantships. Updated: 3/28/05.

Jacksonville State University. Educational Resources, 700 Pelham Road N., Jacksonville, AL 36265. (256) 782-5096. Fax: (256) 782 5872. Web site: http://www.jsu.edu. Dr. Martha Merrill, Coord., Instructional Media Program (mmerrill@jsucc.jsu.edu). *Specialization:* M.S. in Education with emphasis in Library Media. Add-on Certification in Library Media. Technology, Management, Literature, Reference. *Admission Requirements:* Bachelor's degree in Education. *Degree Requirements:* 36–39 semester hours including 24 hours in library media. *Students:* 2 full-time and 30 full- and part-time. Updated: 3/11/05.

University of Alabama. School of Library and Information Studies, Box 870252. Tuscaloosa, AL 35487-0252. (205) 348-4610. Fax: (205) 348-3746. Web site: http://www.slis.ua.edu. Joan Atkinson, Director; Gordy Coleman, Coordinator of School Media Program. jatkinso@slis.ua.edu; gcoleman@slis.ua.edu. *Specialization:* MLIS degrees in a varied program including school, public, academic, and special libraries. Ph.D. in the larger College of Communication and Information Sciences; flexibility in creating individual programs of study. Also a Master of Fine Arts Program in Book Arts (including history of the book). MLIS is 1 of 56 accredited programs in the United States and Canada. *Admission Requirements:* MLIS: 3.0 GPA; 50 MAT or 1000 GRE and an acceptable score on Analytical Writing. Doctoral: 3.0 GPA; 60 MAT or 1200 GRE and acceptable score on Analytical Writing. *Degree Requirements:* Master's: 36 semester hours. Doctoral: 48–60 semester hours plus 24 hours dissertation research. *Faculty:* 10 full-time; five part-time. *Students:* Master's, 45 full-time, 140 part-time; doctoral, 1 full-time, 3 part-time. *Financial Assistance:* assistantships, grants, student loans, scholarships, work assistance, campus work. *Degrees Awarded 2003:* 88 MLIS; 4 educational specialist; 3 MFA in Book Arts. Updated: 6/9/03.

University of South Alabama. Department of Behavioral Studies and Educational Technology, College of Education. University Commons 3700, Mobile, AL 36688. (251) 380-2861. Fax: (251) 380-2713. Web site: http://www.southalabama.edu/coe/bset/. Daniel W. Surry, IDD Program Coord.; Mary Ann Robinson, Ed Media Program Coord. dsurry@ usouthal.edu. *Specializations:* M.S. and Ph.D. in Instructional Design and Development. M.Ed. in Educational Media (Ed Media). Online master's degrees in ED Media and IDD are available for qualified students. For information about online master's degree programs, http://usaonline.southalabama.edu. *Features:* The IDD master's and doctoral programs emphasize extensive education and training in the instructional design process, human performance technology and multimedia- and online-based training. The IDD doctoral program has an additional emphasis in research design and statistical analysis. The Ed Media master's program prepares students in planning, designing, and administering library/media centers at most levels of education, including higher education. *Admission Requirements:* For the ED Media & IDD master's: undergraduate degree in appropriate academic field from an accredited university or college; admission to graduate school; satisfactory score on the GRE. ED Media students must have completed requirements for a certificate at the baccalaureate or master's level in a teaching field. For IDD Ph.D.: master's degree, all undergraduate and graduate transcripts, three letters of recommendation, written statement of purpose for pursuing Ph.D. in IDD, satisfactory score on GRE. *Degree Requirements:* Ed Media master's: satisfactorily complete program requirements (minimum 33 semester hours), 3.0 or better GPA, satisfactory score on comprehensive exam. IDD master's: satisfactorily complete program requirements (minimum 40 semester hours), 3.0 or better GPA; satisfactory complete comprehensive exam. Ph.D.: satisfactorily complete program requirements (minimum 82 semester hours of approved graduate courses), one-year residency, satisfactory score on examinations (research and statistical exam and comprehensive exam), approved dissertation completed. Any additional requirements will be determined by students doctoral advisory committee. *Faculty:* 17 full-time in department; 8 part-time faculty. *Students:* 68 IDD master's, 100 Ph.D., 44 Ed Media master's, 26 Ed Media certificate. *Financial Assistance:* 10 graduate assistantships. *Degrees Awarded 2003:* 12 Ed Media master's; 10 IDD master's; 5 IDD doctoral. Updated: 5/19/04.

Arizona

Arizona State University. Educational Technology Program. Division of Psychology in Education, Box 870611, Tempe, AZ 85287-0611. (480) 965-3384. Fax: (480) 965-0300. Web site: http://coe.asu.edu/psyched. James D. Klein, Professor; Nancy Archer, Admissions Secretary (dpe@asu.edu). *Specialization:* The Educational Technology program at Arizona State University offers M.Ed. and Ph.D. degrees that focus on the design, development, and evaluation of instructional systems and educational technology applications to support learning. *Features:* The program offers courses in a variety of areas such as instructional design technology, media development, technology integration, performance improvement, evaluation, and distance education. The doctoral program emphasizes research using educational technology in applied settings. *Admission Requirements:* for admission to the M.Ed. program, a 4-year undergraduate GPA of 3.0 or above and a score of either 500 or above on verbal section of the GRE or 50 or above on the MAT are required. A score of 550 or above on the paper-based TOEFL (or 213 on the computer-based test) is also required for students who do not speak English as their first language. Requirements for admission to the Ph.D. program include a 4-year undergraduate GPA of 3.20 or above and a combined score of 1200 or above on the verbal and quantitative sections of the GRE. A score of 600 or above on the paper-based TOEFL (or 250 on the computer-based test) is also required for students who do not speak English as their first language. *Degree Requirements:* The M.Ed. degree requires completion of a minimum of 30 credit hours including 18 credit hours of required course work and a minimum of 12 credit hours of electives. M.Ed. students also must complete an internship and a comprehensive examination. The Ph.D. degree requires a minimum of 84 semester hours beyond the bachelor's degree. At least 54 of these hours must be taken at ASU after admission to the program. Ph.D. students must fulfill a residence requirement and are required to be continuously enrolled in the program. Students also take a comprehensive examination and must satisfy a publication requirement prior to beginning work on their dissertation. *Faculty:* 6 full-time. *Students:* 30 M.Ed. and 30 Ph.D. *Financial assistance:* scholarships, fellowships, graduate assistantships, loans, and professional work opportunities are available to qualified applicants. *Degrees Awarded 2004:* 14 M.Ed. degrees and 1 Ph.D. Updated: 3/28/05.

University of Arizona. School of Information Resources and Library Science. 1515 E. First St., Tucson, AZ 85719. (520) 621-3565. Fax: (520) 621-3279. Web site: http://www.sir.arizona.edu. Susan Irwin (sirwin@u.arizona.edu). *Specializations:* The School of Information Resources and Library Science offers courses focusing on the study of information and its impact as a social phenomenon. *Features:* The School offers a virtual education program via the Internet. Between two and three courses are offered per semester. *Admission Requirements:* Very competitive for both degrees. Minimum criteria include undergraduate GPA of 3.0 or better; competitive GRE scores; two letters of recommendation reflecting the writer's opinion of the applicants potential as a graduate student; a resume of work and educational experience; written statement of intent. The school receives a large number of applications and accepts the best-qualified students. Admission to the doctoral program may require a personal interview and a faculty member must indicate willingness to work with the student. *Degree Requirements:* M.A.: a minimum of 36 units of graduate credit. Students may elect the thesis option replacing 6 units of coursework. Ph.D.: at least 48 hours of coursework in the major, a substantial number of hours in a minor subject supporting the major, dissertation. The university has a 6-unit residency requirement that may be completed in the summer or in a regular semester. More detailed descriptions of the program are available at the school's Web site. *Faculty:* 8 full-time. *Students:* 220 total; M.A.: 51 full-time; Ph.D.: 12 full-time. *Financial Assistance:* scholarships, teaching assistantships, tuition fee waivers. *Degrees Awarded 2003:* 75. Updated: 4/27/04.

Arkansas

Arkansas Tech University Curriculum and Instruction. 308 Crabaugh, Russellville, AR 72801-2222. (501) 968-0434. Fax: (501) 964-0811. Web site: http://education.atu.edu/. Connie Zimmer, Assoc. Professor of Secondary Education, Coord. (Connie.Zimmer @mail.atu.edu). *Specialization:* Master of Education in Instructional Technology with specializations in library media education, instructional design, and instructional technology. *Features:* NCATE accredited institution. A standards-based program meeting the requirements of the Arkansas State Department of Education licensure requirements for school library media specialist. Classrooms have the latest technology available. GRE or MAT, 2.5 undergraduate GPA, bachelor's degree. Teaching Licensure required for the school library media specialization. 36 semester hours, B average in major hours, action research project. *Faculty:* 2 full-time. *Students:* 5 full-time, 72 part-time. *Financial Assistance:* graduate assistantships, work-study, student loans. *Degrees Awarded 2003:* 45. Updated: 2/18/05.

University of Central Arkansas. Middle/Secondary Education and Instructional Technologies, 201 Donaghey, Conway, AR 72035. (501) 450-3177. Fax: (501) 450-5680. Web site: http://www.uca.edu/. Stephanie Huffman, Program Director of the Library Media and Information Technologies Program (steph@uca.edu). *Specialization:* M.S. in Library Media and Information Technologies Tracks: School Library Media and Public Information Agencies. *Admission Requirements:* Specialization in school library media: Transcripts, GRE scores, and a copy of the candidates teaching certificate (if enrolled in School Library Media Track). *Degree Requirements:* 36 semester hours, practicum (for School Library Media), and a professional portfolio. *Faculty:* 3 full-time, 3 part-time. *Students:* 6 full-time, 51 part-time. *Financial Assistance:* 3 to 4 graduate assistantships each year. *Degrees Awarded 2004:* 35. Updated: 2/22/05.

California

Alliant University. School of Education. 10455 Pomerado Rd., San Diego, CA 92131-1799. (619) 635-4715. Fax: (619) 635-4714. Web site: http://www.alliant.edu/gsoe/. Karen Schuster Webb, Systemwide Dean for the Graduate School of Education. lbanerjee@alliant.edu. *Specializations:* master's in Designing Technology for Learning, Planning Technology for Learning, and Technology Leadership for Learning. Ed.D. in Technology and Learning offers three specializations: Designing Technology for Learning, Planning Technology for Learning, and Technology Leadership for Learning. *Features:* interactive multimedia, cognitive approach to integrating technology and learning. *Admission Requirements:* master's, English proficiency, interview, 3.0 GPA with 1900 GRE or 2.0 GPA with satisfactory MAT score. *Degree Requirements:* Ed.D.: 88 graduate quarter units, dissertation. *Faculty:* 2 full-time, 4 part-time. *Students:* master's, 32 full-time, 12 part-time; doctoral, 6 full-time, 1 part-time. *Financial Assistance:* internships, graduate assistantships, grants, student loans, scholarships.

Azusa Pacific University. EDUCABS—Advanced Studies, 901 E. Alosta, Azusa, CA 91702. (626) 815-5355. Fax: (626) 815-5416. Web site: http://www.apu.edu. Kathleen Bacer, online program; Joanne Gilbreath, site-based program; kbacer@apu.edu. *Specialization:* Educational Technology, site-based and online programs. Master of Arts in Educational Technology and Learning Program offered at five locations (Azusa, Inland, Menifee, Orange, Ventura). *Admission Requirements:* Online Master of Arts in Educational Technology program offered nationally: undergraduate degree from accredited institution with at least 12 units in education, 3.0 GPA, ownership of a designated laptop computer and software. *Degree Requirements:* 36 unit program. *Faculty:* 2 full-time, 16 part-time. *Students:* 180 part-time. *Financial Aid:* student loans. *Degrees awarded 2004:* 89. Updated: 3/13/05.

California State University—Dominguez Hills. Graduate Education. 1000 E. Victoria St., Carson, CA 90747. (310) 243-3524. Fax: (310) 243-3518. Web site: http://www. csudh.soe.edu. Peter Desberg, Prof., Coord., Technology-Based Education Program. pdesberg@csudh.edu. *Specializations:* M.A. and Certificate in Technology-Based Education. *Features:* M.A. and Certificate in Technology-Based Education. *Admission Requirements:* 2.75 GPA. *Degree Requirements:* M.A.: 30 semester hours including project. Certificate: 15 hours. *Faculty:* 2 full-time, 2 part-time. *Students:* 60 full-time, 40 part-time. *Financial Assistance:* Available. *Degrees Awarded 2003:* 30. Updated: 3/5/04.

California State University—Los Angeles. Division of Educational Foundations and Interdivisional Studies. 5151 State University Drive, Los Angeles, CA 90032. (323) 343-4330. Fax: (323) 343-5336. Web site: http://www.calstatela.edu/dept/efis/. Dr. Fernando A. Hernandez, Division Chairperson. efis@calstatela.edu. *Specializations:* Our four major programmatic areas include Educational Foundations, which offers a graduate degree in Educational Foundations focusing on Educational Sociology, Educational Psychology, Urban Education, or the Philosophy of Education; Instructional Technology and Computer Education, which offers graduate degrees in Instructional Technology and Computer Education; TESOL, which offers a graduate degree in Teaching as a Secondary Language (for more information, see the TESOL homepage); and Educational Research, Evaluation, and Statistics, which offers service courses to other Education degree programs in statistics, educational research, and evaluation. *Features:* M.A. degree in Education, option in New Media Design and Production; Computer Education and Leadership; Joint Ph.D. in Special Education with UCLA. *Degree Requirements:* 2.75 GPA in last 90 quarter units, 45 quarter units, comprehensive written exam or thesis or project. Must also pass Writing Proficiency Examination (WPE), a California State University—Los Angeles requirement. *Faculty:* 7 full-time. Updated: 3/25/03.

California State University—San Bernardino. Dept. of Science, Mathematics, and Technology Education, 5500 University Parkway, San Bernardino, CA 92407-2397. (909) 880-5290. Fax: (909) 880-7522. Web site: http://coe.csusb.edu/etec/index.html. Olga E. Cordero, Administrative Support Coordinator (ocordero@csusb.edu). *Specializations:* Technology integration, online instruction, instructional design. Preparing educators in K–12, corporate, and higher education. *Admission Requirements:* Bachelor's degree, appropriate work experience, 3.0 GPA ("B") , completion of introductory computer course, and a graduate entrance expository writing course. *Degree Requirements:* 48 units including a master's project (33 units completed in residence); a grade point average of 3.0 ("B") in course work taken to satisfy the master's of arts degree requirements and grades of "C" (2.0) or better in all courses in the program. *Faculty:* 5 full-time, 7 part-time. *Students:* 106. Contact Office of Graduate Studies (909) 880-5058. Updated: 2/21/05.

San Diego State University. Educational Technology. 5500 Campanile Dr., San Diego, CA 92182-1182. (619) 594-6718. Fax: (619) 594-6376. Web site: http://edtec.sdsu.edu/. Dr. Donn Ritchie, Prof., Chair. dritchie@mail.sdsu.edu. *Specializations:* Certificate in Instructional Technology. Advanced Certificate in Distance Learning. Master's in Education with an emphasis in Educational Technology. Doctorate in Education with an emphasis in Educational Technology (a joint program with the University of San Diego). *Features:* Combining theory and practice in relevant, real-world experiences. Both campus and online programs. *Admission Requirements:* Please refer to SDSU Graduate bulletin at http://libWeb.sdsu.edu/bulletin/. Requirements include 950 GRE (verbal + quantitative) and GRE Writing Assessment Exam with score of 4.5 or better. Grades of B+ or better in EDTEC 540 and EDTEC 541. *Degree Requirements:* 36 semester hours for the master's (including 6 prerequisite hours). 15 semester hours for the certificates. *Faculty:* 9 full-time, 5 part-time. *Students:* 120 in campus program; 100 in online program. *Financial Assistance:* graduate assistantships. *Degrees Awarded 2003:* 40. Updated: 3/11/05.

San Francisco State University. College of Education, Department of Instructional Technology. 1600 Holloway Ave., San Francisco, CA 94132. (415) 338-1509. Fax: (415) 338-0510. Web site: http://www.itec.sfsu.edu. Dr. Kim Foreman, Chair; Anna Kozubek, Office Coord. kforeman@sfsu.edu. *Specializations:* master's degree with emphasis on Instructional Multimedia Design, Training and Designing Development, and Instructional Computing. The school also offers an 18-unit Graduate Certificate in Training Systems Development, which can be incorporated into the master's degree. *Features:* This program emphasizes the instructional systems approach, cognitivist principles of learning design, practical design experience, and project-based courses. *Admission Requirements:* bachelor's degree, appropriate work experience, 2.5 GPA, purpose statement, 2 letters of recommendation, interview with the department chair. *Degree Requirements:* 30 semester hours, field study project, or thesis. Three to nine units of prerequisites, assessed at entrance to the program/. *Faculty:* 4 full-time, 16 part-time. *Students:* 250-300. *Financial Assistance:* Contact Office of Financial Aid. *Degrees Awarded 2003:* 60.

San Jose State University. Instructional Technology. One Washington Square, San Jose, CA 95192-0076. (408) 924-3620. Fax: (408) 924-3713. Web site: http://sweeneyhall. sjsu.edu/depts/it. Dr. Roberta Barba, Program Chair. rbarba@email.sjsu.edu. *Specializations:* master's degree. *Features:* MA in Education with an emphasis on Instructional Technology. *Admission Requirements:* Baccalaureate degree from approved university, appropriate work experience, minimum GPA of 2.5, and minimum score of 550 on TOEFL (Test of English as a Foreign Language). Thirty-six semester hours (which includes 6 prerequisite hours). *Degree Requirements:* 30 units of approved graduate studies. *Faculty:* 4 full-time, 12 part-time. *Students:* 50 full-time master's students, 260 part-time. *Financial Assistance:* Assistantships, grants, student loans and scholarships. *Degrees Awarded 2003:* 42.Updated: 2/18/05.

University of Southern California. Instructional Technology, Division of Learning and Instruction. 502C W.P.H., 502C W.P.H., Rossier School of Education, Los Angeles, CA 90089-0031. (213) 740-3288. Fax: (213) 740-3889. Web site: http://www.usc.edu/dept/ education/index2.html. Dr. Richard Clark, Prof., doctoral programs; Dr. Edward J. Kazlauskas, Prof., Program Chair, master's programs in Instructional Technology. kazlausk@usc.edu. *Specializations:* M.A., Ed.D., Ph.D. to prepare individuals to teach instructional technology; manage educational media and training programs in business, industry, research and development organizations, schools, and higher education institutions; perform research in instructional technology and media; and deal with computer-driven technology. *Features:* Special emphasis on instructional design, human performance at work, systems analysis, and computer-based training. *Admission Requirements:* bachelor's degree, 1000 GRE. *Degree Requirements:* M.A.: 28 semester hours, thesis optional. Doctoral: 67 units, 20 of which can be transferred from a previous master's degree. Requirements for degree completion vary according to type of degree and individual interest. Ph.D. requires an outside field in addition to coursework in instructional technology and education, more methodology and statistics work, and coursework in an outside field. *Faculty:* 3 full-time, 2 part-time. *Students:* M.A., 5 full-time, 15 part-time; doctoral, 5 full-time, 20 part-time. *Financial Assistance:* Part-time, instructional technology-related work available in the Los Angeles area and on campus, some scholarship monies available. Full support for Ph.D. students. *Degrees Awarded 2003:* 28. Updated: 2/19/05.

Colorado

University of Colorado at Denver. School of Education. Campus Box 106, P.O. Box 173364, Denver, CO 80217-3364. (303) 556-4478. Fax: (303) 556-4479. Web site: http://www.cudenver.edu/ilt. Brent Wilson, Program Coordinator, Information and Learning Technologies, Division of Technology and Special Services. brent.wilson@ cudenver.edu. *Specializations:* M.A. in Information and Learning Technologies; Ph.D. in Educational Leadership and Innovation with emphasis in Learning Technologies. *Features:* design and use of learning technologies; instructional design. Ph.D. students complete 12 semester hours of doctoral labs (small groups collaborating with faculty on difficult problems of practice). Throughout the program, students complete a product portfolio of research, design, teaching, and applied projects. The program is cross-disciplinary, drawing on expertise in technology, adult learning, systemic change, research methods, reflective practice, and cultural studies. *Admission Requirements:* M.A. and Ph.D.: satisfactory GPA, GRE (for low GPA), writing sample, letters of recommendation, transcripts. See Web site for more detail. *Degree Requirements:* M.A.: 36 semester hours including 28 hours of core coursework; professional portfolio; field experience. Ph.D.: 50 semester hours of coursework and labs, plus 20 dissertation hours; portfolio; dissertation. *Faculty:* 5 full-time, several part-time (see Web). *Students:* M.A., 15 full-time, 80 part-time; Ph.D., 3 full-time, 8 part-time. *Financial Assistance:* assistantships, internships. *Degrees awarded in 2004:* 43. Updated: 2/22/05.

University of Northern Colorado. Educational Technology. College of Education, Greeley, CO 80639. (970) 351-2816. Fax: (970) 351-1622. Web site: http://www. coe.unco.edu/edtech/. Kay Persichitte, Professor, Department Chair, Educational Technology. kay.persichitte@unco.edu. *Specializations:* M.A. in Educational Technology; M.A. in Educational Media; Nondegree endorsement for school library media specialists; Ph.D. in Educational Technology with emphases in Distance Education, Instructional Development/Design, Interactive Technology, and Technology Integration. *Features:* Graduates are prepared for careers as instructional technologists, course designers, trainers, instructional developers, media specialists, and human resource managers. Graduates typically follow employment paths into K–12 education, higher education, business, industry, and occasionally the military. *Admission Requirements:* M.A.: bachelor's degree, 3.0 undergraduate GPA, 1000 GRE verbal and quantitative and 3.5 on the written/analytical, 3 letters of recommendation, statement of career goals. Endorsement: Same as MA but no GRE. Ph.D.: 3.2 GPA in last 60 hours of coursework, three letters of recommendation, congruency between applicants statement of career goals and program goals, 1100 GRE verbal and quantitative and 3.5 on the written/analytical, interview with faculty. *Degree Requirements:* MA-Ed Tech: 30 semester hours (min), MA-Ed Media: 36–39 semester hours (min) Endorsement: 30–33 semester hours (min), Ph.D.: 67 semester hours (min). *Faculty:* 6 full-time. *Students:* M.A., 20 full-time, 130 part-time; Ph.D., 20 full-time, 25 part-time. *Financial Assistance:* Assistantships, grant development, student loans, fellowships, scholarships through the Graduate School. Very competitive with first consideration to full-time doctoral students. *Degrees Awarded 2003:* >30 MA; 3 Ph.D. Updated: 3/5/03.

Connecticut

Central Connecticut State University. Educational Technology. 1615 Stanley St., New Britain, CT 06050. (860) 832-2139. Fax: (860) 832-2109. Web site: http://www.ccsu.edu. Farough Abed, Director., Educational Technology Program. abedf@ccsu.ctstateu.edu. *Specializations:* M.S. in Educational Technology. Curriculum emphases include instructional technology, instructional design, message design, and computer technologies. Degree applies to Public School, Business-Training and Development, and College teaching position. *Features:* The program supports the Center for Innovation in Teaching and Technology to link students with client-based projects. Hands-on experience with emphasis on design, production, and evaluation. Students work as teams in their second year. *Admission Requirements:* bachelor's degree, 2.7 undergraduate GPA, two letters of reference, and goal statement. *Degree Requirements:* 36 semester hours, optional thesis or master's final project (3 credits). *Faculty:* 2 full-time, 4 part-time. *Students:* Full 3, Part time 45. *Financial Assistance:* graduate assistant position. *Degrees Awarded 2003:* 28. Updated: 7/7/04.

Fairfield University. Educational Technology, N. Benson Road, Fairfield, CT 06824. (203) 254-4000. Fax: (203) 254-4047. Web site: http://www.fairfield.edu. Dr. Ibrahim M. Hefzallah, Prof., Chair., Educational Technology Department; Dr. Justin Ahn, Assistant Professor of Educational Technology. ihefzallah@mail.fairfield.edu, jahn@mail.fairfield.edu. *Specializations:* M.A. and a certificate of Advanced Studies in Educational Technology in one of five areas of concentrations: Computers-in-Education, Instructional Development, School Media Specialist, Applied Educational Technology in Content Areas, and Television Production; customized course of study also available. *Features:* emphasis on theory, practice, and new instructional developments in computers in education, multimedia, school/media, and applied technology in education. *Admission Requirements:* bachelor's degree from accredited institution with 2.67 GPA. *Degree Requirements:* 33 credits. *Faculty:* 2 full-time, 8 part-time. *Students:* 4 full-time, 74 part-time. *Financial Assistance:* assistantships, student loans. *Degrees Awarded 2004:* 15. Updated: 3/15/05.

Southern Connecticut State University. Information and Library Science. 501 Crescent St., New Haven, CT 06515. (203) 392-5781. Fax: (203) 392-5780. Web site: http://www.southernct.edu/. Arlene Bielefield, JD, Chairperson; Edward Harris, Ph.D., Dean. mckayl1@southernct.edu. *Specializations:* M.S. in Instructional Technology; Sixth-Year Professional Diploma Library—Information Studies (student may select area of specialization in Instructional Technology). *Features:* Courses in instructional design and technology and in corporate training and development. *Admission Requirements:* bachelor's degree from an institution accredited by a recognized regional accrediting agency in the United States. Degrees from outside the U.S. must be evaluated by an accredited evaluating agency. Undergraduate cumulative average of at least 2.5 on a scale of A = 4. Initial teacher certification programs require a minimum of 2.7. Recommendation of the graduate program coordinator. *Degree Requirements:* for Instructional Technology only, 36 semester hours. For sixth-year degree: 30 credit hours with 6 credit hours of core requirements, 9–15 credit hours in specialization. *Faculty:* 1 full-time; 4 part-time. *Students:* 3 full-time and 38 part-time in M.S./IT program. *Financial Assistance:* graduate assistantship (salary $1,800 per semester; assistants pay tuition and a general university fee sufficient to defray cost of student accident insurance). Updated: 3/5/04.

University of Connecticut. Educational Psychology. 249 Glenbrook Rd, Unit 2064, Storrs, CT 06269-2064. (860) 486-0182. Fax: (860) 486-0180. Web site: http://www.epsy.uconn.edu/. Michael Young, program coordinator. myoung@UConnvm.UConn.edu. *Specializations:* M.A. in Educational Technology (portfolio or thesis options), one-year partially online master's (summer, fall, spring, summer), 6th Year certificate in Educational Technology and Ph.D. in Learning Technology. *Features:* MA can be on-campus or two Summers (on campus) and Fall–Spring (Online) that can be completed in a year. The Ph.D. emphasis in Learning Technology is a unique program at UConn. It strongly emphasizes Cognitive Science and how technology can be used to enhance the way people think and learn. The Program seeks to provide students with knowledge of theory and applications regarding the use of advanced technology to enhance learning and thinking. Campus facilities include $2 billion 21st-Century UConn enhancement to campus infrastructure, including a new wing to the Neag School of Education. Faculty research interests include interactive video for anchored instruction and situated learning, telecommunications for cognitive apprenticeship, technology-mediated interactivity for learning by design activities, and in cooperation with the National Research Center for Gifted and Talented, research on the use of technology to enhance cooperative learning and the development of gifted performance in all students. *Admission Requirements:* admission to the graduate school at UConn, GRE scores (or other evidence of success at the graduate level). Previous experience in a related area of technology, education, or experience in education or training. *Degree Requirements:* completion of plan of study coursework, comprehensive exam (portfolio-based with multiple requirements), and completion of an approved dissertation. *Faculty:* The program in Cognition and Instruction has 7 full-time faculty; 3 full-time faculty administer the emphasis in Educational Technology. *Students:* 8 M.A., 10 Ph.D. *Financial Assistance:* graduate assistantships, research fellowships, teaching assistantships, and federal and minority scholarships are available competitively. *Degrees Awarded 2003:* 4 MA, 2 Ph.D. Updated: 5/19/03.

District of Columbia

George Washington University. School of Education and Human Development. Washington, DC 20052. (202) 994-1701. Fax: (202) 994-2145. Web site: http://www. gwu.edu/~etl. Dr. William Lynch, Educational Technology Leadership Program. Program is offered through Jones Education Company (JEC). Contact student advisors at (800) 777-MIND. unirel@www.gwu.edu. *Specializations:* M.A. in Education and Human Development with a major in Educational Technology Leadership. *Admission Requirements:* application fee, transcripts, GRE or MAT scores (50th percentile), two letters of recommendation from academic professionals, computer access, undergraduate degree with 2.75 GPA. *Degree Requirements:* 36 credit hours (including 24 required hours). Required courses include computer application management, media and technology application, software implementation and design, public education policy, and quantitative research methods. *Faculty:* Courses are taught by GWU faculty. *Financial Assistance:* For information, contact the Office of Student Financial Assistance, GWU. Some cable systems that carry JEC offer local scholarships.

Florida

Barry University. Department of Educational Computing and Technology, School of Education. 11300 N.E. Second Ave., Miami Shores, FL 33161. (305) 899-3608. Fax: (305) 899-3718. Web site: http://www.barry.edu/ed/programs/master's/ect/default.htm. Donna Lenaghan, Dir. dlenaghan@bu4090.barry.edu. *Specializations:* M.S. and Ed.S. in Educational Technology Applications and Ph.D. degree in Educational Technology Leadership. *Features:* These programs and courses prepares educators to integrate computer/technologies in their disciplines and/or train individuals to use computers/technologies. The focus is on improving the teaching and learning process thought integration of technologies into curricula and learning activities. *Admission Requirements:* GRE scores, letters of recommendation, GPA, interview, achievements. *Degree Requirements:* M.S. or Ed. S.: 36 semester credit hours. Ph.D.: 54 credits beyond the master's including dissertation credits. *Faculty:* 5 full-time, 10 part-time. *Students:* M.S., 8 full-time, 181 part-time; Ed.S., 5 full-time, 44 part-time; Ph.D., 3 full-time, 15 part-time. *Financial Assistance:* assistantships, student loans. *Degrees Awarded 2003:* 75. Updated: 5/19/03.

Florida Institute of Technology. Science Education Department, 150 University Blvd., Melbourne, FL 32901-6975. (321) 674-8126. Fax: (321) 674-7598. Web site: http://www.fit.edu/catalog/sci-lib/comp-edu.html#master-info. Dr. David Cook, Dept. Head. dcook@fit.edu. *Specializations:* master's degree options in Computer Education and Instructional Technology; Ph.D. degree options in Computer Education and Instructional Technology. *Features:* Flexible program depending on student experience. *Admission Requirements:* master's: 3.0 GPA for regular admission; 2.75 for provisional admission. Ph.D.: master's degree and 3.2 GPA *Degree Requirements:* master's: 33 semester hours (15 in computer or and technology education, 9 in education, 9 electives); practicum; no thesis or internship required. Ph.D.: 48 semester hours (12 in computer and technology education, 12 in education, 24 dissertation and research). *Faculty:* 4 full-time. *Students:* 11 full-time, 10 part-time. *Financial Assistance:* loans, limited graduate student assistantships (full tuition plus stipend) available. *Degrees Awarded 2003:* 5. Updated: 5/5/04.

Florida State University. Educational Psychology and Learning Systems. 305 Stone Bldg., Tallahassee, FL 32306. (850) 644-4592. Fax: (850) 644-8776. Web site: http://www. epls.fsu.edu/is/index.htm. Mary Kate McKee, Program Coordinator. MMcKee@oddl. fsu.edu. *Specializations:* M.S., Ed.S, Ph.D. in Instructional Systems with specializations for persons planning to work in academia, business, industry, government, or military, both in the United States and in International settings. *Features:* Core courses include systems and materials development, development of multimedia, project management, psychological foundations, current trends in instructional design, and research and statistics. Internships are recommended. *Admission Requirements:* M.S.: 3.0 GPA in last two years of undergraduate program, 1000 GRE (verbal plus quantitative), 550 TOEFL (for international applicants). Ph.D.: 1100 GRE (V+Q), 3.5 GPA in last two years; international students, 550 TOEFL. *Degree Requirements:* M.S.: 36 semester hours, 2-4 hour internship, comprehensive exam preparation of professional portfolio. *Faculty:* 7 full-time, 4 part-time. *Students:* M.S., 50; Ph.D., 50. *Financial Assistance:* Graduate research and teaching assistantships on faculty grants and contracts; Program, college, and university fellowships. Updated: 3/5/04.

Jacksonville University. Division of Education. 2800 University Boulevard North, Jacksonville, FL 32211. (904) 745-7132. Fax: (904) 745-7159. Dr. Margaret Janz, Interim Dir., School of Education, or Dr. June Main, Coordinator of MAT in Integrated Learning with Educational Technology. mjanz@mail.ju.edu. *Specializations:* The Master's in Educational Technology and Integrated Learning is an innovative program designed to guide certified teachers in the use and application of educational technologies in the classroom. It is based on emerging views of how we learn, of our growing understanding of multiple intelligences, and of the many ways to incorporate technology in teaching and learning. Activity-based classes emphasize instructional design for a multimedia environment to reach all students. M.A.T. degrees in Computer Education and in Integrated Learning with Educational Technology. *Features:* The M.A.T. in Computer Education is for teachers who are already certified in an area of education, for those who wish to be certified in Computer Education, kindergarten through community college level. *Degree Requirements:* M.A.T. in Computer Education and in Integrated Learning with Educational Technology: 36 semester hours, including 9–12 hours in core education graduate courses and the rest in computer education with comprehensive exam in last semester of program. Master's in Educational Technology and Integrated Learning: 36 semester hours, including 9 in core graduate education courses, 6 in integrated learning, and the rest in educational technology. Comprehensive exam is to develop a practical group of multimedia applications. *Financial Assistance:* student loans and discounts to graduate education students. *Students:* Computer Education, 8; Integrated Learning with Educational Technology, 20.

Nova Southeastern University—Fischler Graduate School of Education and Human Services. Programs in Instructional Technology and Distance Education (ITDE). 1750 NE 167th Street, North Miami Beach, FL 33162. (954) 262-8572. (800) 986-3223, ext. 8572. Fax: (954) 262-3905. Web site: itde.nova.edu. Marsha L. Burmeister, Recruitment Coordinator and Program Professor ITDE. itdeinfo@nova.edu. *Specializations:* M.S. and Ed.D in Instructional Technology and Distance Education. *Features:* M.S. 21 months (M.S. ITDE program graduates may continue with the Ed.D. program as second year students). Ed.D. 36 months, M.S. and Ed.D. combined: 4+ years, Blended/hybrid delivery model with limited face-to-face and via instruction at-a-distance using Web-based technologies. *Admission Requirements:*

- Active employment in the field of instructional technology/distance education.

- Completion of bachelor's degree for M.S. program (2.5 minimum GPA); master's degree required for admission to Ed.D. program (3.0 minimum GPA).

- Miller Analogies Test (MAT) score (test taken within last 5 years)

- Submission of application/supplementary materials

- Approval of Skills Checklist (application)

- Three letters of recommendation

- Official copies of transcripts for all graduate work

- Resume

- Oral interview (via telephone)

- Demonstrated potential for successful completion of the program via acceptance of application

- Internet service provider; laptop computer

Degree Requirements: M.S. 21 months and 30 semester credits. Ed.D. 3 years and 65 semester credits. M.S. program: 3 "extended weekends": one extended weekend in the fall (5 days), one extended weekend in the spring (4 days), one summer instructional session (4–5 days; July), final term online delivery. Ed.D. program: same as above, continues throughout the 3 years (3 sessions in first year, 2 sessions in the second year, and one instructional session in the third year for a total of six face-to-face sessions). *Faculty:* 6 full-time and 20 adjuncts. *Students:* 300 full-time. *Financial Assistance:* Student loans; apply to Nova Southeastern University Office of Student Financial Assistance: http://www.nova.edu/cwis/finaid/index.html. All ITDE students are considered full-time students for the purposes of financial aid. *Degrees Awarded 2003:* 100. Updated: 3/19/03.

University of Central Florida. College of Education, ERTL, 4000 Central Florida Blvd., Orlando, FL 32816-1250. (407) 823-1760. Fax: (407) 823-4880. Web site: http://insttech.education.ucf.edu. Atsusi Hirumi, Instructional Systems; Glenda Gunter, Educational Technology (hirumi@mail.ucf.edu and ggunter@pegasus.cc.ucf.edu.) *Specializations:* Graduate Certificates in Educational Technology, Instructional Design for Simulations, and e-Learning. Master's of Arts in Professional Tracks, Educational Technology, Instructional Systems, e-Learning. Doctoral Programs: Ph.D. in Education with specialization in Instructional Technology; Ed.D. in Curriculum and Instruction with concentration in Instructional Technology. *Features:* All programs rely heavily on understanding of fundamental competencies as reflected by ASTD, AECT, AASL, and ISTE. There is an emphasis on the practical application of theory through intensive hands-on experiences. Orlando and the surrounding area is home to a plethora of high-tech companies, military training and simulation organizations, and tourist attractions. UCF, established in 1963, now has in excess of 36,000 students, representing more than 90 countries. It has been ranked as one of the leading "most-wired" universities in North America. *Admission requirements:* GRE score of 840 if last 60 hours of undergraduate degree is 3.0 or above, 1000 if less; TOEFL of 550 (270 computer-based version) if English is not first language; three letters of recommendation; resume, statement of goals; residency statement, and health record. Financial statement if coming from overseas. *Degree Requirements:* Graduate Certificates, 15 semester credit hours; M.A. 39–42 semester credit; Ph.D. and Ed.D. require between 58–69 hours beyond the master's for completion. *Faculty:* 4 full-time, 1 part-time. *Students:* 35 full-time, 50 part-time. *Financial Aid:* Competitive graduate assistantships in department and college, numerous paid internships, limited number of doctoral fellowships. *Degrees awarded in 2004:* 21. Updated: 3/29/05.

University of Florida. School of Teaching and Learning. 2403 Norman Hall, Gainesville, FL 32611-7048. (352) 392-9191 ext. 261. Fax: (352) 392-9193. Web site: http://www. coe.ufl.edu/Courses/EdTech/index.html. Kara Dawson. dawson@coe.ufl.edu. *Specializations:* Educational technology students may earn M.S., Ed.S., Ed.D. or Ph.D. degrees and have an opportunity to specialize in one of three tracks: (1) teaching and teacher education, (2) production, or (3) instructional design. Teacher education students and students in other degree programs may also elect to specialize in Educational Technology. *Features:* Students take core courses listed on our Educational Technology Web site and then select an area of specialization. *Admission Requirements:* Please see the Educational Technology Web site for the most up-to-date information. Current admission requirements are as follows: Obtain a GRE score of 1000 or more on the verbal and quantitative components of the GRE. Applicants must have a score of 450 or higher for each component (verbal and quantitative). Submit a written document outlining (1) your career goals and (2) the track you wish to specialize in the Educational Technology program. *Degree Requirements:* Please see the Educational Technology Web site for the most up-to-date information. Program and college requirements must be met but there is considerable flexibility for doctoral students to plan an appropriate program with their advisors. *Faculty:* 3 full-time faculty members; 2 faculty members teach part-time within the program. *Students:* approximately 50 students are enrolled in our Educational Technology. *Financial Assistance:* A limited number of graduate assistantships are available. Interested students should submit an assistantship application with their admissions application. Students should also check the Web site for information about available assistantships. Updated: 2/27/05.

University of South Florida. Instructional Technology Program, Secondary Education Department, College of Education. 4202 E. Fowler Avenue, EDU162, Tampa, FL 33620-5650. (813) 974-3533. Fax: (813) 974-3837. Web site: http://www.coedu.usf.edu/it. Dr. William Kealy, Graduate Certificates; Dr. Frank Breit, Master's program; Dr. Ann Barron, Education Specialist program; Dr. James White, Doctoral program. See http://www.coedu.usf.edu/it. *Specializations:* Graduate Certificates in Web Design, Instructional Design, Multimedia Design, School Networks, and Distance Education M.Ed., Ed.S., and Ph.D. in Curriculum and Instruction with emphasis in Instructional Technology. *Features:* Many students gain practical experience in the Florida Center for Instructional Technology (FCIT), which provides services to the Department of Education and other grants and contracts; the Virtual Instructional Team for the Advancement of Learning (VITAL), which provides USF faculty with course development services; and Educational Outreach. The College of Education is one of the largest in the United States in terms of enrollment and facilities. As of Fall 1997, a new, technically state-of-the-art building was put into service. The University of South Florida has been classified by the Carnegie Foundation as a Doctoral/Research University—Extensive. *Admission Requirements:* See http://www. coedu.usf.edu/it. *Degree Requirements:* See http://www.coedu.usf.edu/it. *Faculty:* 4 full-time, 6 part-time. *Students:* 120 full-time, 255 part-time. *Financial Assistance:* some assistantships, grants, loans, scholarships, and fellowships. *Degrees Awarded 2003:* 60+. Updated: 5/20/03.

Georgia

Georgia Southern University. College of Education. Box 8131, Statesboro, GA 30460-8131. (912) 681-5307. Fax: (912) 486-7104. Web site: http://coe.georgiasouthern. edu/eltr/tech/inst_tech/index.htm. Judi Repman. Professor, Dept. of Leadership, Technology, and Human Development. jrepman@georgiasouthern.edu. *Specializations:* M.Ed. and GA certification for School Library Media Specialist. An Instructional Technology strand is available in the Ed.S. in Teaching and Learning Program and in the Ed.D. program in Curriculum Studies. *Features:* GA Special Technology Certification course available strong emphasis on technology. *Admission Requirements:* BS (teacher certification not required), MAT score of 44 or GRE score of 450 verbal and 450 quantitative for Regular admission. Provisional admission requires lower scores but also requires letters of intent/reference. *Degree Requirements:* 36 semester hours, including a varying number of hours of media for individual students. *Faculty:* 3 full-time. *Students:* 100 part-time. *Financial Assistance:* See graduate catalog for general financial aid information. *Degrees Awarded 2003:* 20. Updated: 2/25/05.

Georgia State University. Middle-Secondary Education and Instructional Technology. University Plaza, Atlanta, GA 30303. (404) 651-2510. Fax: (404) 651-2546. Web site: http://www.gsu.edu/~wwwmst/. Dr. Stephen W. Harmon, contact person. swharmon@gsu.edu. *Specializations:* M.S., Ed.S., and Ph.D. in Instructional Technology or Library Media. *Features:* focus on research and practical application of instructional technology in educational and corporate settings. *Admission Requirements:* M.S.: bachelor's degree, 2.5 undergraduate GPA, 800 GRE, 550 TOEFL. Ed.S.: master's degree, teaching certificate, 3.25 graduate GPA, 48 MAT or 900 GRE. Ph.D.: master's degree, 3.30 graduate GPA, 53 MAT or 500 verbal plus 500 quantitative GRE or 500 analytical GRE. *Degree Requirements:* M.S.: 36 semester hours, internship, portfolio, comprehensive examination. Ed.S.: 30 semester hours, internship, and scholarly project. Ph.D.: 66 semester hours, internship, comprehensive examination, dissertation. *Faculty:* 8 full-time, 3 part-time. *Students:* 200 M.S., 40 Ph.D. *Financial Assistance:* assistantships, grants, student loans. *Degrees Awarded 2003:* 44 M.S., 6 Ed.S., 5 Ph.D. Updated: 2/27/03.

University of Georgia. Department of Educational Psychology and Instructional Technology, College of Education, Athens, GA 30602. (706) 542-3810. Fax: (706) 542-4032. Web site: http://it.coe.uga.edu.Dr. Randy Kamphaus, Department Head, rkamp@uga.edu. *Specializations:* M.Ed., Ed.S. and Ph.D. in Instructional Technology. The program offers advanced study for individuals with previous preparation in instructional media and technology, as well as a preparation for personnel in other professional fields requiring a specialty in instructional systems or instructional technology. Representative career fields for graduates include designing new courses, tutorial programs, instructional materials in state and local school systems, higher education, business and industry, research and non-profit settings. *Features:* Minor areas of study available in a variety of other departments. Personalized programs are planned around a common core of courses and include practica or internships. Research activities include grant-related activities and applied projects, as well as dissertation studies. *Admission Requirements,* all degrees: application to graduate school, satisfactory GRE score, other criteria as outlined in Graduate School Bulletin and on the program Web site. M.Ed.: 36 semester hours with 3.0 GPA, portfolio with oral exam. Ed.S.: 30 semester hours with 3.0 GPA and project exam. Ph.D.: three full years of study beyond the Master's degree, two consecutive semesters full-time residency, comprehensive exam with oral defense, internship, dissertation with oral defense. *Faculty:* 11 full-time, 3 part-time. *Students:* M.Ed 150; Ed.S. 60; Ph.D. 42. *Financial Assistance:* Graduate assistantships available. *Degrees awarded in 2004:* 60. Updated: 2/26/05, Janette R. Hill, janette@coe.uga.edu

University of West Georgia. Department of Media and Instructional Technology. 138 Education Annex, Carrollton, GA 30118. (770) 836-6558 or 836-4442. Fax: (770) 838-3088. Web site: http://coe.westga.edu/mit/index.html. Dr. Barbara K. McKenzie, Professor and Chair. bmckenzi@westga.edu. *Specializations:* M.Ed. with specializations in Media and Instructional Technology and Add-On certification for students with master's degrees in other disciplines. The Department also offers an Ed.S. program in Media with two options, Media Specialist or Instructional Technology. The program strongly emphasizes technology integration in the schools. *Features:* master's degree students and initial certification students are required to complete a practicum. *Admission Requirements:* M.Ed.: 800 GRE, 44 MAT, 550 NTE Core, 2.5 undergraduate GPA. Ed.S.: 900 GRE, 48 MAT, or 575 NTE and 3.25 graduate GPA. *Degree Requirements:* 36 semester hours for M.Ed. 27 semester hours for Ed.S. *Faculty:* 6 full-time in Media/Technology; 1 full-time instructor in Instructional Technology; 2 part-time in Media/Instructional Technology. *Students:* Approximately 460, part-time. *Financial Assistance:* two graduate research assistantships for the department. *Degrees Awarded 2004:* Approximately 70 across both levels. Updated: 2/18/05.

Valdosta State University. Curriculum & Instructional Technology, 1500 N. Patterson St., Valdosta, GA 31698. (229) 333-5927. Fax: (229) 333-7167. Web site: http://education.valdosta.edu/info/cait/. Catherine B. Price, Professor/Dept. Head, cprice@valdosta.edu. Gayle Brooks, gbrooks@valdosta.edu. *Specializations:* M.Ed. in Instructional Technology with two tracks: Library/Media or Technology Applications; Online Ed.S. in Instructional Technology; Ed.D. in Curriculum and Instruction. *Features:* The program has a strong emphasis on systematic design and technology in M.Ed., Ed.S., and Ed.D. Strong emphasis on change leadership, reflective practice, applied research in Ed.S and Ed.D. *Admission Requirements:* M.Ed.: 2.5 GPA, 800 GRE. Ed.S.: master's degree, 3 years of experience, 3.0 GPA, 850 GRE, MAT 36 and less than 5 years old. Ed.D.: master's degree, 3 years of experience, 3.50 GPA, 1000 GRE. *Degree Requirements:* M.Ed.: 33 semester hours. Ed.S.: 27 semester hours. Ed.D.: 54 semester hours. *Faculty:* 6 full-time, 4 part-time. *Students:* 94 master's, 86 specialist, 25 doctoral students. *Financial Assistance:* graduate assistantships, student loans, scholarships. Updated: 2/21/05.

Hawaii

University of Hawaii—Manoa. Department of Educational Technology, 1776 University Ave., Honolulu, HI 96822-2463. (808) 956-7671. Fax: (808) 956-3905. Web site: http://etec.hawaii.edu. Curtis P. Ho, Ph.D., Chair (edtech-dept@hawaii.edu). *Specialization:* M.Ed. in Educational Technology, min. 36 semester hours, including 3 in practicum, thesis and non-thesis available. *Admission Requirements:* Bachelor's degree in any field, B average (3.0 GPA). *Degree Requirements:* 36 semester hours (plus 3 semester hours of prerequisites if needed). *Faculty:* 7 full-time (state funded), 2 full-time (grant-funded). *Students:* 14 full-time, 32 part-time. *Financial Assistance:* Consideration given to meritorious second-year students for tuition waivers and scholarship applications. *Degrees Awarded 2004 Idaho:* 16. Updated: 2/18/05.

Idaho

Boise State University. Instructional and Performance Technology. 1910 University Drive, ET-338, Boise, ID 83725. (208) 424-5135; (800) 824-7017 ext. 4457. Fax: (208) 426-1970. Web site: http://ipt.boisestate.edu/. Dr. David Cox, IPT Program Dir.; Jo Ann Fenner, IPT Program Developer and distance program contact person. bsuipt@boisestate.edu. *Specializations:* M.S. in Instructional and Performance Technology is available in a traditional campus setting or via asynchronous computer conferencing to students located anywhere there is access to the Internet. The program is fully accredited by the Northwest Commission of Colleges and Universities and is the recipient of an NUCEA award for Outstanding Credit Program offered by distance education methods. *Features:* Leading experts in learning styles, evaluation, and leadership principles serve as adjunct faculty in the program via computer and modem from their various remote locations. For details, visit our faculty Web page at http://ipt.boisestate.edu/faculty.htm. *Admission Requirements:* undergraduate degree with 3.0 GPA, one-to-two page essay describing why the applicant wants to pursue this program and how it will contribute to his or her personal and professional development, and a resume of personal qualifications and work experience. For more information, visit http://ipt.boisestate.edu/application_admission.htm *Degree Requirements:* 36 semester hours in instructional and performance technology and related coursework; project or thesis available for on-campus program and an oral comprehensive exam required for distance program (included in 36 credit hours). *Faculty:* 5 full-time, 10 part-time. *Students:* 190 part-time. *Financial Assistance:* DANTES funding for some military personnel, low-interest loans to eligible students, graduate assistantships for on-campus enrollees. *Degrees Awarded 2003:* 47. Updated: 2/25/05.

Illinois

Chicago State University. Department of Library Science and Communications Media, Chicago, IL 60628. (312) 995-2278; (312) 995-2503. Fax: (312) 995-2473. Janice Bolt, Prof., Chair, Dept. of Library Science and Communications Media. l-robinson@csu.edu. *Specializations:* master's degree in School Media. Program has been approved by NCATE: AECT/AASL through accreditation of University College of Education; State of Illinois Entitlement Program. *Admission Requirements:* teacher's certification or bachelor's in education; any B.A. or B.S. *Degree Requirements:* 36 semester hours; thesis optional. *Faculty:* 2 full-time, 5 part-time. *Students:* 88 part-time. *Financial Assistance:* assistantships, grants, student loans.

Governors State University. College of Arts and Sciences. University Drive, University Park, IL 60466. (708) 534-4082. Fax: (708) 534-7895. m-stelnicki@govst.edu. Michael Stelnicki, Prof., Human Performance and Training. m-stelni@govst.edu. *Specializations:* M.A. in Communication and Training with Human Performance and Training major. Program concentrates on building instructional design skills. *Features:* Emphasizes three professional areas: Instructional Design, Performance Analysis, and Design Logistics. *Admission Requirements:* Undergraduate degree in any field. *Degree Requirements:* 36 credit hours (trimester), all in instructional and performance technology; internship or advanced field project required. Metropolitan Chicago–area based. *Faculty:* 2 full-time. *Students:* 30 part-time. *Financial Assistance:* Contact Student Assistance. *Degrees Awarded 2004:* 10. Updated: 4/19/05.

Northern Illinois University. Educational Technology, Research and Assessment. 208 Gabel Hall, DeKalb, IL 60115. (815) 753-9339. Fax: (815) 753-9388. Web site: http://www.cedu.niu.edu/etra. Dr. Jeffrey B. Hecht, Department Chair. etra@niu.edu. *Specializations:* M.S.Ed. in Instructional Technology with concentrations in Instructional Design, Distance Education, Educational Computing, and Media Administration; Ed.D. in Instructional Technology, emphasizing instructional design and development, computer education, media administration, and preparation for careers in business, industry, and higher education. In addition, Illinois state certification in school library media is offered in conjunction with either degree or alone. *Features:* Program is highly individualized. All facilities remodeled and modernized in 2002–2003 featuring five smart classrooms and over 110 student use desktop and laptop computers. Specialized equipment for digital audio and video editing, Web site and CD creation, and presentations. All students are encouraged to create portfolios highlighting personal accomplishments and works (required at master's). Master's program started in 1968, doctorate in 1970. *Admission Requirements:* M.S.Ed.: 2.75 undergraduate GPA, GRE verbal and quantitative scores, two references. Ed.D.: 3.25 M.S. GPA, writing sample, three references, interview. *Degree Requirements:* M.S.Ed.: 39 hours, including 30 in instructional technology; portfolio. Ed.D.: 63 hours beyond master's, including 15 hours for dissertation. *Faculty:* 8 full-time, 18 part-time. *Students:* M.S., 185 part-time; Ed.D., 135 part-time. *Financial Assistance:* Assistantships available at times in various departments, scholarships, and minority assistance. *Degrees Awarded 2003:* 104 degrees awarded: 93 M.S.Ed. in IT; 11 Ed.D. in IT. Updated: 5/27/03.

Southern Illinois University at Carbondale. Department of Curriculum and Instruction, Carbondale, IL 62901-4610. (618) 536-2441. Fax: (618) 453-4244. Web site: http://www. siu.edu/~currinst/index.html. Sharon Shrock, Coord., Instructional Technology/Development. sashrock@siu.edu. *Specializations:* M.S. in Education with specializations in Instructional Development and Instructional Technology; Ph.D. in Education including specialization in Instructional Technology. *Features:* All specializations are oriented to multiple education settings. The ID program emphasizes nonschool (primarily corporate) learning environments. *Admission Requirements:* M.S.: bachelor's degree, 2.7 undergraduate GPA, transcripts. Ph.D.: master's degree, 3.25 GPA, MAT or GRE scores, letters of recommendation, transcripts, writing sample. *Degree Requirements:* M.S., 32 credit hours with thesis; 36 credit hours without thesis; Ph.D., 40 credit hours beyond the master's degree in courses, 24 credit hours for the dissertation. *Faculty:* 5 full-time, 2 part-time. *Students:* M.S., 35 full-time, 45 part-time; Ph.D., 8 full-time, 19 part-time. *Financial Assistance:* some graduate assistantships and scholarships available to qualified students.

Southern Illinois University at Edwardsville. Instructional Technology Program. School of Education, Edwardsville, IL 62026-1125. (618) 692-3277. Fax: (618) 692-3359. Web site: http://www.siue.edu. Dr. Charles E. Nelson, Dir., Dept. of Educational Leadership. cnelson@siue.edu. *Specializations:* M.S. in Education with concentrations in (1) Instructional Design and (2) Teaching, Learning, and Technology. *Features:* evening classes only. *Degree Requirements:* 36 semester hours; thesis optional. *Faculty:* 6 part-time. *Students:* 125.

University of Illinois at Urbana-Champaign. Department of Educational Psychology. 210 Education Bldg.1310 S. 6th St., Champaign, IL 61820. (217) 333-2245. Fax: (217) 244-7620. Charles K. West, Prof., Div. of Learning and Instruction, Dept. of Educational Psychology. c-west@uiuc.edu. *Specializations:* M.A., M.S., and Ed.M. with emphasis in Instructional Design and Educational Computing. Ph.D. in Educational Psychology with emphasis in Instructional Design and Educational Computing. *Features:* Ph.D. program is individually tailored and strongly research-oriented with emphasis on applications of cognitive science to instruction. *Admission Requirements:* excellent academic record, high GRE scores, and strong letters of recommendation. *Degree Requirements:* 8 units for Ed.M., 6 units and thesis for M.A. or M.S. Ph.D.: 8 units coursework, approx. 4 units of research methods courses, minimum 8 hours of written qualifying exams, 8 units Thesis credits. *Faculty:* 8 full-time, 5 part-time. *Students:* 31 full-time, 7 part-time. *Financial Assistance:* scholarships, research assistantships, and teaching assistantships available; fellowships for very highly academically talented; some tuition waivers.

Western Illinois University. Instructional Technology and Telecommunications. 37 Harrabin Hall, Macomb, IL 61455. (309) 298-1952. Fax: (309) 298-2978. Web site: http://www.wiu.edu/users/miitt/. M.H. Hassan, Chair. mh-hassan@wiu.edu. *Specialization:* master's degree. *Features:* New program approved by Illinois Board of Higher Education in January 1996 with emphases in Instructional Technology, Telecommunications, Interactive Technologies, and Distance Education. Selected courses delivered via satellite TV and compressed video. *Admission Requirements:* bachelor's degree 3.0/4.0 GRE score. *Degree Requirements:* 32 semester hours, thesis or applied project, or 35 semester hours with portfolio. Certificate Program in Instructional Technology Specialization. Graphic applications, training development, video production. Each track option is made of 5 courses or a total of 15 semester hours. *Faculty:* 8 full-time. *Students:* 35 full-time, 150 part-time. *Financial Assistance:* graduate and research assistantships, internships, residence hall assistants, veterans' benefits, loans, and part-time employment.

Indiana

Indiana University. School of Education. W. W. Wright Education Bldg., Rm. 2276, 201 N. Rose Ave., Bloomington, IN 47405-1006. (812) 856-8451. Fax: (812) 856-8239. Web site: http://education.indiana.edu/~ist/. Elizabeth Boling, Chair, Dept. of Instructional Systems Technology. istdept@indiana.edu. *Specializations:* M.S. and Ed.S. degrees designed for individuals seeking to be practitioners in the field of Instructional Technology. M.S. degree also offered in Web-based format with instructional product and portfolio requirements. Offers Ph.D. degree with four program focus areas: Foundations; Instructional Analysis, Design, and Development; Instructional Development and Production; and Implementation and Management. *Features:* Requires computer skills as a prerequisite and makes technology utilization an integral part of the curriculum; eliminates separation of various media formats; and establishes a series of courses of increasing complexity integrating production and development. The latest in technical capabilities have been incorporated, including teaching, computer, and laptop-ready laboratories, a multimedia laboratory, and video and audio production studios. *Admission Requirements:* M.S.: bachelor's degree from an accredited institution, 1350 GRE (3 tests required) or 900 plus 3.5 analytical writing (new format), 2.75 undergraduate GPA. Ed.S. and Ph.D.: 1650 GRE (3 tests required) or 1100 plus 4.5 analytical writing (new format), 3.5 graduate GPA. *Degree Requirements:* M.S.: 36 credit hours (including 15 credits in required courses); colloquia; an instructional product; and 9 credits in outside electives, and portfolio. Ed.S.: 65 hours, capstone project with written report and a portfolio. Ph.D.: 90 hours, portfolio, and thesis. *Faculty:* 11 full-time, 2 part-time. *Students:* 240 (includes full-time, part-time, and ABDs). *Financial Assistance:* assistantships, fellowships. *Degrees Awarded 2003:* 48 M.S.; 2 Ed.S.; 10 Ph.D. (2002). Updated: 2/28/03.

Indiana State University. Dept. of Curriculum, Instruction, and Media Technology, Terre Haute, IN 47809. (812) 237-2937. Fax: (812) 237-4348. Dr. James E. Thompson, Program Coord. efthomp@befac.indstate.edu. *Specializations:* master's degree in Instructional Technology with education focus or with non-education focus; Specialist Degree program in Instructional Technology; Ph.D. in Curriculum, Instruction with specialization in Media Technology. *Degree Requirements:* master's: 32 semester hours, including 18 in media; thesis optional; Ed.S.: 60 semester hours beyond bachelor's degree; Ph.D.: approximately 100 hours beyond bachelor's degree. *Faculty:* 5 full-time. *Students:* 17 full-time, 13 part-time. *Financial Assistance:* 7 assistantships.

Purdue University. School of Education, Department of Curriculum and Instruction, 100 N. University St., W. Lafayette, IN 47907-2098. (765) 494-5669. Fax: (765) 496-1622. Web site: http://www.edci.purdue.edu/et/. Dr. Tim Newby, Prof. of Educational Technology (edtech@COE.purdue.edu). *Specializations:* Master's degree and Ph.D. in Educational Technology. *Features:* Vision Statement—The Educational Technology Program at Purdue University nurtures graduates who are effective designers of learning experiences and environments that incorporate technology to engage learners and improve learning. *Admission Requirements:* master's and Ph.D.: 3.0 GPA, three letters of recommendation, statement of personal goals. A score of 550 (paper-based) or 213 (computer-based) or above on the Test of English as a Foreign Language (TOEFL) for individuals whose first language is not English. Ph.D. Additional Requirement: 1000 GRE (verbal + quantitative); verbal score of at least 500 preferred. *Degree Requirements:* master's: minimum of 32 semester hours (17 in educational technology, 6–9 in research, development, and exit requirements, 6–9 electives); thesis optional. Ph.D.: 60 semester hours beyond the master's degree (15–18 in educational technology, 27–30 in education and supporting areas; 15 dissertation research hours). *Faculty:* 6 full-time; 1 part-time. *Students:* M.S., 24; Ph.D., 31. *Financial Assistance:* assistantships and fellowships. *Degrees Awarded 2004:* 8. Updated: 2/18/05, Aggie Ward, aggie@purdue.edu

Iowa

Clarke College. Graduate Studies. 1550 Clarke Drive, Dubuque, IA 52001. (563) 588-8180. Fax: (563) 584-8604. Web site: http://www.clarke.edu. Margaret Lynn Lester. llester@clarke.edu. *Specializations:* M.A. in Technology and Education. *Features:* This program offers hybrid courses in educational technology. Courses are offered through WebCT and face-to-face. Course objectives are aligned with the National Educational Technology Standards. *Admission Requirements:* 2.5 GPA, GRE (verbal + quantitative) or MAT, $25 application fee, two letters of recommendation *Degree Requirements:* 12 hours of core courses and 18–21 hours in technology courses for teachers. *Faculty:* 1 full-time, 1–2 part-time. *Students:* 10 part-time. *Financial Assistance:* scholarships, student loans. *Degrees Awarded 2004:* 5. Updated: 3/28/05.

Iowa State University. College of Education. E262 Lagomarcino Hall, Ames, IA 50011. (515) 294-7021. Fax: (515) 294-6260. Web site: http://www.educ.iastate.edu/. Niki Davis, Director, Center for Technology in Learning and Teaching. nedavis@iastate.edu. *Specializations:* M.Ed., M.S., and Ph.D. in Curriculum and Instructional Technology. *Features:* Prepares candidates as practitioners and researchers in the field of curriculum and instructional technology. All areas of specialization emphasize appropriate and effective applications of technology in teacher education. M.Ed. program also offered at a distance (online and face-to-face learning experiences). Practicum experiences related to professional objectives, supervised study and research projects tied to long-term studies within the program, development and implementation of new techniques, teaching strategies, and operational procedures in instructional resources centers and computer labs, program emphasis on technologies for teachers. *Admission Requirements:* M.Ed. and M.S.: bachelor's degree, top half of undergraduate class, official transcripts, three letters, autobiography. Ph.D.: top half of undergraduate class, official transcripts, three letters, autobiography, GRE scores, scholarly writing sample. *Degree Requirements:* M.Ed. 32 credit hours (7 research, 12 foundations, 13 applications and leadership in instructional technology); and action research project. M.S. 36 credit hours (16 research, 12 foundations, 8 applications and leadership in instructional technology); and thesis. Ph.D. 78 credit hours (minimum of 12 research, minimum of 15 foundations, additional core credits in conceptual, technical and advanced specialization areas, minimum of 12 dissertation);portfolio, and dissertation. *Faculty:* 9 full-time faculty leading technology; many more in curriculum and instruction. *Students:* M.Ed. and M.S.: 80. Ph.D.: 45. *Financial Assistance:* Assistantships and fellowships; study abroad support; annual conference attendance support. *Degrees awarded 2004:* Approximately 14 M.Ed./M.S and 2 Ph.D. Updated: 2/18/05.

University of Iowa. Division of Psychological and Quantitative Foundations. College of Education, Iowa City, IA 52242. (319) 335-5519. Fax: (319) 335-5386. Web site: http://www.uiowa.edu/~coe2/facstaff/salessi.htm. Stephen Alessi, 361 Lindquist Center. provost-office@uiowa.edu. *Specializations:* M.A. and Ph.D. with specializations in Training and Human Resources Development, Computer Applications, and Media Design and Production (MA only). *Features:* flexibility in planning to fit individual needs, backgrounds, and career goals. The program is interdisciplinary, involving courses within divisions of the College of Education, as well as in the schools of Business, Library Science, Radio and Television, Linguistics, and Psychology. *Admission Requirements:* MA: 2.8 undergraduate GPA, 500 GRE (verbal + quantitative), personal letter of interest. Ph.D.: master's degree, 1000 GRE (verbal + quantitative), 3.2 GPA on all previous graduate work for regular admission. Conditional admission may be granted. Teaching or relevant experience may be helpful. *Degree Requirements:* MA: 35 semester hours, 3.0 GPA, final project or thesis, comprehensive exam. Ph.D.: 90 semester hours, comprehensive exams, dissertation. *Faculty:* 4 full-time, 3 part-time. *Financial Assistance:* assistantships, grants, student loans, and scholarships.

University of Northern Iowa. Educational Technology Program. 618 Schinder Education Center, Cedar Falls, IA 50614-0606. (319) 273-3250. Fax: (319) 273-5886. Web site: http://ci.coe.uni.edu/edtech/index.html. Sharon E. Smaldino. Sharon.Smaldino@UNI.edu. *Specializations:* M.A. in Curriculum and Instruction: Educational Technology, M.A. in Performance and Training Technology. *Features:* The master's degrees are designed to meet the AECT/ECIT standards and are focused on addressing specific career choices. The Educational Technology master's is designed to prepare educators for a variety of professional positions in educational settings, including: school building level, school district level, vocational-technical school, community college, and university. The Performance and Training Technology master's is designed for persons planning to work in nonschool settings. Majors in this area will complete a basic core of coursework applicable to all preparing for work as media specialists, trainers in industry and business, or communications designers. Specific areas of interest will determine the supporting electives. Licensure as a teacher is not required for admission to either master's in Iowa. The bachelor's degree may be in any field. *Admission Requirements:* bachelor's degree, 3.0 undergraduate GPA, 500 TOEFL. *Degree Requirements:* 38 semester credits, optional thesis worth 6 credits or alternative research paper of project, comprehensive exam. *Faculty:* 4 full-time, 6 part-time. *Students:* 120. *Financial Assistance:* assistantships, grants, student loans, scholarships, student employment. *Degrees Awarded 2003:* 32.

Kansas

Emporia State University. Instructional Design and Technology (IDT). 1200 Commercial St., Campus Box 4037, Emporia, KS 66801. (620) 341-5829. Fax: (620) 341-5785. Web site: http://idt.emporia.edu. Dr. Marcus D. Childress, Chair. marcus.childress@emporia. edu. *Specializations:* distance education, Web-based education, corporate education. *Features:* All required courses available via the Internet. All forms and application materials available at the Web site: http://idt.emporia.edu. *Admission Requirements:* 2.75 undergrad. GPA; resume; two recommendations; writing competency. Two admission approval dates each year: September 15 (for spring semester admission) and February 15 (for fall semester admission). Only applicants with completed admission packets will be considered. An IDT admission committee will meet to review admission materials. Applicants will be admitted to the IDT graduate program based on the selection process. Those applicants who are not admitted may request that their names be placed on a waiting list for the next semester. *Degree Requirements:* 36 semester hours: 19 credits core, 6 credits research, 11 credits electives. *Faculty:* 5.5 full-time. *Students:* 10 full-time; 140 part-time. *Financial Assistance:* 4 GTA positions per year. *Degrees awarded 2004-05:* 43. Updated: 3/21/05.

Emporia State University. School of Library and Information Management. 1200 Commercial, P.O. Box 4025, Emporia, KS 66801. (800) 552-4770. Fax: (620) 341-5233. Web site: http://slim.emporia.edu. Daniel Roland, Director of Communications. sliminfo@emporia.edu. *Specializations:* Master's of Library Science (ALA accredited program); Master's in Legal Information Management, in partnership with the University of Kansas School of Law, 50 semester hours or 15-hour certificate. School Library Certification program, which includes 27 hours of the M.L.S. program; Ph.D. in Library and Information Management; B.S. in Information Resource Studies; Information Management Certificate: 18 hours of MLS curriculum; Library Services Certificates: 6 separate 12-hour programs of undergraduate work available for credit or noncredit. Areas include Information Sources and Services; Collection Management; Technology; Administration; Youth Services; and Generalist. *Features:* The Master of Library Science program is also delivered to satellite campus sites in Denver, Salt Lake City, Portland, Oregon. New programs tend to start every three years in each location. New programs include Denver, Summer 2004; Portland, Spring 2005, Salt Lake City, Fall 2005. *Admission Requirements:* Undergrad GPA of 3.0 or better for master's degrees, 3.5 or better for Ph.D. GRE score of 1,000 points combined in Verbal and Analytical sections for master's degrees, 1,100 for Ph.D. GRE can be waived for students already holding a graduate degree in which they earned a 3.75 GPA or better. Admission interview. *Degree Requirements:* M.L.S.: 42 semester hours. Ph.D.: total of 55-59 semester hours beyond the master's. *Faculty:* 10 full-time, 25 part-time. *Students:* 71 full-time, 297 part-time. *Financial Assistance:* assistantships, grants, student loans, scholarships, doctoral fellowships. *Degrees Awarded 2003:* 127 master's degrees, 2 doctoral degrees. Updated: 3/4/04.

Kansas State University. Educational Computing, Design, and Online Learning. 363 Bluemont Hall, Manhattan, KS 66506. (785) 532-7686. Fax: (785) 532-7304. Web site: http://coe.ksu.edu/ecdol. Dr. Diane McGrath. dmcgrath@ksu.edu. *Specializations:* M.S. in Curriculum and Instruction with a specialization in Educational Computing, Design, and Online Learning; Ph.D. and Ed.D. in Curriculum & Instruction with a specialization in Educational Computing, Design, and Online Learning. Master's program started in 1982; doctoral in 1987. *Features:* Coursework focuses on research, theory, practice, ethics, and design of learning environments. Students work in a project-based learning environment much of the time but also read, discuss, write, and present papers. The program does not focus on how to do particular applications, but rather on how and why one might use technology to improve the learning environment. Some courses focus on the K–12 learning environment (generally MS coursework) and others on lifelong learning. *Admission Requirements:* M.S.: B average in undergraduate work, one programming language, 590 TOEFL. Ed.D. and Ph.D.: B average in undergraduate and graduate work, one programming language, GRE or MAT, three letters of recommendation, experience or course in educational computing. *Degree Requirements:* M.S.: 33 semester hours (minimum of 15 in Educational Computing); thesis, internship, or practicum not required, but all three are possible. Capstone project or research is required. Ed.D.: 94 semester hours (minimum of 18 hours in Educational Computing or related area approved by committee, 16 hours dissertation research, 12 hours internship); thesis. Ph.D.: 90 semester hours (minimum of 21 hours in Educational Computing, Design, and Online Learning or related area approved by committee, 30 hours for dissertation research); thesis; internship or practicum not required but available. *Faculty:* 1 full-time, 2 part-time, other faculty available to serve on committees. *Students:* M.S., 0 full-time, est. 30 part-time; doctoral, 20 full-time, 10 part-time. *Financial Assistance:* 2–3 assistantships typically go to people associated with the program; 3 assistantships on a related grant project; other assistantships sometimes available in other departments. *Degrees awarded 2004:* 5 Ph.Ds. Updated: 3/14/05.

Kentucky

University of Louisville. College of Education and Human Development. Belknap Campus, Louisville, KY 40292. (502) 852-6667. Fax: (502) 852-4563. Web site: http://www.louisville.edu/edu. Carolyn Rude-Parkins, Chair of Leadership, Foundations, Human Resource Education. cparkins@louisville.edu. *Specializations:* Master's in Instructional Technology (appropriate for K–12 teacher and for trainers / adult educators), post-master's/Rank 1 in Instructional Technology (K–12 teachers). Doctoral strand in Instructional Technology Leadership. Technology Leadership Institute Cohort for Jefferson County Schools offered onsite. *Features:* Appropriate for business or school audiences. Program is based on ISTE and ASTD standards, as well as Kentucky Experienced Teacher Standards. *Admission Requirements:* 2.75 GPA, 800 GRE, 2 letters of recommendation, application fee. *Degree Requirements:* 30 semester hours, internship. *Faculty:* 2 full-time, 6 part-time. *Students:* 75 part-time students. *Financial Assistance:* graduate assistantships. *Degrees Awarded 2003:* 20 M.Ed. Updated: 3/11/05.

Louisiana

Louisiana State University. School of Library and Information Science. 267 Coates Hall, Baton Rouge, LA 70803. (225) 578-3158. Fax: (225) 578-4581. Web site: http://slis.lsu.edu. Beth Paskoff, Dean, Assoc. Prof., School of Library and Information Science. bpaskoff@lsu.edu. *Specializations:* MLIS, CLIS (post-master's certificate), Louisiana School Library Certification. An advanced certificate program is available. *Features:* none. *Admission Requirements:* bachelor's degree, with 3.00 average. *Degree Requirements:* MLIS: 40 hours, comprehensive exam, one semester full-time residence, completion of degree program in five years. *Faculty:* 10 full-time. *Students:* 84 full-time, 86 part-time. *Financial Assistance:* A large number of graduate assistantships are available to qualified students. *Degrees Awarded 2003:* 90. Updated: 3/28/05.

Maryland

The Johns Hopkins University. Graduate Division of Education, Technology for Educators Program. Columbia Gateway Park, 6740 Alexander Bell Drive, Columbia, MD 21046. (410) 309-9537. Fax: (410) 312-3868. Web site: http://www.spsbe.jhu.edu. Dr. Linda

Tsantis, Program Coordinator; Dr. John Castellani, Program Coordinator. tsantis@jhu.edu. *Specializations:* The Department of Technology for Education offers programs leading to the M.S. degree in Education, the M.S. in Special Education, and four specialized advanced Graduate Certificates: Technology for Multimedia and Internet-Based Instruction; Instructional Technology for Online Professional Development and Training; Data-Driven Decision-Making; and Assistive Technology for Communication and Social Interaction. *Features:* Focuses on training educators to become decision makers and leaders in the use of technology, with competencies in the design, development, and application of emerging technologies for teaching and learning. Incorporates basic elements that take into account the needs of adult learners, the constantly changing nature of technology, and the need for schools and universities to work together for schoolwide change. The Center for Technology in Education works in partnership with the graduate program linking research and teaching of the University with the leadership and policy direction of the Maryland State Department of Education. *Admission Requirements:* bachelor's degree with strong background in teaching, curriculum and instruction, special education, or a related service field. *Degree Requirements:* 36 Credit hour part-time program, Electronic Portfolio in place of comprehensive exams. *Faculty:* 2 full-time, 30 part-time. *Students:* 300 part-time. *Financial Assistance:* grants, student loans, scholarships. *Degrees Awarded 2003:* 48. Updated: 6/16/03.

McDaniel College (formerly Western Maryland College). Department of Education,. 2 College Hill, Westminster, MD 21157. (410) 857-2507. Fax: (410) 857-2515. Web site: http://www.mcdaniel.edu. Dr. Ramona N. Kerby, Coord., School Library Media Program, Dept. of Education. rkerby@mcdaniel.edu. *Specializations:* M.S. in Education with an emphasis in School Library Media. *Features:* School librarianship. *Admission Requirements:* 3.0 Undergraduate GPA, 3 reference checklist forms from principal and other school personnel, acceptable application essay, acceptable Praxis test scores. *Degree Requirements:* 34 credit hours, including professional digital portfolio. *Faculty:* 1 full-time, 7 part-time. *Students:* 140, most part-time. Updated: 2/18/05.

Towson University. College of Education. Hawkins Hall, Towson, MD 21252. (410) 704-6268. Fax: (410) 704-4227. Web site: http://wwwnew.towson.edu/coe/rset/insttech/. Dr. David R. Wizer, Associate Professor. Dept.: Reading, Special Education, & Instructional Technology. wizer@towson.edu. *Specializations:* M.S. degrees in Instructional Development, Educational Technology and School Library Media. Ed. D. degrees in Instructional Technology. *Features:* Excellent labs. Strong practical hands-on classes. Focus of MS program: Students produce useful multimedia projects for use in their teaching and training. Many group activities within courses. Innovative Ed. D. program with online hybrid courses and strong mix of theory and practical discussions. *Admission Requirements:* bachelor's degree from accredited institution with 3.0 GPA. (Conditional admission granted for many applicants with a GPA over 2.75.) *Degree Requirements:* MS degree is 36 graduate semester hours without thesis. Ed. D. is 63 hours beyond the MS degree. *Faculty:* 10 full-time, 5 adjunct. *Students:* 20 full-time, 190 part-time [approximately]. *Financial Assistance:* graduate assistantships, work study, scholarships, loans. *Degrees Awarded 2003:* 25 in master's degree program. Updated: 2/21/05.

University of Maryland. College of Library and Information Services. 4105 Hornbake Library Bldg., South Wing, College Park, MD 20742-4345. (301) 405-2038. Fax: (301) 314-9145. Ann Prentice, Dean and Program Chair. ap57@umail.umd.edu. *Specializations:* Master's of Library Science, including specialization in School Library Media; doctorate in Library and Information Services including specialization in Educational Technology/Instructional Communication. *Features:* Program is broadly conceived and interdisciplinary in nature, using the resources of the entire campus. The student and the advisor design a program of study and research to fit the student's background, interests, and professional objectives. Students prepare for careers in teaching and research in information science and librarianship and elect concentrations including Educational Technology and Instructional

Communication. *Admission Requirements:* doctoral: bachelor's degree (the majority of doctoral students enter with master's degrees in Library Science, Educational Technology, or other relevant disciplines), GRE general tests, three letters of recommendation, statement of purpose. Interviews required when feasible for doctoral applicants. *Degree Requirements:* M.L.S.: 36 semester hours; thesis optional. *Faculty:* 15 full-time, 8 part-time. *Students:* master's, 106 full-time, 149 part-time; doctoral, 5 full-time, 11 part-time. *Financial Assistance:* assistantships, grants, student loans, scholarships, fellowships.

University of Maryland Baltimore County (UMBC). Department of Education. 1000 Hilltop Circle, Baltimore, MD 21250. (410) 455-2310. Fax: (410) 455-3986. Web site: http://www.research.umbc.edu/~eholly/ceduc/isd/. Greg Williams, Ed.D, Program Director. isd-td@umbc.edu. *Specializations:* M.A. degrees in School Instructional Systems, Post-Baccalaureate Teacher Certification, Training in Business and Industry, Experienced Teacher—Advanced Degree, ESOL/Bilingual. *Features:* Programs are configured with evening courses to accommodate students who are changing careers. Maryland teacher certification is earned two-thirds of the way through the postbaccalaureate program. *Admission Requirements:* 3.0 undergraduate GPA, GRE scores. *Degree Requirements:* 36 semester hours (including 18 in systems development for each program); internship. *Faculty:* 18 full-time, 25 part-time. *Students:* 59 full-time, 254 part-time. *Financial Assistance:* assistantships, scholarships. *Degrees Awarded 2003:* 75. Updated: 3/11/05.

Massachusetts

Boston University. School of Education. Two Sherborn St., Boston, MA 02215-1605. (617) 353-3181. Fax:(617) 353-3924. Web site: http://Web.bu.edu/EDUCATION. David B. Whittier, Asst. Professor and Coord., Program in Educational Media and Technology. whittier@bu.edu. *Specializations:* Ed.M., CAGS (Certificate of Advanced Graduate Study) in Educational Media and Technology; Ed.D. in Curriculum and Teaching, Specializing in Educational Media and Technology; preparation for Massachusetts public school certificates as Instructional Technology Specialist. *Features:* The master's program prepares graduates for professional careers as educators, instructional designers, developers of educational materials, and managers of the human and technology-based resources necessary to support education and training with technology. Graduates are employed in K–12 schools, higher education, industry, medicine, government, and publishing. Students come to the program from many backgrounds and with a wide range of professional goals. The doctoral program sets the study of Educational Media and Technology within the context of education and educational research in general, and curriculum and teaching in particular. In addition to advanced work in the field of Educational Media and Technology, students examine and conduct research and study the history of educational thought and practice relating to teaching and learning. Graduates make careers in education as professors and researchers, technology directors and managers, and as developers of technology-based materials and systems. Graduates also make careers in medicine, government, business, and industry as instructional designers, program developers, project managers, and training directors. Graduates who work in both educational and noneducational organizations are often responsible for managing the human and technological resources required to create learning experiences that include the development and delivery of technology-based materials and distance education. *Admission Requirements:* Ed.M.: recommendations, minimum 2.7 undergraduate GPA, graduate test scores are required and either the GRE or MAT must be completed within past five years. CAGs: Ed.M., recommendations, 2.7 undergraduate GPA, graduate test scores are required and either the GRE or MAT must be completed within past five years. Ed.D.: 3 letters of recommendation, MAT or GRE scores, transcripts, writing samples, statement of goals and qualifications, analytical essay, minimum 2.7 GPA. *Degree Requirements:* Ed.M.: 36 credit hours (including 24 hours from required core curriculum, 12 from electives). CAGs: 32 credits beyond Ed.M., one of which must be a curriculum and teaching course and a mini-comprehensive exam. Ed.D.: 60 credit hours of courses in Educational Media and Technology, curriculum and teaching, and educational thought and practice with comprehensive exams; coursework and apprenticeship in research; dissertation. *Faculty:* 1 full-time, 1 half-time, 10 part-time. *Students:* 20 full-time, 25 part-time. *Financial Assistance:* U.S. Government sponsored work study, assistantships, grants, student loans, scholarships. *Degrees Awarded 2003:* Ed.M. 17; Ed.D. 2.

Bridgewater State College. Library Media Program. Hart Hall, Rm. 219, Bridgewater, MA 02325. (508) 697-1320. Fax: (508) 697-1771. Web site: http://www.bridgew.edu. Mary Frances Zilonis, Coord., Library Media Program. Specialization: M.Ed. in Library Media Studies. fzilonis@bridgew.edu. *Features:* This program heavily emphasizes teaching and technology. *Degree Requirements:* 39 semester hours; comprehensive exam. *Faculty:* 2 full-time, 6 part-time. *Students:* 58 in degree program, 30 nondegree. *Financial Assistance:* Graduate assistantships, graduate internships.

Fitchburg State College. Division of Graduate and Continuing Education. 160 Pearl Street, Fitchburg, MA 01420. (978) 665-3544. Fax: (978) 665-3055. Web site: http://www.fsc.edu. Dr. Randy Howe, Chair. rhowe@fsc.edu. *Specializations:* M.S. in Communications Media with specializations in Applied Communication, Instructional Technology, and Library Media. *Features:* Collaborating with professionals working in the field both for organizations and as independent producers, Fitchburg offers a unique M.S. program. The objective of the Master of Science in Communications/Media Degree Programs is to develop in candidates the knowledge and skills for the effective implementation of communication within business, industry, government, not-for-profit agencies, health services, and education. *Admission Requirements:* MAT or GRE scores, official transcript(s) of a baccalaureate degree, two or more years of experience in communications or media, department interview and portfolio presentation, three letters of recommendation. *Degree Requirements:* 36 semester credit hours. *Faculty:* 1 full-time, 7 part-time. *Students:* 48 part-time. *Financial Assistance:* assistantships, student loans, scholarships. *Degrees Awarded 2003:* 7 MS in Communications/Media. Updated: 4/6/05.

Harvard University. Graduate School of Education. Appian Way, Cambridge, MA 02138. (617) 495-3541. Fax: (617) 495-3626. Web site: http://www.gse.harvard.edu/tie. Joseph Blatt, director, Technology in Education Program; Kristen DeAmicis, program coordinator, Technology in Education Program. deamickr@gse.harvard.edu. *Specializations:* Available degrees: Ed.M. in Technology in Education; Certificate of Advanced Study in Technology in Education; Ed.D. in Learning and Teaching, with research focus in technology in education. *Features:* Courses in design, technology policy and leadership, research and evaluation. Access to other courses throughout Harvard University, and at MIT. Internship opportunities. *Admission Requirements:* bachelor's degree, MAT or GRE scores, 600 TOEFL, 3 recommendations. Students interested in further information about the TIE Program should visit the Web site (URL above), which includes a link to the Harvard Graduate School of Education online application. *Degree Requirements:* 32 semester credits. *Faculty:* 5 full-time, 4 part-time. *Students:* approx. 55: 45 full-time, 10 part-time. *Financial Assistance:* Determined by Harvard policies. *Degrees Awarded 2003:* 45. Updated: 2/18/05.

Lesley University. Technology In Education. 29 Everett St., Cambridge, MA 02138-2790. (617) 349-8419. Fax: (617) 349-8169. Web site: http://www.lesley.edu/soe/111tech.html. Dr. Isa Kaftal Zimmerman, Division Director. ikzimmer@lesley.edu. *Specializations:* M.Ed. in Technology in Education GAGS in Technology in Education. Ph.D. in Educational Studies with specialization in Technology in Education. *Features:* M.Ed. program is offered off-campus at 70+ sites in 21 states; contact (617) 349-8311 for information. The degree is also offered completely online. Contact Maureen Yoder, myoder@lesley.edu, or (617) 348-8421 for information. Or check our Web site (URL above). *Admission Requirements:* Completed bachelor's degree. *Degree Requirements:* M.Ed.: 33 semester hours in technology, integrative final project in lieu of thesis, no internship or practicum. C.A.G.S.:

36 semester hours. Ph.D. requirements available on request. *Faculty:* 12 full-time and 2 part-time core, approximately 200 part-time adjuncts on the Master's and doctorate levels. *Students:* 1500+ part-time. Information available from Admissions Office. *Degrees Awarded April 2004 to March 2005:* 475. Updated: 3/30/05.

Simmons College. Graduate School of Library and Information Science. 300 The Fenway, Boston, MA 02115-5898. (617) 521-2800. Fax: (617) 521-3192. Web site: http://www.simmons.edu/gslis/. Dr. James C. Baughman, Prof. jbaughman@simmons. edu. *Specializations:* M.S. Dual degrees: M.L.S./M.A. in Education (for School Library Media Specialists); M.L.S./M.A. in History (Archives Management Program). A Doctor of Arts in Administration is also offered. *Features:* The program prepares individuals for a variety of careers, media technology emphasis being only one. There are special programs for School Library Media Specialist and Archives Management with strengths in Information Science/Systems, Media Management. *Admission Requirements:* B.A. or B.S. degree with 3.0 GPA, statement, three letters of reference. *Degree Requirements:* 36 semester hours. *Faculty:* 18 full-time. *Students:* 104 full-time, 591 part-time. *Financial Aid:* assistantships, grants, student loans, scholarships. *Degrees Awarded in 2004:* 230. Updated: 2/18/05.

University of Massachusetts—Boston. Graduate College of Education. 100 Morrissey Blvd, Boston, MA 02125. (617) 287-5980. Fax: (617) 287-7664. Web site: http://www. umb.edu. Donald D. Babcock, Graduate Program Dir. babcock@umbsky.cc.umb.edu. *Specializations:* M.Ed. in Instructional Design. *Admission Requirements:* MAT or previous master's degree, goal statement, three letters of recommendation, resume, interview. *Degree Requirements:* 36 semester hours, thesis or project. *Faculty:* 1 full-time, 9 part-time. *Students:* 8 full-time, 102 part-time. *Financial Assistance:* graduate assistantships providing tuition plus stipend.

University of Massachusetts—Lowell. Graduate School of Education. 255 Princeton Street, North Chelmsford, MA 01863. (508) 934-4601. Fax (508) 934-3005. Web site: http://gse.uml.edu/. Vera Ossen, Coordinator, Graduate Program in Teaching. vera_ossen@uml.edu. *Specializations:* M.Ed., CAGS, and Ed.D. concentrations in Educational Technology may be pursued in the context of any degree program area (Leadership, Administration and Policy; Curriculum and Instruction; Math and Science Education; Reading, Language Arts and Literacy). The M.Ed. program in Curriculum and Instruction has a specialization strand in educational technology. The Certificate of Advanced Graduate Study (CAGS), equivalent to 30 credits beyond a M.Ed., is also offered. *Features:* As part of the U Mass Lowell "CyberEd" online learning initiative, a new Web-based M.Ed./state certification program in educational administration was launched in 2001 and is now in full swing. The school also manages an extensive video network that links the university with other campuses in the state higher education system and with area public schools. Technology is heavily infused into the teacher preparation and school support programs, where new initiatives have been supported by grants from several federal and non-federal sources. *Admission Requirements:* For admission at the master's level, a bachelor's degree from an accredited institution in an academic discipline is required, along with a completed application form, recent GRE scores, a narrative statement of purpose, and three written recommendations. Additional admission requirements and conditions are described in the UMass Lowell Graduate Catalog. *Degree Requirements:* M.Ed. 30 credits beyond bachelor's; Ed.D. 60 credits beyond master's plus dissertation based on original research and demonstration of comprehensive mastery in relevant fields of inquiry. *Faculty:* Various full-time and part-time faculty members teach educational technology courses in the school. *Students:* FTE approximately 500. *Financial Assistance:* Assistantships; work-study; student loans; occasional scholarships. *Degrees Awarded 2003:* Approximately 75. Updated: 7/7/04.

Michigan

Eastern Michigan University. Teacher Education. 313 John W. Porter Building, Ypsilanti, MI 48197. (734) 487-3260. Fax: (734) 487-2101. Web site: http://www. emich.edu. Toni Stokes Jones, Ph.D., Assistant Professor/Graduate Coordinator. tsjones@ online.emich.edu. *Specializations:* M.A. in Educational Psychology with concentration in Educational Technology. The mission of this program is to prepare professionals who are capable of facilitating student learning in a variety of settings. The program is designed to provide students with both the knowledge base and the application skills that are required to use technology effectively in education. Focusing on the design, development, utilization, management and evaluation of instructional systems moves us toward achieving this mission. Students who complete the educational technology concentration will be able to (a) provide a rationale for using technology in the educational process; (b) identify contributions of major leaders in the field of educational media technology and instructional theory, and the impact that each leader has had on the field; (c) assess current trends in the area of educational media technology and relate the trends to past events and future implications; (d) integrate technology into instructional programs; (e) teach the operation and various uses of educational technology in instruction; (f) act as consultants/facilitators in educational media technology; (g) design and develop instructional products to meet specified needs; and (h) evaluate the effectiveness of instructional materials and systems. *Features:* Courses in our 30 credit hour Educational Media and Technology (EDMT) program include technology and the reflective teacher, technology and student-centered learning, technology enhanced learning environments, issues and emerging technologies, instructional design, internet for educators, advanced technologies, psychology of the adult learning, principles of classroom learning, curriculum foundations, research seminar and seminar in educational technology. Effective Spring 2003, all of the EDMT courses will be taught online. In some EDMT courses, students may be asked to come to campus only 3 times during the semester. Students who do not want to receive a master's degree can apply for admission to our 18-credit-hour Educational Media and Technology certificate. The EDMT courses for the certificate are also offered online. *Admission Requirements:* Individuals seeking admission to this program must:

1. comply with the Graduates School admission requirements.

2. score 550 or better on the TOEFL and 5 or better on TWE, if a nonnative speaker of English.

3. have a 2.75 undergraduate grade point average, or a 3.30 grade point average in 12 hours or more of work in a master's program.

4. solicit three letters of reference.

5. submit a statement of professional goals.

Degree Requirements: To graduate, each student is expected to:

1. complete all work on an approved program of study (30 semester hours).

2. maintain a B (3.0 GPA) average or better on coursework taken within the program.

3. get a recommendation from the faculty adviser.

4. fill out an application for graduation and obtain the advisers recommendation.

5. meet all other requirements for a master's degree adopted by the Graduate School of Eastern Michigan University.

6. complete a culminating experience (research, instructional development or evaluation project) as determined by the student and faculty adviser.

Faculty: 5 full-time; 3 part-time. *Students:* 75. *Financial Assistance:* graduate assistantship. *Degrees Awarded 2003:* 10. Updated: 3/31/03. Toni Stokes Jones, toni.jones@emich.edu

Michigan State University. College of Education. 513E Erickson, East Lansing, MI 48824. (517) 353-0637. Fax: (517) 353-6393. Web site: http://edutech.educ.msu.edu/master's /TLTEL.htm. Susan Way. ways@msu.edu. *Specializations:* M.A. in Educational Technology with Learning, Design and Technology specialization. *Features:* Extensive opportunities to work with faculty in designing online courses and online learning environments. Several courses available online. *Admission Requirements:* bachelor's degree, two letters of recommendation, goal statement. *Degree Requirements:* 30 semester hours, Web-based portfolio. *Faculty:* 14 full-time. *Students:* approximately 60. *Financial Assistance:* some assistantships for highly qualified students. *Degrees Awarded 2003:* 6. Updated: 3/21/03.

University of Michigan. Department of Educational Studies. 610 East University, Ann Arbor, MI 48109-1259. (734) 763-7500. Fax: (734) 615-1290. Web site: http://www.soe. umich.edu/learningtechnologies/. Barry J. Fishman. fishman@umich.edu. *Specializations:* M.A., M.S., Ph.D. in Learning Technologies. *Features:* The Learning Technologies Program at the University of Michigan integrates the study of technology with a focus in a substantive content area. A unique aspect of the program is that your learning and research will engage you in real-world educational contexts. You will find that understanding issues related to a specific content area provides an essential context for meaningful research in learning. Your understanding of technology, school contexts, and a content area will place you among the leaders who design and conduct research on advanced technological systems that change education and schooling. The doctoral specialization in Learning Technologies must be taken in conjunction with a substantive concentration designed in consultation with your advisor. Current active concentrations include: Science, Literacy, Culture and Gender, Teacher Education, Design and Human-Computer Interaction, Policy, and Social Studies. Other areas are possible. The Master's Degree in Learning Technologies at the University of Michigan prepares professionals for leadership roles in the design, development, implementation, and research of powerful technologies to enhance learning. Our approach to design links current knowledge and research about how people learn with technological tools that enable new means of organizing and evaluating learning environments. Course and project work reflects the latest knowledge and practice in learning, teaching, and technology. Core courses prepare students to use current understandings about learning theory, design principles, research methodologies, and evaluation strategies in educational settings ranging from classrooms to Web-based and distributed learning environments. Faculty work with students to shape programs that meet individual interests. Practical experience is offered through internships with area educational institutions. *Admission Requirements:* GRE, B.A. for M.A., M.S., or Ph.D.; TOEFL for students from countries where English is not the primary language. *Degree Requirements:* M.A. and M.S.: 30 hours beyond B.A. Ph.D.: 60 hours beyond B.A. or 30 hours beyond master's plus research paper/qualifying examination, and dissertation. *Faculty:* 3 full-time, 6 part-time. *Students:* 35 full-time, 1 part-time. *Financial Assistance:* assistantships, grants, student loans, scholarships, internships. *Degrees Awarded 2003:* 10. Updated: 2/21/05.

Wayne State University. 381 Education, Detroit, MI 48202. (313) 577-1728. Fax: (313) 577-1693. Web site: http://www.coe.wayne.edu/InstructionalTechnology. Rita C. Richey, Prof., Program Coord., Instructional Technology Programs, Div. of Administrative and Organizational Studies, College of Education. rrichey@coe.wayne.edu. *Specializations:* M.Ed. degrees in Performance Improvement and Training, K–12 Educational Technology, and Interactive Technologies. Ed.D. and Ph.D. programs to prepare individuals for leadership in business, industry, health care, and the K–12 school setting as instructional design and development specialists; media or learning resources managers or consultants; specialists in instructional video; and computer-assisted instruction and multimedia specialists. The school also offers a six-year specialist degree program in Instructional Technology. *Features:* Guided experiences in instructional design and development activities in business and industry are available. *Admission Requirements:* Ph.D.: master's degree, 3.5 GPA, GRE, MAT, strong professional recommendations, interview. *Degree Requirements:* M.Ed.: 36 semester hours, including required project; internship recommended. *Faculty:* 6 full-time, 5 part-time. *Students:* 525 M.Ed.; 95 doctoral, most part-time. *Financial Assistance:* student loans, scholarships, and paid internships.

Minnesota

Minnesota State University. Educational Leadership, College of Education. MSU 313 Armstrong Hall, Mankato, MN 56001. (507) 389-1965. Fax: (507) 389-5751. Web site: http://www.coled.mnsu.edu/coled_new_home/coe_new.htm. Dr. P. Gushwa. prudence. gushwa@mnsu.edu. *Specializations:* M.S. in Educational Technology with three tracks; M.S. in Library Media Specialist; SP in Library Media Education. *Features:* Educational Technology certificates, Licensure program in Library Media. *Admission Requirements:* bachelor's degree, 2.75/4.0 for last 2 years of undergraduate work. *Degree Requirements:* 32 semester hour credits, comprehensive exam. *Faculty:* 4 full-time. *Students:* About 75. *Financial Assistance:* Contact Financial Aid Office. Updated: 5/28/03.

St. Cloud State University. College of Education, St. Cloud, MN 56301-4498. (612) 255-2022. Fax: (612) 255-4778. John G. Berling, Prof., Dir., Center for Information Media. jberling@tigger.stcloud.msus.edu. *Specializations:* master's degrees in Information Technologies, Educational Media, and Human Resources Development/Training. A Specialist degree is also offered. *Admission Requirements:* acceptance to Graduate School, written preliminary examination, interview. *Degree Requirements:* master's: 51 quarter hours with thesis; 54 quarter hours, Plan B; 57 quarter hours, portfolio; 200-hour practicum is required for media generalist licensure. Coursework applies to Educational Media Master's program. *Faculty:* 7 full-time. *Students:* 15 full-time, 150 part-time. *Financial Assistance:* assistantships and scholarships.

Walden University. 155 5th Avenue South, Minneapolis, MN 55401. (800) 444-6795. Web site: http://www.waldenu.edu; http://www.waldenu.edu/ecti/ecti.html. Dr. Gwen Hillesheim, Chair. www@waldenu.edu or info@waldenu.edu. *Specializations:* M.S. in Educational Change and Technology Innovation. Ph.D. in Education in Learning and Teaching with specialization in Educational Technology. In 1998 a specialization in Distance Learning will be added. In addition, there is a generalist Ph.D. in Education in which students may choose and design their own areas of specialization. *Features:* delivered primarily on-line. *Admission Requirements:* accredited bachelor's. Ph.D.: accredited master's, goal statement, letters of recommendation. *Degree Requirements:* master's: 45 credit curriculum, 2 brief residencies, master's project. *Faculty:* 18 part-time. *Students:* 50 full-time, 53 part-time in master's program. *Financial Assistance:* student loans, 3 fellowships with annual review.

Missouri

Fontbonne College. 6800 Wydown Blvd., St. Louis, MO 63105. (314) 889-1497. Fax: (314) 889-1451. Dr. Mary K. Abkemeier, Chair. mabkemei@fontbonne.edu. *Specializations:* M.S. in Computer Education. *Features:* small classes and coursework immediately applicable to the classroom. *Admission Requirements:* 2.5 undergraduate GPA, 3 letters of recommendation. *Degree Requirements:* 33 semester hours, 3.0 GPA. *Faculty:* 2 full-time, 12 part-time. *Students:* 4 full-time, 90 part-time. *Financial Assistance:* grants.

Northwest Missouri State University. Department of Computer Science/Information Systems. 800 University Ave., Maryville, MO 64468. (660) 562-1600. Fax: (660) 562-1963. Web site: http://www.nwmissouri.edu/~csis. Dr. Phillip Heeler, Chairperson. pheeler@ mail.nwmissouri.edu. *Specializations:* M.S.Ed. in Instructional Technology. Certificate program in Instructional Technology. *Features:* These degrees are designed for industry trainers and computer educators at the elementary, middle school, high school, and junior college level. *Admission Requirements:* 3.0 undergraduate GPA, 700 GRE (V+Q). *Degree Requirements:* 32 semester hours of graduate courses in computer science education and instructional technology courses. Fifteen hours of computer education and instructional technology courses for the Certificate. *Faculty:* 12 full-time. *Students:* 5 full-time, 20 part-time. *Financial Assistance:* assistantships, grants, student loans, and scholarships. *Degrees Awarded 2003:* 10. Updated: 2/18/05.

University of Missouri—Columbia. College of Education. 303 Townsend Hall, Columbia, MO 65211. (573) 882-4546. Fax: (573) 884-2917. Web site: http://sislt.missouri.edu. John Wedman. wedmanj@missouri.edu. *Specializations:* The Educational Technology program takes a theory-based approach to designing, developing, implementing, and researching computer-mediated environments to support human activity. We seek individuals who are committed to life-long learning and who aspire to use advanced technology to improve human learning and performance. Graduates of the program will find opportunities to use their knowledge and competencies as classroom teachers, media specialists, district technology specialists and coordinators, designers and developers of technology-based learning and information systems, training specialists for businesses, medical settings, and public institutions, as well as other creative positions.

The curriculum has three focus areas: Technology in Schools; Network Learning Systems; Designing and Developing Learning Systems; with coursework tailored to each focus area. *Features:* Entire master's program is available online. Visit our Web site at: MUEdTech.Missouri.edu. *Admission Requirements:* master's: bachelor's degree, 1500 GRE score. Ph.D.: 3.2 graduate GPA, 1500 GRE, letter of recommendation, statement of purpose. *Degree Requirements:* Minimum of 30–35 graduate credit hours required for the degree. Minimum of 15 credit hours of upper division (400/9000) coursework. Maximum of 6 hours of transfer credit. *Faculty:* 9 Full time; ~10 part-time. *Students:* master's ~200; Ph.D. 55. *Financial Assistance:* master's: assistantships, grants, student loans, scholarships. Ph.D.: graduate assistantships with tuition waivers; numerous academic scholarships ranging from $200 to $18,000. *Degrees Awarded 2003:* 55.

University of Missouri—Columbia. School of Information Science & Learning Technologies. 303 Townsend Hall, Columbia, MO 65211. (573) 882-4546. Fax: (573) 884-2917. Web site: http://www.coe.missouri.edu/~sislt. John Wedman. wedmanj@missouri.edu. *Specializations:* The Educational Technology emphasis area prepares educators and technologists for excellence and leadership in the design, development, and implementation of technology in education, training, and performance support. The program offers three focus areas: Technology in Schools, Networked Learning Systems, and Training Design and Development Each focus area has its own set of competencies, coursework, and processes. *Features:* All three focus areas are available online via the Internet or on the MU campus. The Technology in Schools focus area is based on the ISTE competencies and culminates in an online portfolio based on these competencies. Several courses are augmented by technical resources developed at MU, including a technology integration knowledge repository and online collaboration tools. The Networked Learning Systems focus area offers a truly challenging and innovative set of technical learning experiences. Students have opportunities to work on large-scale software development projects, acquiring valuable experience and broadening their skill-set. The Digital Media ZONE supports anytime/anywhere technical skill development.

The Training and Development focus area links to business, military, and government contexts. The curriculum is offered by faculty with extensive experience in these contexts and is grounded in the problems and processes of today's workplace. Ed.S. and Ph.D. programs are also available. *Admission Requirements:* bachelor's degree with 3.0 in last 60 credit hours of coursework. GRE (V>500; A>500; W>3.5); TOEFL of 540 (207 computer-based test) (if native language is not English); letters of reference. *Degree Requirements:* master's: 30–34 credit hours; 15 hours at 400 level. Specific course requirements vary by focus area. *Faculty:* 8 full-time; 20 part-time. *Students:* 30 full-time; 210 part-time. *Financial Assistance:* Numerous graduate assistantships are available. Assistantships include stipend and tuition waiver. *Degrees Awarded 2003:* 72. Updated: 3/12/05.

Southwest Missouri State University. School of Teacher Education. 901 S. National, Springfield, MO 65804. (417) 836-5280. Fax: (417) 836-6252. Web site: http://www. smsu.edu/. Dr. Roger Tipling. RogerTipling@smsu.edu. *Specializations:* M.S. in Education. Emphasis areas: Technology Coordinator strand; Building Level Technology Specialist strand; School Library Media Specialist strand; Business/Industrial/Medical strand. *Features:* Production, Administration, Instructional Design, Selection and Utilization, Networking, Web Based Education, Hardware and Software Troubleshooting, Library Certification Courses, Building Level Technology Specialist Certificate Research Practicum. *Admission Requirements:* Graduate College Admission Standards, three letters of reference, autobiography, *Degree Requirements:* Minimum of 33 hrs. in Instructional Design and Technology, major research paper or project, Comprehensive Exam, practicum (dependent upon emphasis). *Faculty:* Three full-time, two part-time. *Students:* Five to ten full-time students, more than 50 part-time students. *Financial Assistance:* Graduate assistantships. *Degrees Awarded 2003:* 6.

Webster University. Learning and Communication Arts, College of Education, St. Louis, MO 63119. (314) 968-7490. Fax: (314) 968-7118. Web site: http://www.Webster.edu/gradcatalog/ed_tech.html. Dr. Phyllis Wilkinson. wilkinsp@Webster.edu. *Specializations:* master's degree (M.A.T.); State Certification in Media Technology is a program option. *Admission Requirements:* bachelor's degree with 2.5 GPA *Degree Requirements:* 33 semester hours (including 24 in media); internship required. *Faculty:* 5. *Students:* 7 full-time, 28 part-time. *Financial Assistance:* partial scholarships, minority scholarships, government loans, and limited state aid. Updated: 5/28/03.

Montana

University of Montana. School of Education. 32 Campus Drive, Missoula, MT 59812. (406) 243-5785. Fax: (406) 243-4908. Web site: http://www.umt.edu. Dr. Carolyn Lott, Professor of Library/Media. carolyn.lott@mso.umt.edu. *Specializations:* M.Ed. and Specialist degrees; K–12 School Library Media specialization with School Library Media Certification endorsement. *Features:* 22 of 25 credits online. Combined program with University of Montana-Western in Dilon, MT. *Admission Requirements:* (both degrees): GRE, letters of recommendation, 2.5 GPA *Degree Requirements:* M.Ed.: 37 semester credit hours (18 overlap with library media endorsement). Specialist: 28 semester hours (18 overlap). *Faculty:* 2 full-time. *Students:* 5 full-time, 20 part-time. *Financial Assistance:* assistantships; contact the University of Montana Financial Aid Office. *Degrees Awarded 2003:* 1. Updated: 2/27/03.

Nebraska

University of Nebraska—Kearney. Teacher Education. 905 West 25th Street, Kearney, NE 68849-5540. (308) 865-8833. Fax: (308) 865-8097. Web site: http://www.unk.edu/departments/pte. Dr. Scott Fredrickson, Professor and Chair of the Instructional Technology Graduate Program. fredricksons@unk.edu. *Specializations:* M.S.ED in Instructional Technology, M.S.ED in Educational Media. *Features:* Four emphasis areas—Instructional Technology; Multimedia Development; Educational Media; Assistive Technology. *Admis-*

sion Requirements: M.S. GRE (or electronic portfolio meeting dept. requirements), acceptance into graduate school, approval of Instructional Technology Committee *Degree Requirements:* M.S.: 36 credit hours, Instructional technology project or field study. *Faculty:* 5 full-time, 10 part-time. *Students:* 130 full-time equivalent. *Financial Assistance:* assistantships, grants, student loans. *Degrees Awarded 2004:* 30. Updated: 3/29/05.

University of Nebraska—Omaha. Department of Teacher Education. College of Education, Kayser Hall 208D, Omaha, NE 68182. (402) 554-2119. Fax: (402) 554-2125. Web site: http://www.unomaha.edu/~edmedia. Dr. R. J. Pasco. rpasco@mail.unomaha.edu. *Specializations:* Library Media Endorsement (undergraduate and graduate); M.S. in Secondary and Elementary Education, M.A. in Secondary and Elementary Education, both with Library Media concentration; M.S. in Reading with Library Media concentration; M.S. in Educational Administration, with Library Media concentration; Master's in Library Science Program (Cooperative program with University of Missouri at Columbia); Instructional Technology Certificate—Graduate program only. *Features:* Library Media Endorsement (Undergraduate and Graduate); M.S. in Secondary and Elementary Education, M.A. in Secondary and Elementary Education, both with Library Media concentration; M.S. in Reading with Library Media concentration; M.S. in Educational Administration, with Educational Media concentration; Master's in Library Science Program (Cooperative program with University of Missouri at Columbia); Instructional Technology Certificate—Graduate program only. *Admission Requirements:* As per University of Nebraska at Omaha undergraduate and graduate requirements. *Degree Requirements:* Library Media Endorsement (Undergraduate and Graduate)—33 hours M.S. in Secondary and Elementary Education, M.A. in Secondary and Elementary Education, both with Library Media concentration—36 hours; M.S. in Reading with Library Media concentration—45 hours; M.S. in Educational Administration, with Educational Media concentration; Master's in Library Science Program (Cooperative program with University of Missouri at Columbia)—42 hours. *Faculty:* 1 full-time, 4 part-time (adjunct). *Students:* 21 undergraduates; 157 graduate students (mix of part-time and full-time). *Financial Assistance:* Contact Financial Aid Office. *Degrees Awarded 2003:* 23. Updated: 2/20/05.

Nevada

University of Nevada. Counseling and Educational Psychology Dept. College of Education, Reno, NV 89557. (702) 784-6327. Fax: (702) 784-1990. Web site: http://www.unr.edu/unr/colleges/educ/cep/cepindex.html. Dr. LaMont Johnson, Program Coord., Information Technology in Education. Marlowe Smaby, Dept. Chair. ljohnson@unr.edu. *Specializations:* M.S. and Ph.D. *Admission Requirements:* bachelor's degree, 2.75 undergraduate GPA, 750 GRE (V+Q). *Degree Requirements:* 36 semester credits, optional thesis worth 6 credits, comprehensive exam. *Faculty:* 2 full-time, 1 part-time. *Students:* M.S., 15; Ph.D., 10.

New Jersey

Montclair State University. Department of Curriculum & Teaching. 1 Normal Avenue, Montclair, NJ 07043. (973) 655-5187. Fax: (973) 655-7084. Web site: http://www.monclair.edu/pages/edmedia. Dr. Vanessa Domine, Professor of Educational Technology. dominev@mail.montclair.edu. *Specializations:* MSU offers two post-baccalaureate certification programs for Associate Educational Media Specialist Certification and (advanced) Educational Media Specialist Certification. A new master of education degree program in Educational Technology will take effect Fall 2005. Educational Technology courses will be offered beginning Fall 2004. *Features:* The Media Specialist programs provide instruction for persons preparing to function as directors of school media centers and programs at three levels: district, secondary and elementary. The curriculum focuses on the role of instructional context and the necessity to recognize and respect perceptions and views of the individual learner. Theory and practice are combined in the curriculum to afford students opportunities for productive roles in various educational and multicultural contexts. *Admission Requirements:* The advanced program provides certification (endorsement) as a Media Specialist for certified teachers who possess a master's degree in a related educational field. The Associate Educational Media Specialists certificate requires a bachelor's degree and a standard New Jersey teaching certificate. Potential candidates submit applications to the Graduate School office for review and evaluation. Approved applications will be forwarded to the Department of Curriculum and Teaching for review and the scheduling of interviews. *Degree Requirements:* Certification Requirements:18–21 semester hours of media and technology are required for the AEMS program and 30–33 hours for the EDMS program. *Faculty:* 3 full-time, 5 part-time. *Students:* 220. *Financial Assistance:* n/a. Updated: 3/19/04.

Rutgers–The State University of New Jersey. Ph.D. Program in Communication, Information, and Library Studies, The Graduate School, New Brunswick, NJ 08901-1071. (732) 932-7447. Fax: (732) 932-6916. Web site: http://www.scils.rutgers.edu/. Dr. Lea P. Stewart, Director, Master's Program, Dept. of Library and Information Studies, School of Communication, Information and Library Studies. (732) 932-9717. Fax: (732) 932-2644. Dr. Carol Kuhlthan, Chair. lstewart@scils.rutgers.edu. *Specializations:* M.L.S. degree with specializations in Information Retrieval, Technical and Automated Services, Reference, School Media Services, Youth Services, Management and Policy Issues, and Generalist Studies. Ph.D. programs in Communication; Media Studies; Information Systems, Structures, and Users; Information and Communication Policy and Technology; and Library and Information Services. The school also offers a six-year specialist certificate program. *Features:* Ph.D. Program provides doctoral-level coursework for students seeking theoretical and research skills for scholarly and professional leadership in the information and communication fields. A course on multimedia structure, organization, access, and production is offered. *Admission Requirements:* Ph.D.: master's degree in Information Studies, Communication, Library Science, or related field; 3.0 undergraduate GPA; GRE scores; TOEFL (for applicants whose native language is not English). *Degree Requirements:* M.L.S.: 36 semester hours, in which the hours for media vary for individual students; practicum of 150 hours. *Faculty:* M.L.S., 15 full-time, 12 adjunct; Ph.D., 43. *Students:* M.L.S., 97 full-time, 199 part-time; Ph.D., 104. *Financial Assistance:* M.L.S.: scholarships, fellowships, and graduate assistantships. Ph.D.: assistantships. Updated: 5/19/03.

William Paterson University. College of Education. 300 Pompton Rd., Wayne, NJ 07470. (973) 720-2140. Fax: (973) 720-2585. Web site: http://pwcWeb.wilpaterson.edu/wpcpages/library/default.htp. Dr. Amy G. Job, Librarian, Assoc. Prof., Coord., Program in Library/Media, Elementary and Early Childhood Dept. joba@wpunj.edu. *Specializations:* M.Ed. for Educational Media Specialist, Associate Media Specialist, Ed.S. *Features:* Provides training for New Jersey certified Educational Media Specialists and Associate Media Specialists. *Admission Requirements:* teaching certificate, 2.75 GPA, MAT or GRE scores, 1 year teaching experience. Assoc.Ed.S.: certificate, 2.75 GPA. *Degree Requirements:* M.Ed.: 33 semester hours, including research projects and practicum. Assoc.Ed.S.: 18 semester hours. *Faculty:* 6 full-time, 2 part-time. *Students:* 30 part-time. *Financial Assistance:* limited. *Degrees Awarded 2003:* 6. Updated: 2/22/05.

New York

Buffalo State College. CIS Department. 1300 Elmwood Ave., Buffalo, NY 14222-1095. (716) 878-4923. Fax: (716) 878-6677. Web site: http://www.buffalostate.edu/depts/edcomputing/. Dr. Anthony J. Nowakowski, Program Coordinator. nowakoaj@buffalostate.edu. *Specializations:* M.S. in Education in Educational Computing. *Features:* This program is designed for educators who wish to develop and expand their skills in the educational application of computers. Emphasis is given to the use of computers in the instructional process. *Admission Requirements:* bachelor's degree from accredited institution, 3.0 GPA in last 60 hours, 3 letters of recommendation. *Degree Requirements:* 33 semester hours (15 hours in computers, 12-15 hours in education, 3-6 electives); thesis or project (see: http://www.buffalostate.edu/edc). *Faculty:* 5 part-time. *Students:* 3 full-time, 98 part-time.

Fordham University. Department of Communication and Media Studies. Rose Hill Campus, 441 E. Fordham Rd., Bronx, NY 10458. (718) 817-4860. Fax: (718) 817-4868. Web site: http://www.fordham.edu. Robin Andersen, Department Chair, James Capo, Director of Graduate Studies. andersen@fordham.edu. *Specializations:* MA in Communications. *Features:* Internship or thesis option; full-time students can complete program in twelve months. *Admission Requirements:* 3.0 undergraduate GPA. *Degree Requirements:* 10 courses plus internship or thesis. *Faculty:* 8 full-time, 2 part-time. *Students:* 8 full-time, 22 part-time. *Financial Assistance:* assistantships, student loans, scholarships.

Ithaca College. School of Communications, Park Hall, Ithaca, NY 14850. (607) 274-1025. Fax: (607) 274-7076. Web site: http://www.ithaca.edu/ocld. Gordon Rowland, Professor, Chair, Graduate Program in Communications; Roy H. Park, School of Communications (rowland@ithaca.edu). *Specializations:* M.S. in Communications. Students in this program find employment in such areas as instructional design/training, multimedia/Web development, corporate/community/public relations and marketing, and employee communication. The program can be tailored to individual career goals. *Features:* Program is interdisciplinary, incorporating organizational communication, instructional design, management, and technology. *Admission Requirements:* 3.0 GPA, recommendations, statement of purpose, resume, application forms and transcripts, TOEFL 550 (or 213 computer-scored) where applicable. *Degree Requirements:* 36 semester hours including capstone seminar. *Faculty:* 8 full-time. *Students:* approx. 20 full-time, 10 part-time. *Financial Assistance:* graduate assistantships, research fellowships (for continuing students). *Degrees Awarded 2003:* 15. Updated: 2/22/05.

New York Institute of Technology. Dept. of Instructional Technology. Tower House, Old Westbury, NY 11568. (516) 686-7777. Fax: (516) 686-7655. Web site: http://www.nyit.edu. Davenport Plumer, Chair, Depts. of Instructional Technology and Elementary Education—preservice and inservice. dplumer460@aol.com. *Specializations:* M.S. in Instructional Technology; M.S. in Elementary Education; Specialist Certificates in Computers in Education, Distance Learning, and Multimedia (not degrees, but are earned after the first 18 credits of the master's degree). *Features:* computer integration in virtually all courses; online courses; evening, weekend, and summer courses. *Admission Requirements:* bachelor's degree from accredited college with 3.0 cumulative average. *Degree Requirements:* 36 credits with 3.0 GPA for M.S., 18 credits with 3.0 GPA for certificates. *Faculty:* 11 full-time, 42 part-time. *Students:* 112 full-time, 720 part-time. *Financial Assistance:* graduate assistantships, institutional and alumni scholarships, student loans.

New York University. Educational Communication and Technology Program, Steinhardt School of Education. 239 Greene St., Suite 300, New York, NY 10003. (212) 998-5520. Fax: (212) 995-4041. Web site: http://www.nyu.edu/education/alt/ectprogram. Francine Shuchat-Shaw, Assoc. Prof. (MA Advisor), Dir.; W. Michael Reed, Prof. (Doctoral Advisor). sm24@nyu.edu. *Specializations:* M.A., Ed.D., and Ph.D. in Education—for the preparation of individuals as instructional media designers, developers, media producers, and/or researchers in education, business and industry, health and medicine, community services, government, museums and other cultural institutions; and to teach or become involved in administration in educational communications and instructional technology programs in higher education, including instructional television, microcomputers, multi-media, Internet and telecommunications. The program also offers a post-M.A. 30-point Certificate of Advanced Study in Education. *Features:* emphasizes theoretical foundations, especially a cognitive science perspective of learning and instruction, and their implications for designing media-based learning environments and materials. All efforts focus on video, multimedia, instructional television, Web-based technology and telecommunications; participation in special research and production projects and field internships. Web site: http://create.alt.ed.nyu.edu. Consortium for Research and Evaluation of Advanced Technologies in Education—uses an apprenticeship model to provide doctoral students and advanced MA students with research opportunities in collaboration with faculty. *Admission Requirements:* M.A.: 3.0 undergraduate GPA, responses to essay questions, interview related to academic and professional goals. Ph.D.: 3.0 GPA, 1000 GRE, responses to essay questions, interview related to academic or professional preparation and career goals. For international students, 600 TOEFL and TWE. *Degree Requirements:* M.A.: 36 semester hours including specialization, elective courses, thesis, English Essay Examination. Ph.D.: 57 semester hours beyond MA, including specialization, foundations, research, content seminar, and elective coursework; candidacy papers; dissertation; English Essay Examination. *Faculty:* 4 full-time, 6 part-time. *Students:* M.A.: 40 full-time, 35 part-time. Ph.D.: 14 full-time, 20 part-time. *Financial Assistance:* graduate and research assistantships, student loans, fellowships, scholarships, and work assistance programs. Updated: 3/8/04.

Pace University. School of Education. 861 Bedford Road, Pleasantville, NY 10570. (914) 773-3200, (914) 773-3870. Fax: (915) 773-3871. Web site: http://www.pace.edu. Janet McDonald, Dean and Professor of Education. jmcdonald@pace.edu. *Specializations:* M.Ed. in Educational Technology (leads to New York State Certification as an Educational Technology Specialist.) Advanced Certificate in Educational Technology (leads to New York State Certification as an Educational Technology Specialist.) Pace certificate in Computing for Teachers. *Features:* Results in New York State Educational Technology Specialist Certification (2/2004). Program is individualized to meet the needs of two distinct populations: those with an education background or those with a technology background. Some courses are delivered through a distance learning platform. *Admission Requirements:* bachelor's degree or higher from an accredited institution; Minimum GPA of at least 3.0 (upon the recommendation of the Dean, Graduate Faculty Admissions Committee or the Director of Student Support Services, candidates whose GPA is less than 3.0 may be admitted on a conditional basis, provided that it is determined that the candidate has the necessary knowledge and skills to complete the program successfully.) A transcript review is required of all candidates to determine if any Arts and Sciences content knowledge required for certification are unmet. If unmet requirements exist, they must be met during the course of the program; however, the credit hours earned completing them may not be counted toward the graduate degree. Transcript review demonstrating Arts and Sciences and Content Area background comparable to New York State requirements including preparation to teach to the New York State Learning Standards. Completion of the application process, including an essay, two letters of recommendation, personal statement and, in some cases, an interview. *Degree Requirements:* 36–39 semester hours. *Faculty:* 8 full-time, 50 part-time. *Students:* 60–70 part-time. *Financial Assistance:* assistantships, internships, scholarships. *Degrees Awarded 2003:* Program is new and was implemented as of September 2001. Updated: 7/7/04.

St. Johns University. Division of Library and Information Science. 8000 Utopia Parkway, Jamaica, NY 11439. (718) 990-6200. Fax: (718) 990-2071. Web site: http://www.stjohns.edu/libraryscience. Elizabeth B. Pollicino, Associate Director. libis@stjohns.edu. *Specializations:* M.L.S. with specialization in School Media. The school also offers a 24-credit Advanced Certificate program in which students may also take School Media and Technology courses. *Features:* small class size, personal advisement, student lounge and computer lab, high-tech classrooms. *Admission Requirements:* 3.0 GPA, 2 letters of reference, statement of professional goals. GRE (General) required for assistantships. *Degree Requirements:* 36 semester hours, comprehensive exam, practicum. *Faculty:* 6 full-time, 10 part-time. *Students:* 30 full-time, 77 part-time. *Financial Assistance:* 4 assistantships in DLIS; others available in University Library. Rev. Brian J. O'Connell, CM Library Studies

Scholarships (for incoming students with superior academic records). *Degrees Awarded 2003:* 29. Updated: 6/11/03.

State University College of Arts and Science at Potsdam. Information and Communication Technology. 302 Satterlee Hall, Potsdam, NY 13676. (315) 267-2525. Fax: (315) 267-2987. Web site: http://www.potsdam.edu/EDUC/gradpages/MSEdPrograms/ICTHome. html. Dr. Anthony Betrus, Chair, Information and Communications Technology. betrusak@potsdam.edu. *Specializations:* M.S. in Education in Instructional Technology with concentrations in: Educational Technology Specialist, Human Performance Technology, Information Technology, and Organizational Leadership. *Features:* A progressive, forward looking program with a balance of theoretical and hands-on practical coursework. *Admission Requirements:* (1) Submission of an official transcript of an earned baccalaureate degree from an accredited institution. (2) A minimum GPA of 2.75 (4.0 scale) in the most recent 60 credit hours of coursework. (3) Submission of the Application for Graduate Study (w/ $50 nonrefundable fee). (4) For students seeking the Educational Technology Specialist Certification, a valid NYS Teaching Certificate is required. *Degree Requirements:* 36–39 semester hours, including internship or practicum; culminating project required. *Faculty:* 3 full-time, 3 part-time. *Students:* 33 full-time, 92 part-time. *Financial Assistance:* student loans, student work study, graduate assistantship. *Degrees Awarded 2003:* 28. Updated: 4/27/04.

State University of New York at Albany. School of Education. 1400 Washington Ave., Albany, NY 12222. (518) 442-5032. Fax: (518) 442-5008. Karen Swan (ED114A), contact person. swan@cnsunix.albany.edu. *Specializations:* M.Ed. and Ph.D. in Curriculum and Instruction with specializations in Instructional Theory, Design, and Technology. M.Ed. offered entirely online over the World Wide Web. *Admission Requirements:* bachelor's degree, GPA close to 3.0; transcript, three letters of recommendation. Students desiring New York State permanent teaching certification should possess preliminary certification. *Degree Requirements:* M.Ed.: 30 semester hours with 15-18 credits in specialization. Ph.D.: 78 semester hours, internship, portfolio certification, thesis. *Faculty:* 13 full-time, 7 part-time. *Students:* 100 full-time, 350 part-time. *Financial Assistance:* fellowships, assistantships, grant, student loans, minority fellowships.

State University of New York at Stony Brook. Technology and Society. College of Engineering and Applied Sciences, SUNY at Stony Brook, Stony Brook, NY 11794-3760. Carole (631) 632-8765,(631) 632-8770, (631) 632-8765 Rita (631) 632-1057. Fax: (631) 632-7809. Web site: http://www.stonybrook.edu/est/. Carole Rose. Carole.Rose@ stonybrook.edu. *Specializations:* master's degree in Technological Systems Management with concentration in Educational Computing (30 credits). Students may simultaneously earn an Advanced Graduate Certificate (ACG) in Educational Computing (18 credits). *Features:* Students develop the skills to be effective educational leaders and decision-makers. Graduates manage technology-based learning environments and integrate technology into education in meaningful and innovative ways. Our program emphasizes the (a) design of standard-based learning modules, (b) research, and evaluation of educational technologies, and (c) development of prototype learning technologies and learning activities. *Admission Requirements:* bachelor's degree in engineering, natural sciences, social sciences, mathematics, or closely related area; 3.0 undergraduate GPA, have taken the GRE, experience with computer applications or use of computers in teaching. *Degree Requirements:* 30 semester credits, including two general technology core courses, 5 required educational computing courses, and 3 eligible electives. *Faculty:* 5 full-time, 8 part-time. *Students:* 15 full-time, 30 part-time. *Financial Assistance:* assistantships, grants, student loans. *Degrees Awarded 2003:* 14. Updated: 6/9/03.

Syracuse University. Instructional Design, Development, and Evaluation Program, School of Education. 330 Huntington Hall, Syracuse, NY 13244-2340. (315) 443-3703. Fax: (315) 443-1218. Web site: http://idde.syr.edu. J. Michael Spector, Professor and Chair.

lltucker@syr.edu. *Specializations:* Certificates in Educational Technology and Adult Lifelong Learning and M.S., C.A.S., and Ph.D. degree programs for Instructional Design, Educational Evaluation, Human Issues in Instructional Development, Technology Integration, and Educational Research and Theory (learning theory, application of theory, and educational media research). Graduates are prepared to serve as curriculum developers, instructional designers, program and product evaluators, researchers, resource center administrators, technology coordinators, distance learning design delivery specialists, trainers and training managers, and higher education faculty. *Features:* The courses are typically project centered. Collaborative project experience, field work and internships are emphasized throughout. There are special issues seminars, as well as student- and faculty-initiated mini-courses, seminars and guest lecturers, faculty-student formulation of department policies, and multiple international perspectives. International collaborations are an ongoing feature of the program in IDD&E. The graduate student population is highly diverse. *Admission Requirements:* M.S.: undergraduate transcripts, recommendations, personal statement, interview recommended; TOEFL for international applicants; GRE recommended. Doctoral: Relevant master's degree from accredited institution or equivalent, GRE scores, recommendations, personal statement, TOEFL for international applicants; interview strongly encouraged. *Degree Requirements:* M.S.: 36 semester hours, comprehensive exam and portfolio required. Ph.D.: 90 semester hours, research apprenticeship, portfolio, qualifying exams and dissertation required. *Degrees awarded in* 2004: 13 MS; 2 Ph.D. Updated: 3/2/05.

North Carolina

Appalachian State University. Department of Curriculum and Instruction. College of Education, Boone, NC 28608. (828) 262-2277. Fax: (828) 262-2686. Web site: http://edtech.ced. appstate.edu. Robert Muffoletto. muffoletto@appstate.edu. *Specializations:* M.A. in Educational Media and Technology with three areas of concentration: Computers, Media Literacy, and Media Production. A plan of study in Internet distance teaching is offered online. Two certificate programs: (1) Distance Learning—Internet delivered; (2) Media Literacy. *Features:* Business, university, community college, and public school partnership offers unusual opportunities for learning. The programs are focused on developing learning environments over instructional environments. *Admission Requirements:* Undergraduate degree. *Degree Requirements:* 36 graduate semester hours. We also have certificates in (1) Distance Learning and (2) Media Literacy. *Faculty:* 6 full-time faculty. *Students:* 35. *Financial Assistance:* assistantships, grants, student loans. *Degrees Awarded 2003:* 5. Updated: 2/24/05.

East Carolina University. Department of Library Science and Instructional Technology, 1103 Joyner Library, Greenville, NC 27858-4353. (252) 328-4373. Fax: (252) 328-4368. lsit.coe.ecu.edu. Dr. P. Alston Jones, Assoc. Prof., Interim Chair (mathisk@mail.ecu.edu). *Specializations:* Master of Library Science; Certificate of Advanced Study (Library Science); Master of Arts in Education (North Carolina Instructional Technology Specialist licensure); Master of Science in Instructional Technology; Certificate of Tele-learning; Certificate of Virtual Reality in Education and Training; Certificate for Special Endorsement in Computer Education. *Features:* M.L.S. graduates are eligible for North Carolina School Media Coord. certification and for NC Public Library Certification; C.A.S. graduates are eligible for North Carolina School Media Supervisor certification; M.A.Ed. graduates are eligible for North Carolina Instructional Technology certification; Cert. for Special Endorsement in Computer Education for North Carolina Licensure as Technology Facilitator. All programs available 100% online. *Admission Requirements:* M.S., M.A.ED., and M.L.S.: bachelor's degree; C.A.S.: M.L.S. or equivalent degree. Admission to Graduate School. *Degree Requirements:* M.L.S.: 39 semester hours; M.A.Ed.: 39 semester hours; M.S.: 39 semester hours; C.A.S.: 30 semester hours. *Faculty:* 14 full-time; 3 part-time. *Stu-*

dents: 7 full-time, 250 part-time. *Financial Assistance:* graduate assistantships. *Degrees Awarded 2003:* 35 MLS; 16 MAED; 15 MS. Updated: 2/18/05.

North Carolina Central University. School of Education. 1801 Fayetteville St., Durham, NC 27707. (919) 560-6692. Fax: (919) 560-5279. Dr. James N. Colt, Assoc. Prof., Coordinator., Graduate Program in Educational Technology. bWebb@nccu.edu. *Specializations:* M.A. with special emphasis on Instructional Development/Design. *Features:* Graduates are prepared to implement and utilize a variety of technologies applicable to many professional ventures, including institutions of higher education (college resource centers), business, industry, and professional schools such as medicine, law, dentistry, and nursing. *Admission Requirements:* undergraduate degree, GRE. *Degree Requirements:* 33 semester hours (including thesis). *Faculty:* 2 full-time, 2 part-time. *Students:* 19 full-time, 18 part-time. *Financial Assistance:* assistantships, grants, student loans.

North Carolina State University. Department of Curriculum and Instruction. P.O. Box 7801, Raleigh, NC 27695-7801. (919) 515-1779. Fax: (919) 515-6978. Web site: http://www.ncsu.edu/ced/ci/. Dr. Ellen Vasu, Professor. Ellen_Vasu@ncsu.edu. *Specializations:* M.Ed. and M.S. in Instructional Technology-Computers (program track within one master's in Curriculum and Instruction). Ph.D. in Curriculum and Instruction with focus on Instructional Technology as well as other areas. *Admission Requirements:* master's: undergraduate degree from an accredited institution, 3.0 GPA in major or in latest graduate degree program; transcripts; GRE or MAT scores; 3 references; goal statement. Ph.D.: undergraduate degree from accredited institution, 3.0 GPA in major or latest graduate program; transcripts; recent GRE scores, writing sample, interview, three references, vita, goal statement (see http://www2.acs.ncsu.edu/grad/prospect.htm). *Degree Requirements:* master's: 36 semester hours, practicum, thesis optional; Ph.D.: 72 hours beyond bachelor's (minimum 33 in Curriculum and Instruction core, 27 in Research); other information available on request. *Faculty:* 2 full-time, 2 part-time. *Students:* master's, 15 part-time; Ph.D., 6 part-time, 1 full-time. *Financial Assistance:* some assistantships available on a limited basis. *Degrees Awarded 2004:* 6 master's degrees. Updated: 2/22/05. Ellen Vasu, Ellen_Vasu@ncsu.edu

University of North Carolina. School of Information and Library Science, CB#3360, Chapel Hill, NC 27599-3360. (919) 962-8062, 962-8366. Fax: (919) 962-8071. Web site: http://www.ils.unc.edu/. Evelyn H. Daniel, Prof., Coord., School Media Program (daniel @ils.unc.edu). *Specializations:* Master of Science Degree in Library Science (M.S.L.S.) with specialization in school library media work. Post-master's certification program. *Features:* Rigorous academic program plus teaching practicum requirement; excellent placement record. Many courses offered online. *Admission Requirements:* Competitive admission based on all three GRE components (quantitative, qualitative, analytical), undergraduate GPA (plus graduate work if any), letters of recommendation, and student statement of career interest and school choice. *Degree Requirements:* 48 semester hours, practicum, comprehensive exam, master's paper. *Faculty:* 22 full-time, 10 part-time. *Students:* 300 full-time, 50 part-time (about 30 students specialize in SLMC). *Financial Aid:* Grants, assistantships, student loans. *Degrees Awarded in 2004:* 130, 30 for school library media certification. Updated: 3/12/05.

North Dakota

Minot State University. Graduate School, 500 University Ave. W., Minot, ND 58707. (701) 858-3250. Fax: (701) 839-6933 Web site: www.minotstateu.edu. Dr. Jack L. Rasmussen, Dean of the Graduate School (butler@minotstateu.edu). *Specializations:* M.S. in Elementary Education (including work in educational computing); M.S. in Special Education with Specialization in Severe Multiple-Handicaps, Early Childhood Special Education, Education of the Deaf, and Learning Disabilities; M.S. in Communication Disorders,

Specializations in Audiology and Speech Language Pathology. *Features:* All programs include involvement in computer applications appropriate to the area of study, including assistive technologies for persons with disabilities. Computer laboratories are available for student use in the library and various departments. Some courses are offered through the Interactive Video Network, which connects all universities in North Dakota. All programs have a rural focus and are designed to offer a multitude of practical experiences. *Admission Requirements:* $35 fee, three letters of recommendation, 300-word autobiography, transcripts, GRE in Communication Disorders or GMAT for M.S. in Management. *Degree Requirements:* 30 semester hours (hours in computers, education, and outside education vary according to program); written comprehensive exams; oral exams; thesis or project. *Faculty:* 10 full-time. *Students:* 61 full-time, 63 part-time. *Financial Aid:* loans, assistantships, scholarships. Updated: 4/9/02.

University of North Dakota. Instructional Design & Technology, Box 7189, Grand Forks, ND 58202. (701) 777-3574. Fax: (701) 777-3246 (idt.und.edu). Richard Van Eck(richardvaneck@und.com). *Specializations:* K–12 Technology Integration; Computer/ Web-Based Instruction; Human Performance Technology; Simulations & Games. Founded as a collaborative effort of the College of Education, Psychology Department, and John D. Odegard School of Aerospace Sciences, the IDT program has trained instructional designers to work in schools as curriculum developers and technology facilitators, and to work in corporate settings as trainers and developers of print-, computer-, and web-based instruction. *Features:* The program was modified in 2005 to reflect the needs of modern schools and the training workplace, with nine new courses in instructional design, human-performance technology, and technology-based instruction. This new curriculum is based on the AECT/NCATE curriculum standards for instructional design programs, and is competitive with the best graduate programs in IDT. What makes the IDT program at UND stand out, however, is its interdisciplinary nature, access to cutting edge simulation and video production resources, and the personal, one-to-one learning, research, and development experiences our students enjoy. *Admission Requirements:* General admission requirements can be viewed at http://www.und.edu/dept/grad/genrequ.html. You must first complete an application to the program (http://www.und.edu/dept/grad/admissns.html) and then submit a statement outlining your goals and objectives for seeking the graduate degree in IDT. Specifically, what is it that attracts you to this field, and what do you hope to do with the degree professionally. Other requirements are outlined in the application process, including letters of recommendation. *Degree Requirements:* The IDT master's degree programs offer three options: the M.Ed., the M.S. (independent study option), and the M.S. (thesis option). These programs are comprised of 34 (M.Ed. and M.S. independent study option) or 36 (M.S. thesis option) credits. These credit hours consist of 9 hours of core coursework in instructional design and technology, 6 (M.Ed.) to 9 (M.S.) additional hours of coursework in instructional design and technology as an area of emphasis, 3 (M.Ed) to 6 (M.S.) hours of foundations coursework in education and psychology, 3 (M.Ed) to 6 (M.S.) hours of coursework in the Scholarly Tools/Research option, 3 (M.S.) to 6 (M.Ed) hours of elective coursework in some area of specialization, 2 hours of internship, and 2 hours of independent study credit (M.Ed. and M.S. independent study option) or 4 hours of thesis (M.S. thesis option). The IDT degree options are based on the same set of program components:

- Program core component: New courses presenting IDT content

- Research component: Development of research skills

- Foundations component: Fundamental background in psychology

- Area of Emphasis in IDT: Opportunity for area or skill specialization within IDT

The IDT course requirements are organized within a major, foundations area research and scholarly tools area. The major consists of the IDT core and the area of emphasis in IDT.

Students in both the M.Ed. and M.S. options will be required to complete 15 (M.Ed.) to 18(M.S.) hours of coursework in IDT subject matter. The Master of Education (M.Ed.) degree is primarily intended for students who plan to work in an education environment, either the K–12 schools or higher education. Individuals pursuing this degree will work primarily as technology facilitators or curriculum specialists. As technology facilitators, they are likely to work with instructors in assisting them to appropriately, effectively, and successfully integrate technology into their instruction. They are also likely to do some direct work with students in teaching skills associated with the use of technology. As curriculum specialists, they are likely to work at the school, district, or state levels to design curriculum for public education. Students pursuing this degree will learn the theoretical issues associated with technologically supported instruction but their emphasis will be in the application of this knowledge in terms of best practice. An independent study project (research) is required and is considered a capstone experience. The independent study may address a practical problem or address a theoretical construct in the same way that a thesis does. The Master of Science (M.S.) degree is primarily intended for students who plan to work in business, government, and industry developing and delivering technologically supported curriculum. Students from backgrounds other than education, e.g., nursing, engineering, aerospace, may prefer this option. This degree is available in two tracks. The M.S. (thesis option) is intended for those students who want to develop and utilize research skills in their work context. The M.S. (independent study option) is intended for those students who prefer to emphasize the development and evaluation of application and practice. Required coursework within the two options is consistent with this distinction between an emphasis on research or practice. *Faculty:* Two full-time faculty, one with dual teaching role in Psychology; one full-time faculty hire for Fall 2005. *Students:* 15 part-time. *Financial Aid:* Graduate assistantships with full tuition waiver and standard financial aid packages available. Contact program for addition information. Updated: 4/1/05.

Ohio

Kent State University. Instructional Technology. 405 White Hall, Kent, OH 44242. (330) 672-2294. Fax: (330) 672-2512. Web site: http://itec.educ.kent.edu. Dr. David Dalton, Coord., Instructional Technology Program. ddalton@kent.edu. *Specializations:* M.Ed. or M.A. in Instructional Technology, Computing/Technology, and Library/Media Specialist; Ph.D. in Educational Psychology with emphasis in Instructional Technology. *Features:* Programs are planned individually to prepare students for careers in elementary, secondary, or higher education, business, industry, government agencies, or health facilities. Students may take advantage of independent research, individual study, practica, and internships. *Admission Requirements:* master's: bachelor's degree with 2.75 undergraduate GPA. *Degree Requirements:* master's: 37–43 semester hours. *Faculty:* 4 full-time, 7 part-time. *Students:* 75. *Financial Assistance:* 6 graduate assistantships, John Mitchell and Marie McMahan Awards, 5 teaching fellowships. *Degrees Awarded 2003:* 25.

Ohio University. Educational Studies. 250 McCracken Hall, Athens, OH 45701-2979. (740) 593-4561. Fax: (740) 593-0477. Web site: http://www.ohiou.edu/edstudies/comped.html. Teresa Franklin, Instructional Technology Program Coordinator. franklit@ohio.edu. *Specializations:* M.Ed. in Computer Education and Technology. Ph.D. in Curriculum and Instruction with a specialization in Instructional Technology also available; call for details or visit the Web site: http://www.ohiou.edu/edstudies/tech/DOC.HTM. *Features:* master's program is a blended online and face-to-face delivery. *Admission Requirements:* bachelor's degree, 3.0 undergraduate GPA, 35 MAT, 550 TOEFL for International applicants, three letters of recommendation, official transcripts, and a letter which states how personal goals relate to the goals of the CET program. Ph.D. admission requirements are 3 letters of recommendations, a short autobiography that states how your personal goals relate to goals of the program, GRE 1000 or MAT 35, GPA 3.0, 550 TOEFL for International applicants, Master's degree, and official transcripts from each institution attended. *Degree Requirements:* Master's—49–52 qtr. credits, electronic portfolio or optional thesis worth 2–10 credits or alternative seminar paper. Ph.D.—109 hours with 15 hours being dissertation work see our Web site for the Program of Study. Web site: http://www.ohio.edu/education/dept/es/it/dept-es-it-phdsci.cfm. *Faculty:* 3 full-time tenure track faculty, 1 part-time instructor. *Students:* M.Ed.: 32 Ph.D.: 18. *Financial Aid:* Graduate Associateships or Teaching Assistantships. *Degrees Awarded 2004:* 18 MED, 9 Ph.D. Updated: 2/24/05.

University of Cincinnati. College of Education, 401 Teachers College, ML002, Cincinnati, OH 45221-0002. (513) 556-3579. Fax: (513) 556-1001. Web site: http://www.uc.edu/. Richard Kretschmer (richard.kretschmer@uc.edu). *Specializations:* Ed.D. in Special Education with an emphasis on Language/Literacy with Special Needs Children. *Features:* Contact division for features. *Admission Requirements:* Master's degree from accredited institution, 2.8 undergraduate GPA; GRE 1500 or better. *Degree Requirements:* 135 credit hours, core courses in the division of Teacher Education, and in the area of special education, two comprehensive papers, one completed at the end of the first academic year and the second at the end of the second academic year, and dissertation. *Faculty:* 3 full-time. *Students:* In the Ed.D. program there are 10 students. *Financial Assistance:* scholarships, assistantships, grants. *Degrees Awarded in 2004:* 2 Ed.D.s in Language/Literacy in Special Needs Children. Updated: 3/14/05.

University of Toledo. Curriculum & Instruction. MS 924, Carver Education Center, Toledo, OH 43606. (419) 530-2837. Fax: (419) 530-2466. Web site: http://www. utoledo.edu/~rsulliv/. Robert F. Sullivan, Ph.D. Robert.Sullivan@utoledo.edu. *Specializations:* Technology Using Educator/Technology Coordinator, Instructional Designer, and Performance Technologist. *Features:* Graduate students may concentrate in one of the three primary "roles," or may choose a blended program of study. Program was completely redesigned in 2004. *Admission Requirements:* master's: 3.0 undergrad. GPA, GRE (if undergrad. GPA < 2.7), recommendations; doctorate: master's degree, GRE, TOEFL (as necessary), recommendations, entrance writing samples, and interview. *Degree Requirements:* master's: 36 semester hours, culminating project; doctorate: 76 semester hours (after master's), major/minor exams, dissertation. *Faculty:* 4 full-time, 1 part-time (Fall 2004). *Students:* master's, 12 full-time, 50 part-time; doctoral, 4 full-time, 25 part-time (approximate). *Financial Assistance:* assistantships, scholarships, fellowships, and fee waivers (extremely competitive); student loans. *Degrees Awarded in 2004:* approximately 17 (graduate). Updated: 2/21/05.

Wright State University. College of Education and Human Services, Dept. of Educational Leadership. 421 Allyn Hall, 3640 Colonel Glenn Highway, Dayton, OH 45435. (937) 775-2509 or (937) 775-2821. Fax: (937) 775-4485. Web site: http:// www.ed.wright.edu. Dr. Bonnie K. Mathies, Associate Dean; Dr. Roger Carlsen, Program Coordinator. bonnie.mathies@wright.edu. *Specializations:* M.Ed. in Computer/Technology, Library Media, or Administrative Specialist—Technology Leader; M.A. in Educational Media or Computer Education; Specialist degree in Curriculum and Instruction with a focus on Educational Technology; Specialist degree in Higher Education with a focus on Educational Technology. *Features:* Ohio licensure available in Multi-age library media (ages 3–21); Computer/technology endorsement; Administrative Specialist—Curriculum, Instruction, Professional Development—Technology. Above licensure only available on a graduate basis and with teaching credentials. *Admission Requirements:* Completed application with nonrefundable application fee, bachelor's degree from accredited institution, official transcripts, 2.7 overall GPA for regular status (conditional acceptance possible), statement of purpose, satisfactory scores on MAT or GRE; however, if undergraduate GPA was a 3.0 or above there is no test requirement. *Degree Requirements:* M.Ed. requires a comprehensive portfolio; M.A. requires a 6-hour thesis. *Faculty:* 2 full-time, 10 part-time, including other university full-time faculty and staff. *Students:* approx. 4 full-time, approx. 120 part-time. *Financial Assistance:* 2 graduate assistantships in the College's Educational Resource Center; plus graduate fellowships for full-time students available; limited number of small graduate scholarships. *Degrees Awarded 2004:* 14; we also work with numerous students who are seeking Ohio licensure.

Oklahoma

Southwestern Oklahoma State University. School of Education. 100 Campus Drive, Weatherford, OK 73096. (405) 774-3140. Fax: (405) 774-7043. Web site: http://www. swosu.edu. Gregory Moss, Asst. Prof., Chair, Dept of School Service Programs. mossg@ swosu.edu. *Specializations:* M.Ed. in Library/Media Education. *Admission Requirements:* 2.5 GPA, GRE or GMAT scores, letter of recommendation, GPA 150 + GRE = 1100. *Degree Requirements:* 32 semester hours (including 24 in library media). *Faculty:* 1 full-time, 4 part-time. *Students:* 17 part-time.

The University of Oklahoma. Instructional Psychology and Technology, Department of Educational Psychology, 321 Collings Hall, Norman, OK 73019. (405) 325-5974. Fax: (405) 325-6655. Web site: http://www.ou.edu/education/edpsy/iptwww/iptwww.html. Dr. Raymond B. Miller, Area Head (rmiller@ou.edu). *Specializations:* Master's degree with emphases in Instructional Technology, Design & Development of Computer Software, Instructional Design, Instructional Psychology & Technology. Doctoral degree in Instructional Psychology and Technology. Strong interweaving of principles of instructional psychology with design and development of Instructional Technology. Application of IP&T in K–12, vocational education, higher education, business and industry, and governmental agencies. *Admission Requirements:* Master's: acceptance by IPT program and Graduate College based on minimum 3.00 GPA for last 60 hours of undergraduate work or last 12 hours of graduate work; written statement that indicates goals and interests compatible with program goals. Doctoral: 3.0 in last 60 hours undergraduate, 3.25 GPA, GRE scores, written statement of background and goals. *Degree Requirements:* Master's: approx. 36 hours course work with 3.0 GPA; successful completion of thesis or comprehensive exam. Doctorate: see program description from institution or http://www.ou.edu/education/edpsy/iptwww/iptwww.html. *Faculty:* 9 full-time. *Students:* Master's, 10 full-time, 200 part-time; doctoral, 10 full-time, 50 part-time. *Financial Assistance:* assistantships, grants, student loans, scholarships. *Degrees Awarded 2003:* 14. Updated: 3/11/05.

Oregon

Western Oregon State College. Teacher Education. 345 N. Monmouth Ave., Monmouth, OR 97361. (503) 838-8471. Fax: (503) 838-8228. Web site: http://www.wou.edu/education/elms/msed.html. Dr. Dana Ulveland, Coordinator for Information Technology. ulvelad @wou.edu. *Specializations:* M.S. in Information Technology. *Features:* offers advanced courses in library management, instructional development, multimedia, and computer technology. Additional course offerings in distance delivery of instruction and computer-interactive video instruction. *Admission Requirements:* 3.0 GPA, GRE or MAT. *Degree Requirements:* 45 quarter hours; thesis optional. *Faculty:* 3 full-time, 6 part-time. *Students:* 6 full-time, 131 part-time. *Financial Assistance:* assistantships, grants, student loans, scholarship, work assistance. Updated: 6/30/03.

Pennsylvania

Bloomsburg University. Institute for Interactive Technologies—Instructional Technology. 1210 McCormick Bldg., Bloomsburg, PA 17815. (717) 389-4506. Fax: (717) 389-4943. Web site: http://iit.bloomu.edu. Dr. Timothy L. Phillips, contact person. tphillip@bloomu.edu. *Specializations:* M.S. in Instructional Technology with emphasis on preparing for careers as interactive media specialists. The program is closely associated with the Institute for Interactive Technologies. *Features:* instructional design, authoring languages and systems, media integration, managing multimedia projects. *Admission Requirements:* bachelor's degree. *Degree Requirements:* 33 semester credits (27 credits + 6 credit thesis, or 30 credits + three credit internship). *Faculty:* 4 full-time. *Students:* 53 full-time, 50 part-time. *Financial Assistance:* assistantships, grants, student loans. Updated: 5/28/03.

Clarion University of Pennsylvania. Library Science. 209 Carlson Library Building, Clarion, PA 16214. (814) 393-2271. Fax: (814) 393-2150. Web site: http://www.clarion. edu/libsci. Dr. Andrea L. Miller, Chair. amiller@clarion.edu. *Specializations:* Master of Science in Library Science; Master of Science in Library Science with Pennsylvania School Library Media Certification; Certificate of Advanced Studies. Students may specialize in various areas of library science as determined by program of study. Clarion has a Rural Libraries program and began an online cohort program with a focus on rural and small libraries in January of 2004. In January of 2005, an online cohort program with a master's of Library Science with Pennsylvania School Library Media Certification will begin. *Features:* The graduate program in library science provides professional study encompassing the principles and techniques common to all types of libraries and information centers with the opportunity for advanced work in areas of special interest. The curriculum reflects today's applications of information technology in libraries and information centers. The master's program at Clarion University was initiated in 1967 and has the distinction of being the first graduate library science program offered within the State System of Higher Education. The program has been accredited by the American Library Association since 1976. As part of its commitment to meeting the needs of all residents of the Commonwealth of Pennsylvania, the Department of Library Science offers a variety of distance education programs. These programs utilize various delivery techniques, including on-site instruction, interactive television (ITV), and Web-based delivery. ITV delivery involves two or more sections of the same course that are taught simultaneously by the same instructor from a central location. Students at remote sites participate in the class via two-way audio and video. Courses offered via the World Wide Web may, at the instructors discretion, require some on-campus meetings. Clarion presently offers the program at the Dixon Center in Harrisburg, PA and at the Free Library in Philadelphia. In January of 2004, Clarion began offering an Web-based online cohort program with a focus on rural and small libraries. In January of 2005, Clarion will offer a Web-based online cohort program, Master of Science in Library Science with Pennsylvania School Library Media Certification. *Admission Requirements:* Applicants for admission to the Master of Science in Library Science degree program must meet Division of Graduate Studies admission requirements with the following additions: M.S.L.S.

1. An overall quality-point average for the baccalaureate degree of at least 3.00 on a 4.00 scale; or

2. A 3.00 quality-point average for the last 60 credits of the baccalaureate degree with an overall quality-point average of at least 2.75; or

3. A 2.75 to 2.99 overall quality-point average for the baccalaureate degree with a score of at least 50 on the Miller Analogies Test or a combined score of at least 1,000 on the quantitative and verbal sections of the Graduate Record Examination; or

4. A graduate degree in another discipline with an overall quality-point average of at least 3.00 and an overall undergraduate quality-point average of at least 2.75. International students are required to achieve a minimum score of 550 on the TOEFL. M.S.L.S. with Pennsylvania School Library Media Certification.

In addition to the above, students who begin their M.S.L.S. with Pennsylvania School Library Media Certification program in spring 2002 or later must meet the following additional requirements:

1. completion of at least six credits of college-level mathematics; and

2. completion of at least six credits of college-level English composition and literature.

Applicants without valid teacher certification must also pass the Praxis I pre-professional skills tests. State law limits the number of applicants with an overall quality-point average for the baccalaureate degree of less then 3.00 on a 4.00 scale who can be admitted to the School Library Media Certification program. *Degree Requirements:* The degree of Master of Science in Library Science is conferred upon the candidate who has met the following requirements: The completion of 36 hours of approved graduate study, including five required core courses (LS 500, 501, 502, 504, and 550), one management course (LS 530, 531, 532, 533, or 569), and six elective courses. The maintenance of a cumulative average of 3.00 or higher. A student who receives a grade of "C" or lower in two or more courses is disqualified as a candidate in the degree program unless special permission to continue is obtained from the dean of the College of Education and Human Services and the coordinator of Graduate Studies. The completion of all degree requirements within a six-year period. Coursework over six years old may not be applied toward the degree. Master of Science in Library Science Degree with Pennsylvania School Library Media Certification

A student wishing to obtain Pennsylvania School Library Media Certification, K–12, must hold a valid teaching certificate (or meet the requirements for preliminary certification by taking required undergraduate courses); complete 36 semester hours of an approved curriculum in library science; and complete three semester hours of internship in a school library media center. Students without prior certification will substitute twelve semester hours of student teaching for the internship requirement; students with emergency Pennsylvania School Library Media Certification may petition the department to substitute a site visit and portfolio for the internship requirement. Required courses for the Master of Science in Library Science degree with Pennsylvania School Library Media Certification, K–12, include: LS 459g, 490g, 500, 501, 502, 504, 532, 550, 577, 570, 583, 589, and one elective course. Praxis Series: Professional Assessments for Beginning Teachers®, The Commonwealth of Pennsylvania requires that all candidates for teacher certification take and pass specified tests in the Praxis Series, which is administered by the Educational Testing Service (ETS). Students without prior certification take the Praxis I, Academic Skills Assessments, to qualify for entry into teacher certification programs administered by the College of Education and Human Services. Tests in the Praxis II Series, Subject Assessments, are required of all students for licensure. These include Elementary Education, Content Knowledge (10014) and, for Pennsylvania School Library Media Certification, K–12, Library Media Specialist (10310). Students must pass the latter test with a minimum score of 620. Starting in spring 2004, students without prior certification must pass these tests prior to student teaching. The departments certification curricula are designed to cover topics found on this test. Click on the following link for a list of topics and the courses in which they are covered. Master of Science in Library Science/Juris Doctor Program. The department offers a joint M.S.L.S./J.D. program in cooperation with Widener University School of Laws Harrisburg, Pennsylvania, campus. Students must be admitted to both programs separately. Any six credits of coursework taken as part of a students J.D. program may be applied to that students M.S.L.S. program, and vice versa. These courses will be chosen in consultation with the students faculty advisors. Effective spring 2002. Certificate of Advanced Studies: The Certificate of Advanced Studies program is designed to provide the post-master's student an opportunity to expand and update professional skills and competencies through a structured pattern of continuing education. Study may be either full- or part-time. On a full-time basis, the certificate may be completed in two semesters. Requirements include a written statement of personal/professional goals, completion of a program of 24 graduate credits within a four-year period, and maintenance of a 3.00, (B) quality-point average. *Faculty:* 6 full-time and a large number of professional part-time faculty. *Students:* 47 full-time; 202 part-time *Financial Assistance:* Assistantships and various scholarships and awards. *Degrees Awarded 2004:* 77. Updated: 3/1/05.

Drexel University. College of Information Science and Technology, 3141 Chestnut Street, Philadelphia, PA 19104-2875. (215) 895-2474. Fax: (215) 895-2494. Web site: http://www.cis.drexel.edu. Dr. David E. Fenske, Dean (info@cis.drexel.edu). *Specializations:* M.S. Master of Science (Library and Information Science); M.S.I.S. Master of Science in Information Systems; M.S.S.E. Master of Science in Software Engineering; Ph.D. *Features:* On-campus and online degree programs for M.S. and M.S.I.S. *Admission Requirements:* Graduate application. Official final transcripts from ALL colleges/universities attended. Two letters of recommendation. Essay/Statement of purpose. Current resume. Official Graduate Record Exam (GRE) Scores (may be waived with a 3.2 GPA CUM or in the last half (credits) of the undergraduate degree; department decision. Official Test of English as a Foreign Language (TOEFL) Scores, international applicants only. I-20 form and accompanying bank documents, international applicants only. In addition to above, Ph.D. degree admission requirements also include knowledge of introductory descriptive and inferential statistics. All applicants to the Ph.D. program are required to submit GRE scores. Ph.D. applicants are not eligible for a waiver of the GRE requirement. *Faculty:* 32 full-time, 25–30 active adjuncts per term. *Students:* Graduate, 88 full-time; 508 part-time. *Financial Assistance:* The College of Information Science and Technology awards scholarships once a year in the Fall term only, and only accepts online applications from the Web site. IST offers many different types of assistance, including research assistantships for new, full-time Ph.D. students (there are no assistantships for Master's level students), endowed scholarships, Dean's Fellowships, and IST Alumni loan funds. All eligible, degree-seeking, continuing students and newly accepted, degree-seeking applicants are encouraged to apply. The IST scholarship committee generally awards the scholarships evenly between continuing and new students. There is no distinction made between online vs. on-campus students; all who are eligible are encouraged to apply. Please visit our Web site at www.cis.drexel.edu for complete information, deadlines and additional criteria. *Degrees Awarded 2004:* 137 graduate degrees. Updated: 4/28/05.

Lehigh University. College of Education, 111 Research Drive, Bethlehem, PA 18015. (610) 758-4794. Fax: (610) 758-3243. Web site: http://www.lehigh.edu. Ward Cates, Coord., Educational Technology Program (ward.cates@LEHIGH.edu). *Specializations:* M.S. in Instructional Design and Development: Emphasizes how to create technology products for teaching and learning in diverse settings. M.S. in Educational Technology: Degree aimed at our international program, emphasizing implementation of technology in International Schools abroad. Ed.D. in Educational Technology: Emphasizes design, development, implementation, and evaluation of technology-based teaching and learning products in a variety of settings. *Features:* Heavy emphasis on instructional design and interface design. Coursework in Web and resource development. Practical, professional-level design and development work. All work cross-platform and cross-browser. Both master's and doctoral students collaborate with faculty on projects and studies (including national presentation and publication). The Educational Technology program has a high level of collaboration with Technology-based Teacher Education. We are working on a new Learning, Sciences, and Technology Ph.D. degree program that will involve university-wide collaboration with departments in all four colleges of the university. This program will ultimately replace our current ed tech doctorate. *Admission Requirements:* M.S. (competitive): 3.0 undergraduate GPA or 3.0 graduate GPA, GREs recommended, transcripts, at least 2 letters of recommendation, statement of personal and professional goals, application fee. Application deadlines: July 15 for fall admission, Dec. 1 for spring admission, Apr. 30 for summer admission. Ed.D. (highly competitive): 3.5 graduate GPA, GREs required. Copy of two extended pieces of writing (or publications); statement of future professional goals; statement of why Ed Tech at Lehigh is the best place to meet those goals; identification of which presentations, publications, or research by Lehigh faculty attracted applicant to Lehigh. Application deadline: February 1 (admission only once per year from competitive pool). *Degree Requirements:* M.S.: 30 semester hours; thesis option. Ed.D.: 48 hours past the master's plus dissertation. *Faculty:* 3 full-time, 1 part-time. *Students:* M.S.: 8 full-time, 35 part-time; Ed.D.: 4 full-time, 8 part-time. *Financial Assistance:* University graduate and research assistantships, graduate student support as participants in R&D projects, paid internships in local businesses and schools doing design and development. *Degrees Awarded 2004:* 10. Updated: 2/19/05.

Pennsylvania State University. Instructional Systems. 314 Keller Bldg., University Park, PA 16802. (814) 865-0473. Fax: (814) 865-0128. Web site: http://www.ed.psu.edu/insys/. Alison Carr-Chellman, Associate Professor of Education, Professor in Charge of Instructional Systems. ali.carr@psu.edu. *Specializations:* M.Ed., M.S., D.Ed., and Ph.D. in Instructional Systems. Current teaching emphases are on Corporate Training, Interactive Learning Technologies, and Educational Systems Design. Research interests include multimedia, visual learning, educational reform, emerging technologies, constructivist learning, open-ended learning environments, scaffolding, technology integration in classrooms, technology in higher education, change and diffusion of innovations. *Features:* A common thread throughout all programs is that candidates have basic competencies in the understanding of human learning; instructional design, development, and evaluation; and research procedures. Practical experience is available in mediated independent learning, research, instructional development, computer-based education, and dissemination projects. Exceptional opportunities for collaboration with faculty (30%+ of publications and presentations are collaborative between faculty and students). *Admission Requirements:* D.Ed., Ph.D.: GRE (including written GRE), TOEFL, transcript, three letters of recommendation, writing sample, vita or resume, and letter of application detailing rationale for interest in the degree, matched with interests of faculty. *Degree Requirements:* M.Ed.: 33 semester hours; M.S.: 36 hours, including either a thesis or project paper; doctoral: candidacy exam, courses, residency, comprehensives, dissertation. *Faculty:* 9 full-time, 1 joint appointment in Information Sciences, 4 affiliate and 1 adjunct. *Students:* master's, approx. 46; doctoral, 103. *Financial Assistance:* assistantships, graduate fellowships, student aid loans, internships; assistantships on grants, contracts, and projects. *Degrees Awarded 2003:* Ph.D., D.Ed., M.S., M.Ed.

Rosemont College. Graduate Studies in Education, 1400 Montgomery Ave., Rosemont, PA 19010-1699. (610) 526-2982; (800) 531-9431. Fax: (610) 526-2964. Web site: http://www.rosemont.edu/root/main/gs/prog/tech.htm. Dr. Robert Siegfried, Director, Graduate Program in Technology and Education (rsiegfried@rosemont.edu). *Specializations:* M.Ed. in Technology in Education, Certificate in Professional Study in Technology in Education. *Admission Requirements:* GRE or MAT scores. *Degree Requirements:* Completion of 12 units (36 credits) and comprehensive exam. *Faculty:* 7 full-time, 10 part-time. *Students:* 110 full- and part-time. *Financial Assistance:* graduate student grants, assistantships, Federal Stafford Loan Program. Updated: 3/11/05.

Temple University. Department of Psychological Studies in Education, 1301 Cecil B. Moore Avenue Philadelphia, PA 19122. (215) 204-4497. Fax: (215) 204-6013. Web site: http://ilt.temple.edu/. Susan Miller, Ph.D. (susan.miller@temple.edu). *Specializations:* Instructional and Learning Technology (ILT) is a new master's program within the Educational Psychology Program in the Department of Psychological Studies in Education. As such, ILT is designed to address conceptual as well as technical issues in using technology for teaching and learning. Program areas include (a) instructional theory and design issues, (b) application of technology, and (c) management issues. *Features:* Instructional Theory and Design topics includes psychology of the learner, cognitive processes, instructional theories, human development, and individual differences as well as psychological and educational characteristics of technology resources, and identification of strengths and weaknesses of instructional technology resources. The Application of Technology area focuses on clarification of instructional objectives, identification of resources to facilitate learning, operation and application of current and emergent technologies, facility using graphic design, multimedia, video, distributed learning resources, Internet, and print publishing. Management and Consultation is structured around defining instructional needs, monitoring progress, and evaluating outcomes, designing technology delivery systems, preparing policy statements, budgets, and facility design criteria, managing skill assessment and training, understanding legal and ethical issues, and managing and maintaining facilities. *Admission Requirements:* bachelor's degree from an accredited institution, GRE (MAT) scores, 3 letters of recommendation, transcripts from each institution of higher learning attended (undergraduate and graduate), goal statement. *Degree Requirements:* Coursework (33 hours: 5 core courses, 3 technology electives, 3 cognate area courses). Practicum in students area of interest, Comprehensive Exam, Portfolio of Certification Competencies (for students interested in PA Dept. of Ed Certification as Instructional Technology Specialist). *Faculty:* 2 full-time, 1 part- time (plus educational psychology faculty). *Financial Assistance:* Presidential, Russell Conwell, and University Fellowships, Graduate School Tuition and Fellowship Funds, Graduate Teaching Assistantships and Assistantships in Administrative Offices, CASHE (College Aid Sources for Higher Education). Updated: 6/18/05

Rhode Island

The University of Rhode Island. Graduate School of Library and Information Studies. Rodman Hall, 94 W. Alumni Ave., Kingston, RI 02881-0815. (401) 874-2947. Fax: (401) 874-4964. Web site: http://www.uri.edu/artsci/lsc. W. Michael Havener, Ph.D., Director. mhavener@uri.edu. *Specializations:* M.L.I.S. degree with specialties in School Library Media Services, Youth Services Librarianship, Public Librarianship, Academic Librarianship, and Special Library Services. *Admission Requirements:* undergraduate GPA of 3.0, score in 50th percentile or higher on SAT or MAT, statement of purpose, current resume, letters of reference. *Degree Requirements:* 42 semester-credit program offered in Rhode Island and regionally in Amherst and Worcester, MA, and Durham, NH. *Faculty:* 8 full-time, 30 part-time. *Students:* 247. *Financial Assistance:* graduate assistantships, some scholarship aid, student loans. *Degrees Awarded 2003:* 80. Updated: 3/29/05.

South Carolina

University of South Carolina Aiken and University of South Carolina Columbia. Aiken: School of Education, Columbia: Department of Educational Psychology. 471 University Parkway, Aiken, SC 29801. (803) 641.3489. Fax: (803) 641.3720. Web site: http://edtech.usca.edu. Dr. Thomas Smyth, Professor, Program Director. smyth@usca.edu. *Specializations:* Master of Education in Educational Technology (A Joint Program of The University of South Carolina, Aiken and Columbia). *Features:* The master's degree in Educational Technology is designed to provide advanced professional studies in graduate level coursework to develop capabilities essential to the effective design, evaluation, and delivery of technology-based instruction and training (e.g., software development, multimedia development, assistive technology modifications, Web-based development, and distance learning). The program is intended (1) to prepare educators to assume leadership roles in the integration of educational technology into the school curriculum, and (2) to provide graduate-level instructional opportunities for several populations (e.g., classroom teachers, corporate trainers, educational software developers) that need to acquire both technological competencies and understanding of sound instructional design principles and techniques.

Several course offerings will be delivered from only one campus, though students on both campuses will enroll in the courses. These will include Web-based courses, two-way video courses, and courses that include a combination of Web-based, two-way video, and face-to-face meetings. *Admission Requirements:* Application to the Educational Technology Program can be made after completion of at least the bachelor's degree from a college or university accredited by a regional accrediting agency. The standard for admission will be based on a total profile for the applicant. The successful applicant should have an undergraduate grade point average of at least 3.0, a score of 45 on the Miller's Analogies Test or scores of 450 on both the verbal and quantitative portions of the Graduate Record Exam, a well-written letter of intent that matches the objectives of the program and includes a description of previous technology experience, and positive letters of recommendation from individuals who know the professional characteristics of the applicant. Any exceptions for students failing to meet these standards shall be referred to the Admissions Committee for review and final decision. *Degree Requirements:* 36 semester hours, including instructional theory, computer design, and integrated media. *Faculty:* 4 FT, 11 PT. *Students:* 39. *Financial Assistance:* Graduate Assistantships are available. *Degrees Awarded 2003:* This is a new program that began Fall 2002. Updated: 2/20/05.

Tennessee

East Tennessee State University. College of Education, Dept. of Curriculum and Instruction. Box 70684, Johnson City, TN 37614-0684. (423) 439-7843. Fax: (423) 439-8362. Web site: http://coe.etsu.edu/department/cuai/meda.htm. Harold Lee Daniels. danielsh@etsu.edu. *Specializations:* 1) M. Ed. in School Library Media; 2) M.Ed. in Educational Technology; 3) 24 hour School Library media specialist add on for those with current teaching license and a master's degree.; 4) M.Ed. in Classroom Technology for those with teaching license. *Features:* Two (MAC &PC) dedicated computer labs (45+ computers) Online and evening course offerings for part-time, commuter, and employed students. Student pricing/campus licensing on popular software (MS, Adobe, Macromedia, etc.) Off-site cohort programs for classroom teachers. Extensive software library (900+ titles) with review/checkout privileges. *Admission Requirements:* bachelor's degree from accredited institution, transcripts, personal essay; in some cases, GRE and/or interview. *Degree Requirements:* 36 semester hours, including 12 hours in common core of instructional technology and media, 18 professional content hours and 5 credit hour practicum (200 field experience hours). *Faculty:* 3 full-time, 4 part-time. *Students:* 15 full-time, 50 part-time. *Financial Assistance:* Scholarships, assistantships, aid for disabled. *Degrees Awarded 2003:* 8. Updated: 3/11/05.

University of Memphis. Instruction and Curriculum Leadership/Instructional Design & Technology, 406 Ball Hall, Memphis, TN 38152. (901) 678-2365. Fax: (901) 678-3881. Web site: http://idt.memphis.edu. Dr. Deborah Lowther (dlowther@memphis.edu). *Specializations:* Instructional Design, Web-based instruction, Computer-based instruction, Digital Video, K–12 NTeQ technology integration model, Instructional Games, Pedagogical Agents. *Features:* The Advanced Instructional Media (AIM) lab, staffed and run by IDT faculty and students, serves as an R&D space for coursework and research involving technologies such as digital media, WBT/CBT (Dreamweaver, Flash, Authorware, WebCT, DV cameras, DV editing, DVD authoring, etc.), pedagogical agents, gaming and simulation. The AIM lab and IDT program is connected to the Center for Multimedia Arts in the FedEx Institute of Technology. The AIM Lab brings in outside contract work from corporate partners to provide real-world experience to students. We have also partnered with the Institute for Intelligent Systems and the Tutoring Research Group (www.autotutor.org) to work on intelligent agent development and research. *Admission Requirements:* Minimum standards which identify a pool of master's level applicants from which each department selects students to be admitted: An official transcript showing a bachelor's degree awarded by an accredited college or university with a minimum GPA of 2.0 on a 4.0 scale, competitive MAT or GRE scores, GRE writing test, two letters of recommendation, graduate school and departmental application. Doctoral students must also be interviewed by at least two members of the program. *Degree Requirements:* M.S.: 36 hours, internship, master's project or thesis, 3.0 GPA. Ed.D: 54 hours, 45 in major, 9 in research; residency project; comprehensive exams; dissertation. *Faculty:* 4 full-time, 6 part-time. *Students:* 10 full-time, 50 part-time. *Financial Assistance:* Teaching Assistantships (Two classes, full tuition waiver plus stipend). Graduate Assistantships (20 hours per week, full tuition plus stipend). *Degrees Awarded 2003:* 2002/2003: 8 doctoral, 10 master's. 2003/2004: 5 doctoral, 10 master's. Updated: 4/1/05.

University of Tennessee—Knoxville. Instructional Technology and Educational Studies, College of Education. A535 Claxton Addition, Knoxville, TN 37996-3456. (423) 974-5037. Web site: http://Web.utk.edu/~itce/. Dr. Michael L. Waugh. waugh@utk.edu. *Specializations:* M.S. Ed.S. and Ph.D. in Ed. Concentrations in Curriculum/Evaluation/Research and Instructional Technology; M.S. and Ph.D. in Ed. Concentration in Cultural Studies in Education. *Features:* coursework in media production and management, advanced software production, utilization, research, theory, instructional computing, and instructional development. *Admission Requirements:* Send for Graduate Catalog, The University of Tennessee *Degree Requirements:* See Graduate Catalog for current program requirements. *Faculty:* 12 full-time. *Students:* M.S., 80; Ed.S., 30 ; Ed.D., 40; Ph.D., 50. *Degrees Awarded 2003:* approximately 20 across all levels.

Texas

Texas A&M University. Educational Technology Program, Dept. of Educational Psychology. College of Education and Human Development, College Station, TX 77843-4225. (979) 845-7276. Fax: (979) 862-1256. Web site: http://educ.coe.tamu.edu/~edtc. Ronald D. Zellner, Assoc. Prof., Coord. Program information. Carol Wagner for admissions materials. zellner@tamu.edu/c-wagner@tamu.edu. *Specializations:* M.Ed. in Educational Technology; EDCI Ph.D. program with specializations in Educational Technology and in Distance Education; Ph.D. in Educational Psychology Foundations: Learning and Technology. The purpose of the Educational Technology Program is to prepare educators with the competencies required to improve the quality and effectiveness of instructional programs at all levels. A major emphasis is placed on multimedia instructional materials development and techniques for effective distance education and communication. Teacher preparation with a focus on field-based instruction and school to university collaboration is also a major component. The program goal is to prepare graduates with a wide range of skills to work as professionals and leaders in a variety of settings, including education, business, industry, and the military. *Features:* Program facilities include laboratories for teaching, resource development, and production. Computer, video, and multimedia development are supported in a number of facilities. The college and university also maintain facilities for distance education materials development and fully equipped classrooms for course delivery to nearby collaborative school districts and sites throughout the state. *Admission Requirements:* M.Ed.: bachelor's degree, (range of scores, no specific cutoffs), 400 GRE Verbal, 550 (213 computer version) TOEFL; Ph.D.: 3.0 GPA, 450 GRE Verbal. Composite score from GRE verbal & Quantitative and GPA, letters of recommendation, general background, and student goal statement. *Degree Requirements:* M.Ed.: 39 semester credits, oral exam; Ph.D.: coursework varies with student goals; degree is a Ph.D. in Educational Psychology Foundations with specialization in educational technology. *Faculty:* 3 full-time; several associated faculty from related programs in EPSY. *Students:* M.Ed., 25 full-time, 15 part-time; Ph.D., 12 full-time, 10 part-time. *Financial Assistance:* several graduate assistantships and teaching assistantships. *Degrees Awarded 2004:* M.Ed. 21, Ph.D. 3. Updated: 2/18/05. Ron Zellner, zellner@tamu.edu

Texas A&M University—Commerce. Department of Secondary and Higher Education. PO Box 3011, Commerce, TX 75429-3011. (903) 886-5607. Fax: (903) 886-5603. Web site: http://www.tamu-commerce.edu/. Dr. Sue Espinoza, Associate Professor, Program Coordinator. Sue_Espinoza@tamu-commerce.edu. *Specializations:* M.S. or M.Ed. degree in Learning Technology and Information Systems with emphases in Educational Computing, Educational Media and Technology, and Library and Information Science. Certifications offered: School Librarian, and Technology Applications, both approved by the Texas State Board for Educator Certification. *Features:* Courses are offered in a variety of formats, including traditional classroom/lab based, and distance education, via video teleconferencing and/or online. Most courses are taught in only one of these, but some include multiple delivery methods. *Degree Requirements:* 36 hours for each master's degree; Educational Computing includes 30 hours of required courses, and 6 hours of electives; Media & Technology includes 21 hours of required courses, and 15 hours of electives, selected in consultation with advisor; Library includes courses in Library, Educational Technology, and Education. *Faculty:* 3 full-time, 5 part-time. *Students:* 30 full-time, 150 part-time. *Financial Assistance:* graduate assistantships in teaching and research, scholarships, federal aid program. *Degrees Awarded 2003:* 15.

Texas Tech University. College of Education. Box 41071,TTU, Lubbock, TX 79409. (806) 742-1997, ext. 287. Fax: (806) 742-2179. Web site: http://www.educ.ttu.edu/edit. Dr. Nancy Maushak, Program Coordinator, Instructional Technology. nancy.maushak @ttu.edu. *Specializations:* M.Ed. in Instructional Technology; completely online M.Ed. in Instructional Technology; Ed.D. in Instructional Technology. *Features:* Program is NCATE accredited and follows ISTE and AECT guidelines. *Admission Requirements:* holistic evaluation based on GRE scores, GPA, student goals and writing samples. *Degree Requirements:* M.Ed.: 39 hours (30 hours in educational technology, 6 hours in education, 3 hours electives). Ed.D.: 93 hours (60 hours in educational technology, 21 hours in education or resource area, 12 hours dissertation). *Faculty:* 5 full-time, 1 part-time, 6 teaching assistants. *Students:* M.Ed.:10 full-time, 30 part-time; Ed.D.:15 full-time, 15 part-time. *Financial Assistance:* teaching and research assistantships available ($9,000 for 9 months); small scholarships. *Degrees Awarded 2003:* 6 M.Ed, 2 Ed.D. Updated: 3/19/05.

University of Houston. Curriculum & Instruction, 256 Farish, Houston, TX 77204. (713) 743-4950; 713-743-4990. Web site: http://www.it.coe.uh.edu/. Melissa Pierson, Program Area Coordinator (mpierson@uh.edu). *Specializations:* urban community partnerships enhanced by technology, integration of technology in teaching, visual representation of information, collaborative design teams, innovative uses of technology in instruction, digital storytelling, digital photography, intercultural uses of technology, technology for STEM Education. *Features:* The IT Program at the University of Houston can be distinguished from other IT programs at other institutions through our unique philosophy based on a strong commitment to the broad representations of community, the individual, and the collaboration that strengthens the two. We broadly perceive community to include our college, the university, and the local Houston environment. The community is a rich context and resource from which we can solicit authentic learning tasks and clients, and to which we can contribute new perspectives and meaningful products. Our students graduate with real-world experience that can only be gained by experience with extended and coordinated community-based projects, not by contrived course requirements. Our program actively seeks outside funding to promote and continue such authentic projects because we so strongly believe it is the best context in which our students can develop expertise in the field.

We recognize that each student brings to our program a range of formal training, career experience, and future goals. Thus, no longer can we be satisfied with presenting a single, static curriculum and still effectively prepare students for a competitive marketplace. Our beliefs have led us to develop a program that recognizes and celebrates student individuality and diversity. Students work with advisors to develop a degree plan that begins from their existing knowledge and strives toward intended career goals. We aim to teach not specific software or hardware operations, but instead focus on transferable technical skills couched in solid problem-solving experiences, theoretical discussions, and a team-oriented atmosphere. Students work throughout the program to critically evaluate their own work for the purpose of compiling a performance portfolio that will accurately and comprehensively portray their individual abilities to themselves, faculty, and future employers.

Completing our philosophical foundation is a continuous goal of collaboration. Our faculty operates from a broad collaborative understanding that recognizes how everyone involved in any process brings unique and valuable experiences and perspectives. Within the IT program, faculty, staff, and students rely on each other to contribute relevant expertise. Faculty members regularly seek collaboration with other faculty in the College of Education, especially those involved with teacher education, as well as with faculty in other schools across campus. Collaboration is a focus that has been infused through the design of our courses and our relationships with students.

Admission Requirements: Admission information for graduate programs can be found at http://www.it.coe.uh.edu/. Master's program: 3.0 grade point average (GPA) for unconditional admission or a 2.6 GPA or above for conditional admission over the last 60 hours of coursework attempted. GRE or MAT scores: The 30 percentile on each section (Verbal, Quantitative, and Analytic) of the GRE serves as the minimum guideline for admission to all Master's programs in the College of Education. A score of 35 on the MAT serves as the minimum guideline for admissions to all Master's programs in the College of Education. The GRE or the MAT must have been taken within five (5) years of the date of application for admission to any Graduate program in the College of Education. Doctoral program: Each applicant must normally have earned a master's degree or have completed 36 semester hours of appropriate graduate work with a minimum GPA of 3.0 (A = 4.0). GRE: The 35th percentile on each section (Verbal, Quantitative, and Analytic) of the GRE serves as the minimum guideline for admission to all Doctoral programs in the College of Education. The GRE or the MAT must have been taken within five (5) years of the date of application for admission to any Graduate program in the College of Education. *Degree Requirements:* Students with backgrounds in educational technology can complete the master's program with 36 hours of coursework. For the typical student, the M.Ed. in Instructional Technology consists of 9 semester hours of core courses required by the College of Education, and an additional 18 hour core in Instructional Technology as well as 9 hours that are determined by the students career goals (K–12, higher education, business and industry). Students take a written comprehensive examination over the program, coursework, and experiences. The minimum hours required in the doctoral program is 66. More details about the courses and requirements can be found on the IT Web site: http://www.it.coe.uh.edu/. *Faculty:* 7 full time. *Students:* 20 full time, 120 part time. *Financial Assistance:* Graduate assistantships (20 hours week); university and college scholarships. *Degrees Awarded in 2004:* approximately 30. Updated: 3/28/05.

University of North Texas. Technology & Cognition (College of Education). Box 311337, Denton, TX 76203-1337. (940) 565-2057. Fax: (940) 565-2185. Web site: http://www.cecs.unt.edu. Dr. Mark Mortensen & Mrs. Donna Walton, Computer Education and Cognitive Systems. Dr. Jon Young, Chair, Dept. of Technology and Cognition. coeinfo@coefs.coe.unt.edu. *Specializations:* M.S. in Computer Education and Cognitive Systems—two emphasis areas: (1) Instructional Systems Technology and Teaching and (2) Learning with Technology. Ph.D. in Educational Computing. See www.cecs.unt.edu. *Fea-*

tures: Unique applications of theory through research and practice in curriculum integration of technology, digital media production, and Web development. See www.cecs. unt.edu. *Admission Requirements:* Toulouse Graduate School Requirements, 18 hours in education, acceptable GRE: 405 V,489 A, 3 Analytical Writing for M.S. Degree. Increased requirements for Ph.D. program. *Degree Requirements:* 36 semester hours (12 hour core, 12 hour program course requirement based on M.S. track, 12 hour electives; see www.cecs.unt.edu). *Faculty:* 8 full-time, 1 part-time. *Students:* 300+ actively enrolled students in M.S. Highly selective Ph.D. program. *Financial Assistance:* Please see http://essc.unt.edu/finaid/index.htm. *Degrees Awarded 2003:* 10-30.

The University of Texas at Austin. Curriculum & Instruction. 406 Sanchez Building, Austin, TX 78712-1294. (512) 471-5211. Fax: (512) 471-8460. Web site: http://jabba. edb.utexas.edu/it/. Min Liu, Ed.D., Associate Professor and IT Program Area Coordinator/Graduate Advisor. Mliu@mail.utexas.edu. *Specializations:* The Instructional Technology Program at the University of Texas—Austin is a graduate program and offers degrees at the master and doctoral levels. This comprehensive program prepares professionals for various positions in education and industry. Master's degrees (M.A. and M.Ed.) in Instructional Technology focus on the processes of systematic planning, design and development of instruction. Since IT requires more than skill in the production of instructional materials and use of machines, the instructional technologist emerging from our program uses knowledge of learning theory, curriculum development, instructional systems, communications theory, and evaluation to support appropriate uses of instructional resources.

The doctoral programs in Instructional Technology are comprehensive and research-oriented, providing knowledge and skills in areas such as instructional systems design, learning and instructional theories, instructional materials development and design of learning environments using various technology-based systems and tools. Graduates assume academic, administrative, and other leadership positions such as instructional evaluators, managers of instructional systems, and professors and researchers of instructional design and performance technology. *Features:* The program is interdisciplinary in nature, although certain competencies are required of all students. Programs of study and dissertation research are based on individual needs and career goals. Learning resources include a model Learning Technology Center, computer labs and classrooms, a television studio, and interactive multimedia lab. Students can take courses offered by other departments, including Radio-TV Film, School of Information, Computer Science, and Educational Psychology. *Admission Requirements:* 95% of the current students and recent graduates admission materials included the following: master's: 3.5 GPA; 450 GRE Verbal, 1150 GRE Verbal + Quantitative; strong letters of recommendation; statement of study goals that can be satisfied with existing program offerings and resources. Doctoral: 3.5 GPA; 500 GRE Verbal, 1250 GRE Verbal + Quantitative; strong letters of recommendation; statement of study goals that can be satisfied with existing program offerings and resources *Degree Requirements:* see http://jabba.edb.utexas.edu/it/ for details. *Faculty:* 3 full-time. *Students:* 19 master's, 36 doctoral. *Financial Assistance:* Different forms of financial aid are often available to develop instructional materials, supervise student teachers in local schools, and assist with research/service projects. *Degrees Awarded Fall 2003–Summer 2004:* 2 master's; 2 doctoral, 5 master's; 6 doctoral. Updated: 2/20/05.

Utah

Brigham Young University. Department of Instructional Psychology and Technology. 150 MCKB, BYU, Provo, UT 84602. (801) 422-5097. Fax: (801) 422-0314. Web site: http://www.byu.edu/ipt. Russell Osguthorpe, Prof., Chair. russ_osguthorpe@byu.edu. *Specializations:* M.S. degrees in Instructional Design, Research and Evaluation, and Multimedia Production. Ph.D. degrees in Instructional Design, and Research and Evaluation. *Features:* Course offerings include principles of learning, instructional design, assessing learning outcomes, evaluation in education, empirical inquiry in education, project management, quantitative reasoning, microcomputer materials production, multimedia production, naturalistic inquiry, and more. Students participate in internships and projects related to development, evaluation, measurement, and research. *Admission Requirements:* both degrees: transcript, 3 letters of recommendation, letter of intent, GRE scores. Apply by Feb 1. Students agree to live by the BYU Honor Code as a condition for admission. *Degree Requirements:* Master's: 36 semester hours, including core courses (17 hours), specialization (9 hours), seminar (1 hour), internship (3 hours), thesis or project (6 hours) with oral defense. Ph.D.: 72 semester hours beyond the Bachelor's degree, including: prerequisite courses (3 hours), required core courses (13 hours), specialization (18 hours), seminar (2 hours), internship (12 hours), two projects (6 hours), and dissertation (18 hours). The dissertation must be orally defended. At least two consecutive 9-hour semesters (Fall and Winter) must be completed in residence. *Faculty:* 10 full-time. *Students:* master's, 30 full-time; Ph.D., 50 full-time. *Financial Assistance:* internships, tuition scholarships, loans, and travel to present papers. *Degrees Awarded:* Average 9–12 per year. Updated: 4/27/05.

Utah State University. Department of Instructional Technology, College of Education. 2830 Old Main Hill, Logan, UT 84322-2830. (435) 797-2694. Fax: (435) 797-2693. Web site: http://www.coe.usu:edu/it/. Dr. Byron R. Burnham, Prof., Chair. byron. burnham@ usu.edu. *Specializations:* M.S. and Ed.S. with concentrations in the areas of Instructional Development, Multimedia, Educational Technology, and Information Technology/School Library Media Administration. Ph.D. in Instructional Technology is offered for individuals seeking to become professionally involved in instructional development in corporate education, public schools, community colleges, and universities. Teaching and research in higher education is another career avenue for graduates of the program. *Features:* M.S. and Ed.S. programs in Information Technology/School Library Media Administration and Educational Technology are also delivered via an electronic distance education system. The doctoral program is built on a strong master's and specialists program in Instructional Technology. All doctoral students complete a core with the remainder of the course selection individualized, based upon career goals. *Admission Requirements:* M.S. and Ed.S.: 3.0 GPA, a verbal and quantitative score at the 40th percentile on the GRE or 43 MAT, three written recommendations. Ph.D.: master's degree in Instructional Technology, 3.0 GPA, verbal and quantitative score at the 40th percentile on the GRE, three written recommendations. *Degree Requirements:* M.S.: 39 semester hours; thesis or project option. Ed.S.: 30 semester hours if M.S. is in the field, 40 hours if not. Ph.D.: 62 total hours, dissertation, 3-semester residency, and comprehensive examination. *Faculty:* 11 full-time, 7 part-time. *Students:* M.S., 70 FT, 119 PT; Ed.S., 6 full-time, 9 part-time; Ph.D., 60. *Financial Assistance:* approx. 18 to 26 assistantships (apply by April 1). *Degrees Awarded 2004:* 19 M.S.; 42 M.Ed.; 4 Ph.D. Updated: 2/22/05.

Virginia

George Mason University. Instructional Technology Programs. Mail Stop 5D6, 4400 University Dr., Fairfax, VA 22030-4444. (703) 993-3798. Fax: (703) 993-2722. Web site: http://it.gse.gmu.edu/. Dr. Eamonn Kelly, Coord. of Instructional Technology Academic Programs. akelly1@gmu.edu. *Specializations:* Ph.D. specializations in Instructional Design and Development; Integration of Technology in Schools; Assistive Technology; master's degrees in Curriculum and Instruction with emphasis in Instructional Technology: Track I—Instructional Design and Development; Track II—Integration of Technology in Schools; Track III—Assistive Technology; Track IV—Technology Innovations in Education. Graduate Certificates: Multimedia Development; Integration of Technology in Schools; Assistive Technology. *Features:* The Instructional Technology program promotes the theory-based design of learning opportunities that maximize the teaching and learning process using a range of technology applications. Program efforts span a range of audiences, meeting the needs of diverse learners—school-aged, adult learners, and learners with disabilities—in public and private settings. Within this framework, the program emphasizes research, reflection, collaboration, leadership, and implementation and delivery models. The Instructional Technology (IT) program provides professionals with the specialized knowledge and skills needed to apply today's computer and telecommunications technologies to educational goals within school, community and corporate settings. The IT program serves professional educators as well as those involved in instructional design, development and training in government and private sectors. Master degrees and certificates can be earned in each of three program tracks. Refer to the IT Web site (http://it.gse.gmu.edu/) for detailed information on admissions.

Track 1—Instructional Design and Development (IDD)—Students are prepared to craft effective solutions within public, private and educational contexts to instructional challenges by using the latest information technologies in the design and development of instructional materials.

Track II: Integration of Technology in Schools (ITS)—Students are prepared to effectively integrate technology in the K–12 learning environment. Graduates frequently become the local expert and change agent for technology in schools.

Track III: Assistive/Special Education Technology (A/SET)—Graduates will use technology to assist individuals to function more effectively in school, home, work and community environments. Graduates are prepared to incorporate technology into the roles of educators, related service providers, Assistive Technology consultants, hardware/software designers and school based technology coordinators.

Track IV: TIE focuses on the following concepts and practical applications of technology in educational environments: Emerging educational trends and innovations in technology and their potential impact on learning, policy and leadership issues, creating community partnerships, distance learning and its present and future impact on education. This program is intended for students who are already familiar with technology and are looking to expand their knowledge and skills. The program will combine instructional design activities with integration in K–12, higher education, and corporate learning environments. Exciting aspects of the program include the building and programming of robots using Lego Mindstorms, designing and creating an innovative project and then evaluating its effectiveness for learning, developing partnerships with the Museum of Art and serving as online mentors for pre-service teachers. *Admission Requirements:* Teaching or training experience, undergrad GPA of 3.0,TOEFL of 575(written) /230(computer), three letters of recommendation, goal statement. *Degree Requirements:* M.Ed. in Curriculum and Instruction: 39 hours; practicum, internship, or project. M.Ed. in Special Education: 36–42 hours. Ph.D.: 56–62 hours beyond master's degree for either specialization. Certificate programs: 12–15 hours. *Faculty:* 8 full-time, 15 part-time. *Students:* M.Ed. full-time, 75; M.Ed., part-time, 150; certificate programs, 300. *Financial Assistance:* Information on assistantships, fellowships, loans and other types of financial aid is available through the Office of Student Financial Aid at (703) 993-2353 or at apollo.gmu.edu/finaid. The IDD cohort offers tuition assistance. *Degrees Awarded 2003:* 130. Updated: 2/21/05.

Radford University. Educational Studies Department, College of Education and Human Development. P.O. Box 6959, Radford,, VA 24142. (540) 831-5302. Fax: (540) 831-5059. Web site: http://www.radford.edu. Dr. Martin S. Aylesworth, Acting Dept. Chair. mayleswo@radford.edu. *Specializations:* M.S. in Education with Educational Media/Technology emphasis. *Features:* School Library Media Specialist licensure. *Admission Requirements:* bachelor's degree, 2.7 undergraduate GPA. *Degree Requirements:* 33 semester hours, practicum; thesis optional. *Faculty:* 2 full-time, 3 part-time. *Students:* 2

full-time, 23 part-time. *Financial Assistance:* assistantships, grants, student loans, scholarships. Updated: 5/28/03.

University of Virginia. Department of Leadership, Foundations, and Policy, Curry School of Education. Ruffner Hall, Charlottesville, VA 22903. (434) 924-7471. Fax: (434) 924-0747. Web site: http://curry.edschool.virginia.edu/curry/dept/edlf/instrtech/. John B. Bunch, Assoc. Prof., Coord., Instructional Technology Program, Dept. of Leadership, Foundations and Policy Studies. jbbunch@virginia.edu. *Specializations:* M.Ed., Ed.S., Ed.D, and Ph.D. degrees with focal areas in Media Production, Interactive Multimedia, e-Learning/Distance learning and K–12 Educational Technologies. *Features:* The IT program is situated in a major research university with linkages to multiple disciplines. Graduate Students have the opportunity to work with faculty across the Curry School and the University. *Admission Requirements:* undergraduate degree from accredited institution in any field, undergraduate GPA 3.0, 1000 GRE (V+Q), 600 TOEFL. Financial aid application deadline is March 1st of each year for the fall semester for both master's and doctoral degrees; admission is rolling. *Degree Requirements:* M.Ed.: 36 semester hours, comprehensive examination. Ed.S.: 60 semester hours beyond undergraduate degree. Ed.D.: 54 semester hours, dissertation, at least one conference presentation or juried publication, comprehensive examination, residency; Ph.D.: same as Ed.S. with the addition of 18 semester hours. For specific degree requirements, see Web site, write to the address above, or refer to the UVA. *Faculty:* 5 full-time, 2 part-time. *Students:* M.Ed. 9/11 Ed.D, 1/3; Ph.D., 16/11. *Financial Assistance:* Graduate assistantships and scholarships are available on a competitive basis. *Degrees Awarded 2004:* 6 M.Ed., 6 Ph.D. Updated: 3/28/05.

Virginia Polytechnic Institute and State University. College of Liberal Arts and Human Sciences. 220 War Memorial Hall, Blacksburg, VA 24061-0341. (540) 231-5587. Fax: (540) 231-9075. Web site: http://www.tandl.vt.edu/it/default.htm. Katherine Cennamo, Program Area Leader, Instructional Technology, Dept. of Teaching and Learning. cennamo@vt.edu. *Specializations:* M.A., Ed.S. Ed.D., and Ph.D. in Instructional Technology. Preparation for education, higher education, faculty development, business, and industry. *Features:* Areas of emphasis are Instructional Design, Distance Education, and Multimedia Development. Facilities include two computer labs, extensive digital video and audio equipment, distance education classroom, and computer graphics production areas. *Admission Requirements:* Ed.D. and Ph.D.: 3.3 GPA from master's degree, GRE scores, writing sample, three letters of recommendation, transcripts. MA.: 3.0 GPA Undergraduate. *Degree Requirements:* Ph.D.: 96 hrs above B.S., 2-year residency, 12 hrs. research classes, 30 hrs. dissertation; Ed.D.: 90 hrs. above B.S., 1 year residency, 12 hrs. research classes; MA.: 30 hrs. above B.S. *Faculty:* 6 full-time, 2 part-time. *Students:* 35 FT and 10 PT, doctoral level. 15 FT and 200 PT (online) master's. *Financial Assistance:* 10 assistantships, limited tuition scholarships. *Degrees Awarded 2003:* 9 Ph.D. and 50 MS. Updated: 3/2/05.

Virginia State University. School of Graduate Studies, Research and Outreach. 1 Hayden Drive, Box 9402, Petersburg, VA 23806. (804) 524-5377. Fax: (804) 524-5104. Web site: http://www.vsu.edu. Vykuntapathi Thota, Chair, Dept. of Education. *Specializations:* M.S., M.Ed. in Educational Technology. *Features:* Video Conferencing Center and PLATO Laboratory, internship in ABC and NBC channels. *Admission Requirements:* See Web site. *Degree Requirements:* 30 semester hours plus thesis for M.S.; 33 semester hours plus project for M.Ed.; comprehensive exam. *Faculty:* 1 full-time, 2 part-time. *Students:* 8 full-time, 50 part-time. *Financial Assistance:* Scholarships through the School of Graduate Studies. Updated: 5/19/03.

Washington

Eastern Washington University. Department of Computer Science. 202 Computer Science Building, Cheney, WA 99004-2412. (509) 359-6260. Fax: (509) 359-2215. Web site: http://acm.ewu.edu/csd/. Ray O Hamel, Ph.D., Linda Kieffer, Ph.D. compsci@ mailserver.ewu.edu. *Specializations:* M.Ed. in Computer and Technology Supported Education; M.S. Interdisciplinary. Master's program started in 1983. *Features:* Many projects involve the use of high-level authoring systems to develop educational products, technology driven curriculum, and Web projects. *Admission Requirements:* 3.0 GPA for last 90 graded undergraduate quarter credits. *Degree Requirements:* M.S Interdisciplinary.: 52 quarter hours (30 hours in computers, 15 hours outside education; the hours do not total to 52 because of freedom to choose where Methods of Research is taken, where 12 credits of supporting courses are taken, and where additional electives are taken); research project with formal report. M.Ed.: 52 quarter hours (28 hours in computer education, 16 hours in education, 8 hours outside education). *Faculty:* 1 full-time. *Students:* approx. 25. *Financial Assistance:* some research and teaching fellowships. Updated: 5/3003.

University of Washington. College of Education. 115 Miller Hall, Box 353600, Seattle, WA 98195-3600. (206) 543-1847. Fax: (206) 543-8439. Web site: http://www.educ. washington.edu/COE/c-and-i/c_and_i_med_ed_tech.htm. William Winn, Prof. of Education. billwinn@u.washington.edu. *Specializations:* M.Ed., Ed.D, and Ph.D. for individuals in business, industry, higher education, public schools, and organizations concerned with education or communication (broadly defined). *Features:* Emphasis on design of materials and programs to encourage learning and development in school and non-school settings; research and related activity in such areas as interactive instruction, Web-based learning, virtual environments, use of video as a tool for design and development. Close collaboration with program in Cognitive Studies. *Admission Requirements:* M.Ed.: goal statement (2-3pp.), writing sample, 1000 GRE (verbal plus quantitative), undergraduate GPA indicating potential to successfully accomplish graduate work. Doctoral: GRE scores, letters of reference, transcripts, personal statement, master's degree or equivalent in field appropriate to the specialization with 3.5 GPA, two years of successful professional experience and/or experience related to program goals. *Degree Requirements:* M.Ed.: 45 quarter hours (including 24 in technology); thesis or project recommended, exam optional. Ed.D.: see http://www.educ.washington.edu/COEWebsite/programs/ci/EdD.html. Ph.D.: http://www. educ.washington.edu/COEWebsite/students/prospective/phdDescrip.html. *Faculty:* 4 full-time, 2 part-time. *Students:* 12 full-time, 32 part-time; 20 M.Ed., 10 doctoral. *Financial Assistance:* assistantships awarded competitively and on basis of program needs; other assistantships available depending on grant activity in any given year. *Degrees Awarded 2003:* 2. Updated: 3/14/05.

Western Washington University. Woodring College of Education, Instructional Technology. MS 9087, Bellingham, WA 98225-9087. (360) 650-3387. Fax: (360) 650-6526. Web site: http://www.wce.wwu.edu/depts/IT. Dr. Les Blackwell, Prof., Department Chair. Les.Blackwell@wwu.edu. *Specializations:* M.Ed. with emphasis in Instructional Technology in Adult Education, Special Education, Elementary Education, and Secondary Education. *Admission Requirements:* 3.0 GPA in last 45 quarter credit hours, GRE or MAT scores, 3 letters of recommendation, and, in some cases, 3 years of teaching experience. *Degree Requirements:* 48–52 quarter hours (24–28 hours in instructional technology; 24 hours in education-related courses, thesis required; internship and practicum possible). *Faculty:* 6 full-time, 8 part-time. *Students:* 5 full-time, 10 part-time. *Financial Assistance:* assistantships, student loans, scholarships.

Wisconsin

Edgewood College. Department of Education. 1000 Edgewood College Drive, Madison, WI 53711-1997. (608) 663-2293. Fax: (608) 663-6727. Web site: http://www. edgewood.edu. Dr. Joseph E. Schmiedicke, Chair, Dept. of Education. schmied@ edgewood.edu. *Specializations:* M.A. in Education with emphasis on Instructional Technology. Master's program started in 1987. *Features:* classes conducted in laboratory setting with emphasis on applications and software. *Admission Requirements:* 2.75 GPA *Degree Requirements:* 36 semester hours. *Faculty:* 2 full-time, 3 part-time. *Students:* 5 full-time, 150 part-time. *Financial Assistance:* grants, student loans. *Degrees Awarded 2003:* 8.

University of Wisconsin—La Crosse. Educational Media Program. Rm. 235C, Morris Hall, La Crosse, WI 54601. (608) 785-8121. Fax: (608) 785-8128. Web site: http://www.uwlax.edu/mediaservices/soe/html/soe-about.htm. Ronald Rochon, Ph. D., Interim Associate Dean, Director of School of Education. rochon.rona@uwlax.edu. *Specializations:* M.S. in Professional Development with specializations in Initial Instructional Library Specialist, License 901; Instructional Library Media Specialist, License 902 (39 credits). *Degree Requirements:* 30 semester hours, including 15 in media; no thesis. *Faculty:* 2 full-time, 4 part-time. *Students:* 21. *Financial Assistance:* guaranteed student loans, graduate assistantships.

University of Wisconsin—Madison. Curriculum and Instruction, School of Education. 225 North Mills Street, Madison, WI 53706. 608) 263-4670. Fax: (608) 263-9992. Web site: http://www.education.wisc.edu/ci/. Michael J. Streibel. streibel@education.wisc.edu. *Specializations:* M.S. and Ph.D. degree programs to prepare college and university faculty. On-going research in photography and visual culture in education as well as educational game design and design experiments in education. *Features:* Traditional instructional technology courses are processed through social, cultural, and historical frames of reference. Current curriculum emphasizes new media theories, critical cultural and visual culture theories, and constructivist theories of instructional design and development. Many courses offered in the evening. *Admission Requirements:* Master's and Ph.D.: previous experience in Instructional Technology preferred, previous teaching experience, 3.0 GPA on last 60 undergraduate credits, acceptable scores on GRE, 3.0 GPA on all graduate work. *Degree Requirements:* M.S.: 24 credits plus thesis and exam (an additional 12 credits of Educational Foundations if no previous educational background); Ph.D.: 1 year of residency beyond the bachelor's, major, minor, and research requirements, preliminary exam, dissertation, and oral exam. *Faculty:* 2 full-time, 1 part-time. *Students:* M.S., 24; Ph.D., 12. *Financial Assistance:* TA and PA positions are available. *Degrees Awarded 2003:* 5 M.S.

Foreign Institutions

Universiti Sains Malaysia. Centre for Instructional Technology and Multimedia, Centre for Instructional Tech and Multimedia, Universiti Sains Malaysia, Minden, Pg 11800, Malaysia. (+604) 6533222. Fax: (+604) 6576749. Web site: http://www.ptpm.usm.my. Zarina Samsudin, Director. ina@usm.my. *Specializations:* instructional design, Web/Internet instruction and learning, educational training/resource management instructional training technology/evaluation, instructional system development, design and development of multimedia/video/training materials, instructional and training technology, constructivism in instructional technology. A new master's in instructional technology program started in 2004–2005 (duration: full-time, 1–2 years; part-time, 2–4 years).

Teaching Programs—Postgraduate programs and research; consultancy—services on the application of educational technology in teaching learning; training and diffusion—

Diploma in Multimedia, Certificate in Training Technology and Continuing Education; Academic Support Services—services to support research, teaching and learning activities and centers within the University. *Admission Requirements:* bachelor's and master's degree from accredited institution. *Faculty:* 13 full-time. *Students:* Postgraduate students: 30 full-time, 60 part-time. *Financial Assistance:* None. Updated: 3/3/04.

Part Six
Mediagraphy

Introduction

Chun-Min Wang, Editor

CONTENTS

This resource lists media-related journals, books, ERIC documents, journal articles, and nonprint media resources of interest to practitioners, researchers, students, and others concerned with educational technology and educational media. The primary goal of this section is to list current publications in the field. The majority of materials cited here were published in fall 2004 or spring 2005. Media-related journals include those listed in past issues of *EMTY* and new entries in the field. A thorough list of journals in the educational technology field has been updated for the 2005 edition using Ulrich's Periodical Index Online and journal Web sites. This section is not intended to serve as a specific resource location tool, although it may be used for that purpose in the absence of database access. Rather, readers are encouraged to peruse the categories of interest in this chapter to gain an idea of recent developments within the field. For archival purposes, this chapter serves as a snapshot of the field in 2005. Readers must bear in mind that technological developments occur well in advance of publication and should take that fact into consideration when judging the timeliness of resources listed in this chapter.

SELECTION

Items were selected for the Mediagraphy in several ways. The EBSCO Host Databases were used to locate most of the journal citations. Others were reviewed directly by the editors. Items were chosen for this list when they met one or more of the following criteria: reputable publisher, broad circulation, coverage by indexing services, peer review, and coverage of a gap in the literature. The editors chose items on subjects that seem to reflect the instructional technology field as it is today. Because of the increasing tendency for media producers to package their products in more that one format and for single titles to contain mixed media, titles are no longer separated by media type. The editors make no claims as to the comprehensiveness of this list. It is, instead, intended to be representative.

OBTAINING RESOURCES

Media-Related Periodicals and Books: Publisher, price, and ordering/subscription address are listed wherever available.

ERIC Documents: As of December 31, 2003, ERIC was no longer funded. However, ERIC documents can still be read and copied from their microfiche form at any library holding an ERIC microfiche collection. The identification number beginning with ED (for example, ED 332 677) locates the document in the collection. Document delivery services and copies of most ERIC documents can also continue to be available from the ERIC Document Reproduction Service. Prices charged depend upon format chosen (microfiche or paper copy), length of the document, and method of shipping. Online orders, fax orders, and expedited delivery are available.

To find the closest library with an ERIC microfiche collection, contact: ACCESS ERIC, 1600 Research Blvd., Rockville, MD 20850-3172; (800) LET-ERIC (538-3742); e-mail: acceric@inet.ed.gov

To order ERIC documents, contact:

ERIC Document Reproduction Service (EDRS)
7420 Fullerton Rd., Suite 110, Springfield, VA 22153-2852
(800) 443-ERIC (443-3742); (703) 440-1400
fax: (703) 440-1408
e-mail: service@edrs.com.

Journal articles: Photocopies of journal articles can be obtained in one of the following ways: (1) from a library subscribing to the title, (2) through interlibrary loan, (3) through the purchase of a back issue from the journal publisher, or (4) from an article reprint service such as UMI.

UMI Information Store, 500 Sansome Street, Suite 400
San Francisco, CA 94111
(800) 248-0360 (toll-free in U.S. and Canada); (415) 433-5500 (outside U.S. and Canada)
E-mail: orders@infostore.com

Journal articles can also be obtained through the Institute for Scientific Information (ISI).

ISI Document Solution
P.O. Box 7649
Philadelphia, PA 19104-3389
(215) 386-4399
Fax (215) 222-0840 or (215)386-4343
E-mail: ids@isinet.com

ARRANGEMENT

Mediagraphy entries are classified according to major subject emphasis under the following headings:

- Artificial Intelligence, Robotics, and Electronic Performance Support Systems
- Computer-Assisted Instruction
- Distance Education
- Educational Research
- Educational Technology
- Information Science and Technology
- Innovation
- Instructional Design and Development
- Interactive Multimedia
- Libraries and Media Centers
- Media Technologies
- Professional Development
- Simulation, Gaming, and Virtual Reality
- Special Education and Disabilities
- Telecommunications and Networking

Mediagraphy

ARTIFICIAL INTELLIGENCE, ROBOTICS, AND ELECTRONIC PERFORMANCE SUPPORT SYSTEMS

AI Magazine [online]. AAAI Press, American Association for Artificial Intelligence, 445 Burgess Drive, Menlo Park, CA 94025-3442, www.aaai.org, www.aaai.org/Magazine/magazine.html [4/yr., $50 indiv., $65 inst.]. Proclaimed "journal of record for the AI community," *AI Magazine* provides full=length articles on research, new literature but is written to allow access to those reading outside their area of expertise.

Artificial Intelligence Review. Kluwer Academic Publishers, 101 Philip Drive, Norwell, MA 02061, customer.service@springer-sbm.com, www.wkap.nl/journalhome.htm/0269-2821 [6 issues/yr, $635 inst. for print and online eds.]. Publishes commentary on issues and development in artificial intelligence foundations and current research.

International Journal of Robotics Research. Sage Science Press, http://www.sagepub.com/ [mo., indiv., $151, $1,263.36 inst., available online]. Interdisciplinary approach to the study of robotics for researchers, scientists, and students. The first scholarly publication on robotics research.

Journal of Intelligent and Robotic Systems. Springer Science+Business Media B.V Publishers, PO Box 14302 14197 Berlin, Germany, www.wkap.nl/journalhome.htm/0921-0296 [mo., $1258 inst., for print *or* online format]. The main objective is to provide a forum for the fruitful interaction of ideas and techniques that combine systems and control science with artificial intelligence—and other related computer science—concepts. It bridges the gap between theory and practice.

Journal of Interactive Learning Research. Association for Advancement of Computing in Education, Box 2966, Charlottesville, VA 22902-2966, aace@virginia.edu, www.aace.org [q.; $140 inst., $155 foreign inst., $40 student., $55 foreign student]. International journal publishes articles on how intelligent computer technologies can be used in education to enhance learning and teaching. Reports on research and developments, integration, and applications of artificial intelligence in education.

Knowledge-Based Systems. Elsevier BV, 6277 Sea Harbor Drive Orlando, FL 32887-4800 USA, e-mail: usjcs@elsevier.com, www.elsevier.com/locate/knosys [8 issues/yr, $1,000 inst., except in Europe and Japan]. Interdisciplinary applications-oriented journal on fifth-generation computing, expert systems, and knowledge-based methods in system design.

Martínez-Miranda, J., & Aldea, A. (2005, March). Emotions in human and artificial intelligence. *Computers in Human Behavior, 21*(2), 323–341. This paper presents a review of recent research that shows the importance of the emotions in human intelligence and the research that has been carried out into the incorporation of emotions to intelligent systems.

Minds and Machines: Journal for Artificial Intelligence, Philosophy and Cognitive Science. Kluwer Academic Publishers, 101 Philip Drive, Norwell, MA 02061 [q., $545 inst.]. Discusses issues concerning machines and mentality, artificial intelligence, epistemology, simulation, and modeling.

Pfeifer, R., Iida, F., & Bongard, J. (2005, winter). New robotics: Design principles for intelligent systems. *Artificial Life, 11*(1/2), 99–120. This article provides an overview of all the principles for intelligent systems design with the focus on the ecological balance.

Prasad, S. M., Prasad, S. M., Maniar, H. S., Chu, C., Schuessler, R. B., & Damiano, R. J. (2004, December). Surgical robotics: Impact of motion scaling on task performance. *Journal of the American College of Surgeons, 199*(6), 863–868. This study compares the surgical accuracy between conventional laparoscopic instruments and a robotic surgical system and evaluate the importance of tremor filtration (TF) and motion scaling (MS) in these robotic systems.

Robinson, M. (2005, February). Robotics-driven activities: Can they improve middle school science learning? *Bulletin of Science, Technology & Society, 25*(1), 73–84. This article shows that robotics can promote inquiry, make physics more interesting, and help students learn and practice new words in English.

Ruiz-del-Solar, J., & Aviles, R. (2004, November). Robotics courses for children as a motivation tool: The Chilean experience. *IEEE Transactions on Education, 47*(4), 474–480. This article reviews the authors' experience concerning practical robotics courses for children developed since 2000.

Ziemke, T., Bergfeldt, N., Buason, G., Susi, T., & Svensson, H. (2004, December). Evolving cognitive scaffolding and environment adaptation: A new research direction for evolutionary robotics. *Connection Science, 16*(4), 339–350. This article examines how the evolution of environment adaptation can sent to provide cognitive scaffolding that reduces the requirements for individual agents. Besides, the theoretical implications, open questions, and future research directions for evolutionary robotics are also discussed.

COMPUTER-ASSISTED INSTRUCTION

Australian Educational Computing. Australian Council for Computers in Education. PO Box 1255, Belconnen, ACT 2616, Australia. Available online at www.acce.edu.au, secretary@acce.edu.au [irregular publishing, online]. Educational computer issues forum.

Brett, P., & Nagra, J. (2005, March). An investigation into students' use of a computer-based social learning space: Lessons for facilitating collaborative approaches to learning. *British Journal of Educational Technology, 36*(2), 281–292. The results of this study inform how higher education institutions might best provide computer access to learners to encourage collaborative working and positively affect student approaches to their learning.

CALICO Journal. Computer Assisted Language Instruction Consortium (CALICO), 214 Centennial Hall, 601 University Drive, San Marcos, TX 78666, info@calico.org, www.calico.org [3/yr., $ 35 indiv., $ 45 indiv. in Canada and Mexico, $60 elsewhere; $ 70 inst. $80 inst. in Canada and Mexico, $95 elsewhere]. Provides information on the applications of technology in teaching and learning languages.

Chiang, A. C.-C., & Fung, I. P.-W. (2004, December). Redesigning chat forum for critical thinking in a problem-based learning environment. *Internet & Higher Education, 7*(4), 311–328. This article introduces a model that supports problem-based learning (PBL) and enhances critical thinking skills in discussion-based Internet forums.

Children's Technology Review. CSR, 120 Main Street, Flemington, NJ 08822; www.childrenssoftware.com [4/yr., $26, $42 in Canada, $ 59 elsewhere]. Provides reviews and other information about software to help parents and educators more effectively use computers with children.

Computer Education. K.K. Roy, Ltd., 55 Gariahat Rd., PO Box 10210, Calcutta, West Bengal 700 019, India, Ed. K.K. Roy. Tel. 91-33-475-4872 [Bi-monthly, $35 US]. Discusses how schools and universities are using educational software. Profiles and reviews new educational software n the market in content areas such as science, social science, and the humanities.

Computer Education. Staffordshire University, Computer Education Group, c/o CEG Treasurer, Beaconside, Staffs, ST18 0AD, United Kingdom, Ed. S. Kennewell [3/yr., 25 GBP to US]. Covers Educational Computer application for students 11–18 years of age.

Computer Learning. Computer Learning Foundation, PO Box 60007, Palo Alto, CA 94306-0007, clf@computerlearning.org, http://www.computerlearning.org. Free. Focuses people's attention on the importance of technology in children's learning. Includes tips for parents and teachers.

Computers and Composition. Elsevier Ltd., 6277 Sea Harbor Drive Orlando, FL 32887-4800 USA [4/yr., $72 indiv., $296 inst.]. International journal for teachers of writing focuses on the use of computers in writing instruction and related research and dialogue.

Computers & Education. Elsevier, Regional Sales Office, Customer Service Department, 6277 Sea Harbor Drive, Orlando, FL 32887-4800 USA [8/yr., $183 indiv., $1,478 inst.]. Presents technical papers covering a broad range of subjects for users of analog, digital, and hybrid computers in all aspects of higher education.

Computers in Education Journal. American Society for Engineering Education, Computers in Education Decision, PO Box 68, Port Royal Sq, Port Royal, VA 22535, Ed. W.W. Everett, Jr. [q., $45 US, $65 foreign]. Covers transactions, scholarly research papers, application notes, and teaching methods.

Computers in Human Behavior. Elsevier, Customer Service Department, 6277 Sea Harbor Drive, Orlando, FL 32887-4800 USA [6/yr., $252 indiv., $1,158 inst.]. Scholarly journal dedicated to examining the use of computers from a psychological perspective.

Computers in the Schools. Haworth Press, 10 Alice St., Binghamton, NY 13904-1580, (800) HAWORTH, fax (800) 895-0582, getinfo@haworthpressinc.com, www. haworthpress.com [q., $75 indiv., $150 inst., $420 libraries]. Features articles that combine theory and practical applications of small computers in schools for educators and school administrators.

Converge Online. E. Republic, Inc., 100 Blue Ravine, Folsom, CA 95630, toll free (877) 487-7377. cz@convergemag.com, www.convergemag.com/ [free]. Explores the revolution of technology in education.

Curriculum-Technology Quarterly. Association for Supervision and Curriculum Development, Education & Technology Resource Center, 1703 N Beauregard St., Alexandria, VA 22311, (800) 933-2723, member@ascd.org, www.ascd.org. Ed. Rick Allen [q., $10 per issue]. Explores strategies for using technology for enhancing classroom instruction. Includes pullout sections on curriculum content areas. For K–12 teachers and curriculum developers.

Dr. Dobb's Journal. C M P Media LLC, Dr. Dobb's Journal PO Box 56188, Boulder, CO 80322-6188, (800) 456-1215, www.djj.com/djj [mo., $25 US, $35 Mexico and Canada, $50 elsewhere]. Articles on the latest in operating systems, programming languages, algorithms, hardware design and architecture, data structures, and telecommunications; in-depth hardware and software reviews.

Education Technology News. Business Publishers, Inc., 8737 Colesville Rd., 10th floor, Silver Spring, MD 20910-3928, (800) 274-6737, bpinews@bpinews.com, http://www. bpinews.com. Ed. Rasheda Childress [bi-w., $217/yr.]. For teachers and other persons interested in the educational uses of computers in the classroom. Includes future articles on application, educational software, and pertinent programs.

Educational Software Review. Growth Systems, Inc. 855 Normandy Rd., Encinitas, CA 92024, Ed. Stewart Walton [M., $33.75]. A newsletter designed for parents to choose software for children.

Educational Technology and Society. International Forum of Educational Technology and Society. IEEE Computer Society, Learning Technology Task Force, kinshuk@ieee.org, http://ifets.gmd.de/periodical. Eds. Ashok Patel and Reinhard Oppermann [q., free]. Explores issues concerning educational software developers and educators.

Educational Technology Review. Association for the Advancement of Computing in Education, PO Box 2966, Charlottesville, VA 22902-2966, info@aace.org, http://www. aace.org. Ed. Gary H Marks [q., $40 domestic to nonmembers, $50 to nonmembers]. Publishes articles dealing with the issues in instructional technology application.

Electronic Education Report. SIMBA Information, 60 Long Ridge Road, Suite 300, Stamford, CT 06902, (203) 325-8193, info@simbanet.com, http://www.simbanet.com. Ed. Kathleen Martucci [bi-w., $599/yr., $1198/yr., print and online eds.]. Newsletter discussing software and multimedia educational technologies.

Electronic School. National School Boards Association, 1680 Duke Street, Alexandria VA 22314, subscriptions@electronic-school.com, http://www.electronic-school.com/ Ed. Sally Zakariya [q.] Trade publication that discusses trends and strategies for integrating technology into primary and secondary education.

Eriksen, O. (2004, October). Experiences from ICT-based teacher education: technology as a foundation for active learning. *Journal of Educational Media, 29*(3), 201–211. This article presents a case study of ICT implementation within a teacher education programme in Norway.

e-WEEK. Ziff-Davis Publishing Co., 28 East 28th Street, 11th Floor, New York, NY 10016, (212) 503-3500; fax: (212) 503-5680 [W., $195, Canada and Mexico $250, free to qualified personnel]. Provides current information on the IBM PC, including hardware, software, industry news, business strategies, and reviews of hardware and software.

Hadjerrouit, S. (2005, February). Learner-centered Web-based instruction in software engineering. *IEEE Transactions on Education, 48,* 99–104). This paper presents a new approach called learner-centered Web-based instruction in software engineering that can be used to educate skilled engineers.

Information Technology in Childhood Education. Association for the Advancement for Computing in Education, PO Box 3728, Norfolk, VA 22902-2966. infor@aace.org, http://www.aace.org, Ed. Daniel Shade [q., $55 domestic to individual members, $70 to foreign to individual members, $95 domestic to inst., $110 foreign to inst., $40 domestic to students, $55 foreign to students]. Scholarly trade publication reporting on research and investigations into the applications of instructional technology.

InfoWorld. InfoWorld Publishing, 155 Bovet Rd., 501 Second Street, San Francisco, CA 94107. (847) 291-5217, customerservice@infoworld.com [W., $195]. News and reviews of PC hardware, software, peripherals, and networking.

Instructor. Scholastic Inc., PO Box 420235 Palm Coast, FL 32142-0235. (866) 436-2455 [8/yr., $9.99]. Features articles on applications and advances of technology in education for K–12 and college educators and administrators.

INTERACTIVE. Question Publishing Company, Ltd., 27 Frederick St., Hockley, Birmingham, Warks, B1 3HH, United Kingdom, tel. +44 121-212-0919, fax +44 121-212 1959 [5/yr., GBP 25 subscription per year domestic to individuals GBP 33 subscription per year foreign to individuals, GBP 40 subscription per year domestic to institutions, GBP 60 subscription per year foreign to institutions]. Designed to help all primary and secondary teachers get the most from information technology in the classroom.

Interactive Learning Environments. Taylor & Francis (The Netherlands), beverley.acreman@tandf.co.uk, http://www.tandf.co.uk/journals/titles/10494820.asp [3/yr., GBP 62, USD 102 combined subscription per year to individuals print and online eds. GBP 185, USD 306 combined subscription per year to institutions print and online eds.]. Explores the implications of the Internet and multimedia presentation software in education and training environments.

Internet & Personal Computing Abstracts (IPCA). EBSCO Publishing, 10 Estes Street, Ipswich, MA 01938, (978) 356-6500, (800) 653-2726 [4/yr., USD 269 subscription per year domestic, USD 281 subscription per year in Canada/Mexico, USD 297 subscription per year elsewhere]. Abstracts literature on the use of microcomputers in business, education, and the home, covering over 175 publications.

Journal of Computer Assisted Learning. Blackwell Scientific Ltd., subscrip@bos.blackwellpublishing.com, www.blackwell-science.com [bi-m., $166 indiv., $867 inst.]. Articles and research on the use of computer-assisted learning.

Journal of Educational Computing Research. Baywood Publishing Co., 26 Austin Ave., PO Box 337, Amityville, NY 11701 [8/yr. $145 subscription per year to individuals, $400 subscription per year domestic to institutions, $415 subscription per year foreign to institutions]. Presents original research papers, critical analyses, reports on research in progress, design and development studies, article reviews, and grant award listings.

Journal of Educational Multimedia and Hypermedia. Association for the Advancement of Computing in Education, Box 2966, Charlottesville, VA 22902-2966, aace@virginia.edu, www.aace.org [q., $130 inst.]. A multidisciplinary information source presenting research about and applications for multimedia and hypermedia tools.

Journal of Research on Technology in Education. ISTE, University of Oregon, 1787 Agate St., Eugene, OR 97403-1923, (800) 336-5191, cust_svc@ccmail.uoregon.edu, www.iste.org [q., $38 1 year, $73 2 years, $108 3 years]. Contains articles reporting on the latest research findings related to classroom and administrative uses of technology, including system and project evaluations.

Language Resources and Evaluation. Kluwer Academic Publishers, Order Department, PO Box 358, Accord Station, Hingham, MA 02018-0358 [q., inst. $528, print and online eds.]. Contains papers on computer-aided studies, applications, automation, and computer-assisted instruction.

Learning and Leading with Technology. ISTE, Membership Services: iste@iste.org, (800) 336.5191, www.iste.org [8/yr., subscription included with membership]. Focuses on the use of technology, coordination, and leadership; written by educators for educators. Appropriate for classroom teachers, lab teachers, technology coordinators, and teacher educators.

Lenard, M. (2005). Dealing with online selves: Ethos issues in computer-assisted teaching and learning. *Pedagogy, 5*(1), 77–95. This article addresses several issues such as dealing with ethos issues in computer-assisted teaching and learning, using computers in college English classrooms, and the focus of many studies of computer-assisted instruction as well as the idea behind an electronically enforced egalitarianism.

MacWorld. MacWorld Communications, Mac Publishing, 501 Second Street San Francisco, CA 94107, (415) 978-3158, www.macworld.com [mo., $19.97 subscription per year domestic, $44.97 subscription per year foreign, $7.99 newsstand/cover]. Describes hardware, software, tutorials, and applications for users of the Macintosh microcomputer.

Masiello, I., Ramberg, R., & Lonka, K. (2005, September). Attitudes to the application of a Web-based learning system in a microbiology course. *Computers & Education, 45*(2), 171–185. This study argues that for a computer-based system to be effective, it must be designed and implemented with care, otherwise it may lower students' interests and activation.

Mathur, S., Stanton, S., & Reid, W. D. (2005, March). Canadian physical therapists' interest in Web-based and computer-assisted continuing education. *Physical Therapy, 85*(3), 226–237. The purposes of this study were (1) to determine the interest of Canadian physical therapists in participating in continuing education using CAL methods and (2) to determine whether interest in CAL was related to type of employment, area of practice, education, computer skill and access, and other demographic variables.

Miller, L. M. (2005). Using learning styles to evaluate computer-based instruction. *Computers in Human Behavior, 21*(2), 287–306. This study compares two instruments while evaluating the effects of learning style on performance when using a computer-based instruction (CBI) system to teach introductory probability and statistics.

OnCUE. Computer Using Educators, Inc., 2150 Mariner Square Drive, Suite 100, Alameda, CA 94501, cueinc@cue.org, www.cue.org, Ed. Maria McDonough [bi-m., $40 domestic, $65 foreign, $30 students]. Contains articles, news items, and trade advertisements addressing computer-based education.

The One-Computer Classroom [video, 36 min., $109.95]. Films for the humanities and sciences, www.films.com. Explores how a single computer in the classroom can be used as a workstation, a presentation device, and a tool used for interactive learning.

PC Magazine. Ziff-Davis Publishing Co., (866) 879-9144, svaldez@fostereprints.com [bi-w., $ $34.97, $70.97 foreign]. Comparative reviews of computer hardware and general business software programs.

Pol, H., Harskamp, E., & Suhre, C. (2005). Solving physics problems with the help of computer-assisted instruction. *International Journal of Science Education, 27*(4), 451–469. This article describes about a computer program that contains hints for various different episodes of problem solving. The result appears that pupils involved in the experiment made better use of their declarative knowledge in solving problems than pupils from the control group.

Qayumi, A. K., Kurihara, Y., Imai, M., Pachev, G., Seo, H., Hoshino, Y., et al. (2004, October). Comparison of computer-assisted instruction (CAI) versus traditional textbook methods for training in abdominal examination (Japanese experience). *Medical Education, 38*(10), 1080–1088. The results suggest that computer-assisted learning methods will be of greater help to students who do not find the traditional methods effective.

Ringstaff, L. (2005, February). Innovative solutions: Developing computer-based instruction for the nursing unit computers. *Dimensions of Critical Care Nursing, 24*(1), 35–36. This short article describes one hospital's efforts to develop a computer-based instruction program for critical care nurses who care for patients undergoing increased intracranial pressure monitoring.

Sime, D., & Priestley, M. (2005, April). Student teachers' first reflections on information and communications technology and classroom learning: Implications for initial teacher education. *Journal of Computer Assisted Learning, 21*(2), 130–142. This article explores student teachers' views of the use of information and communication technologies (ICT) in schools.

Social Science Computer Review. Sage Publications, Inc., 2455 Teller Rd., Thousand Oaks, CA 91320, order@sagepub.com, www.sagepub.com [q., $91 indiv., $463.68 inst., $483 inst., print and online]. Features include software reviews, new product announcements, and tutorials for beginners.

Software Magazine. Wiesner Publishing, LLC, PO Box 135, E. Walpole, MA 02032, subscriptions@softwaremag.com [6/yr., $42 US, $58 Canada, $140 elsewhere, free to qualified personnel]. Provides information on software and industry developments for business and professional users; announces new software packages.

Stahl, G. (2005, April). Group cognition in computer-assisted collaborative learning. *Journal of Computer Assisted Learning, 21*(2), 79–90. This paper takes a critical look at the concept of shared meaning as it is generally used and proposes an empirical study of how group cognition is constituted in practice.

Technology and Learning. C M P Media LLC, 600 Harrison St., San Francisco, CA 94107, (415) 947-6746, www.techlearning.com [10/yr., $29.95 US, $39.95 Can and Mexico, $69.95 elsewhere]. Features discussions of innovations in educational hardware and software.

Wireless Networks: The Journal of Mobile Communication, Computation and Information. Springer Science+Business Media B.V., PO Box 14302 14197, Berlin, Germany [6/yr., $442 Euro, $458 USD institution, $278 GPB]. A journal devoted to the technological innovations that result from the mobility allowed by wireless technology. Refereed and research-based publication.

DISTANCE EDUCATION

American Journal of Distance Education. Lawrence Erlbaum Associates, Inc., Michael G. Moore, Ed., College of Education, The State University of Pennsylvania, 411C Keller Building, University Park, PA 16802-3202, www.ajde.com [3/yr.; $55 indiv.; $120 inst.]. Created to disseminate information and act as a forum for criticism and debate about research in and practice of systems, management and administration of distance education.

Bernard, R. M., Abrami, P. C., Lou, Y., & Borokhovski, E. (2004, October). A methodological morass? How we can improve quantitative research in distance education. *Distance Education, 25*(2), 175–198. This article discusses about the quantitative research practices and methodologies used in distance education.

Bower, B. L., & Hardy, K. P. (2004, winter). From correspondence to cyberspace: Changes and challenges in distance education. *New Directions for Community Colleges, 128,* 5–12. This paper traces the evolution of distance learning and provides an overview of some of the challenges inherent in learning in an online environment.

Chim, H., & Chen, L. (2004, Dec.). The design and implementation of a Web-based teaching assistant system. *International Journal of Information Technology & Decision Making, 3*(4), 663–672. This paper introduces a Web-based learning system that provides a dynamic interaction environment for the students to share their information with each other.

DEOS News. (Distance Education Online Symposium). Penn State University, College of Education, American Center for the Study of Distance Education, 411 Keller Building, University Park, PA 16802-13032, acsde@psuvm.psu.edu, www.ed.psu.edu/acsde/deos/deosnews/deosarchives.asp [Online]. Posts information on distance education research and practice and is the most widely referenced online journal in the field.

Distance Education Clearinghouse. A highly maintained and frequently updated Web site that provides a wide range of information about distance education and related resources. It is managed and maintained by Instructional Communications Systems, University of Wisconsin-Extension. www.uwex.edu/disted/journals.html

Distance Education Report. Magna Publications, Inc., 2718 Dryden Dr., Madison, WI 53704 [24/yr., $399]. Digests periodical, Internet, and conference information into monthly reports.

Dupin-Bryant, P. A. (2004). Pre-entry variables related to retention in online distance education. *American Journal of Distance Education, 18*(4), 199–206. The results of this study indicate that prior educational experience and prior computer training may help distinguish between individuals who complete university online distance education courses and those who do not.

Elgamal, A., Fraser, M., & McMartin, F. (2005). On-line educational shake table experiments. *Journal of Professional Issues in Engineering Education & Practice, 131*(1), 41–49. This article describes the application of Internet technologies to allow real-time video monitoring, control, and execution of bench-top shake table experiments.

Goodfellow, R. (2004). Online literacies and learning: Operational, cultural and critical dimensions. *Language & Education, 18*(5), 379–399. This paper addresses the nature of literacy practices in online distance learning environments, specifically those involved in text-based collaborative discussion at post-compulsory level.

Grant, M. M. (2004, December). Learning to teach with the Web: Factors influencing teacher education faculty. *Internet & Higher Education, 7*(4), 329–341. This paper explores the ways in which teacher education faculty members were influenced to participate in decentralized professional development focused on learning to teach with WebCT.

Hyde, A., & Murray, M. (2005, Jan). Nurses' experiences of distance education programmes. *Journal of Advanced Nursing, 49*(1), 87–95. This paper reports on a study exploring the experiences of nurses undertaking distance education (DE) programmes.

Jones, N., & O'Shea, J. (2004, October). Challenging hierarchies: The impact of e-learning. *Higher Education, 48*(3), 379–395. The paper reflects on the university's strategic planning process and outlines the development process of an e-learning initiative.

Journal of Distance Education. Canadian Association for Distance Education, http://cade.athabascau.ca/ Aims to promote and encourage scholarly work of empirical and theoretical nature relating to distance education in Canada and throughout the world.

Journal of Library and Information Services in Distance Learning. 2710 University Drive, Richland, WA 99352-1671, (509) 372-7204, Haworth Information Press, http://www.HaworthPress.com [q., $48 indiv., $150 inst., $150 libraries.] Contains peer-reviewed articles, essays, narratives, current events, and letters from distance learning and information science experts.

Journal of Research on Technology in Education. International Society for Technology in Education. SIG, 1787 Agate St. Eugene, OR, 97403-1923, tel (800) 336-5191, fax (541) 302-3778, Ed. Lynn Schrum [q., $48 domestic to members, $28 to students and retired persons.]. This peer-reviewed publication presents communications technology, projects, research findings, publication references, and international contact information in instructional technology.

Koper, R., & Tattersall, C. (2004, November). New directions for lifelong learning using network technologies. *British Journal of Educational Technology, 35*(6), 689–700. This article presents an integrated model and architecture to serve as the basis for the realization of networked learning technologies serving the specific needs and characteristics of lifelong learners.

Koszalka, T. A., & Ganesan, R. (2004, October). Designing online courses: a taxonomy to guide strategic use of features available in course management systems (CMS) in distance education. *Distance Education, 25*(2), 243–256. This paper describes a taxonomy that strategically guides the use of appropriate CMS features to integrate informational, instructional, and learning elements into online courses to support designers in the development of quality of online instruction.

Lee, C. S., Tiong Hok Tan, D., & Goh, W. S. (2004, December). The next generation of e-learning: Strategies for media rich online teaching and engaged learning. *International Journal of Distance Education Technologies, 2*(4), 1–17. This paper reviews the processes Nanyang Technological University (NTU) in Singapore adopted in adding the human touch to traditional e-learning projects and serves as a good case study for other institutions with a similar aim to achieve interactive and engaged online learning.

Mackintosh, W., Mason, R., & Oblinger, D. (2005, February). An ODL perspective on learning objects. *Open Learning, 20,* 5–13. This article explores the relevance of learning objects for open and distance learning (ODL).

Mupinga, D. M. (2005, Jan.). Distance education in high schools. *Clearing House, 78*(3), 105–108. This article provides information on distance education in high schools.

Open Learning. Taylor & Frances Group, Open University, Editor: Anne Gaskell, The Open University in the East of England, Cintra House, 12 Hills Road, Cambridge, CB2 1PF [3/yr., $79 indiv., $246 inst.]. Academic, scholarly publication on aspects of open and distance learning anywhere in the world. Includes issues for debate and research notes.

Restauri, S. L. (2004, Nov/December). Creating an effective online distance education program using targeted support factors. *TechTrends: Linking Research & Practice to Improve Learning, 48*(6), 32–39. In this article, two major models are provided to illustrate the institutional support for online instruction.

Richardson, J. (2005, Feb.). Students' perceptions of academic quality and approaches to studying in distance education. *British Educational Research Journal, 31*(1), 7–27. The results of this study show that students' perceptions of the academic quality of courses in distance education are strongly associated with the approaches to studying that they adopt on those courses.

Russo, T. C., & Campbell, S. W. (2004, Oct.). Perceptions of mediated presence in an asynchronous online course: Interplay of communication behaviors and medium. *Distance Education, 25*(2), 215–232. This paper investigates students' perceptions of mediated presence in an online college class.

Sachs, S. G. (2004, winter). Institutional issues when distance learning joins the mainstream. *New Directions for Community Colleges, 128,* 23–30. This paper describes the best practices that helped the Extended Learning Institute at Northern Virginia Community College evolve into a mature distance-learning program that is successfully integrated into the institution.

USDLA Journal. United States Distance Learning Association, Winter St., Suite 508, Boston, MA 02108, www.usdla.org/html/membership/publications.htm [mo., free]. The publication for USDLA publishes articles on research and practice on the many areas related to distance education and online learning. These areas include administrative issues, teaching practices, student concerns, international applications, and more.

EDUCATIONAL RESEARCH

American Educational Research Journal. American Educational Research Association, 1230 17th St., NW, Washington, DC 20036-3078 [4/yr, $48 indiv., $140 inst.]. Reports original research, both empirical and theoretical, and brief synopses of research.

Current Index to Journals in Education (CIJE). Oryx Press, 4041 N. Central at Indian School Rd., Phoenix, AZ 85012-3397 [mo., $245 ($280 outside North America); semi-annual cumulations $250 ($285 foreign); combination $475]. A guide to articles published in some 830 education and education-related journals. Includes complete bibliographic information, annotations, and indexes. Semiannual cumulations available. Contents are produced by the ERIC (Educational Resources Information Center) system, Office of Educational Research and Improvement, and the US Department of Education.

Education Index. H. W. Wilson, 950 University Ave., Bronx, NY 10452 [mo., except July and August; $1,295 for CD-ROM, including accumulations]. Author-subject index to educational publications in the English language. Cumulated quarterly and annually.

Educational Research. www.tandf.co.uk [3/yr., $101 indiv., $298 inst.]. Reports on current educational research, evaluation, and applications.

Educational Researcher. American Educational Research Association, 1230 17th St., NW, Washington, DC 20036-3078 [9/yr., $48 indiv., $150 inst.]. Contains news and features of general significance in educational research.

Johnson, R. B., & Onwuegbuzie, A. J. (2004, October). Mixed methods research: A research paradigm whose time has come. *Educational Researcher, 33*(7), 14–26. This paper provides specific sets of designs and applications for mixed research.

Journal of Interactive Learning Research. Association for the Advancement of Computing in Education, PO Box 3728, Norfolk, VA 23514, info@aace.org, www.aace.org [q., $95 domestic indiv., $140 domestic inst.]. Publishes articles pertaining to theory, implementation, and overall impact of interactive learning environments in education.

Learning Technology. IEEE Computer Society, Learning Technology Task Force, Private Bag 11-222, Massey University, Palmerston North, New Zealand. http://lttf.ieee.org/learn_tech [q., online]. Reports developments, projects, conferences, and findings of the Learning Technology Task Force.

Logo Exchange. International Society for Technology in Education, Special Interest Group for Logo-Using Educators, 1787 Agate St., Eugene, OR 97403-1923. Ed. Gary Stager [q., $24/year for ISTE Members, $34 for nonmembers. Add $10 (US) for overseas subscriptions]. Provides current information on research, lesson plans, and methods related to LOGO.

MERIDIAN (RALEIGH). c/o Edwin Gerler, College of Education and Psychology, North Carolina State University, Box 7801, Raleigh, NC 27695-7801. meridian@poe. coe.ncsu.edu. http://www.ncsu.edu/meridian. Ed. Cheryl Mason [semi-annual, online]. Online journal dedicated to research in middle school educational technology use.

Research in Science & Technological Education. Taylor & Francis Group, 11 New Fetter Lane, London EC4P 4EE, www.tandf.co.uk [2/yr., $171 indiv., $864 inst.]. Publication of original research in the science and technological fields. Includes articles on psychological, sociological, economic, and organizational aspects of technological education.

Resources in Education (RIE). Superintendent of Documents, US Government Printing Office, PO Box 371954, Pittsburgh, PA 15250-7954, www.access.gpo.gov [mo., USD 102]. Announcement of research reports and other documents in education, including abstracts and indexes by subject, author, and institution. Contents produced by the ERIC (Educational Resources Information Center) system, Office of Educational Research and Improvement, and the US Department of Education.

TESS (The Educational Software Selector). Educational Products Information Exchange (EPIE) Institute, 103 3 W Montauk Hwy., 3, Hampton, NY, 11946-4006, (516) 728-9100, fax (516)728-9228 [ann., $82.50 base volume (1996), $ 32.50 for update]. A guide listing annotated references to educational software for preschool through postgraduate education.

Educational Technology

Appropriate Technology. Research Information Ltd., 222 Maylands Avenue Hemel Hempstead, Herts. HP2 7TD, UK, www.researchinformation.co.uk, info@ researchinformation.co.uk [q., $84 indiv., $275 inst.]. Articles on less technologically advanced but more environmentally sustainable solutions to problems in developing countries.

British Journal of Educational Technology. Blackwell Publishing Ltd., www. blackwellpublishing.com [bi-m., $628 inst. to Americas and Caribbean, print and online eds.]. Published by the National Council for Educational Technology, this journal includes articles on education and training, especially theory, applications, and development of educational technology and communications.

Canadian Journal of Learning and Technology. Association for Media and Technology in Education in Canada, 3-1750 The Queensway, Suite 1318, Etobicoke, ON M9C 5H5, Canada, www.cjlt.ca/ [3/yr., no cost]. Concerned with all aspects of educational systems and technology.

Dede, C. (2004, October). Enabling distributed learning communities via emerging technologies—Part Two. *T H E Journal, 32*(3), 16–26. This article focuses on the role of emerging technologies in augmented reality and ubiquitous computing interfaces in a distributed learning community.

Dori, Y. J., & Belcher, J. (2004). How does technology-enabled active learning affect undergraduate students' understanding of electromagnetism concepts? *Journal of the Learning Sciences, 14*(2), 243–279. This article discusses how educational technology supports meaningful learning and enables the presentation of spatial and dynamic images, which portray relationships among complex concepts.

Educational Technology. Educational Technology Publications, Inc., 700 Palisade Ave., Englewood Cliffs, NJ 07632-0564, (800) 952-BOOK [bi-mo., $139 US, $159 elsewhere]. Covers telecommunications, computer-aided instruction, information retrieval, educational television, and electronic media in the classroom.

Educational Technology Abstracts. Taylor & Francis Group, 11 New Fetter Lane, London EC4P 4EE, www.tandf.co.uk [6/yr., $1211inst. for print and online eds.]. An international publication of abstracts of recently published material in the field of educational and training technology.

Educational Technology Research and Development. AECT, ETR&D Subscription Dept., 1800 N. Stonelake Dr., Suite 2, Bloomington, IN 47404, www.aect.org [q., indiv. $55 US, $63 foreign; inst. $150 US, $175 elsewhere]. Focuses on research, instructional development, and applied theory in the field of educational technology; peer-reviewed.

Heath, M. (2005, April/May). Are you ready to go digital? The pros and cons of electronic portfolio development. *Library Media Connection, 23*(7), 66–70. This article describes the pros and cons of electronic portfolio development.

Iding, M., & Skouge, J. (2005, Feb.). Educational technology and the World Wide Web in the Pacific Islands. *TechTrends: Linking Research & Practice to Improve Learning, 49,* 14–18. This article describes technology issues that educators, teacher educators, and students in the Pacific Islands confront.

International Journal of Technology and Design Education. Kluwer Academic Publishers, 101 Philip Drive, Norwell, MA 02061, (617) 871-6600, fax (617) 871-6528, kluwer@wkap.com [3/yr., $230 inst. for print and online eds.]. Publishes research reports and scholarly writing about aspects of technology and design education.

Kerfoot, B. P., Masser, B. A., & Hafler, J. P. (2005, April). Influence of new educational technology on problem-based learning at Harvard Medical School. *Medical Education, 39*(4), 380–387. This study investigates how the introduction of the educational technology employed in this study impacted on the problem-based learning tutorials.

Jewell, V. (2005, March). Continuing the classroom community: Suggestions for using online discussion boards. *English Journal, 94*(4), 83–87. Deals with the utilization of online discussion boards in literature classes. Level of student participation in online discussions compared with the classroom setting; guidelines in group discussion boards; benefits of online discussion boards.

Jones, A., & Issroff, K. (2005, May). Learning technologies: Affective and social issues in computer-supported collaborative learning. *Computers & Education, 44*(4), 395–408. This paper is concerned with affective issues in learning technologies in a collaborative context.

Journal of Computing in Higher Education. Norris Publishers, Journal of Computing in Higher Education, Box 2593, Amherst, MA 01004-2593. cmacknight@oit.umass.edu, www.jchesite.org. Ed. Carol B MacKnight [semi-ann., $40 US indiv., $45 Canada indiv; $65 foreign indiv., $80 domestic to inst., $85 in Canada to inst., $95 foreign to inst.]. Publishes scholarly essays, case studies, and research that discuss instructional technologies.

Journal of Educational Technology Systems. Society for Applied Learning Technology, Baywood Publishing Co., Inc., 26 Austin Ave, Box 337, Amityville, NY 11701

Baywood@baywood.com, http://baywood.com [q., $274 US inst. &282 foreign inst.]. Discusses educational hardware and software.

Journal of Interactive Media in Education. Open University, Knowledge Media Institute, Milton Keynes, MK7 6AA United Kingdom, Eds. Simon Buckingham Shum and Tamara Sumner [online, full text, free]. A multidisciplinary forum for debate and idea sharing concerning the practical aspects of interactive media and instructional technology.

Journal of Science Education and Technology. Kluwer Academic/Plenum Publishers/Springer, 233 Spring Street, New York, NY 10013, (800) SPRINGER [6/yr., $748 institution]. Publishes studies aimed at improving science education at all levels in the US.

Maidment, J. (2005, Mar.). Teaching social work online: Dilemmas and debates. *Social Work Education, 24*(2), 185–195. This article provides an overview of the literature related to online learning in social work.

Mann, S. J. (2005, Feb.). Alienation in the learning environment: A failure of community? *Studies in Higher Education, 30*(1), 43–55. This paper argues that our focus may need to be more on supporting dialogue within the learning environment rather than seeking to establish belonging in a learning community.

MultiMedia & Internet@Schools. Information Today, Inc., 213 Danbury Rd., Wilton, CT 06897-4006, custserv@info today.com, www.infotoday.com/MMSchools/. Ed. David Hoffman, Kathie Felix [online, full-text, 6/yr., $39.95 US, $54 Canada/Mexico, $63 other]. Reviews and evaluates hardware and software. Presents information pertaining to basic troubleshooting skills.

Riffell, S., & Sibley, D. (2005, April). Using Web-based instruction to improve large undergraduate biology courses: An evaluation of a hybrid course format. *Computers & Education, 44*(3), 217–235. This paper evaluates a hybrid course format (part online, part face-to-face) to deliver a high-enrollment undergraduate biology courses.

Science Communication (formerly **Knowledge: Creation, Diffusion, Utilization**). Sage Publications, Inc., 2455 Teller Rd., Thousand Oaks, CA 91320, order@sagepub.com, www.sagepub.com [q., $119indiv., $554.88 inst. $578 inst. print and online eds.]. An international, interdisciplinary journal examining the nature of expertise and the translation of knowledge into practice and policy.

SIGTC Connections. ISTE, University of Oregon, 1787 Agate St., Eugene, OR 97403-1923, (800) 336-5191, cust_svc@ccmail.uoregon.edu, www.iste.org [q., $29, $39 intl., $42 intl. air]. Provides forum to identify problems and solutions and to share information on issues facing technology coordinators.

Social Science Computer Review. North Carolina State University, Social Science Research and Instructional Computing Lab, Sage Publications, inc., 2455 Teller Rd., Thousand Oaks, CA, 91320 info@sagepub.com, http://hcl.chass.ncsu.edu/sscore/sscore.htm Ed. David Garson [q., $91 indiv., $463.68 inst., $483 inst., print and online eds.]. Presents research and practical applications of instructional technology in social science.

Surry, D. W., Ensminger, D. C., & Haab, M. (2005, March). A model for integrating instructional technology into higher education. *British Journal of Educational Technology, 36*(2), 327–329. The article presents a model for integrating instructional technology into higher education.

TECHNOS Quarterly. Agency for Instructional Technology, Box A, 1800 North Stonelake Drive, Bloomington, IN 47402-0120 [q., free]. A forum for discussion of ideas about the use of technology in education, with a focus on reform.

TechTrends. AECT, 1800 N Stonelake Dr., Suite 2, Bloomington, IN 47404, www.aect.org [6/yr., $55 US, $75 elsewhere]. Targeted at leaders in education and training; features authoritative, practical articles about technology and its integration into the learning environment.

T.H.E. Journal (Technological Horizons in Education). ETC Group LLC, 17501 17th St., Suite 230, Tustin, CA 92780 [mo., $29 US]. For educators of all levels. Focuses on a specific topic for each issue as well as technological innovations as they apply to education.

van Merrienboer, J. J. G., & Brand-Gruwel, S. (2005, May). The pedagogical use of information and communication technology in education: A Dutch perspective. *Computers in Human Behavior, 21*(3), 407–415. This article discusses Dutch research on information and communication technology in education.

Weaver, B. E., & Nilson, L. B. (2005, spring). Laptops in class: What are they good for? What can you do with them? *New Directions for Teaching & Learning* (101), 3–13. This article describes Clemson University's Laptop Faculty Development Program and its assessment, offering the program as one model for designing faculty development to implement laptop mandates successfully.

INFORMATION SCIENCE AND TECHNOLOGY

Boekhorst, A. K., & Britz, J. J. (2004). Information literacy at school level: A comparative study between the Netherlands and South Africa. *South African Journal of Library & Information Science, 70*(2), 63–71. This article investigates, on a comparative basis, the current status of information literacy at school level in both the Netherlands and in South Africa.

Canadian Journal of Information and Library Science. CAIS, University of Toronto Press, Journals Dept., 5201 Dufferin St., Downsview, ON M3H 5T8, Canada [q., $65 indiv., $95 inst., orders outside Canada +$15]. Published by the Canadian Association for Information Science to contribute to the advancement of library and information science in Canada.

CD-ROM Databases. Worldwide Videotex, Box 3273, Boynton Beach, FL 33424-3273 [mo., $150 US, $190 elsewhere]. Descriptive listing of all databases being marketed on CD-ROM with vendor and system information.

Dofan, G., & Getz, I. (2005, winter). library directors' perceptions of the desirable US education for library service to schoolchildren. *Journal of Education for Library & Information Science, 46*(1), 59–76. This study identifies the professional knowledge and skills deemed necessary for the education and training of library and information science (US) specialists who provide services to school students, both in school and public libraries.

EContent. Online, Inc. 88 Danbury Road Suite 1D, Wilton, CT 06897-4007 (203) 761-1466, (800) 248-8466 [10/yr., $115 US, $126 Canada/Mexico, $151 intl. airmail]. Features articles on topics of interest to online database users; includes database search aids.

Gale Directory of Databases (in 2 vols: Vol. 1, Online Databases; Vol. 2, CD-ROM, Diskette, Magnetic Tape Batch Access, and Handheld Database Products). The Gale Group, PO Box 9187, Farmington Hills, MI 48333-9187 [ann. plus semi-ann. update $490 per vol.]. Contains information on database selection and database descriptions, including producers and their addresses.

Information Processing and Management. Pergamon Press, 660 White Plains Rd., Tarrytown, NY 10591-5153 [bi-mo., USD 1,495 subscription per year to institutions Except Europe and Japan, USD 313 subscription per year to qualified personnel except Europe and Japan]. International journal covering data processing, database building, and retrieval.

Information Services & Use. I.O.S. Press, 5795-G Burke Centre Parkway Burke, VA 22015 [4/yr., $350, print and online eds.]. An international journal for those in the information management field. Includes online and offline systems, library automation, micrographics, videotex, and telecommunications.

The Information Society. Taylor & Francis Group, www.tandf.co.uk, beverley. acreman@tandf.co.uk [5/yr., $336 inst., print and online eds.]. Provides a forum for discussion of the world of information, including transborder data flow, regulatory issues, and the impact of the information industry.

Information Technology and Libraries. American Library Association, ALA Editions, 50 East Huron St., Chicago, IL 60611-2795, (800) 545-2433, fax (312) 836-9958 [q., $55 US, $60 Canada/Mexico; $65 elsewhere]. Articles on library automation, communication technology, cable systems, computerized information processing, and video technologies.

Information Today. 143 Old Marlton Pike, Medford, NJ 08055, 609-654-6266 [11/yr., $72.95; Canada and Mexico, $97; outside North America, $107]. Newspaper for users and producers of electronic information services. Articles and news about the industry, calendar of events, and product information.

Information Management. IDEA Group, 701 E. Chocolate Avenue, Suite 200, Hershey, PA, 17033-1117, (866) 342-6657 www.idea-group.com [semi-ann., $50 indiv., $70 inst.]. This semiannual newsletter includes essays on current topics in information science, expert reviews of information management products, and updates on professional conferences and events.

Information Technology Newsletter. IDEA Group, 701 E. Chocolate Avenue, Suite 200, Hershey, PA, 17033-1117, (866) 342-6657, www.idea-group.com [bi-ann., $30 indiv., $45 inst.]. Designed for library information specialists, this biannual newsletter presents current issues and trends in information science presented by and for specialists in the field.

Internet Reference Service Quarterly. Haworth Information Press, The Haworth Press Inc., 10 Alice St. Binghamton, NY 13904 (800) 429-6784, www.HaworthPress.com [q., $40 indiv., $110 inst., $110 libraries.] Discusses multidisciplinary aspects of incorporating the Internet as a tool for reference service.

Journal of the American Society for Information Science & Technology. American Society for Information Science, 8720 Georgia Avenue, Suite 501, Silver Spring, Maryland 20910-3602, (301) 495-0900, www.asis.org [14/yr., inst. rate: $1,715 US, $2,059, print and online eds.; $1,855 Canada/Mexico, $2,199 print and online eds.; $1,974 Outside North America, $2,318, print and online eds.]. Provides an overall forum for new research in information transfer and communication processes, with particular attention paid to the context of recorded knowledge.

Journal of Database Management. IDEA Group, 701 E. Chocolate Avenue, Suite 200, Hershey, PA, 17033-1117, (866) 342-6657, www.idea-group.com [q., $95 indiv., $315 inst.]. Provides state-of-the-art research to those who design, develop, and administer DBMS-based information systems.

Journal of Documentation. Emerald Group Publishing Ltd., 60/62 Toller Lane Bradford England BD8 9BY, +44 (0)1274 777700, feedback@emeraldinsight.com [bi-mo., $709 in N. America]. Focuses on theories, concepts, models, frameworks and philosophies in the information sciences.

Journal of Access Services. Haworth Information Press, 10 Alice St. Binghamton, NY 13904, (800) 429-6784, www.HaworthPress.com [q., $150 US inst. print and online eds., $202.5 Canada inst. print and online eds., $217.5 elsewhere inst. print and online eds.]. Explores topics and issues surrounding the organization, administration, and development of information technology on access services and resources.

Journal of Internet Cataloging. Haworth Information Press, 10 Alice St. Binghamton, NY 13904, (800) 429-6784, www.HaworthPress.com [q., print and online eds.: $170 US inst., $229.5 Canada inst., $246.5 elsewhere inst.]. Gives library-cataloging experts a system for managing Internet reference resources in the library catalog.

Karagiorgi, Y. (2005, March). Throwing light into the black box of implementation: ICT in Cyprus elementary schools. *Educational Media International, 42*(1), 19–32. This study examines the implementation of information and communication technologies in a number of Cypriot elementary schools.

Lytras, M. D., Naeve, A., & Pouloudi, A. (2005 April/June). Knowledge management as a reference theory for e-learning: A conceptual and technological perspective. *International Journal of Distance Education Technologies, 3*(2), 1–12. This paper emphasizes the role of knowledge management as a reference theory for e-learning.

Mackey, T. P. (2005, winter). Web development in information science undergraduate education: Integrating information literacy and information technology. *Journal of Education for Library & Information Science, 46*(1), 21–35. This article examines the impact of Web development on information literacy (IL) and information technology (IT) skills in an undergraduate information science (IS) course.

Pardue, D. (2005, March). CD cover art as cultural literacy and hip-hop design in Brazil. *Education, Communication & Information, 5*(1), 61–81. This article focuses on the material of rap music CD cover art as a space where local Brazilian hip-hoppers create powerful links between idea and image.

Resource Sharing & Information Networks. Haworth Information Press, 10 Alice St. Binghamton, NY 13904 United States, (800) 429-6784, www.HaworthPress.com [2/yr., q., $275 US inst. print and online eds., $317.25 Canada inst. print and online eds., $298.75 elsewhere inst. print and online eds.]. A forum for ideas on the basic theoretical and practical problems faced by planners, practitioners, and users of network services.

Rossetti, R. J. F., & Liu, R. (2005, JanuaryMarch). An agent-based approach to assess drivers' interaction with pre-trip information systems. *Journal of Intelligent Transportation Systems, 9*(1), 1–10. This article reports on the practical use of a multiagent microsimulation framework to address the issue of assessing drivers' responses to pretrip information systems.

Sharma, R. N. (2005, winter). Development of library and information science education in South Asia with emphasis on India: Strengths, problems and suggestions. *Journal of Education for Library & Information Science, 46*(1), 77–91. This article traces the history of

US education developments about library and information science (LIS) education in all South Asian countries with emphasis on India.

Web Feet. Rock Hill Communications, 14 Rock Hill Road, Bala Cynwyd, PA 19004, (888) ROCK HIL, fax (610) 667-2291, www.webfeetguides.com/ [12/yr., $225]. Indexes Web sites for general interest, classroom use, and research; reviews Web sites for quality, curricular relevance, timeliness, and interest.

Winston, M. D., & Hoffman, T. (2005). Project management in libraries. *Journal of Library Administration, 42*(1), 51–61. This article addresses the importance of project management in libraries and the extent to which graduate programs in library and information science provide such preparation.

INSTRUCTIONAL DESIGN AND DEVELOPMENT

Ausburn, L. J. (2004, December). Course design elements most valued by adult learners in blended online education environments: An American perspective. *Educational Media International, 41*(4), 327–337. This research describes course design elements most valued by adult learners in blended learning environments that combine face-to-lace contact with Web-based learning, as well as the applications for adult learners in higher education.

Bermejo, S. (2005, February). Cooperative electronic learning in virtual laboratories through forums. *IEEE Transactions on Education, 48*(1), 140–149. This work demonstrates how to design cooperative learning activities on the Internet by using basic principles derived from contemporary pedagogical research results.

Elen, J. (2004, winter). Turning electronic learning environments into useful and influential "instructional design anchor points." *Educational Technology Research & Development, 52*(4), 67–73. This article argues that instructional design anchor points (IDAPs) are the basis for making educational research more useful and influential.

Human–Computer Interaction. Lawrence Erlbaum Associates, 10 Industrial Avenue Mahwah, NJ 07430-2262, (201) 258-2200, www.leaonline.com [q., $60 indiv. US and Canada, $90 elsewhere, $495 inst., $525 elsewhere]. A journal of theoretical, empirical, and methodological issues of user science and of system design.

Instructional Science. Springer Science+Business Media B.V, PO-Box 14302 14197 Berlin, Germany, Eds. Peter Goodyear and Patricia Alexander [bi-mo., $558 inst., online and print eds.]. Promotes a deeper understanding of the nature, theory, and practice of the instructional process and the learning resulting from this process.

International Journal of Human-Computer Interaction. Lawrence Erlbaum Associates, 10 Industrial Avenue Mahwah, NJ 07430-2262, (201) 258-2200, www.leaonline.com [bi-mo., print and online eds.: $565 inst. US & Canada, $610 inst. elsewhere, $595 inst. in US/Canada, $640 inst. elsewhere]. A journal that addresses the cognitive, social, health, and ergonomic aspects of work with computers. It also emphasizes both the human and computer science aspects of the effective design and use of computer interactive systems.

Journal of Educational Technology Systems. Baywood Publishing Co., Inc., 26 Austin Avenue Box 337 Amityville, NY 11701, (631) 691-1270 [q., $274 inst. US $282 inst. foreign]. JETS deals with systems in which technology and education interface and is designed to inform educators who are interested in making optimum use of technology.

Journal of Instructional Delivery Systems. Learning Technology Institute, Society for Applied Learning Technology, 50 Culpepper St., Warrenton, VA 20186 [q., $60 domestic,

$80 foreign]. JIDS is devoted to the issues, problems, and applications of instructional delivery systems in education, training, and job performance.

Journal of Interactive Instruction Development. Learning Technology Institute, Society for Applied Learning Technology, 50 Culpepper St., Warrenton, VA 20186 [q., $40 member, $60 nonmember; add $20 postage outside N. America]. A showcase of successful programs that will heighten awareness of innovative, creative, and effective approaches to courseware development for interactive technology.

Journal of Technical Writing and Communication. Baywood Publishing Co., 26 Austin Ave., Box 337, Amityville, NY 11701 [q., $67 indiv., $274 inst., $282 inst. foreign]. Essays on oral and written communication, for purposes ranging from pure research to needs of business and industry.

Journal of Visual Literacy. International Visual Literacy Association, c/o John C. Belland, 122 Ramseyer Hall, 29 West Woodruff Ave., Ohio State University, Columbus, OH 43210 [bi-ann., $40 US & Canada to membership, $45 elsewhere to membership, $20 subscription per year to students]. Explores empirical, theoretical, practical or applied aspects of visual literacy and communication.

Keller, J. M., & Suzuki, K. (2004, October). Learner motivation and E-learning design: A multinationally validated process. *Journal of Educational Media, 29*(3), 229–239. In this article, a general model for motivational design of instruction is described and reviewed in terms of its application to e-learning contexts.

Koszalka, T. A., & Ganesan, R. (2004, October). Designing online courses: A taxonomy to guide strategic use of features available in course management systems (CMS) in distance education. *Distance Education, 25*(2), 243–256. A taxonomy of the instructional value for CMS features and how it could used to improve the quality of distance education are discussed in this article.

Performance Improvement Journal. International Society for Performance Improvement, 1300 L St. NW, Suite 1250, Washington, DC 20005 [10/yr., $69 nonmembers, $119 nonmembers foreign, free to members]. Journal of ISPI; promotes performance science and technology. Contains articles, research, and case studies relating to improving human performance.

Performance Improvement Quarterly. International Society for Performance Improvement, 1300 L St. NW, Suite 1250, Washington, DC 20005 [q., $50 domestic, $70 foreign]. Presents the cutting edge in research and theory in performance technology.

Philip East, J. (2004, December). Applying software design methodology to instructional design. *Computer Science Education, 14*(4), 257–276. This article argues that software design processes employed in computer science for developing software can be used for planning instruction and should improve instruction in much the same manner that design processes appear to have improved software.

Thornton, D., Armstrong, S. W., & Aguilar, M. (2004, December). Using an Internet-controlled robot to facilitate learning. *TechTrends: Linking Research & Practice to Improve Learning, 48*(6), 61–64. This article describes an instructional design using the Internet-controlled robot to aid teachers in achieving their curriculum goals by keeping their students interested and actively involved in learning.

Tietjen, P., Southard, S., & Bates, C. (2005, February). Applying instructional design theories to improve efficacy of technology-assisted presentations. *Technical Communication,*

52(1), 107. This article explores application of instructional design theories for the purpose of developing effective technology-assisted presentations using the context of an Information Security course.

Training. V N U Business Publications, www.vnuemedia.com/ [mo., $78 US, $88 Canada, $154 elsewhere]. Covers all aspects of training, management, and organizational development, motivation, and performance improvement.

Yanes, M. J. (2004, winter). Distance education in traditional classes. *Quarterly Review of Distance Education, 5*(4), 265–276. This article describes an approach to increasing opportunities for peer feedback for preservice teachers in a traditional face-to-face course using a hybrid instructional design that combines distance education teaching methods with traditional instruction.

LIBRARIES AND MEDIA CENTERS

Abram, S. (2004, December). Twenty ways for all librarians to be successful with e-Learning. *Information Outlook, 8,* 42–44. This article provides e-learning and distance education guidelines for librarians.

Annbell, M. (2005, March). Encouraging image-savvy imagination: Creative and ethical student use of graphics. *Library Media Connection, 23*(6), 55–57. This article provides the perspective of encouraging image-savvy imagination of students and offers the result of joint planning between their art teacher, technology teacher, and library media specialist.

Baumbach, D. J. (2005, January/February). The School Library Media Center Web Page. *Knowledge Quest, 33,* 8–12. This article focuses on the random selection of school library media Web sites in the U.S. in 2004 to investigate the use of a spreadsheet as well as the provision of a complete scope and sequence of information skills and activities.

Boehner, K., Gay, G., & Larkin, C. (2005, May). Drawing evaluation into design for mobile computing: a case study of the Renwick Gallery's Hand Held Education Project. *International Journal on Digital Libraries, 5*(3), 219–230. This article presents a case study about the design, launch, and evaluation of a handheld mobile computing guide for visitors to the Smithsonian American Art Museum's Renwick Gallery. It also discusses the crossover between physical navigation of museum spaces and information navigation of online museum data.

Breeding, M. (2005, May). Looking toward the future of library technology. *Computers in Libraries, 25*(5), 39–41. This article presents forecasts about library technology as of May 2005.

Callison, D. (2005, February). Professional Assessment. *School Library Media Activities Monthly, 21,* 35–41. Presents information on several program assessments for school library media specialists. Statements that can serve as a foundation for a progressive teaching philosophy

Collection Building. Emerald Group Publishing Ltd., 60/62 Toller Ln., Bradford, W. Yorks. BD8 9BY, England, http://ariel.emeraldinsight.com/ [q., $1149 in N. America]. Provides well-researched and authoritative information on collection maintenance and development for librarians in all sectors.

Computers in Libraries. Information Today, Inc., 213 Danbury Rd., Wilton, CT 06897-4006, custserv@info today.com [10/yr., $99.95 US; $114 Canada/Mexico; $124

outside North America]. Covers practical applications of microcomputers to library situations and recent news items.

Ebersole, S. E. (2005, spring). On their own: Students' academic use of the commercialized Web. *Library Trends, 53*(4), 530–538. This article reviews research conducted in 1998–1999 examining students' perceptions and uses of the World Wide Web for academic purposes.

The Electronic Library. Emerald, 60/62 Toller Ln., Bradford, W. Yorks. BD8 9BY, UK, www.emeraldinsight.com/journals/ [bi-mo., $519 U.S.]. International journal for minicomputer, microcomputer, and software applications in libraries; independently assesses current and forthcoming information technologies.

Gotz, D., & Mayer-Patel, K. (2005, May). A framework for scalable delivery of digitized spaces. *International Journal on Digital Libraries, 5*(3), 205–218. This article presents a framework for scalable delivery of digitized environments to large groups of independent digital museum visitors.

Government Information Quarterly. Elsevier Science/Regional Sales Office, Customer Support Department—JAI Books, PO Box 945, New York, NY 10159-0945 [q., $147 indiv., $269 inst.]. International journal of resources, services, policies, and practices.

Griffiths, J. R., & Brophy, P. (2005, spring). Student searching behavior and the Web: Use of Academic Resources and Google. *Library Trends, 53*(4), 539–554. This study focuses on student searching behavior and shows that commercial Internet search engines dominate students' information-seeking strategy.

Huffman, S., Thurman, G., & Thomas, L. K. (2005, spring). An investigation of block scheduling and school library media centers. *Reading Improvement, 42*(1), 3–15. This article examines the effects of block scheduling on secondary school library media centers across the state of Arkansas.

Hutchinson, H. B., Rose, A., Bederson, B. B., Weeks, A. C., & Druin, A. (2005, March). The International Children's Digital Library: A case study in designing for a multilingual, multicultural, multigenerational audience. *Information Technology & Libraries, 24*(1), 4–12. This article addresses the challenges encountered in building the International Children's Digital Library (ICDL), a freely available online library of children's literature are described.

Information Outlook (formerly Special Libraries). Special Libraries Association, 331 South Patrick Street Alexandria, VA 22314-3501 USA, (703) 647-4900, www.sla.org [mo., $125]. Discusses administration, organization, and operations. Includes reports on research, technology, and professional standards.

The Journal of Academic Librarianship. Elsevier Science/Regional Sales Office, Customer Support Department—JAI Books, PO Box 945, New York, NY 10159-0945 [6/yr., $266 inst. except Europe and Japan, $105 qualified personnel except Europe and Japan]. Results of significant research, issues and problems facing academic libraries, book reviews, and innovations in academic libraries.

Journal of Government Information. Elsevier Science Ltd., Journals Division, 6277 Sea Harbor Drive Orlando, FL 32887-4800, usjcs@elsevier.com, (877) 839-7126 [6/yr., $653]. An international journal covering production, distribution, bibliographic control, accessibility, and use of government information in all formats and at all levels.

Journal of Librarianship and Information Science. Sage Publications Ltd., 1 Oliver's Yard, 55 City Road, London EC1Y 1SP, +44 (0)20 7324 8500 [q., $439 indiv., $438.72 inst., $457 inst., print and online eds.]. Deals with all aspects of library and information work in the United Kingdom and reviews literature from international sources.

Journal of Library Administration. Haworth Press, 10 Alice St., Binghamton, NY 13904-1580, (800)-HAWORTH, fax (800) 895-0582, getinfo@haworth.com, www. haworthpress.com [q., $75 indiv., $101 Canada to indiv., $109 elsewhere to indiv., $265 domestic to institutions and libraries, $384 elsewhere to institutions and libraries]. Provides information on all aspects of effective library management, with emphasis on practical applications.

Kelly, B., Closier, A., & Hiom, D. (2005, spring). Gateway standardization: A quality assurance framework for metadata. *Library Trends, 53*(4), 637–650. This article describes a quality assurance methodology that has been developed to support digital library programs in the United Kingdom higher and further education sectors.

Koohang, A., & Ondracek, J. (2005, May). Users' views about the usability of digital libraries. *British Journal of Educational Technology, 36*(3), 407–423. By using the survey, this study examines the users' view about the digital library. Some issues such as usability and future directions are also discussed.

Kovacs, D. K. (2004, Fall). Why develop Web-based health information workshops for consumers? *Library Trends, 53*(2), 348–359. The article describes in detail the application of good instructional design in developing Web-based training for health care consumers, creating usable Web-based training, and the ongoing evaluation and maintenance of Web-based training.

Larive, C. K., Kuwana, T., & Chalk, S. (2004, Nov.). A Web-based resource for the analytical novice and the seasoned practitioner. *Analytical Chemistry, 76*(21), 398A–402A. This article introduces the Analytical Science Digital Library (ASDL), which is a collection of peer-reviewed Web sites targeted at a diverse, multidisciplinary audience consisting primarily of educators, students, and practitioners.

Lawson, K. G. (2005). Using eclectic digital resources to enhance instructional methods for adult learners. *OCLC Systems & Services, 21*(1), 49–60. The purpose of this article is to demonstrate that adult learning can be improved through the use of eclectic digital resources to enhance instructional methods rather than through learning skills in isolation.

Library and Information Science Research Information Today, Inc., 213 Danbury Rd., Wilton, CT 06897-4006, custserv@info today.com, Elsevier B.V., Customer Service Department, 6277 Sea Harbor Drive, Orlando, FL 32887-4800, usjcs@elsevier.com [q., $124 indiv. excerpt for Europe and Japan, $332 inst. except for Europe and Japan]. Research articles, dissertation reviews, and book reviews on issues concerning information resources management.

Library Computing. Emerald Group Publishing Ltd., 60/62 Toller Lane Bradford BD8 9BY, England, america@emeraldinsight.com [q., $65 indiv., $255 US inst.]. Emphasizes practical aspects of library computing for libraries of all types, including reviews of automated systems ranging from large-scale mainframe-based systems to microcomputer-based systems, and both library-specific and general-purpose software used in libraries.

Library Hi Tech. Emerald Group Publishing Ltd., 60/62 Toller Lane Bradford BD8 9BY, England, america@emeraldinsight.com [q., $349 in N. America, $649 in N. America combined Library Hi Tech News]. Concentrates on reporting on the selection, installation, maintenance, and integration of systems and hardware.

Library Hi Tech News. Emerald Group Publishing Ltd., 60/62 Toller Lane Bradford BD8 9BY, England. america@emeraldinsight.com [q., $429 in N. America, $649 in N. America combined Library Hi Tech News]. Supplements *Library Hi Tech* and updates many of the issues addressed in-depth in the journal and keeps you fully informed of the latest developments in library automation, new products, network news, new software and hardware, and people in technology.

Library Journal. Reed Business Information. Corporate Headquarters, (646) 746-6400, corporatecommunications@reedbusiness.com [20/yr., $141US, $163 Canada, $221 elsewhere]. A professional periodical for librarians, with current issues and news, professional reading, a lengthy book review section, and classified advertisements.

Library Media Connection. Linworth Publishing, 480 E. Wilson Bridge Rd., Suite L., Worthington, OH 43085-2372, (800) 786-5017, fax (614) 436-9490, orders@linworth.com, linworth.com [7/yr., $69 US, $91 in Canada]. Journal for junior and senior high school librarians provides articles, tips, and ideas for day-to-day school library management, as well as reviews of audiovisuals and software, all written by school librarians.

Library Quarterly. The University of Chicago Press, Journals Division, PO Box 37005, Chicago, IL 60637, (773) 753-3347 or toll-free in U.S. and Canada (877) 705-1878 [q., $42 indiv., $140 inst.]. Scholarly articles of interest to librarians.

Library Resources and Technical Services. Association for Library Collections and Technical Services, 50 E. Huron St., Chicago, IL 60611-2795. (800) 545-2433 x 5037 [q., $75 nonmembers]. Scholarly papers on bibliographic access and control, preservation, conservation, and reproduction of library materials.

Library Trends. University of Illinois Press, Journals Dept., 1325 S. Oak St., Champaign, IL 61820 [q., $75 indiv.; $82 indiv. foreign; $105 inst.; $112 inst. foreign]. Each issue is concerned with one aspect of library and information science, analyzing current thought and practice and examining ideas that hold the greatest potential for the field.

LISA: Library and Information Science Abstracts. CSA, 3rd Floor, Farrington House, Wood Street, East Grinstead, West Sussex RH19 1UZ, UK, sales@csa.com [13/yr., $1120]. More than 500 abstracts per issue from more than 500 periodicals, reports, books, and conference proceedings.

Mitchell, S. (2005). Collaboration enabling Internet resource collection-building software and technologies. *Library Trends, 53*(4), 604–619. This article introduces an open-source software and projects that represent appropriate technologies and sustainable strategies to meet the needs for scholars and educators.

Pelikan, M. (2004, October). Problem-based learning in the library: Evolving a realistic approach. *Portal: Libraries & the Academy, 4*(4), 509–520. This article examines issues encountered over a two-year period by a faculty librarian at the Pennsylvania State University Libraries while developing and delivering course-related library instruction employing problem-based learning (PBL).

The Public-Access Computer Systems Review. An electronic journal published on an irregular basis by the University Libraries, University of Houston, Houston, TX 77204-2091, LThompson@uh.edu, http://info.lib.uh.edu/pr/pacsrev.html [free to libraries]. Contains articles about all types of computer systems that libraries make available to their patrons and technologies to implement these systems.

Public Libraries. Public Library Association, American Library Association, ALA Editions, 50 East Huron St., Chicago, IL 60611-2795; (800) 545-2433; fax (312) 836-9958 [Bi-mo., $50 US nonmembers, $60 elsewhere, $10 single copy]. News and articles of interest to public librarians.

Public Library Quarterly. Haworth Press, 10 Alice St., Binghamton, NY 13904-1580, (800)-HAWORTH, fax (800) 895-0582, getinfo@haworth.com, www.haworthpress.com [q., $60 indiv. US, $81 indiv. Canada, $87 indiv. elsewhere; $265 inst. print and online eds. US, $357.75 inst. print and online eds. Canada, $384.25 inst. print and online eds. elsewhere]. Addresses the major administrative challenges and opportunities that face the nation's public libraries.

The Reference Librarian. Haworth Press, 10 Alice St., Binghamton, NY 13904-1580, (800)-HAWORTH, fax (800)895-0582, getinfo@haworth.com, www.haworthpress.com [2/yr.; $75 indiv. US, $101 indiv. Canada, $109 indiv. elsewhere; $345 inst. print and online eds. US, $465.75 inst. print and online eds.; Canada, $500.25 inst.; print and online eds. elsewhere]. Each issue focuses on a topic of current concern, interest, or practical value to reference librarians.

Reference and User Services Quarterly. Reference and Adult Services Association, American Library Association, ALA Editions, 50 East Huron St., Chicago, IL 60611-2795; (800) 545-2433; fax (312) 836-9958 [q., $60 nonmembers, $65 nonmembers Canada/Mexico, $70 elsewhere, $15 single copy]. Disseminates information of interest to reference librarians, bibliographers, adult services librarians, those in collection development and selection, and others interested in public services; double-blind refereed.

Reference Services Review. Haworth Press, 10 Alice St., Binghamton, NY 13904-1580, (800)-HAWORTH, fax (800) 895-0582, getinfo@haworth.com, www.haworthpress.com [2/yr.; EUR 357.79 in Europe, USD 359 in North America, AUD 469 in Australasia, GBP 238.16 in UK and Elsewhere]. Dedicated to the enrichment of reference knowledge and the advancement of reference services. It prepares its readers to understand and embrace current and emerging technologies affecting reference functions and information needs of library users.

School Library Journal. Reed Business Information, Reed Business Information, 360 Park Avenue South, New York, NY 10014 [mo., $124 US, $170 Canada, $181 elsewhere, $11 per issue]. For school and youth service librarians. Reviews about 4,000 children's books and 1,000 educational media titles annually.

School Library Media Activities Monthly. LMS Associates LLC, 17 E. Henrietta St., Baltimore, MD 21230-3190 [10/yr., $49 US, $55 elsewhere]. A vehicle for distributing ideas for teaching library media skills and for the development and implementation of library media skills programs.

School Library Media Research. American Association of School Librarians, American Library Association [available online, www.ala.org/aasl/SLMR/index.html]. For library media specialists, district supervisors, and others concerned with the selection and purchase of print and nonprint media and with the development of programs and services for preschool through high school libraries.

Sumner, T., Ahmad, F., Bhushan, S., Gu, Q., Molina, F., Willard, S., et al. (2005, March). Linking learning goals and educational resources through interactive concept map visualizations. *International Journal on Digital Libraries,* 5(1), 18–24. This article explores the library interface the Strand Map for users to navigate interactive visualizations of related learning goals and to request digital library resources aligned with learning goals. Preliminary findings suggest that these library interfaces appear to help users stay focused on the scientific content of their information discovery task, as opposed to focusing on the mechanics of searching.

Teacher Librarian. Box 34069, Dept. 284, Seattle, WA 98124-1069, TL@rockland.com [5/yr., $54]. "The journal for school library professionals," previously known as *Emergency Librarian.* Articles, review columns, and critical analyses of management and programming issues for children's and young adult librarians.

The Unabashed Librarian. Maurice J. Freedman, ed. and pub. [q., $65.5 US, $73.5 elsewhere]. Down-to-earth library items: procedures, forms, programs, cataloging, booklists, software reviews.

Wareesa-ard, A. (2004, November). The role of academic libraries in developing an automated library network in Thailand. *Journal of Academic Librarianship, 30*(6), 502–506. This article focuses on the role of academic libraries in developing an automated library network in Thailand

MEDIA TECHNOLOGIES

Broadcasting and Cable. Reed Business Information, (800) 554-5729, broadcastingcable @espcomp.com, www.broadcastingcable.com/ [w., $189/yr. US print and online, $249 Canada, $360 elsewhere]. All-inclusive newsweekly for radio, television, cable, and allied business.

Dennis, E. E. (2004, October). Out of sight and out of mind: The media literacy needs of grown-ups. *American Behavioral Scientist, 48*(2), 202–211. The expanding concept of literacy in relationship to media platforms and technologies is considered, as are college-level and postcollege approaches.

Flack, J. (2005). Phones, games and virtual worlds. *Screen Education,* 74–79. This article argues too little space is given to new media in the curriculum.

Multichannel News. Reed Business Information, (888) 343-5563, multichannelnews @espcomp.com, www.broadcastingcable.com [semi-mo.; $149 US, print and online, $219 elsewhere]. A newsmagazine for the cable television industry. Covers programming, marketing, advertising, business, and other topics.

Communication Abstracts. Sage Publications, Inc., 2455 Teller Rd., Thousand Oaks, CA 91320, order@sagepub.com, www.sagepub.com [bi-mo., $266 US indiv., $1,258 inst.]. Abstracts communication-related articles, reports, and books. Cumulated annually.

Education, Communication & Information. Routledge, 11 New Fetter Lane, London EC49.4EE, UK, www.tandf.co.uk/journals/titles/1463631X.asp [3/yr., USD 110 indiv., USD 298 inst.]. A major new journal dedicated to exploring the interaction of innovations in educational theory, practice, and technologies. It features international research, theoretical debates, and analyses of effective practices.

Educational Media International. Routledge, 11 New Fetter Lane, London EC49.4EE, UK, www.tandf.co.uk/journals/routledge/09523987.html [q., $98 indiv., $379 inst.]. The official journal of the International Council for Educational Media.

Federal Communications Commission Reports. Superintendent of Documents, Government Printing Office, Box 371954, Pittsburgh, PA 15250-7954, www.fcc.gov/ [*Daily Digest, Weekly Update,* online, no cost]. Decisions, public notices, and other documents pertaining to FCC activities.

Historical Journal of Film, Radio, and Television. Routledge. 270 Madison Avenue, New York, NY 10016-0602, Sales Department, (212) 216-7800 [q., $284 indiv., $814 inst.]. Articles by international experts in the field, news and notices, and book reviews concerning the impact of mass communications on political and social history of the 20th century.

International Digital Media and Arts Association Journal. International Digital Media and Arts Association, Florida State University, PO Box 1150,Tallahassee, FL 32306-1150 [2/yr., $95 US] For more information contact Conrad Gleber, editor. cgleber@mailer.fsu.edu, (850) 766-0188. Focuses on both the use of and the administration of new an emerging technologies such as mobile computing (GPS, personal digital assistants, cell phones), ubiquitous computing ("smart houses," "information appliances") , interactive television, online role-playing games, virtual reality, and distributed collaborations.

International Journal of Instructional Media. Westwood Press, Inc., ll8 Five Mile River Road, Darien, CT 06820 [q., $186 US, $196 foreign]. Focuses on quality research; ongoing programs in instructional media for education, distance learning, computer technology, instructional media and technology, telecommunications, interactive video, management, media research and evaluation, and utilization.

Journal of Broadcasting and Electronic Media. Broadcast Education Association, (888) 380-7222, beainfo@beaweb.org, 1771 N St., NW, Washington, DC 20036-2891 [q., print and online eds.: $50 indiv., $120 inst. US/Canada, $80 indiv., $150 elsewhere]. Includes articles, book reviews, research reports, and analyses. Provides a forum for research relating to telecommunications and related fields.

Journal of Educational Multimedia and Hypermedia. Association for the Advancement of Computing in Education, PO Box 3728, Norfolk, VA 23514, info@aace.org, www.aace.org. Ed. Gary H. Marks, R&P Sarah D Williams [q., $35 indiv. member, $130 domestic to inst., $145 foreign to inst.]. Presents research and applications on multimedia and hypermedia tolls that allow one to integrate images and sound into educational software.

Journal of Popular Film and Television. Heldref Publications, 1319 Eighteenth St., NW, Washington, DC 20036-1802, (800) 365-9753 [q., indiv. $51 US, $65 foreign; inst. $104 US, $118 foreign; $26 per issue]. Articles on film and television, book reviews, and theory. Dedicated to popular film and television in the broadest sense. Concentrates on commercial cinema and television, film and television theory or criticism, filmographies, and bibliographies. Edited at the College of Arts and Sciences of Northern Michigan University and the Department of Popular Culture, Bowling Green State University.

Lamb, A., & Callison, D. (2005, May). Online learning and virtual schools. *School Library Media Activities Monthly, 21,* 29–35. This article discusses the fundamentals of online education and virtual schools.

Learning, Media & Technology. Taylor & Francis Group/Routledge, 270 Madison Avenue, New York, NY 10016-0602, Sales Department, (212) 216-7800, specialsales@taylorandfrancis.com [3/yr., $223 indiv., $833 inst.]. This journal of the Educational Television Association serves as an international forum for discussions and reports on developments in the field of television and related media in teaching, learning, and training.

Library Talk. Linworth Publishing, 480 E. Wilson Bridge Rd., Suite L., Worthington, OH 43085-2372, (800) 786-5017, fax (614) 436-9490, orders@linworth.com, linworth.com [6/yr., $49 US, $67 Canada, $71 elsewhere, $7 single copy]. The only magazine published for the elementary school library media and technology specialist. A forum for K–12 educators who use technology as an educational resource, this journal includes information on what works and what does not, new product reviews, tips and pointers, and emerging technology.

Media and Methods. Educational products, technologies, and programs for schools and universities. American Society of Educators, 1429 Walnut Street, Philadelphia, PA 19102, www.media-methods.com. Ed. Christine Weiser [5/yr., $33.50 US, $51.50 foreign]. This educational magazine offers practical information regarding instructional technologies.

MultiMedia & Internet@Schools. Information Today, 143 Old Marlton Pike, Medford, NJ 08055, www.infotoday.com/MMSchools/default.shtml, (800) 300-9868 [6/yr., $39.95 US; $54 Canada/Mexico, $63 elsewhere]. Reviews new titles, evaluates hardware and software, offers technical advice and troubleshooting tips, and profiles high-tech installations.

Multimedia Systems. Springer-Verlag New York Inc., Secaucus, NJ 07096-2485, USA, (800) SPRINGER, www.bertelsmannspringer.de/, custserv@springer-ny.com [6/yr., EUR 448, inst. print and online eds.]. Publishes original research articles and serves as a forum for stimulating and disseminating innovative research ideas, emerging technologies, state-of-the-art methods and tools in all aspects of multimedia computing, communication, storage, and applications among researchers, engineers, and practitioners.

Film & Video Finder (National Information Center for Educational Media). NICEM, PO Box 8640, Albuquerque, NM 87198-8640. (505) 265-3591, (800) 926-8328, fax (505) 256-1080, www.nicem.com/index.html, nicem@nicem.com. A custom search service to help those without access to the existing NICEM products. The NICEM database of 425,000 records, updated quarterly, provides information on non-print media for all levels of education and instruction in all academic areas. Fees are $500 user or multiple user pricing.

Ricer, R. E., Filak, A. T., & Short, J. (2005, spring). Does a high tech (computerized, animated, PowerPoint) presentation increase retention of material compared to a low tech (black on clear overheads) presentation? *Teaching & Learning in Medicine, 17*(2), 107 11. The purpose of this study was to determine if differences in (a) subjective evaluation, (b) short-term retention of material, and (c) long-term retention of material occurred with the use of static overheads versus computerized, animated PowerPoint for a presentation to medical students.

Russo, J. P. (2004, December). New media, new era. *Bulletin of Science, Technology & Society, 24*(6), 500–508. This article explores the impact of the new communications technologies on the generation born in the 1980s, the first to grow up under the dominance of the computer.

Sefton-Green, J. (2005, March). Timelines, timeframes and special effects: Software and creative media production. *Education, Communication & Information, 5*(1), 99–110. This article argues that software frequently used in the production of digital media by young people structures the way young authors conceptualize the medium.

Sorensen, E. K., & Murchu, D. (2004, October). Designing online learning communities of practice: A democratic perspective. *Journal of Educational Media, 29*(3), 189–200. This study addresses the problem of designing an appropriate learning space or architecture for distributed online courses using net-based communication technologies.

Telematics and Informatics. Elsevier Science Regional Sales Office, Customer Support Department, PO Box 945, New York, NY 10159-0945, www.elsevier.com/inca/publications/store/7/0/3/index.htt, (888) 4ES-INFO, usinfo-f@elsevier.com [q., $987 inst. except Europe and Japan]. Publishes research and review articles in applied telecommunications and information sciences in business, industry, government, and educational establishments. Focuses on important current technologies including microelectronics, computer graphics, speech synthesis and voice recognition, database management, data encryption, satellite television, artificial intelligence, and the ongoing computer revolution. Contributors and readers include professionals in business and industry, as well as in government and academia, needing to keep abreast of current technologies and their diverse applications.

Videography. C M P Information, Inc., Entertainment Technology Group. Creative Planet Communities, 1551 S. Robertson Blvd., Ste. 201, Los Angeles, CA 90035, (310) 284-3418, www.uemedia.com/CPC/videography/ [$72 US, $102 Canada, $153 elsewhere]. For the video professional; covers techniques, applications, equipment, technology, and video art.

Willett, R., Burn, A., & Buckingham, D. (2005, March). New media, production practices, learning spaces. *Education, Communication & Information, 5*(1), 1–3. This article discusses the creative potential of new media technologies for children.

PROFESSIONAL DEVELOPMENT

Annetta, L., & Minogue, J. (2004, December). The effect teaching experience has on perceived effectiveness of interactive television as a distance education model for elementary school science teacher's professional development: Another digital divide? *Journal of Science Education & Technology, 13*(4), 485–494. This article presents the relationship between the effect of a professional development project and years of teaching experience.

Continuing Professional Development. Virtual University Press, Brookes University, School of Hotel and Restaurant Management, Gipsy Ln., Headington, Oxford, Oxon OX3 0BP, U.K., (+44) 1642-751168, www.openhouse.org.uk/virtual-university-press/cpd/welcome.htm. Ed. Nigel Hammington [q., Great Britain $30, US $ $50, US $185 with online access.] Contains book reviews concerning online opportunities for continuing education.

Grant, M. M. (2004, Dec.). Learning to teach with the web: Factors influencing teacher education faculty. *Internet & Higher Education, 7*(4), 329–341. This study explored the ways in which teacher education faculty members were influenced to participate in decentralized professional development focused on learning to teach with WebCT.

Journal of Computing in Teacher Education. ISTE, University of Oregon, 1787 Agate St., Eugene, OR 97403-1923, (800) 336-5191, cust_svc@ccmail.uoregon.edu, www.iste.org [q., $65 US to membership, $85 Canada to membership, $89.55 elsewhere to membership]. Contains refereed articles on preservice and inservice training, research in computer education and certification issues, and reviews of training materials and texts.

Journal of Technology and Teacher Education. Association for the Advancement of Computing in Education (AACE), PO Box 2966, Charlottesville, VA 22902, AACE@virginia.edu, www.aace.org [q., indiv. members $55 US, $70 foreign; inst. $140 US, $155 foreign]. Serves as an international forum to report research and applications of technology in preservice, inservice, and graduate teacher education.

King, K. P. (2004, winter). Both sides now: Examining transformative learning and professional development of educators. *Innovative Higher Education, 29*(2), 155–174. The purpose of this mixed method research is to understand and support educators' continuing learning and growth better by using a lens of transformative learning to examine their experience and professional development practice and responsibility.

Society for Applied Learning Technology. Society for Applied Learning Technology, 50 Culpepper St., Warrenton, VA 20186 info@salt.org, http://www.salt.org, Ed. Raymond D Fox [q.]. Provides news, publication reviews, and conference updates for instructional technology professionals

Stevenson, H. J. (2004, winter). Teachers' informal collaboration regarding technology. *Journal of Research on Technology in Education, 37*(2), 129–144. This article includes information pertaining to teachers' perceptions of informal collaboration, factors that influence conversations, and with whom and for what purpose participants informally collaborate.

Triggs, P., & John, P. (2004, December). From transaction to transformation: Information and communication technology, professional development and the formation of communities of practice., *Journal of Computer Assisted Learning, 20,* 426–439). The purpose of this article is to challenge the linearity embedded in much of the professional development processes associated with ICT and to re-model the relationship between practice and research.

Voogt, J., Almekinders, M., van den Akker, J., & Moonen, B. (2005, May). A "blended" in-service arrangement for classroom technology integration: Impacts on teachers and students. *Computers in Human Behavior, 21*(3), 523–539. The article describes and discusses two studies that applied and evaluated the "blended" approach to teacher professional development.

Yang, S. C., & Liu, S. F. (2004, November). Case study of online workshop for the professional development of teachers. *Computers in Human Behavior, 20*(6), 733–761. The study investigates the value and effectiveness of online workshops as a tool for creating professional learning communities.

SIMULATION, GAMING, AND VIRTUAL REALITY

Chiu, S.-I., Lee, J.-Z., & Huang, D.-H. (2004, October). Video game addiction in children and teenagers in Taiwan. *CyberPsychology & Behavior, 7*(5), 571–581. This study suggests that video game addiction can be statistically predicted on measures of hostility, and a group with high video game addiction has more hostility than others.

Cruz, B. R. C., & Patterson, J. (2005). Cross-cultural simulations in teacher education: Developing empathy and understanding. *Multicultural Perspectives, 7*(2), 40–47. This article discusses how cross-cultural simulations could help to build a holistic teacher education program.

Foreman, J. (2004, September/October). Game-based learning how to delight and instruct in the 21st century. *Educause Review, 39*(5), 50–66. This article presents a discussion on the influence of video games on higher education.

Inglis, S., Sammon, S., Justice, C., Cuneo, C., Miller, S., Rice, J., et al. (2004, December). Cross-cultural simulation to advance student inquiry. *Simulation & Gaming, 35*(4), 476–487. This article reviews how and why the authors have used the cross-cultural simulation BAFA BAFA in a 1st-year social sciences inquiry course on social identity.

International Digital Media and Arts Association Journal. International Digital Media and Arts Association, Florida State University, PO Box 1150,Tallahassee, FL 32306-1150 [2/yr., $95 US] For more information contact Conrad Gleber, Ed., cgleber@mailer.fsu.edu,

(850) 766-0188. Focuses on both the use of and the administration of new an emerging technologies such as mobile computing (GPS, personal digital assistants, cell phones), ubiquitous computing ("smart houses," "information appliances") , interactive television, online role playing games, virtual reality, distributed collaborations.

Kokol, P., Kokol, M., & Dinevski, D. (2005, May). Teaching evolution using visual simulations. *British Journal of Educational Technology, 36*(3), 563–566. The article focuses on teaching evolution using visual simulations.

Mangan, K. S. (2005, February). Joysticks in the classroom: Game-design programs take off. *Chronicle of Higher Education, 51,* A29-A31. This article provides information on graduate-level video-game-design program being offered by Southern Methodist University in Dallas.

Martens, R. L., Gulikers, J., & Bastiaens, T. (2004, October). The impact of intrinsic motivation on e-learning in authentic computer tasks. *Journal of Computer Assisted Learning, 20*(5), 368–376. The present study investigated what students actually did in an electronic learning environment that was designed as a game-like realistic simulation in which students had to play the role of a junior consultant.

Maxwell, N. L., Mergendoller, J. R., & Bellisimo, Y. (2004, December). Developing a problem-based learning simulation: An economics unit on trade. *Simulation & Gaming, 35*(4), 488–498. This article argues that the merger of simulations and problem-based learning (PBL) can enhance both active-learning strategies.

Monaghan, P. (2004, October). Real fear, virtually overcome. *Chronicle of Higher Education, 51,* A12–A13. This article discuss about the effectiveness of virtual reality technology in treating common phobias and traumas.

Ong, S. K., & Mannan, M. A. (2004, December). Virtual reality simulations and animations in a web-based interactive manufacturing engineering module. *Computers & Education, 43*(4), 361–382. This paper presents a Web-based interactive teaching package that provides a comprehensive and interactive environment for a module on automated machine tools.

Popovici, D.-M., Gerval, J.-P., Chevaillier, P., Tisseau, J., Serbanati, L.-D., & Gueguen, P. (2004, October). Educative distributed virtual environments for children. *International Journal of Distance Education Technologies, 2*(4), 18–40. This paper presents a distributed virtual reality environment for children called EVE—Environnements Virtuels pour Enfants.

Porter, T. S., Riley, T. M., & Ruffer, R. L. (2004, winter). A review of the use of simulations in teaching economics. *Social Science Computer Review, 22*(4), 426–443. This article reviews the literature on the use of simulations and describes some of the simulations currently being distributed.

Ramasundaram, V., Grunwald, S., Mangeot, A., Comerford, N. B., & Bliss, C. M. (2005, Aug). Development of an environmental virtual field laboratory. *Computers & Education, 45*(1), 21–34. This article describes the development of an environmental virtual field laboratory to study environmental properties and processes that stimulate the higher-order cognitive skills of students.

Robertson, J., & Good, J. (2005, Jan). Story creation in virtual game worlds. *Communications of the ACM, 48*(1), 61–65. The article discusses how the process of game creation fosters children's programming skills.

Simulation and Gaming. Sage Publications, Inc., 2455 Teller Rd., Thousand Oaks, CA 91320, order@sagepub.com, www.sagepub.com [q., $ 105, indiv., $519.36, inst., $541, inst., print and online]. An international journal of theory, design, and research focusing on issues in simulation, gaming, modeling, role-play, and experiential learning.

van Joolingen, W. R., de Jong, T., Lazonder, A. W., Savelsbergh, E. R., & Manlove, S. (2005, July). Co-Lab: Research and development of an online learning environment for collaborative scientific discovery learning. *Computers in Human Behavior, 21*(4), 671–688. This article describes an overview of how the challenges happened in collaborative learning could be addressed within Co-Lab, a collaborative learning environment in which groups of learners can experiment through simulations and remote laboratories, and express acquired understanding in a runnable computer model.

Winston, I., & Szarek, J. L. (2005, May). Problem-based learning using a human patient simulator. *Medical Education, 39*(5), 526–527. This article describes a problem-based learning activity for medical students using a human patient simulator.

SPECIAL EDUCATION AND DISABILITIES

Journal of Special Education Technology. Department of Special Education, UNLV, 4505 Maryland Parkway, Box 453014, Las Vegas, NV 89154-3014, (615) 322-8150, http://jset.unlv.edu/shared/volsmenu.html, Eds. Kyle Higgins and Randall Boone [q., $40 indiv., $89 inst.]. *The Journal of Special Education Technology* provides "information, research, and reports of innovative practices regarding the application of educational technology toward the education of exceptional children."

Harrysson, B., Svensk, A., & Johansson, G. I. (2004, September). How people with developmental disabilities navigate the Internet. *British Journal of Special Education, 31*(3), 138–142. This article makes a series of recommendations for developments that would facilitate ease of access and independence in the use of the Internet for people with developmental disabilities.

Lintz, J. (2004, November). CNC technology brings out hidden talents in disabled children. *Tech Directions, 64,* 19–21. This article relates how computerized numerical control (CNC) technology helped the disabled students in the Hialeah Middle School in Miami-Dade County, Florida.

Parette, P., & Wojcik, B. W. (2004, fall). Creating a technology toolkit for students with mental retardation: A systematic approach. *Journal of Special Education Technology E Journal 19* (4). Retrieved May 10, 2005, from http://jset.unlv.edu/19.4T/PARETTE/first.html. This article focuses specifically on the creation of a toolkit about assistive technology designed for use with students with mental retardation.

Wehmeyer, M. L., Smith, S. J., Palmer, S. B., & Davies, D. K. (2004, fall). Technology use by students with intellectual disabilities: An overview. *Journal of Special Education Technology E Journal 19* (4). Retrieved May 10, 2005 from http://jset.unlv.edu/19.4T/WEHMEYER/first.html. This article overviews technology use by students with intellectual disabilities, with a particular focus on electronic and information technologies, such as computers, that are widely used in education. Issues pertaining to barriers to such use for this population are also examined.

TELECOMMUNICATIONS AND NETWORKING

Brown, D. G. (2005, spring). Concluding comments: Laptop learning communities. *New Directions for Teaching & Learning, 101,* 89–94. This article describes how increasingly sophisticated computer enhancements of the curriculum create more and more learning possibilities.

Canadian Journal of Learning and Technology. Association for Media and Technology in Education in Canada, 3-1750 The Queensway, Suite 1318, Etobicoke, ON M9C 5H5, Canada [3/yr., $75]. Concerned with all aspects of educational systems and technology.

Caverly, D. C., & MacDonald, L. (2005, spring). Techtalk: Wireless networking. *Journal of Developmental Education, 28*(3), 38–39. This short article discusses key issues concerning wireless networking.

Computer Communications. Elsevier Science, Inc., PO Box 882, Madison Square Station, New York, NY 10159-0882 [18/yr., $1,342 inst.]. Focuses on networking and distributed computing techniques, communications hardware and software, and standardization.

Connected Newsletter. Classroom Connect, 8000 Marina Blvd. Suite 400 Brisbane, CA 94005, (650) 351-5100 Fax: (650) 351-5250 [9/yr., $59]. Provides pointers to sources of lesson plans for K–12 educators as well as descriptions of new Web sites, addresses for on-line "keypals," Internet basics for new users, classroom management tips for using the Internet, and online global projects. Each issue offers Internet adventures for every grade and subject.

EDUCAUSE Review. EDUCAUSE, 1112 Sixteenth St., NW, Suite 600, Washington, DC 20036-4823, (800) 254-4770, info@educause.edu [bi-mo., $24 US/Canada/Mexico, $48 elsewhere]. Features articles on current issues and applications of computing and communications technology in higher education. Reports of EDUCAUSE consortium activities.

Firth, L., & Mellor, D. (2005, March). Broadband: benefits and problems. *Telecommunications Policy, 29*(2/3), 223–236. This article identifies a core set of controversies regarding broadband at the national, individual and organizational levels, and calls for diversity of analysis of possible broadband outcomes.

Grignano, D. (2004, October). 12 tips for launching a wireless laptop program. *Technology & Learning, 25,* 37–40. As mentioned in the title, this article offers tips for launching a wireless laptop program in schools.

Heyman, J. D., Swertlow, F., Ballard, M., Barnes, S., Duffy, T., Gray, L., et al. (2005, January). Pssst . . . WHAT'S THE ANSWER? *People, 63,* 108–111. This article looks at cheating in the classroom and how high-tech electronics are making it easier than ever before.

International Journal of E-Learning. Association for the Advancement of Computing in Education, PO Box 2966, Charlottesville, VA 22901, (804) 973-3987, fax (804) 978-7449, AACE@virginia.edu, www.aace.org [q., $55 domestic individual members, $70 foreign individual members, $140 domestic inst., $155 foreign inst.]. Reports on current theory, research, development, and practice of telecommunications in education at all levels.

The Internet and Higher Education. Elsevier Science/Regional Sales Office, Customer Support Department—JAI Books, PO Box 945, New York, NY 10159-0945 [q., $90 indiv., $288 inst. Except for Europe and Japan]. Designed to reach faculty, staff, and administrators responsible for enhancing instructional practices and productivity via the use of information technology and the Internet in their institutions.

Internet Reference Services Quarterly. Haworth Press, 10 Alice St., Binghamton, NY 13904-1580, (800) HAWORTH, fax (800) 895-0582, getinfo@haworth.com, www.haworthpress.com [q., indiv.: $40 US, $54 Canada, $58 elsewhere; inst. print and online eds: $95 US, $128.25 Canada, $137.75 elsewhere]. Describes innovative information practice, technologies, and practice. For librarians of all kinds.

Internet Research. Emerald Group Publishing Ltd., 60-62 Toller Ln., Bradford, W. Yorks. BD8 9BY, England [5/yr, $2029 in N. America]. A cross-disciplinary journal presenting research findings related to electronic networks, analyses of policy issues related to networking, and descriptions of current and potential applications of electronic networking for communication, computation, and provision of information services.

Network Magazine. CMP Media INC, 600 Harrison St., San Francisco, CA 94107, www.networkmagazine.com [mo., $135 domestic, $175 foreign]. Provides users with news and analysis of changing technology for the networking of computers.

Nicol, D. J., & MacLeod, I. A. (2005, May). Using a shared workspace and wireless laptops to improve collaborative project learning in an engineering design class. *Computers & Education, 44*(4), 459–475. The paper discusses the importance of embedding supportive technologies and the different forms of learner collaboration mediated by each technology.

Online. Information Today, Inc., 143 Old Marlton Pike, Medford, NJ 08055-8750, (609) 654-6266, www.infotoday.com/online/ [6/yr., $115 US, $116 Canada/Mexico, $151 elsewhere]. For online information system users. Articles cover a variety of online applications for general and business use.

Savill-Smith, C. (2005, May). The use of palmtop computers for learning: a review of the literature. *British Journal of Educational Technology, 36*(3), 567–568. The major findings in this literature review are that the palmtop computers assist students' motivation, help organizational skills, and encourage a sense of responsibility.

Scarpa, S. (2004, November). Philly to become biggest wireless "hot zone" in nation. *District Administration, 40,* 15. This article is a short report about the steps taken by Philadelphia, Pennsylvania, to build the largest wireless network in the United States.

Sikora, A. (2004, October). Design challenges for short-range wireless networks. *IEE Proceedings—Communications, 151*(5), 473–479. The paper points out three major challenges, which include topology, device, and security issues, and also suggests different solutions for these challenges, especially in the field of security.

Telecommunications. Horizon House Publications, Inc., 685 Canton St., Norwood, MA 02062 [mo., $145 US, $230 elsewhere, free to qualified individuals]. Feature articles and news for the field of telecommunications.

Index

Abram, S., 399
Abrami, P. C., 387
Academic achievement and creativity, 227
Academy of Motion Picture Arts and Sciences
  (AMPAS), 257
Acceptance and use of technology,
  constraints on
  in corporate training and development,
    11–12
  in higher education, 16–19
  in K–12 education, 27–28
Access, equity in
  in higher education, 58
  in K–12 education, 26–27
Access Network, 316
Accessibility for students with disabilities in
  higher education, 19–20
Adaptech Research Network, 316–17
ADDIE (Analysis, Design, Development,
  Implementation, and Evaluation)
  impact on research and teaching, 47
  limitations, 36
  origin of, 36
  purpose of, 36–37, 40
  strengths, 35–36
Administrative issues in higher education, 16
Adult learning theory, 58
AEL, Inc., 257
Aeve, A., 396
Affective skills, 228
Affinity charts, 190
Agency for Instructional Technology (AIT),
  257
Aguilar, M., 398
Ahmad, F., 403–4
AI Magazine, 381
Alabama State University, 323
Aldea, A., 381
Alexander, Christopher, 43, 44
Alliant University, 326
Almekinders, M., 408
Ambiguity, 229
American Association for the Advancement of
  Science (AAAS), 171
American Association of Colleges for Teacher
  Education (AACTE), 257–58
American Association of Community Colleges
  (AACC), 258
  Community College Satellite Network
    (CCSN), 258
American Association of School Librarians
  (AASL), 169, 172, 199, 206, 258–59
American Association of State Colleges and
  Universities (AASCU), 259

American Behavioral Scientist, 404
American Civil Liberties Union, 29
American Educational Research Association
  (AERA), 259
American Educational Research Journal, 390
American Foundation for the Blind (AFB),
  259–60
American Journal of Distance Education, 387,
  388
American Library Association (ALA), 172,
  260
American Library Trustee Association
  (ALTA), 260
American Life Project, 28
American Management Association
  International (AMA), 260–61
American Montessori Society (AMS), 261
American Society for Training and
  Development (ASTD), 4, 261–62
American Society of Cinematographers (ASC),
  262
American Society of Educators (ASE), 262–63
American Telecommunications Group (ATG),
  263
American Women in Radio and Television
  (AWRT), 263
Americans with Disabilities Act (1990), 19
Analog audiovisual (AV) collections in K–12
  education, 23
Analytical Chemistry, 401
Anesthesiology, 109–17
Annbell, M., 399
Annetta, L., 407
Annotations, Web resource database, 98–108
Anthony, K., 42, 43
Anthropology Film Center (AFC), 263–64
Appalachian State University, 357
Appropriate Technology, 391
Architecture, 41
Arizona State University, 325
Arkansas Tech University Curriculum and
  Instruction, 326
Armstrong, S. W., 398
Artifacts, design, 45–47
Artificial intelligence, mediagraphy, 381–82
Artificial Intelligence Review, 381
Artificial Life, 382
Aryee, S., 158
Assessment
  and computers in K–12 education, 21
  and language barriers, 69
  of students in science education, 174
  of technology by staff and students,
    180–81

About the Editors

MICHAEL OREY is Associate Professor in the Department of Educational Psychology and Instructional Technology at the University of Georgia.

V. J. MCCLENDON is a doctoral candidate in the Department of Educational Psychology and Instructional Technology at the University of Georgia. Spanning two decades, her experience includes K–12 teacher, college instructor, and academic librarian. Her research focuses on faculty collaboration online.

ROBERT MARIBE BRANCH is Professor of Instructional Design in the Department of Educational Psychology and Instructional Technology at the University of Georgia.